THE WAR AMPUTATIONS OF CANADA

KEY TAG SERVICE

140 Merton Street, Toronto, Ontario M4S 1A5

Tel. (416) 488-0600

Dial Toll Free Area Codes 519, 613, 705:
1-800-268-8821
All other codes: 1-800-268-8917

CHILD AMPUTEE PROGRAM

January 22, 1987

Don Hall
Box 1492 Main P.O.
Kingston, Ontario
K7L 5C7

Dear Mr. Hall:

Thank you so much for your request. We are pleased indeed to send you herewith copy of our DIGEST about Billy Bishop.

It is hoped that you find it interesting and challenging. My feeling is that although the National Film Board is a government agency, this is not a political matter. On the contrary, there is a major public issue involved.

If we were to allow this type of unprincipled attack to continue, who knows where it might end? In the film, veterans are pictured as blood-thirsty killers -- or worse.

At the same time, I do not think that in the DIGEST I am attacking the Film Board on those grounds, but merely attempting to put all of the information out in the open so that Canadians can decide for themselves.

Getting out the DIGEST was a bit of work -- but nonetheless a labour of love.

Should you have any comments, I would be delighted to have them ... yes, including criticisms.

Thank you for your interest.

H. Clifford Chadderton, OC, CAE
Chief Executive Officer

Encl.

D1126990

Charitable Institution Registration No. 0286831 09 10

Hanging a Legend:
The NFB's Shameful Attempt
To Discredit Billy Bishop, VC

Hanging a Legend:
The NFB's Shameful Attempt
To Discredit Billy Bishop, VC

by H. Clifford Chadderton, OC, CAE
Chief Executive Officer
The War Amputations of Canada
2827 Riverside Drive, Ottawa, Canada K1V 0C4

Published as a public service and distributed free of charge.

ISBN 0-921391-06-4

Contents

Part II   Senate Sub-Committee Material

Part III   Malloch-Chadderton: An Interesting Exchange of Letters

Part IV   Research Documents

DREAMS

Some fellows are out to make money in shoals
And some to win races and some to shoot goals,
But I sit in my study and breathlessly read
Of McCudden and Mannock and their deathless breed.

Of Boelcke and Bishop, Richthofen and Ball,
Yes, by name and by fame I'm acquainted with all;
And sometimes the study fades out from sight
And high over Flanders I'm swooping to fight.

I've raked a tall Fokker from cockpit to rudder
And drawing away I've bagged yet another.
Then a noise from the engine says something is wrong,
And I'm crashed from the clouds by the old dinner gong!

J.N.H. Brennan

Foreword

I never imagined that it would be necessary for me to speak on behalf of my grandfather, the late Billy Bishop, VC. Paul Cowan and the National Film Board, with its ridiculous documentary *THE KID WHO COULDN'T MISS*, changed all of that.

If I ever had any doubt about the need to say something, it quickly evaporated when I read a letter written by a Katie Malloch who uses the same street address as that shown in the Montreal telephone book for Paul Cowan, the film's producer. (See letters appended.)

In a letter to the author of this *Digest* Ms. Malloch says: "As for the injury to the feelings of the Bishop family, father, grandfather, father-in-law, or whatever he may be to them . . . They have doubtless reaped the rewards of the situation—please don't tell me that the Bishop pedigree hasn't opened doors and aroused admiration! Now they're taking the bumps that go with the roses. If they have any evidence that all doubts about the Bishop legend are groundless, then let them come forward. If they can't, or won't, that is their choice. Frankly, I can't work up much sympathy for the Bishop clan!"

I would not dignify those remarks by replying to them.

It is noted, however, that there is a Katie Malloch who has a credit in the NFB film as music consultant. Her comments on the Bishop family would appear to say something about the people around Paul Cowan.

Be that as it may, my wish is that Canadians, both present and future, should know what kind of person my grandfather was—both as an aviator and as a human being.

As a child, I had reason to know of the strength, the courage and depth of feeling that marked Billy Bishop for greatness. In fact, most Canadians who met him felt nothing but admiration.

On June 2, 1917 in Flanders, when he carried out a single-handed raid against a heavily armed German aerodrome, he became a legend. On that day he destroyed his 25th enemy aircraft. He continued to carry the fight in the air and was credited with another 47 victories before he was ordered out of the combat zone to organize a Canadian Air Force.

Billy Bishop made a significant contribution to aeronautics in Canada in the 20s and early 30s and then, sensing that another war was in the offing, he re-joined what was by then the Royal Canadian Air Force. Once again, he served his country, this time as Air Marshall Bishop, in charge of recruiting and training combat pilots for the Commonwealth.

In the end, the risk that he was willing to take for his country eventually caught up to him. As always, it was

Cliff Chadderton and Catherine Willis-O'Connor

his choice. Canada remembered Billy Bishop with a 21-gun salute.

I have been moved by the tremendous support of Canadians in all walks of life, who have gone out of their way to let me know of their distasteful feelings evoked by the National Film Board production of *THE KID WHO COULDN'T MISS*.

I feel a deep sorrow (and maybe a little anger) that the film contains so many inaccuracies—and attempts to portray a totally insupportable and uncalled-for profile of a man who was as big as, if not bigger than, the legend that his life represented.

I should like to take this opportunity of expressing my appreciation. I have the utmost admiration for The War Amputations of Canada and for the publication of this *Digest* and for its author, Cliff Chadderton, whose dedication is evident in its pages.

The heroic saga of Billy Bishop will never die, but we cannot run the risk that some day the doubts expressed by Paul Cowan and the National Film Board could once again surface. They must be consigned to obscurity for all time.

This *Digest* should leave no doubt in anyone's mind concerning what kind of person Billy Bishop really was. His remarkable war record and his place in the history of this country stands intact.

The attempts to malign and discredit William Avery Bishop, VC, DSO and BAR, MC, DFC will pass into history; a shameful episode nonetheless.

Catherine Willis-O'Connor
Ottawa, October 1986

Prologue
Just a Brief, Personal Note to Begin

This is a *Digest*—it consists of personal commentary, together with other written material: Senate Sub-Committee documents; correspondence; background articles and research documents.

The author has taken an intense interest in the Billy Bishop controversy since the National Film Board (NFB) production *THE KID WHO COULDN'T MISS* began to stir the public consciousness. Unfortunately, as the story unfolded in the print and broadcast media, it was apparent that "the baby was being thrown out with the bathwater!"

The serious, underlying issues were being all but ignored. Those who understood what Billy Bishop did—and why—got some play but so did the producers of this film, which is an insulting and disgraceful profile of a national war hero. It was evident that we had a classic situation where confusion reigned supreme. For whatever reason, many media-types were being swept along on well-meaning waves of protest against the enquiry into the film, spouting catch words like "censorship" and sounding dire warnings about "government control over public institutions such as the National Film Board."

This *Digest* is an attempt to consolidate, between two covers, all of the relevant material pertaining to this issue. The author is an executive of a veterans organization which is also a charitable institution. This *Digest* has the full support of this organization (The War Amputations of Canada). It is important to state, however, that charitable funds have not been used to produce the *Digest*.

John Percival has recently published a book entitled *For Valour* in the United Kingdom. It was based on an award-winning documentary produced by Thames Television.

Concerning the awarding of the Victoria Cross, Percival states: "The process whereby a Victoria Cross is awarded is always shrouded in mystery, and to avoid invidious lobbying it is just as well that this should be so."

The fact that the Victoria Cross was awarded to Bishop without confirmation of his airfield raid seems to be at the centre of the controversy. It would appear that the first mistake was made by the British military authorities, in seizing upon this particular exploit for the basis of the recommendation that Billy Bishop be awarded the Victoria Cross. He had, by that time, already shot down more than 20 enemy aircraft. (Hindsight is better than 20-20... if only they had waited, there would have been no controversy for the NFB to seize on.)

Hopefully the point is clear! As we will show later, there may have been no hard evidence of confirmation of Bishop's raid on the German Squadron on June 2, 1917 (although we will, in this *Digest*, indicate proof of a circumstantial nature). As we will point out, however, it has been universally accepted by all established military historians that the raid did, in fact, take place.

You might ask, then, what was the basis of the NFB's allegations which cast doubt upon the record of Billy Bishop? The producer of the film stated that he could find no proof that the raid did take place... and on this premise he decided to challenge and destroy the legend and the reputation of our finest Canadian airman... a man whose significance has been written into and who has become a major part of our history, if we accept that Canada became a nation during those terrible and dark days of the First Great War.

Some historians who have appeared before the Senate Sub-Committee have suggested that this controversy could be settled if more "primary" research were carried out, that is if, through research, additional or new evidence could be uncovered regarding the Bishop raid.

This is most unlikely. It is known that much of the German material is no longer available and the historians presumably have most, if not all, of the British and Canadian data. What seems to be required now is an exercise in judgement. That is, all of the information must be assembled and commented upon by those who support the Bishop claim and those who do not. It seems possible, then, to suggest that there are more factors supporting the raid than those which can be assembled to indicate that it did not take place. The Bishop supporters seem to agree that there is "no evidence" to confirm the raid but the historical factors do make it possible to come to the logical assumption that Bishop's claims were true.

Just a word about identification of source material. The written comments contain many quoted references. Purposely, I have not identified these references in the text itself. There were two reasons in not doing so: firstly, for the reader it is a constant irritation and secondly, to fully understand the reference material itself, it should be read in full. (In any event, most of it is, I think, both informative and entertaining.)

The format used herein will allow a person to find his or her own answers to the present controversy surrounding Billy Bishop. We are not expressing an opinion—and in this regard no apology is offered. There is no simple, direct way to prove that Bishop did what he, generally, is accepted as having done.

The *Digest* will include the evidence. The riddle as

to whether Billy Bishop was a fraud or a true hero has all the earmarks of a mystery story. This *Digest* provides the opportunity of solving it.

Remember though, in support of Bishop, we have the official record, the history books and, of course, the award of the Victoria Cross. Contrariwise, Paul Cowan, the writer-director-producer, has cited a number of sources such as Fry, James, Warne and Ferko (all identified later in this text) who appear to take an anti-Bishop stance.

It is not suggested that, in seeking the truth, it is reasonable merely to fall back on historical acceptance; neither will it be prudent, presumably to accept the NFB version at first blush.

It is important, however, to find the truth. The deeds of valor which have had much to do with our birthright must be analysed. If these deeds were falsified for political or other reasons, are we a nation deserving of the respect of the world?

Make no mistake. This is not a simple matter of one man's place in history. Paul Cowan himself made that clear. He was challenging not only how heroes are made, but why a country needs heroes anyway.

If we, as Canadians, allow Paul Cowan to get away with his attempt to destroy Billy Bishop, perhaps we are paving the way for those who would re-arrange our history and ignore the struggle to build this nation, and the ongoing challenge to keep it free.

At the commencement of this project, my feelings regarding Paul Cowan ran somewhere between pity and ridicule. As the research developed, however, it became apparent that Mr. Cowan would have had available to him the same sources which I was able to uncover in my spare time. I began to wonder, then, whether he in fact did examine the documents which indicate that Bishop's record was reasonably accurate; in particular, that the VC raid did take place.

To be honest, I cannot see how Cowan would have missed this information if he did any serious research. He must have come across enough factual data to support the legend of Billy Bishop.

It is pure conjecture on my part, admittedly, but I cannot escape the nagging feeling that he decided to ignore all of the positive material and to use the fragmentary and often prejudiced view that the Bishop legend was a monumental hoax.

At this point, my feelings toward Paul Cowan veered somewhat towards rage and disdain. I would be less than candid if I did not admit this. If I have been something less than impartial it is because I feel that Cowan's attempt to destroy Billy Bishop's name must be challenged.

I am not a professional researcher. Still, the evidence on which this *Digest* is based was located mostly by me, as an extra-curricular task—and the entire project took less than a month. I believe the work is accurate. I mention this specifically to show that Paul Cowan could have done the same thing; but better. I can only assume that he did not look in the right places; or if he did, he did not like what he found.

H. Clifford Chadderton, OC, CAE
Ottawa, Canada
October 1986

Acknowledgements

The author is indebted to the historians and authors who have been freely quoted in this *Digest*, in an attempt to restore the record of Billy Bishop. For valuable assistance in the preparation of this publication, thanks are also due to Task Force Co-ordinator Margaret Harvey Melenhorst, to Production Co-ordinator Wendy DeMos Robinson, and to Communications Director Shelley Henderson for editorial support.

A copy of the script, *THE KID WHO COULDN'T MISS*, can be obtained by writing to: The National Film Board, P.O. Box 6100, Station 'A', Montreal, Quebec, H3C 3H5. There is no cost for the script.

Part I
Digest

Chapter 1

In The Public Interest?

Paul Cowan and the NFB vs
William Avery Bishop, VC, DSO and BAR, MC, DFC*

Billy Bishop, as he has so fondly been known by Canadians for nearly 70 years, is officially credited with having shot down 72 enemy aircraft in the battles over Flanders in World War I.

The National Film Board (NFB) made *THE KID WHO COULDN'T MISS*, originally designated as a documentary, in 1982. It is important to keep in mind that the NFB has a mandate to make films which are in the public interest, and which are designed to portray Canadians in a positive way.

The NFB film was temporarily withdrawn and finally released again in 1984. It has been the subject of intense controversy since that time.

The film is largely the work of Paul Cowan, Canadian by birth, educated in the United States and now working for the NFB in Montreal. The film was examined by the Sub-Committee on Veterans Affairs of the Standing Senate Committee on Social Affairs, Science and Technology late in 1985, which subsequently released a recommendation that the film be allowed to remain in existence with a notation that it was a docu-drama. This recommendation was not satisfactory to the Senate as a whole and the matter was sent back to the Committee for further investigation (see Senate Sub-Committee Material).

This poses two problems. Firstly, the Senate itself may not have the authority to deal with the matter. Secondly, the NFB is claiming, by its mandate, that it has an "arms-length" relationship with Parliament.

This is, in any event, purely academic. Billy Bishop has been a favourite public figure and has been part of the history of this country for many years. The decision as to the final disposition of this film cannot be left to Parliament or to the media. **It is for the public to decide—hence this *Digest*.**

---

*Billy Bishop was awarded the CB (Order of the Bath) in the 1944 King's Birthday list. He received the news with mixed feelings. The CB would come immediately after his VC thus breaking up his string of combat medals. We refer in this *Digest* only to what he called his "fighting row"—VC, DSO and Bar, MC, DFC.

Chapter 2
What Billy Bishop Did

There are several ways to tell the story of Billy Bishop. We have his own biography *Winged Warfare* written in 1917 when he came back to Canada to get married between his two stints at the front as a fighter pilot in World War I (see excerpts in Research Documents).

We have the excellent biography *The Courage of the Early Morning* written by his son, Arthur W. Bishop, published in 1965.

We have the references written about Bishop in a number of excellent histories, the most recent of which is Carleton University (Ottawa) Professor Steven Wise's fascinating tome *Canada's Airmen and the First World War*.

This *Digest* chooses, however, to go back in history to another author. The Honourable George Drew, who served his country well in wartime and later as Premier of Ontario and as Leader of the Opposition in the Federal Parliament wrote an authoritative volume entitled *Canada's Fighting Airmen*, published in 1930.

George Drew knew Billy Bishop; more importantly, he knew Bishop's contemporaries and he was part of the "living history" of those Canadians who fought in the First Great War. George Drew knew how people felt about Billy Bishop then and, with uncanny wisdom and prophesy, he stated the place in history that those men would occupy...and its importance in the development of our country.

Quoted herewith from George Drew's book are some fascinating introductory remarks followed by segments of his book which deal with Billy Bishop. Here, then, is Billy Bishop from the perspective of George Drew, author, historian and statesman.

Excerpt from:
Canada's Fighting Airmen
by: Lieut. Colonel George A. Drew (1930)

In this almost incredible story of British achievement Canadians played a tremendous part.

Canada's share individually and collectively was out of all proportion to her population.

It is unfortunate that so little has been told of their wonderful story, that a generation has already grown up to whom their names are almost unknown. Their exploits should be an inspiration to young Canadians for all time, because at the height of their glory these men were mere boys, and what Canadian boys did then forever avoids the necessity of seeking beyond the borders of Canada for examples of the highest bravery, devotion to duty and self-sacrifice. The reason that so little is known is not hard to find. John Buchan, the British historian, tells us why in a few words. "The Germans and the French made no secret of their heroes, but rather encouraged the advertisement of their names; but the Royal Flying Corps* true to its traditions contented itself with a bare recital of the deed, until an occasional VC lifted the veil of anonymity."

Opinions differ as to the wisdom of this course but there is no question about the result. It was not until the *London Gazette* announced in terse official sentences that Captain Albert Ball had destroyed nearly fifty enemy machines that the British public throughout the Empire awoke to the fact that British airmen were the peers of any in the world. Canadians, throughout the war, had no separate unit in the Royal Air Force (RFC) and Canadians were therefore equally ignorant of what their flying men were doing. It was a VC which lifted the veil of anonymity from the greatest Canadian pilot.

Canadians read with pride that Captain William Avery Bishop, of Owen Sound, had been awarded the most coveted decoration for valour in the world, the Victoria Cross, "for most conspicuous bravery, determination and skill." Unknown to most Canadians at home he had already won the Military Cross and Distinguished Service Order for deeds of great bravery.

In the course of time Bishop's record stood beside those of the great British aviators, Ball, McCudden and Mannock, and finally well above them. As the months of 1918 passed, other Canadians rose to claim a place in that select company. Collishaw, Barker and MacLaren were not far behind and there were many others whose exploits marked them as among the greatest pilots in the war.

A comparison of the number of aeroplanes destroyed by the four leading pilots of various nations forcibly demonstrates the high rank attained by Canadians.

Canadian		American	
Bishop	72	Rickenbacker	21
Collishaw	60	Lufberry	17
Barker	50	Vaughn	12
MacLaren	48	Springs	12
Other British Pilots		**German**	
McCudden	54	Richthofen	80
Mannock	50	Udet	62
Fullard	45	Lowenhardt	56
Ball	43	Voss	48
French			
Fonck	75		
Guynemeyer	53		
Nungesser	45		
Madon	41		

*Forerunner of the Royal Air Force.

From these figures, which refer only to aeroplanes and do not include balloons destroyed, it will be seen that only one German and one Frenchman surpassed Bishop's record, and that . . . four of the first ten from all nations of the world were Canadians.

As between Richthofen and the British pilots there was a vast difference in the manner of their fighting which must be remembered when considering their records. Richthofen scarcely ever fought alone. He was a calculating defensive fighter, seldom attacking machines of equal fighting strength unless accompanied by several of his squadron. He was a deadly shot and unquestionably a fearless fighter, but we find few instances in his combat reports where he sought single-handed combat with British scouts and fewer still where he followed an enemy far over the British lines. On the other hand, Bishop, Collishaw, McCudden, Barker, Mannock, MacLaren, Ball and hundreds of other British pilots were constantly attacking German formations alone and most of their fighting was done over German territory.

This had two important effects. In the first place, there could not fail to be uncertainty at times as to which pilot had fired the fatal shots when a whole squadron attacked. . . . In the second place, the fact that nearly all the fighting took place far behind the German lines had a very important bearing on the results. . . . An examination of Richthofen's reports shows that several of his victories were over machines which were forced to land without being seriously damaged. On the other hand, Bishop forced many machines down on their own side of the lines which landed safely and were not counted as victories.

But it is well that bravery such as theirs should be remembered, as well as that of hundreds of thousands of their countrymen, because in that memory lies a tradition which means much in building the character of a nation.

These words are carved on the wall of the beautiful memorial chamber in the Parliament Buildings at Ottawa: "They are too near to be great but our children shall understand when and how our fate was changed and by whose hand." To those who knew them well, and still see some of them from day to day, these men are, perhaps, "too near to be great", but already a generation has reached maturity, of those who were too young at the time to remember the events described (1930). They should be taught with pride that these young Canadians—mere boys, most of them—were more than equal to the task they faced in the most appalling conflict of all history, and that in the particular sphere of their war efforts, were among the truly great men of the world.

Bishop

Lieut.-Col. William Avery Bishop, VC, DSO and Bar, MC, DFC, Chevalier of the Legion of Honour, Croix de Guerre with Palm, who destroyed more German aeroplanes during the Great War than any other British pilot, was probably the most spectacular fighter in the world. No other pilot of any nation even approached his almost incredible record of shooting down twenty-five enemy machines in ten days. With orders to return to England, to assume administrative duties, in his pocket, he went up on his last day in France for one final effort and in a few hours of meteoric fighting added five more victims to his list. All the time he was at the front he took fearful chances, never hesitating to accept battle against the greatest odds and yet he was never even wounded.

His was, indeed, a charmed life. Time and time again he found himself in the midst of a whirling maelstrom of enemy machines,

in which a greater danger than the flaming bullets was the chance of a collision. Yet when the "dog fight" cleared away, Bishop's machine, riddled with bullets, would wing its way safely home while a smoking heap of wreckage behind the German lines told the watching armies that the master marksman had won again.

Bishop was born at Owen Sound, Ontario, on February 8, 1894. He passed through the ordinary educational routine of a Canadian boy until he entered the Royal Military College in 1912, and had just completed his second year when the war began in 1914. Beyond the fact that he had been an excellent shot with a rifle since he was a young boy he showed no particular indication during his school years of those qualities which made him one of the world's greatest airmen.

He enlisted at Toronto in 1914 with the 4th Battalion, Canadian Mounted Rifles, and proceeded shortly afterwards to England, where fate, in the form of the British War Office, directed this unit to a particularly muddy training-camp. Mud caused the death of many men during the war. Indirectly, it brought death to more than a hundred German airmen because it was mud that persuaded Bishop to join the Flying Corps.

Bishop applied immediately for his transfer and got it. A few months later he had qualified as an observer and was in France.

He spent four months in action as an observer. During this period he carried out the customary routine of observation, photography and bombing. This four months was a marked contrast with his later experiences, for although he was almost daily over the German lines he did not have a single fight. He was forced to return to England because of an injury to his knee when his pilot made a bad landing. He was laid up for several months on account of this—his only injury during the war and not a serious one—and then, his sick leave over, was given his chance to become a pilot.

He spent the winter of 1916-17 in training, going through the usual steps from a ground school up to night flying, during which he served on the Zeppelin patrols. Early in March, 1917, . . . he reported to the headquarters of the Royal Flying Corps for his orders to proceed to France as a pilot. At last he was ready for the great adventure in which he was destined to make so proud a name.

At the time of Bishop's arrival, the 60th Squadron was equipped with the Nieuport Scout, a small fast single-seated machine designed essentially for fighting. It was fitted with a single Lewis machine gun fixed above the upper plane and firing over the propeller. The sights however were immediately in front of the pilot's head so that he sighted his gun without changing his position and fired by pressing a trigger on the control stick. This called for a nice balance of shooting and flying skill as it was necessary to point the whole machine in the required direction to bring the sights on the target.

His first visit to German territory, flying his own machine was in an observation patrol with five others. This was no more eventful than his earlier experiences as an observer had been, as the report of the patrol for the day discloses. "While on observation patrol two machines engaged five Albatross Scouts. One other was chased. Clouds and wind prevented decisive results," he reported.

On March 25, he had his first real fight, and very nearly his last. The great strategical retreat of the German armies to the Hindenburg line was in full swing and the British airmen were constantly at work observing enemy movements, bombing their supply centres, and photographing the country over which the advancing forces must pass. The scouts bore a vital part in this important work, protecting the slower observing and bombing machines from hostile aircraft during their flights over the enemy's lines. On the 25th,

Bishop was on a patrol with three other scouts when they encountered three German Albatrosses. What followed is described in the briefest sort of outline by his combat report for the day.

COMBATS IN THE AIR

SQUADRON:	No. 60
TYPE and No. of AEROPLANE:	Nieuport Scout A-306
ARMAMENT:	1 Lewis Gun
DATE:	25-3-17
TIME:	5.00 p.m.
DUTY:	Defensive Patrol
PILOT:	Lieut. W. A. Bishop
LOCALITY:	Between St. Leger and Arras
HEIGHT:	9,000 feet

REMARKS ON HOSTILE MACHINE: TYPE, ARMAMENT, SPEED, ETC.

Albatross Scout

Narrative

While on Defensive Patrol, 3 Albatross Scouts approached us; one separating from the rest lost height and attempted to come up behind our 2nd to the rear machine. I dived and fired about 12 to 15 rounds. Tracers went all around his machine. He dived steeply for about 600 ft. and flattened out. I followed him and opened fire from 40 to 50 yds. range, firing 40 to 50 rounds. A group of tracers went into the fuselage and centre section, one being seen entering immediately behind the pilot's seat, and one seemed to hit himself. The machine then fell out of control in a spinning nose dive. I dived after him firing. When I reached 1500 or 2000 feet, my engine had oiled up and I glided just over the line. The Albatross Scout when last seen by me was going vertically downwards at a height of 500 to 600 ft. evidently out of control and appeared to crash at—

(Signed) **Lt. W.A. Bishop**

It will be noticed that Bishop was not sure of the exact location where the enemy machine had crashed and in fact was not apparently absolutely certain that it had been destroyed. The reason for this appears in his report. "My engine had oiled up and I glided just over the line." He had something else to think about than the German machine. There was, however, no doubt about it, as the complete destruction of the machine had been observed by other pilots and he was officially given credit for his first victory.

The brief report gives an outline which the imagination must complete. It does not tell us of the rushing machines, spinning, twisting and looping, nearly two miles above the ground, nor of the mad dives at perhaps 200 miles an hour with the engine roaring under a wide-open throttle. And then above the roar of the engine would sound the deadly chatter of the machine guns as they spat forth their streams of tell-tale, smoking bullets. It is, however, enough to give us a fairly accurate picture of the fight. As the two patrols met, Bishop got "on the tail" of one of the German machines, dived

down and fired twelve or fifteen rounds. Apparently the German airman was not seriously hit, but dived steeply for about 600 feet in an effort to get out of his dangerous position under Bishop's gun. Bishop followed him down, however, and, as the lower machine flattened out, closed to within forty or fifty yards and fired another burst of tracers into the fuselage which appeared to hit the pilot. The German machine then fell in a spinning nosedive. But this might be only a trick to get away from the hopeless position in which he had placed himself, because once an enemy machine was above and behind at close range, or "on his tail" as the airmen expressed it, only luck or bad shooting could save him. Bishop was taking no chances of letting his quarry escape, however. Down he went in a great dive of nearly 7000 feet firing all the way, and then when he had reached 1500 or 2000 feet from the ground, with a dead engine and the enemy trenches bristling with machine guns, there was every prospect that his first flight was to be his last and that the best he could hope for was to spend the remainder of the war in a prison camp. There was nothing to do but glide in the direction of his own lines and hope for the best. His luck, however, was with him when he needed it most. He "glided just over the line."

It was one of those strokes of chance which were so important a factor in the success of even the greatest pilots. Richthofen had a similar experience while flying as an observer on the Russian front late in 1915, long before he had a victory to his credit. His pilot flew over a burning town and the engine became choked with smoke. With very little idea of where they were, they barely succeeded in reaching their own troops. In either case, just a little less height, a little less speed, an adverse wind or a lucky shot from the machine guns which the infantry turned on them and the names of Bishop and Richthofen would never have been known.

On March 25, 1917, Bishop's record of one machine looked small beside those of the leaders of that time. Earlier on the same day Richthofen, who had been a fighting pilot for six months, had shot down his 31st victim. Guynemer, the great Frenchman, had thirty-five to his credit and Ball, twenty-nine. Probably Bishop was the last to think that he would very soon exceed those figures.

Those were busy days for the air force. The British artillery was busy all along the line, and particularly around Vimy Ridge where the great Canadian attack was to be launched on April 9. Fights followed daily for Bishop as he and the other machines in his squadron escorted photography and observation planes over the German lines. On March 31 he won his second victory. His report for the day was typically brief but it told all that was necessary to his superiors.

COMBATS IN THE AIR

SQUADRON:	No. 60
TYPE and No. of AEROPLANE:	Nieuport A-6769
ARMAMENT:	Lewis Gun
PILOT:	Lieut. W.A. Bishop
LOCALITY:	10 miles N.E. of Arras
DATE:	31-3-17
TIME:	7.30
DUTY:	Escort
HEIGHT:	15,000 ft.

REMARKS ON HOSTILE MACHINE: TYPE, ARMAMENT, SPEED, ETC.

Albatross Scouts
5 seen
1 engaged

Narrative

While on escort, I went to the assistance of another Nieuport being attacked by an Albatross Scout. I opened fire twice, the last time 50 yrds. range, my tracers were seen to hit his machine in the centre section. Albatross seemed to fall out of control, as he was in a spinning nosedive with his engine on. Albatross crashed at 7.30: Ref. 51B. 29-30.

(Signed) **Lt. W.A. Bishop.**

I was behind Lt. Bishop and saw the Albatross Scout go down in a spinning nose dive.

(Signed) **2nd. Lt. L.H. Leckie.**

The above is confirmed by A.A. (Anti-Aircraft Battery).

Again the destruction of the machine was confirmed by another pilot and the Anti-Aircraft observers as the footnotes indicate. The notation "10 miles N. E. of Arras" indicates that the fight took place far behind the German lines.

A few days more of escort work protecting the bombers which were dropping tons of high explosives on the enemy defenses, the photographers and the artillery observation machines, and then a new duty was added. The German observation machines and balloons which would detect the great concentration of British troops, were to be driven from the sky. This meant almost continuous fighting for the scouts and gave Bishop the chance he always sought to go over the lines alone in search of enemy machines.

On Saturday, April 7, 1917, Bishop was ordered to destroy a particular observation balloon about five miles behind the German lines. As he was about to dive on the balloon, he was attacked by an enemy scout which he drove down after a short fight. Then he proceeded to finish the job he had started on. While he had been engaged with the enemy airplane, the balloon had been hauled down, but he went down after it, firing bursts of tracer bullets into the bag, and at the crew on the ground. Again his engine failed, for the second time in a few days, and he was very nearly forced to land miles within enemy territory. However, when only a few feet from the ground his engine came to life again and he was able to get safely home. It was learned afterward that the balloon had been completely destroyed by fire. Bishop won his first decoration for this exploit, the following concise official notice appearing in the London Gazette on May 26, 1917:

"His Majesty the King has been graciously pleased to confer the Military Cross on the undermentioned Officers and Warrant Officers in recognition of their gallantry and devotion to duty in the Field:

SQUADRON:	No. 60
TYPE and No. of AEROPLANE:	Nieuport No. A-6769
ARMAMENT:	1 Lewis Gun
PILOT:	Lt. W. A. Bishop
DATE:	8-4-17
TIME:	9.30 to 10.15
DUTY:	Offensive Patrol
HEIGHT:	10,000 ft.

REMARKS ON HOSTILE MACHINE: TYPE, ARMAMENT, SPEED, ETC.

1 Double-Seater
1 Albatross Scout
1 Balloon
1 Albatross Scout
2 Single-Seaters
2 Albatross Scouts
and 1 Double-Seater

"Canadian Force
Lt. William Avery Bishop,
Can. Cav. and R.F.C.

"For conspicuous gallantry and devotion to duty. He attacked a hostile balloon on the ground, dispersed its crew and destroyed the balloon, and also drove down a hostile machine which attacked him. He has on several other occasions brought down hostile machines."

The day following the fight for which he had received the Military Cross, was Easter Sunday, but it was not to be a day of rest, for Easter Monday was the day set for the great attack on Vimy Ridge. It was a beautiful, clear day and at nine o'clock in the morning he crossed the lines with an offensive patrol of six machines under his squadron leader, Major Scott. They flew for miles behind the German lines before meeting the enemy they sought. Bishop became separated from the others in the course of the first fight and his report for the day in a few words describes what most men would consider more than enough fighting for a lifetime, to say nothing of having it packed into about three-quarters of an hour on Easter Sunday morning.

Narrative

While on Offensive Patrol at 9.30, I dived after Major Scott, on a two-seater, opening fire twice as he was already diving. Then I engaged a single-seater, he flew away eastwards after I had fired 40 rounds at him, tracers hit his machine in fuselage and planes. I then dived at a balloon from 5,000 feet and drove it down to the ground. It did not smoke. I climbed to 4,000 and engaged an Albatross Scout, fired the remainder of my drum at him, dodged away and put a new drum on, and engaged him again. After two bursts he dived vertically and was still in a nosedive when about 500 feet from the ground. I then climbed to 10,000 and 5 miles N. E. of Arras I engaged 2 single-seaters flying toward our lines. 3 more machines were above and behind. I fired the remainder of my drum into the pair, one burst of 15 at one and the rest at the 2nd one. The former turned and flew away with his nose well down, the 2nd one went down in a spinning nosedive, my tracers hit all round the pilot's seat and I think he must have been hit. Then I climbed and got behind the other three about the vicinity of Vitry, I engaged them and one double-seater went down in a nosedive but I think partly under control, I engaged the remaining 2 and finished my third drum at them. They both flew away eastwards.

(Signed) **W.A. Bishop**

It was afterwards learned that two of these machines had been completely destroyed. His record was mounting fast and it was still only two weeks since his first fight.

On Easter Monday morning, April 9, 1917, the Canadian Corps won a brilliant victory when they swept over the formidable Vimy Ridge which had withstood so many earlier British and French assaults. Then followed days of attacks and counter-attacks as the opposing troops fought beyond the ridge, during which all the British machines were actively engaged. Flying low over the enemy lines, the scouts attacked infantry formations on the ground with machine gun fire, frequently dispersing counter-attacks before they had been launched. Bishop had several engagements during this period but his work was more with the enemy troops on the ground than with hostile aircraft.

On April 20 he won his next victory, the enemy machine on this occasion being the first he had destroyed in flames. His report tells the story in a few words:

SQUADRON:	60
TYPE and No. of AEROPLANE:	N.S.B. 1566
ARMAMENT:	1 Lewis Gun
PILOT:	Lt. W.A. Bishop
LOCALITY:	
DATE:	20-4-17
TIME:	2.58 p.m.
DUTY:	Hostile Aircraft
HEIGHT:	2,000 ft.

REMARKS ON HOSTILE MACHINE: TYPE, ARMAMENT, SPEED, ETC.

No. 329
1 Two-Seater

Narrative

I engaged a two-seater by getting under him and firing with my gun pulled down at a range of 10 to 20 yds. I fired about 10 to 15 rounds, then dived twice, firing from 100 yds. range. I dived a third time, opening fire at 30 yds. range, and looking back after passing, saw smoke was coming out around the pilot's seat. In a few seconds flames were visible and the machine fell in a volume of smoke. I fired 80 rounds in all.

(Signed) **Lt. W.A. Bishop**

Then followed a period of almost incredible activity. Day by day Bishop's reports recorded fight after fight with an ever-increasing toll of German aeroplanes and balloons. At this time he was flying as much as seven and a half hours between sunrise and sunset and scarcely a day passed without several engagements. When one reads with astonishment today of some venturesome flight and wonders at the courage which such a risk demands, it is well to maintain some sense of proportion, and remember that more than ten years ago men like Bishop were day by day and hour by hour for months at a time facing a more certain prospect of death than even the most daring of pilots are forced to contemplate today, and there was nothing beyond the flight but the recognition of a duty performed.

It is impossible in this brief story to go into the details of all of Bishop's fighting but a few of his reports at this time are well worth reading, as they show not only what Bishop was doing but also give a fair idea of what was being done by many other Canadian pilots.

On April 24, he attacked a balloon near Vitry, several miles behind the German lines. His report for the day tells of this without embellishment. "I attacked balloon on ground firing 20 rounds from 800 feet. Gun stopped and I flew away. I came back about five minutes later and again attacked from 800 feet to 300 feet, firing remainder of drum. Bullets were seen hitting balloon but no smoke or flame was visible." This was not the result which he was coming to expect, so he went back after it again three days later. His report for the 27th tells us that "While proceeding to attack the Vitry Balloon I lost my way in the clouds. I discovered a balloon about 800 yds. west of me about 600 ft. up. I attacked it and fired about 60 rounds of Buskingham into it. I passed over and turned to finish my drum, but saw the balloon smoking. I then fired about 10 rounds into the basket as I had seen no one jump out. I flew South then for a few minutes and came to Vitry where another balloon was up. I fired the remainder of my drum at it, but cannot say whether I hit it or not."

The following day, Bishop received notice of the award of the Military Cross and was promoted to the rank of Captain only six weeks after he had joined the squadron. He signalized his quick promotion by shooting down another machine in flames the next day. His report shows how little he had any intention of resting on his laurels.

SQUADRON:	No. 60
TYPE and No. of AEROPLANE:	N.S. B1566
ARMAMENT:	One Lewis Gun
PILOT:	Capt. Bishop
LOCALITY:	Epinoy, E. of
DATE:	29-4-17
TIME:	11.55
DUTY:	Hostile Aircraft
HEIGHT:	14,500 ft.

REMARKS ON HOSTILE MACHINE: TYPE, ARMAMENT, SPEED, ETC.

(1) 1 Single-Seater
(2) 1 Single-Seater
(3) 1 Single-Seater

Narrative

(1) While flying at 17,000 feet, I saw one hostile aircraft 8,000 feet below me. I dived at him from the sun side, opening fire at 150 yds. I fired in bursts of 3's and after about 12 shots he went down in a spin. I followed and fired the remainder of my drum with the exception of about 10 rounds at him. At about 11,000 ft. he burst into flames.
(2) I climbed again to 15,000 ft. and dived at another single-seater. He dived away and I fired about 30 shots at him with no apparent result.
(3) I then saw another hostile aircraft on my own level. I climbed above him and dived from the sun but he dived away before I could get within 400 yds. I fired the remainder of my drum at long range, but could observe no apparent result.

(Signed) **Capt. W. A. Bishop**

It all sounds so ridiculously easy when reported in this simple form that it is well to remember how comparatively few pilots brought down more than five or six enemy machines.

Bishop was now reaching the point where he might have some hope of overtaking Ball who had returned from leave in England and was adding almost daily to his record. This personal rivalry was a tremendous incentive in the flying corps and introduced a sporting element into the work which relieved it to a great extent of its more sombre aspect. Twenty-five machines destroyed was more like a score in some wildly exciting game than the cold record of the death of probably forty men killed in personal combat. Bishop was now filled with ambition to become the leading British pilot and almost daily he spent as much time as possible when off duty practicing on the Petit Bosche. This was a target on the ground representing the vital parts of an aeroplane. The pilot would dive steeply at this target firing as he would at an enemy. He could see where his bullets hit, which gave valuable experience and an opportunity to correct defects in his sighting. This practice was not without dangers that in peace time might in themselves be considered formidable, as it was necessary to plunge at full speed to within a few feet of the earth before flattening out, the whole procedure duplicating the course followed when a pilot was successful in getting "on the tail" of an enemy machine. To the skill acquired in many hours of work on the Petit Bosche Bishop himself attributed most of his success.

On the last day of April, Bishop had nine fights during which he destroyed one enemy machine and forced two others to land. The latter landed on their own side of the lines as the fighting, as usual, was far over German territory. His report shows not only the almost incredible amount of fighting through which he came unscathed, but also gives some idea of the number of fights in which the best pilots engaged without decisive results on either side. It helps one to understand the magnitude of the effort which his ultimate record of machines destroyed really represents.

SQUADRON:	No. 60
TYPE and No. of AEROPLANE:	N.S.B. 1566
ARMAMENT:	One Lewis Gun
PILOT:	Capt. W.A. Bishop, M.C.
LOCALITY:	Lens, Monchy le Preux, Wancourt
DATE:	30-4-17
TIME:	9.45 a.m. 12.15 p.m.
DUTY:	Offensive Patrol
HEIGHT:	

REMARKS ON HOSTILE MACHINE: TYPE, ARMAMENT, SPEED, ETC.

Two-Seaters
Halberstadt Scouts

Narrative

At 10.00 a.m. South of Lens at 10,000 ft. while leading offensive patrol, dived at hostile aircraft and fired 15 rounds with no apparent result. Hostile aircraft dived away Eastwards.

At 10.10 North of Lens at 11,000 ft. climbed up to 2 two-seater hostile aircraft on our side of the line. I fired at one from underneath, firing 15 rounds. Wire cocking device caught in slide, and I returned to aerodrome to adjust it.

At 11.08 South of Lens not having found the patrol I attacked 2 two-seaters doing artillery observation. I dived on the leader and fired 10 rounds at him. He dived away and flew under 5 Halberstadt Scouts. I was 500 ft. above these so I attacked them from above, firing 20 rounds. I then flew away as they had almost reached my level.

At 11.15 South of Lens at 8,000 ft. the three hostile aircraft doing artillery observation returned. I attacked them firing 20 rounds into 2nd machine. He went into a spin and I turned and attacked the last machine. He dived away and I followed finishing my drum into him. He continued diving Eastwards. I could now see 2nd machine still in a spin and only about 1,000 ft. from the ground. The last one evidently landed as he didn't come back.

At 11.25 East of Monchy at 6,000 ft. I attacked from above 5 Halberstadt Scouts who were flying as if to attack the B.E.'s. I dived at them three times and fired in all about 20 rounds. They flew away East.

At 11.30 East of Wancourt at 5,000 ft. I attacked two machines doing artillery observation firing at the rear one. They flew away East. I followed them to Vitry and again opened fire with no result. They came back to East of Monchy and I again attacked, finishing my drum into one.

At 11.45 North of Monchy, I attacked one of the above pair firing at him head on, he flew away East losing height and neither of them came back.

At 12.08 South of Lens at 11,000 ft. I dived on one hostile aircraft doing artillery observation and fired about 60 rounds finishing my last drum into him. He dived away East and landed about Sheet 36C, V 19, in a field.

(Signed) **Capt. W.A. Bishop.**

Even that wasn't enough for one day and at 3 o'clock he was up again and handed in a second report for the same day which showed that he engaged four Albatross scouts at a height of 11,000 feet. "I attacked four hostile aircraft from behind and above. I fired two bursts of 5 rounds each at the leader who had turned. I then fired ten rounds at the rear man with no apparent result. Seeing four more machines diving from above I zoomed up and found they were triplanes. The four hostile aircraft then disappeared."

The nine fights recorded in Bishop's remarkable combat report for April 30, 1917, took place in a little more than two hours in the air. They not only set up a new high record of activity for this extremely active pilot, but also furnished a wide variety of fighting. The report is worth examining again as it requires very little imagination to understand the vivid story which it tells.

At ten o'clock he was leading an offensive patrol over the lines south of Lens at a height of 10,000 feet when he saw an enemy machine below him. Down he went after the enemy, firing fifteen rounds at close range with no apparent result. The enemy dived eastward for home and safety. "No apparent result," may mean much or little. Every bullet may have found its target, the pilot himself may have been wounded but still able to fly, the machine may have been seriously damaged but still under control. No result of his firing was, however, apparent to Bishop.

Only ten minutes after this first fight he was north of Lens on his own side of the lines climbing up to two hostile aircraft at 11,000 feet. He opened fire on one of these from underneath as he climbed up to it, but after fifteen rounds his machine gun jammed and he found he could not adjust it in the air, so was forced to return to his aerodrome some miles away. These were two very large machines which Bishop afterward identified as the first of the great Gothas which were later to become so well known in the daylight raids on London. He was naturally chagrined at the failure of his gun just when it seemed that he had one of the largest of the enemy machines at his mercy.

He was soon up in the air again, and less than an hour later was back over the lines alone south of Lens attacking two-seated observation machines which were serving as eyes for the German artillery. He got ten rounds away at the leader, who then sought protection by diving under five Halberstadt scouts. Bishop then turned his attention to the scouts, firing twenty rounds as he dived at them, but without result. Having lost his advantage of height he flew away.

Only seven minutes later he again encountered the three artillery observation machines which had evidently decided that it was reasonably safe to proceed with the work of ranging their batteries. Bishop immediately attacked, firing twenty rounds into the second of the three machines. It went down in a spinning nosedive completely out of control. As soon as his victim went down, Bishop turned and attacked the third machine. Evidently its pilot had lost heart, as he dived away and Bishop followed, emptying the remainder of the drum of bullets on his gun into him. The third machine also disppeared, so that in a few minutes' fighting the particular batteries which these machines were serving had lost their eyes, and some target behind the British lines was for the time being relieved from enemy shell fire.

The record of these fights in Bishop's reports sounds so uneventful that it is well to remember that a fight with three enemy planes, each of which mounted two machine guns, was a very formidable undertaking because each of these German machines had an observer with a gun which he could fire in any direction and to which he was able to devote his whole attention while the pilot manoeuvred for position. True, Bishop had the advantage of speed, but with bullets pouring at him from six guns, many of which passed through the wings and body of his machine, the odds were far from being wholly in his favor. A single chance shot among the hundreds of smoking bullets that were streaming past him and he would have been the victim instead of the victor.

Having disposed of the artillery observers, Bishop flew south to Monchy where ten minutes later he found the same five Halberstadt scouts, which he had already engaged, about to attack some B. E.s which were observing for the British guns. He was higher than the German machines and had the advantage of position. He dived at them, opening fire when very close, then zoomed up with the speed he had gained in his descent and dived again. This he repeated three times, when the German scouts found it too hot for them and turned for home, leaving the slow moving B. E.s to continue their work for the artillery.

These last two fights which had taken place in the brief space of ten minutes vividly demonstrate the role of the fighting scouts and the tremendous importance of their work to the troops far below. In the fight near Lens he had driven the German observers from the sky, thus protecting the particular British targets upon which they had undertaken to range their batteries, while in the fight at Monchy, ten minutes later, he had engaged enemy scouts which contemplated the same treatment for the B. E.s. Bishop's single-handed success in driving off the Halberstadts made it possible for the old Bleriot Experimentals to carry on with the ranging of the British guns.

In those busy days in the spring of 1917, a scout cruising over the lines at ninety miles an hour rushed from one stirring incident to the next in less time than it takes to tell it, particularly if he sought battle as Bishop did. Only five minutes after he had driven off the five Halberstadts he attacked two two-seated machines observing for the artillery at a height of 5,000 feet east of Wancourt. They flew to the rear and he followed them as far as Vitry, more than five miles behind the German lines where he again fired at them. They were persistent, however, and flew back toward the lines again, and this time he finished the remainder of his second drum of ammunition into one of them without apparent result.

After putting a fresh drum on his machine gun he again attacked, and this time singling out one of the enemy he flew at him head-on, both of them firing as they approached. This proved too much for the Germans, who dived out of the fight and did not come back.

About twenty minutes later he climbed to 11,000 feet when he discovered another artillery observation machine below him south of Lens. He got about it and then dived vertically, opening fire at close range. The German dived steeply, to the east and Bishop followed, firing in all some sixty rounds which finished his last drum. During this time the observer in the German machine was, of course, returning the fire. This machine was forced to land in a field not far behind the German lines.

In one hour from 11.08 to 12.08 Bishop had single-handed engaged eleven different enemy planes, five of which were fighting scouts. The fact that in that length of time he had forced six enemy two-seaters to discontinue their artillery observation, had destroyed one machine, thus killing two of the enemy, and forced another to land, at the same time making it possible for the British observers at Monchy to continue their flight by driving off the threatened attack of the five Halberstadts, gives some estimate of his immense value as an individual fighting unit in the British army.

Nor was his fighting over for the day. After lunch at his aerodrome, he and his squadron commander, Major Scott, went over the lines together at three o'clock. Before long they encountered four Albatrosses at a height of 11,000 feet. Bishop climbed above them and then dived at the leader, firing short bursts of five rounds each. The fight continued, with Bishop and the Major firing as they saw their chance, but with no apparent result. Seeing four more machines diving from above, Bishop "zoomed" up out of the fight to see whether they were friend or enemy and found they were triplanes of one of the British naval squadrons which had just come to that part of the front. The four Albatrosses evidently decided the odds were too much against them and disappeared.

These German machines were painted a brilliant red which indicated that they belonged to Richthofen's squadron of skilled pilots. Bishop believed that Richthofen himself was the leader whom he had engaged and there is reason to believe that he was correct, as Richthofen at this time frequently flew with three others of his squadron, his brother Lothar, Schaeffer and Wolff. In any event it is almost certain that these two must have come together at some time during that month of April when both of them were fighting many times a day nearly every day on the same part of the front.

The colouring of the German aeroplanes was an interesting development of 1917. Early in the spring the German fighting machines began to appear in startling hues. Richthofen had adopted red as his distinctive colour which was the source of the names by which he became popularly known. On the British side he was commonly called "The Red Devil", while to the world at large he has since become known as "The Red Knight." Others quickly followed his lead without any apparent limitation on the expression of individual taste.

Doubtless the colouring of the wings and bodies of the aeroplanes was in the first place simply part of the effort to camouflage the machines, but these experiments met with comparatively little success and it is likely that the later efforts, when every colour of the rainbow flashed across the sky, had less to do with camouflage than with that light-hearted braggadocio which characterized the airmen of both sides. After all the colouring of the rainbow had been employed, fantastic combinations gave considerable scope to individual ingenuity and the Teuton pilots pursued their errands of death on gaudy wings whose vivid tints outshone the brightest of their feathered friends of the air. Pink planes with green noses; black planes with yellow bodies; blue bodies and orange wings; silver planes with gold noses; there was no end to the possibilities of this spring fancy of the German airmen.

The British did not follow the Germans in the painting of their machines, although many of the pilots wanted to do it, and for once the Teuton mind had an opportunity to display a lighter side in the war. In spite of the many variations of colouring, Richthofen's squadron generally used red machines with smaller distinctive markings. At first only Richthofen himself used an all-red machine, but eventually all of his squadron employed the same colour.

April had been a month of intense fighting for both Bishop and Richthofen. On May 1, Richthofen left the front for a six-week holiday with the then unheard of total of fifty-two machines to his credit. Bishop on the other hand began an even more active period of fighting. May 1 was comparatively uneventful but May 2 was a day of almost continuous fighting during which he won his second decoration.

The second fight recorded in the first of three reports earned for him the Distinguished Service Order. The following brief official citation covering this award appeared in the *London Gazette* on June 18, 1917.

"His Majesty the King has been graciously pleased to approve of the appointment of the undermentioned officers to be Companions of the Distinguished Service Order in recognition of their gallantry and devotion to duty in the Field:

Captain Willian Avery Bishop, Canadian Cavalry and R.F.C.

"For conspicuous gallantry and devotion to duty. While in a single-seater he attacked three hostile machines, two of which he brought down, although in the meantime he was himself attacked by four other hostile machines. His courage and determination have set a fine example to others."

His first fight had been on March 25. Thus in less than six weeks of fighting he had won both the Distinguished Service Order and the Military Cross "for conspicuous gallantry and devotion to duty," had been promoted to the rank of Captain, and had destroyed many German aeroplanes and balloons.

The report of the fight on May 2, for which he was decorated, contains a naive statement which once more emphasizes the fact that Bishop was always the pursuer. "I manoeuvred to catch one party of three when just west of the Queant-Drocourt line, as that was the nearest they were coming to our lines." Bishop was not boasting. It was a simple statement of the fact that no matter how far back the enemy observers chose to do their work, that was where they must be attacked.

These three reports are worth examining closely to appreciate what this twenty-three-year-old Canadian, whose courage and determination had "set a fine example to others," was really doing. They disclose that in that one day he had engaged twenty-three different German aircraft, had completely destroyed two two-seaters and thus killed four of the enemy, had fired seven drums of machine gun ammunition, and must have had several thousand rounds fired at him.

Two days later he brought down his next victim. The story loses none of its dramatic effect in the brief statement contained in his report. After the word "Duty" appear the two letters H. A. The duty of Captain Bishop and Lieutenant Fry who accompanied him was to engage Hostile Aircraft. This they did.

SQUADRON:	No. 60
TYPE and No. of AEROPLANE:	N. S. B. 1566 and B. 1597
ARMAMENT:	Lewis Guns
PILOT:	Capt. W. A. Bishop, M. C., Lieut. W. W. Fry.
LOCALITY:	Brebières
DATE:	4-5-17
TIME:	1.30
DUTY:	H. A.
HEIGHT:	5,500

REMARKS ON HOSTILE MACHINE: TYPE, ARMAMENT, SPEED, ETC.

Two two-seaters

Narrative

With Lieut. Fry following me I dived at two two-seaters. I fired twenty rounds at one and turned off, Lieut. Fry diving on and firing. I dived again as he stopped firing and fired about forty rounds, in the course of which the observer stopped firing. The machine did two turns of a spin and then nosedived to earth where we saw him crash. I fired a short burst at long range at the second one which flew away and did not return.

(Signed) **Capt. W. A. Bishop.**

The observers on the ground saw something with their glasses which Bishop and Fry did not see, and a footnote was added to Bishop's report by the ground observers that during the fight five enemy scouts "were 1,500 feet above Capt. Bishop and Lieut. Fry, but during all this time they did not come down." From Bishop's reports and official citations it is quite certain that had the situation been reversed Bishop and Fry would have been streaking down to attack the five Germans.

His next victory came on May 7 after three more days of heavy fighting, when he brought down one of the fast Albatross scouts in flames.

Narrative

I dived from the sun at one H. A. (Hostile Aircraft) going N., and with the speed from my dive I overtook him flying underneath. I pulled my gun down and opened fire from fifteen yards range firing twenty rounds, all of which entered his fuselage. He fell in a spin and smoke was coming from the machine.

(Signed) **Capt. W. A. Bishop.**

May 7 had been favorable to Bishop, but it was a blue day for the 60th Squadron and the whole Royal Flying Corps. Late in the afternoon Captain Albert Ball, the leading British pilot at that time, was killed during a fight with Richthofen's squadron.

A few days after Ball's death, Bishop left for two weeks leave in England, having destroyed more than twenty machines in a little over six weeks fighting. His airmanship, shooting and fighting tactics were steadily improving and his reports indicate that he had also begun to avoid taking unnecessary risks where nothing was to be gained. He returned from leave with fresh vigor and a fixed ambition to become the leading British pilot.

When Bishop rejoined his squadron late in May, 1917, he found a new and exacting task facing the scouts. After the German retreat to the Hindenburg line, the artillery on both sides required continual assistance from the air force in ranging their guns on the vital points within their new zones of fire. This was trying work for the artillery observation machines which were bound to "carry on" in spite of frequent attacks by the scouts and a severe shelling by the anti-aircraft guns whenever they approached the enemy lines. It was also trying work for the scouts.

When not attacking the artillery observation machines, Bishop was as busy as ever over the lines and destroyed three more of the enemy before the end of May. He was now planning an expedition which he had contemplated for some time, having decided to make a single-handed attack on a German aerodrome at dawn in the hope of surprising the enemy as they were preparing to take off for the morning's work. He finally chose June 2 for this extremely hazardous adventure.

He rose before sunrise and just as the first light of dawn was brightening the sky he was speeding over the enemy lines. He flew straight to the aerodrome he had decided to attack but; when he reached it, was disappointed to find no sign of life. He had, however, come too far to give up without an effort and he turned his machine to the southeast in the hope of finding a target. About three miles from the first aerodrome he came to another, but this time the scene was very different. Passing over it at about three hundred feet he saw seven machines out of their hangars with busy groups of mechanics getting them ready for flight. Several of the machines already had their engines running.

He swooped down, raking the length of the aerodrome with his bullets as he passed over. When he turned he saw that one of the enemy was "taxiing" along the ground and about to take off. This was the very chance for which he had waited and often imagined while planning the flight. With his greater speed he was soon immediately above and behind the rising plane and a short burst of fifteen rounds was enough to send it crashing back to the ground. As he turned back toward the aerodrome he found another machine had just taken off. This time he fired thirty rounds at a range of one hundred and fifty yards and the German aeroplane crashed into a tree near the aerodrome. As he turned back again he found two of the machines in the air. He had now lost the advantage of height but he did not hesitate to continue the fight. He attacked one of these machines at a height of 1,000 feet, finishing his drum of ammunition into it before it crashed close to its aerodrome. He then placed a fresh drum of ammunition in his gun and attacked the fourth machine, finishing the whole drum before he flew away.

During all the time that Bishop had been flying back and forth over the aerodrome, he had been subjected to terrific fire from machine guns on the ground in addition to that which he faced from the machines in the air, and his faithful Nieuport was literally riddled with bullets. When he finally turned for home he still was far from safety, for his own aerodrome was a good twenty miles away and his machine and engine had been under a severe strain. For some time he was followed by four enemy scouts which flew directly over him, but to his surprise they did not attack and in spite of heavy rifle and machine gun fire from the trenches, which he crossed at a height of less than 100 feet, he landed safely at his own aerodrome.

This daring exploit won for Bishop the greatest of all decorations for valour, the Victoria Cross. The significance of this award may be realized when it is remembered that of the sixteen thousand Canadians who served with such distinction in the Royal Air Force or its predecessors, the Royal Flying Corps and the Royal Naval Air Service, only two others, Barker and McLeod, were awarded the V.C. Bishop was the first Canadian airman who wore the dull crimson ribbon which means so much to those who served in France in any branch of the service.

The public announcement of the award, which did not appear until more than two months later, for once lost some of the cold official brevity which characterized most of the British citations for bravery.

"*London Gazette* No. 30228
11th August, 1917
War Office

"His Majesty the King has been graciously pleased to approve of the award of the Victoria Cross to the undermentioned Officer:

Captain William Avery Bishop, D.S.O., M.C.,
Canadian Cavalry and Royal Flying Corps.

"For most conspicuous bravery, determination and skill.

"Captain Bishop, who had been sent out to work independently, flew first of all to an enemy aerodrome; finding no machines about, he flew on to another aerodrome about three miles southeast, which was at least twelve miles the other side of the line. Seven machines, some with their engines running, were on the ground. He attacked these from about fifty feet, and a mechanic, who was starting one of the engines, was seen to fall. One of the machines got off the ground, but at a height of sixty feet Captain Bishop fired fifteen rounds into it at very close range, and it crashed to the ground.

"A second machine got off the ground, into which he fired thirty rounds at 150 yards range, and it fell into a tree.

"Two more machines then rose from the aerodrome. One of these he engaged at the height of 1,000 feet, emptying the rest of his drum of ammunition. This machine crashed 300 yards from the aerodrome, after which Captain Bishop emptied a whole drum into the fourth hostile machine, and then flew back to his station.

"Four hostile scouts were about 1,000 feet above him for about a mile of his return journey, but they would not attack.

"His machine was very badly shot about by machine gun fire from the ground."

It was six days later, on the eighth of June, before he won his next victory, although he had been in numerous fights in the meantime. The Germans were employing a new formation which often trapped inexperienced pilots. Six machines would fly together in three layers of two machines each, with perhaps three or four thousand feet between each layer. If either of the lower layers was attacked the machines would dive down and usually catch the enemy, who was most concerned with the fight on hand, completely by surprise. Bishop spotted one of these layer flights and climbed carefully above the top pair getting "on the tail" of one of them before they were aware of any danger. After a few rounds the German went into a spinning nosedive and crashed far below.

All through the summer Bishop was fighting almost every day and sometimes many times a day, but the fights were so similar to those already described that there is no occasion to review them in detail.

From the beginning of the war, superiority in fighting machines had see-sawed from one side to the other. At first the airmen engaged each other with rifles and revolvers. Then some enterprising British observers began strapping machine guns—usually against orders—on their none-too-stable craft and for a while were able to make some show of real fighting. When the Germans developed really efficient mountings for their guns, the British had a very poor time until they were similarly equipped. And so on it went. In the latter part of 1916, the British had faster machines and almost drove the Germans from the sky. Early in 1917, however, the tide turned when the Albatrosses were able to show their heels to the Nieuports. In July of 1917 the tide turned once more when the fighting squadrons received the new S.E.5 which was perhaps twenty-five miles an hour faster than the Nieuport.

The 60th Squadron received their new machines in the latter part of July. Like the Albatross they mounted two machine guns which, quite apart from the greater speed, gave them a marked advantage over the Nieuport with its single gun. This inspired added confidence and fighting spirit in the pilots, and Bishop's victories began to mount even faster than before.

Bishop was undoubtedly one of the greatest aerial marksmen of the war. He was a wonderful shot with a rifle before he took up aviation, and this, with constant practice at the Petit Bosche, developed a deadly accuracy which became more and more infallible as the months passed by.

When he returned to England in August, 1917, he already had a remarkable record. He had destroyed forty-seven enemy aeroplanes and several balloons, had driven down many more with which he was not officially credited, as there was no absolute proof of their destruction, had numberless narrow escapes including a fall of 4,000 feet with his machine in flames, and wore on his breast the ribbons of the Victoria Cross, the Distinguished Service Order and the Military Cross—distinction which had been conferred on no other Canadian hitherto. His record of forty-seven machines also placed him in the forefront of living British airmen, as Ball had been killed in the spring and McCudden had not yet reached the peak of his record of more than fifty.

Shortly after his return to England, he attended an investiture at Buckingham Palace when King George pinned on his breast the three decorations for bravery which he had won. A week later he was promoted to the rank of major and heard that he had been awarded a Bar to the Distinguished Service Order which was equivalent to a second award of the same decoration. The citation accompanying the official announcement indicates that the recommendation for this award was made only a few days before he left France, as at the time of the recommendation he is shown to have destroyed forty-five machines.

"War Office, 26th September, 1917.

"His Majesty the King has been pleased to confer the undermentioned reward for gallantry and distinguished service in the field.

Awarded a Bar to the Distinguished Service Order

"Captain William Avery Bishop, V.C., D.S.O., M.C., Canadian Cavalry and Royal Flying Corps.

"For conspicuous gallantry and devotion to duty when engaging hostile aircraft. His consistent dash and great fearlessness have set a magnificent example to the pilots of his squadron. He has destroyed no fewer than forty-five hostile machines within the past five months, frequently attacking enemy formations single-handed, and on all occasions displaying a fighting spirit and determination to get to close quarters with his opponents, which have earned the admiration of all in contact with him."

No higher words of praise could possibly be written than the simple declaration by the traditionally conservative War Office that this young Canadian had on all occasions displayed a fighting spirit and determination to get to close quarters with his opponents, which had earned the admiration of all in contact with him.

A few days after his promotion to the rank of major and the award of the Bar to the Distinguished Service Order, he received word that he had been granted leave to visit Canada and on September 27 he arrived in Toronto where he received a tumultuous civic welcome.

His visit to Canada was scarcely leave in the usual sense of the word. He was continually before the public and his presence in person provided a tremendous stimulus to recruiting for the rapidly growing training-centres of the Royal Flying Corps which had sprung up in Canada during the preceding few months under the direction of the Imperial Munitions Board. Young men and boys, scarcely of military age, saw before them an amiable youth of twenty-three who, after less than six months with a fighting squadron, had risen from lieutenant to the rank of major, wore on his breast the three premier officers' decorations for valour, and now had more machines to his credit than any living aviator in the Allied armies....

After spending little more than a week with his family in Owen Sound he visited the Royal Military College at Kingston where he had been a cadet when the war began and naturally received an enthusiastic welcome. A few days later he was married to Miss Margaret Burden, of Toronto, a niece of the late Sir John Eaton.

He continued to appear at various gatherings and occasionally to do a little flying which aroused considerable public interest, as people realized that the machine which they saw flying gracefully above them carried the greatest living British aviator. Early in 1918, he returned to England and joined the School of Aircraft Gunnery to which he had been attached. He continued to perform valuable services in an instructional capacity until he again had the chance to demonstrate his extraordinary fighting spirit and deadly marksmanship when he was given command of the 85th Squadron on May 22, 1918, and proceeded to the front for the third time.

For a while Bishop's work was part of the general routine which the close co-operation that now existed between the airmen and the line became fairly well established and the work of the air force resumed its more normal role, he started on a carnival of destruction which had no parallel in the annals of aviation.

It is true that Richthofen and Fonck exceeded his total by a few machines, but in the short period of his active service during 1918 he proved himself beyond question the most brilliant aerial duellist the world has known.

He was only in France about four weeks on this final visit to the front and while he had many encounters from the beginning, in the last twelve days he seemed to go fighting mad, and the official citation accompanying the award of the Distinguished Flying Cross tells a story of indomitable courage, fighting spirit and sheer flying skill beside which the most daring of the post-war flights seem comparatively uneventful.

"London Gazette No. 30827
3rd August, 1918
Air Ministry.

"His Majesty the King has been graciously pleased to confer the undermentioned reward on Officers of the Royal Air Force, in recognition of gallantry in flying operations against the enemy:

Awarded the Distinguished Flying Cross

Capt. (temp. Maj.) William Avery Bishop, V.C., D.S.O. M.C., (formerly Canadian Cavalry).

"A most successful and fearless fighter in the air, whose acts of outstanding bravery have already been recognized by the awards of the Victoria Cross, Distinguished Service Order, Bar to the Distinguished Order and Military Cross.

"For the award of the Distinguished Flying Cross now conferred upon him he has rendered signally valuable services in personally destroying twenty-five enemy machines in twelve days—five of which he destroyed on the last day of his service at the front.

"The total number of machines destroyed by this distinguished officer is seventy-two and his value as a moral factor to the Royal Air Force cannot be overestimated."

It is difficult to visualize what this brief official summary really means. In twelve days Bishop had destroyed four more machines than Rickenbacker, the leading American pilot, did in the whole of his five months at the front. On his last day in France, as many of the enemy fell under his guns as were brought down by the whole of the Royal Flying Corps in the first month of the war. The record of seventy-two machines, which no airman then living had equalled, did not include a very large number which had been driven down but not seen to crash, and there can be no doubt that many of these were also destroyed. Nor did it include several observation balloons brought down in flames. With these facts in mind one understands how full of meaning was the frank official statement that "his value as a moral factor to the Royal Air Force cannot be overestimated."

Perhaps nothing more vividly emphasizes the phenomenal development of aviation during the war than a comparison of the above citation with a quotation from Sir John French's first official dispatch on September 7, 1914. "I wish particularly to bring to your Lordships' notice the admirable work done by the Royal Flying Corps under Sir David Henderson. Their skill, energy, and perseverance has been beyond all praise. They have furnished me with most complete and accurate information, which has been of incalculable value in the conduct of operations. Fired at constantly by friend and foe, and not hesitating to fly in every kind of weather, they have remained undaunted throughout. Further, by actually fighting in the air, they have succeeded in destroying five of the enemy's machines."

It was a long cry from that day to the spring of 1918 when Richthofen's mighty circus of some sixty skilled fighters flew in one devastating swarm and it could be recorded that one airman in the face of such a menace had destroyed twenty-five enemy machines in twelve days. The war in the air had changed vastly in those four years. There was little similarity between the fleet, powerful aircraft of 1918 which often engaged each other at 20,000 feet and the first army machines as described by Major J.T.B. McCudden. "About August 22, 1914, a strange aeroplane flew over us at about 4,000 feet, and the aerodrome look-out reported it to be a German machine, the first we had seen in the war. We all turned out armed with rifles, and about six machines got ready to go up in pursuit. All the machines which went up were loaded with hand-grenades, as the intention then was to bring a hostile aeroplane down by dropping bombs on it."

Development in aircraft having kept pace fairly evenly on both sides, the ever increasing number of machines with their continual improvements in offensive equipment greatly increased the danger. Bishop's survival, unscratched, through those wild days of June, 1918, is therefore all the more remarkable.

Bishop was appointed to the staff of the Air Ministry in June, 1918. About this time it was decided to form a separate Canadian branch of the Royal Air Force and with the organization of this force in view he was transferred to Canadian Headquarters on August 5, 1918. Although plans had been completed, the Canadian Air Force did not come into actual existence before the Armistice, and Bishop therefore saw no more service at the front.

In the meantime he had been promoted to the rank of Lieutenant-Colonel and on November 2, 1918, the *London Gazette* contained the following announcement.

"The undermentioned officer of the Royal Air Force has been awarded the Decorations specified, in recognition of distinguished services rendered:

Conferred by the Government of the French Republic.
Croix de Chevalier, Legion of Honour.
Croix de Guerre with Palm.
"Lieutenant-Colonel William Avery Bishop, V.C., D.S.O., M.C., D.F.C., Canadian Cavalry and Aviation Service."

Thus when the war ended, Bishop at the age of twenty-four was a Lieutenant-Colonel, and had been awarded practically every decoration for valour conferred by the British and French Governments.

Perhaps no finer words have been written of the brave youths of all nations who joined this new fighting service than those of a German, Von Gessler. They are well worth quoting, not only for the splendid sentiment they express, but also as a fitting conclusion to this short history of Bishop's fighting career, since they show so clearly the international recognition of his high place among the greatest airmen of the war.

"History will provide few examples of greater courage and self-sacrifice than that written into the annals of the World War by the daring spirits of all sides who followed their duties and found their fate in the air. They fought in an element new to war; they accepted and braved dangers unknown before; they were the young, the quick, and the keen of all who fought, and admiration for their deeds is non-partisan.

"Into the strife they brought the high ideal of chivalry. Their solicitude for a fallen foe that had won their admiration was almost the same as for a fallen friend. Their deeds have won for them the respect of all who admire sterling valour.

"They came from homes of all countries that participated in the struggle. From the French came Fonck, Guynemeyer and Nungesser. From the British came Bishop, Ball and Hawker. From America came Rickenbacker and his comrades who had succeeded him in the French and British services.

"From our own ranks came Immelmann, Boelcke, and Richthofen, and to Germans their names will always remain dear as the names and deeds of French, British, and American flying aces will always stand out in the records of their own countries.

"But bigger than the national fame that these heroes, friend and foe alike, won as patriots to conflicting causes is the growing international recognition of their achievements, not as partisans, but as men who gave to the world new and unprecedented examples of the highest form of physical and moral courage. Respect for human qualities of this high order knows no frontier."

The sincerity of these words was proved in 1928 when Bishop was the guest of honour at a gathering of German airmen in Berlin and was made an honorary member of their association. Germans have been similarly received in London. In each case sincere tribute was paid to the courage and achievements of former enemies. "Respect for human qualities of this high order knows no frontier."

THIS ACCOUNT BY A LEADING STATESMAN, HISTORIAN AND EX-SOLDIER WAS WRITTEN IN 1930. THERE HAD BEEN TIME ENOUGH FOR BISHOP'S RECORD TO BE SCRUTINIZED; BUT MEMORIES HAD NOT BECOME FUZZY WITH THE PASSAGE OF THE YEARS EITHER. (The author.)

Chapter 3
Praise from Foreign Shores

For any "doubting Thomases" who might dismiss the late George Drew's book on the basis of Canadian self-interest, there are publications in both Great Britain and the United States which indicate, unquestionably, that Billy Bishop was recognized as one of the "greats"...if not *the* greatest!

The United States

The air historians who reside and write in the U.S.A. seem to have no doubts whatsoever about Billy Bishop. In their authoritative periodical, the *Cross & Cockade Journal*, published by the Society of Air Historians, an article appeared by George Shiras in the Winter 1963 issue entitled "Who Is the British Ace of Aces?" The article talks about fighter pilots Ball, Mannock and others and suggests at the conclusion that the greatest may well have been Billy Bishop. It is of interest that Ed Ferko, now being cited by Paul Cowan as "anti-Bishop," is quoted in the article as having read and approved it. (See Research Documents.)

Great Britain

Here also, are seen few derogatory comments about Billy Bishop's record—that is, in the written material by what might be termed legitimate sources. We make reference to several articles complementary in nature, from *Popular Flying*—an authoritative publication in the U.K. from the Thirties. (See Research Documents.)

What about Recent Publications?

One of the newer reference books on fighter pilots was *The First of the Few* by Denis Winter, published in Great Britain in 1982. It is well to remember that this was *after* Paul Cowan conducted his research which led him to question Billy Bishop's record. Winter's book, as the subtitle says, was about fighter pilots of the First World War. He certainly had a great deal of praise for Billy Bishop.

Winter's book deals with a side of Bishop that seems, somehow, to have been overlooked. Bishop's success was measured in the number of victories he had in the air, but he was widely known throughout the RFC as a tactician. Winter refers to an excerpt from an RFC handbook, speaking about indoctrination of new pilots.

In the meantime the CO would be checking progress in an office until he approached the point specified by Major William Bishop:

"To be able to fight well, a pilot must be able to have absolute control over his machine. He must know by the feel of it how the machine is, what position it is in and how it is flying so that he may manoeuvre rapidly and at the same time watch his opponent. He must be able to loop, turn his machine over on to its back and do various other stunts—not that these are actually necessary during a combat but from the fact that he has done these things several times he gets absolute confidence and when the fight comes along, he is not worrying about how the machine will act. He can devote all his time to fighting. The flying part of it will come instinctively."

There was something about him that left one feeling that he perferred to live as he fought, in a rather hard, brittle world of his own.

Winter was, in fact, quoting Air Vice Marshall Sholto Douglas, Deputy Chief of Staff with the Royal Air Force, who was himself a fighter pilot in WWI.

Speaking of Bishop's ability as a flier, Winter uses another quotation:

Good flying has never killed a Hun yet. You just get on with sighting your guns. What counted above all was not flying the airplane but converting it into a flying rifle, held steady to the pilot's shoulder. Such skill might find flamboyant expression.

Bishop suggested a balance between these skills (hiding, seeing, evaluating and diving). He suggested:

"By this time (1917) I had learned nearly all the fundamental principles of fighting in the air and had decided upon exactly what tactics were best for me to use. I had learned that the most important thing in fighting was shooting. Next, the various tactics in coming into the fight. Last of all, flying ability itself."

Bishop said:

I have come to the conclusion that to be successful in fighting in the air, two things were required above all. One was accuracy in shooting and the second was to use one's head and take no unnecessary risks.

Concerning Bishop's marksmanship, Winter quotes Bishop as saying:

I became more and more expert at it with the result that I finally had great confidence in myself and knew for certain that if

I could get a shot in from one or two of my favorite positions, I would be successful in downing an opponent.

Winter goes on to say:

> With this object Bishop had his own personal ground target for practice—his Petit Bosche.

The First of the Few places Bishop as one of the "greats" along with Ball, McCudden, Barker, McLeod, Nungesser, Fonck, Guynemer, von Richthofen and Boelcke. Winter's research must have satisfied him regarding Bishop's place in history as late as 1982.

And, his position was still secure three years later. For example, and this is quoted from Robert Jackson's book *The RAF in Action: From Flanders to the Falklands,* published in 1985:

> His (Bishop's) first combat report described the action:
>
> 10:25 a.m. Staden Hooglede 18,000 feet.
> (i)   Between Staden and Hooglede, 18,000 feet at 10:25 a.m., I turned back a two seater who was approaching our lines, finally closing to 75 yards. After 20 rounds he burst into flame.
> 10:50 a.m. Sailly-Sur Lys 4,000 feet.
> (ii) Over Sailly-Sur Lys, 4,000 feet at 10:50 a.m., seeing one Albatros I zoomed into the edge of a cloud. Albatros passed cloud and I secured position on tail. After 20 rounds he burst into flames.
> 10:55 a.m. Laventie (near) 2,000 feet.
> (iii) After attacking (ii) I saw a two seater EA quite low. I dived at him from the east but he turned and got east of me. After

second burst of 20 rounds he fell in a turning dive, then crashed between Laventie and main road.

Jackson's book goes on to state:

> Bishop's last day in action was even more dramatic. Patrolling near Ypres he saw and attacked three Pfalz fighters, one of which he destroyed quickly. As the others turned to attack him, two more Pfalz dropped out of the clouds and a dogfight developed. Two of the Pfalz suddenly dove toward Bishop, who saw his chance and dived between them. The Pfalz tightened their turns in an effort to get on his tail and collided, whereupon the other two turned away towards their own lines. Bishop went after them, opening fire on one from 200 yards. It went down in flames; the other escaped into a cloud. Next day, Bishop left France for good. He had destroyed 72 enemy aircraft in just over a year of air combat. No other fighter pilot in the 1914-1918 war had achieved as much in such a comparatively short time and in this top scoring bracket only one other—the Frenchman, René Fonck—was destined to survive the conflict.

The dust jacket gives the following information concerning Jackson's book:

> The book also offers an operational history of the Squadrons and all types of aircraft and operations across the world. Using original research from official sources and personal records, Robert Jackson is able to give a totally new perspective on life and action in the front line.
>
> Robert Jackson is a widely published professional writer specializing in military and aviation history. Recent books include *Acro Vulcan, Military Aircraft Since 1945, History of Air Combat* and *RAF Bomber Command 1936-1945*.

Chapter 4

What Paul Cowan Did

T his is a sad and sorry tale. Paul Cowan is employed on the Canadian government payroll with the NFB. He produced, wrote and directed a film entitled *THE KID WHO COULDN'T MISS*. It concerns the war record of the late William Avery Bishop, winner of the Victoria Cross along with every other medal which could be given by the British to an officer engaged as a combat pilot in World War I, together with the coveted Croix de Guerre and the rest of the meaningful decorations of the French government.

According to testimony given before the prestigious Sub-Committee of the Senate Committee on Social Affairs, Science and Technology. . .this is what Paul Cowan did.

The Proposal

He submitted a proposal to his superiors in the NFB, requesting that he be allowed to make a documentary film, telling the heroic story of Billy Bishop. He received approval, together with a budget of $400,000. (See Senate Sub-Committee Material for copy of the proposal.)

Research

He set about to do the research but apparently did not consult any recognized historical sources in Canada, including the Directorate of History of the Department of National Defence; Mr. S.R. Taylor, Official Historian of the Canadian World War One Flyers who comprised the Canadian element in the Royal Flying Corps of the British Army in WWI; or Professor Steven Wise, Director of the Canadian Institute for Historical Studies and author of a recently published 800-page volume entitled *Canadian Airmen and the First World War*.

Instead, he went to Great Britain. He talked to Willy Fry, (an English fighter pilot and a very brave airman) who had flown and fought with Billy Bishop but is now anti-Bishop, possibly for ulterior motives. When Bishop asked Fry to go along on the pre-dawn raid, Fry refused. This may well have created a stigma for Fry which he still carries with him.

Cowan listened to a 1972 tape of Archibald James, a pilot who flew in another Squadron and whose memoires were recorded in an interview for the Imperial War Museum in London, England. The tape contains some rambling suggestions that Bishop's "kills" were inflated. It seems James did not know Bishop, and was not in the same Squa-

dron. James has a reputation, however, for dealing in unsubstantiated rumours.

Cowan contacted Squadron Leader (retired) Joe Warne who served with 60 Squadron in the post-World War II era and became the Squadron's amateur historian (although a later Commanding Officer of 60 Squadron made some unflattering remarks about Warne).

In the research area, it is more important to consider what Paul Cowan did *not* do. A magazine entitled *Popular Flying* published in England had a very great interest in the WWI flying aces. Copies of the magazine are readily available to researchers (including me) and contain a great deal of information about Billy Bishop—all of it favourable. The same can be said for the authoritative American version, named *Popular Aviation*. A reading of this material indicates that most of the pilots who flew with Billy Bishop had a very warm affection for him and had nothing but praise and pride for his exploits. They considered him among the best. (Excerpts from *Popular Flying* and *Popular Aviation* can be found in the Research Documents.)

His Doubts

According to Paul Cowan's testimony, these sources in England gave him reason to doubt Billy Bishop's record and he decided to use the taxpayer's money to make a film, the focal point of which would revolve around the suggestions inspired by Bishop's detractors—few in number though they be. In the movie, the English contacts theorized that Billy Bishop's record of enemy planes downed was inflated—and that in particular the claim concerning a raid on a German aerodrome for which Billy Bishop was awarded the Victoria Cross, was fraudulent.

His Decision

Paul Cowan then proceeded to make his film, slanting it to discredit Bishop. The evidence before the Senate Committee seems to imply, however, that at no time did he obtain new, specific written instructions from his superiors at the NFB. Presumably producers are given wide latitude. Possibly he felt content that they would still let him have his $400,000 even though now, instead of a "great guy" version, he intended to show Billy Bishop as a liar, a cheat and a fraud. He ignored or perhaps never bothered to find out that Billy Bishop stands as one of the most prominent aerial duelists from a generation that bred the likes of Ball, McCudden (U.K.), von Richthofen (Germany), Guynemer, Nungesser (France), and other Canadians such as Collishaw, Barker and MacLaren.

Why?

The obvious question, then, is why? Paul Cowan unabashedly provides the reasons himself. He had some personal views, according to his testimony before the Senate Sub-Committee, about HOW HEROES ARE MADE and WHY A COUNTRY NEEDS HEROES. So, again according to the evidence, he decided on a one-man campaign to discredit wars in general and gallantry in particular by launching his attack on our greatest wartime legend—Billy Bishop, VC.

His Reaction

It is interesting to examine the reaction of Paul Cowan when the public outcry began to be heard. He was in an indefensible position. The film was shot through with half-truths, insinuations and pure fabrications. No problem. Change the category from documentary to docu-drama and it no longer mattered whether Mr. Cowan's premise would stand muster.

The change of designation to docu-drama must obviously be taken to mean that the NFB had made a tremendous error—and the film could no longer be taken seriously.

It remains in circulation, however, replete with a bold-face type disclaimer added to every print which states: "The film you are about to see is a docu-drama. It is a perspective on the nature of heroism and the legend of Billy Bishop. It contains both actual documentary footage and dramatized segments."

This explanatory note flashes by in a few seconds but the viewer is then left with 80 minutes in which Paul Cowan's innuendos assault the eyes and the ears of the audience. The disclaimer recommended by the Senate was much stronger.

What is a Docu-Drama?

What is meant by the word docu-drama? In the film business, it is used to describe actual events, making use of actors and dialogue to dramatize them. In re-categorizing *THE KID WHO COULDN'T MISS*, the NFB is simply compounding the error. A docu-drama must still be based on the truth. Mr. Cowan's film attempts to establish a hypothesis for which he has no hard evidence at all—and in the process he resorts to practically every known trick in the book. To illustrate:

Actual film footage: He has gone to the archives for some footage—but only *one* scene is identified in which Billy

Bishop might appear. (A winter scene is taken from a Russian World War II film!)

Dramatized events: Mr. Cowan is entitled to use poetic licence to show a twelve-year-old Billy Bishop shooting wild game. There is, however, something very seriously wrong with other dramatized events using actors—particularly when he resorts to putting words of sinister criticism about Bishop into the mouth of the man who history records as being Bishop's beloved mechanic...and a man who still revered Bishop many years after WWI (as will be shown later in this *Digest*).

Interviews: These also are permissible in a docu-drama but Mr. Cowan uses the interviews to serve his own purposes in two ways. Firstly, he has the interviewer off-camera suggesting that Bishop's claims were fraudulent and asking the interviewee to comment. Secondly, he takes the comments of persons being interviewed completely out of context. For example, immediately following the suggestion that Bishop was submitting false claims for victories he has Bishop's son, Arthur, on-camera saying that his father was very *competitive*!

Hollywood Film Sequences: Mr. Cowan's film contains some exciting scenes of WWI aerial dogfights, presumably purchased from film studios in Hollywood or elsewhere. In a docu-drama?

Narrative

This is where the writer (Mr. Cowan, according to the credits) does much of his damage. The narration suggests, in a number of segments, that Bishop's claims were fraudulent and that the records were faked. This would be in extremely poor taste, even if it was a thinly disguised piece of fiction; it is inexcusable in a docu-drama which supposedly is based on proven research.

It should be borne in mind that in defaming the name of Billy Bishop, Paul Cowan is challenging:

- The recollections of other Canadian fighter pilots who served with Billy Bishop;
- Every published history book in the schools and libraries throughout Canada;
- The word of Jack Scott, a noted English barrister who was Billy Bishop's Squadron Commander;
- The credibility of the British War Office;
- The process under which the VC, one of the world's outstanding medals for courage, is awarded and even the King of England in whose name the Victoria Cross was given.

Billy Bishop Goes To War

John Gray wrote a successful play entitled *Billy Bishop Goes To War*. This play is in the nature of a musical comedy and the central figure is an actor playing the role of Billy Bishop. It makes no pretense, however, of being a documentary—or docu-drama for that matter.

It portrays Billy Bishop, not always in a favourable light, but at least as a character with a sense of humour, and with tremendous courage...the type of profile that many of his friends remember. Some of the criticism we have heard of the play is that it has Bishop using ungrammatical language which, given his family background and education, would hardly be accurate.

Paul Cowan Gets His Second Wind

Public outrage reached the boiling point when the media began reporting on the Senate Sub-Committee hearings which commenced in October 1985. Cowan and other officials of the NFB made their first appearance before the Sub-Committee on November 28, 1985. They returned for a second time on December 10, after the Sub-Committee had heard from Colonel A. Bauer, Chairman of the Billy Bishop Heritage Trust; and from historians Professors S. Wise, A. Kear and Stewart Taylor.

By this time, the NFB apparently realized Cowan was in considerable difficulty, in regard to *THE KID WHO COULDN'T MISS*. A close scrutiny of the Responses prepared by the NFB, in an attempt to explain some of the supporting data submitted by the pro-Bishop forces, is interesting. The Responses are referred to in some detail in Chapter 11 and are reprinted in full as part of the Senate Sub-Committee material appended.

It is strange indeed that, when put on the defensive, all of a sudden the NFB decides to do a little serious research—but where do they go? The official historians have already spoken their piece. To them, Bishop's record is unassailable! No problem—back to the amateurs, Warne and Fry. These two, who had been trying for several years to punch holes in Bishop's record, must have jumped for joy when they were first contacted by Cowan. His proposed film would give them their chance to "go public" with their anti-Bishop hatred.

Later, when the film comes in for some scathing criticism and Paul Cowan is looking very bad in public, he again turns to his original sources. Fry apparently says he will back up his statements against Bishop, but puts nothing in writing. Warne prepares a lame and ambiguous report, to which reference will be made later in this *Digest*.

Cowan also contacted Ed Ferko, another amateur historian, living in the United States who had fallen heir to some rare documents from German Air Units of WWI and who now sees an opportunity for a little personal aggrandizement. He readily joins Cowan's team of amateurs.

Cowan has done his best in the film, to destroy the legend of Billy Bishop through innuendo and unfounded criticism. Cowan lashes out at those who dare to expose him. He insults Senators. He enlists the aid of his colleagues in the media. He attempts to construct a defence based on foolish hypotheses...Bishop did not have enough fuel to carry out the raid!...Bishop's exploits were suspect by his Squadron mates!...Bishop's contemporaries refused to support a Billy Bishop VC stamp 60 years after his VC raid, etc. The litany of puerile, immature, manufactured attempts to defend his film go on. The ridiculousness of his assertions will become apparent later in this *Digest*.

What of the $400,000?

In reviewing the elements which went to make up the film *THE KID WHO COULDN'T MISS* some 22 minutes was shot as actual footage from the play. Paul Cowan used the sequences from the play "out of context" and John Gray said so—publicly.

This leads to the question as to how the NFB could have spent $400,000 on an 80-minute film. Presumably Cowan needed some of the money to go to England for research, but why? Billy Bishop is one of the best-known historical figures in Canada. As we have said earlier, Paul Cowan did not bother to check with reliable sources in Canada. Could it be that they would not have given him the angle he was seeking? Instead, he must have gone to the U.K. to locate the type of reference sources which would give him the story he apparently felt he needed so badly: "evidence" that Canada's most decorated hero was a fraud and a cheat.

Dates Rearranged

It is common knowledge, of course, that Cowan played fast and loose with history. He changed dates, places and events...all presumably to suit his theme. There are two authentic reports which delineate the countless errors in the film. They make for interesting reading. (See Research Documents.)

To understand the real thrust of the anti-Bishop posture throughout the film, however, one needs to look closely at the most significant date of all—that of the VC raid. It took place on June 2, 1917, while Bishop had 22 victories to his credit. Cowan decided, however, to ignore chronology and his film portrays the raid as taking place just before Bishop was sent back to England for the last time.

The obvious conclusion here is that the filmmaker wanted it to appear that, in one final effort to add to his score, Bishop decided to fabricate the raid on the German aerodrome and, incidentally, to get that one medal which had still eluded him—the prestigious Victoria Cross. It all sounds a little devious, does it not?

Is There Any Damage Done?

''What Paul Cowan Did'' is the title of this Chapter. Perhaps it is time to ask whether it is serious. Of course it is! The heroism of great men has been the very stuff from which the fabric of a country can be woven. Our neighbours to the South have never hesitated to adopt, as part of their heritage, the deeds of war heroes such as Eddie Rickenbacker and Alvin York. England's part in WWI, and WWII's Battle of Britain, will ever be taught to school children in the U.K. through the exploits of Albert Ball, Jimmy McCudden, Guy Gibson and Douglas Bader. There is a von Richthofen museum in Germany! Would these countries allow tampering with their most revered heroes? Of course not—and neither should we. Stories of similar attempts to besmirch the reputations of Ball and von Richthofen will be found later in this *Digest*.

Cowan's Qualifications to Change History

Back to Mr. Cowan for a moment. He is not a scholar, in the ordinary sense of that word. He is not a historian. He is not a researcher. What qualifications does he have to throw out this challenge and, in the process defile the memory of a great man; to cast serious doubts upon the institutions that have made this country great; and last but not least, to heap untold misery upon Billy Bishop's family and friends?

Did he know something that was not known to others? He must have realized the controversy which his film would create, but controversy is not new for a government-sponsored film corporation which has made films about AIDS; nuclear disarmament; pornography; child custody for lesbian mothers; Nicaraguan politics and Maoism.

Also, Paul Cowan quite probably realized that much of the media would come to his defence, whether he was right or wrong. They would defend his actions...and why?

Firstly, Paul Cowan would guess that the media has a conditioned response to any suggestion that published material should be changed, edited or withdrawn. They call it censorship.

Secondly, in the eyes of much of the media the NFB is another of those sacred cows, which operate at the expense of the taxpayer but which must remain unaccountable—else it would lose its objectivity. (Here is a beautiful piece of irony! If *THE KID WHO COULDN'T MISS* is an example of objectivity then Kaiser Wilhelm, Benito Mussolini, Adolf Hitler and Hirohito were out to save the world!)

Chapter 5

The NFB's Circumstantial Case

When one stops to think of it, the maker of a documentary film (and it is not suggested that *THE KID WHO COULDN'T MISS* is) has a very great advantage over the author of a written essay or reference book. The filmmaker doesn't have to include footnotes, annotations or sources. It is usually sufficient to do a few interviews and throw in the occasional quotation.

It was only when Paul Cowan appeared before the Senate Sub-Committee that the public learned just how he had gone about constructing his case against Billy Bishop.

His thinking apparently went something like this:

Witnesses to the VC Raid

There were no "friendly" witnesses—how could there be: it was a single-handed raid carried out when few if any other aircraft were in the sky, at a location at least twelve miles inside the German front lines. As to German witnesses and our own balloon observers—more later!

Fuel Endurance

Bishop didn't have enough fuel to fly the distances he claimed. His accusers in this regard probably didn't know that the Nieuport Scout had a much longer endurance capability in the air than most other planes: two and one-half hours as opposed to the Spad XIII (one and three-quarter hours) or the Nieuport 28 (one and one-half hours).

The Missing Lewis Gun

It seems true that Bishop returned to base without his Lewis gun and the hypothecators have jumped on this, suggesting without proof that, instead of raiding the German airfield, he put down in a safe place, dismantled his Lewis gun, fired it from a "hand-held" position into his own plane, threw away the gun and flew back to his base, shooting off the customary flares and indicating he had had some success.

In the film, Paul Cowan made the flare episode look like a bit of bravado whereas, as the biographers of Billy Bishop attest, he had adopted this as his own little bit of showmanship—and who would blame him? He would have just risked his neck, single-handedly again, to take on the deadly German Jastas (Squadrons), which included the most feared air fighters ever known. Paul Cowan makes it look as if the "Bishop salute" was an infantile trick, designed to pave the way for the story which he would proceed to

invent. In any event the evidence is that he did it at the request of his Squadron mechanics!

Bullet Holes in Bishop's Plane

The official records show that his plane had many bullet holes in it. This was confirmed by Jack Scott, his Commanding Officer (CO) and reconfirmed by Grid Caldwell, who took over as CO a few weeks later when the British authorities at a higher level had asked for further details on the raid.

IT WAS ALSO CONFIRMED BY WHAT IS PROBABLY THE MOST AUTHENTIC SOURCE AVAILABLE TO US—AND ONE WHICH HAS NOT AS YET BEEN MENTIONED IN THE CONTROVERSY: THAT IS, BY AN NCO MECHANIC BY THE NAME OF SGT. MAJ. A.A. NICOD WHO WAS SERVING IN 60 SQUADRON AT THE TIME.

Notwithstanding the official reports, Paul Cowan, stretching poetic licence to its fullest, puts words in the mouth of an actor, portraying the part of Walter Bourne—Billy Bishop's mechanic and longtime friend. The actor suggests as "proof" that Bishop landed and shot up his own plane, a pathetic tale about a very neat "grouping" of bullet holes in the tail plane. This is purely a figment of the imagination of Paul Cowan and is countermanded by every legitimate source—but a neat bit of trickery, all the same.

Unknowledgeable viewers of the film could not be blamed if they came to the conclusion which Paul Cowan was aiming at: that is, that instead of his plane being shot up in a number of places as Billy Bishop (and official sources) were to claim, the words of the phony mechanic could make it look as if Bishop had, in fact, fired the neat "grouping" of bullets into his own plane, to create the illusion that he had been fired upon in the enemy airfield.

There is ample evidence to indicate the validity of the official version that the plane was shot up in many places. Later, we will draw a hypothesis of our own which seems to indicate that Cowan's version is pure fabrication. For now, suffice it to say that the angle of the line of fire would simply have made it impossible to put the bullet holes where Cowan's film said they were.

The Condition of the Plane

This is a further development by Cowan of his "bullet hole" theory. In the film, Cowan makes a big issue of the fact that, if the plane were badly shot up, how would it have been possible for Bishop to take off later the same day on another flight? (It is known from the records, and from Bishop's own statements, that he did this.)

Firstly, Mr. Cowan has a lot to learn about how quickly bullet holes in canvas can be repaired so long as there is no structural damage to the plane—and the official reports indicate that there was not!

But one does not need to look for any official proof of the correct story. IN THE MILLION OR SO WORDS THAT HAVE BEEN WRITTEN ON THE CONTROVERSY SINCE THE FILM WAS RELEASED, NO ONE SEEMS TO HAVE APPLIED A VERY COMMON SENSE, SIMPLE AND PRACTICAL LINE OF THINKING!

Consider this: The official version was that there were many bullet holes in the plane. This seems to be amply verified by observers.

Cowan, in his film, indicates that there was only a neat "grouping" of bullet holes put there by Bishop himself and suggests that if the plane was so badly shot about, then how was it possible to repair it in time for Bishop to take off again the same day; and why were there no written reports of the damage, and the repairing thereof?

No one apparently stopped to remember that, although the plane may have been full of bullet holes, Bishop was still able to *fly it back and land it*! If his aeroplane was still airworthy *after* the raid, despite the fact that the fuselage, wings and tail assembly may have been full of holes, it would have been a rather simple matter for his ground crew to apply glue and fabric and have his precious Nieuport ready to fly again within a few hours.

Site of the German Aerodrome

There has always been some confusion as to the actual aerodrome whose aircraft were caught in the deadly fire of Billy Bishop's gun on that morning of June 2, 1917. Bishop, himself, says he was not sure. The maps in those days were primitive, and who could read one anyway in an open cockpit, all the time keeping an eye out for the wily Hun!

Also, the ceiling when he took off was 500 feet and there was some mist around early on that morning. Bishop's own version was that he located an airport which he thought was Estourmel, found no activity there and turned southeast. He spotted another airport where planes were on the ground with engines running. He believed it to be Esnes or Awoignt. Cowan attempts to make use of this confusion, presumably as a means of casting further doubt as to whether the raid took place at all.

German Records

Here, Cowan pulls out all the stops! The film states that German records (meticulously kept) were thoroughly researched in later years and no one was able to come up with any German reports on the raid.

If the viewer wishes to accept Cowan's "broad brush" treatment, so be it! We will show later, however, that there are some very reasonable explanations. Firstly, despite popular conception, air historians are in unanimous agreement that the Germans did *not* keep accurate records. Secondly, records were not maintained at German aerodromes; only by the Jastas (or Squadrons).

Herman Goering, for whatever reason, issued a strict order that the records of the German pilots were to be consolidated in one area in the Thirties and access to them restricted. (Some air historians give, as the reason, Goering's wish to keep his own record as a German fighter pilot from public scrutiny. After all, he was being sold to the German public, and the world, as the successor to von Richthofen, the Red Baron.)

Thirdly, credible air historians agree that the raid was very likely on the Esnes aerodrome which, at that time, was occupied by Jasta 20. Here, the records are important for what they do *not* show. Bishop's detractors have seized upon the fact that the Jasta 20 records are silent for a period of more than a month, between late May and early July. "Ah ha," they claimed, "there was no record of Bishop's raid."

Air historians (professional ones) take a different interpretation. They suggest that it would not have been in the interests of the German Commanding Officer to admit that his Jasta 20 had been caught napping by a single British pilot. Further, the absence of activity of Jasta 20 would have been exactly what one would expect, if in fact Billy Bishop had disabled three or more of its planes and killed some of its pilots and ground crew.

One significant bit of evidence in support of Bishop is the fact that the names of three German pilots, who were on strength of Jasta 20 in late May, disappeared from the records when once again reports of Jasta 20 show up in early July.

In defence of his film, Paul Cowan quotes Ed Ferko, an amateur air historian in the United States on the matter of the German aerodrome. (More about Mr. Ferko later.)

It seems apparent that the mystery may never be solved. Historian Stewart Taylor has contributed more information on the subject, in a letter to the author dated September 19, 1986, in which he states:

More recent research concludes that Awoignt is a prime candidate. Some researchers have theorized that Bishop may have attacked Estourmel and other such Jasta aerodromes much further southeast as Wassigny, Bohain, and even Guise, close to the Somme.

Bishop had never previously flown operational patrols in that area. Just weeks before he left 21 Squadron as an observer in May 1916, his squadron did move down to the Somme area. However, it is doubtful he flew on any missions before his transfer back to England.

As most of the official allied records covering the periods of Bishop's service flying, both as an observer and later a pilot with 21, 60 and 85 Squadrons RFC/RAF, were either lost or destroyed during and after WWI, historians are dealing with a real dearth of documentation. The same problem exists with German WWI records. During the war a huge amount of documentation was removed from official archives of the three north German cities to protect them from allied bombing. They were stored in mine shafts in Bernberg, between Magdeburg and Halle, in present day East Germany and that which survived the war was shipped to the Soviet Union. Some were shipped back to East Germany in the 1950s but no one in the West has any idea if any WWI aviation material exists amongst these archives.

It is realized that this information offers little by way of proof of what aerodrome was attacked. At the same time, it further complicates the task of those who wish to raise doubts about the raid. If professional historians have not been able to solve the vexing question of "which aero-drome" one must wonder how Paul Cowan can be positive in stating that no evidence exists in German records concerning Bishop's early morning foray?

This *Digest* attempts to report on the "evidence" which Paul Cowan states he used to come to his conclusions. Any material which is available, and which is known to have been used by Mr. Cowan is included. To balance the scales, other written material will be published.

At about this time the reader should (hopefully) get the feeling that he or she is sitting in judgement. That is exactly what is intended.

The NFB film tells one side of the story, supported by Cowan's own statements before the Senate Sub-Committee and in the media. On the other hand, the lengthy and interesting documentation in this *Digest* may well suggest that the Billy Bishop legend is not only true, but deserves now to be even better known by Canadians.

Chapter 6
Comments on the Witnesses for the "Prosecution"

The public is being asked by Mr. Cowan to accept his condemnation of Billy Bishop. Surely then this same public has the right to examine the reliability of those whose "testimony" is used by the NFB to attempt to accomplish this ridiculous task.

While there is some hesitation in making reference to the personalities who have been, wittingly or unwittingly, drawn into this controversy, the credibility of the "witnesses" relied upon by Paul Cowan must be carefully scrutinized.

Joe Warne

It would seem, in reviewing the documentation, that Joe Warne plays a good guy/bad guy role. He is the historian of 60 Squadron with which he served, insofar as we can determine, after World War II. He is known to have co-authored a history of 60 Squadron, in which he has no hesitation about crediting Bishop with seventy-two air victories, including the controversial raid on the German airfield. In fact, he acknowledges Bishop's victories No. 23, 24 and 25 (the planes downed in the raid).

Yet the same Joe Warne, when interviewed by Cowan in preparation for his NFB film, apparently cast serious doubts upon Bishop's claims, including the raid on the German airfield on June 2, 1917. Mr. Warne does a further 180° when, after seeing the film, he brands it as being full of inaccuracies. In a court of law, Mr. Warne could hardly be considered as a reliable witness in support of Mr. Cowan's cause.

Warne adds to his feeble and poisonous innuendos by stating that books and articles about the better-known aces appear in the market or in special aviation journals "except in the case of Billy Bishop." Wrong, Mr. Warne— the proof is published in the Research Documents herewith. Periodicals published in both the United Kingdom and the United States dealt with the war record of Billy Bishop in a most complimentary manner.

Joe Warne's report contains the most ridiculous statement one could possibly imagine. After writing some three and one-half pages (small print by the way) of a report which is critical of Billy Bishop in the severest possible terms, Mr. Warne states: "I have no intention of publishing anything derogatory about Billy Bishop or any other member of 60 Squadron."

How could Joe Warne possibly have been expected to be taken seriously?

The memorandum from Warne, filed with the Senate Sub-Committee, makes reference to a fund-raising activity of the Royal Air Force Museum in Hendon, England—an activity which produces and sells stamped specialized envelopes. The organizers decided to issue a "cover" commemorating Billy Bishop's VC raid. (Incidentally, an indication in itself of how the people around the RAF Museum think about Billy Bishop.) Warne states that some of Bishop's contemporaries refused a request to endorse the Bishop "cover" (although *it was* endorsed by Edgar Percival, a former member of 60 Squadron). Apparently one of those who refused to sign was Grid Caldwell. This was the man who:

- Signed a report as temporary commanding officer, 60 Squadron, providing further details of Bishop's VC raid. Apparently Caldwell had no reservations at that time;
- Commented favourably about Bishop on at least two occasions; one was in connection with an article written *about* Caldwell...the other being a commentary on another article which asks the question, "Who *is* the British Ace of Aces?" and ended up with the suggestion that it was Billy Bishop (see Research Documents).

The only motive which comes to mind, if indeed any of Bishop's contemporaries did refuse to endorse the commemorative stamp, is so tasteless that the author hesitates to mention it. Still, having regard for the hatchet job which the NFB attempts to do on Billy Bishop, it must be said: Were Bishop's contemporaries, out of jealousy, saying about the stamp: "Why him? Why not me?"

Willy Fry

Here again we have a source heavily relied upon by Cowan, but one where the man contradicts himself. Willy Fry wrote a book called *Air of Battle*. He faithfully records Billy Bishop's raid and makes no suggestion that it was fabricated. Still, when consulted by Mr. Cowan on his research expedition to England, Willy Fry, then a man well into his eighties, suggested blatantly that Bishop's claims could not be believed, and that Bishop had inflated his "kills."

In judging Fry's "evidence" it is of significance that Bishop asked him to take part in the raid. He apparently agreed before going to bed but when awakened by Bishop early in the morning of June 2 he declined to go. Make of that what you will!

Fry's account at least establishes one factor. Billy Bishop certainly did intend to go on the raid; otherwise he would not have invited anyone else to go along with him.

It is an interesting reflection on the reliability of Fry as a source to see, right in the film itself, an "on camera" interview with another pilot from 60 Squadron—a bright, healthy-looking elderly gentleman by the name of Cecil Knight, who also flew with Billy Bishop. In a somewhat clumsy attempt to put words in Cecil Knight's mouth, the "off camera" interviewer refers to comments by Archibald James to the effect that Bishop was inflating his claims. Cecil Knight, who gives every appearance of being totally reliable, suggests any such rumour is nonsense. "Not in the character of Bishop as I knew him," was Cecil Knight's summation.

Archibald James' Tapes

Cowan makes reference to these tapes in the film. They were part of an eight-hour interview conducted by David Lance who was interested in getting onto the taped records of the Imperial War Museum, some recollections of RFC pilots from WWI.

It is true, of course, that the aging Archibald James did suggest, on tape, that Bishop was a fraud. The records show, however, that James did not serve in 60 Squadron with Bishop; was not in France at the time of the raid on the German Jasta 20 and may well have been the source of the rumours which began to fly about Billy Bishop's claims in certain circles in the U.K., somewhere around the 1960s. Once again, should we consider Archibald James as a credible witness in support of Cowan's theorizing?

Remember (as we will show later) there certainly was prejudice against Canadians in the RFC—and no wonder. Pilots like Bishop, William Barker, Roy Brown, Raymond Collishaw—colonials all from Canada—were garnering far more than their share of the triumphs. Be that as it may, is it reasonable for Paul Cowan to take the recollections of Archibald James, who will be seen later to come under a certain amount of skepticism by the Director of the Imperial War Museum in London, England, as sufficient grounds to destroy the Bishop legend? Can the meanderings of Archibald James stand up against the recollections of Bishop's own comrades, the investigation of the British War Office and the thorough documentation of historians in the sixty-plus years that have followed?

Ed Ferko and the Amateur Historians in the United States

In the mid-thirties, there was considerable interest in the United States in regard to the exploits of U.S. airmen in the skies over Flanders in WWI. Part of this was based on a desire for the American public to become better informed about their war heroes like Eddie Rickenbacker, and in general about the adventuresome Americans in the French Lafayette Escadrille and the U.S. Army's own aero squadrons.

No doubt the interest was fueled, also, by some excellent Hollywood films such as *Dawn Patrol*. Eventually a number of amateur historical societies officially came together under the title of the Cross and Cockade Society, which, according to its constitution, was a "society of World War I Aero Historians." The purpose: to establish "an informal organization composed of serious World War I aviation enthusiasts."

Prior to this the aviation magazine entitled *Popular Aviation* published many articles of historical significance in regard to WWI flyers of all nations. In fact, *Popular Aviation* did a series of articles on the Air Aces from WWI including Billy Bishop.

We must come now, however, to an assessment of the role played by Ed Ferko in the current controversy. Ferko—a member of the Cross and Cockade Society—produced some information which Paul Cowan reported to the Senate Sub-Committee. The gist of that information is simply that the records of the German's Squadrons known to have been within flying distance of the Filescamp aerodrome at which 60 Squadron RFC was stationed, and from which Billy Bishop took off on his June 2 raid, showed no reports of the raid.

Ed Ferko was contacted by telephone. He confirmed exactly what those who have followed this intriguing attempt to defame Bishop suspected. Ferko inherited some records from a Mr. William Puglisi which had been purchased from a German air historian by the name of Tornhuss. The records are handwritten copies.

Apparently Tornhuss had been given access, in the 1930s, to some of the reference documents held in the archives of the German Air Force. As pointed out earlier, the German records are "silent" in regard to any reference to the Bishop raid. Is this "evidence?"

Also Ed Ferko reportedly did some amateurish detective work. He is said to have calculated the distance back and forth from the Filescamp to the German aerodromes in what is generally known as the Cambrai area and deduced that Bishop could not have been in the air long enough to cover this mileage. He is apparently suggesting that, instead, Bishop found some safe haven on which to land behind his own lines, shot up his plane and flew back claiming victory.

Ferko's theory doesn't stand up. For example, one wonders whether Ed Ferko was aware that the Nieuport Scout flown by Bishop had sufficient fuel for a flight endurance of two and one-half hours—much higher than many of the one-seaters of the day. Bishop's official log shows that on June 2 he took off at 3:57 hours and returned at

5:40 hours; plenty of time to get to the first aerodrome which he found unoccupied, find the second, zero-in on the enemy aircraft in three or four lightning-like thrusts and fly back to safety. (Flying time for Bishop: 1 hour, 43 minutes. Fuel endurance: 2 hours, 30 minutes.)

Somehow Mr. Cowan's "witnesses for the prosecution" seemed to show a remarkable lack of consistency. For example, the same Ed Ferko is quoted in an article entitled "The Two Faces of Chivalry in the Air War" by George Shiras, *Cross & Cockade Journal*, Volume 5, Number 4, Winter 1964, in the following terms: "Ed Ferko read the first draft of this article and made several important suggestions." As will be seen later, the article says some very flattering things about Billy Bishop—and not one derogatory comment.

Air Historians:
The Professionals Versus
the Amateur "Enthusiasts"

This seems to be an important element in the Billy Bishop controversy. Professional historians with academic degrees in history which prepare them for the important work of research (but which make little or no provision for flights of fancy), must locate, study, analyse and put down their conclusions based on evidence. It is, as the term implies, a professional occupation.

Then there are the amateur historians. Usually great guys, well-motivated, who have decided, as an avocation, to take an interest in a specific area. The history of aerial warfare in WWI is a very fertile field for this type of endeavour—with the special attraction of primitive aircraft, makeshift gunnery and observation balloons. There were, too, differing ideas as to the tactical usefulness of aerial warfare and, last but not least, there were the intriguing personalities of those brave few, flying the flimsy kites and engaging in what must certainly have been the last vestiges of the knights of old.

Imagine the delight when an amateur air historian gets his hands on some documents which were long thought to be lost for all time. These people thoroughly enjoyed their "armchair" investigations, but it is well to remember that, with them, it was a game! They were not qualified to express any expert opinion. A debt is owed for preserving the memory of what little chivalry there was in a World War which was for the most part, a slaughterhouse in the mud of France. The amateur historians do represent, however, an area which is ripe for rumour—and even prejudice!

In earlier times, as we will show, the legends of Britain's great Albert Ball and Mick Mannock were challenged by the amateurs. Yes, and there was even controversy about the Red Baron, Manfred von Richthofen himself. And yet, even among the amateur historians (again as we will show) there was nothing but praise for Billy Bishop. In the writings of most of these air warfare hobbyists in both Great Britain and the United States, Billy Bishop's record stood, unimpeachable. To many, he was the greatest of them all.

How really tragic it is that along comes Paul Cowan, speaks to a few of these amateurs who themselves have either been discredited (or even worse have discredited themselves by being inconsistent) and in a film heralded by an agency of the Canadian government, Bishop is shown as a charlatan—and worse.

Chapter 7
Jack Scott on Billy Bishop

So much of the continuing saga of Billy Bishop revolves around interviews, reminiscences on a tape recorder and the speculations of a few latecomers who pride themselves on turning some bit of idle speculation into a whole 80-minute film, damning our greatest legend from the skies over France in the 1914-18 War.

Yet, none of the researchers seemed to think of going back to the writings of the one man who knew Bishop best of all—a man who flew with Bishop. He lived with Bishop in the quarters at Filescamp aerodrome while they were not out looking for the enemy, and he had the responsibility of signing that final certification stating that he concurred in Bishop's report of the famous VC raid on the German Jasta.

Fortunately, Major Jack Scott, MC wrote it all down and he published his personal account of 60 Squadron in 1919.

Let Jack Scott tell us, in his own words, what *he* thought about Billy Bishop. The quotes are directly from Scott's book: *Sixty Squadron RAF*.

At the beginning of this month (on the day before Graves's death, to be exact) W.A. Bishop joined. The son of a well-known family in Montreal, he had passed through the Royal Military College and had joined the Canadian Cavalry, coming over with his regiment with the first Canadian contingent. On arrival in England he very soon applied to join the Flying Corps, and was posted as an observer to No. 7 Squadron. After a tour of duty in France in this capacity he went home to learn to fly, and was posted to us almost as soon as he had got his wings.

It was curious to notice how quick the mechanics of the squadron were to recognise Bishop's quality. Only a few days after his arrival at the squadron the sergeants gave a musical evening to which the officers were invited, and it was observed that one of the very few toasts which were proposed by them was that of Bishop's health, although at this time he had only destroyed one enemy machine, and none of his fellow-officers had, as yet, any idea of the brilliant career that was in store for him. This occasion, on which he got his first Hun, was remarkable for the fact that his engine failed, and forced him to land very near the front-line trenches. He only, in fact, just succeeded in scraping over. The failure of the engine was due to his inexperience in allowing it to choke while diving. Having landed in a very unhealthy spot, he got rapidly into a dugout occupied by some field gunners, and, with their help, moved his machine every half-hour to prevent the German artillery shelling it. During the night he borrowed a toothbrush from the gunner officer, and with this contrived to clean the sparking plugs of his engine. Having heard nothing of him, the squadron had already reported him missing, when he succeeded in getting a telephone message through to say that he was safe.

The next day, Sunday, 'B' Flight, five strong, lost two pilots: one, Milot, a French-Canadian Major, who was killed; the other, Hervey, who had already gained two Military Crosses as an observer and promised very well, was forced to land on the other side by anti-aircraft fire. On this patrol Bishop, who had just been promoted captain, got two Huns and a balloon, having had five or six combats. On Monday 'C' Flight (Bishop's) went out without the flight commander, and only one, Young, returned; this meant that in three days ten out of eighteen pilots were lost, and had to be replaced from England by officers who had never flown this particular type of machine, because there were none in England. . . .

Hostile balloons also were constantly attacked during April and May, and Bishop, Ross, Molesworth, and Penny did considerable execution.

Hardly a day passed during April and May without Bishop destroying at least one Hun machine, and on June 2, 1917, he visited an enemy aerodrome near Cambrai—a long way over—by himself at dawn and found seven machines on the ground with their engines running. They began to take off and he destroyed four, returning safely with *his machine considerably shot about by machine-gun fire from the ground*. For this exploit, *after three months* of remarkably fine work, he was awarded the Victoria Cross.

Scott quotes a report from "one of the pilots" from 60 Squadron, as follows:

The work has been fairly hard lately: two patrols in the morning, one generally at dawn and the other about noon, with 'wireless interruption' in the afternoon. The latter is rather a strenuous job. This is how we work it: When a Hun two-seater begins to register on any part of our front, a telephone message, giving his height and locality, is immediately sent through to the wireless squadron. Each scout squadron in the wing takes it in turn. As soon as the Recording Officer receives the message, he sounds a horn. Three of us who are standing by in readiness immediately jump into our machines, and the leader gets hold of the position and height of the Hun. Then we push off as quickly as possible to the lines, and a sort of 'hide-and-seek' begins. We try if possible to hide in the clouds and approach the Hun when he is off his guard. He, on the other hand, departs hurriedly into Hunland when he spots us, and as soon as we go he comes back to carry on his job. We then turn on him again, but he is off like a flash, and so it goes on until the next three machines relieve us. It is really quite amusing at times, and, although we do not often bring our man down, we give him such a devil of a time that he hasn't much of it to spare for his companions on the ground. Our 'stunt merchant' (Bishop) is good at this game, and continues to add to his score, seldom coming back without firing his red light. He works by himself a lot now, preferring to surprise the Hun by hiding rather than by trying to get him in a scrap. Wish I could do the same. I always feel so fagged after a patrol, that I haven't got the energy or the patience to sit up in the clouds waiting for a chance to bag a 'lone Hun.'

Quoting again from a squadron mate's letter, Scott says:

The Major seemed pleased to have me back, and they all had great stories to tell about our 'stunt merchant,' who had been putting up a jolly good show by bringing down umpteen Huns. His star turn was the shooting up of an aerodrome. He started off at dawn by himself and arrived over the aerodrome he had planned to attack. Finding that there was nothing doing here, he pushed off to look for trouble elsewhere. Suddenly he saw the hangars of another aerodrome. He attacked these with much gusto, and when the Huns came up to do him down, he crashed two of them and drove another into the trees. He also managed to flatten out a large number of mechanics and put pukka wind up the rest. You can imagine how the fat old Huns ran, as nothing like this had ever happened to them before. I believe his name has been put in for something big in the decoration line.

Scott continues, in his book, to speak favourably of Bishop, as follows:

By this time, Bishop was back in France commanding No. 85 Squadron and was doing wonders. Much of his success was due now, as always, to his extremely accurate shooting, the importance of which in aerial fighting it is almost impossible to exaggerate.

The significance of the comments of Major Scott cannot be underestimated. He was a prominent barrister from an excellent family background. It is scarcely conceivable that he would lie! Admittedly, Scott cannot provide proof that the aerodrome raid took place. He was prepared, however, to sign a document that told of the many bullet holes in Billy Bishop's plane. THAT in itself should be sufficient to disqualify all of the theories about the raid put forward in Paul Cowan's film.

Note should be taken, as well, of the reports, excerpts of which appear above, which were written by Bishop's contemporaries in 60 Squadron. Their tone is obviously one of good fellowship, mixed in with some little awe at Bishop's deeds.

What is the relevance of Major Scott's book in regard to the current Billy Bishop controversy? That is a deduction left to others. This *Digest* attempts to put forward all of the data. . . anything that might have a bearing on whether Billy Bishop was a superb air fighter and whether his report on the German aerodome raid is truth or fantasy.

Chapter 8

Further Circumstantial Evidence Confirming Bishop's Raid

Some six years after the publication of George Drew's book, *Canada's Fighting Airmen*, he wrote an article for *Popular Flying* magazine (England) published in March 1936.

Paul Cowan keeps on saying there was no confirmation. In his article George Drew (bless his heart) took the time to describe how it was that he and others received all the necessary confirmation they needed. George Drew stated in his article, in that part dealing with Billy Bishop's raid, as follows: ''This daring exploit, *which was confirmed in the next few days by German pilots*, who were taken prisoner, won for Bishop the greatest of all decorations for valour, the Victoria Cross.''

George Drew also tells a heck of a lot about Billy Bishop, in describing what took place when Bishop returned to the combat zone, this time in command of 85 Squadron. By this time he was a precious commodity and his death would have been a severe blow to morale; and of course to his family. The Drew article states:

Under instructions, he flew very little during his first ten days at the Front but even though he confined his activities largely to executive duties, he added two more victories to his list. Then he threw caution to the winds and in the next 12 days demonstrated beyond all question that he was the greatest aerial fighter the world has known.

In those 12 days, he destroyed 25 German aircraft, 12 of them falling under his guns in the last three days. He was then ordered to return to England immediately and appointed to the staff of the Air Ministry. Those in authority thought he was too valuable as a living example to young pilots to take any more chances with his life.

Now seriously, does this sound like the attitude which the British High Command would take towards a pilot, about whom, as a few insignificant detractors said in later years, ''everyone knew that he was cheating on his kills'' (a quotation attributed to Archibald James).

As George Drew says in his conclusion to his article:

Bishop has been successful in peace as in war, but he is still the same cheerful, lovable Billy Bishop that he was during those hectic years when the Royal Air Force was made up of mere boys, and in days of single combat, when a pilot's life was pitched on a higher plane of excitement than will probably ever be possible again.

The George Drew article will be found among the Research Documents. It makes for great reading and should, for all time, spell ''finale'' to the dismal attack upon Bishop and his record by Paul Cowan and the NFB.

Chapter 9
The Clincher

There should not have been any question about the validity of Billy Bishop's claim in regard to the raid on the German airfield. Paul Cowan, however, decided to raise doubts which even to him must have seemed flimsy.

As a result, it has been necessary to go through the lengthy exercise of bringing forth the extensive circumstantial evidence so that the theories advanced in the NFB film would be shown for what they are: hollow, pitiful, tragic, sinister and without a shred of substance.

In the unlikely event, however, that there could be any reasonable person who might still believe the innuendo and downright lies in the film, it was felt that somewhere, some place there would be that incontrovertible piece of evidence—that final and uncontradictable argument—which would clinch the case.

It exists; and it was so obvious that it was nearly missed! Paul Cowan's claim hinges, largely, on the proposition that the holes in Bishop's Nieuport were put there by Bishop himself who, instead of carrying out the raid, landed in a convenient field, unhooked his Lewis gun, shot a neat circle of holes in the tail of his aircraft, threw away the gun and came back to Filescamp aerodrome, shooting off flares and claiming that he had raided a German Jasta and shot down three planes.

Enter Mr. Bob Bradford, Director of the National Aviation Museum in Ottawa, Ontario. The museum contains a replica of the Nieuport used by Billy Bishop while he was with 60 Squadron. Mr. Bradford is an acknowledged expert in vintage aircraft and, as such, is thoroughly familiar with this particular Nieuport.

The author visited the museum on September 17, 1986 to discuss the characteristics of the Nieuport. Mr. Bradford was, of course, fully aware of the NFB film. He stated, willingly and unequivocably, that the version which Cowan would have us believe is *just not possible*. The Nieuport, if landed in a field, *could not take off again* without assistance from ground personnel!

The facts are unbelievably simple:

- The plane could land in a field (although those who have studied the terrain in the area south of Arras in 1917 will realize that most of the ground was either torn up with shell fire or was being used for support trenches or ammunition dumps);
- Once landed, the pilot would have a devil of a time bringing the plane to a full stop, because the Nieuport had *no brakes*;

- If the pilot were to shut off his engine, his chances of starting it again unassisted would be nil;
- If the pilot were to dismount leaving the engine at idle speed the plane would continue to move forward or nose-dive into the ground.

Assuming, if we still wish to fantasize, that Bishop disengaged his gun, jumped some six feet to the ground, fired off rounds into the tail and was able, somehow, to get back into the cockpit he would still have an insurmountable problem.

Why? Well, even on a smooth field the tail of the Nieuport tended to rise in the air when the pilot revved up the motor to commence taxiing for takeoff. (In fact, Cowan manages very nicely to demonstrate this right in his own film in several scenes where Nieuports are taking off and there are at least two ground personnel steadying them until the plane starts to roll.) It is difficult to see how, in the light of this expert opinion from the Director of the National Aviation Museum, anyone could take any part of Paul Cowan's film seriously.

To be doubly sure, the author screened all available film footage of Nieuports in the takeoff mode. In every single instance, the takeoffs were assisted by ground personnel. Moreover, the violent sideways and up-and-down movement of the tail section of the plane was clearly evident.

This, of course, has to be the clincher.

Mr. Bradford confirmed also another point about which there may have been some contention. That is, the possibility that Billy Bishop could have disengaged the Lewis gun from its mount in flight, which seems to be the most plausible explanation as to how he arrived back at Filescamp minus the gun.

Mr. Bradford stated, unquestionably, that, although it would be difficult, the feat certainly could be accomplished, particularly by someone who was very familiar with the gun's mechanism. Billy Bishop was an acknowledged expert with firearms, while he was still in grade school. He was one of two pilots in 60 Squadron who were known to put in inordinately long hours at target practice. It seeems he could have done it easily!

It should be noted that there is some confusion regarding the particular Nieuport flown by Billy Bishop while he was with 60 Squadron. The plaque in the Canadian Aviation Museum indicates that it was a Nieuport 17. Armorer's reports indicate, however, that the Nieuport 17 was equipped with one Vickers and one Lewis gun. It is known for certain that the plane flown by Bishop, in the early part of his war when he was with 60 Squadron, was equipped with only one Lewis gun.

The only other notable differences between the two planes were in the matters of speed and endurance. The Nieuport II had a maximum speed of a little more than 90 miles an hour with endurance in the air of two and one-half hours. The Nieuport 17 is shown as having a maximum speed of approximately 110 miles an hour with an endurance of two hours. There is some evidence that some 17s had only the Lewis gun.

Author's Note: Having presented 'The Clincher' is there any need to say more? Yes indeed! Cowan has succeeded in 'muddying the waters' in regard to Billy Bishop to a very serious degree. You are being asked to arrive at a decision. There are still some areas to explore before you can be sure you know the truth!

Chapter 10
British and Colonial Prejudice

There is always some hesitation about using the very word prejudice! It seems justified, however, in this instance. Remote as it might seem, the attitude of the British towards "Colonials" may be of more than casual significance in sorting out what went wrong in the Billy Bishop matter.

First, a personal anecdote. My own regiment—The Royal Winnipeg Rifles—landed in England in September of 1940, and went immediately to Aldershot Camp, which to many represents the heart and soul of the British Army. "Another batch of Colonials," was the greeting from both the military and civilian population. This was my first brush with the Britishers who used expressions like "Imperial" and who ignored the fact that Canada had been independent since 1867, when the BNA Act was passed in the English Parliament.

That was in 1940. One can imagine how it was for that generation of Canadians who went to fight for the Mother Country some 25 years earlier.

The attitude towards Canadians in the Royal Flying Corps is described in an exchange between Senator Hartland Molson and Dr. Steven Wise at a meeting of the Senate Sub-Committee on November 17, 1985:

Senator Molson: Does that not suggest that there are perhaps causes of jealousy other than the disbelief in the (Bishop's) record?

Dr. Wise: There is much evidence of that, Senator. Bishop was one of about seven thousand Canadians who transferred from the CEF to the Royal Flying Corps...In the first days of the war they were looking for the hunting and shooting kind of person; but flying became a deadly and important business by the mid-years of the war, and although it is true that the Canadians, as Colonials, often met with a rather mixed reception in RFC and RAF messes, by mid-1918 we have it on British testimony that a third of the aircrew on the Western Front was Canadian.... I do not for a moment doubt that there was a good deal of tension and antagonism between Canadians and the Australians and their British counterparts.

The Senate Sub-Committee received an excellent, informative report from the Royal Military College Club of Manitoba (see Senate Sub-Committee Material). The submission was prepared by several qualified historians. In regard to Bishop's relationship with the Royal Flying Corps, it stated:

Bishop flew for the Royal Flying Corps, even though he was a Canadian. The Canadians did not have a separate air force at that time. The British flyers were all gentlemen, drawn from the upper class. Gentlemen, although well-known for their chivalry, were not generally raised to be tough and competitive. Bishop was typically un-British. He was not from the upper class, he had a highly competitive, very determined personality with an intense desire to increase his score and obtain recognition. Regardless of his abilities as a fighter pilot, he could never have been accepted as one of the British upper class.

Bishop's relationship with Lady St. Helier (an English dowager who opened her home for hospitalized servicemen) could easily have instilled jealousy and anger. Why was she helping a Colonial rather than one of the English pilots, such as McCudden or Ball?

Bishop was a loner. He had few close friends, so there were no allies to help him defeat any unwarranted negative publicity. The very nature of being a loner tends to create enemies of people who do not understand.

Bishop set his goal at being number one. This required the dethroning of other aces; a very effective way to make enemies.

Of the British Empire's top seven aces, the first and second were Canadians, Bishop was the first and Collishaw was second. Of the remaining five, two more were Canadian, one Australian, one South African and one British. This record alone is enough to damage British pride.

Furthermore, there is evidence that Bishop may not have been alone in being disliked by British pilots. Canada was making a major contribution to the air war and by 1918...was sending two hundred pilots over monthly, and by the end of the war a Dominion with ten percent of the Empire's population was producing a third of the British air force. For this major contribution little attention is given in *War in the Air* (British official history of air war published in six volumes) to the contributions made by airmen from the Colonies.

Looking at Jones' action, and at the British pride, seeing the way that the British air history treated Canadians, and reviewing the dismal record of top ace positions held by England, the potential is definitely there for Bishop to have enough enemies, in his Squadron, in the press, or back in Britain to be sources of derogatory rumours.

An excerpt from the preface of Dr. Wise's book, *Canadian Airmen and the First World War*, lends further credence to the RMC Association's submission:

From a Canadian perspective there is another deficiency in *War in the Air* of which its authors, Sir Walter Raleigh and H.A. Jones, were probably quite unconscious. British air forces of the First World War—the Royal Naval Air Service, the Royal Flying Corps, and the Royal Air Force—were multi-national in composition, drawn mainly from the British Isles but also, and to a substantial extent, from many parts of what was then the British Empire. Raleigh and Jones may have assumed, with Sir David Henderson, a wartime commander of the RFC, that 'the more people of British origin are mixed up together in this war the better'; at any rate, little attention is given in *War in the Air* to the contributions made by airmen from the colonies.

The attitude towards Colonials in general—and Bishop in particular in view of his spectacular record—seems well established. In view of this, how much credibility can we give to the statements of Willy Fry, an Englishman who flew with Bishop?

By the same token, Joe Warne, who provided Paul Cowan with much of the data used to discredit Bishop, obtained his data from British pilots and British sources—including the admittedly prejudiced Ira Jones. (See text later.)

Incidentally, this same Joe Warne claimed, in his statement filed with the Senate Sub-Committee, that British periodicals—and the British version of the *Cross & Cockade Journal* in particular—had refused to print articles about Bishop. Our Research Documents prove differently. One is led to surmise that Warne's utterance might be just some more of the British prejudice, carrying over from the long-dead attitude towards Colonials (or is it dead?).

Chapter 11

Rebuttal

The rebuttal of the NFB's case against Bishop should be a relatively simple, straightforward matter. It is recognized, however, that in setting aside the arguments used by Paul Cowan more than a few simple statements are needed. Therefore, this Rebuttal is fully supported in the Research Documents published herewith.

THE KID WHO COULDN'T MISS

The film says Bishop was cheating on his claims. To support this proposition, Cowan used the statements of Archibald James made in the tape to the Imperial War Museum, together with some rather vague statements attributed to Joe Warne. In addition, a former pilot, Willy Fry, made a few veiled suggestions.

Who Stands for Bishop

Firstly, no one *needs* to stand for Billy Bishop, in regard to his Victoria Cross. This award stands by itself. It is given by the reigning monarch of Great Britain on recommendation of his or her advisers. There has been too much written about the awards of the Victoria Cross to ignore the validity of that award! At the date of this writing we have been unable to gain access to the records of the Victoria Cross custodians. It is not that they do not wish to cooperate. It is partly tradition and partly the fact that they simply cannot believe that anyone would doubt the veracity of the Commonwealth's highest decoration for valour.

The author of this *Digest* has, however, been in communication with Sir Godfrey Place, VC, CB, DSC who is the Chairman of the Victoria Cross and George Cross Association, Old Admiralty Building, Whitehall, London, England. In a letter dated September 12, 1986, Sir Godfrey states:

Air Marshall Bishop died just as this Association was being formed so I am afraid we really have no more information about him than is to be found in the various standard works on the VC or the First World War. Such archives as we get of holders of the VC are normally handed to the Imperial War Museum with whom I expect you have been in correspondence.

Sir Godfrey Place, who won his VC for a raid in Norway in a midget submarine, made a further statement in this letter which has tremendous significance. He writes:

In case it is of interest to you, this Association has always taken the view that there is no 'grading' of VCs—none should be considered 'greater' or 'lesser' than any other: simply, that *those at the time in a position to judge the deed took great pains to collect all the evidence and deemed it appropriate to make the award. And so it should remain with Air Marshal Bishop*.

Hopefully, the real import of Sir Godfrey Place's statement will be understood. IF COWAN'S INNUENDOS AGAINST BILLY BISHOP ARE ALLOWED TO STAND, THEN THEY REPRESENT A SLUR AND DEFAMATION OF ALL HOLDERS OF THE VICTORIA CROSS—PAST AND PRESENT.

Who else stands for Bishop—most of the pilots who served with him and the Chief Aeroplane Mechanic (Sergeant Major Nicod) of 60 Squadron.

Who else stands for Bishop—every writer of every article we could find written about Bishop from the Thirties to the Sixties—and right through until 1985.

No Confirmation

This is a misuse of words. Of course there *was* confirmation in the sense that, in his best judgement, Bishop's Commanding Officer (Major Jack Scott) was willing to certify that the raid which earned Bishop the Victoria Cross took place. We can assume that the British War Office made its own investigation, in accordance with required custom. Is this not confirmation?

Now, if Cowan was talking about *eye witnesses*, even there the record is interesting. A careful search of the documents will find that, at least in one instance, some of the ground crew stated that they had been advised by observers in balloons of the Allied Forces that they had watched the raid and had reported back by telephone.

Cowan, in defence later, attempted to say that this could not be true as Bishop had taken off in poor visibility and the German aerodrome could not be seen from the balloons. Yes, but it would have taken him half an hour to reach his objective and the weather reports indicate that by the time the raid would have taken place, conditions had improved. Also it was nearing the summer solstice. There would have been an early sunrise. One would have to study the controversy in regard to the balloon observations and make one's own decision as to who is correct on this particular matter.

The Holes in Bishop's Aircraft

Once again Cowan challenges Bishop's version at having been shot at by implying that the holes were self-inflicted. The Chief Aero Mechanic of the Squadron, Sergeant Major Nicod, speaks of numerous bullet holes in the plane. Jack Scott included similar information in his official report. Grid Caldwell, who took over from Jack Scott and was asked to submit a further confirmation, repeated in his report that the aircraft was full of holes.

We believe we know the source of Cowan's suggestion that there was a neat grouping of bullet holes, as if from Bishop's own gun. Apparently there was such a grouping, and these were very close to the back of Bishop's headrest. This was reported by Sergeant Major Nicod and also by E.W. Molesworth, who was a fellow pilot in Bishop's Squadron at the time.

Nowhere, however, does it state that this small grouping were the *only* bullet holes in Bishop's plane. In any event, Cowan has absolutely no backup for the theory which is put forth in the words of an actor but which is meant to imply, of course, that Bishop landed and shot the holes in his own plane.

The removal of Bishop's Lewis gun from his plane in flight is a major cornerstone in Cowan's argument. Cowan seems to feel that if he could prove that it was not possible for a pilot to remove the Lewis gun in flight, then Bishop must have landed and shot up his own aircraft.

Really now! How much evidence does one need to rebut this silly theory being put forward in the NFB film? Well firstly take a very good look at the actual photographs of the gun mount. In firing position, the gun rested on top of the upper wing. When the pilot wanted to change drums (which was practically every time he was in the air fighting) he had to drag the Lewis down into the cockpit. If the pilot could replace the drum, he could also twist the thumbscrew or turnbuckle and release the mounting. In fact, in the instructions for a pilot before he took off, he was warned to ensure that this particular thumbscrew or turnbuckle was properly tightened.

Admittedly, it might be difficult to remove the Lewis gun in flight—but this is a long way from what Paul Cowan is implying...that it is impossible!!

Experts in the field will say, "but what about the Bowden cable which went from the joy stick up to the trigger mechanism?" Sorry to deflate anyone who wants to argue the point...but the author of this *Digest* personally saw this type of cable disengaged in seconds flat.

If, as many people believe, in the haste of getting away from the airfield, and in the excitement following the raid, Bishop tried to reload an ammunition drum, it is likely that he got into a real foul-up. It would have been prudent to get the Lewis gun out of his way as the easiest solution to the dilemma. This, then, would have left him free to make his escape.

Supposition? Maybe. But certainly as believable as the cockamamy story that Cowan would have us swallow!

Fortunately, there exists an excellent picture of Billy Bishop checking the mechanism of his Lewis gun (see Research Documents). The Nieuport pilots went up with three ammunition drums carrying 97 rounds in each drum. In flight, they often had to change drums and they did this by holding the joy stick (which controlled the aircraft) between their knees, as changing the Ammo magazine was a job which called for both hands.

If Billy Bishop could pull the gun down into his cockpit, as seen in the picture, and remove the ammunition drum, it would probably have been even easier for him to twist the turnbuckle and remove the gun altogether.

This seems to shoot holes in Paul Cowan's theory, as mouthed by the actor playing the part of Bishop's mechanic, in which the latter states, rather positively, that it would be impossible for the pilot to remove the Lewis gun, while the plane was in flight.

Another theory concerning what might have happened to Bishop's machine gun was outlined in Denis Winter's book, *The First of the Few*, as follows:

Ira Jones (fighter pilot with 74 Squadron) noted his bewilderment on being allowed to fly away when his single Lewis gun had been ripped from his machine by slip stream.

This is the same Ira Jones who showed something of an anti-Bishop attitude in his book, *Tiger Squadron*.

Billy Bishop has never mentioned what happened to his machine gun but Paul Cowan's film makes the suggestion that Bishop landed and took off his gun to shoot up his own plane. If Ira Jones' Lewis gun, mounted on the upper wing of his Nieuport, could be "ripped from his machine by slip stream" would it not be reasonable to suggest that the same thing may have happened to Bishop's Lewis gun?

Time Enough?

We understand now, from what might be a very authoritative source from within Cowan's milieu, that no less an authority than Mr. Ed Ferko has come up with the theory, after studying the maps, that Bishop simply did not have enough fuel to carry out the raid. (If true, a somewhat belated attempt to buttress the weak arguments put forward in the film.)

Sorry again for the doubters. Published herewith is

an actual map. The flying time to complete the whole raid was somewhere around an hour and 43 minutes. The mileage, round trip, was 81 miles. The actual timings as reported by Grid Caldwell in a follow-up report for the RFC were:

Time left aerodrome . . . . 3:57 am
Time arrived at hostile aerodrome . . . . . . 4:24 am
Time arrived back . . . . 5:40 am

The map shows that the distance from Filescamp to Estourmel is approximately thirty-nine miles. Esnes, now generally accepted as the site of the raid, is four miles south of Estourmel. The mileage from Esnes back to Filescamp is approximately thirty-eight miles; hence, Bishop must have covered approximately eighty-one miles of "direct line" flying, plus a few miles circling and diving on the aeroport. Assuming he was "tanked-up" he would have had enough fuel for more than 200 miles.

So much for the suggestion from Mr. Cowan's side, that Bishop would not have been able to fly the distance he claimed, due to the short endurance of his aircraft.

See map of B.E.F. operations 1917 on next page.

B.E.F. Operations 1917

Filescamp to Estourmel 39
to Esnes 4
to Filescamp 38
—————
81

Flying time   54 minutes
Endurance—Nieuport Scout   2 to 2-1/2 hours

In his report filed with the Senate Sub-Committee Joe Warne makes two obvious errors in regard to the time-in-air and Bishop's fuel supply. He states that Bishop left the Filescamp Airport at 3:57 a.m. and landed back at his base at 5:40 a.m.—a total of 1 hour and 43 minutes. His statement then indicates that Bishop "logged two hours flying." There appears to be an error of 17 minutes in Warne's calculation.

In the same statement Warne says that "it is likely that the Nieuport would have exhausted its fuel supply in about 1 hour and 20 minutes." We have the official flight endurance performance charts which showed the Nieuport II at 2-1/2 hours and the Nieuport 17 at 2 hours. Bishop was certainly flying a Nieuport Scout Model with 1 Lewis gun as armament; this is shown as having fuel for 2-1/2 hours in the air. (See Performance Chart in Research Documents.)

Mr. Warne's calculations were made very recently. In its task of verifying Bishop's raid, the RFC would have checked the matter of fuel capacity very closely. One could hardly imagine that the British authorities would overlook these simple, easily-checked factors. They would not have wanted to be caught out in a recommendation which had

to stand full scrutiny through military channels, all the way up to the King himself.

Later in the same paper Warne puts forward another totally unfounded hypothesis. He is speaking of whether Bishop landed in the French sector and suggests that: "If he switched off his engine, this could have confirmed the fact that he wouldn't have had sufficient fuel for the stated length of the flight." Perhaps Joe Warne could be excused for not knowing, but it was not difficult for this author, as reported elsewhere in this *Digest*, to determine that a pilot could not hope to land a Nieuport Scout, and take off again, without assistance!

The Jasta 20 Records

Most leading military historians now believe that the Bishop raid was carried out on a temporary airfield at a place called Esnes. It is known that, on June 2, 1917 this location was occupied by Jasta 20, comprising approximately 15 pilots.

The film suggests that the German records were "scoured" after the war and no trace could be found of any raid. It is a fact that the historical records of much of the German Air Force in WWI were destroyed while placed in storage in Dresden, Germany in World War II. It seems factual, however, that a German historian by the name of Tornhuss managed, through an arrangement with Air Marshall Herman Goering, to have access to the German Air Force material in the 1930s.

Ed Ferko notes that the Jasta 20 records were "silent" for a period of some 24 days following June 2, 1917—the date of the Bishop raid on the airfield. He suggests that the Germans were meticulous record keepers and would certainly have recorded the loss of planes and men. This may be a valid assumption.

On the other side of the argument, however, some inferences can be drawn. For example, a Jasta comprised of some 12 planes has four of its vehicles knocked out, with a number of its personnel killed or wounded. Can we really expect that particular Jasta would be in a position to make reports, considering the amount of loss and devastation from Billy Bishop's gun? Also, we have evidence to indicate that Jasta 20 was at the Esnes airport on a temporary basis and was en route to a destination further north. Being in a mobile state, this Jasta may not have been keeping its records up to date.

Another supposition (and we consider it to be a fair one) is that, to coincide with Ed Ferko's information to the effect that there was no activity reported, the possibility exists that Jasta 20 was put out of action by Bishop's raid; hence, there certainly would have been no activity to report.

To refute Ed Ferko's line of argument that the absence of records would indicate that no raid took place, there is now some strong evidence to the effect that the names of

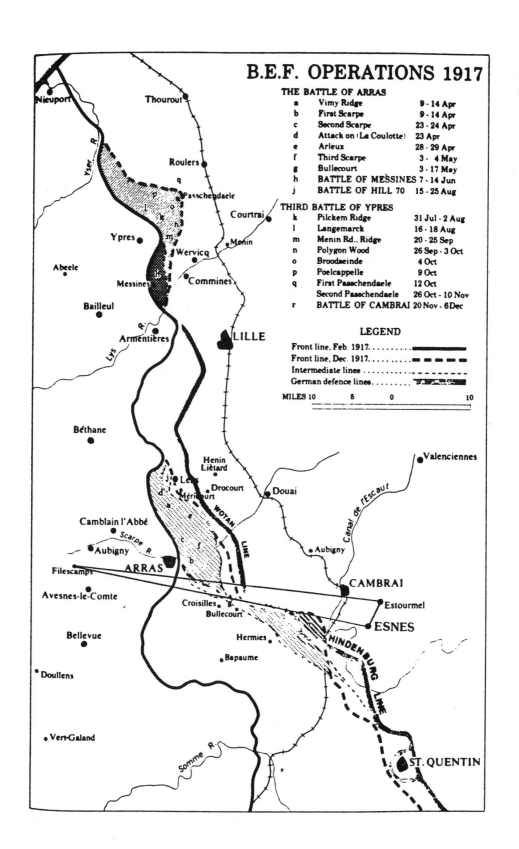

B.E.F. OPERATIONS 1917

THE BATTLE OF ARRAS

a	Vimy Ridge	9 - 14 Apr
b	First Scarpe	9 - 14 Apr
c	Second Scarpe	23 - 24 Apr
d	Attack on (La Coulotte)	23 Apr
e	Arleux	28 - 29 Apr
f	Third Scarpe	3 - 4 May
g	Bullecourt	3 - 17 May
h	BATTLE OF MESSINES	7 - 14 Jun
j	BATTLE OF HILL 70	15 - 25 Aug

THIRD BATTLE OF YPRES

k	Pilckem Ridge	31 Jul - 2 Aug
l	Langemarck	16 - 18 Aug
m	Menin Rd., Ridge	20 - 25 Sep
n	Polygon Wood	26 Sep - 3 Oct
o	Broodseinde	4 Oct
p	Poelcappelle	9 Oct
q	First Passchendaele	12 Oct
	Second Passchendaele	26 Oct - 10 Nov
r	BATTLE OF CAMBRAI	20 Nov - 6 Dec

LEGEND

Front line, Feb. 1917 . . . .
Front line, Dec. 1917 . . . .
Intermediate lines . . . .
German defence lines . . . .

MILES 10   5   0   10

three German pilots disappeared from the records of Jasta 20 during the period in question.

In support of the Bishop raid, surely the disappearance of the names of three pilots from the records, during the period just after Bishop shot up the airfield and its planes, allows one to conclude that these may well have been the personnel who were killed and injured during the raid. The German pilots have been identified as Baurose, Giessler and Heiss. Data provided by Major E. Guth, German Military Historical Department, Frieberg, Germany states implicitly that no other details on Jasta 20 exists. (This data is in the Proceedings of the Senate Sub-Committee.)

Theoretically, one can take the assumption from Ferko's records that no activity took place. Theoretically, also, one can take the assumption that, because Jasta 20 did not report any activity, Bishop's objective of neutralizing a German unit was successful. As well, some reasonable explanation would have to be given for the fact that three German pilots were struck off strength of the Jasta 20 during this particular period of time.

We are indebted to Wing Commander Ira (Taffy) Jones, DSO, MC, DFC, MM for at least one favourable comment indirectly supporting Billy Bishop (although it is well known that Taffy Jones was a strong supporter of Mick Mannock in his rivalry with Bishop to be the top Ace). In his book, *Tiger Squadron*, Jones talks of an incident where he told the official air historian (U.K.), the late Mr. H.A. Jones, that little credence could be placed in the German information.

A quote from his book follows:

After some discussion, we put to them the best of known facts.
On June 19, 1918 Major (later Colonel) Billy Bishop, VC, DSO, MC, DFC, who was then commanding 85 Squadron, shot down five Huns before breakfast, and Captain Cobby, DSO, MC, DFC, No. 1 Australian Squadron, shot down one Hun after tea. These were the only victories claimed that day by the Royal Air Force.
In reply to our query, the German Air Ministry said they had lost neither pilots nor aircraft on June 19th. I know for a fact that that statement was a lie. Captain Cobby's victim was lying, riddled with bullets, in my hangar at Clamarais North aerodrome, near Saint Omer, on the evening in question.

So much for the accuracy of German statistics.

Squadron Leader (retired) D.W. Warne

In his statement, Joe Warne gives information concerning his own background, indicating that he has had a personal interest in RAF history dating back prior to 1941. He states: "I am considered to be the expert on 60 Squadron history." It should be noted in this regard, that Warne's reputation as Squadron historian was questioned by S/L J. Maddocks, the current (1985) CO of 60 Squadron. (See reference later in this chapter.)

Warne states, in regard to Albert Ball: "...virtually all of Ball's claims whilst with 60 had been substantiated..." It is difficult to reconcile this with evidence given to the Sub-Committee by historian Stewart Taylor (proceedings of the Sub-Committee on Veterans Affairs of the Standing Senate Committee on Social Affairs, Science and Technology, October 17, 1985, appendix VA-1-B, page 3A:5) as follows:

When one considers the great difficulty the first biographer of Albert Ball had in the late Thirties while attempting to identify Ball's victories it is somewhat satisfying to know that it has been possible to corrolate a higher percentage of admitted German casualties with specific claims made by Billy Bishop almost 50 years later.
Historians have been able to identify thirteen of Ball's total of forty-four victories, nineteen of Mannock's seventy-three victories and eighteen of McCudden's fifty-seven victories.

Remaining with generalities for the moment, it is wondered how Warne can justify his statement published as an Appendix to the Senate Sub-Committee Hearings—a statement which condemns Billy Bishop and in which Warne raises considerable doubts as to whether the raid took place—with other statements attributed to Warne.

For example, one must wonder how Warne harmonizes his doubts about the raid with the information he apparently gave to the NFB, in his position as "Official Historian" of 60 Squadron RFC, to the effect that Bishop's victories number 23, 24, 25 are admitted. These are the three German aircraft which Bishop reported as destroyed during the raid which Warne presumably disputes!

Historian Stewart Taylor reports in his evidence before the Senate Sub-Committee on October 17, 1985 concerning Joe Warne as follows: "I have a confidential letter Joe Warne wrote to me. This is a critique on his 60 Squadron article and never mentions Billy Bishop, but he did say this: '—which leads me to the Bishop film by the National Film Board of Canada. I enjoy that film more each time I see it, in practise! Initially, I tried to count the historical/factual/chronological errors but gave up.' "

This is the same Joe Warne whose evidence is now being used by Paul Cowan to support the contentions made in the film!

A conversation, reported in the *Toronto Star* on April 17, 1985, might very well place the statements of Joe Warne in their true perspective. The same Squadron in which Billy Bishop served in the early part of the war—that is, 60 Squadron of the Royal Flying Corps—is still today a unit in the Royal Air Force. The CO in 1985 was Squadron Leader John Maddocks.

Warne is said to have told Paul Cowan that "It was common knowledge that Billy Bishop faked some of his claims in regard to enemy planes shot down.'' To this, Squadron Leader Maddocks replied that 60 Squadron has ''no doubt whatsoever'' about Billy Bishop's integrity and bravery and ''we are very proud that he was in our Squadron.''

Maddocks reported to the *Toronto Star* that he had talked to Warne, who told him that ''The producers' opinions are entirely their own.'' Maddocks wrote to Billy Bishop's son, Arthur, stating:

''It does seem to me perhaps to be another case of the media trying to down the name of a great man, when he is no longer around to defend his corner. I'm sure there were occasions when your father's gallantry went unrecorded and undocumented, occasions which would have merited further recognition.''

Willy Fry

Reference is made to an incident in which Willy Fry was invited, by Bishop, to take part in the raid on the enemy aerodrome. This is mentioned in a comment by Senator Hartland Molson (Proceedings 7-11-85 page 5:13) as follows:

Senator Molson: It seemed to me that, in the National Film Board film, there was a lot of evidence which seems to come from Willy Fry. Have you read Willy Fry's book *Air of Battle*?

Dr. Wise: Yes, I read it some time ago.

Senator Molson: In that, he describes that Bishop, at a mess party the night before, invited him to go with him as Ball was no longer available. Willy Fry said he was not interested. According to the book, in the morning, on his way out around 3 o'clock, Bishop stopped at Willy Fry's room and asked him if he was coming and Willy Fry's response was that he had a hangover and he turned over.

One cannot help wondering, hearing since then that Willy Fry has spoken to many people and expressed his doubts about this whole thing, if, having refused to go on that raid, which turned out to be a great success, Willy Fry has not regretted it for the rest of his life; perhaps it made it a little difficult for him to say what a wonderful exploit it must have been, when he could have been on it and was not.

According to the testimony of Senator Molson, Willy Fry in his book apparently makes no mention of any questions concerning the veracity of the reports in regard to Billy Bishop's raid. Senator Molson stated: ''. . . he makes no mention of this question. His book was printed and published in 1964, and he goes through the whole business of the Bishop raid; he does not say that he thinks it was fraudulent. He said that afterwards, in his older age, for reasons best known to him.''

Paul Cowan's film suggests, as a major issue, the close grouping of bullets in the tail plane of Bishop's Nieuport. Unfortunately Mr. Cowan must have been somewhat less than thorough in his research. He readily points to William Fry, one of Bishop's Squadron mates, as a source of criticism of Bishop. Yet, Fry in his book, *Air of Battle* gives a very explicit explanation of that small cluster of bullet holes. Fry remembers ''clearly seeing a group of about five bullet holes in the rear half of his tail plane, the elevator, within a circle of not more than six inches in diameter at the most. Whatever machine was on his tail must have been very close indeed to achieve that group.''

It might be argued that Fry was being cynical, but there is no reason to suggest that was so. As has been stated elsewhere in this *Digest*, Fry's book, *Air of Battle*, is complimentary, wherever reference to Billy Bishop is included.

It seems safe to conclude that, in referring to the bullet holes in the tail plane, Fry was saying in his 1964 book that Bishop must have had a very narrow escape from an enemy plane which was within a few yards of him when the pilot fired his guns.

Perhaps, with the passage of time, the memory really does start to play tricks. Willy Fry may well have told Paul Cowan, in 1981, that he had some doubts about Bishop's record—and the aerodrome raid in particular. On the other hand, in *Air of Battle*, Fry seemed to have no reservations at all about the raid. He stated, regarding Billy Bishop's award for the aerodrome attack:

This must surely be a very unusual case of a Victoria Cross or any high honour being awarded on the word of the recipient only as to his exploit and without any witnesses or participants. Our CO (Jack Scott) knew Bishop so well as to believe in him implicitly, as did the whole Squadron and higher authority.

Perhaps special emphasis should be directed towards Fry's use of the words ''the whole Squadron.'' This is hardly consistent with the comments of Archibald James, given in his tape to the Imperial War Museum; and, neither for that matter, would Fry's comments in his book be in accord with the damaging statements he is said to have made later concerning Billy Bishop's integrity.

Another reference which might impute an ulterior motive to Willy Fry is stated by Stewart Taylor in discussion concerning Billy's ability as a Flight Commander (Proceedings Senate Sub-Committee 17.10.85): ''Yet, the occasion on which he did not lead his flight and it was led by Willy Fry, they ran into real trouble and could not handle it.''

Concerning Fry's presumed reluctance to accompany Bishop on the raid, Mr. Taylor states:

Everybody in Bishop's Squadron knew that he wanted to attempt this flight. Willy Fry says in his book that Bishop came to him the night before and said that he was going to do it, and Fry said that was fine. Bishop arose early that morning at about three o'clock—and Fry was Bishop's flight leader—and asked if Fry was coming. Fry turned over and went back to sleep. In a situation like that you are separating the men and Fry did not want to have anything to do with it.

The statements supposedly made by William Fry should probably be weighed against those made by Jack Scott, Bishop's Squadron Commander.

Common sense would indicate that Fry may very well have had a motive to condemn Bishop. It is hard to suggest any motive on the part of Major Scott, unless it would be that of "reflected glory" in that Bishop was a member of his Squadron.

Scott had no reason to acquire additional credit; his own war record was of a most exemplary nature and he had won gallantry awards. Scott was a well-known barrister who came from a prominent family and had earned an enviable reputation in legal circles in the United Kingdom.

He was hardly the type of person who would knowingly falsify records, or for that matter, who would enter into a conspiracy with Billy Bishop or anyone else, in regard to the certification of official reports. Scott is quoted, in two separate instances, as having given an opinion in writing to the effect that the raid actually took place.

Another interesting reference, by way of evidence supporting the contention that the raid took place, may be found in what is described as a "confidential report" made to the Headquarters of 13th Wing, that was the formation of which 60 Squadron was part, dated June 30, 1917 (some 28 days after the raid) signed by Captain Grid Caldwell who succeeded Scott as Commander of 60 Squadron which reads as follows:

> Reference our telephone conversation of today, herewith is information required. Time left aerodrome 3:57 a.m.; time arrived at hostile aerodrome 4:25 a.m.; time arrived back 5:40 a.m. Personal evidence only. Damage done: 17 bullet holes. Trailing edge of lower plane shot away in two bays. Distance: 30 miles. Aerodrome south of Cambrai.

The contradictions are significant, to say the least. Fry suggests the raid never took place; Scott is prepared to sign a certification that it did. Taking into consideration motive, known reputation of Scott and Scott's position, the probability seems to rest on the side of Scott. Caldwell substantiates Scott's statement.

Ed Ferko

This amateur historian did not enter the picture until long after the film was released. According to our information, however, he apparently made some statements which were reported by Paul Cowan to the Senate Sub-Committee and which are reviewed now in this chapter.

The Ferko statement provides information concerning the reporting system involving the Jastas or Jagdstaffeln (air fighting units) of the German army. The point at issue is whether there would have been a record containing evidence of an attack on June 2, 1917 from the German unit involved, in regard to the raid carried out by Billy Bishop.

The Ferko statement deals, in part, with the activities at Jasta 20 and attempts to rebut with evidence given to the Senate Sub-Committee earlier by Air Historian Stewart Taylor, suggesting that Jasta 20 was, in fact, out of action for a considerable period following the Billy Bishop raid. The Ferko statement:

> The J. 20 KTB. (work diary) notes failed to show much activity between May 27 and July 11 of 1917. It is not because the Staffel had been severely damaged on June 2, but rather that when Tornhuss took the notes from the original Jasta 20 KTB, there was nothing of worth there....

This is a personal judgement of Ferko. There are no grounds! Ferko provides no explanation for his comment! He is apparently historically sound in that Jasta 20 made no combat reports for 44 days from May 27 to July 11, including 39 days immediately following the raid by Billy Bishop. This was at a stage in the war when, presumably, the German High Command would have been expecting a maximum effort from their flying units.

Mr. Ferko suggests that the absence of any combat notes from Jasta 20 during this period was because "there was nothing of worth there other than personnel movement in and out of the unit." This is hardly credible. Ferko's statement does suggest that German reports presumably covering this period of time, clearly show the "lack of activity near the channel." Under ordinary circumstances, one might be expected to weigh the statement and decide whether it has any substance or not. It should be remembered, however, that this statement is being offered in evidence to refute another statement which is crucial to any adjudication on the question of whether the raid did or did not take place.

The absence of combat activity on the part of Jasta 20 for a period of some 39 days immediately following the Bishop raid represents strong circumstantial evidence that, for some reason, Jasta 20 was put out of action; and a reasonable assumption is that the Bishop raid had some adverse effect upon Jasta 20's ability to engage in combat.

Ferko would have us believe that this absence of reports was due to a lack of activity and this was a general condition in that part of the war zone at that time. His suggestion lacks sufficient substance bearing in mind that it is being made in an attempt to refute the claim of a man who had already established his reputation as one of the greatest combat fliers of WWI; and a man who, by that time had already established a record of 22 confirmed victories over enemy aircraft.

Ferko's statement must be considered also in light of three factors:

- Extensive testimony before the Senate Sub-Committee, from noted historians, indicated that much of the material comprising the German records of air activity in WWI were destroyed and/or were no longer available;

- The official historian for the WWI fliers in Canada, Mr. Stewart Taylor, indicated that in fact he does have a record of pilots who left Jasta 20 on or shortly after June 2, 1917. (Further evidence concerning this statement is available later.);
- In the final paragraph of his statement, Ferko suggests that the records of Jasta 20 "are extensive and quite complete." It certainly would have been helpful to the Senate Sub-Committee if, as part of his statement, Mr. Ferko had produced evidence that such records exist, or did exist.

Ferko's Letter

Paul Cowan uses Ed Ferko as a source of information. It would appear that Ferko was not consulted before or during the making of *THE KID WHO COULDN'T MISS.* So far as we can determine, he became involved only after the NFB film was publicly challenged.

Ferko wrote a letter to Paul Cowan, from his home in Salem, Ohio. That letter, dated November 22, 1985, offers crude criticisms of Colonel Bauer, and historians Stewart Taylor and Professor A.R. Kear. About the Senators he says: "Strange behavior by supposedly educated people who should know better."

He refers to a comment in the evidence by Stewart Taylor that, "Billy Bishop had a mission when he went to France. That was to shoot down enemy machines." Ferko dismisses this as, "Sheer bullshit! Bishop hadn't the slightest idea of shooting down German machines when he went to France."

Ferko's letter of November 1985 regurgitates a lot of information about German aerodromes. It apparently matters to Ferko, because he states he has records involving some aerodromes—but not all. In this regard, Arthur Bishop's Book *The Courage of the Early Morning*, written about his father and based on conversations and family papers, states:

Bishop had no idea where he was. He had lost his way in the cloud and had flown further into enemy territory than he intended. When he descended from the overcast he found himself over a deserted aerodrome. So he hunted around for another field and a few minutes later he sighted the shadowy shapes of hangar buildings away to the right.

Ferko then, in his letter to Paul Cowan, attempts to recreate the Bishop raid. "If you can find a good map of the Cambrai area it would help you to visualize what was going on," he states.

Ferko sketches out what he states is "Bishop's alleged route" saying that it is "likely he followed the straight line old Roman Road from Arras to Cambrai, etc." Aerial photographs of the area, which are easily found, indicate rather clearly that Mr. Ferko has no idea of the so-called "navigating" which the World War I pilots were required to do.

Most roads, villages and farms had long ago been obliterated by shellfire. Usually, the pilots headed in the general direction of German territory. When they finished they hightailed it for home, hoping to pick up their own aerodrome or, as is frequently quoted in the reports of the time, they landed at any convenient friendly aerodrome and asked for directions.

Ferko goes to some length to rake what might be called an "old chestnut out of the fire." That is, the suggestion that the German Air Service Intelligence became irritated by reports in Allied newspapers and magazines of the Bishop raid. According to Ferko, the Germans conducted an investigation and reported that no such raid had been carried out. Surely Mr. Ferko has heard of the saying 'all's fair in love and war'?

The Bishop airfield raid had great morale effect. Also, as we have shown elsewhere in this *Digest,* British Intelligence were convinced sufficiently of its effectiveness to order similar raids throughout the rest of the war. One can well imagine, then, why the Germans did not want to admit that one of their crack Jastas had been caught napping by a lone British (Canadian) airman.

Ferko's suggestion that German Intelligence reports denied Bishop's claims is hardly compatible with the known fact that, in March 1928, he was feted at a luncheon in the Berlin Aero Club. Billy Bishop was made the first and only foreign member of the German Aces Association.

There are two other comments in Ferko's letter which might give some clue as to Ferko's reliability. In one place he is speaking of a Canadian historian and says, "Perhaps he is an exponent of the school which believes if you can't blind them with brilliance, baffle them with bull...t." In another section, he introduces some German "data" about Bishop's claims, saying: "Regards Bishop's dream list."

Incidentally, Ferko *does* state in his letter, "I am no respecter of titles or degrees...I am neither an historian nor an expert or authority."

The Phelan Book

It would seem that much of Paul Cowan's case rests on evidence provided by Ferko, who proudly describes himself as a member of the Cross and Cockade Society (U.S.). In this *Digest*, an attempt has been made to countermand the efforts put forward by Mr. Ferko, who concluded, in a letter to Paul Cowan dated November 22, 1985: "Nothing even remotely suggests there is any evidence W.A. Bishop did what he is said to have done on 2 June, 1917."

There is no wish to discredit Mr. Ferko publicly, but he leaves little or no alternative. In 1966, Joseph A. Phelan, a United States Air Force veteran and "a member of that dedicated group of WWI enthusiasts, the Cross and Cockade Society," published a book entitled *Heroes and*

Aeroplanes of the Great War in 1914-1918 (Grosset and Dunlap). He devotes a section to: Air Marshall, William Avery Bishop, VC, CB, DSO, BAR, MC, DFC.

The only other WWI aces profiled in the Phelan book were: Roland Garros, Max Immelman, Albert Ball, Jean Navarre, Werner Voss, and Charles Nungesser.

Joseph Phelan provides an account of the aerodrome raid in exact detail. He suggests the aerodrome was Estourmel occupied by Jasta V. The excerpt from Phelan's book will be found in the Research Documents.

Incidentally, the book is, by any standards, one of the most authoritative from the point of view of detail, personalities and sketches that exists in the libraries in the United Kingdom, the United States and Canada. (No, Mr. Cowan. Mr. Phelan's account is not ''proof'' but having been written from his background of many, many years of study of WWI aeronautics, it certainly makes *THE KID WHO COULDN'T MISS* look like an incompetent bit of bungling.)

Mr. Phelan writes with authenticity about Frenchmen Roland Garros, Jean Navarre, Armand Pinsard, Rene Cigognes, Charles Nungesser, Alfred Heurtaux, Rene Fonck and the immortal George Guynemer; about Britishers like Albert Ball, Mick Mannock and Jimmy McCudden; about Canadians such as Billy Bishop, Collishaw, MacLaren, Barker, Claxton, Bell-Irving, MacLanachan, Richardson and Mullock; about Americans such as Captain Eddie Rickenbacker, Frank Luke, Elliott Springs; and of all the enemy fighter pilots including of course von Richthofen, Ernst Udet and Werner Voss; and the Belgian ace, Willie Coppens.

Phelan can describe all of the military orders and decorations including those of Great Britain. He knows the intimate details of every aircraft that flew in WWI, from the British Sopwith Baby to the French Nieuports and Spads, the Russian Sikorskys, to the dozen or so German craft, including the Fokkers, the Albatros, the Pfalz and the Rumplers. As frosting on the cake, he can sketch and describe in detail all of the insignias.

It is elementary, but one wonders if Mr. Cowan, for example, could describe why the RFC ROUNDEL (sometimes called the Cockade) came into being. Mr. Phelan knows. It was simply that, from the air, the Union Jack was difficult to distinguish from the German Iron Cross.

Cecil Knight

The narrator suggests that pilots who flew with Bishop doubted his claims. The film quotes a ''Mr. James'' who apparently made a tape, in 1972, which Mr. Cowan heard at the Imperial War Museum in London, England saying something to the effect that everyone knew that Bishop was falsifying his claims.

It is interesting that one of the pilots who flew with Bishop (and this has been confirmed in Bishop's own book,

Winged Warfare), was Cecil Knight. Knight is interviewed on camera in the NFB film. The NFB talker presumably tried to draw him (that is Knight) out by referring to the tape made by a pilot by the name of James and here we quote the narrative: ''He (James) said that Bishop's record was fraudulent. He did not, in fact, have that number of kills. He thought that Bishop was a very ambitious man and was cheating on his kills and it was generally known in the RFC that Bishop was cheating. Have you heard that?'' Cecil Knight's very positive response was ''Never! I would doubt it! It was not in the character of Bishop as I knew him to do a thing like that!''

It should be noted that the only reliable source interviewed in the film, Cecil Knight, positively refutes Cowan's theory that Bishop was making fraudulent claims. Admittedly there are two viewpoints; James said on tape that Bishop was a fraud but Knight said, right on film, that he was not!

Author's Note: It is deemed necessary, on occasion, to repeat certain points of information. It is not enough to destroy Cowan's speculations. It is essential to furnish an explanation of some of the uncertainty which Cowan has managed to create!

The NFB Responses

In a paper prepared for, and submitted to the Senate Sub-Committee, dated November 28, 1985, a number of Responses to questions raised by the witnesses summoned by the Sub-Committee are outlined. The experts challenged in the NFB paper are Dr. Steven Wise, Mr. Stewart Taylor and Professor A. Kear—all well-respected historians—together with Col. Arnold Bauer, Chairman of the Billy Bishop Trust.

It will be necessary to deal with several of the Responses in this *Digest*, by heading.

German Records: The subject was the German Squadron war diaries. The NFB re-stated its position. *There was no reference in the German diaries to a number of Bishop's claims. Therefore the claims are suspect.* The NFB Response fails to take into account one significant factor, stated as a question: Was the absence of confirmation in German records due to the fact that no planes were shot down, or is it that the specific records from the German Squadrons are missing?

The NFB's information on German aerodromes was apparently compiled by William Puglisi of the United States Cross and Cockade Society. Puglisi died several years ago but apparently turned over his records to another Society member, Ed Ferko.

In effect, the Response from the NFB pits the records of William Puglisi against the research of Professor Wise and Stewart Taylor. And it must be remembered that the late Mr. Puglisi was an amateur historian, obviously enjoying himself but with, so far as we have been able to determine, no professional qualifications.

Spencer Horne: The NFB Response concerns comments attributed to Mr. Spencer Horne, a man now in his 80s or better who flew with Billy Bishop in 60 Squadron. Horne was quoted in Arthur Bishop's book, *The Courage of the Early Morning*, as saying that he flew over Estourmel aerodrome to confirm that the raid had taken place. The flight was carried out on the orders of Jack Scott, the Squadron Commander. *The Response says: "We know that no other aircraft crossed the German lines that day to Estourmel or anywhere else."* Strange, isn't it, that the activity reports of 60 Squadron show four combat patrols on June 2, 1917. Also, another report states that Spencer Horne's flight over the enemy aerodrome took place "two days after" Billy Bishop's aerodrome raid.

The references to Spencer Horne came up in the controversy which raged after the film was released and criticized. The first mention seen of this man—who flew with Billy Bishop in 60 Squadron—was in the book by Arthur Bishop, Billy Bishop's son. In that book, the author mentions having met with Spencer Horne when he was doing his research for his book. Spencer Horne apparently told Arthur Bishop that he had flown over the aerodrome and had seen evidence of the damage. (Incidentally Arthur Bishop states that his book was endorsed by both the RCAF and the RAF.)

In attempting to refute this, the NFB representatives in testimony before the Senate Sub-Committee stated that Spencer Horne was "anti-Bishop" and had denied ever having taken the flight over the aerodrome.

Whose word do we take? That of Arthur Bishop, a highly respected executive who wrote a book, based on his father's own papers, historical records and a wealth of other material OR do we accept the unsubstantiated version of Paul Cowan and his associates who may or may not have spoken with Spencer Horne—but who, by that time, were feeling badly beleaguered in their attempts to salvage a very questionable premise raised in their film?

Incidentally, in March 1918, at Bishop's invitation, Horne joined him as a flight commander in 85 Squadron. This is confirmed in a diary kept by Mac Grider, published by the well-known American pilot, Elliott Springs. Grider's diary (as reported in Arthur Bishop's book) stated:

> Springs and Callahan came down from Ayr with me and Captain Horne, who is a flight commander at Hounslow in the Squadron that the great Major Bishop, VC, DSO, MC, etc., is organizing to take overseas, took us out to see him. He wants the three of us to go with him. They are letting Bishop pick his own pilots and he went with us to the U.S. headquarters to try and arrange it. A Colonel Morrow told us it couldn't be done. The whole staff nearly lost their eyes staring at us when we strolled out, arm in arm with the great Bishop.

Horne fought under Bishop, and was involved in flying sorties with him until he (Bishop) left 85 Squadron on June 19, 1918. Does it seem possible that 61 years later Spencer Horne would become "anti-Bishop" as Warne claims?

The Lewis Gun: Concerning the matter of removing the Lewis gun the Response states: *"But to stop the gun falling out of the bottom of its guiderail was a stop, the removal of which enabled the gun to be taken off the aircraft."* Wrong gentlemen: no such mechanism as a "stop" existed. The Lewis gun was held in the guide by a through-and-through bolt and nut mechanism. Also the guide rail had no opening at the bottom.

The Response suggests the removal of the Lewis gun would have given no advantage in speed . Who can say why Bishop wanted to remove the Lewis gun? Maybe it was to increase his speed but it could be suggested with equal plausibility that he was having trouble loading the drum. The gun was in his way; hence his decision to jettison it!

Balloon Observers: Information was given that balloonists saw the raid. The NFB Response dismisses the possibility of a balloonist seeing the raid because *"heavy clouds hung at 500 feet. . . ."* Come on now! The balloons would have remained below the cloud ceiling. Also weather reports indicate that the ceiling lifted.

Bishop's Colleagues: The Response suggests there were doubts being expressed by Bishop's colleagues "before the so-called VC raid, which in itself created major misgivings. . . ." Please read the Research Documents. *Bishop was a "hero's hero" in the eyes of his contemporaries. Just to name a few: Barker; Molesworth; Crompton; Sir William Stephenson (Intrepid); Rutherford, and even Willy Fry, in his earlier memoirs.*

Letter from Grid Caldwell: A letter from Grid Caldwell written to another senior Air Force Officer on July 30, 1966 indicated a problem concerning verification of Billy Bishop's claims. The Response from the NFB mentions this specifically. *It is noted, however, that Caldwell's doubts were based on the inability to "do cross-checking with the German archives. . ."* There is ample evidence in this *Digest* to indicate the unreliability of German records. . .or the absence thereof. If Caldwell had known the full story of the German records he may not have been so eager to suggest that some of Bishop's claims were inflated. Certainly Caldwell gave no evidence of an anti-Bishop attitude in his earlier writings.

The "No Confirmation" Issue: One particular Response from the NFB earns top marks for sarcasm. Stewart Taylor stated that the Victoria Cross was awarded without confirmation. *The NFB Response states with obvious glee: "Finally, it is admitted!"* We deal with the "confirmation" question elsewhere; suffice it here to say that there are other ways to come to a conclusion that the raid took place, without it being confirmed by eye witnesses.

Taylor/Warne: The NFB criticizes Stewart Taylor for not having contacted Joe Warne. This is said in the Response to a comment by Mr. Taylor that over the years he has met many pilots and observers, some who actually flew with Billy Bishop in World War I. *The Response is suggesting that if Taylor had spoken with Warne he (Taylor) would have heard information that among Bishop's fellow pilots there were "whisperings" about the validity of the Bishop combat reports.* Yes—but what proof did Warne have that this suspicion existed! Also, why would Taylor contact Warne? Taylor does primary research by speaking with people who have knowledge of the facts because they were either there or were associated with the circumstances. Warne came along some time after WWII! The NFB Responses in full will be found in the Senate Sub-Committee material attached.

A Final Comment, In Rebuttal

The film fails to distinguish between Bourne and Knight. Bourne is an actor; Knight is an actual person—but who is to tell? The whole film weaves in fiction, fantasy, actual film footage, clips from Hollywood films, actors portraying parts and actual persons being interviewed. It is virtually impossible, in watching the film, to know which is which.

To label the film a docu-drama is a joke. To the public, the term implies that the events actually took place,

although in order to tell the story, some dramatization has been used. In the final analysis, however, it is the *narrative* that tells the big lie. Let's leave it to others to resort to *dizinformacia*.

As Canadians, let us not, through a government film agency, drag through the mud the memory of a man who military historians say, without reservation, was the greatest single aerial combat pilot of them all.

Reviewing the published material, who speaks for **Billy Bishop**?:

George Drew: *Canada's Fighting Air Men (and articles)*
Denis Winter: *The First of the Few*
Robert Jackson: *RAF—Flanders to the Falklands*
Arthur Bishop: *The Courage of the Early Morning*
Steven Wise: *Canadian Airmen and the First World War*
Willy Fry: *Air of Battle*
Pierre Berton: *Vimy*
Jack Scott: *Sixty Squadron*
Joseph Phelan: *Heroes and Airplanes of the Great War 1914-1918*
John Norman Harris: *Knights of the Air*
K.M. Molson, G.A. Fuller, J.A. Griffin: *125 Years of Canadian Aeronautics*, published by the Canadian Aviation Historical Society. (Published in 1983 by this prestigious society, the book makes several references to the significant contribution of Billy Bishop.)
William D. Mathieson: *My Grandfather's War* (This book, published in 1981, contains some touching extracts from Bishop's letters home. Noted particularly is Bishop's "ambivalence" about his success.)
Steven Longstreet: *The Canvas Falcons*
Edmund Cosgrove: *Canada's Fighting Pilots*

Chapter 12
Summation

The crux of the matter is that Paul Cowan and the NFB did a film which challenges the basis upon which the Victoria Cross was awarded to Billy Bishop. Mr. Cowan believes that he has the right to attempt to destroy the legend on the grounds that there was no confirmation that the raid upon the German aerodrome, for which the Victoria Cross was granted, in fact took place.

Mr. Cowan's defence, in his appearances before the Senate Sub-Committee, appeared to boil down to this one "no confirmation" contention. His view? There is no proof; therefore, he (Cowan) has every right to make the assumption, in his film, that Bishop's claim was fraudulent.

The question to be examined now is whether Paul Cowan was entitled to come to this conclusion. He cannot say, simply, that there *was no confirmation, therefore the raid did not take place*!

The onus is on Mr. Cowan to substantiate his charges! Billy Bishop made his report on the raid, as required by RFC procedures. His CO gave the report his seal of approval. By the very process of a Gallantry Award, there would have been an investigation by British Military authorities who must have been satisfied with the evidence, and processed the recommendation through to His Majesty King George V.

Admittedly, it is usual procedure to make an award of the Victoria Cross only where there is some confirmation. There is, however, no hard rule to this effect! By the very standards which are known to be applied, Bishop's claim deserves the stamp of credibility and acceptance.

There would have to be a great preponderance of evidence, to support Mr. Cowan's suggestion that the claim is fraudulent. In other words, it surely is not enough for Cowan to state that there is no confirmation. There are substantial grounds to support the contention that the claim is valid, even if there is no direct confirmation.

The point being made here, however, is that Mr. Cowan's hypothesis should never have been the subject of consideration at all! Mr. Cowan, during questioning by Senator Gildas Molgat in the Senate Sub-Committee hearing of December 12, 1985 states: "But I would also say that no information has come forward to disprove what the film says." There is much significance in this comment by Mr. Cowan. Surely it is his responsibility to prove the allegations which the film makes against Bishop's reputation. There is no requirement for anyone to "disprove what the film says."

Bishop's record has been one of long-standing historical acceptance. If Mr. Cowan wishes to challenge that record, he must have some evidence. He cannot challenge the record and then state that it is someone's responsibility to disprove what they are saying! With respect, the shoe is still on the other foot!

It is ludicrous to think that he could make a film of this importance, simply on the grounds that there was no confirmation that the raid took place. He has failed to produce credible evidence. Therefore, the film should be withdrawn from circulation. Incidently, no amount of re-editing could possibly render the film acceptable. Too many notable historians have challenged its accuracy in too many areas.

No apology should be contemplated even though the Bishop family would have every reason to expect one.

No redress of the grievance would be practical. The distrust and suspicion which this film has raised in the public mind can be put to rest in only one way; the film entitled *THE KID WHO COULDN'T MISS* must be destroyed.

No one can right the wrongs that have been done, or expunge the agonies which certain people have experienced by reason of this film. It is all part of a sad experience which has left its scars. The withdrawal and destruction of the film, however, should leave no room for future doubt, and in so far as may be possible, should restore, in the public consciousness, the reputation of William Avery Bishop, VC, DSO and Bar, MC, DFC.

Although the author holds the position of Chairman of the National Council of Veteran Associations and Chief Executive Officer of The War Amputations of Canada, the support for Bishop is not on behalf of veterans. That statement may surprise some and will possibly require clarification.

The main issue does, of course, involve Gallantry Awards and service to one's country in time of war. The potential audience for the film, however, is general, and comprises the public generally; with special appeal for children.

Organized war veterans come into the picture because they are presumably qualified to speak to the public at large. They are knowledgeable about the subject of war and those who fought in them—and their families!

Putting it another way, one could not expect that the general public, per se, would have all of the necessary background knowledge and first-hand experience to understand Billy Bishop and what he did. Our cause should not be seen as one which is serving the self-interest of veterans. Rather, it should be perceived as a duty—an obligation to place matters in perspective—to interpret the situation so that the public is aware of all of the issues.

If it can be said that Mr. Cowan and the NFB are ''prosecuting'' Bishop (and there seems to be some indication that they are) then, hopefully, the public will see the need to present the other side of the story; that is, the opposite view to that expressed in the film. *THE KID WHO COULDN'T MISS* is an anti-Bishop statement. That cannot be left unchallenged. The public deserves the facts; then the public can decide.

N.B.: If anyone wishes to know where we stand on war and glory, see our current *NEVER AGAIN* film series. Call our 1-800 lines: area codes 519, 613, 705 dial 1-800-268-8821; all other area codes dial 1-800-268-8917.

Chapter 13
The NFB Disclaimer

The film, as now issued by the NFB, contains a written explanation at the start, stating that it is a docu-drama; and that some parts of the film are documentary in nature and some are dramatizations.

Surely this is not good enough. Some of the dramatizations, for which there is no evidence at all, are harmful to the reputation of Billy Bishop. That is bad enough!

It is, however, the narration (spoken by an unidentified male) which spews out most of the damage. At one point, the narrator says, "...the only dark spot is that some members of 60 Squadron are now whispering that Bishop is getting credit for a lot of kills for which there is no confirmation." At another point, the narrator again alludes to the fact that Bishop is cheating on his kills in the following words: "Meanwhile doubts about Bishop are increasing."

Straight talk
to the National Film Board

Gentlemen, your explanatory note is a very weak attempt to keep the film in circulation. No amount of explanation can eliminate the fact that the narration itself is the worst kind of innuendo.

To most viewers the disclaimer would go unnoticed. Suppose, however that some persons watching the film do keep in mind your introductory comment. They would look at the dramatization of Walter Bourne, Bishop's mechanic, (who is portrayed as suggesting Bishop's claims are fraudulent, and that the raid on Estourmel never took place) and say: "Yes, but that is a dramatization!" They might still consider the essence of the statement was true! Using the docu-drama technique, it is permissible for the script writer to put words in an actor's mouth; but only if there is some proof that the words may actually have been spoken.

Usually the dramatization is employed to make the event seem more interesting. The event itself should have actually occurred!

Quit kidding the public. There is no evidence that Walter Bourne, the mechanic, ever said those words. In fact, many years after WWI, Bourne did communicate with Bishop. That communication still exists and it indicates nothing but sincere love and respect for the man who flew that flimsy 875-pound Nieuport Scout that Bourne kept in flying condition. Walter Bourne was so fond of Billy Bishop that, in 1942, when Bishop was critically ill, he wrote:

Get well soon, sir. Train us men and we will beat them as we did in the old days. Here is good luck—I am enclosing something which has travelled with me all these years.

Remember the time your gun jammed (April 30, 1917 in the attack against the Gothas) and you had to get away. Well, sir, here is the bullet that might have ended your career. You can see the mark on it where I gripped it in the vice to get it free.

Back to the theme. Suppose that people seeing the film and remembering the NFB's disclaimer do in fact discredit Bourne's comments on the grounds that it is only a dramatization of an event that never took place.

There is still the narrative. That is to say, the "disclaimer" does not comment on the narration. The audience is left with the impression that the "behind the scenes" voice is *history* speaking.

The disclaimer is not only useless, it is dangerous because it still leaves the suggestion that the general "thrust" of the film is true.

Chapter 14
Bishop As Seen By a Squadron Mechanic

The Cowan film relies heavily on fictitious film sequences during which an actor playing the part of Walter Bourne, who was Billy Bishop's mechanic, makes some sweeping condemnations...Bishop was faking his claims; there was great doubt that the raid took place, etc.

The words, which were never uttered by the real Walter Bourne, were created by Cowan and spoken by an actor—and just to be a little more convincing, the interview with the actor gives the appearance of having taken place at a WWI aerodrome. It is shot in black and white (1918?). The film even shows a specially doctored photograph of the actor, to look as if it came from the Bourne family album.

Fortunately for the record, our research has turned up an article by former Sergeant Major A.A. Nicod entitled "Memories of 60 Squadron R.F.C." Nicod was a senior mechanic of the Squadron and served with Bishop. The article is illustrated with some great pictures of Billy Bishop engaged in horseplay with Squadron mates, including the late Jack Rutherford of Montreal.

For those who just may have some doubts about Billy Bishop, read what Sergeant Major Nicod had to say:

The coming of Captain Bishop helped matters considerably and it was here that his memorable exploit over Cambrai gained for him the coveted VC.

And further:

What with the skillful reorganization of our new CO (Major Jack Scott) the wonderful deeds of Captain Bishop and the excellent work performed by Captain Grid Caldwell, Lieutenant Meintjes, Lieutenant Rutherford, Lieutenant Fry, and other pilots of this period, we entered upon the most triumphant period of the history of the Squadron.

Sergeant Major Nicod speaks further about Billy Bishop in NCO's terms. He speaks of how the ground crew would "surge around his machine on landing." Apparently, it was standard procedure for the ground staff to find out how the renowned Bishop had done. He also confirms Bishop's trademark of firing off a Verey pistol if he had achieved success.

Concerning what Sergeant Major Nicod calls "Captain Bishop's stupendous feat over Cambrai Aerodrome for which he was awarded the VC," Nicod's description is graphic...and he leaves the impression that, from his point of view, it certainly was genuine.

He gives also some first-hand evidence concerning the bullet holes and indicates that, not only the officers celebrated the victory but that Billy Bishop was tendered a special dinner in the Sergeant's mess—a rare tribute indeed.

The Nicod article will be found in the Research Documents.

Sergeant Major Nicod wrote another article for *Popular Flying* magazine which was published in January, 1936 under the title of "Reunion Memories." Again he speaks fondly of Bishop.

If, as Paul Cowan seems to imply in his film, Bishop was a braggart, a liar, a man cheating on his kills...does anyone with an ounce of common sense really believe that eighteen years later, in writing about reunion memories, one of the senior NCOs would speak of Billy Bishop with the warmth and affection that is apparent? (By the way, it is possible to determine from his writings that Nicod is no dummy—not the type to be taken in by a charlatan making highly exaggerated and bombastic claims.)

Sergeant Major Nicod's second article, which is also available in the Research Documents herewith, makes for most interesting reading. Only a brief quote or two are included here, but the entire article should be read.

A memorable night that no one who was present will ever forget was the celebration of Captain Bishop's winning the VC for his wonderful show at Cambrai...what a night! We thought the whole place was going up in flames. Many of us stood by with troops armed with fire extinguishers while the "great man" (Bishop) went about like a piece of paper in a gale.

Nicod, incidentally, confirms that Bishop's plane was riddled with bullet holes.

Chapter 15
Bishop: The Humanitarian

Among the less-palatable features of Paul Cowan's film is the portrait he paints of Billy Bishop. One gets the impression, early in the film, of a very young boy who delights in shooting helpless waterfowl. Later, Cowan's profile turns more sinister . . . and Bishop is seen glorifying in his new-found occupation—killing Huns.

It would appear that the real story is something quite different. In our research, one particular article was located which would seem, for all time, to spell denial to the unsavory picture of the Bishop which runs throughout *THE KID WHO COULDN'T MISS*.

It is an article published in the English magazine *Popular Flying* (October 1934 issue) which was written by Billy Bishop himself. In the article he talks about this "feeling almost of friendship" on both sides and that it was possible for fighter pilots to "regard our work as a game and not as war."

In the article Bishop tells a touching story of the "flying pig" . . . a German observer-gunner who was so fat he could scarcely fit into the cockpit. He was handicapped by having with him what Bishop called a "far from good pilot." The observer-gunner had, however, shown great bravery and 60 Squadron began to look upon the unfortunate German as a pet mascot, granting him immunity. Later, a new British pilot who did not recognize the "flying pig," shot him down. That night 60 Squadron held a mess dinner in his (the German's) honour.

Bishop's article indicates, also, his well-known sense of humour. He tells of the incident when he was being entertained in Berlin ten or so years after the war as a special guest of a large number of German war pilots. The room was decorated with paintings, showing (what else) British fighters being shot down by a German Fokker or an Albatros. Bishop said, jokingly, that the artists had gotten it all wrong. He remarked that, so far as he knew, no such thing had ever occurred!

Seriously, anyone who wishes to have a little insight into the real Billy Bishop should read this article. It will be found among the Research Documents. It is entitled "Chivalry in the Air."

Also, read Senator Molson's address in the documentation entitled "Senate Sub-Committee Material". The Senator knew Billy Bishop personally.

Chapter 16
Tempest in a Teapot?

Some media have been dismissing the Billy Bishop controversy as the proverbial "tempest in a teapot." Let's be serious! The NFB, in its film *THE KID WHO COULDN'T MISS* is tampering with history.

And not ordinary history either...but the history of a war where, as has often been quoted, "Canada became a nation."

It is sad enough to contemplate that the NFB film, based solely on innuendo and so-called research (skimpy at best), attempts to destroy the legend of one of Canada's greatest war heroes.

Possibly of far greater significance is the surprising and perhaps sinister discovery that Paul Cowan's real mission was to attack the proud record of Canada's fighting men...and of our country's war effort in general.

What grounds are there for this deduction? One does not have to look very far. In attempting to defend his film, Paul Cowan has stated publicly two objectives:

• To examine why we need heroes; and
• To examine why we go to war at all.

The rebuttal to these observations will be found elsewhere. In this chapter, we are dealing solely with what must be exposed as the ulterior motives behind the production of the film itself.

We are accustomed in Canada to looking for the sensational. Someone, somewhere within the NFB must have come to the conclusion that it would not have been enough to do a film on Billy Bishop. Was it within the hierarchy itself...or was it just Cowan? No matter, someone looked at the Bishop legend and must have said...the same old Horatio Alger scenario. Who needs it! Who would bother to look at it? Ah, but what if the film could destroy the legend. That's the stuff of which award-winning documentaries are made! This would be acceptable—but only if the evidence is conclusive—not fragmentary or even non-existent as is the case in *THE KID WHO COULDN'T MISS!*

No...the Billy Bishop story is not a tempest in a teapot. It is probably one of the most important (and most interesting) issues in the public domain today.

Just to recap where we are right now with this story, the chronological summary is as follows:

1982: NFB film *THE KID WHO COULDN'T MISS* is released.

1983-84: The controversy commences. Some reviewers liked it as a film. Most historians suggested it be subject-ed to the same fate as the 72 enemy aircraft who fell to the guns of Billy Bishop—fighter pilot extraordinaire. It should be shot down in flames.

1985: The issue is referred to the Senate Sub-Committee on Veterans Affairs. The media picks up the issue in earnest. Some supported the film, principally on four bases:

• To circumvent distribution of the film would be censorship;
• The independence of the NFB from government control must be maintained;
• "Revisionists" are sometimes right...and should be given an opportunity to challenge historical accounts;
• Most of the opposition was being voiced by Senators (whose capabilities are often underestimated by the media).

The media who concurred in the criticisms of the film made a number of points too. They said:

• The NFB witnesses were not credible;
• The public should believe the supporters for Bishop including historians such as Dr. Steven Wise, Head of the Institute for Canadian Studies at Carleton University (Ottawa) and the author of a recent (1980) 800-page history entitled *Canadian Airmen and the First World War*; Stewart Taylor, the official historian of Canada's WWI Flyers and A.M. Kear, a professor of History at the University of Manitoba;
• The awarding of the Victoria Cross must necessarily be given credence, in that the responsible authorities in the British government who make the recommendation to the King, are known to do so only after thorough investigation of the facts.

1986: The next major development was the report of the Senate Sub-Committee which made some lukewarm recommendations suggesting disclaimers or "riders" be added to the film, stating that it was not historically accurate and should be called a docu-drama. The report was not accepted by the Senate and the issue was to have been reconsidered by the Senate in the fall of 1986. In the meantime Parliament was prorogued and the matter "died on the Order Paper."

ALL THAT HAS GONE BEFORE MIGHT BE CONSIDERED AS ROUND ONE. ROUND TWO IS

UNDERWAY. This time there are a number of important factors:

• The Senate hearings may not be renewed;
• The matter may be referred to the House of Commons Standing Committee on Veterans Affairs—doubtful;
• The information which will be available to the media will be much more detailed in support of Billy Bishop. Round two will, however, be in the nature of an ''open debate'' and presumably if there is any further evidence to substantiate the stand taken by the NFB it will come out;
• The final arbiter in the Billy Bishop issue should be the Canadian public—and obviously will be;
• Another possibility: a legal injunction prohibiting exhibition of the film.

It can certainly be expected that round two will again be interesting and informative. It should establish for all time that Billy Bishop was indeed a great, if not our greatest, war hero.

Conjecture: Can anyone imagine the furor if a government-supported film were released in the United States, questioning the record of Sgt. York? Or in Britain, vilifying Sir Douglas Bader? Or in Germany saying that von Richthofen was a fraud? Imagine the reaction of Snoopy if the German government had done a film portraying the Red Baron as a Bertrüger!

Chapter 17
Hero Bashing

There is plenty of evidence to indicate that "hero bashing" becomes a bit of a national sport, if the sensation-seekers are allowed to get away with it.

Albert Ball

Probably the first to suffer was none other than Albert Ball, VC, the eccentric, fearless young English hero. Albert was the son of a prominent family and his father was the Lord Mayor of Nottingham. Albert was a quiet, studious youngster who, between sorties as a member of the famed 60 Squadron, played his violin and tended a flower garden which he planted beside a small hut near the hangar which housed his aeroplane. He is credited with 43 victories.

He liked his own company. He was by no means a snob, but preferred to live in the privacy of his own quarters, where he could be surrounded with the pictures of his family. (The fascinating story of Albert Ball is set out in the Research Documents.)

Shortly after WWI, an educator in Great Britain, who fancied himself as a bit of a historian, published a book in which he suggested that Albert Ball's claims stretched the truth somewhat. There was an immediate and violent public reaction. Albert's father threatened legal action and we quote from an article in the British aviation magazine *Popular Flying* (Fall '69) as follows:

Captain Ball's Victories

R.H. Kierman, in compiling his summary of Captain Ball's victories, caused a great deal of resentment in both the local and national press over his attitude to the number of victories claimed and credited to Captain Ball. A report published in the *Manchester Evening News*, dated September 28, 1933, was typical:

Book Slur on Air VC
'I will fight it', says Sir Albert Ball.
Shot 47 Planes Down.

"Sir Albert Ball, father of the late Captain Albert Ball, VC, the British Air Ace, vigorously denied allegations made in a book published today that Captain Ball's death came at a time when the world's news was full of Richthofen's deeds and gossip said that Royal Flying Corps Headquarters were stampeded into exaggerating Ball's material success in order to create an English air fighter of status to the German."

The book, *Captain Albert Ball, VC, DSO*, was written by Mr. R.H. Kierman, a Birmingham school master, and also states:

"From April 22 to noon May 7, 1917, he had engaged 35 German aeroplanes, forced one to land and destroyed 11. These, added to those forced down, sent down out of control and destroyed in 1916, give the VC citation of 43. Forty-three victories, but not 43 German aeroplanes destroyed."

"It seems to have been a careless error in expression that made Headquarters appear to grant him in death more material success than had been officially allowed him in life; more than Ball claimed for himself."

Today, Sir Albert Ball said:

"This book must be stopped. I will not stand by and see my dead son attacked in this way. I will see my solicitors at once and ask them to get in touch with the publishers. Who is Mr. Kierman? He is a school teacher at a school in Birmingham. He knows nothing about my son. I have letters in my possession from officers who fought with my son, including one from Lord Trenchard in which he said: 'As you know, he was the most daring and successful pilot the Royal Flying Corps has ever had...I have never met a man who has been so successful as he was in such a short time, and who was so reliable.'

"In the record of the 'VC and DSO' edited by the late Sir O'Moore Cragh, VC, it states: 'In his last eleven days, he was in 26 fights. Altogether he was in well over a 100 fights. Though the precise number of enemy machines he brought down in his short career is not known, there are records of 47 aeroplanes and one balloon.'

Surely, said Sir Albert, this is evidence enough. I think the statements in the book are a slur, not only on my son, but on the whole Royal Flying Corps and the Royal Air Force. It is a slur I will fight!

Von Richthofen

Manfred von Richthofen was a great hero in Germany. Long before he had racked up his 80 victories, he became a national figure.

There was controversy surrounding his death. Roy Brown, a Canadian from Carleton Place, Ontario fighting in the RFC, was chasing von Richthofen and certainly put some bullets into the German's aircraft. Simultaneously, an Australian Battery was spraying von Richthofen's aircraft with machine gun bullets from the ground. Both the RFC in Roy Brown's name, and the Australians, claimed victory. Presumably no one will really know but von Richthofen's craft was salvaged by the Australians and he was given a military funeral, with all honours.

We are including what seems to us to be an impartial review concerning von Richthofen as part of our Research Documents. His story, too, will speak for itself.

In view of his fame, however, it was a foregone conclusion that someone would challenge the Red Baron. In

THE RED KNIGHT OF GERMANY

RITTMEISTER BARON MANFRED VON RICHTHOFEN.

The German Ace of Aces. Victor of 80 combats. Leader of the Richthofen
Circus. Killed in action, May 21, 1918.

CAPTAIN ALBERT BALL, V.C., D.S.O., M.C.

Born August 21st, 1896   —   Killed in Action May 7th, 1917

a 1935 series of newspaper articles in the U.K., Ira Jones, former RFC pilot and prominent writer, implied that von Richthofen would usually fight only if he had his opponent at a great disadvantage. (N.B.: Ira Jones didn't like Billy Bishop either.)

Some of the assertions in the English newspaper articles were:

• English airmen were forced to fly over von Richthofen's aerodome to look for him;

• Von Richthofen wrote in his diary: "It is better to let one's customers come to one's shop than to go running after them'';

• Von Richthofen was purely a defensive fighter and seldom fought on the British side of the front;

• Most of the one-seaters he shot down were no match for the German aircraft von Richthofen flew and of the ones that were he "shot down only very few!"

The British magazine *Popular Flying* published what is called: "A Necessary Answer to an Incredible Slander on the Dead Hero of the Air'' written by Ernst Udet, who fought and flew with von Richthofen.

Von Richthofen was an incredible fighting airman; a fact known to the world. It is probably less well-known that Ira Jones attempted to defile von Richthofen.

The British writer's attempt to vilify the German hero, compared the English two-seaters to "a sparrow fledgling which had strayed from its nest'' up against Richthofen, portrayed as a "hunting falcon.'' The English article went on to suggest that "there was no great song to be made about his (von Richthofen's) victories.''

Ira Jones' attempt to besmirch the record of von Richthofen was answered rather adroitly by one of the world's most honoured airmen...the famed Ernst Udet who himself was able to claim 62 victories and survive. Though an anti-Nazi, he became an advisor to the German Luftwaffe in WWII.

An added bonus: During research for this *Digest* an English publication of the Thirties surfaced. In it there is favourable mention of Billy Bishop in Ernst Udet's defence of the Red Baron. Udet finishes up his article by citing comments of Billy Bishop, whose record 50 years later is the subject of a controversial and slanderous attack by film journalist Paul Cowan in Canada.

This is how Ernst Udet concluded his article: "My friend and comrade Bishop, who is the greatest English Scouting Ace, and his splendid Squadron, had many battles with Richthofen. What he (Bishop) has told me of my dead Commander is in accordance with the picture of that heroic, undaunted, honourable airman which the whole world honours and esteems in our Manfred von Richthofen.''

What say you to that, Paul Cowan! The criticisms of the Red Baron may have some basis in fact. The matter is raised here for one purpose; to indicate the extent that desperate and ambitious journalists might go "to get a story!''

There's more: interesting, isn't it, that biographers of Rittmeister Manfred von Richthofen state that the Red Baron himself was described as "not a very good cavalry officer.''

The article goes on to say: "He (Richthofen) admits he was not an apt pupil, and it is difficult to reconcile his early attempts to fly with the masterly ability that came to him later. It must have dumbfounded his instructors.'' (For further details see articles on von Richthofen in the Research Documents.)

Sounds familiar? Seems the NFB film makes similar assumptions about Billy Bishop.

Mick Mannock

Another major instance of hero bashing concerns Mick Mannock, an Irishman who served with RFC Squadrons. In some circles (including British writer Ira Jones) he is credited with 73 victories—somewhat ironically, one more than Billy Bishop! Other air historians who have scrutinized the records give him no more than 54. Billy Bishop, being the true sportsman that he was, never uttered one word on the matter, even though it did begin to appear in the Twenties, that some British authorities were trying very hard to push Mannock's claims ahead of Bishop's.

This controversy is cited for two reasons:

• Firstly, the exact number of aircraft shot down by any one of these early aerial duelists can never really be known, despite the system of checks and balances used by the military authorities for the reporting of 'kills' confirmations and 'possibles.' The inexactness of the confirmation system does, however, create for the amateur historians a fiendish opportunity to practice their detective work;

• The fact that Mannock was eventually given credit for 73 victories; and that this record was openly challenged (and has remained so ever since) should be a warning to all. Be wary of the amateurs who seem to relish in questioning the official records—and in the process the reputations—of a group of fearless men who created history.

Research Documents

As background, the Research Documents contain a number of leading articles on the life and times of these fearless airmen of an earlier era. They are taken from aviation journals published after WWI and include: "Who is the British Ace of Aces?'' *Cross & Cockade Journal,* Winter 1963; "Victory Lists of Leading Aces,'' *Cross & Cockade Journal,* Winter 1973; "Grid Caldwell,'' *Cross*

& Cockade Journal, Summer 1964; ''Collishaw-Caldwell Comments,'' *Cross & Cockade Journal*.

The Collishaw-Caldwell comments are interesting. Cowan and/or his *supporters* insinuated, in statements reported in the proceedings of the Senate Sub-Committee, that Bishop was a fake, suggesting that his claims were the subject of criticism by both Raymond Collishaw and Grid Caldwell.

Collishaw would have had good reason to withhold endorsement of Bishop's record. It was common knowledge that the Royal Naval Air Service, with which Collishaw fought, was reticent about the exploits of their pilots. Hence, Collishaw may have thought that his number of kills equalled or even surpassed Bishop's. Yet, Bishop got the public acclaim, not because he sought it, but because by 1917 the RFC was actively publicizing the exploits of its most famous Aces.

(For a detailed account of the RNAF's attitude read the extract from John Norman Harris' *Knights of the Air* in the Research Documents.)

The excellent article on Grid Caldwell mentions Bishop quite favourably and includes a very positive note about Bishop. The article was reviewed by Caldwell himself.

A positive statement in the Caldwell article is noted as well about Jack Scott, Bishop's CO, who also has been made to look like a villain in Cowan's film. The comment on Scott, which Caldwell endorsed, was as follows: ''His old CO of 60 Squadron, Colonel A.L.J. Scott, who above all was a marvellous judge of a man's capabilities as a fighter....''

The article on Caldwell is a classic portrayal of the life of a fighter pilot at the front in those hectic days towards the close of WWI. (It is published in the Research Documents in full.)

Chapter 18
Revisionism

A recent book by Professor S.F. Wise entitled *Canadian Airmen and the First World War* is, as he states in the preface, "...primarily an attempt to restore a phase of our military history—and, indeed, of our national history—that has been all but lost."

Professor Wise's book is now the latest, acknowledged history of Canada's participation in the air in WWI.

We note the following references to Billy Bishop in the preface: "Most of this collection was organized into biographical files, and included papers of such notable airmen as W.A. Bishop, Ray Collishaw, W.G. Barker, Lloyd Breadner, and R.H. Mulock."

In speaking of the pioneers of the idea of a special Canadian force Professor Wise mentions Bishop and states: "One of these was W.A. Bishop. As a young pilot officer I passed under the cold blue reviewing eye of Air Vice Marshall Bishop, VC, DSO, MC, DFC, Croix de Guerre, an experience shared with many thousands of graduates of the British Commonwealth Air Training Plan. His presence was a visible demonstration to us that our service, young as it was, had a tradition of high accomplishment."

A review of the WWI history books used in at least six of the ten provinces of Canada indicate considerable reference to the exploits of Billy Bishop including, of course, his raid on the German aerodrome. What are we going to do with the history books, if we accept the version in the NFB film? Is Paul Cowan's evidence strong enough to suggest that the history books should now contain a notation to the effect that there is some doubt that the raid ever took place?

If so, what sources could be used to support such doubts? There was some reference in the Senate Sub-Committee Hearings to the matter of "revisionism" and undoubtedly there is a valid place for the findings of the "revisionists." In other words, one cannot change history, but if those who wrote about the history in earlier days were wrong, and the "revisionists" can prove it, surely we have to be open-minded enough to accept the authenticity of new accounts.

So there we have it. Professor Wise is taking the stance of a "revisionist." What qualifications does *he* have? Here is a short biography:

S.F. Wise, a pilot in the Royal Canadian Air Force during the Second World War, is a former National Defence Director of History. Among his published works is *Men in Arms: A History of the Interrelationship of Warfare and Western Society* (4th edition, 1979) written with R.A. Preston. He is a past president of the Canadian Historical Association and of the Social Science Federation of Canada. Currently he is Professor of History and Director of the Insti-

tute of Canadian Studies at Carleton University and Chairman of the Ontario Heritage Foundation.

It seems reasonable that we could accept Professor Wise's interpretation of the Billy Bishop air raid, as supported by the extensive research done. Professor Wise states, in regard to this research:

To reconstruct the 1914-18 air war from a Canadian perspective has been a research task of some complexity. The starting point was the thousands of record cards compiled by Captain MacAdams and his clerks in 1919 from records of the RAF and the headquarters of the overseas Military Forces of Canada in London. On each card was written the name of the airman, his rank, trade, decorations, place of origin in Canada (or place of enlistment), records of service, and, occasionally, occupation prior to enlistment.

Gradually, as the result of Hitchins' work, (Dr. Fred Hitchins, noted historian who investigated the work of Canadians in the Royal Flying Corps, the Royal Naval Air Service and the RAF) later carried on by the Directorate of History, there was accumulated a large body of documentation of the most varied kind: logbooks, diaries, letters, photographs, and taped interviews with former airmen.

All the records collected in this war were indexed and organized to make them accessible for research and to link them to the biographical collection. In sum, the body of evidence ordinarily immediately available for the writing of Canadian service history had first to be generated before a history could actually be written.

Some of the reference sources used by Professor Wise include: Public Archives of Canada; The Keeper of the Records and Officials of the Public Record Office, London; The Director and Staff of the Imperial War Museum, London; The Curator and Staff of the Canadian War Museum and the Aviation and Space Division of the National Museum of Science and Technology; The Staff of the National Aeronautical Collection (Canada); and The Archivist of the University of Toronto.

So it was not the "revisionists" who were calling for Billy Bishop's scalp! The "revisionists" have already given considerable thought and attention to the role of Canadian airmen in WWI including, of course, the most notable of them all—then Captain W.A. Bishop.

To suggest that Paul Cowan and others who produced the NFB film were, in fact, "revisionists" is giving to them a role which, in the light of hard evidence, it seems they were ill equipped to assume.

The official record of Billy Bishop's part in the air war in World War I stands; and it is well supported by the "revisionist" history of Professor Wise, first published in 1980. The book—*Canadian Airmen and the First World War*—makes fascinating reading.

Chapter 19

Interesting Sidelights

Jack Scott

Obviously, Paul Cowan and his associates didn't care about whom they might hurt. Not only did they attempt to tarnish the reputation of Billy Bishop, but in the process they managed to call one of Britain's most cherished (if unsung) heroes an outright liar. That person was Major Jack Scott, Bishop's CO in 60 Squadron.

Major Scott came from a prominent family in the U.K. He had already made a reputation for himself as a barrister and then proceeded to become an outstanding war hero. Severely wounded in both legs, he continued to serve in RFC as a Squadron Commander; and although officially barred from flying, he defied the order and continued to lead his men in the air. Eventually, Sir John Trenchard, head of the RFC who happened to be a personal family friend, recalled Jack Scott from combat and he ended the war ''flying a desk.'' He died within five years of his discharge from the forces, as a result of the wounds sustained in 1915.

A.C. Mynarski, VC

Billy Bishop's raid was on an airfield in the Cambrai area. It is a coincidence that twenty-seven years later, in the skies over this same Cambrai, Pilot Officer A.C. Mynarski of 419 Squadron, RCAF committed an act of bravery that brought *him* the Victoria Cross. Mynarski was the mid-upper gunner in a Lancaster bomber which had been set on fire by a German night fighter. Surrounded by flames, Mynarski attempted to release the trapped rear gunner who miraculously survived the crash. Mynarski received fatal injuries.

Maybe a Paul Cowan of the future will try to cast doubts on Mynarski's heroism? You remember Cowan's particular paranoia—how heroes are made and why a country needs heroes anyway?

Opinions of Other Fliers

Here again is an opportunity to weigh the evidence. The NFB quotes Willy Fry, and D.W. Warne who is reported to have obtained opinions from other pilots who either flew with Bishop or who knew him.

On the other side, no one as yet seems to have brought up the name of Bill Barker, VC, certainly one of the best known contemporaries of Bishop among Canadian pilots who flew with the RFC. Barker apparently had enough confidence in Billy Bishop to go into business with him after the 1914-18 war.

A rare insight into how Billy Bishop's contemporaries felt about him is outlined in a letter from Air Marshall Leigh F. Stevenson of Vancouver to Senator Hartland Molson, quoted in the minutes of the Senate Sub-Committee of October 30, 1985 and repeated hereunder:

Dear Senator,

I was astounded to learn that there is a campaign afoot to discredit the name of Air Marshall A. Bishop, VC, DSO, MC, DFC and question his entitlement to the Honours and Decorations he was awarded in World War I. I was more astounded to hear that the National Film Board of Canada was considering production of a film supporting this campaign.

If there was any question as to Air Marshall Bishop's creditability or entitlement to his honours, why was it left until this late date when he and most of his contemporaries are dead and few left to defend his good name. There are only a few of us left, nearly all in an organization called ''World War One Flyers'' which perhaps held its last meeting in May this year.

I talked with Major Don MacLaren, Nick Carter and George Howsam within the last few days, all Fighter Pilots in France and well decorated for their achievements, they are amazed that a campaign to discredit Bishop should arise, let alone receive support from a government agency.

There is not only a reflection on Air Marshall Bishop but on every recipient of Honours and Awards, on all Commanders recommending such awards, and even on His Majesty the King who finally gave the awards.

The recent play ''Billy Bishop Goes to War'' was in fact a theatrical cartoon which did nothing to enhance the image of Air Marshall Bishop, and now this new venture to further destroy the image of a gallant fighter pilot.

Commanders in the Field are meticulous in scrutinizing recommendations for Honours and Awards before passing them on to the Commander in Chief for final approval and eventually to His Majesty.

I did not know Bishop during the First War but met him immediately after. From that time until his death we were friends and he was a friend of all those with whom he fought in World War I. They were the Officers who called him back to the RCAF to assist in the Commonwealth Air Training Plan. Never was there a suggestion that he was not entitled to Honours and Awards with which he was decorated. And no one ever questioned his bravery.

I was in the Infantry during the first three years of the First War but during my 28 years in the RFC, the RAF and the RCAF I got to know a great many pilots who served in France with Air Marshall Bishop and between the Wars and during the last War met and knew personally most of the Commanders who served in France during the First War. These included Marshall of the Royal Air Force, Lord Trenchard, Air Chief Marshall Lord Portal, Air Chief Marshall Sir Shalto Douglas and never did I hear anything but the most complimentary remarks about Air Marshall Bishop. They were the men through whose hands recommendations for Honours and Awards would pass. They were all men of high integrity.

You, Senator are the best person I know to step in and stop this nonsense about Air Marshall Bishop. You were a fighter pilot in World War II, highly respected in business, social and military circles, and, in the Senate of Canada. Your voice would be heard.

If there is anything we, surviving pilots of World War I can do, please call upon us. I am afraid you will have to move quickly as we are all in our nineties and time is running out.

Another dynamic piece of information was given to the Senate Committee from William Stevenson, author of the book *Intrepid* . . . The story of Sir William Stephenson, the Secret-Service agent who, among other things, negotiated between Sir Winston Churchill and President Franklin D. Roosevelt during World War II.

Firstly, a telex addressed to Senator Hartland Molson as follows:

Bill Stevenson (the writer) telephoned re Billy Bishop. Have confirmed to him my knowledge of and confidence in Bishop to pass on to you. Glad to learn you are pursuing the subject of nefarious unwarranted posthumous attacks on Billy. Trust you will persist in your course. All good wishes and admiration.
Signed **Bill Stephenson** (Intrepid)

This telex was followed by a letter from William Stevenson, the author, quoting Sir William Stephenson; that is, Intrepid. The letter reads:

Dear Senator Molson,
I spoke to Sir William Stephenson again today, and he repeated what he had told me two or three weeks ago with respect to his knowledge of Billy Bishop in the 1914-18 war. "We were flying the same type of fighter aircraft in the same sector," Sir William says. "In the last most active periods of the air war against the Germans, I got to know Billy Bishop by reputation and then through personal contact. To my certain knowledge, Billy Bishop was held in the highest regard by all those Canadian and British airmen who flew in combat at the same (time) as he did. All his words and actions were regarded as beyond reproach, and representative of professional fliers of the time. We were a close-knit group. Nobody could have tried to mislead us about his individual actions

without the truth becoming very quickly known: Billy Bishop never made any kind of false claim, to my certain knowledge. On one occasion, when the Germans were preparing for their last great offensive, we pilots were told there would be a weekend in Blighty for the top-scorers. Billy and I flew back to England for that prize weekend, and we flew back to the front greatly refreshed, and with an even closer knowledge of one another. I have the clearest recollection of finding Billy Bishop a gentleman who played, as he fought, according to a code of honour that makes it utterly inconceivable that he would have made claims he could not substantiate. And furthermore, that was the reputation he enjoyed among those who shared with him the actual fighting. I never heard a whisper of criticism against him, and it is nonsense to suggest that 'it was common knowledge he exaggerated.' Such a comment could only come from someone who had no experience in the air. All of us made genuine mistakes at some time or another, inevitable in the swiftness of dogfights or other aerial engagements, but those mistakes generally got sorted out later when the survivors worked with the intelligence officers to crosscheck the details.

Buzz Buerling DSO, DFC, DFM and Bar

A bit of rather interesting information, relating directly to the current controversy over Billy Bishop, is found in the biography *Hero* by Brian Nolan—the story of Buzz Buerling, the Knight of Malta, of Verdun, Quebec.

Nolan's book defines "Ace" as follows: "The term 'Ace' is an unofficial one. It seems to have its origin in the French Escadrilles of the First World War, when anyone who scored ten or more aerial victories earned the honour. After the Americans arrived in France they arbitrarily set the figure at five. There it remains."

Concerning the matter of credit, Nolan said: "Attempting to list victories accurately has become a tedious and frustrating undertaking for aviation writers, since different Air Forces used different methods in recording the kills."

Nolan goes on to say: "There is some confusion regarding Buerling's score. Official records themselves are contradictory, crediting him with a final total of both 31-1/3 and 29-1/3. Some controversy revolves around two of Buerling's 'probably destroyed' enemy aircraft. For this examination the total figure of 31-1/3 is given. The 1/3 figure was credited to Buerling when he and two other pilots attacked an enemy airplane at the same time and it could not be determined who actually shot it down, so all three get part credit."

Buerling was, in any event, the leading Canadian Ace of the Second World War, regardless of whether the figure of 31-1/3 or 29-1/3 is used. The second highest was Vernon C. Woodward, DFC and Bar of Victoria, B.C.

Billy Bishop at RMC

The film makes a big issue about Billy Bishop having left Royal Military College without graduating, suggesting he was caught "cheating on his final exams." This sounds like a terrible condemnation; attempting once again to smear the man's reputation.

It is ironic, however, that when the millions of Canadians were singing his praises as he returned to Canada a much-decorated soldier of aerial warfare, did it matter to anyone that he had cribbed a few notes at examination time at RMC?

The manner in which Billy Bishop departed from RMC was all part of the legend that grew up during and after the First World War. Here was an impetuous scallywag who disdained academic matters, but who had gone to the battlefields of France. Here he engaged in combat with the likes of the Red Baron, and was the first man in history ever to receive three gallantry awards from the King of England at the same time, one of them being the coveted Victoria Cross.

If wars have to be fought, maybe we need more people who disdain academia for that dangerous world where one's very life is on the line, every day...every hour.

Incidentally, the incident involving Billy Bishop and his RMC exams has been blown out of all proportion. One print media story in December 1985 headlined it this way: "Bishop Cheated at RMC." The Senate Sub-Committee that day had heard some two hours of testimony, of which less than a minute was devoted to the RMC exam incident.

Billy Bishop never made any effort to downplay the matter; neither did his family. Why? Because they treated it as a joke...and it was always looked upon this way, even at RMC, until Paul Cowan came along with his accusing finger.

Billy Bishop readily admitted that he had some notes and he was told by the Commandant that he would not be allowed to write his final examinations. With respect, this is a somewhat lesser accusation than the implication in the film that he was caught cheating at his final exams.

As a member of the family (who refuses to be drawn into this controversy and no wonder) has said, the Commandant's ruling was subject to appeal, but the war was on and Billy Bishop had only one desire...to get into uniform and into the fighting as soon as he could.

Today, there is a memorial in Currie Hall at Royal Military College in Kingston. It is a panel dedicated to Billy Bishop, showing him in his aircraft. Paul Cowan may have his own ideas about Billy Bishop's relationship with RMC—but there is no doubt in the minds of the College itself, and its graduates, as to how *they* feel about one of their most honoured students.

That "Still" of King George V

One wonders how low a filmmaker will stoop in an attempt to buttress his argument that Bishop's raid was

merely a calculated ploy on the part of the British High Command to create a hero. Paul Cowan blatantly suggests that the army brass were waiting at the airport for Bishop to return. (It never happened.) The film even shows a still photograph of King George V, presumably standing around with some staff officers.

In our research, the photograph was located. The caption says "King George V talking to a pilot during the war." It is not necessary to have taken a course in photo identification to recognize that the pilot is *certainly not* Billy Bishop. Part of the pilot's profile is seen; also he is well over six feet tall. Billy Bishop was certainly not more than five feet and eight inches tall. A reproduction of the King's picture (albeit not a good one) is included in the Research Documents.

Billy Bishop and the King

Billy Bishop received yet another decoration for bravery after his Victoria Cross for service in 85 Squadron later in the war. Guests at the investiture at Buckingham Palace were rewarded by an incisive bit of humour from King George V. As he pinned the new Distinguished Flying Cross on Bishop he said: "You now have the VC, DSO, MC, DFC *after* your name. If you distinguish yourself again we shall have to give you something to put in front of your name. Perhaps we could call you 'Archbishop.'"

Estourmel or Esnes

It may be true that official reports did not give the actual name of the airfield. This certainly does not entitle Paul Cowan to conclude that the raid did not take place. In fact, it would seem to be rather significant that on June 7, 1917—just five days after Billy Bishop's raid—in the orders issued by Headquarters, No. 9 Wing (which included 60 Squadron) RFC Units were encouraged to carry out, as Professor Wise states in his book, "...low flying attacks on aerodromes of a kind which had not been attempted before Bishop's exploit."

Pierre Berton and *Vimy*

In his brilliant 1986 book—*Vimy*—author-researcher-historian Pierre Berton seems to have no difficulty at all with the Bishop legend.

Speaking of the episode with the German balloon, which resulted in Bishop's award of the Military Cross, Berton says: "Young Billy Bishop of No. 60 Squadron, late of Orillia, became an official ace that day and also won his first decoration...."

Berton then describes Bishop diving on the balloon, shooting down the German aircraft which attempted to intercept him and then returning in an attempt to destroy the balloon "in its bed" after it had been hauled down by the German crew.

He speaks of Bishop's concern that his parents would worry about him and goes on to say: "But like most heroes and all air aces, Bishop was blessed with more than his share of luck."

Billy Bishop gave a graphic description of the Battle of Vimy Ridge from the air and Pierre Berton uses this in the "Overture" section of his book.

This kind of recognition is both pleasing to read and well deserved. No innuendos—just one great Canadian expressing his pride in the feats of another. If Paul Cowan considers himself a journalist, he could learn a great deal from literary giants like Pierre Berton.

By the way, war veterans will see Berton's *Vimy* as a classic—and Berton saw no need to express doubts about how heroes are made and why a country needs them. Berton speaks with justifiable pride of the four Victoria Cross winners from the Vimy action to which he refers in his book.

- Private Bill Milne, of the Canadian Scottish, from Moose Jaw destroyed a machine gun emplacement.
- Ellis Sifton of the Victoria Rifles (Eastern townships) charged an enemy machine gun nest, clubbing and slashing its crew. He was killed minutes later.
- Major Thane MacDowell from Lachute, Quebec, serving with the 38th Battalion from Ottawa, bombed out two machine gun nests and, single-handedly, took prisoner two German officers and seventy-seven members of the Prussian Guard.
- Private John Pattison of the 44th Battalion from Winnipeg charged an enemy stronghold, putting its guns out of action with hand grenades.

John Norman Harris

The question arises as to how Paul Cowan and the NFB could have gone so wrong in attempting to discredit Billy Bishop.

Was the NFB attempting "revisionism?" Why? The Billy Bishop legend has survived. It is not a mixture of myth and fact, as Paul Cowan would have us believe! No legend, if even one part myth, could come through the years unscathed.

Looking back there was Jack Scott's book of 1919. There was George Drew's book of 1930. There were numerous articles in prestigious aviation magazines in the early Thirties, Forties and Fifties. Reference has been made to Dennis Winter's book *The First of the Few* of 1982 and Robert Jackson's book *The RAF from Flanders to the Falklands* of 1985.

Nowhere, however, does one get the feel of what Billy Bishop did better than in John Norman Harris' book *The Knights of the Air* published in 1963.

On the dust cover Harris says: "Billy Bishop was the most famous of all. In his first six weeks of flying he scored 17 victories and won the DSO and the MC. Four weeks later he added the VC."

In the Chapter headed "Bishop: The Black Days," Norman Harris speaks specifically of Bishop's value in the strategic and tactical sense. Much has been written about "Bloody April"—April of 1917—where over Flanders the Royal Flying Corps' losses reached disastrous proportions.

General John Trenchard, Commander of the RFC, laid down the policy known as "the full dinner table." That is, if a pilot were shot down on the dawn patrol his replacement would be sent to the Squadron to take the missing man's place at the dinner table that evening.

By April 5, Bishop had a roving commission. On April 6 and 7, 28 British planes had been shot down. The morale of the RFC was strained to the utmost, and as Harris says: "They were the days calling for utmost fortitude—and they were also the days when Bishop found himself."

Concerning the aerodrome raid, Norman Harris gives an excellent account. He states that he based much of it on the research done by George Drew in 1930, but "wherever possible I have gone back to the sources."

Norman Harris' account of the attack appears in the Research Documents.

Ira "Taffy" Jones

I have no idea how much time Paul Cowan spent in research.

My interest in World War One flyers did not start with the Billy Bishop film. I was *raised* on the history of World War I. My family had a deep personal interest in it—and had lived with the grief of having lost loved ones. Our family library contained many interesting books on the subject.

Hence for me the arguments concerning Mick Mannock's score and the conjecture as to who really brought Richthofen down made for lively "light reading"—I am going back some fifty years now.

Many of my age group have known the "detective games" played by early aviation buffs in regard to the relative "scores" of the air aces of the 1914-18 war. Paul Cowan stumbled on this information, but perhaps he didn't realize that for many it is an interesting hobby—not to be taken too seriously.

Be that as it may, it seems possible to suggest that any bias against Billy Bishop started with the writings of one man. If interested, I suggest you read him! His name was Ira Jones, sometimes known as "Taffy."

He wrote numerous books and articles. They purported to tell the story of the Royal Flying Corps but strangely enough, made very little reference to Canadians—despite the fact that at least a third of the flyers and certainly the very top ones like Bishop, MacLaren, Barker and Collishaw came from Canada.

It is suspected, however, that Ira Jones had a personal animus towards Canadians and even possibly a feeling of hatred towards Billy Bishop. After all, Bishop was the top gun in this brash group of Colonials.

Ira Jones' dislike of Billy Bishop comes out quite clearly in his book *Tiger Squadron*, published in 1954. His book, incidentally, is a glowing tribute to Mick Mannock, the Irish Ace, eulogized by Jones in his book.

The first anti-Bishop reference to be noted was as follows: ''. . . Mick was to go and command 85 Squadron on his return from leave, in place of Bishop. Bishop was returning to England at the request of the Canadian government. They did not want their hero to be killed. This is a precedent in war. Everyone is fed up to the teeth. . . .''

Then he says: ''Their leader (85 Squadron) turned out to be Nigger Horne, not Bishop their CO, who specializes in fighting alone, not in formation.''

In the context in which it was written, Jones is criticizing Bishop for his ''lone wolf'' technique although Billy Bishop was encouraged to seek out the enemy single-handedly; and was given a roving commission to do so.

In another bit of underhanded writing, Jones describes a patrol when there was only an 800-foot ceiling where his flight had returned, empty handed. He goes on to say:

Imagine our surprise when, an hour later, Nigger (Spencer) Horne phoned Grid (the CO) and told him of Bishop's wonderful feat, before going home today, of shooting down four Huns on our Front and at the same time we were up.

We went over to Saint Omer and read his report.

Apparently, he went through the clouds and found a formation of five scouts at 1,500 feet. He attacked them. Two immediately collided. One he shot down. Going down through the clouds, he found another Hun, which he destroyed on his way back from the enemy line. He said he finished up his ammunition by shooting up troops he saw near Kemmel.

What we can't understand is, first, what a formation of Huns were doing above the clouds—a thick layer, with no breaks in it—since they could not see the ground. Secondly, why didn't we see the Huns below the clouds? Luck of the game, I suppose.

The Colonel asked to see me about the show when he visited us this morning. As the general weather conditions were overcast and rain all along the Ypres Salient Front, he exonerated us from our failure to assist Bishop in his heroic achievement.''

Just one comment. Both the Allied and German fighters were capable of flying up to 16,000 feet or higher. One wonders why, in his description, Ira Jones expresses surprise that the German planes should be at 1,500 feet. He then asks why his flight didn't see the Huns below the clouds. That is obvious. The ceiling was at 800 feet while the German planes were flying above the ceiling at 1,500 feet. Perhaps the cause of his annoyance lies in the acknowledged fact that the CO must have been upset at the failure of Ira Jones' flight to find and engage the Germans.

Another snide remark in Jones' book lashes out at Billy Bishop's tendency to fight alone. He says:

The Squadron is very full out. Everyone says they much prefer Mick (Mannock) to Bishop as CO. Mick leads all Squadron patrols and produces the Hun on a plate. Bishop rarely did this. He was an individualist and most of his victories were on lone patrols.

It is well to remember that Bishop's practice of fighting on his own, rather than in formation, was being carried out on direct instructions from the top brass.

Incidentally, in the Appendix to his book *Tiger Squadron*, written in 1954, Ira Jones gave Billy Bishop credit for 72 victories. It is interesting, however, that in the same list, he shows Major E. Mannock with 73 victories. Most historians and others who wrote about World War I airmen, up until that time, had Mick Mannock's ''score'' between 54 and 60.

So there is some suspicion that the rumours of Bishop inflating the reports of his victories, and faking his VC raid on the aerodrome, may well have come originally from the poison pen of Ira Jones. Think about it!

It would seem that the NFB film should be destroyed. Please think about that too!

Chapter 20
Conclusion

Did Paul Cowan and the National Film Board perpetrate a monumental hoax on the unsuspecting Canadian public... and ruin the reputation of one of our most loved and respected heroes in the bargain (Oops, a Freudian slip with a price tag of $400,000)?

This *Digest* has attempted to present all of the evidence. Maybe there is a slant—but only to the extent that the film *THE KID WHO COULDN'T MISS* is slanted in the other direction.

A word about libel: The Senate Sub-Committee Proceedings contain an excellent treatise on the law of defamation, when the person defamed is dead. Billy Bishop cannot sue Paul Cowan. Agreed. What if Cliff Chadderton has libelled Paul Cowan? Unlike Cowan, I have some solid backing for what this *Digest* says... but if I have transgressed the law of libel I am sure Mr. Cowan knows some good lawyers.

Now... as to a conclusion. As was stated at the beginning... this *Digest* is intended to spark debate so as to get at the heart of the issue. Please, draw your own!

A Footnote

The mandate of the National Film Board was described by its Commissioner, François Macerola before the Senate Sub-Committee in the following terms:

The NFB was established by the National Film Act. The NFB is a departmental agency under the direction and control of the Minister of Communications, accountable to Parliament through the Minister! In a practice respected by all governments the final decision-making authority for content and aesthetic judgment has been entrusted to the Government Film Commissioner and the Board of Trustees. I need not mention that since the 1950's a tradition of arm's length, whereby the NFB has remained autonomous in its decisions, both administrative and artistic, has been the order of the day which has governed the relationship between this institution and the government.

Successive governments and Parliaments have protected this tradition which assures the creative and artistic credibility and integrity of the NFB. It is for this reason that the NFB has remained a cultural institution which has come to take an important place in the lives of Canadians and Canadian culture.

I have no doubt that you would agree with me that the programming decisions of our cultural agencies and artists should continue to remain free from political directives. The use of public dollars is clearly protected via accountability for procedures which, in the case of the NFB means annual review of Estimates by Parliament.

Has Paul Cowan, in *THE KID WHO COULDN'T MISS*, taken the NFB past its mandate?

Everyone agrees that there must be no *political* interference with government-financed institutions in the media field. This is guaranteed in their mandate. What happens, however, when the mandate is ignored? The Parliamentary process cannot grapple with the situation. The Sinclair Stevens affair is a prime example. Unlike a Parliamentary Committee, where the questioners are the Parliamentarians themselves, the Public Enquiry is a forum where the questions are asked by highly skilled Counsel. Witnesses can be examined and cross-examined.

If the National Film Board will not admit its gross blunder and recall and destroy the film, perhaps a Public Enquiry is the only way that Canadians can have some say if indeed an independent government agency has gone beyond its intent and purpose as defined by Parliament.

The author

Glossary

AA	Anti-aircraft
CAF	Canadian Air Force
CB	Confined to barracks or Commander of the Bath
CEF	Canadian Expeditionary Force
CO	Commanding Officer
DFC	Distinguished Flying Cross
DSC	Distinguished Service Cross
DSO	Distinguished Service Order
EA	Enemy aircraft
F/S	Flight Sergeant
HEA	Hostile Enemy Aircraft
HQ	Headquarters
Jasta	Squadron
Lt.	Lieutenant
MC	Military Cross
mph	miles per hour
NCO	non-commissioned officer
NFB	National Film Board
OC	Officer Commanding
RAF	Royal Air Force
RCAF	Royal Canadian Air Force
RFC	Royal Flying Corps
RMC	Royal Military College
SE	southeast
SL	Schütte-Lanz
VC	Victoria Cross

The official portrait of Lieutenant-Colonel W.A. Bishop, VC, hangs in the Royal Canadian Air Force Officers' Mess in Ottawa, Canada.

An Allied aerodrome with aircraft (two-seater Samsons) and personnel lined up for review.

An impressive line-up of Nieuports at a French airfield. The planes were covered with Irish linen, as were many planes of that era. Irish linen was an ideal fabric, extremely resilient, yet lightweight and easy to repair.

Members of the Royal Flying Corps receive instruction on the Lewis gun. Bishop, during his Observer Training, attended similar classes.

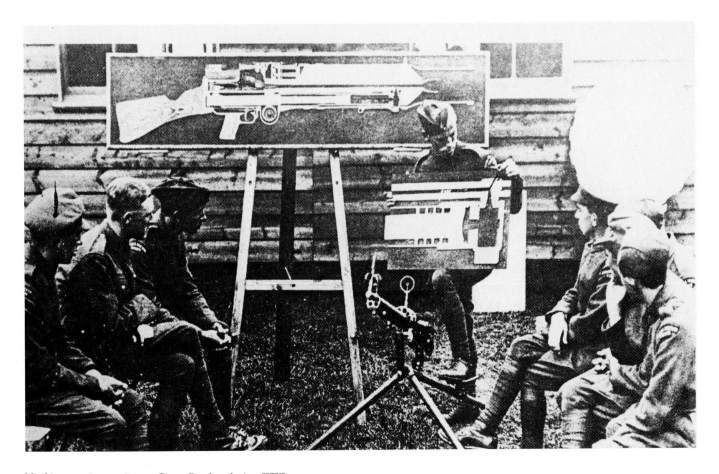

Machine gun instruction at Camp Borden during WWI.

A lineup of Nieuport 17s. Notice the plane on the far right getting ready for take-off: it required the assistance of ground crew during engine run up.

Bishop stands before his favourite Nieuport 17.

A Nieuport 17 in flight over the enemy lines.

Billy Bishop as a cadet at the Royal Military College in Kingston, Ontario.

Lieutenant Bishop wearing the "O" and single wing of an RFC Observer.

The now-famous picture of Lieutenant Bishop in the cockpit of his Nieuport, the WWI aircraft with which he won the Victoria Cross.

Lt. Col. W.G. Barker, VC, DSO, MC

Bishop having some fun with his faithful mascot in France.

The author examines the Lewis gun on an exact replica of Bishop's Nieuport. The plane is housed at the National Aviation Museum in Ottawa, Canada. The Museum's official description of the plane reads:

Nieuport 17
The Nieuport 17 was probably the most successful fighter design of the mid-war period, and was used by the air forces of all the Allies. All the famous French aces of the time used it as well as many well-known aces of the Royal Flying Corps.
This example, a flying replica with an original engine and other equipment, was built from contemporary drawings by C.R. Swanson of Sycamore, Illinois. It is in the markings of B1566, the aircraft in which Lt. W.A. Bishop won his Victoria Cross, when he attacked Esnes Airfield on the 2nd of June 1917, destroying three German aircraft as they took off.

Wing span	26' 10''	Armament	1 Lewis mg.
Length	18' 11''	Maximum speed	107 mph.
Gross weight	1,233 lbs.	Maximum range	155 miles
Engine	Le Rhone 110 hp.	Service ceiling	17,400 ft.

It's worthwhile to note that parachutes were not worn in these aircraft.

During the Second World War Billy Bishop served as an Air Marshall. He worked vigorously in the recruiting field doing much to inspire aircrew undergoing training in the British Commonwealth Air Training Plan.

Part II
Senate Sub-Committee
Material

RMC Critique (narrative)

Author's Note

The minutes of the Senate Sub-Committee for October 30, 1985 contain an almost unbelievable account of the problems encountered by the Manitoba and Northwestern Ontario Branch of the Royal Military College Club of Canada, in attempting to arrange meetings with Mr. François Macerola, NFB Commissioner and with Paul Cowan.

As Professor Kear told the Sub-Committee, three letters and three phone calls to the Commissioner or his office went for naught. The other could not, or did not want to, meet with the RMC Graduate Group in Manitoba.

A letter from Paul Cowan to Professor Kear was even more pointed. Mr. Cowan, in his reply to Professor Kear, pointed out that he had ''made a trip out West talking about the film, and I have written many responses to those who wrote to me. . .I think I have been open and candid, but enough is enough and I am moving on to other things.''

The critique prepared for the RMC Club (Manitoba) follows.

CRITIQUE

of

THE KID WHO COULDN'T MISS

Principal Authors

    T.A. MCMANUS BA, MBA, CFA

    D.J. MCMANUS RN

Produced by request of the
Manitoba Branch of the
Royal Military College Club of Canada

In Association with

    B. RUTHERFORD, BSc, LLB

    Professor A. KEAR, BA, BA, MA

April, 1984

THE KID WHO COULDN'T MISS

"Every year on November 11, Billy Bishop is
remembered once again. And with the passing
of years, it becomes harder to know what part
of his legend is myth and what part truth.
But one thing is clear, heroism, like war
itself is neither as simple or as glorious
as we would like."[1]

"The Kid Who Couldn't Miss" is marketed as an
historical documentary about Billy Bishop. In actual fact, Bishop's
story has been used to present the author's more subtle anti-war,
anti-hero theme. Billy Bishop is a hero. If the author can
destroy the legend of Bishop, he can destroy the concept of a hero.
What an excellent way to present a theme!

Although I have no objection to anyone presenting
an anti-war, anti-hero theme, it has always been my expectation
that the theme should evolve from the facts. In this case, the
author has been so devoted to his theme, that the facts were
altered to illustrate the theme.

The objective of reviewing this movie is to show
that there are such serious inaccuracies in the presentation,
that the film should be withdrawn. Furthermore, money should
be made available for further research on Bishop, hopefully primary
research, including a thorough search of German records, letters
and diaries. This material should be made available to a film
company interested in producing an unbiased movie about Billy Bishop.

It is well known that this production is not the
first about Billy Bishop. The stage production "Billy Bishop Goes
to War" was widely played across Canada. It is interesting to
note here that there was an underlying anti-war theme there as
well, showing the excited new recruit gradually being disillusioned
by war. The difference is that, in "Billy Bishop Goes to War",
the author managed to follow the course of history in presenting
that theme. Bishop and the audience are disillusioned together,
so we are not left feeling scornful of whatever sentiments motivate
a young man to do unusual things during war.

I suspect that this stage production, along with its
success, is the reason for the course taken by the author of
"The Kid Who Couldn't Miss". Merely making a stage production
into a movie, is not an artistic challenge, nor will it make a
name for its producers. It is understandable that the authors would
have searched for a new angle, some fresh insight into the story,
before agreeing to produce the movie. It is also understandable
that the controversy about the aerodrome raid deserved investigation.
However, it is not understandable that the author has allowed himself
to be drawn so far from the course of history for the sake of his own
glory. I find it rather ironic that the suggestion in the movie is
that Billy Bishop faked the aerodrome raid in the quest of glory.
I now suggest that the film's authors have falsified this production
for the same reason.

Billy Bishop was a hero from the first World War. He

was a Canadian fighting ace, the top scorer in the Royal Flying Corps of all the aces-British, Canadian or other nationalities. No matter what our opinions may be regarding war, Bishop did what we asked of him, and did it to the best of his ability. He received at least four medals for various acts of bravery and commendable behaviour. It is the events leading up to the awarding of one of these medals that form the basis of the controversy in this film.

There are rumors that this aerodrome raid has never been documented, leading to questions about whether in fact it was ever carried out as described. In the search for a controversial new outlook from which to present this film, the author has used this controversy as the climax of the film. He has emphasized it, and given it the status of a crime. This documentary is not Bishop's life story, its his trial, and Bishop is guilty until proven innocent. Any other details of Bishop's life, either before or after the raid in question, are related only if they will help the prosecution prove its case.

There is nothing wrong with putting any figure on trial when there is a significant event that needs investigation. But Bishop deserves a fair trial. Both sides of the case should be presented. Documented fact should be separated from speculation and conjecture. Psychological manipulation should be omitted. The authors of this production have done none of these.

Firstly, the defense is never called upon to speak. This presentation contains only details that will contribute in some way to the prosecution's case.

The real criticisms of the case become apparent when we start to analyze the facts presented. There are so many factual errors in this presentation, that the film should not be allowed to continue being shown on this basis alone. Some of the errors are small, with no apparent significance to the authors' story. Some of them are of obvious significance and have undoubtedly been altered to enhance the plot. For example, the presentation of the aerodrome raid at the end of Bishop's career, instead of during the early stages of it, is nothing more than an artistic ploy to increase its significance, and to change its relevance by altering the circumstances in which it took place. (See page 23 for further discussion.) In fact, by doing this, the author has used events which happened as a result of the raid, to help create the motive for faking the raid.

When Bishop returned to Canada on leave in September, 1917, "he experiences for the first time what it means to be a hero"[2], and he likes being a celebrity. (Who among us would not?) This   love of glory, and the awareness that his actions are becoming famous in the press, is built up to be the motive for faking the aerodrome raid. "Such celebrity also pushes one to take insane risks."[3] The raid on the German aerodrome occurred before Bishop went on leave to Canada, and before the press started to glorify the air war and make the pilots famous. It was a result of the raid, and the subsequent Victoria Cross that Bishop became so well known that the crowds came out to cheer him when he returned to Canada.

The author has used this fame to provide a motive for the events that created it. That is quite a reversal, and definitely not evidence that we should allow to be submitted against any defendant.

A discussion of the factual errors in the movie is included in the detailed critique attached to this paper. I do not pretend that this list is complete. In fact, more errors have been pointed out since the list was compiled. The items discussed compare the movie's presentation with the information available in history texts. The significance of each item is included to discuss the advantage(s) of each change to the authors' objective. I have not returned to primary sources for verification of the details of Bishop's career, though I do hope that in future this will be done.

There is of course the question of whether the author has had access to new and revealing documents not contained in conventional texts. I do not have the ability to answer this question definitively. However, I can say that the attention to accuracy in this film has been of such low quality on details that could be verified easily, that it is unlikely that time has been spent on researching the facts before commencing production. Furthermore, if new evidence with the power to convict Bishop had been found, the author would not have bothered to falsify history in attempts to obtain that conviction.

Another point here, is that the author has never gone so far as to state outright that Bishop is guilty. The technique has been to build the case on erroneous details and circumstantial evidence. In fact, the author has shown a great talent for using innuendo, the power of suggestion, and emotive terms to manipulate us psychologically, and lead us step by step toward the guilty verdict. The plot has been constructed with admirable talent to produce these responses without putting the suggestions into words. The audience, in coming to view the film expect to be entertained and to have a history lesson in the process. They should in fact, be warned that they are Bishop's judge and jury and that they should be prepared to be analytical; to look past the manipulation techniques in making a decision about this potential crime in Bishop's life.

There is another point on which the audience should be warned as well. The prosecution's star witness is Walter Bourne, Bishop's mechanic in 60 Squadron. Bourne is supposedly interviewed several times throughout the movie, and several of the points he submits are his opinions, not fact. It is he who alleges that Bishop's intention to conduct the raid was so well advertised that Bourne thought that the king was coming (quite a motive for not wanting to fail). Bourne informs us that Bishop could not remove his Lewis gun in flight, and that the plane had only a neat circle of bullet holes in it, not the tattered remains that are described in the literature. This is very damning evidence against Bishop. Bourne is a strategic figure in convincing the audience that there are too many discrepancies between the "facts" and the historical records to have any doubts that the raid was faked. However, although

Walter Bourne was the name of Bishop's mechanic, this witness is
not the real Walter Bourne. His opinions hold no validity, and
his "facts", far from being a firsthand account, are pure fiction.
I would be getting a bit dramatic with my own imagery if I stated
that the author has perjured himself by creating this witness
and allowing him to testify, in order to augment the prosecution's
argument. In any case, the point should be stressed that this figure
is fictional and should not be present in a historical documentary.
(Walter Bourne is discussed at some length in the detailed critique,
pages 7, 8, 14, 26, 28 and 37). The part of Bourne was played by the
same actor who played Bishop in both the stage play and the film.

        I have referred to the rumors that exist regarding
Bishop's career. Did he in fact have 72 kills on his score as the
record states, did he single-handedly attack a German aerodrome
and did he deserve the Victoria Cross? I do not have the answers
to these questions. They could only be obtained by returning to
the primary records. The purpose of this paper is to show that the
author does not have the answers either. If I am not qualified to
speak in Bishop's defense, the film's producers are even less
qualified to prosecute him. They have demonstrated themselves
to be unethical and unprincipled in their reporting and arguments,
and therefore unworthy of credibility.

        What about these rumors. I think that it is
appropriate to reflect for a few moments upon the nature of heroes,

and the possible sources of rumors about them. Most of the air aces have some rumors connected with their records, some may be deserved, some not. What about Bishop's situation? Where, or from whom could these rumors originate?

Bishop flew for the Royal Flying Corps, even though he was a Canadian. The Canadians did not have a separate air force at that time. The British fliers were all gentlemen, drawn from the upper class. Gentlemen, although well known for their chivalry, were not generally raised to be tough and competitive. Bishop was typically unBritish. He was not from the upper class, he had a highly competitive, very determined personality with an intense desire to increase his score and obtain recognition. Regardless of his abilities as a fighter pilot, he could never have been accepted as one of the British upper class.

Bishop's relationship with Lady St Helier could easily have instilled jealousy and anger. Why was she helping a Colonial rather than one of the English pilots, such as McCudden or Ball?

Bishop was a loner. He had few close friends, so there were no allies to help him defeat any unwarranted negative publicity. The very nature of being a loner tends to create enemies of people who do not understand.

Bishop set his goal at being number one. This required the dethroning of other aces, a very effective way to make enemies.

For his aerodrome raid Bishop asked two people to join him.[4] Both refused. Were these people sufficiently angered by all the publicity and the receipt of the Victoria Cross after the raid that they decided to plant rumors? Did other pilots turn vindictive because Bishop did not offer them a chance at glory?

Of the British Empire's top seven aces, the first and second were Canadians, Bishop was first and Collishaw was second. Of the remaining five, two more were Canadian, one Australian, one South African, and one British.[5] This record alone is enough to damage British pride.

Furthermore, there is evidence that Bishop may not have been alone in being disliked by British pilots. Canada made a major contribution to the air war and "by 1918...was sending 200 pilots over monthly, and by the end of the war a Dominion with 10% of the Empire's population was producing a third of the British airforce."[6] For this major contribution "little attention is given in 'War in Air' (British Official History of Air War published in 6 volumes) to the contributions made by airmen from the colonies."[7]

It should be noted here that there is a dispute over these top ace positions. In referring to the British ace Edward Mannock, Christopher Shores states "After the war he was awarded a Victoria Cross, the citation indicating that he had some 50 victories, but subsequently his biography written by 74 Squadron ace, JIT Jones, quoted his score as 73-one above Bishop whom

Jones obviously disliked and disapproved of".[8] (Jones' dislike of Bishop can be found on pages 129, 140, 141, and 152 of his book, "Tiger Squadron").[9] It must have been a very powerful sentiment that motivated Jones to make such a drastic change in Mannock's score.

Looking at Jones' action, and at the British pride, seeing the way that the British air history treated Canadians, and reviewing the dismal record of top ace positions held by England, the potential is definitely there for Bishop to have enough enemies, in his squadron, in the press, or back in Britain to be sources of derogatory rumors. Perhaps the film's author has been a susceptible victim of these sour grapes arguments, allowing these reports to colour the facts.

These reflections do not clear Bishop of the charges against him, but they do explain why the existence of rumors does not prove that he is guilty either. Bishop was no saint, he never pretended to be. But then that is not the definition of a hero either. The pity is that we, as Canadians, often demand sainthood of our heroes. We must allow the man to be eccentric. After all, what we were asking him to do was a far cry from your typical white collar job. No matter what our opinions are of war, we cannot condemn the man for getting involved in his job, or for growing to enjoy it. Our assessment of him as a hero must take his actions in the context in which they occurred. In peace time, acts of war are looked down upon. But Bishop was

at war. He put all of his energies into helping the Allies win
that war and undoubtedly performed many acts of bravery in that
cause. Even if we exclude the aerodrome raid, and its ensuing
Victoria Cross, he still won the Distinguished Service Order,
the Military Cross and the Distinguished Flying Cross. His
reputation is not based on one event alone. Regardless of the
results of any research in that regard, his hero status should not
be revoked.

Billy Bishop has been "used" in this film production
to destroy the glory of being a hero. As well as trying to
demonstrate Bishop himself as unworthy of this title, the author
has woven into the film the message that "heroism, like war itself
is neither as simple or as glorious as we would like."[10] The
suggestion is that the air ace was invented as a propaganda tool.
The publicity of the romantic air war was used to keep the public's
mind off the miserable ground war. Did the press exploit the
air war? If they did, does that negate any contribution that the
air war made in the country's defense? Did it make the fights or
the raids that were conducted any less lethal, any less brave, or
any less heroic?

The result of this discussion is the downgrading of
the presenting of medals during war. The presentation of the
Victoria Cross for an undocumented raid was "virtually unheard of".
The explanation is offered that "The king has said that the one
thing he has always wanted is to give the three awards (the V.C.,
the D.S.O. and the M.C.) at the same time and the king generally
gets what he wants."[11] The glory, the pride and the reward value

are turned into a joke.

Billy Bishop is a Canadian hero. I freely admit
that my indignation over this film is based not only on the
destruction of Bishop's reputation but on the destruction of
a Canadian hero. We, as Canadians, have so few heroes, I object
to having one dethroned for no other motive than an author's
glory, and by such unethical techniques. The National Film
Board should be helping us to identify ourselves as Canadians,
and helping us find sources of pride in our history rather than
setting out to destroy the ones we have.

Billy Bishop was put on trial in "The Kid Who
Couldn't Miss". The prosecution has presented its case. This
paper has been produced to refute that case. Now it's time to
prepare the case for the defense. It is our hope that someone
will take up the challenge of returning to primary sources to
investigate. We owe it to Billy Bishop, we owe it to ourselves
as Canadians, and we owe it to all our heroes, both past and
future.

FOOTNOTES

1. "The Kid Who Couldn't Miss", The National Film Board.

2. "The Kid Who Couldn't Miss", The National Film Board.

3. "The Kid Who Couldn't Miss", The National Film Board.

4. Winged Warfare, p. 157.

5. Air Aces, p. 43.

6. The First of the Few, p. 21.

7. Canadian Airmen and the First World War, Preface, px.

8. Air Aces, p. 24.

9. Tiger Squadron, p. 129, 140, 141, 152.

10. "The Kid Who Couldn't Miss", The National Film Board.

11. "The Kid Who Couldn't Miss", The National Film Board.

RMC Detailed Critique (film)

NOTE: The events listed in this critique, follow the order of presentation in the movie. They do not follow in the order of the significance of the errors. The quotations from the movie were transcribed from a tape recording of the film's sound track.

INCIDENT=BILLY_BISHOP'S_BOYHOOD

Nature_of_the_Error=_Inaccurate_Information

Movie

> "It's cold and miserable this Fall of 1904, and just outside of Owen Sound, William Avery Bishop is stalking the last of the honkers....He's after the two bits his father will pay him for each bird brought down."

Fact

As a young man, Bishop probably did shoot down birds. But what is important though is that in "The Courage of the Early Morning", Art Bishop, Billy's son, indicates that it was squirrels that provided Bishop's allowance.

> "Billy's father had given him a .22 rifle one Christmas and offered him twenty-five cents for every squirrel he shot. Will Bishop did not expect the offer to cost him much. He knew it was extremely difficult to kill a wary squirrel high on a tree with a single, low powered .22 bullet, but the difficulty would give Billy good practise, and might even scare off some of the squirrels that damaged the fruit trees in his garden by gnawing their bark.

> That offer was to cost Will Bishop many dollars....When the surviving squirrel population no longer invaded the Bishop garden, Billy expanded his operation into other gardens and orchards, at the standard rate of twenty-five cents per squirrel. The 'Sun' recorded the phenomenon of the scarcity of squirrels in town and

dubbed Billy 'the Pied Piper of Owen
Sound'."(1)

Significance

This first distortion of fact probably falls within the limits of artistic license. It is recorded here because it is
just the beginning of a long list of errors that exceed such
an acceptable limit.

Having seen the movie, it is obvious why the film's authors
decided to use birds instead of squirrels. The term "birds"
is slang for airplanes. The authors of the film were thus
able to show a young boy shooting down airplanes, ie birds.
To have presented such a scene after mentioning squirrels,
would have been artistically illogical.

INCIDENT - BISHOP'S ENTRANCE INTO RMC

Nature of the Error - Inaccurate Information

Movie

The film moves onto Billy Bishop's entrance to the Royal
Military College. "In desparation," Billy's father, "packs
him off to the Royal Military College in Kingston, Ontario
where Bishop's lack of academic inclination will pass unnoticed."

Fact

There is some evidence that Bishop's parents "sent" him off
to RMC, but I certainly know of no evidence to support the
contention that RMC accepted low academic standards of performance, even in 1911. RMC has always demanded very high
academic standards.(2)

The film in discussing Bishop's career at RMC (1911-1914),
purports to show scenes of college life and college training. I would suggest that the scenes shown are neither.

Significance

1   The Courage of the Early Morning p14.
2   Winged Warfare p22.

These comments inaccurately degrade RMC, and by association the college's graduates. This will help promote the anti-war theme by casting doubts upon the graduates' competence as officers in the Armed Forces.

INCIDENT - BISHOP CHEATS ON FINAL EXAMS

Nature of the Error - Inaccurate Information

Movie

The movie nears the completion of Bishop's time at RMC and the following statement is made. "When the other cadets are rehearsing for final graduation, Billy Bishop isn't with them. He's cheated on his final exams and is to be expelled."

Fact

Although Bishop did cheat on his exams held in May 1914, there is no evidence that supports the statement that the decision had been made to expel him.

> "In May 1914, when he sat his examinations, he was caught cheating....With Billy once more up before him, Adjutant Perreau had only a few terse words for the culprit; the punishment would be held in abeyance during the summer holidays... It was almost certain that the verdict would be dismissal."(3)

It would seem presumptuous to state that Bishop "is to be expelled" when no verdict had been rendered, even though the probability of this event was high.

Fortunately, or unfortunately, for Bishop, the decision was never made as World War I broke out and he left RMC to join the Mississauga Horse, and later the Seventh Canadian Mounted Rifles.

Significance

3   The Courage of the Early Morning p18.

This is the first presentation of Bishop as a cheat, a theme that is recurrent throughout the whole movie and is the foundation for the anti-hero message.

The authors can again probably argue artistic license because the cheating incident is documented and it really sounds so much more impressive to suggest that he was really expelled, rather than only at risk of being expelled. The former implies a crime of much greater magnitude. It will be interesting to see the records of the incident at RMC, to discover whether in fact, the decision was ever made, although not handed down.

INCIDENT - BISHOP'S ENROLLMENT INTO THE ARMY

Nature of the Error - Guilt by Association

Movie

The script continues and describes the conditions existing in Canada in regards to the enrollment of officers for the army. The statements themselves may hold truth, but when read with Bishop's photo on the screen, the suggestion is effectively made that the statement is not a general one, but designed to describe Bishop in particular.

> "The declaration of war has induced the Canadian Army to commission even its poorest prospects. So in September Billy Bishop is commissioned a Lieutenant and starts serious training."

Fact

No one knows yet whether or not Bishop will make a good officer. It takes more than one indiscretion as a student to earn the title of the "poorest prospect." In actual fact, the three years of military training at RMC probably made Bishop very desirable to the recruiters, who were faced with multitudes of untrained individuals.

Significance

The movie is laying the groundwork for presenting Bishop as an undesireable character, so that later arguments and rumors will be accepted more easily by the viewer.

INCIDENT - BISHOP SAILS TO ENGLAND

Nature of the Error - Incorrect Dates

Movie

> "As Canadian boys embark for the front in 1914, they cried glory without embarrassment. And in November, Billy Bishop mounts the gangplank of the SS Caledonia."

Fact

This statement is contradicted by Art Bishop in "The Courage of the Early Morning".

> "Early in June...the Seventh got its orders to sail for England.... In Montreal a week later the Seventh and their seven hundred horses crowded aboard the cattleship Caledonia. The Atlantic voyage lasted fourteen days...The Caledonia ... sailed unscathed into Plymouth harbour in thick fog at four o'clock on the morning of June 23,1915." (4)

Significance

Repeatedly throughout the movie the timing of events has been altered. Some of the changes are so minor that the question could be raised as to whether they were intentional errors or merely the visible result of sloppy research. On the other hand, there are visible motives for some of the time changes and reordering of history.

This particular time change advances Bishop's arrival into England by six months. This will give the authors more time in which to rearrange the later sequences.

INCIDENT - LIFE IN THE TRENCHES IN FRANCE, CHRISTMAS 1914

Nature of the Error - Incorrect Information

4   The Courage of the Early Morning p23.

Movie

The movie goes on to state that Bishop goes to France as a soldier and that,

> "On Christmas Day 1914 the opposing forc-
> es crossed the trenches and joined each
> other for a smoke; they exchanged gifts;
> then they go back to killing each other.
> It is during this period that Bishop
> finds himself and his horse mired in the
> awful French muck....It is then that he
> sees his first tiny airplane....In a
> flash, Bishop realises the only way he
> can escape the trenches is to fly." (Said
> over the sound of gunfire.)

Fact

The Christmas exchanges did occur and are well documented,
among the ironies of war. However, Bishop did not leave
Canada until June 1915. Thus he was certainly not in France
in December 1914. Furthermore, Bishop did not go to France
at all during his time in the army. The described experiences in the French muck were actually in the English muck
while training with the Seventh Canadian Mounted Rifles.
This point is documented in Bishop's own book, "Winged Warfare", and in Art Bishop's book, "The Courage of the Early
Morning".(5) Also documented is Bishop's reaction to the
sight of his first airplane.

> "At first we were sent to a very sandy
> camp on the coast, and from there to.a
> very muddy camp somewhere else in the
> British Isles. It was to this camp that
> the aeroplane came that stormy day in
> July. A week later my plans were in
> motion. I met a friend in the Royal Fly-
> ing Corps and confided in him my ambition
> to fly."(6)

Significance

5   Winged Warfare pp22-23. The Courage of the Early Morning
        pp23-24.
6   Winged Warfare p23.

—112—

The Christmas exchange in France is such a contradiction to our moral standards, that any reporting of the incident leaves us wondering what type of callous personalities could have a friendly visit, then immediately go back to killing each other. Presenting this incident in the film is useful to the author's anti-war theme.

In placing Bishop at the scene, the film's authors are able to make a clear statement about his personality. Guilt by association.

Furthermore the picture of Bishop seeing his first airplane from these physically unpleasant and dangerous trenches, suggests that he is running away rather than being fasci-nated by flight. The impact of escaping muddy training trenches in England would not have made as powerful a state-ment as this does in showing flying as Bishop's only real hope to escape this form of war.

INCIDENT - CORPORAL WALTER BOURNE IS ASSIGNED AS BISHOP'S MECHANIC

Nature of the Error - Undocumented Information

Movie

After Bishop is transferred to the Royal Flying Corps as an observer, the film states that,

> "Each plane in 21 squadron is assigned a mechanic. Corporal Walter Bourne is in charge of Bishop's machine. As Bishop's mechanic, Bourne will later play his part in the making of the Billy Bishop leg-end."

Fact

It seems most unusual to hear that a mechanic is in charge of an observer's plane. In most cases that I am aware of, a mechanic would be in charge of a pilot's plane. One does not refer to a plane as belonging to an observer, but to a pilot.

In Bishop's own book, "Winged Warfare", he makes no mention of meeting Bourne when he was an observer.(7) In Art Bishop's book, "The Courage of the Early Morning", the first

7   Winged Warfare pp24-30.

mention of Bourne is in March 1917 after Bishop became a pilot at 60 Squadron.(8)

Thus although I can neither prove, nor disprove the film's claims, I would think that these remarks are probably not true. Research would have to be done on Bourne's service record to determine if he was at 21 Squadron at the same time as Bishop.

Significance

By introducing Bourne to Bishop, at what appears to be ahead of reality, the film's authors are attempting to lengthen the period of time that Bourne knew Bishop, and hence give greater credibility to the dramatizations. The statement, "Bourne will later play his part in the making of the Billy Bishop legend", is the first of the author's attempts to lay the groundwork for convincing the viewer that Bourne is a credible source. The film uses Bourne as its major weapon in destroying the Billy Bishop legend.

INCIDENT - INTRODUCTION OF WALTER BOURNE

Nature of the Error - Misleading Authority

Movie

The film sequence here is particularly intriguing. The actor Eric Peterson, who performed as Billy Bishop in the stage play "Billy Bishop Goes to War", dramatizes the role of Walter Bourne. To present Bourne, the technique used is to take pictures of Eric Peterson, colour them brown to give the appearance of authenticity, and then to present these "stills" as Bourne in the early days.

Fact

The film's authors do not appear to have, or want to use, any live film or photos of Walter Bourne.

Significance

8   The Courage of the Early Morning p55.

—114—

Later on, when Bourne's role is dramatized by Peterson, the haunting look-alike between the actor and the browned stills is very powerful. This lends authority to Bourne when he delivers the most incriminating evidence against Bishop.

INCIDENT - BISHOP'S TIME WITH 21 SQUADRON IN FRANCE

Nature of the Error - Inaccurate Information (2 Errors)

Movie

The movie states,"after three very undistinguished months with 21 Squadron Bishop's nerves are shot, and he is being sent to London to recuperate."

Fact

Bishop's nerves were shot, and he was being sent to London to recuperate. But the remaining information is wrong. Bishop spent four, not three months with 21 Squadron and they were probably not undistinguished.

In "Winged Warfare", Bishop states, "altogether I spent four months in France as a observer."(9)

In "The Courage of the Early Morning", Art Bishop states,

> "Twenty-one Squadron was supposed to take delivery of its new improved planes in time for departure to France on New Year's Day, 1916, but they had not arrived when the squadron crossed the Channel." (10)

And,

> "The full scale performance was held on the morning of May 2, 1916, the day that Bishop and a group of others from the Suicide Squadron were to go on leave."(11)

The period described covers slightly in excess of four months.

9   Winged Warfare p31.
10   The Courage of the Early Morning p31.
11   The Courage of the Early Morning pp37-38.

The second error in the movie's statement was the referral to Bishop's undistinguished accomplishments.

While training in England as an observer, Bishop took "photographs so expertly that the War Office used them as standards of excellence."(12)

It is not logical to assume without further references that a man with this much talent, and given his later accomplishments and demonstrations of courage, would not have continued to perform as expertly in France as he had in England.

In France, Art Bishop documents, that from an airplane Bishop was able to "drop the bag (a practise smoke bomb) within eighteen paces of the target. A hit anywhere within sixty yards was considered accurate."(13) Again this is hardly an undistinguished accomplishment given the crude bombing sights used in World War I.

Significance

The advantage to the movie's theme of changing the tour from four to three months is not obvious. It is in fact a minor detail, but an error nonetheless. There are two possibilities.

The idea that the error is due to sloppy research is unlikely. The references are found in two major works about Bishop and could easily have been checked. Also, the authors do not appear sloppy, for each "change" seems to be calculated to add more weight to the idea that Bishop is an unpleasant fraud. It is possible that the film's authors shortened Bishop's tour of duty to suggest that he was a man whose nerves could deteriorate in a shorter period of time.

The second point under discussion is the significance of the comment on the undistinguished accomplishments. The advantages to film's authors in stating this are more obvious. It is not logical to compliment a character you wish to denigrate. The technique of stressing flaws and "black-washing" strengths, achieves that goal more effectively — even if it is at the expense of accuracy.

INCIDENT – BISHOP'S HOSPITALIAZTION WHILE ON LEAVE IN ENGLAND

Nature of the Error – Inaccurate Information

12   The Courage of the Early Morning p30.
13   The Courage of the Early Morning p37.

Movie

The movie relates that,

> "Shortly after he finished his first
> three months in 21 Squadron, Bishop on
> leave, coming out at night from the Savoy
> Hotel, fell down the steps and broke his
> arm."

The movie then goes on to relate a story that supposedly the King was coming to visit the hospital where Bishop was taken, and that Bishop would have to fake a head wound, since falling down at the Savoy Hotel and breaking an arm was not good enough to tell the King. (This story is related by a pilot named Cecil Knight.)

Fact

I have been unable to validate this story. I would appreciate knowing Cecil Knight's sources for this information. It appears from my reading, that Bishop, prior to going on leave, had an aircraft accident in France in which he injured his knee.(14)

While disembarking from the ship at the start of his leave, Bishop fell getting off the gangplank and hurt that same knee again.(15)

It was only on the last day of his leave that he went to hospital to have his knee checked by a doctor.

There is no mention of Bishop breaking his arm or faking injuries for the King.

Significance

Why would the film's authors report a broken arm instead of an injured knee? The answer is not obvious.

The change of the location of the injuries from an airfield in France and the gangplank of a naval vessel, to the steps of the Savoy Hotel is quite significant. Bishop's reputation falls from that of a dutiful airmen to that of a drunken bum. His injury is no longer war related, it is self-induced. When this is combined with the the fact that

14   Winged Warfare p31.   The Courage of the Early Morning
     p37.
15   The Courage of the Early Morning p38.

—117—

the injury is so shameful that Bishop must lie to the King, the film's authors make another very derogatory statement about Bishop without putting it into words.

INCIDENT - THE BATTLE OF VERDUN

Nature of the Error - Incorrect Dates

Movie

During the discussion of Bishop's time training as a pilot, the movie digresses to discuss the overall progress of the war, specifically the Battle of Verdun.

> "In June, the Germans attack the French
> fortress of Verdun....The useless fort
> was saved at a cost of a million men, and
> the mutiny of most of the French army."

We are lead to believe that it is now June, 1917, since the movie was recently discussing February 1917. It does seem logical to assume that an historical presentation would fol-low chronological order.

Fact

In reviewing the history of World War I, the following can be noted. The major battle for Verdun began in February 1916 and basically ended around year end 1916.(16) A major German attack occurred on 23 June 1916.(17)

Furthermore, the French army mutinied in April, May, and June of 1917, back in time with the dates in the movie, but a full year after the Battle of Verdun and the defense of the "useless fort" that was accused of having instigated the rebellion.

It is also an interesting inaccuracy to note that the troops portrayed in the film as fighting in the Battle of Verdun were British, when in fact the script acknowledges that they were French.

Significance

16 A History of the Great War 1914 - 1918 p243 and p252.
17 A History of the Great War 1914 - 1918 p251.

The reordering of historical events has no obvious significance here, unless it was done to facilitate the association between the battle and the mutiny. The stress on the mortality rate, the poor motives of the commanders, and the association with the mutiny, have advantages in promoting the anti-war theme.

The inaccurate portrayal of the nationality of the soldiers in the battle is unlikely to be more than carelessness or naivete, or an appreciation for good footage which just happens to suit the author's needs.

INCIDENT - BILLY BISHOP'S FIRST KILLS

Nature of the Error - Incorrect Information

Movie

Following Bishop's career as a pilot the film states, "Billy Bishop is learning how to fight. He gets victory number two the day after his first."

Fact

Bishop's first kill was on 25 March 1917. His second was on 31 March 1917, 6 days later.(18)

Significance

The point is small, but it is inaccurate. It could have been easily verified. It is another example of careless research — or does one day's lapse really sound that much more impressive than six day's lapse?

INCIDENT - DOUBTS ABOUT THE ACCURACY OF BISHOP'S SCORE

Nature of the Error - Misleading Authority and Error by Omission

Movie

The movie next introduces the idea of Bishop cheating on his score. The narrator reports that a pilot by the name of A.

18 Winged Warfare p249.

James, whose identity and qualifications as a source are not mentioned,

> "Thought that Bishop's record was fraudulent... He did not in fact have that number of kills... He thought that Bishop was a very ambitious man and was cheating on his kills... it was generally known in the RFC that Bishop was cheating."

When interviewed in the film, a veteran of World War I, responded to the question,"Have you ever heard that?", by stating firmly,"Never, I would doubt it... It was not in the character of Bishop as I knew him to do a thing like that."

Another opinion on the topic is offered by Eric Peterson, playing the part of Walter Bourne, who uses the first person to add authority to his message. Bourne's basic point is that if a quiet bloke like Carlyle believed that Bishop was cheating, then it must be true.

Fact

A. James has been presented as an authority, but in fact, "Colonel Arnie Bauer, a retired Group Captain and Chairman of Billy Bishop Heritage, who went through the files at the British Public Records office, casts doubt on the accuracy of James' knowledge."(19)

The use of the term "cheated", is not necessarily appropriate, even if discrepancies were documented. It is probably more correct to state that there are differences between what a flyer stated he achieved and that on the official record. Given the nature of aerial combat, the difficulty in verifying records, and the lack of witnesses, the discrepancies will probably exist with no fault on either side.

In terms of Bishop's kills, Art Bishop notes,

> "It is true that in 1917, when Bishop returned to Canada after his first tour of duty, the British War Office admitted that, in addition to his 47 confirmed victories, he had 23 'probable but unconfirmed' kills."(20)

It is interesting to note here that Richthofen's score, has been questioned by others. Stephen Longstreet indicates that,

19 Toronto Star 6 January 1984 p A13.
20 The Courage of the Early Morning p144.

"The British official experts stated that twenty-one of Von Richthofen's victories are not listed on any documents or records in the Berlin Archives."(21)

Although the movie discusses Richthofen's score, it raise no questions of any controversy.

Significance

This discussion about Bishop cheating is a major character assassination. The authors are well aware here, of the powerful impact carried by the idea that one of our heroes cheats. They are aware of this, and have made a major effort to make sure that we are convinced. The theory is presented by the third hand information of an unknown figure - A. James. The discussion by Eric Peterson is fiction, but is presented authoritatively as fact. Eric Peterson is not Walter Bourne. There are no direct quotes from Walter Bourne, and no indication that Bourne has authorized Peterson to speak on his behalf. However, Peterson's acting is good, and we believe him as if he were Bourne.

Furthermore, the use of the emotion packed word, "cheat", is also more convincing than the word discrepancies. It is also interesting to note here that the authors are specifically out to destroy Bishop's reputation, leaving other aces unscathed, even though as much, if not more, question surrounds their records.

INCIDENT - BISHOP'S KILLS RECORD IN 60 SQUADRON

Nature of the Error - Inaccurate Information

Movie

"...In his first 60 days, he has had 60 fights, and brought down 36 planes."

Fact

Bishop arrived at 60 Squadron on 17 March 1917.(22)

21 The Canvas Falcons p31.
22 The Courage of the Early Morning p53.

Sixty days later would be 16 May 1917. By 16 May 1917, Bishop had only 19 kills.(23)

He did not reach 36 kills until 20 July 1917 - ie he reached 36 kills in his first 125 days.(24)

Significance

This error will assist the authors in rearranging Bishop's life to help present the theme. It is interesting that the authors have just spent considerable time convincing us that Bishop "cheated" on his score. Now, the authors inflate it by twice Bishop's actual number of kills. I find this ironic and unethical in a production marketed as a documentary film.

INCIDENT-BISHOP FIGHTS RICHTHOFEN

Nature of the Error - Incorrect Dates

Movie

> "Although no one knows it yet, May 10th will be a very special day. For it is on this day, when the two most daring fighters will finally meet - Billy Bishop and Manfred Von Richthofen."

Von Richthofen's brother Lothar is portrayed as also being part of this fight.

Fact

The fight between Bishop and Richthofen did not occur on 10 May 1917. The literature only records one known fight between the two, and that occurred on 30 Apr 1917.(25)

23   Winged Warfare p249. The Courage of the Early Morning
      p203.
24   Winged Warfare p250. The Courage of the Early Morning
      p203.
25   The Canvas Falcons p338. Winged Warfare pp117 - 125. The
      Courage of the Early Morning pp80 - 82.

On 7 May 1917 Bishop went on two weeks leave to England.(26)He did not return to France until 22 May 1917.(27)

Von Richthofen went on leave on 1 May 1917, and was to be away for six weeks.(28)I would think that it is difficult for two people to have a fight when one is away in England on leave and the other is away in Germany on leave!

As additional proof that this date is unlikely, Lothar was in hospital on 5 May 1917 suffering from hip and leg wounds received that day in combat.(29)I rather doubt that Lothar would be flying on 10 May 1917, only 5 days later.

Significance

I can see no advantage to the author's story in making this small change. Careless research seems to be a possibility, when the facts are so easily checked in so many books. It appears that the authors did not care enough about historical details to bother checking.

INCIDENT - BISHOP FIGHTS VON RICHTHOFEN

Nature of the Error - Undocumented Information

Movie

During a description of the battle between Bishop and Von Richthofen, the following incident is described:

> "Out of the corner of his (Von Richthofen's) eye, he sees his brother Lothar hit. Von Richthofen is horrified at the sight of Lothar's smoking DR 7. This lapse allows Bishop, who has used the old German trick of dousing his cylinders with oil, to get on Richthofen's tail..."

26   Winged Warfare p139. The Courage of the Early Morning pp89 - 92.
27   Winged Warfare p139. The Courage of the Early Morning p95.
28   Richthofen - A True History of the Red Baron pp147 - 149. The Courage of the Early Morning p82.
29   They Fought for the Sky p136. The Red Baron p97. Air Aces p23.

Fact

There is no record in Von Richthofen's autobiography of Lothar being hit or feared hit on 30 April 1917, the actual date of the fight.(30) If the Red Baron was so distressed, surely he would have made a passing remark in his autobiography.

Furthermore, if these two brothers had accepted the obvious risks of flying together, one would expect that they would have become somewhat prepared for this type of incident.

Significance

The authors are manipulating our emotions with some carefully chosen phrasing. Our sympathy is completely with Bishop's enemy in his time of sorrow, as he watches his brother head down. The fact that Bishop takes advantage of this man in his weak moment, causes us to turn to Bishop in shocked anger.

INCIDENT - VON RICHTHOFEN'S CAREER

Nature of the Error - Incorrect Dates (4 Errors), Incorrect Information

Movie

> "The Red Baron now has 80 kills, and at least that many offers of marriage.....But on June 10th, he's hit badly in the head, and barely survives an emergency operation. A month later, barely recovered, the baron starts his comeback on a routine patrol. His departure is however marred, when a camera man takes his picture, which all pilots consider an ill omen. He is eleven days short of his 26th birthday."

The film proceeds to describe the Red Baron's last fight and states,

> "While the Red Baron tries desparately to get May, another Canadian, Roy Brown, puts one bullet into Von Richthofen's back."

30   The Red Baron pp87 - 91.

The Red Baron is dead.

Fact

The film portrays this injury as occurring in June 1917. Von Richthofen was wounded in 1917, but on 6 July, not 10 June.(31)

At the time of his wound, Von Richthofen had only 57 kills, not 80.(32)

The head wound described above is heavily exaggerated . In "Richthofen - A True History of the Red Baron", Burrows' description does not sound like "barely surviving".

> "Woodbridge's bullet had left a four inch crease in Richthofen's head, furrowing deeply enough so that after the blood was washed off, his skull was plainly visible. So were several bone splinters."

And later,

> "Less than a week after he was admitted to St Nicholas's, Manfred was able to sit up in frogged silk pajamas to be photographed..."(33)

The next point of discrepancy is that Von Richthofen was not out of the air a month as stated, but only 19 days. He returned to the front on 25 July 1917.(34)

Concerning the date of Richthofen's death, the authors demostrate their ability to mislead without actually putting it into words. The time sequence of Von Richthofen's come-back on that routine patrol, and his death are clearly por-trayed as one event. In fact there were nine months between the two. The amusing point here is that the authors state that he died just "eleven days short of his 26th birthday". This statement is accurate. Von Richthofen's birthday was on 2 May 1892.(35) He was killed on 21 April 18, an interval of

31   Richthofen - A True History of the Red Baron pp159 - 160. The Red Baron p106. Air Aces p14. The Canvas Fal-cons p221.
32   The Red Baron p169. The Canvas Falcons p370.
33   Richthofen - A True History of the Red Baron pp163 - 164.
34   Richthofen - A True History of the Red Baron p166.
35   The Canvas Falcons p99.

eleven days before his 26th birthday.(36) Since there is no way that the audience would know Von Richthofen's birthday, the authors have had no fear that this piece of information would contradict the earlier statements.

One further point is shown in error when it is realized that the interval between the Red Baron's death and his return to the air after his head injury was nine months, not one month. Stephen Longstreet, on the subject of the wound notes,

> "This was a scalp wound from which Von Richthofen developed, FOR A TIME, (emphasis added) very bad headaches."(37)

And later,

> "But by September he had recovered most of his old timing to claim his sixtieth kill.(38)

Since Von Richthofen was killed on 21 April 1918, and scored another 20 kills between September and April, we can refute the claim that the Red Baron was still in ill health when he died and hence deserves our sympathy.

Significance

The authors have again altered the course of history to suit their story. It is convenient to have Von Richthofen's death occur before Bishop's aerodrome raid, that will soon be presented. And, since Von Richthofen's death has been moved up, this explains why the movie has falsified the date on which he recorded his 80th kill. This type of sensationalizing can be expected in an artistic presentation.

The story has been related to make us feel sympathy for the Red Baron. He "barely survived" the operation. He was "barely recovered" when he returned to the air. He even had bad luck as someone took his picture before takeoff.

The relevant point here is that the German ace, from the Canadian point of view, was the enemy. The authors are being consistent in their tendencies to exaggerate negatively toward Bishop, but always favorably toward the enemy.

36   The Canvas Falcons p372. Air Aces p14, p22.   They Fought for the Sky p200. Richthofen — A True History of the Red Baron pp195 — 201.
37   The Canvas Falcons p222.
38   The Canvas Falcons p371.

INCIDENT – VON RICHTHOFEN'S DEATH

Nature of the Error – Incorrect Information

Movie

The narrator states,

> "While the Red Baron tries desparately to
> get May, another Canadian, Roy Brown,
> puts one bullet into Von Richthofen's
> back."

Fact

The Red Baron was not shot in the back, but in the chest.
William Burrows in "Richthofen – A True History of the Red
Baron", states,

> "The autopsy showed that a single bullet
> entered the right side of Richthofen's
> chest, ricocheted off his spine, and came
> out two inches higher on the left side of
> his chest. The bullet was never
> found."(39)

Furthermore, credit for Richthofen's death may not go to Roy
Brown. Stephen Longstreet states,

> "Captain Brown never claimed he actually
> downed the Baron, just that he fired at
> him and that the pilots of his flight had
> seen the scarlet plane go down. Claims
> were later put in for the kill by some
> Australians manning a Lewis gun post near
> the road protecting a battery armed with
> 18 – pound field guns."(40)

Art Bishop states,

> "Strangely enough no one has ever been
> given offical credit for the kill. Most
> people – certainly all Canadian airmen –
> credit Roy Brown,....On the other hand
> Australians have always maintained that
> Richthofen was brought down by a single

39   Richthofen – A True History of the Red Baron
     p201.
40   The Canvas Falcons p373.

lucky shot fired by Robert Buie, an Australian infantryman."(41)

Christopher Shores states,

"The very next day he (Von Richthofen)
was shot down and killed in combat...
though whether by fire from Camel ace A.
Roy Brown or from Australian machine-gun-
ners on the ground has never been finally
resolved."(42)

Significance

The authors are again manipulating our emotions to achieve
their objectives. Shooting someone in the back is an act of
a coward even in war. By changing this small piece of information, censure has been given to the murderer and sympathy
has been given to the Red Baron. We see this interesting
custom again of criticising the Canadian in favor of what
was then the enemy.

There appear to be two relevant points about awarding the
kill to Roy Brown. The first is consistent with the point
above. The anti-Canadian theme is more easily served by not
mentioning the Australian machine gunners.

The second point is also consistent with the practice of the
authors when discussing Bishop's career. Although the story
line of the movie was probably chosen in order to create
controversy, when controversial items have arisen, the
authors have made the decision as to the outcome according
to their own views, and presented the situation as undis-
puted. (The other examples of this are the questions of
Bishop cheating on his score and the events surrounding the
Estourmel raid.)

INCIDENT - RICHTHOFEN'S FUNERAL

Nature of the Error - Incorrect Information

Movie

"Despite the Red Baron's death there are no happy faces at
60 Squadron. And Bishop writes..."

41 The Courage of the Early Morning p142.
42 Air Aces p22.

The dates for Richthofen's death were discussed above as being presented in July 1917.

Fact

On the suggested date, the movie indicates that Bishop was at 60 Squadron. However, on the actual date of Richthofen's funeral, 22 April 1918, Bishop was in England as the Commanding Officer of 85 Squadron, training it for war. (This part of his career is totally omitted from his story on the screen.)

Significance

Again the authors show talent for misleading without lying directly. They do not say that Bishop was at 60 Squadron, though the implication is clear that it is Bishop that we are discussing. Because the film's authors have reordered so completely the course of historical events, it has been necessary for them to consistently alter other details to coincide.

INCIDENT=COURSE_OF_EVENTS_LEADING_UP_TO_THE_AERODROME_RAID

Nature_of_the_Error_=_Incorrect_Dates

Movie

The time course through this next section of the movie is very confused. The authors have very cunningly related dates as month and day, omitting the year, thereby hiding from the viewer the fact that the events are not presented in chronological order.

The last firm date on which Bishop was mentioned in the script was at the Bishop - Richthofen air battle, 10 May 1917. It was implied however, that Bishop was at 60 Squadron on Von Richthofen's death in July 1917.

The next sequence of events states that Bishop went on leave (no dates), was married (no dates), and remained in Canada for an undetermined length of time. Following this, Bishop is said to have returned to the front on 14 June (no year). And finally, August 11, 1917, a date is recorded as the date on which Bishop received the Victoria Cross for the aerodrome raid (the date of the raid is also not given).

If we follow these events through in sequence, analyzing the available dates, it becomes obvious that all these events

—129—

could not have occurred before the aerodrome raid and the receiving of the VC on 11 August 1917. Without even knowing the correct dates, it is obvious that the authors have altered the course of history, and have no expectations that the viewer will be able to realize it.

Fact

The aerodrome raid was, in fact, the first of the listed events, not the last.(43) The raid occurred 33 days after the Bishop - Von Richthofen battle, and even before Richthofen received his initial head wound. The raid occurred on Bishop's first tour of duty in France as a pilot, not at the end of his second. At the time of the raid he had only 22 kills on his score.(44) In other words, compared to the 72 kills he had when his career climaxed, he was still a novice.

The Victoria Cross was awarded to Bishop by the King in August 1917, around the 23rd of the month, not the 11th as stated in the film.(45) On 11 August 1917, Bishop was still in France.(46) The 11 August 1917 date, is the date of the gazette record for Bishop's Victoria Cross.(47)

Bishop went on leave to Canada after he received the VC, not before he received it.(48) The date of his proceeding on leave was September 1917. He was married in October of 1917, and remained in Canada for 4 - 5 months.(49) He served as Commanding Officer of 85 Squadron in England and France from January - February 1918 until June 1918.(50)

Bishop returned to the front in late May 1918, not on June 14, as the movie states.(51)

Because of the time manipulation, the movie omits Bishop's brilliant career with 85 Squadron. For instance there is no mention of his final flight in which he scored 5 kills in 15 minutes, "his greatest triumph".(52) This act assisted him in winning the Distinguished Flying Cross. However, we must remember that the authors appear to have a policy against relating complimentary events in Bishop's career.

43 The Courage of the Early Morning p99. Winged Warfare p155.
44 Winged Warfare p249.
45 The Courage of the Early Morning pp122 - 125.
46 The Courage of the Early Morning p122.
47 The Story of the Victoria Cross 1856 - 1963 p260.
48 The Courage of the Early Morning p128.
49 The Courage of the Early Morning pp131 - 133.
50 The Courage of the Early Morning p136, p161.
51 The Courage of the Early Morning p145.
52 The Courage of the Early Morning p163.

Bishop left France again on 20 June 1918, only three to four weeks later, but with 25 more kills recorded.(53)

At this point the movie stated that in October, Bishop was fighting again. It is interesting to note here, that Bishop did not fight in October of any year. In October 1914, he was in Canada. In October 1915, he was training observers in England. In October 1916, he was training to be a pilot. In October of 1917, he was on leave in Canada. In October of 1918, his wife and he were returning to Canada.

Significance

What is the point of all these confusing details? The authors have reordered the course of history to suit their story line in the movie. They needed a climax to the movie, to make it sensational, and artistically sound. This move is of major significance, going far beyond the bounds of artistic license. The significance of the aerodrome raid is altered by being taken out of context.

By rearranging the course of events, the author's argument suggests that the only likely motive for Bishop's action was personal glory. The movie portrays a very competitive man, finishing off his second tour of duty as an ace, about to be pulled out of active fighting. He wants to do that one big stunt, the aerodrome raid. When he returns, the movie says that the plane has highly suspicious, self-inflicted damage. We are lead to believe that the man wanted glory badly enough, here, at the end of his career, that he would rather be a fraud than a failure. In spite of what are portrayed as suspicious events, he still receives the VC for the raid.

Arthur Bishop suggests that it was frustration, rather than the need for glory that motivated the aerodrome raid. The Germans had changed their flying patterns, and the pilots of 60 Squadron were having trouble battling them in the air.

> "The next Friday, June 1, 60 Squadron
> continued its futile and hazardous chase
> of the German two-seaters.'What a com-
> plete waste of time,' Bishop complained
> to Jack Scott at lunch.'My mind is made
> up. I'm going after those aerodromes
> tomorrow morning, rain or shine.' "(54)

The point that is being made here, is that this raid occur-ring in June 1917, took place when the war was still accel-erating, and when there were very real strategic advantages to any ace, and therefore to Bishop himself, of having the

53 The Courage of the Early Morning p160, pp204 - 205
54 The Courage of the Early Morning pp98 - 99.

—131—

aerodromes inactivated. By moving the event to the end of Bishop's career, the strategic advantages are negated, and personal glory is the only resulting motive.

Therefore, as the authors create the motive for the crime, it is easier to promote the suggestion that Bishop was desparate enough for the glory, to shoot up his own plane, rather than come back as a failure.

INCIDENT - BISHOP RETURNS FROM THE RAID WITH THE LEWIS GUN MISSING AND HIS PLANE SHOT UP

Nature of the Error - Use of Misleading Authority and Undocumented Information

Movie

> "Later there will be many doubts about the Estourmel raid, although no pilot from 60 Squadron will ever publicly discuss the issue. One of the most baffling questions is why Bishop's Nieuport returned with its Lewis gun missing."

The Bourne dramatization continues,

> "Its a bit of a mystery isn't it. I mean it didn't have its Lewis gun, you know. I mean, he said he chucked it on the way back, you know,to lighten up the plane, for added speed, you see. I mean, well, I'd like to see somebody take one of those off in the air, you know, while flying... well I ought to know, I put 'em on."

The reporter here is Walter Bourne, or rather Eric Peterson acting the part of Bourne, and reading a fictional script. The movie has worked very hard to give the actor credibility, so that his opinion will be respected by the audience.

Fact

I have been unable to definitely refute the accusation that it is impossible to remove a Lewis gun in flight. However, there are several relevant points here that suggest that Bishop may have been able to do what other pilots could not do.

Bishop practised incessantly with his Lewis gun, and his level of skill with all aspects of the gun would therefore be significantly higher than that of the less trained pilots.

There is evidence that the Lewis gun could be moved around the cockpit during flight. Ira Jones, an observer, in his book entitled "Tiger Squadron", states,

> "Now, there were four socket mountings on the B.E. (type of aircraft), intended to cover a wide field of fire. To get a shot at the enemy, when his pilot was outmanoeuvred, the observer had to keep changing the Lewis gun from one socket to another. If a plane got under your belly, none of the sockets was any good. You just couldn't get at him. Seeing this blighter and being unable to do anything about it, was more than I could stand. I yanked the gun out of the rear socket, leaned over the right side of the cockpit, and holding the Lewis like a rifle, let go with a burst."(55)

The plane and mount in this example are different from that of Bishop's situation. However, the gun is a Lewis gun, and if Ira Jones could move a Lewis gun around an airplane during flight, it is possible that Bishop could have as well.

In terms of man-handling the Lewis gun, while in flight, and using the same mount as Bishop would have had on his plane on 2 June 1917, the following demonstrates that it was a difficult, but possible task.

In the "First of the Few", Denis Winter states, in reference to the Lewis gun,

> "Their problem was one of loading, for even the largest double-capacity ammunition drum held only ninety-seven rounds to 500 for each Vickers. Re-loading was therefore a frequent exercise and a difficult one. The safety catch had first to be released and the gun slid down over a virtual right angle bend in the aluminium mounting quadrant before the spent drum was lifted off its spike and another fitted against a slipstream of over 100 miles per hour (this would of course depend upon the speed of the plane). At best, the operation required three sepa-

55 Tiger Squadron p38.

rate movements in five seconds during
which time the machine had to be flown
with the hands off the controls and the
eyes disengaged from enemy activity."(56)

Bishop, in fact did change magazines in the air. In "Winged
Warfare", he states,

"Then suddenly I managed to get a chance
from an angle I knew very well, and
opened fire. He immediately dropped out
of control and I dived after him firing
as he fell. Having finished one drum of
ammunition, I had to come out of the dive
to put on a new one. The other scout and
two-seater were still in the same place,
so getting above them I tried two dives
but without result."(57)

Therefore, there are two points here, that need to be
stressed. The quotations above suggest that there is a distinct possibility that an expert like Bishop may be able to
remove the Lewis gun from its mount and throw it overboard.
The second point, is that the authority that the movie uses
- Eric Peterson acting the part of Bourne - is a fictional
insert into an historical work. His opinion does not deserve
the respect that we are asked to give it.

Significance

This suggestion that it is impossible to remove the Lewis
gun from its housing without landing the plane, is a major
point in the argument against Bishop. If the audience can be
convinced on this point then, we must also believe that
Bishop deliberately set out to deceive us, and that he
accepted the VC for an act of bravery that did not occur.

INCIDENT_-_BISHOP_RETURNS_FROM_THE_RAID_WITH_HIS_LEWIS_GUN_MISSING
AND_HIS_PLANE_SHOT_UP

Nature_of_the_Error_-_Inaccurate_Information_and_Misleading
Authority

Movie

56   The First of the Few p41.
57   Winged Warfare p186.

After discussing the Lewis gun, the narrator continues,

> "In the accounts of the raid, Bishop's plane is described as returning in tatters. This isn't so."

The Bourné dramatization continues,

> "In the tail, there's, there's about 17 bullet holes, you see, all in a nice little group like that, you know. Well, I mean, I've seen a lot of planes shot up, but I mean, nobody can shoot a plane like that, you know. No, no, quite a mystery."

Fact

Art Bishop writes,

> "Bourne as usual turned his attention to the plane as soon as he saw Bishop was unhurt. He took in the innumerable holes and slashes in the wings, fuselage, and tail and uttered an incredulous whistle. 'Beats me how the thing stayed in one piece, Sir!' "(58)

In all honesty, Art Bishop is, potentially, not an unbiased source in this discussion. But the point here is that the movie does not appear to be using any sources at all. Again the authors use an actor, and a fictitious script, to present an opinion that contradicts "the accounts of the raid".

In a recent article in the Toronto Star, Ron Lowman writes,

> "Of the movie's suggestion that Bishop never did attack a German airfield all by himself and instead and (sic) shot his own plane's tail full of holes on the ground, Bauer (a retired Group Captain and chairman of Billy Bishop Heritage) said, 'There were more than 100 holes in the plane. Cowan (the film's producer) doesn't mention that at all.' "(59)

I would also suggest that the authors have made the details of 17 bullet holes in a nice little group, just a little too neat to be believeable. Bishop had been in enough air battles to know that if he wanted people to believe that he had

58 The Courage of the Early Morning p103.
59 Toronto Star 6 Jan 1984 p A13.

a horrendous battle, that he would need more than one circle of holes to be convincing.

Furthermore, Bishop must also have been aware of the dangers that could have resulted from landing the plane, then shooting up the tail – where some of the controls are located – and possibly grounding it. This possibility of immobilizing the plane, or having someone witness the incident, seems an unwarranted risk for a pilot that had plenty of opportunity to have his plane damaged in the air.

Significance

This is the second half of the argument that Bishop shot up his own plane. When analyzed, the argument seems illogical, but the authors have gone to great lengths to create unquestioning faith in Bourne's report. It is no accident that we forget that these damning statements come from the actor and not the real mechanic.

INCIDENT – DOCUMENTATION OF THE ESTOURMEL RAID

Nature of the Error – Inaccurate Information

Movie

> "The Germans keep meticulous records at all their aerodromes. Historians will later find Estourmel's records, and there will be no mention of any raid. They will also scour the records of other aerodromes in the area with the same result. The brass who are waiting for Bishop however, harbor no doubts. They will recommend him for the Victoria Cross even though they can discover no confirmation whatsoever of the raid. A recommendation for the VC without such confirmation is virtually unheard of."

Fact

There are several small technical points that must be made here, before discussing the actual documentation for the raid.

The Germans may have kept meticulous records most of the time, but from the film's authors past reporting, I doubt that they have the knowledge to speak authoritatively on the subject.

The aerodrome raid occurred almost a year and a half before the end of the war. There are numerous ways that those records could have been damaged or destroyed. Since it is not stated at what point the records were supposed to have been scoured, it is also possible that many more years have elapsed, and many more mishaps have befallen the records. Even World War II may have occurred before the records were evaluated for Bishop's raid.

Furthermore, what were the objectives of the historians as they scoured the German records? Was their interest solely in Billy Bishop, causing them to check and cross check references for this particular raid? Or in fact, were they reviewing, with all the events of the war in mind, leading them to record what was available without searching for less obvious clues that may have been linked to Bishop?

In actual fact, the possibilities are endless. The aerodrome may not have been Estourmel itself, but another one in the area. Is it possible that the field was abandoned after the raid, and that no records were found because by the end of the war, an abandoned airfield was overlooked and ignored?

The answers to these questions will only be provided by returning to primary sources. I do not have access to these sources and it is my suspicion that the authors have made no attempt to obtain access to them.

The authors have also used a trick that has been used for years to give credibility to undocumented information - the anonymous "they", or in this case the unidentified "historians". If these historians deserve credibility, they would have been identified, because their reputations would add weight to the argument. The authors have again supplied information without giving us their references.

As to the raid, was it in fact undocumented? In my research I have found three items that suggest that the raid may have been confirmed. The Toronto Star reports,

> "Bishop's son Arthur, a Toronto pulicist who was a World War II fighter pilot, said the solo raid by his father was confirmed by a pilot named Spencer Horn who flew over later and saw the damage Bishop had wrought."(60)

60   Toronto Star Jan 1984 p A13.

The second reference to the raid can be inferred from this statement made by Stephen Longstreet in "The Canvas Falcons",

> "The Germans questioned William Bishop's record of three planes shot down and three damaged on a raid on a German airfield, stating that he left in such a hurry he had no way of knowing what he had destroyed and what merely fired on."(61)

This quotation does show the enemy admitting that Bishop was at the scene of the raid. Longstreet should be questioned on the source of his information.

The final reference is found in a book called "Canada's Fighting Pilots" by Edmund Cosgrove. He writes that when Bishop returned after the raid,

> "He was greeted by a crowd of excited airmen; they had learned of the fight from observers in the British balloon line who had seen the whole affair from their swaying baskets. When Bishop was asked how many machines he had shot down, he replied with unconscious modesty: 'Only three. One got away.'

> "Later investigation revealed that he had severely damaged a number of other planes on the ground and had wounded the pilot of the fourth German fighter which had 'got away.' Bishop's report of the mission against the enemy aerodrome was carefully scrutinized before, on August 11, 1917, he was informed by the Commander of the air contingents in France that he had been awarded the Victoria Cross..."(62)

This is quite a definitive statement, which if true would completely invalidate the movie. Because this is such an important point in the discussion, the statement must be scrutinized closely.

This book is not a particularly authoritative source, and the author does not report his sources of information.

What can be done is to examine the details and evaluate whether it is possible to confirm a raid from a balloon.

61 The Canvas Falcons p31.
62 Canada's Fighting Pilots p79.

Would the balloonists be up between 3.00 a.m. and 6.00 a.m., when the raid was conducted? Could a balloonist see far enough behind enemy lines to assess an air battle? What was the weather like that morning? If it was raining, would balloons be up in the rain?

Balloons could have been airborne between 3.00 a.m. and 6.00 a.m. In a book called "The Balloonatics", by Alan Morris, the following statements are made in reference to balloons in World War I,

> "Before replacement its aeronauts were to be airborne for 1468 hours, provide 1369 intelligence reports, and make 1146 corrections to artillery."(63)

> "The brass hats had been forced to note the advantages that balloonists enjoyed over power-pilots with Morse transmitters. They could,
> 1. Stay up any length of time.
> 2. Work by day and night.
> 3. ..."
> (64)

> "Accordingly in the gusty 5.15 a.m. light of September 25 the balloons bobbed up to aim the preliminary bombardment..."(65)

> "Omitting a few minutes for relief of observers, this balloon remained up all night."(66)

Thus a balloon could have been up at the time that Bishop executed his raid.

Did balloons go up even in the rain? Yes. Sholto Douglas in his book "Years of Combat", states in reference to attacking balloons,

> "The state of the weather was also an important factor. If it was raining or the atmosphere was moist, it was almost impossible to set fire to a balloon."(67)

Thus balloons must have been up in the rain.

63 The Balloonatics p7.
64 The Balloonatics p15.
65 The Balloonatics p19.
66 The Balloonatics p29.
67 Years of Combat p319.

The third consideration is the ability of the balloonist to see the aerodrome, and therefore act as a witness. Denis Winter, in the "First of the Few", writes,

> "With his telescope he surveyed a horizon
> of twenty-eight miles away from a height
> of just 600 feet. In practise the custom-
> ary height was 7000 feet about four miles
> from the front line."(68)

Estourmel aerodrome was probably only 21 miles from the assumed balloon line, well within the twenty-eight mile range that the balloons could view at 600 feet. (This distance was measured on a map.)

If the balloons were up, the aerodrome would have been in sight if the weather permitted. Did the weather interfere with vision that morning?

When Bishop took off there was a light drizzle and heavy clouds were at 500 feet, but the ceiling over Arras was higher than at Bishop's home base at Filescamp Farm.(69) On Bishop's return,

> "The clouds had broken and here and there
> shafts of sunlight shone through... Fur-
> ther west the clouds disappeared and the
> five planes were flying in a clear
> sky."(70)

And as Bishop was about to land,

> "It was exactly fifteen minutes after
> five. The sky was calm and crystal
> clear..."(71)

Thus balloons could have been up at dawn, even in the rain. The aerodrome could have been in sight. Although the state of the weather may have been questionable, it is possible though that the weather did clear sufficiently, so that the aerodrome was visible, if balloons were flying that morning.

This detective work does not prove Cosgrove's statements that the incident was confirmed, but it does make it a possibility, and demonstrate that the incident requires further research.

Significance

68   The First of the Few p121.
69   The Courage of the Early Morning p99.
70   The Courage of the Early Morning p102.
71   The Courage of the Early Morning p103.

The author's statement that the raid was undocumented is the final proof that Bishop did not ever carry out the raid as claimed. I cannot contradict the statements, but I think that the three incidents listed here require further research to find the true answer to the controversy. The very least that should be done is an investigation to record what primary sources are available, so that the viewer can know whether the raid was ever recorded, or whether no one ever really searched the records.

INCIDENT - BISHOP IS GREETED ON HIS RETURN FROM THE AERODROME RAID

Nature of the Error - Inaccurate Information

Movie

> "The brass who are waiting for Bishop however, harbor no doubts. They will recommend him for the Victoria Cross even though they can discover no confirmation whatsoever of the raid. A recommendation for the VC without such confirmation is virtually unheard of."

On the screen we see King George V, among the brass waiting for Bishop's return.

Fact

King George's presence on the landing strip in France during war time is so ridiculous as to be laughable. Did they fly him into an active theatre of war every time someone was expected to pull off a daring stunt?

Art Bishop writes,

> "At half past five Bishop was over Files-camp Farm...The aerodrome was still asleep as he had just left it an hour and a half before... Jubilantly he fired off light after light from his Very pistol to signal his triumph and arouse the slumberers below. A crowd of ground crewmen led by Corporal Walter Bourne ran to greet him..."(72)

72 The Courage of the Early Morning p103.

And Bishop himself writes in "Winged Warfare",

> "I landed and my sergeant immediately
> rushed out and asked me how many I had
> bagged. When I told him three, he was
> greatly pleased, and yelled it back to
> the mechanics who were waiting by the
> shed."(73)

The movie was right in the fact that Bishop was greeted when
he landed, but mechanics and ground crewmen are not usually
described as "brass".

Significance

The movie's implication that such a distinguished group is
waiting to receive Bishop, confident that he will have succeeded, increases his motive for faking the aerodrome raid.
The authors have been very cunning in building their case.

INCIDENT - BISHOP ENTERS WORLD WAR II

Nature of the Error - Inaccurate Information

Movie

"In 1939, Billy Bishop is once again in uniform. He's one of
the brass now - a Lieutenant-Colonel."

Fact

In 1939 Bishop was an Air Vice-Marshal, not a Lieutenant-Colonel.

Bishop ended World War I with the rank of Lieutenant-Colonel. Art Bishop writes,

> "Bishop became the first commanding offi-
> cer designate of the Canadian wing with
> the rank of lieutenant-colonel."(74)

This occurred between June and October of 1918.

Art Bishop continues,

73 Winged Warfare p161.
74 The Courage of the Early Morning p164.

"Shortly after the liberal government
came to power in Canada under William
Lyon MacKenzie King in 1935 my father was
created an Air Vice-Marshal of the
RCAF...On August 10, 1938, he (Defense
Minister Ian MacKenzie) appointed my
father Honorary Air Marshal, the highest
rank in the country at the time."(75)

Significance

It is understandable that after all the derogatory comments
that have been made in the movie, that the authors would not
want to mention that Bishop had already received the rank of
Lieutenant-Colonel by the end of World War I. In spite of
this, there seems to be no advantage in lowering his rank in
1939. Perhaps the authors were not wanting the audience to
be too impressed by his rank. Perhaps they did not bother to
research the details here. Or, perhaps the authors know so
little about the military that they do not recognise the
difference in ranks. If this latter case is true, I can only
say that no author has the right to work on a subject about
which he knows so little.

INCIDENT - RELATIONSHIP BETWEEN BISHOP AND WALTER BOURNE

Nature of the Error - Inaccurate Information

Movie

In the movie, the heaviest criticisms of Billy Bishop come
from Walter Bourne. He is shown as rather scornful of Bishop
as he discusses the discrepancies in Bishop's scores, and
the evidence regarding the aerodrome raid. In short, the
suggestion is strong that Bourne has not much respect for
Bishop.

Fact

Art Bishop writes, that while Bishop was critically ill during 1942,

> "Corporal Walter Bourne, his (Bishop's)
> guardian angel of World War I days wrote
> from an RAF base where he was serving out
> his second war: 'Get well soon, Sir.

75 The Courage of the Early Morning p182, p185.

Train us men and we will beat them as we
did in the old days. Here is good luck —
I AM ENCLOSING SOMETHING WHICH HAS TRAV-
ELLED WITH ME ALL THESE YEARS. (empasis
added) Remember the time your gun jammed
(April 30, 1917 in the attack against the
Gothas) and you had to get away. Well,
Sir, here is the bullet that might have
ended your career. You can see the mark
on it where I gripped it in the vice to
get it free.' "(76)

This letter, written by the real Walter Bourne, seems to
contradict the tone of the movie, and in fact, sounds as if
the writer does indeed have much respect for Bishop. Even
if we consider that the concern may be a result of mellowing
over the intervening years, the fact that Bourne was moved
enough to save the bullet from a fight that almost ended
Bishop's life, suggests again that Bourne held Bishop in
high regard.

Significance

The dramatization of Walter Bourne throughout the movie has
been one of the author's tools in convincing the audience of
Bishop's guilt. Bourne was introduced into the movie much
earlier in Bishop's career than history introduced the two,
thereby increasing Bourne's credibility due to their long-
standing relationship. The "old photos" of Bourne were
browned pictures of Eric Peterson, again giving more credibility to the actor in the later interviews, as he pretends
to give "Bourne's" first hand opinion of Bishop cheating.

I suggest that this fiction has no basis in fact, and that
it also has no place in a movie that is marketed as an historical documentary.

CONCLUSION

"As with any legend, the Bishop saga will
comprise some truth and some myth. And no
one, not even Bishop's learned class-
mates, will ever know the whole story of
'The Kid Who Couldn't Miss.'"(77)

I hope that someone will take up the challenge to ensure
that we do know the whole story. Regardless of the conclu-

76 The Courage of the Early Morning p196.
77 The National Film Board Film — The Kid Who
     Couldn't Miss

sions about the aerodrome raid, Billy Bishop's career contained many acts of bravery. He deserves a fair trial before his hero status is destroyed for the sake of a movie author's glory.

We owe it to Billy Bishop; we owe it to ourselves as Canadians; and we owe it to all heroes, past and future.

BIBLIOGRAPHY OF WORKS RESEARCHED
IN THE
PREPARATION OF THIS PAPER

* Bishop, William Arthur. The Courage of the Early Morning. Toronto: McClelland and Stewart Ltd., 1965, (reprinted 1981).

* Bishop, William Avery. Winged Warfare. Edited by Stanley M. Ulanoff. New York: Arco Publishing Inc., 1981.

* Burrows, William E. Richthofen - A True History of the Red Baron. New York: Harcourt, Brace and World Inc., 1969.

* Cosgrove, Edmund. Canada's Fighting Pilots. Toronto: Clarke Irwin and Company Ltd., 1965.

* Cruttwell, C.R.M.F. A History of the Great War 1914 - 1918. Great Britain: Oxford at the Clarendon Press. Second Edition 1936. Reprinted Edition, Rexdale Ontario: Granada Publishing Ltd., 1982.

* Douglas, Sholto. Years of Combat. London, England: Collins, 1963.

Drew, George. Canada's Fighting Airmen. Toronto: The MacLean Publishing Co Ltd., 1931.

* Jones, Ira. Tiger Squadron. London, England: White Lion Publishers Ltd., 1954, (reprinted 1972).

* Longstreet, Stephen. The Canvas Falcons. New York: Ballantine Books, 1972, (reprinted 1983).

* Lowman, Ron. "Angry Airmen Want Billy Bishop Film Banned". Toronto Star. 6 January 1984, p A13.

Lynch, John William. Princess Patricia's Canadian Light Infantry 1917 - 1919. New York: Exposition Press, 1976.

MacMillan, Norman. Tales of Two Air Wars. London, England: G. Bell and Sons Ltd., 1963.

Mathieson, William D. My Grandfather's War. Toronto: Macmillan of Canada, 1981.

* Morris, Alan. The Balloonatics. London, England: Jarrolds Publishers Ltd., 1970.

Oughton, Frederick and Smyth, Vernon. Ace With One Eye. London, England: Frederick Muller ltd., 1963.

Preston, Arthur. Canada's R.M.C. Toronto: University of Toronto Press, 1969, (reprinted 1982).

* Reynolds, Quentin. They Fought For The Sky. New York: Bantam Books, 1958, (reprinted — Bantam Pathfinder Edition 1963).

* Richthofen, Manfred Von. The Red Baron. Translated by Peter Kilduff, Edited by Stanley M. Ulanoff. Fallbrook, California: Aero Publishers Inc., Second Edition, 1980.

* Shores, Christopher. Air Aces. Greenwich, Connecticut: Bison Books Corp., 1983.

* Smyth, John. The Story of the Victoria Cross 1856 - 1963. London, England: Frederick Muller Ltd., 1963.

* Winter, Denis. The First of the Few. London, England: Penguin Books Ltd., 1982.

* Wise, S.F. Canadian Airmen and the First World War. Toronto: University of Toronto Press, 1980.

Notes

1. In all cases, the most recent date of printing was the edition used.

2. Sources quoted in the paper are indicated by an asterisk.

Appendix "VA-2-E"

Recommended corrections to the NFB Production
" The Kid Who Couldn't Miss", by Stewart K. Taylor
Official Historian of "World War One Flyers"

Recommended corrections to the NFB Production
" The Kid Who Couldn't Miss", by Stewart K. Taylor
Official Historian of " World War One Flyers"

Page 5 - Narrator (line 8)

Quotation: In September Billy Bishop is commissioned a lieutenant
                   and starts serious training with Toronto's and Mississauga horse.

Correction: Bishop joined the 7th Canadian Mounted Rifles in
                   London, Ontario, September 1914.

Page 8 - Narrator (line 8)

Quotation: It is during this period that Bishop finds himself and his horse
                   mired in the awful French mud.

Correction: Bishop was mired in English mud on Salisbury Plain.
                   He did not serve in France with the 7th Canadian Mounted Rifles.

Page 9 - Narrator (line 16)

Quotation: Bishop as observer and Roger Neville as pilot,
                   faithfully recorded the slaughter.

Correction: There was no slaughter on the Flanders and Lille Fronts over
                   which Bishop and his pilots flew in the early spring of 1916
                   as both British and German lines remained static.

Page 11 - Voice (line 11)

Quotation: Yeah..Yeah, it was..it was a lad called Walsley -
                   An Australian bloke. He had come back, you know, after the
                   morning patrol and I mean, aw well he was just shot to
                   pieces, you know, he was mincemeat.

Correction: 21 Squadron, RFC, suffered only one casualty during the period
                   when Bishop flew with them. Capt. D.C. Ware, a pilot, was slightly
                   wounded by Anti-Aircraft shell fragments on the 31st of March, 1916.

Page 12 – Narrator (line 4)

Quotation: After three very undistinguished months with 21 Squadron,
            Bishop's nerves are shot and he is being sent to London to
            recuperate. He is still only an observer and although he
            yearns to become a pilot, his chances are slim.

Correction: As the RE7 aircraft in which Bishop flew could not carry both
            their required load of bombs and an observer at the same time,
            the observers in his flight, who had completed more than two
            month's service in France, were given the option of returning
            to England to commence pilot training while the pilots conducted
            the bombing raids alone.

Page 12 – Narrator (line 9)

Quotation: Pilots come only from the British upper class.
            Colonials need not apply.

Correction: This was true during the early years of the Royal Flying Corps
            from 1912 to 1915. In 1916 pilots were being accepted from
            almost every walk of life. The initial stigma against
            'Colonials' was also lifted at the same time.

Page 15 – Narrator (line 1)

Quotation: It has only been three years since the French pilot brought
            down the first enemy aircraft with a squirrel rifle.

Correction: The RFC actually brought down the first enemy aircraft in France.
            This initial air victory was credited to Lt. Harvey-Kelly,
            assisted by two other pilots of No. 2 Sqdn. RFC on the 25th of
            August 1914. The first French victory occurred on October 5th, 1914.
            The time between the first victory and the period under discussion
            would be two years.

Page 15 - Voice (line 18)

Quotation: Well I've got to take a contradictory a bit there-
          he wasn't a good pilot to begin with. He was a lousy pilot.

Correction: Bishop was a better than average pilot when compared to his
          contemporaries. A quick learner, he flew solo after a meager
          2 hrs. and 30 mins dual instruction on the Maurice-Farman
          Longhorn. This compares quite favourably with the best.
          His pilot training advancement was rapid. When he received
          his pilot's 'Wings' on the 9th of December 1916, he had flown
          a total of 18 hrs. and 15 minutes solo. The average time to
          achieve this milestone in 1916 was 25 hrs.
          He did not break the undercarriage of an aircraft while
          landing until the 27th of February 1917. During his lengthy
          tour with 60 Squadron in France Bishop had three suspect landings
          while flying the Nieuport Scout for the first time in his life.
          When he took delivery of Nieuport B1566 #C5 on the 20th of April
          1917, it was inconceivable that he would fly the same aircraft
          on regular patrols until the 24th of July 1917, for a total of
          153 hrs. and 40 mins. without one serious landing mishap. Few of
          his contemporaries could equal this.

Page 16 - Narrator (line 1)

Quotation: In fact, although he shoots well, Bishop is a lousy pilot. Still,
          like the others, he'll be expected to solo in just four days.

Correction: This was never a prerequisite in the Royal Flying Corps nor the
          Naval counterpart, the Royal Naval Air Service.
          Bishop actually completed his first solo on the third day of
          his pilot training.

Page 18 - Narrator (line 9)

Quotation: On February 16th, 1917, Billy Bishop received the Wings if
          Not the blessings of the R.F.C.

Correction: Bishop received his 'Wings' on the 9th of December, 1916
          at 11 Training Squadron, Northolt, UK.

Page 18 - Narrator (16)

Quotation: It is however a victory of another sort. To divert
             the public's attention from the carnage, the generals
             invent a new hero - the Air Ace.

Correction: Only France and Germany promoted the laurels of their
             exceptional flyers. Britain kept the achievements of their
             outstanding airmen quiet until the spring of 1917. The only
             RFC pilot known to the English public was Albert Ball. It was
             not until the summer of 1918 that the names and photos of other
             outstanding pilots first appeared in the press.
             Both the hierarchy of the British Navy and Army realized how
             the success of the ' air ace' would overshadow the men serving
             at sea and in the trenches. For this reason they suppressed all
             mention by name of outstanding pilots in news releases to the
             public throughout the war. Only the above mentioned ever rated
             close to front page headlines.

Page 19 - Narrator (line 1)

Quotation: An Ace, the generals decide, will be any pilot who shoots
             down five enemy aircraft.

Correction: Only the French and German Generals promoted their ' aces'
             and the number of aircraft they claimed to have shot down.

Page 20 - Narrator (line 3)

Quotation: He brings with him a lamentable record; he has only received
             a slight shrapnel wound; he has never fired on an enemy
             plane and he has committed numerous acts of insubordination.

Correction: Bishop had experienced operational service prior to flying
             as a pilot in France. Most RFC and RNAS pilots had never seen
             France or Belgium before they were required to fly over it.

Page 20 - Narrator (line 8)
Quotation: On his third day, Bishop wrecks a plane while executing
            a   typical landing.
Correction: On the morning of March 14th, Bishop strained the wing of
             his Nieuport when landing. This only the fifth time he had
             flown a Nieuport Scout.

Page 20 - Narrator (line 14)
Quotation: A call is put in to headquarters requesting a new pilot.
            Bishop is to be sent back to England.
Correction: All new pilots, no matter how inept they were at flying the
             squadron's aircraft, were given at least two weeks in the
             squadron to prove their worth. Bishop had only been in 60
             Squadron five days when he strained the wing of his Nieuport.

Page 20 - Narrator (line 16)
Quotation: That afternoon, Walter Bourne tries in vain to reassemble
            Bishop's plane, while Bishop returns to his hut to pack-up
            his troubles.
Correction: Following his landing in which he strained the wing of a
             Nieuport, Bishop was given a Martinsyde scout to fly while
             the Nieuport was being repaired.

Page 21 - Narrator (line 3)
Quotation: The following morning, at five-thirty, the planes are wheeled
            out of the hanger.
Correction: Three days later, March 17th, 1917, the planes are wheeled
             out of their hangars. Each hanger could accomodate
             two aircraft.

Page 21 - Narrator (line 17)
Quotation: The Germans are flying the new Albatross C-3.
Correction: The Germans were flying the relatively new Albatross D111.
             The Albatross C-3 was a two-seater Reconnaissance aircraft.

Page 22 - Narrator (line 9)

Quotation: Then he remembers Scott telling him of the German trick of
              dousing the cylinders with oil to take a hit.

Correction: The Germans developed many tricks while engaged in combat,
              dousing the cylinders was not one of them. When in a tight
              situation the enemy pilots often opened the throttle of their
              160 hp Mercedes D111a water-cooled in-line engines sending
              clouds of bluish smoke into the slipsteam. This ruse often
              worked against novice opponents.

Page 24 - Narrator (line 16)

Quotation: a nineteen-year-old English pilot names Wheeler becomes the
              Baron's 30th kill.

Correction: Manfred v. Richthofen's 30th confirmed victory occured on the
              24th of March , 1917. His victim was Richard Plunkett Baker,
              a 29-year-old Canadian from Vancouver, BC. Lt. Baker was
              taken POW. This was his first trip across the lines.

Page 24 - Narrator (line 17)

Quotation: After his 31st victory von Rochstoven writes - one's heart
              beats more quickly when the adversary, who's face one has just
              seen, goes down in flames. Naturally, little is left of the
              pilot - but I landed and picked-up his I.D. number for my
              collection.

Correction: Lt. C.G. Gilbert flying a Nieuport Scout from 29 Squadron, RFC,
              was brought down on the morning of March 25th, 1917 by Richthofen.
              His aircraft did burn after Lt. Gilbert landed near Tilloy. Gilbert,
              unhurt, was taken POW. Lt. Guy Gilbert survived the war.

Page 25. - Narrator (line 1)

Quotation: Victories 32,33 and 34 came in three days.

Correction: Victories 32,33 and 34 came in the next eight days.

Page 25 - Voice (line 16)

Quotation: although some of them had only got sort of 12 to 14 hours
flying time,.... before they went to the front.

Correction: 20 hours solo was the minimum in 1916 for a pilot who had
been sent to France. In 1917 the total time had increased to
30 hrs. There were a few exceptions, none with less than
20 hours.

Page 26 - Narrator (line 1)

Quotation: Billy Bishop, however, is learning how to fight. He gets
victory number 2 the day after his first.

Correction: His second victory came on the 31st of March, 1917, six
days after his first.

Page 27 - Narrator (line 1)

Quotation: Because of the constant dog-fighting during Bloody April,
other English pilots are also learning how to fight rather
well. In particular, a schoolboy named Edward Albert Ball.

Correction: Albert Ball had claimed his first victory, a hostile kite
balloon, on the 10th of April, 1916. He was a ' seasoned pro'
by August 1916 when flying a much superior Nieuport Scout
against a much inferior German Air force which had few aircraft,
at that time,to oppose him.

Page 27 - Billy Bishop (line 14)

Quotation: I can't fly worth .... compared to someone like Barker or
Ball.

Correction: In the spring of 1917, William Barker was flying an antiquated
BE2e, two-seater reconnaissance machine with 15 Sqn. RFC. Although
he was in command of 'C' flight his flying prowess would have been
unknown at the time.

Page 28 - Narrator (line 10)

Quotation: During Bloody April alone, von Richstoven has shot down
            22 planes and brought his score to 48.

Correction: During Bloody April alone, Richthofen has shot down
            21 planes and brought his score to 52.

Page 28 - Narrator (line 11)

Quotation: The last 10 all burned, he writes.

Correction: The last 4 all burned.

Page 29 - Narrator (line5)

Quotation: The life of a pilot in France was something like
            10 to 20 days.

Correction: During 'Bloody April', the darkest month in the history of
            the RFC, the average life of a pilot in France was six to seven
            weeks (42 to 49 days).

Page 29 - Narrator (line 16)

Quotation: By the end of Bloody April, most of Bishop's friends are wounded
            or dead. Bishop is an emotional lad and the losses hurt him
            deeply. With the exception of Jack Scott,he allows himself no more
            close friends. 'Oh, how I hate the Hun', he writes, 'I'll make
            him pay, I swear.!
            He now has 7 victories.

Correction: At the end of April 1917, Bishop has been credited with
            14 victories.

Page 32 - Narrator (line 7)

Quotation: As the ground war worsens, the politicians turn increasingly
            to the Aces, to divert public attention.

Correction: The French and German politicians did; the British did not
            until the summer of 1918,and then only on a very limited scale.

Page 33 - Narrator (line 1)

Quotation: Billy Bishop is not in the same league with the best of the
Aces, but his score has climbed to 18 and the Owen Sound son
now champions his cause, boasting that he brought down 7 in one
flight, although in fact, it was 3.

Correction: The ' Owen Sound Sun' was Bishop's home town newspaper. The fight
referred to occured on the 30th of April 1917. At the time Bishop
had been credited with 12 aerial victories. During a series of
prolonged scraps with enemy aircraft that began at 9.40 am and
ended at 12.15 pm Bishop had 10 different engagements. He was
credited with 1 enemy aircraft crashed and 2   forced to land.
'The Owen Sound Sun', like many other newspapers at the time,
were only too proud to champion the exloits of their local
heroes. Too often throughout World War One most Canadian newspapers
representing the larger cities printed very little about the
achievements of the Canadian airmen.

Page 35 - Voice (line 15)

Quotation: he said it was generally know in the R.F.C. that Bishop was
cheating.

Correction: Over a period of 20 years, this writer while engaged in research
on all the known 2,360 Canadians who flew in France, Belgium,
Italy and Macedonia during World War One, has interviewed hundreds
of former pilots and some observers who flew with, or near Billy
Bishop during his 2 tours of duty with 60 Squadron in 1917 and 85
Squadron in 1918. Included in this group were 5 veterans who had
actually been in his flight or served in his Squadron (No. 85).
Another 12 had desperately tried to join his 85 Squadron in late
1917 but were refused because the response was enormous. The RFC
had somewhere in the vicinity of 200 applications from pilots who
were eager to join Bishop and fly in his squadron. All of these
men had the highest respect for him; to think that Bishop was a
fraud would have been blasphemy. Only a mere handful, none of whom
ever met, flew with, or served near Bishop, doubted his record.

They appeared to have been privy to the same slanderous rumour.

Page 36 - Narrator (line 7)

Quotation: In his first 60 days, he's had 60 fights and brought down
            36 planes.

Correction: In his first 60 days, he's had 52 fights and brought down
            19 planes.

Page 36 - Narrator (line 8)

Quotation: The only dark spot is that some members of 60 Squadron are
            now whispering that Bishop's getting credit for a lot of kills
            for which there is no confirmation. This is perhaps due to
            jealousy over Bishop's decorations, but the rumours persist.

Correction: Bishop, like Ball his famous predecessor in 60 Squadron, was
            granted a ' roving commission' by Major Jack Scott his Commanding
            Officer. This special duty was only granted to the most outstanding
            pilots in 60 Squadron and was condoned by the R.F.C. hierarchy
            who trusted implicitly the judgement of Jack Scott. Freed from the
            encumbrance of leading a flight these individuals roamed at will
            many miles over the enemy's lines looking for an unsuspecting
            enemy pilot to shoot down. To survive they had to have extra keen
            eyesight, be a deadly shot, and possess impeccable judgement.
            Bishop was blessed with all three.
            As most of their successful combats occured far from the eyes of
            allied witnesses the combat reports they later filled out were taken
            as gospel by the Commanding Officer and his immediate superiors.
            In the summer of 1916 Albert Ball claimed and was credited with
            at least 14 enemy aircraft while flying on a ' roving commission'.
            Most of these ' victories' were not confirmed.

Page 36 - Voice (line 13)

Quotation: When I remember, you know, one of them pilots, Carlisle, I mean
            he got in a right row with Bishop.

Correction: No pilot with the last name of ' Carlisle' ever flew in 60 or 85
            Squadrons. The only known pilot in 60 Squadron to have argued with
            Bishop and Jack Scott was W.M. Fry, MC. He later wrote a book
            titled 'Air of Battle' in which he mentioned having had a disagreement.

Page 37. Narrator (line 4)

Quotation: The day is May 10th, 1917. Final preparations are underway
for a full card of dog-fighting which is now so popular that
the fights and results are published daily throughout the
warring nations. Though no one knows it yet, May 10th will
be a very special day, for it is on this day when the two
most daring fighters will finally meet. Billy Bishop and
Manfred von Richtoven.

The Baron scores first. Bishop kicks his rudder and
dives to escape.

Assured of victory, the Red Baron watches Bishop
plummet.

Correction: Bishop was on leave in London, England from May 8th
to May 22nd, 1917.

Page 37 Narrator (line 18)

Quotation: But then, out of the corner of his eye, he sees his
brother Lother, hit. While Richtoven is horrified at
the sight of Lothar's smoking DR-7 - this lapse allows
Bishop who has used the old German trick of...

Correction: Jasta 11, which included Manfred von Richthofen and his
brother Lothar, was equipped throughout with Albatros D111
and Albatros DVa fighters until early September 1917.
The Fokker D.R.1 Triplane did not appear in the skies of
France until August 30th, 1917.

Page 38 - Narrator (line 1) Continued from bottom of page 37.

Quotation: ...this lapse allows Bishop who has used the old German trick
           of dousing his cylinders with oil, to get on Richtoven's tail.

Correction: When engaged in combat allied pilots flying Nieuport Scouts
            and other rotary-engine aircraft would often enrich the mixture
            of gas, oil & air by means of the hand throttle thereby sending
            out clouds of bluish-oily smoke. Repeated use of this technique
            would eventually gum up the pistons necessitating a premature
            engine overhaul.

Page 40 - Narrator (line 1)

Quotation: Billy Bishop and Jimmy McCudden are now the R.F.C.'s leading
           scorers. Bishop writes: I'm quite famous now.

Correction: When Bishop completed his tour of duty with 60 Squadron in
            August 1917 he was credited with 18 confirmed, 29 driven down
            out of control for a total of 47. At the end of August 1917
            McCudden was credited with 9 enemy machines. There were at least
            10 other RFC pilots with more than 9 enemy machines to their
            credit in August 1917.

Page 40 - Voice (line 11)

Quotation: ...the defence patrols have come back..six or seven machines,
           they hadn't seem anything - nothing. He goes out a little later,
           by himself; comes back in a couple of hours, you know, he's
           firing off his phare guns like it's bleeding Guy Faulks Day,
           claiming he shot down one; two; three planes.

Correction: The defensive patrols only covered the area close to the lines.
            On a good day they may be lucky enough to see 25 miles or slightly
            more above the skies of occupied France and/or Belgium.
            Bishop, while flying alone on a 'roving commission' often covered
            a forty-mile area well into occupied territory were there was
            a much greater opportunity to attack unsuspecting enemy aircraft.

Page 41 - Narrator (line 1)

Quotation: The Red Baron now has 80 kills and at least that many offers of marriage.

Correction: In June 1917,Manfred von Richthofen had 52 victories. He did not gain his 80th victory until April 20th 1918.

Page 44 - Narrator (line 3)

Quotation: Despite the Red Baron's death, there are no happy faces at 60 Squadron.

Correction: The 'Red Baron' was not killed in action until April 21st, 1918. The period under discussion is June 1917.

Page 44 - Voices (line 19)

Quotation: ...looking for the parachute...

Correction: Parachutes were not issued to enemy pilots until April 1918. Parachutes were never issued to allied pilots in World War One. Only the balloon observers were issued with parachutes.

Page 44 - Voices (line 2)

Quotation: I think he fell down for about ten thousand or twenty thousand feet to about two th usand feet...

Correction: No combats were ever fought between allied and enemy aircraft at the height of twenty thousand feet. The oil in the gun synchronization system would congeal at this altitude. After one or two rounds had been fired, the gun(s) would jamb.

Page 45 - Narrator (line 1)

Quotation: Bishop is now ordered on leave to Canada.

Correction: Bishop had finished his tour with 60 Squadron and was given an extended matrimonial leave to Canada.

Page 46 - Narrator (line 5)

Quotation: On June 14th, Bishop departs London for the front.

Correction: Bishop did not fly to France until May 23rd, 1918.

Page 47 – Narrator (line 1)
Quotation: In October, Bishop is fighting again and with McCudden
           dead...
Correction: Bishop never fought in October during World War One.

Page 47 – Narrator (line 3)
Quotation: He is a wreckless fighter now and his plane is often hit.
Correction: Bishop flew SE5a C6490 on operations from May 27th 1918
            to June 6th, 1918 for a total of 23 hours and 25mins.
            He achieved victories #48 to #59 while flying this aircraft.
            During this period SE5a C6490 sustained little, if any,
            combat damage.

            Bishop flew SE5a C1904 on operations from June 10th 1918
            until his recall home to England on the 19th of June 1918.
            He logged 8 hours and 20 minutes over the enemy lines in
            this aircraft and claimed victories #60 to #72 while
            engaged in combat. This aircraft received also received
            very little combat damage and was later flown in combat
            by Capt. S.B. Horn of 85 Squadron after Bishop had returned
            to England.

Page 48 – Narrator (line 5)
Quotation: Knowing he has only a week left, Bishop decides to finally
            attempt the lone raid Ball dreamed of.
Correction: Bishop completed his lone raid on the early morning of
            June 2nd, 1917. He had been with 60 Squadron 56 days. He
            continued to fly on operations with 60 Squadron until the
            28th of August 1917.

Page 48 –Narrator (line 7)
Quotation: He orders extra rounds to be loaded into his Newport.
Correction: Bishop had no extra ammuniton loaded on board his Nieuport
            Scout when he took off to attack an enemy aerodrome.
            In addition to the one drum of Lewis ammunition attached to
            the upper wing mounted Lewis Gun containing 97 rounds he had
            two extra drums, each with 97 rounds, in his cockpit. This was the
            standard amount of ammunition carried on each flight.

Page 49 – Billy Bishop (line 10)

Quotation: A few bursts inside those sheds.

Correction: Neither his combat report or letters he wrote home immediately
after the event mentioned any sheds. Esnes, the advanced landing
ground were Jasta 20 was temporarily located on that morning of
June 2nd, 1917, did not have any permanent wooden hangers.
Although the author of " The Courage Of The Early Morning" mentions
' the shadowy shapes of hanger buildings' on page 100 this is not
correct. The only permanent wooden sheds housing an enemy squadron
was located at Estourmel. Jasta 5, the permanent tenant of this
aerodrome throughout the summer of 1917, did not experience a raid
by a lone enterprising allied pilot on this, or any other morning
throughout 1917.

Page 50 – Narrator (line 16)

Quotation: One of the most baffling questions is why Bishop's Newport
returned with its Lewis gun missing.

Page 51 – Voice (line 1)

Quotation: That's a bit of a mystery, isn't it. I mean, It didn't have its
Lewis gun, you know. I mean he said he chucked it on the way back,
you know, to lighten up the plane for added speed, you see. Well,
I mean, I'd like to see somebody take one of those off in the air,
you know, while flying...

Corrections: Replacing a drum of ammuniton on a Lewis gun while engaged in
to both   combat was an art mastered by very few pilots who flew the Nieuport
questions Scouts with the Foster Mounting on the top wing. Three of the most
50 & #51 noteworthy who could handle this armament, namely Ball, Mannock and
Bishop all experienced trouble in changing the 97-round drum in the
slipstream. It is entirely likely that Bishop jettisoned his drum
and gun overboard when he could not change the drum, after all, he
was being hotly pursued by enemy aircraft and a gun without ammunition
would have been useless and its dead weight would have hampered his
escape.
It would have been relatively simple for him to loosen the screw
on the securing collar, let down the Lewis Gun on the quadrant,
and throw the 15-pound Lewis Gun overboard.

Page 51 Voice (line 14)

Quotation: In the tail, ther's about seventeen bullet holes, you see...
all in a nice little group like that, you know. And, well I
mean I've seen a lot of planes shot up but I mean nobody can
shoot a plane like that, you know.

Correction: Wm. Fry in his book ' Air of Battle' remembers clearly seeing
a group of five bullet holes in the rear half of his tailplane,
the elevator, within a circle if not more than six inches in
diameter at the most.

The 6-inch cluster of five neatly placed holes in the rear of
Bishop's tailplane and elevator had to be the result of close
combat or ground fire. Bishop mentioned that the aerodrome was
armed with one or more machine guns. As Bishop was flying very
close to the ground he had to stall turn a few times to keep
within the radius of the field. During this critical manoeuvre
he would have been an easy target for the ground gunner(s)
firing a wheel mounted high-angle Spandau or Parabellum
machine-gun, the sole means of air-defence against attacking
allied aircraft.

The tail structure of the Nieuport Scout was a delicately-
built structure. Only a fool would have purposefully landed
and sprayed his own tail   with bullets as has been hinted
by Wm. Fry and some of his proponents.

Very, very few allied pilots attempted a solo raid on an enemy
aerodrome during World War One. Had the interviewed witnessed other
allied machines that had survived such an exploit he probably
would have seen more examples of a tight group of bullet holes
strategically located in their fuselage and/or tail assemblies.

Page 52 – Narrator (line 5)

Quotation: The Germans kept meticulous records at all their aerodromes.
Historians will later find Estermel's records and there will
be no mention of any raid. They will also scour the records of
other aerodromes in the area with the same result.

Correction: The Germans did not keep specific records of flying activity at
each aerodrome their units occupied in France or Belgium.
Each German Jasta (fighter squadron) or Flieger-Abteilung
(Artillery-observation squadron) were required to keep a daily
diary. Contrary to accepted belief the German flying unit records
were not comprehensive and did not compare with similar records
kept by the allied squadrons. Often general in nature the German
Aviation War Diaries do not include the exact time that their
airmen were wounded, where exactly this occurred, or in many cases,
the nature of the wound or injury. The actual Jasta War Diaries
examined by this writer do not always take into account the result
of a combat in which the enemy pilot was forced to land, often
damaging his aircraft in the process. As 98% of aerial combats in
World War One occured over enemy-occupied territory the German
pilots could break off a combat at random; they could also descend
with allied aircraft on their tail and land without suffering any
personal injury although the pilot and/or observer could be in a state
of shock. If this occurred in the RFC, RNAS or RAF the affected airmen
would be sent to a Hospital for immediate treatment. In the
Imperial German Air Service they were often kept at the squadron and
given a temporary ground job. None of this would ever be entered in
the Jasta or Flieger-Abteilung War Diary unless the pilot or
observer was temporarily incapacitated. Often damaged enemy aircraft
were repaired at the squadron. If so the high command of the
Imperial German Air Service would never be made privy to this
information.

During the final German retreat in the fall of 1918 a
number of German squadrons lost their War Diaries. Those
that survived were kept in Berlin after World War One.
When Hitler came to power in the thirties he appointed
Goering Chief of the Air Staff. About five years prior to
the outbreak of World War Two, Goering allowed some historians
from around the world to begin corresponding with the Reich
in regards to specific questions pertaining to the World War One
period. He would not allow any researchers or historians from
abroad to examine personally, World War One aviation files
in their archives. One or two German nationals were allowed
the unusual privilege of examining in person specific documents
relating to the more outstanding German fighter squadrons in
World War One. These historians had to copy in long hand any
references elicited from the original documents.
In 1944 Goering requested that all military documents relating
to World War One be sent to a single repository so they would
not fall into allied hands. While temporarily stored in the
city of Dresden they were destroyed by allied bombing. The only
known surviving documents are those kept by the Bavarians in
Munich. They refused to comply with Goering's order and kept their
World War One records in Munich.
With the exception of some additional documentation that may, or
may not survive in East Germany, contemporary historians specializing
in World War One aviation history will have to be content with the
Bavarian documents and the notes, albeit sketchy, of the few
German historians who were granted access to the files of the
Reichsluftfahrtministerium from 1933 to 1936.

Page 54 — Narrator (line 3)

Quotation: Bishop has finally no choice but to leave and early in August
             he completes his last mission, getting an Albatross and a ...

Correction: This statement is out of sequence.

             Bishop completed his first tour of duty with 60 Squadron in
             late August 1917 and was given a two-month matrimonial leave
             to Canada. While commanding Officer of 85 Squadron, Royal Air Force,
             in 1918 he was sent home from France at the request of the
             Air Ministry and the Canadian Government on the 21st of June, 1918.

                        ....

NFB Proposal

APPENDIX "VA-6-A"

The film "Billy Bishop" will be comprised of three elements: excerpts from the play "Billy Bishop Goes to War", stock shots, and interviews with those who knew Bishop.

The play will transpose ideally to the screen: it is a one character narrative of Bishop's life which both structurally and in content is a perfect backbone for the film. Seeing the character Bishop sweating with fear, or consumed by blood lust, or seeing Bishop unable to cope with the international recognition that haunts him after the war will give the film an immediacy and emotional impact otherwise impossible in an historical documentary. Furthermore, the chronological, episodic nature of the play will lend itself well to intercutting with the stock shot and interview sequences. All of the 15 characters mentioned in the play did exist and are factually accurate; many will be seen in the stock shots or referred to in the interviews, a few such as Bishop's wife are still alive and will be interviewed. The connections will integrate the play and will permit smooth transitions in and out of the play sequences. Chronologically the play covers the full spectrum of Bishop's life, from his years as a cadet at RMC to appointment as Vice Air Marshall during the Second World War. In between it touches most of the important events in Bishop's life, so there will be no point in the film where this thread is severed. One final note: Eric Peterson who plays Billy Bishop in the play has an uncanny ressemblance to the real Bishop seen in the stock shots.

The stock shots will be of two varieties: actual historical material and shots from feature films made about the First World War ("Wings", "Aces High", "Dawn Patrol", etc.). Since these films were made shortly after the war their material is virtually indistinguishable from real stock shots (although of course much more dramatic). The actual stockshots will come from several sources: The National Film Board, the Canadian Film Archives, the Royal Aeronautical Society, the German War Archives, amongst other sources. There is not a lot of material on Bishop, but what there is is good. There is excellent material on the planes, on the dog-fights and on the ground war where Bishop got his initiation. There will also be excerpts from the films made after the war where Bishop, then an international hero, played small cameo roles.

There are many people who will be interviewed. Principal among these are Bishop's wife Margret who now resides in Miami, Bishop's daughter, Jackie Willis-O'Connor who is living in Ottawa and who has a considerable collection of Bishop's memorabelia including photographs and his letters home, and Bishop's close personal friend and physician who resides in Montreal. There are also the flyers from Bishop's 60th and 85th Squadron in Canada and England who knew him well and who, for the most part, revered him. Other assorted people will also be interviewed, such an an infantry man who witnessed Bishop's single-handed attack on the German airport. We will also attempt to locate as many as possible of the German flyers who are still living, especially those who might have encountered Bishop.

Throughout the film, it is our intention to keep the material focused as much as possible on Billy Bishop. We are not so much trying to make a war movie as a film about a man who went to war. In that one flyer there is the metamorphosis of most men who have gone to war—the naive kid gleeful at the prospect of encountering the enemy, the blood thirsty killer, the man numbed by fear, and the human being finally horrified by the futility of war. It will be the very intimate story of a rather special hero—it will be also the lament of all fighting men.

Statements: A.E. Ferko; D.W. Warne

STATEMENT BY A. E. FERKO

The flying sections, artillery cooperating flying sections, the fighter units (Jastas or Jagdstaffeln), Bomber units, Escort units and ground attack units all had to maintain daily activity records which were known as their war diaries (Kriegstage buch or simply KTB). Some of these KTBs did survive the two wars but the vast majority did not.

Beyond the field units, the Armee Flug Parks (Army Flying Depots of one which served each armee at the front) had to keep records of all aircraft received and then disposed of (usually to units in this front jurisdiction) by type, date of arrival, from where, whether damaged or destroyed and serial number of machine as well as company work numbers frequently. When moved from the park, the records told where the a/c went, serial number, date of transfer, etc.

Fighter and bomber units were normally assigned directly to Kofl. Every unit reported to Kofl at the close of each day. Kofl then communicated his data to the Armee commander—and to Kogenluft in Berlin. *Thus you can see that a Jastaw would have to report to Kofl each evening with info such as number of patrols flown—how many successes (victories) or losses whether killed, injured or sick—moves if made, or in process, etc.* Not only did Koft receive these reports but the Armee Flug Park also were informed of the status of each unit in the field vis-à-vis aircraft losses and unit readiness—i.e. How many a3C were missing, shot down, damaged in accidents or otherwise unworthy for flying missions at the front. Crews were also supplied by the AFPs— so if losses due to one thing or another such as wounding, sick, injured, killed or missing occurred, the park could send along replacement crews and aircraft. *To suggest that unit commanders engaged in doctoring up the records by failing to show losses of any kind is absolutely absurd—it couldn't or wouldn't be done—far too many checks to adhere to.*

There is no evidence available to prove that W. A. Bishop successfully attacked a German airfield on the morning of 2 June 1917. Extracts from the KTb (war diarys) of Jadgstaffel 2, 5, 6, 20 and 26 as well as Kofl reports for 2 and 6 and 4 German armee, all fail to show evidence of such an attack on 2 June 1917. The above material is all in my files and may be examined if necessary. *The suggestion that Jasta 20 records fail to show a raid resulting in the loss of 3 or 4 of its aircraft while in transit to 4 armee, because there was no need to keep such records, is preposterous.*

The fact that J20 KTB notes fait to show much activity between 27 May and 11.7.17 is not because the Staffel had been severely damaged on 2.6.17, but rather that when Tornuss took the notes from the original Jasta 20 KTB, there was nothing of worth there other than personnel movement in and out of the unit between 7 June and 11 July when Creutzmann scored.

Examination of Kofl 4 reports and victory listings in the Nachrichtenblatt clearly show the lack of activity near the channel. *Thus the allegation that Jasta 20 was unable to function because of Bishop (2 June 1917) has no credence what so ever.*

Jasta Boelcke, Jasta 6, Jasta 5, Jasta 20 and Jasta 26 records are extensive and quite complete. Kofl recorrds are also available and unassailable. Nothing even remotely suggests there is any evidence W. A. Bishop did what he is said to have done on 2 June 1917.

THE BILLY BISHOP CONTROVERSY AS SEEN BY SQN. LDR. D.W. WARNE, MRAeS, RAFRO

1. Personal Involvement as 60 Squadron Historian since 1959 My personal interest in R.A.F. history began even before joining the Air Training Corps in 1941, and has been a hobby ever since, expensive in both time and money. During my subsequent full—and part—time service with the R.A.F., RAFVR(T), RAFRO, etc., I have always taken up the secondary duty of Sqn. historian with my various units. In the case of 60 Sqn., however, I did two tours in the Far East as a NAWF pilot in short succession, totalling over six years; subsequently, I have been on instructional duties, so that 60 was my last operational sqn. and research has been continued ever since. From my research whilst with 60, the Sqn. had a fifty-year history printed in Singapore in time for the fifty-first anniversary for private sale to former members in particular. Upon my return to the U.K. after completion of my second tour in 1966, I embarked on a total revision of the history accumulated in Singapore, using the records in the Public Record Office, R.A.F. Air Historical Branch, etc, not available to me in Singapore. For the next seven years, World War One was investigated in considerable depth, before continuing with further research into later periods. Further, surviving World War One members of 60 were contacted and interviewed if resident in the U.K., and copious correspondence was an outcome in most cases. Inevitably, after some twenty-five years' experience of investigation of the facts and opinions in considerable depth, I am considered to be the expert on 60 Sqn. history. As far as 1916-19 is concerned, my only published work appeared in the Journal of Cross and Cockade (Great Britain), Vol. 11, No. 1, to Vol. 12, No. 1, inclusive (five parts). This represents a major contraction of information actually collected, the narrative merely supporting the annexes of significant interest to other researchers, and is entirely voluntary, unpaid!

2. As a fighter pilot of considerable experience, followed by flying instructional duties including over one thousand hours on the Chipmunk with a performance similar to the Nieuports flown by Bishop for most of his time with 60 Sqn., I considered myself rather more competent to assess Combat Reports than many in that field. When the doubts about Bishop's claims were brought to my attention by some of his contemporaries, a much closer inspection of the records was necessary in the search for facts, free from prejudice. This certainly revealed that some pretty unlikely situations had passed into the legend, unsubstantiated in any way!

3. **General Aspects of Billy Bishop's Tour with 60 Sqn., March to August, 1917**
    For some time before becoming involved with the history of 60 Sqn. I had been made aware of the difficulties in
    reconciling Billy Bishop's claims made both whilst with 60 and with 85 Sqns., in that other air historians had tried
    unsuccessfully to find evidence to support those claims. However, I di not consider that aspect as part of my research
    initially, being entirely concerned with producing a narrative and comprehensive annexes, including one of all claims made
    by all 60 Sqn. pilots in combat. The sources of information used were documentary evidence in the Public Record Office, the
    Air Historian Branch, and other published works and logbooks, backed up by personal recollections from all contactable
    survivors who had served on 60 Sqn. Thus, in the case of Billy Bishop, these sources were Combat Reports, Officers' Record
    Book, 13 Wing and 3 Bde. Diaries, his autobiography *Winged Warfare*, and his logbooks, in addition to other less significant
    publications. Three Air VC's were connected with 60 Sqn., and as they had been written up in several publications
    subsequently, I did not intend to delve much further into the histories of Albert Ball, Billy Bishop, or Jimmy McCudden
    (who was killed en route to take command of 60, so no combat claim were relevant in his case), being more concerned with
    the details of lesser known sqn. members. In any case, virtually all of Ball's claims whilst with 60 had been substantiated,
    either at the time or shortly after the war. At this stage it is appropriate to reject some statements seen in Canadian Press
    cuttings recently—virtually all of Manfred von Richhofen's claims had been matched within a very short time after the war
    by Brisith casualties—very few of his claimed victories did actually escape! Confirmation of R.F.C. claims made east of the
    front lines was inevitably difficult in solid terms, i.e., wreckage on the ground, but post-war research into German flying
    casualties and unit war diaries has produced a lot of matching evidence, in may cases, to substantiate witnessed claims. In
    the dogfighting scene it would have been fatal to watch one's victim all the way down to the ground. Totally impartially,
    then, my examination of Bishop's claims resulted in the list attached, being slightly over-generous to Bishop whenever there
    were discrepancies between initial reports, his logbook, and any follow-up evidence. Thus, whilst official records are used
    where discrepancies occur in quoted dates, the highest standard of claim has been listed, i.e., "Crashed" is quoted if such
    appers elsewhere despite the records made at the time quoted "DOOC."

    The difficulty arises when one attempts to find verification of most of his claims, as they were made as a result of either: solo
    forays or having become separate from his patrol. Hence, no members of 60 were able to confirm the majority of the claims,
    neither did any other R.F.C. observers airborne at the time and in the vicinity; ground observers, mainly the anti-aircraft
    gunners, provided remarkably little confirmation despite the fact that the location of the fight should have been visible to
    someone at the front. Bishop's earlier claims were generally substantiated by other evidence, particularly in view of the fact
    that he was a member of a patrol. Throughout his time on 60, the Sqn. was based at Filescamp Farm near Izel-le-Hameau,
    west of Arras. He survived "Bloody April," when the Sqn. casualty rate was about twenty-five percent and the life
    expectancy of a newly trained scout pilot was about two weeks. Like most other pilots who joined 60 Sqn. at the time, he had
    his initial mishaps whilst learning to fly the Nieuport, but subsequently his record as a "safe" pilot was unsurpassed. He flew
    Niewport 17 B 1566 several times a day for several months until 60 received SE 5 scouts in replacement, when his aircraft A
    8936 again saw him out. He was obviously popular on the Sqn., and there can be no doubt that Maj. Jack Scott, OC 60 for
    most of Bishop's time, considered him a great asset. Letters written home by O.C. "A" Flt. Capt. W. E. Molesworth
    continue to praise his efforts. These letters have been reprinted and published several times since. Gp. Capt. F. O. Soden's
    memoirs make no adverse comments. However, after "Bloody April," the air fighting over the Arras sector diminished
    considerably as the ground action moved north to Flanders, along with the mobile German air support. It was difficult to
    engage any German aircraft for much of the time, despite provocation. There can be no doubt about Bishop's bravery. He
    went off on numerous solo flights endeavouring to catch the opposition by surprise. Other pilots did the same thing but
    rarely found anything within shooting range. There were some advantages in operating alone: the ability to use cloud to
    avoid detection and pick the right moment to attack, and subsequently to hide in the cloud cover; the likelihood of being
    ignored if seen, although the Germans were well aware that Niewports were carrying cameras for photographic
    reconnaissance; once on the fringe of combat, the solo pilot did not have to concern himself with other aircraft of his
    patrol—everything sighted was likely to be hostile. On the other hand, the solo scout pilot had numerous disadvantages too:
    lack of cross cover and mutual support; the German scouts had some performance advantages over the Nieuport; fighting
    east of the lines usually meant having to return to base against the prevailing wind, but there was little chance of finding any
    opposition west of the lines. Maj. Scott was obviously convinced that Capt. Bishop's Combat Reports usually merited the
    subscription "Decisive"—i.e., agreement with the nature of the claim made verbally, despite lack of any corroborating
    evidence. Maj. Scott was a highly respected member of the R.F.C., not only because of his own war record, but also due to
    his numerous political and military contacts in high places stemming from his pre-war profession. He appears not to have
    been too conscientious about Bishop's Combat Reports, however—rarely is the enemy type specified in the sort of detail
    required by Wing Intelligence staff, which doesn't help the historian much (and led to consent from AVM Raymond
    Collishaw attached), and certainly reports by other pilots were rather more specific in such details. In any case, after the
    heavy losses of "Bloody April," the R.F.C. needed more heroes for the public, and Gen Trenchard encouraged aggressive
    policies and sanctioned recommendations for awards readily. This of course continued the trend set in the case of Capt.
    Albert Ball, and no doubt gained further recognition for 60 Sqn. Unfortunately, Gp. Capt. Scott died shortly after the war
    ended and was not able to participate in the aftermath of dubious claims being queried. There is little different to note when
    Maj. Cochran-Patrick replaced Scott as OC 60 with the advent of the SE 5 in July, 1917, although the claims are less
    contentious at that stage.

Thus far it is apparent that R.F.C. records do not help justify many of Bishop's claims in any way. It was by virtue of interviewing his contemporaries, and corresponding with the more remote ones, that I became aware of the strong feelings held among some of the stalwarts. In no case did I bring up the topic for the reasons stated above, but as 60 Sqn. pilot-to-60 Sqn. pilot, I was privileged to hear and read details not available to most researchers. The most critical was Col. Spencer Horn, who served under Bishop in 60 "C" Flt., became his deputy after Lt. Fry returned home, subsequently served as a Fighting Instructor with Bishop, and finally was one of Bishop's Flt. Cdrs. when the latter was OC 85 Sqn. Naturally, all correspondents were reluctant to commit their thoughts on such a controversial issue to paper, but attached are some extracts of relevance. Capt. Geoffrey Pidcock was OC "B" Flt. from mid-April until early May, when he was succeeded by Capt. "Grid" Caldwell, who returned for a further stint with 60. Pidcock remained in the post-war air force, retiring as AVM. Caldwell became the top-scoring New Zealander, thought by many to be the most courageous and aggressive pilot with 60 and more deserving of the top award than anyone else. He rejoined (the R.N.Z.A.F.) in World War Two with the rank of Air Crd. Lt. Willy Fry was deputy "C" Flt. Cdr. to Bishop for most of his second spell with 60 Sqn. He joined the post-war R.A.F. for several years before retiring with an "Exceptional" rating as a heavy-bomber pilot. With the rank of Wg. Cdr., he commanded stations in World War Two. An extract from his book *Air of Battle* is attached. Air. Cdr. Sydney Pope remained in the post-war R.A.F. until the conclusion of World War Two. He spent most of 1917 as a member of 60 "A" Flt. The only significant criticism he voiced concerned his annoyance at being left unprotected whilst carrying out a photographic sortie well over the lines when Bishop departed on some private foray. Capt. Edgar Percival was a Lt. in "C" Flt. under Bishop for a few weeks in April and May, 1917. He volunteered no criticism. All of those contemporaries who made adverse comments about Bishop were themselves decorated "aces" with 60 Sqn. The possibility of "sour grapes" being a factor was soon discarded as all were sincere, humble, well-to-do, successful individuals in their chosen fields. The four who were members of 60 in June, 1917, sowed the seeds of doubt which called for further investigation. Then it became obvious that the historians in the U.K., the U.S.A., and Germany who specialized in analysis of German records were also defeated in their attempts over the years to match Bishop's claims with German losses in the War Diaries of the Jagdstaffein and Jagdgruppe concerned and in the casualty lists, all of which were comprehensive. Wg. Cdr. F. H. Hitchins made a thorough list of German losses in Cross and Cockade (U.S.A.) Journals; Douglass Whetton did specific research into the matching of German claims and losses with my lists; Alex Revell has had similar difficulty trying to find equivalent German losses; no additional matching evidence has resulted from the publication of the 60 Sqn. Claims list in the Journals of Cross and Cockade (G.B.) four years ago as part of the series on 60 Sqn., etc.

4. Bishop's VC Raid

During his time with 60 Sqn., Bishop was awarded the MC, DSO, VC, and a Bar to the DSO, along with several foreign decorations. The recommendation and approval (and Citation) for the award of the VC made no mention of Bishop's previous exploits, though they must have been taken into consideration. However, the focal point of the whole controversy was the solo raid he carried out on 2 June, 1917, which, without any confirmatory evidence of any sort, resulted in the recommendation by Jack Scott, followed up by a personal visit to Gen. Allenby, GOC IIIrd Army, to reinforce the recommendation which went through the normal R.F.C. channels.

It is important to study the available facts and opinions recorded at the time or subsequently. The weather reported over the IIIrd Bde. sector that day was: fine in the morning, clouding over during the afternoon, with storms later. Aircraft of 13 Wing flew over 122 hours that day. 60's patrol activities consisted of "A" Flt. taking off at 06.25 and 10.00 hrs., alternating with "B" Flt. taking off at 08.20 and 12.05 hrs., all for flights of about 1:00 hour in duration on offensive patrol. The other scout Sqn. in the Wing would have filled the gaps in order to maintain continuous offensive scout activity east of the lines. "C" Flt. had a rest day. Bishop took off for his voluntary solo flight (with the declared intention of strafing a German airfield) at 03.57; he reported thirty-seven minutes of combat over an airfield, the identity of which has never been established, between 04.23 and 05.00 hrs., and he landed back at base at 05.40hrs. He logged 2:00 hours flying. Under the reported flight circumstances—low-level, thirty-seven minutes combat, hurried escape—it is likely that the Nieuport would have exhausted its fuel supply in about 1:20 hours! His Combat Report suggests that he made his attack on either Esnes or Awoignt, two of the several airfields around Cambrai. Despite his knowledge of the area after three months flying from Filescamp Farm, it is not too inconceivable that he was lost at low level. What has been established is that the resident scout units in that area were 35.5 at Estourmel and Beoicke 38 at Masnieres. The War Diaries of these units make no reference to any such attack, whilst German Air Casualty records show three fatalities that day, all sustained in training accidents deep inside Germany. Hence there is total lack of confirmatory evidence from these sources.

The mystery deepens when the state of B 1566 upon return to Filescamp Farm is considered. No aircraft Casualty Report was raised for the replacement of his aircraft due to damage sustained. In other words, it was reparable using local resources alone. Recollections of eye witnesses vary somewhat in terms of the location of the bullet holes and the precise number of holes—there is unanimity, however, in that the holes were in close groups. One does not need to be a gunnery expert to appreciate the improbability of a moving target sustaining such damage from machine guns either from the air or from the ground. The damage was obviously only superficial, readily patched up, because Bishop flew the same Nieuport the same afternoon on a visit to 54 Sqn., along with another pilot. *At the time* eyebrows were raised and dissension arose among members of the Sqn. The occurrence had baffled researchers ever since.

Neither the Combat Report nor his account of the raid in *Winged Warfare* makes any reference to the fact that he landed in the French sector to ask for directions back to Filescamp Farm. This is hardly surprising as he was not aware of which airfield he had attacked; if he switched off his engine, this could account for the fact that he wouldn't have had sufficient fuel for the stated length of his flight. However, much more scope for conjecture arises from the other omission in the records; he came back without his machine gun. A subsequent explanation, apparently originating from Bishop himself, is that, being out of ammunition, he threw the gun overboard to reduce his aircraft weight to facilitate his escape. It is well known that Nieuport pilots suffered a grave disadvantage in combat when it became necessary to change ammunition drums on the Foster-mounted Lewis gun; both hands were needed, so the control column was held between the knees. This situation resulted in the loss of several pilots on 60 Sqn. alone. Even if it were possible to remove the gun from its mounting and the trigger cable from the control column in flight (or was it done on the ground in the French sector—when safe from pursuit?), would this have been a logical step? The absence of the gun over the top plane would have been fairly obvious to any keen-eyed JS pilot close enough to consider opening fire, whether the ammunition was exhausted or not. Would any pilot worried about being intercepted with ammunition exhausted really spend time and effort struggling to remove his gun when logically he should have been concentrating on going flat-out for the sanctuary of the lines, beyond which German scouts rarely ventured? Any suggestion of dead weight, or even excess drag, on the performance of the Nieuport under these circumstances must be rejected.

No other "C" Flt. pilot crossed the lines that day, hence the statement in a recent Canadian Press cutting that Spencer Horn flew over the scene of the carnage to confirm the havoc Bishop claimed to have created is rubbish—which airfield could it have been anyway?

World War One historians would have enough to ponder about from the above considerations, but there is more to come. It is noteworthy at this stage that frequently books, booklets, and articles about the better-known "aces" appear on the market or in specialist journals, except in the case of Billy Bishop: Cross and Cockade (G.B.) avoids the controversy by declining to use articles in the Journal with Bishop as a topic!

5. The R.A.F.M. flown cover commemorating Bishop's VC Raid

Among the more lucrative of the essential fund-raising activities of the R.A.F. Museum at Hendon over recent decades has been the production and sale of stamped specialized envelopes with appropriate enclosures, transported by air at some stage in an aircraft with some equivalent connection, generally commemorating the anniversary of some notable event in military or civil flying. These flown covers are of interest to both philatelists and air historians. It is normal to have some of the covers signed by persons connected with the event to enhance their appeal. Obviously, 60 Sqn. was the co-sponsor for the cover commemorating Bishop's VC raid. Flt. Lt. Downey, then a member of 60 Sqn., but also a member of the R.A.F.M. flown-cover sales organization, asked my advice as to which former members contemporary with Bishop might be able to sign the covers. By 1977 few were still alive, but the names and addresses of the survivors were passed on and they were approached by the organizers. The enclosed photostat copy of the front face of the flown cover indicates the result, complemented by the attached extracts from letters. Sixty years after the event, the feelings of Bishop's surviving contemporaries were still so strong that, even for the R.A.F.M. charity, they refused to have anything to do with endorsing the cover, which only substantiated my earlier impressions. Fortuitously, Edgar Percival did sign—he was no longer a member of 60 when the controversial events took place in 1917—which was most appropriate in that 60 was (and still is) flying the Pembroke, a product of the successor to the Percival Aircraft Co., Ltd. Paradoxically, Capt. Percival objected to the enclosure, which gave a brief résumé of his service, his subsequent renown as designer, manufacturer, and racer of light aircraft, based on material he provided to the R.A.F.M. previously. That enclosure was subsequently removed, though no one could fathom his objections.

6. Summary

Billy Bishop was a hero, highly thought of in the main. Both the current 60 Sqn. and its Officers' Dinner Club have made handsome contributions to the Billy Bishop Memorial at Owen Sound. We all wish his name to be respected and see no logic in making public these doubts about the majority of his claims, and it is hardly surprising that Canadians have objected to the NFB film "The Kid who Couldn't Miss" in that these suspicions have been voiced openly for the first time. However, the resulting articles in the Canadian Press have been so weirdly unrealistic that I have gone over all the old ground again to try and introduce some truth into the controversy and dispel some of the legend that has been built up. I do have an axe to grind—to seek the facts concerning 60 Sqn. history, but I have no intention of publishing anything derogatory about Billy Bishop or any other member of 60 Sqn. which I was proud to serve with six years. None of his contemporaries wish to be quoted in detail on such a delicate matter. I respect those wishes and consider the above account and enclosures to be confidential material, not for publication. The absence of all the facts inevitably leads to conjecture, which is a personal matter. But Bishop did publicly declare his intention of becoming the top Commonwealth "ace," and it would appear that his claims were overstated, with the compliance of Maj. Scott.

Naturally, the factual aspects quoted above differ from material published usually by authors who do not do primary research but merely rehash someone else's efforts. A sample is attached.

As the circulation of this paper is severely restricted, I do not expect that it will result in any corroboratory evidence to substantiate Bishop's claims coming to light, but of course I will be delighted to be notified of anything factual that turns up.

Distribution: National Film Board of Canada
                    Billy Bishop Memorial
                    60 Sqn.

[Signed]
Sqn. Ldr. D. W. Warne, MRAeS, RAFRO
79 Valley Road
Melton Mowbray
Leic. LE 13 ODU, U.K.

APPENDIX "VA-6-E"

ERRORS IN TESTIMONY

AN ANALYSIS OF STATEMENTS
MADE TO THE SENATE SUB-COMMITTEE ON VETERANS' AFFAIRS

A. Symansky
P. Cowan
National Film Board of Canada

November 28, 1985

I. *ERRORS REGARDING BISHOP'S RECORD*

1. *Dr. Wise*:

A very high proportion of Bishop's kills, so-called, were, in fact, verified as the result of corroborative testimony.

Response:

American researcher, William Puglisi, obtained voluminous German squadron war diaries from the German historian, Turnuss. Turnuss did his work in the '30' when such records had still not been destroyed. These diaries from opposing squadrons, while listing many casualties, fail in almost every case to confirm Bishop's claims.

2. *Dr. Wise*:

The second factor to be considered in that the records for the German airforce from that period are not complete. We do not have them. They disappeared long ago, well before World War II. We do not know what happened to them. They do not exist. There is, in fact, no possibility so far as I know, of proving from German records whether or not Bishop did what he claimed to have done.

Response:

Dr. Wise is at odds with others here. See following list of 17 planes compiled by Willian Puglisi claimed by Bishop as either 'destroyed', 'crashed', or 'in flames', from March 17 to August 16, 1917. Normally such victories would result in the pilot's death. However, of the 17 claims, only two are 'possibly verifiable' from German records of war dead. In the case of other aces, eg. James McCudden, these types of records have proven to be remarkably accurate.

NL—no loss listed in German record Kofl report

	DATE	TYPE	PLACE	TIME
	25.3.17	Albatross D111	North of St. Leger	17:00
	1.4.17		South of Gravell	07:30
NL	20.4.17	2 seater flames	Biache St. Vast	14:56
NL	29.4.17	Halberstadt D flames	E. of Epinoy	11:55
NL	2.5.17	Alb CIV destroyed	E. of Epinoy	10:10
NL	2.5.17	A16 CIV destroyed	E. of Epinoy	10:10
NL	2.6.17	A16 D 3 crashed		
NL	24.6.17	A16 D111 flames	Beaumont	11:23
NL	26.6.17	A16 D111 flames	Array-Eteing	10:55
NL	17.7.17	A16 D111 flames	Havrincourt	19:43
NL	17.7.17	A16 D111 destroyed	Marquion-Queant	19:55
NL	28.7.17	A16 D111 flames	Phalempic	18:10
NL	6.8.17	A16 D111 crashed	Brebieres	15:45
NL	13.8.17	A16 D111 flames	5 miles S. Dovan	19:02
NL	13.8.17	A16 D111 flames	5 miles S. Dovan	19:05
NL	16.8.17	2 seater crashed	Harnes	19:03
NL	16.8.17	A16 DIV wings came off	Carvin	19:06

Selecting only incidents which should have resulted in deaths of German airmen between 25.3 and 16.8.17 Though such losses would have been described as in flames—or disintegrated in the air—lost wings, etc.

These all were recorded and some published at the time

I was able to find only two possible victories that may have fallen to Bishop—23.4.17 A16 D111 E. Vitry; and 5.8.17—a flamer. ALB D11 vicinity Hendecourt—Monchy at 20:00. Not a very savory record to say the least. For Taylor to suggest that the Germans somehow conspired to rob Bishop of his truly won laurels, especially the 2 June raid, is absolutely ridiculous. For one thing the Germans had no idea when Bishop claimed his victories between late March 17 and August 17 when he left the line with 40 plus victories. So how could they have possibly expunged names and dates from either Unit KTB's AFP KTB, Grufl KTB's or Kofl KTB. To make Bishop out to be a liar? And why? The Kofl 2 records clearly show no such loss of a/c on 2 June 1917—and they would have been declared lost and the wreckage returned to the AFP for either repair or certainly replacement if Bishop's tale was true. Kofl 6 records are equally clear. No airfields attacked by anyone that day. Same for 4th army.

3. *Mr. Taylor*:

Strangely a lot of the German records were not accurate. They were not detailed. We always think of the Germans keeping very good records. They did not. They especially did not keep records of pilots injured, nervous breakdowns, battle damage, other than those who were killed outright—the reason being that the German commanders looked good to their superiors if they could show that they were inflicting damage on allied machines with a minimum of loss to themselves.

Response:

Actually the German system of reporting losses, deaths, injuries, sickness, movement was quite good. It was at two-tired system involving daily reports to Army Flying Depots which kept records of all planes received and disposed of for maintenance reasons, and daily reports to Kofl (the commandant responsible for air power attached to each army). Each unit would have to report to Kofl each evening with information regarding losses (killed, injured, sickness) moves if made, or in process, etc.

4.   *Col. Bauer*:

"The typed pages came to me from the National Film Board and they are a summary of Billy Bishop's record as compiled by a squadron leader, D. W. Warne, who was one of the main researchers of Bishop's record during his tour with 60 Squadron. *He is 60 Squadron's "official historian".* He submitted to the National Film Board that list of Bishop's kills which he recognizes. You will note that the number 47 is exactly the same as the number of officials kills recorded in the official records, again compiled in 1917".

Response:

This is a curious interpretation of what Squadron Leader Warne was saying. In fact, if Col. Bauer had read on he would have noted that Warne was saying he could not find verification for many of these 47 claimed victories. The following is Warne's next statement that Bauer did not include: "The difficulty arises when one attempts to find verification of most of his claims, as they were made as a result of either solo forays, or having become separated from his patrol. Hence, no members of 60 were able to confirm the majority of the claims; neither did any other RFC observer airborne at the time and in the vicinity; Ground observers, mainly the anti-aircraft gunners provided remarkably little confirmation despite the fact that the location of the fight should have been visible to some-one at the front. Bishop's earlier claims were generally substantiated by other evidence, particularly in view of the fact that he was a member of a patrol".

II—ERRORS REGARDING V.C. RAID

1. *Mr. Taylor*:

People have often said, and somewhere along the line Arthur Bishop was misled when he said that his father raided the Estourmel aerodrome. He did not. Even the records and the intelligence reports copies of which I have with me, indicate that it was either Esnes or a place called Awoignt but it is too far east so it is out. People have said that they could not find any records of the German Jagdsta V Squadron being at Esnes. Fortunately, I have been in touch with some very good historians both in Germany and in the United States.

Response:

There is much confusion as to the location of the aerodrome. Mr. Taylor says that "Arthur Bishop was misled when he said that his father raided the Estourmel aerodrome. He did not... it was either Esnes or a place called Awoigt". Curiously, Arthur Bishop is very specific about it being Estourmel, and even cites proof of this that Spencer Horn flew over Estourmel later that afternoon and verified the raid. Mr. Taylor then states that he has been in touch with "some very good historians both in Germany and in the United States" (as if somehow they would extricate him from the difficulty of deciding just which aerodrome they would extricate attacked). He neglects, however, to say who those historians were, and vastly more importantly, what those historians said.

2. *Professor Kear*:

According to Ron Lowman in the "Toronto Star" of April 7, 1984, and I quote: "Art Bishop says it was Horn who confirmed to him, when writing his father's biography, that on the orders of the Squadron's commanding officer, Major Jack Scott, he flew over Estourmel the same afternoon and saw the destroyed aircraft". "Horn said they had to have confirmation for a decoration, in this case the VC", Art Bishop said. "My book was the authentic version of my father's life as it was cleared by the R.A.F. and the R.C.A.F. (Royal Canadian Air Force) plus historians past and present. All his claims are listed in the back".

Response:

This is an extraordinary statement. First of all consider the trail it took before winding up in Hansard. Here we have Professor Kear quoting the Toronto Star quoting Art Bishop quoting Spencer Horn. Now consider the errors included in this one statement. Art Bishop says the aerodrome was Estourmel. Yet S. K. Taylor has said Art Bishop was misled there; it was either Esnes or Awoignt. Then Spencer Horn is described as flying over *Estourmel* that same afternoon when we know that no other aircraft crossed the German lines that day to Estourmel or anywhere else. Then we have Spencer Horn being offered as a confirmation for the raid (although a cursory reading of Horn's quote does not confirm anything at all) when we know from personal statements Horn made to D. W. Warne that Horn was the most anti-Bishop pilot of them all. Finally if such a confirmation exists, why is it nowhere in writing.

3. *Professor Kear*:

In a recent article in the Toronto Star, Ron Lowman writes: Of the movie's suggestion that Bishop never did attack a German airfield all by himself and instead shot his own plane's tail full of holes on the ground, Bauer (a retired Group Captain and Chairman of the Billy Bishop Heritage) said, "There is more than 100 holes in the plane". Cowan (the film's producer) doesn't mention that at all".

I would interject a comment here: if the producer wanted to get across the story, why did he not tell the rest of the facts. Why is the producer of the film selective in the facts?

Reponse:

Again we have Kear quoting the Toronto Star quoting Col. Bauer quoting in turn without attribution. The film version comes from W. M. Frye who examined the plane. It is corroborated by D. W. Warne who spoke to Bishop's contemporaries. At least our facts are not fourth hand.

4. *Col. Bauer*:

Everywhere it was shot about, bullet holes being in almost every part of it, although none luckily two feet of where I sat.

Response:

Col. Bauer, quoting Billy Bishop on the condition of his plane, states: "Everywhere it was shot about, bullet holes being in almost every part of it, although none luckily within two feet of where I sat". Warne states categorically, "Those to whom I have personally spoken over the years speak of figues around a score of bullet holes, mainly in the tail. No aircraft Casualty Report was raised. The damage was repaired on the Sqn. in time for Bishop to fly the aircraft later that day."

5. *Senator Everett*:

Did he, in fact, return without his Lewis gun?

Colonel Bauer: He did; he took it off when he was getting away from the German airplanes that were shadowing him, he thought, although they did not attack. That is an easy thing to do. The gun weighs 17.5 pounds, and anyone of us in the room could probably lift 17.5 pounds from a position where you extend your arms, bring it down in a quadrant, unscrew—for want of a better expression—a Turn-buckle, and cast it aside, throw the gun over the side. That is exactly what he did. It was unusual, but it wasn't unknown in the Royal Flying Corps for this to happen.

Response:

No other cases are cited of a pilot throwing his only gun overboard. Col. Bauer omits to get down to the technical details of the Foster mounting on the over-wing Lewis gun. There was a thumbscrew to enable the pilot to bring the gun down, either to fire upwards, or to fit a new amno. drum. But to stop the gun falling out of the bottom of its guide rail was a stop, the removal of which enabled the gun to be taken off the aircraft. Furthermore, no mention is made of the trigger cable connecting the control column trigger to the gun trigger mechanism.

And then one must ask the question, would removal of the gun have been a logical step, even if possible? The absence of the gun over the top plane would have been fairly obvious to any keen-eyed JS pilot close enough to consider opening fire, whether the ammunition was exhausted or not. Would any pilot worried about being intercepted with ammunition exhausted really spend time and effort struggling to remove his gun when logically he should have been concentrating on going flat-out for the sanctuary of the lines, beyond which German scouts rarely ventured? Any suggestion of dead weight (17.5 pounds) or even excess drag, on the performance of the Nieuport under these circumstances is open to question.

6. *Senator Gigantes*:

"Later there will be many doubts about the Estourmel raid, although no pilot in 60 Squadron will never publicly discuss the incident." Is this true or false?

Colonel Bauer: I cannot see how it can be true. I have never discussed it with any of the contemporary pilots in 60 Squadron because I did not meet them, but I cannot imagine it being true.

Response:

"No. Col. Bauer was not able to discuss Bishop with his contemporaries—I was, but at *their* instigation. And there were many doubts about the Estourmel raid." D. W. Warne

Also Col. Bauer apparently chose not to meet with W. M. Fry the only living 60 Squadron pilot who flew with Bishop.

7. *Professor Kear*:

"Bishop could scarcely have picked a worse time for his raid than that morning of June 2. Heavy clouds hung at five hundred feet and sprinkled the aerodrome with a light drizzle. He gulped a cup of scalding tea and pulled his flying suit over his pyjamas".

Response:

Note the weather—"Heavy clouds hung at five hundred feet and sprinkle the aerodrome with a light drizzle". Compare this with the discussion in the Senate Committee about the possibility of a balloonist seeing perhaps twenty miles or so.

8. *Senator Walker*:

But these pilots, the famous and the not so famous, agreed that he was great and that he shot down what he said he shot down?

Mr. Taylor: There was no question about it. There are all sorts of photographs taken at Filescamp Farm and later when the Squadron moved south of Bishop and these fellows with their arms thrown around each other. These fellows who had their arms thrown around him were also first rate pilots.

Response:

"No one on 60 Sqn. that I have spoken to who flew during Bishop's later months on 60 was still of the opinion that Bishop's claims were all justified. Certainly there are numerous photos of Bishop and colleagues having a jolly time off-duty. He was popular, but the doubts were being voiced before the so-called VC raid, which in itself created the major misgivings because of the observation of B1566 on return. 60 Sqn. did not move anywhere from Filescamp Farm during Bishop's time. The following month, it moved North". D. W. Warne

9. *Senator Molson*:

What about Nigger Horn?

Mr. Taylor: I was just going to bring that up. As a matter of fact, when Bishop went back to England and came to Canada on two months' marriage leave, Horn, a South African, took over Bishop's flight. Two days after this June 2, 1917 raid, Horn went out looking to see what aerodrome it was. They say, I believe, one destroyed German machine on the ground.

Response:

D. W. Warne: "Col. Spencer "Nigger" Horn was an Australian. He was also the most vehement anti-Bishop chap I ever met. He did not find any evidence of the ground in any way confirming the raid! Where was he supposed to look? The aerodrome concerned was never established".

10. *Mr. Taylor*:

I have spoken to five veterans who flew, as I say, with Bishop, one of whom flew with Bishop in 60 Squadron. This was about six weeks after Bishop had finished his airdrome raid. This fellow, J. B. Crompton, from Toronto, originally born in Montreal, when I visited him in 1968 could not say enough about Bishop. When he was first posted to the squadron he was posted to another flight with a chap by the name of Molesworth, an English fellow, also a devotee of Bishop, as was the other flight commander. In other words, each squadron has three flight commanders. The third flight commander was a New Zealander by the name of Grid Caldwell and he could not say enough about Bishop.

Response:

I table the following excerpts from two different letters that Air Commander Caldwell wrote to AVM Pidcock (July 30, 1966): "All references to poor Billy Bishop do raise a problem because some of us know upon cross-checking with German archives that many of B's claims were unreal, including his VC job when no German aircraft were reported lost—it's all very sad, but he is dead". To W. Fry (1977): "I cannot do what they wish: sign and endorse the picture of Bishop doing his VC act, when I have to doubt its authenticity... Trouble is, that the younger generation do not know "the facts of life as they were" and are prepared to accept the book stories as gospel".

11. *Professor Kear*:

Suppose you are an ordinary citizen who knows nothing about war but wants to see a film about Billy Bishop. You look at this film, and what impression do you take away with you? The impression you take away on the evidence that you have seen in the film is that Bishop is a cheat, a liar, and a fraud and that he did not perform the Estourmel raid.

Response:

Kear says you take away from the film the impression that Bishop did not perform the Estourmel raid (note: Estourmel seems to be accepted by this expert, but not Taylor). In fact, the narration says, "There is no confirmation whatsoever of the raid". That statement has already been accepted by S. K. Taylor.

12. *Mr. Taylor*:

There is absolutely not a shadow of a doubt in my mind that the raid happened, but, unfortunately, the records are not available to prove it. Of course, the film uses the fact that the records are not available to prove it as proving that it did not happen.

Senator Everett:

He was awarded the Victoria Cross without confirmation at that time. Is that correct?

Mr. Taylor: Yes, he was.

Response:

Finally, it is admitted!

III—GENERAL ERRORS

1. *Professor Kear*

Certainly, because we have to remember the theme of the film, that Bishop was not a man to be trusted. What we discover when we look at the alleged facts as presented in the film is that the film is not to be trusted, and we are able to demonstrate this by footnotes and so on.
Senator Everett: And that is your case?
Professor Kear: That is our case.
Senator Everett: Since the facts were re-arranged.
Professor Kear: To suit the theme of the author. And the author had the theme in his mind before he made the film.

Response:

Professor Kear states that the facts were re-arranged to "suit the theme of the author. And the author had the theme in his mind before he made the film". I suggest Professor Kear read my original submission to the NFB's program committee if he really wants evidence of what I had in my mind before I made the film.

2. *Senator Perrault*:

I think that the evidence you have brought here tonight is most disturbing. Has anyone established whether Mr. A. James fought for the Royal Flying Corps? What are the facts surrounding these mysterious recordings that have surfaced after 60 years?

Response:

Yes. Sir Archibald James did fight for the RFC and was decorated for it. The recordings are not mysterious at all and have always been available at the Imperial War Museum for anyone who wanted to listen to them.

3. *Col. Bauer*:

If I could go a little further, Mr. Chairman, regarding James, in the 77 hours of tape recordings that the Imperial War Museum has, James is the only individual who has anything disparaging to say about Bishop. I believe there were 34 or 35 subjects.

Response:

Bauer says, that in the 77 hours of tape recordings at the Imperial War Museum, James is the only individual who has anything disparaging to say about Bishop. Bauer neglects to say that James is the only one who had anything at all to say about Bishop.

4. *Mr. Stewart K. Taylor*:

Over those years I met many pilots and observers, some of whom actually flew with Billy Bishop in World War I.

Response:

It is surprising that Mr. Taylor, a thorough historian, apparently did not contact Warne whose interest in Bishop and whose conversations with pilots far pre-dated Mr. Taylor's. If he had, Mr. Taylor would have obtained different information.

5. *Col. Bauer*:

Then on page 57, the narrator says that Bishop ends the war with 72 victories. There is nothing covered in there about the second tour that Bishop had as commanding officer of 85 Squadron.

Response:

Sydney Wise, in his exhaustive book "Canadian Airmen in the First World War" does exactly the same thing—ends his account of Bishop at 60 Squadron, including only a mention of 85 Squadron.

6. *Mr. Taylor*:

The CO did not play favourites with Bishop. Joe Warne, the historian of 60 Squadron, said that anyone who crashed four machines when he first arrived in the squadron should have been sent back. He wondered why Bishop wasn't sent back.

Response:

Warne did not wonder why Bishop was not sent back. He knew very well: there was a desperate shortage of pilots.

7. *Mr. Taylor*:

He should have been washed out two months before he was, but the instructors could see something in him so they allowed him to crash these machines and they were written off. Joe Warne maintains that Bishop crashed four machines, but he burst a tire, destroyed a prop and broke a longherin—that is not crashing four machines. In the official history that this 60 Squadron historian has written, he has maligned Bishop.

Response:

Warne has never publically maligned Bishop, most certainly not in his 60 Squadron history. He challenges Taylor to produce any such statements.

8. *Professor Kear*:

There is evidence that the Lewis gun could be moved around the cockpit during flight. Ira Jones, an observer, in his book entitled: "Tiger Squadron", states: Now, there were four socket mountings on the (B.E. type of aircraft), intended to cover a wide field of fire. To get a shot at the enemy, when his pilot was out manoeuvred, the observer had to keep changing the Lewis gun from one socket to another. If a plane got under your belly, none of the sockets was any good. You just couldn't get at him. Seeing this blighter and being unable to do anything about it, was more than I could stand. I yanked the gun out of the rear socket, leaned over the right side of the cockpit, and holding the Lewis like a rifle, let go with a burst. The source of that is the book entitled "Tiger Squadron", page 38.

Response:

This is a wonderful story of dismantling the Lewis gun while in flight, but in a two-seater machine. The observer would obviously have considerably easier time dismantling the gun than a single pilot who was short of fuel, out of ammunition, alone, and lost in enemy territory.

9. *Professor Kear*:

Bishop, in fact, did change magazines in the air. In "Winged Warfare", Bishop's own autobiography, he states: Then suddenly I managed to get a chance from an angle I knew very well, and open fire. He immediately dropped out of control and I dived after him firing as he fell. Having finished one drum of ammunition, I had to come out of the dive to put on a new one. The other scout and two-seater were still in the same place, so getting above them I tried two dives but without result".

The quotation above suggests that there is a distinct possibility that an expert like Billy Bishop may be able to remove the Lewis gun from its mount and throw it overboard.

Response:

This is another wonderful story. However, it recounts only the removal of the magazine which was *designed* to be removed in mid flight, not the removal of the gun itself which was *not designed* to be so removed.

10. *Mr. Taylor*:

At Estourmel there were wooden permanent hangars like old driving sheds that existed in Canada behind houses built in the 1800s.

Response:

Note that at Estourmel "there were wooden permanent hangars like old driving sheds that existed in Canada behind houses built in the 1800s. This corresponds to what Billy Bishop says in his autobiography, "I was just thinking of turning and going home, or of climbing up to see if there were some Huns in the upper sky, when ahead, and slightly to one side of me, I saw the sheds of another aerodrome. I at once decided here was my change...". This is also the version that Arthur Bishop has accepted in his book. Now, however, since records from the German squadron at Estourmel do not indicate any attack having been carried out, various experts have claimed that it occurred at a temporary aerodrome from a squadron on the move which would of course have no wooden structures. This is meant to explain the fact that no records indicate any attack. Well, which is it? In either case, there is no confirmation whatsoever.

11. *Mr. Taylor*:

It was one of the rare occasion during the First World War where a VC was given without actual confirmation. You must bear in mind that that German unit, Jagdsta XX was in transit, and German aviation units are usually attached to one army or another. This unit was transferring from the Second German Army to the Fourth German Army, and that is the period when they were unattached, so they would not have kept any records and they would not need to do that.

Response:

It is curious that Mr. Taylor states here that Jagdsta XX, one of the possible units Bishop could have attacked, was in transit "so they would not have kept any records". And yet earlier Taylor says he is able to name all seven German pilots at an unknown, ad hoc airfield. And if names are available, why no mention of a raid which would have destroyed almost 50% of the units' machines?

Excerpts from the

Proceedings of the Sub-Committee on

Veterans Affairs

October 17, 1985—December 10, 1985

EVIDENCE

Ottawa, Thursday, October 17, 1985

[*Text*]

The Subcommittee on Veterans Affairs met this day at 3.15 p.m. to examine and report upon the activities of the National Film Board with respect to the production and distribution of the film "The Kid Who Couldn't Miss".

Senator Jack Marshall (*Chairman*) in the Chair.

The Chairman:

In many ways this mandate involves the credibility of two Canadian institutions—the World War 1 flying ace, William Bishop and the National Film Board.

The entry in the Canadian Encyclopedia for Bishop refers to his military exploits as follows:

> He was the top scoring Candian and Imperial ace of WWI, credited with 72 victories. A fellow pilot accurately described him as 'a fantastic shot but a terrible pilot.'

A flamboyant extrovert, he was the first Canadian airman to win a Victoria Cross, awarded him for a single-handed dawn attack on a German airfield on 2 June 1917. His last victory came on 19 June 1918 when he claimed 5 enemy aircraft. In August he was promoted to lt-col and sent to England to help organize an abortive 2-squadron Canadian Air Force.

The National Film Board was established in 1939. According to the encyclopedia, it has:

> . . . pioneered developments in social documentary, animation, documentary drama and direct cinema; and it has been a continuing initiator of new technology. Its films have won hundreds of international awards.

The article concludes that the NFB has contined:

> . . . to maintain its position as the world's most widely respected national film agency.

We have with us today two witnesses, and we thank them for coming. They are Colonel A. J. Bauer and Mr. Stewart K. Taylor.

Colonel Bauer joined the RCAF in 1943. He was a flying instructor in Canada until he left the RCAF in 1946. He enrolled in the University of Western Ontario in journalism, then returned to the RCAF in 1948 until his retirement in 1979. In the RCAF association, he became a vice-president, then president and is now immediate past-president. He is the chairman of the Billy Bishop Heritage, which was established in 1980 as a registered charitable organization dedicated to converting Billy Bishop's boyhood home into a museum honouring Billy Bishop and other airmen of World War I.

In 1960 Mr. Taylor started his research by attempting to contact every living World War I RFC/RNAS and RAF veteran.

In 1976, he was voted official historian of the "World War One Flyers," a unique fraternity of former WWI pilots and observers. He is presently writing two books on all of the known 2,360 Canadians who flew operationally in France, Belgium, Italy and Macedonia during World War I. He interviewed more than 400 pilots and observers and talked by telephone to approximately 170 others. He gathered copies of 61 diaries and 75 privately-printed biographies. He collected 6,300 photographs, hundreds of letters, 310 flying log books, voluminous copies of squadron record books and combat reports.

Colonel A. J. Bauer, Chairman, Billy Bishop Heritage:

I want to say at this point that in all my discussion I will be talking about Billy Bishop only during his time with 60 Squadron. There are several reasons for that, one of which is that the film covers the 60 Squadron time and pays little attention to the 85 Squadron time that Bishop had. Over and above that, in my opinion the largest sin of the film has to do with the Victoria Cross raid of June 2, 1917, and that occurred while Bishop was with 60 Squadron.

_____

I want to direct your attention now to page 36, the middle paragraph of the page, which begins:

> In his first 60 days, he's had 60 fights and brought down 36 planes.

> The only dark spot is that some members of 60 Squadron are now whispering that Bishop's getting credit for a lot of kills for which there is no confirmation. This is perhaps due to jealousy over Bishop's decorations, but the rumours persist.

That paragraph indicates clearly that the film is directed to charging that all of Bishop's kills were not truthful; that is what it boils down to.

Mr. Stewart K. Taylor, Historian, World War I: Honourable senators, never in my wildest imagination would I have visualized a scenario like we are having today when, several years ago, I began my research on all the Canadians who flew in World War I. Over those years I met many pilots and observers, some of whom actually flew with Billy Bishop in World War I.

Getting right to the heart of the matter, during Bishop's tenure with 60 Squadron in 1917 there were only eight other Canadians who flew with him at one time or another. Most of those fellows, greenhorns, lasted two or three weeks. Of the eight who flew with him in France, four returned to Canada. Of those four, two returned to Canada minus some limbs.

I might say that age has not been kind to the men who flew with Billy Bishop nor was it kind to Billy Bishop. He died a comparatively young man.

Jack Rutherford, a Canadian from Montreal flew with Bishop longer than anyone else. He passed away in 1959 in Montreal. I recall vividly Jack Rutherford's son saying, when I was visiting him three years after his father had passed on, that his father's prized possession was a book written in 1921 by Jack Scott, Bishop's former CO of 60 Squadron.

As you get into the history you see that Jack Scott found, soon after Bishop arrived in the squadron, that Bishop was somebody who had the goods. Of course, this is one of the things that you read now about these innuendos and whisperings that began in the squadron about Bishop, because he did, indeed, show the right stuff probably at the right time.

I have spoken to five veterans who flew with Bishop. One of them, J.B. Crompton, flew with Bishop in 60 Squadron. That was about six weeks after Bishop had finished his airdrome raid. Crompton was born in Montreal; when I visited him in Toronto in 1968 he could not say enough about Bishop. When he was first posted to the squadron he was posted to another flight commanded by a chap named Molesworth, an English fellow, who was also a devotee of Bishop; but, then, so was the other third flight commander. Each squadron has three flight commanders. The third flight commander was a New Zealander by the name of Grid Caldwell and he could not say enough about Bishop. Crompton was then posted to Bishop's flight and he said that right away Bishop almost hugged him as another member of the flight. He said very few flight commanders did that, whether they were Canadian flight commanders or not, when they were welcoming a new greenhorn into the flight.

On his third patrol across the lines they ran into some enemy machines. Crompton said he never saw a flight commander—Bishop obviously had fantastic eyesight—spot something so quickly that no one else had seen—not even his deputy flight commander; but Bishop went down on this machine and shot it down and returned to the flight. Crompton said he never felt so comfortable as being posted to a flight with such a capable flight commander.

Bishop has been maligned as not being a good flight commander. No, he was not. He was trying to emulate Albert Ball, the first recognized English ace. Later, when I get into some actual historical criticisms of the transcript, you will find that the author of this, whatever it is, said that the generals had to create aces to keep the war going. That was not true in the British military.

The first mention of English aces was not until June 1918. Very little was written about them in the papers, the reason being that the senior service—the navy—did not want all the publicity going to this new upstart, the Royal Flying Corps.

The Governments of France and Germany did create aces very early—in late 1915 and 1916. The English remained mum throughout the entire war about the exploits of their flyers, with the exception of Albert Ball.

There has also been criticism that a lot of Bishop's claims were not witnessed. No, they were not witnessed because Bishop, like Ball, was given a roving commission in the Royal Flying Corps. This was very rare and only given to the most outstanding pilots, Ball being the first one, Bishop being the second, and a former defence man with the Toronto Maple Leafs, Art Duncan, whom I also knew very well, being given the third roving commission. A few others also had commissions of that type. They could take off and do whatever they wanted to do.

Bishop was such an outstanding pilot that he survived when he went after the enemy, where most pilots played a safe game. Jack Scott, Bishop's CO, was one of the most highly praised men in the Royal Flying Corps. His credentials are beyond criticism. He came from a fairly well to do family, was a practising lawyer before he joined the Royal Flying Corps and attended Sandhurst and some of the finest riding schools in England before he joined the Flying Corps. He was a respected flight commander in an earlier squadron. He was wounded in both legs but managed to crawl into his aircraft and come back. He was given command of 60 Squadron, the one we are talking about which Bishop eventually joined in March 1917.

Jack Scott made that squadron into a first class fighting outfit. It was stationed in a very vulnerable position on the Western Front in March 1917. It faced the very best German pilots, who were flying much superior aircraft. It is difficult to realize that Bishop could survive that holocaust.

In March 1917 the German airforce was at its zenith in the First World War. It was really downhill from then on, with the exception of April 1917 which, in aeronautical history, is known as "Bloody April". More Royal Flying Corps machines were destroyed then than in any other period during the First World War. Interestingly, it is the only period of the Great War when the German airmen flew over our side of the lines. Ninety-nine percent of the aerial fighting took place over enemy lines.

The Germans had high altitude reconnaissance machines that came over around noon hour, because of the weather conditions, to take photographs. They attained such great heights, however, that we could not really catch them. They flew at altitudes of 17,000 to 23,000 feet. They had supercharged Mayback engines and oxygen, a fact that is probably not well known.

Bishop was fighting the cream of the German air force, which was comprised of the Jagdstaffel XI, which stands for "Hunting Squadron." To the east of the Filescamp Farm, where the actual 60 Squadron aerodrome was, about 25 miles due east beyond Arras on what is known as the Douai Plain, a very flat area, the cream of the German fighter squadrons were located within a 35 mile radius. The Jasta XI, led by Baron von Richthofen, was the main thorn in the side of the allies. The Baron, alone, accounted for six or seven machines from 60 Squadron. In recounting this to honourable senators, I am simply setting the scene in which Bishop was required to fight when he first joined the squadron. On his second operational patrol on March 25, 1917 he had a decisive combat. The next day he was given command of a flight. He had only been over the lines twice and he was given command of a flight—that was unheard of. The reason he was given that command was that such bad casualties were suffered and the flight was depleted. There was no one to lead it. However, a seasoned pilot from another flight could have been given command. In all the years of research I have done, I could not find a comparable situation. Naturally, in the first flight that he had over the lines on March 27, two days later, he ran into trouble. No matter how much natural ability he had, he still went for a decoy. The Germans were great for using low flying two-seaters while, lurking in the clouds above, would be four or five Albatros fighters.

Speaking of the German fighting machines, they were far superior to the lightly built Nieuport Scouts that Bishop and the rest of his pilots were flying in 60 Squadron. The German machine had twin machine guns which fired 500 to 600 rounds of ammunition. Those machine guns were synchronized to fire right through the propellor. It was a modern adaptation. The Allied machine, on the other hand, had a strange little Lewis gun mounted on the upper wing. On that Lewis gun was a drum of ammunition which fired 97 rounds. When those 97 rounds were fired, the pilot had to pull the gun into the quadrant and try to change the drum of ammunition. The planes only carried three drums of ammunition so that, at most, we could fire 220 rounds. Trying to change those drums in the slipstream during combat was an art mastered by very few pilots. Honourable senators can imagine trying to keep out of the way of the German fighters while changing the drum on that gun. These drums were not reclaimed or recycled; as they became empty, they were thrown overboard.

The Allied pilots had problems in even hitting a German machine with a gun mounted above the wing, which was an unnatural position, although it was synchronized to fire 75 yards or so before the bullets lost their trajectory and splayed away. When one considers the difference in armament and considers also that the German machines could take terrible punishment when they crashed, one can see the odds that the Allied pilots were up against. The German machines had a solid plywood fuselage. When they went down out of control and crashed, the pilot, because he was cradled in that fuselage, was protected and could walk away, even though the machine might have been destroyed. On the other hand, the Allied machine was built of canvas and wood. Those machines would take no punishment whatsoever.

The Nieuport Scout which Bishop flew was purported to have crashed four times in his first flights during training. That, however, is no intimation that he was a bad flyer. When he arrived in the squadron, he was given an old hack—a sodden old hack that had been around. As a matter of fact, when he first went over the lines with the machine on March 17, 1917, he was flying an aircraft that had been in the squadron since Boxing Day, 1916. It was a real handicap to him, yet he managed to accomplish what he did.

The CO did not play favourites with Bishop. Joe Warne, the historian of 60 Squadron, said that anyone who crashed four machines when he first arrived in the squadron should have been sent back. He wondered why Bishop wasn't sent back. I could point out to him a litany of similar situations. Raymond Collishaw, the noted Canadian flyer, had the devil of a time learning to land. He should have been washed out after two months, but the instructors could see something in him so they allowed him to crash these machines and they were written off. Joe Warne maintains that Bishop crashed four machines, but actually he burst a tire, destroyed a prop and broke a longeron—that is not crashing four machines. In the official history that this 60 Squadron historian has written, he has maligned Bishop.

After Bishop got rid of his initial nerves—and obviously that is what it was—he picked up an aircraft on April 17, 1917—B-1556, the most famous Nieuport Scout ever flown. That lightly built Nieuport had lots of drawbacks. The wings shed because of the type of construction. So you could not dive it too steeply or you might pull the wings off. Bishop flew the same Nieuport from April 20 until July 24, 1917, and that aircraft required only one stop in the shop. It was rerigged only once; and anyone who tries to tell me that Bishop could not fly or was a poor flyer—well, I am sorry, but the records speak for themselves; he was a very good flyer.

Bishop had this plan in his mind. Apparently a month or so before, according to some historians, Albert Ball had suggested to Bishop that they raid a German aerodrome, something that had never been done before—a lone raid on a German aerodrome. Ball never lived to execute that plan. He was killed on the same front early in May. Everybody in Bishop's squadron knew that he wanted to attempt this flight. Bill Fry says in his book that Bishop came to him the night before and said that he was going to do it, and Fry said that that was fine. Bishop arose early that morning at about 3 o'clock—and Fry was Bishop's deputy leader—and asked if Fry was coming. Fry turned over and went back to sleep. In a situation like that you are separating the men and Fry did not want to have anything to do with it. Probably most of the other pilots did not want to have anything to do with it either. So Bishop took off at 4.50 in the morning.

It was very misty, although it turned nice later on. However, the mist was enough to cause him to lose his bearings slightly as he flew south-east over Cambrai appoximately 17 miles. There were three German aerodromes there. The one furthest east was called Estourmel. At that aerodrome was stationed Jagdsta V, an outfit so renowned that it was their job to look after half the Cambrai front, which is quite a sizeable territory.

At Estourmel there were permanent wooden hangers, like the old driving sheds that existed in Canada behind the houses built in the 1800s. There was no activity at that aerodrome. Again Bishop had lost his direction. He had never flown over that particular section of the front. The reason he had flown over that section was that the air activity on his own front—on the Lens front in the Arras area near Vimy Ridge where Canadians made such a name for themselves—had been considerably reduced in May 1917. It had been reduced because the German concentration of air power was then directed to Flanders, where the battle of Ypres was about to commence. All the German outfits, including Jagdsta XI and Jagdsta IV were going north. So, to create some interest and look for some German machines, Bishop flew south over the Cambrai front.

After flying over Estourmel, he flew south, almost southwest, and curving back came to a place called Esnes. In a field nearby he found canvass hangers and seven German Albatros D111s and one LVG two seater on the ground. That is where he shot the squadron up. He dove down to 200 feet, 100 feet and 50 feet. The first German machine to take off was hit and it crashed. The pilot was not hurt but the crash destroyed the machine. Another aircraft took off at 100 feet and spun in. Once again, the pilot would probably not have been hurt. The three machines went in low and the third one crashed into a group of trees at the end of the aerodrome.

People have often said, that Bishop raided Estourmel, and somewhere along the line Arthur Bishop was misled when he said that his father raided the Estourmel aerodrome. He did not. Even the records and the intelligence reports, copies of which I have with me, indicate that it was either Aisne or a place called Awoignt, but Awoignt is too far east so it is out. People have said that they could not find any records of the German Jagdsta V Squadron being at Esnes. Fortunately, I have been in touch with some very good historians both in Germany and in the United States. What records we have were gleaned from the Reich archives between 1934 and 1936. After that Goering said nobody could write to the Reich archives.

The Jagdsta V records are spotty, but we do know where they were located at specific times. What transpired was this, and it is 99.9 per cent true. There was a Jagdsta XX operating from a place called Guise down in the Somme, about as far south as the British troops were located, and the call came from Flanders that they needed reinforcements for the impending allied advance. Jagdsta XX was notified that they had a week to fly north directly across the path of Esnes, up into Flanders to a place called Middelburg where they were to operate. They had their last combat on the Somme front on the 24th of May, 1917. A day later, they commenced to move by kette; in other words, in groups of three, four, five, six or seven. In this case, the weather closed in on the 28th and there was little flying. On the 29th, the weather was bad. Probably the first group of five machines got away on the 1st of June or perhaps the 31st of May. On the night of May 31, the weather was good.

The last group of German machines, seven albatros and one LVG two-seater, left on the 1st of June. They flew as far as Esnes for refuelling and landed on what was almost an emergency landing ground. They figured there would not be any Allied aircraft there because there were only three or four Allied squadrons opposite the Cambrai front at that particular period, so they thought they were safe. The machines were left in the open and when Bishop came along, he saw the seven and it is documented right down. As a matter of fact, I have the names of the German pilots who flew with Jasta XX at that time.

This was, then, the particular outfit involved. If you want specific names of German pilots shot down by Bishop, I can supply them, and that is very rare. Even when you go through the combat reports of Mannock and McCudden, you can only come up with about 10 per cent of the victories being confirmed by names. I have about 22.

The brass really had no doubt about Bishop. Right up to General Allenby, who was commander of the Third British Army, which was the unit that 60 Squadron was attached to, they took his statement at full value. They implicitly trusted him and they implicitly trusted Jack Scott. It was one of the rare occasions during the First World War where a VC was given without actual confirmation. You must bear in mind that that German unit, Jagdsta XX was in transit, and German aviation units are usually attached to one army or another. This unit was transferring from the Second German Army to the Fourth German Army, and that is the period when they were unattached, so they would not have kept any records, other than the Jasta XX War Diary, which was lost during the Allied bombing in 1944.

As a matter of fact, Jagdsta XX were not, because of the loss of machines to Bishop's raids, active until July 18, 1917. By the time some of those pilots had been shot down, they had to make their way north on crowded German trains because the trains were jam-packed with troops from the southern front going to the north.

I have a confidential letter Joe Warne wrote to me. This is a critique on his 60 Squadron article and never mentions Billy Bishop, but he does say this:

—which leads me to the Bishop film by NFB Canada. I enjoy that film more each time I see it, in practice! Initially I tried to count the historical/factual/chronological errors but gave up! I have numerous 60 Squadron connections in Canada from whom I get the press cuttings, particularly Ontario, obviously! (I should mention that I did my pilot training at Centralia 1951-2).

He mentions that certain people discussed with him their criticism of the film, but that is the attitude of a so-called historian and a very biased individual.

EVIDENCE

Ottawa, Wednesday, October 30, 1985

Professor A. R. Kear, President, Manitoba Branch, Royal Military College Club of Canada:

A few years ago, I read *The Courage of the Early Morning*, published by McClelland and Stewart Ltd., Toronto in 1965. It was written by William Arthur Bishop, who lives today in Toronto. The son was very careful to cite his sources of information so he could not be accused of bias. The book is a straightforward account of Bishop's life and of the air tactics he developed and used. Numerous dog fights are described so that the reader gets the feeling of what it was like.

At this point, I would like to read a portion from this book dealing with the Estourmel raid. Page 99 of the book reads:

Early that evening Bishop scrawled on the mess blackboard: "Early call—Capt. Bishop—3.00 A.M." He left the mess just as a party was getting under way, and slept so soundly he didn't even hear Grid Caldwell's noisy arrival from the mess.

Bishop could scarcely have picked a worse time for his raid than that morning of June 2. Heavy clouds hung at five hundred feet and sprinkled the aerodrome with a light drizzle. He gulped a cup of scalding tea and pulled his flying suit over his pyjamas.

Bourne, the only other man out on the aerodrome at that hour, already had the Nieuport engine running. Bishop climbed into the cockpit, still sleepy. Bourne held out his hand under the drizzle as a silent gesture of disapproval. Bishop shrugged without speaking. Bourne pulled the wheel chocks away and waved. Bishop smiled and waved back.

The drizzle became rain as he climbed and he could hardly see through the windscreen. Over Arras the ceiling was a little higher. He turned to the right, saw that he was headed along the Cambrai road, then climbed to just under the clouds.

He experienced a loneliness such as he had never before known. He had a hollow feeling in his stomach—which he suddenly realized was hunger. He wished he had eaten some breakfast before he left.

Chapter 12 begins as follows:

Before first light six Albatros scouts and a two-seater had been wheeled out of the hangars of Estourmel aerodrome, the base of Jagdstaffel V. The scouts' engines were warming up. One pilot was already in his plane preparing to take off. The others were straggling across the field from breakfast in the mess.

Without warning a silver Nieuport with a blue nose streaked over the roof of the hangars, spraying bullets among the waiting planes.

Bishop had no idea where he was. He had lost his way in the cloud and had flown further into enemy territory than he intended. When he descended from the overcast he found himself over a deserted aerodrome. So he hunted around for another field and a few minutes later he sighted the shadowy shapes of hangar buildings away to the right. The aerodrome that Bishop had found was

Estourmel, near Cambrai, although he did not know it at the time. In fact in his report he stated it to be either Esnes or Awoignt. He came down to two hundred feet and turned towards them. As he drew near he saw the line of machines and went into a shallow dive. His first burst carried him to the far edge of the field, where he pulled his Nieuport into a tight climbing turn. He could see men running on to the field and a machine-gun opened fire at him from the ground. Bullets ripped his wingtips. He swerved to dodge the bullets that crackled all around him. The Albatros pilot who was already in his plane had gunned his motor and was gaining speed for take-off. Bishop went after it.

The German fighter was only ten feet off the ground when Bishop pressed the firing button from sixty yards' range. Without enough speed to dodge the attack, the Albatros took the full blast of a burst of fifteen rounds, sideslipped, and crashed. Another Albatros started to roar across the field. Bishop fired at it from a hundred yards and missed, but the attack so unnerved the pilot that he crashed into a tree at the edge of a field, tearing off the right wings. Bishop fired one last volley into the wrecked machine, then hauled back on the control stick and climbed.

Two more machines now started to take off in opposite directions. ("There won't be any wind at that time of the morning and the planes will be able to get off in any direction," Grid Caldwell had warned. "In that case I'll just have to streak for home," Bishop had replied.) But he had no choice but to stay and fight it out.

One Albatros flew away from the aerodrome and hovered at a safe distance, but the other made straight for Bishop, who turned as the German pilot closed in behind him. The enemy tried to follow, taking a fast shot. Bishop saw an opening and fired. Twice the machines circled around each other, but neither pilot could get in a position for a decisive burst.

Once again as in many another battle, the Nieuport's sole advantage over the Albatros—its manoeuvrability—came to Bishop's rescue. He got underneath and at a slight angle to the Albatros, and finished his first drum of ammunition in a long burst. It struck the fuselage just in front of the pilot and put the engine out of action. The Albatros crashed four hundred feet from the aerodrome.

Bishop was now intent on making his escape. No doubt the aerodrome he was attacking had sent an alarm to other nearby fields, and Heaven knew how many fighters were swarming toward the scene. One comfort was that no more planes were attempting to take off from the field.

For the moment he had forgotten the fourth enemy plane, which so far had stayed clear of the fighting, but it now was bearing in. The German pilot opened fire at three hundred yards' range. Bishop saw the flashes from the twin Spandau guns, and turned away sharply. His own ammunition drum was empty.

Changing an ammunition drum while flying a plane was a tricky job at best, and to do it while dodging the bullets of a skilled and tenacious pursuer was a difficult feat of sleight-of-hand. Bishop had practised the procedure endlessly—minus the enemy plane, of course—and somehow he managed it now without giving the Albatros pilot a fatal advantage. Bishop had no intention of continuing the dogfight. His aim was to get away from there as quickly as possible.

But to make his escape he would either have to shoot down the Albatros or chase it away. He pointed the nose of his plane in the general direction of the other machine, pressed his thumb on the Lewis gun's firing button, and kept it there. The German pilot had undoubtedly never had the entire ninety-nine rounds of a Lewis gun's ammunition drum thrown at him in one prolonged burst. He broke off the fight and dived toward his aerodrome.

Bishop did not wait to see his opponent land.

According to Ron Lowman in the *Toronto Star* of April 7, 1984, and I quote:

Art Bishop says it was Horn who confirmed to him, when writing his father's biography, that on the orders of the Squadron's commanding officer, Major Jack Scott, he flew over Estourmel the same afternoon and saw the destroyed aircraft."

"Horn said they had to have confirmation for a decoration, in this case the VC," Art Bishop said. "My book was the authentic version of my father's life as it was cleared by the R.A.F. and the R.C.A.F. (Royal Canadian Air Force) plus historians past and present. All his claims are listed in the back."

Who is to be believed, Bishop's commanding officer at the time of the raid or a film producer putting imaginary words into an actor's mouth more than 60 years later?

Is Bishop, and Bishop's commanding officer, to be believed, or is Paul Cowan to be believed? This is the issue. Where is Paul Cowan's documented evidence to prove his case?

EVIDENCE

THURSDAY, NOVEMBER 7, 1985

Dr. S.F. Wise, Dean, Faculty of Graduate Studies and Research, Professor of History, Carleton University: Mr. Chairman, I am pleased to be here and to have this opportunity to make a brief statement to your committee. I must get my biases out front immediately. I was affronted by the "Kid Who Couldn't Miss" as a professional historian who has himself examined not only the career of Billy Bishop, but the careers of the many thousand other Canadian Airmen who flew during World War I. I noted in the credits for that film that the researchers had gone to the Imperial War Museum, which, it is true, holds a few documents with respect to World War I; but it does not hold many. They did not go to the Public Records Office, which contains voluminous records of the RAF and its predecessors, the Royal Flying Corp and the Royal Naval Air Service. They had gone to the German Bundus Archive, but they did not go to the Directorate of History, Department of National Defence, which holds the most voluminous records on Bishop and on his colleagues. In other words, immediately, when one looks at the credits, one wonders about the research.

I exhibit here a volume my wife calls Canada's most handsome doorstop; it represents ten years of research by myself and a team of professional historians in the Department of National Defence and is entitled: *Canadian Airmen and the First World War.* The research for this book tapped exhaustively not just Canadian sources, but British, German, French, Australian and Italian sources, to arrive at the best possible considered judgment of exactly what did go on in the air war of World War I.

What do historians do when they examine the kinds of incidents detailed in "The Kid Who Couldn't Miss"? First of all, they try to exhaust all of the sources they can for factual information on the given incidents. I am satisfied that the researchers for this particular production did not do that. If this purports to be a revision of received opinion, it has a long way to go before any revisionist position could, in fact, be established. So first of all you collect the data and you do everything you can to make sure that it is complete. Second, you weigh it; you test it for its validity. You look for corroborative evidence. You assess the evidence, just as you would in a court of law, and, finally, you render a judgment. That judgment is bound always to be complex, because historical events are complex, as we all know.

The one element in the Bishop career which does not lend itself effectively to that treatment is the Victoria Cross exploit. That exploit is virtually without example, so far as I know, among V.C. exploits, because there is no possibility of corroboration. Therefore, the event itself could give rise to a variety of interpretations. The producers of "The Kid Who Couldn't Miss" chose one.

What does one do when one encounters an incident like this for which it is impossible to find corroborative testimony? One looks at the whole career. There is a suggestion earlier in the film that other aspects of Bishop's record were fraudulent. In fact, the word is used. I do not know how that judgment was arrived at. Bishop's record has to be examined in the context of his squadron or squadrons, and in the context of the documents which surround it. The basic document is a combat report. We have just about all of Bishop's combat reports. What it is important to recognize is that none of these combat reports stand in isolation. That is to say that there were combat reports from other pilots on the same squadron, taking part in the same action as Bishop, which supplied corroboration. A very high proportion of Bishop's kills, so-called, were, in fact, verified as the result of corroborative testimony. The allegation that there is fraudulence in the Bishop record I find without foundation whatsoever, and I believe I can say that authoritatively, having examined the whole record. Therefore, the assertion early in the film that there is something fraudulent about the record, to my mind as a professional, has no basis.

Therefore, I bring together that whole record against the one event and I ask myself what the possibilities are here. In this particular case, we do not know the airfield that Bishop claims to have attacked. It is stated or implied in the film that the records of the particular airfield, Estourmel, give no indication that that airfield was attacked early in the morning that Bishop was supposed to have done so. We do not know if it was Estourmel. It could have been one of at least three—in fact, it could have been one of half a dozen. Bishop himself says that it was 17 miles behind the lines.

The second factor to be considered is that the records for the German airforce from that period are not complete. We do not have them. They disappeared long ago, well before World War II. We do not know what happened to them. They do not exist. There is, in fact, no possibility, so far as I know, of proving from German records whether or not Bishop did what he claimed to have done.

The third kind of testimony we are given is alleged testimony from his mechanic. I will not dwell on that. I suspect that senators have already considered that. I should add that I am not an expert on the technical details of the possibility of landing in a field, removing a Lewis gun, spraying the empennage of the aircraft and taking off again. I know that there has been a lot of speculation about that, but it is that sort of absurdity that one is led to if one accepts the rather monolithic view of the event put forward by the producers of this particular film.

EVIDENCE

Ottawa, Thursday, November 28, 1985

[*Text*]

The Subcommittee on Veterans Affairs met this day at 9 a.m. to examine and report upon the activities of the National Film Board with respect to the production and distribution of the film "The Kid Who Couldn't Miss".

Senator Jack Marshall (*Chairman*) in the Chair.

The Chairman: Honourable senators, this morning we continue our proceedings on the order of reference dated Tuesday, October 8, 1985, that the Standing Senate Committee on Social Affairs, Science and Technology be authorized to examine and report upon the activities of the National Film Board with respect to the production and distribution of the film "The Kid Who Couldn't Miss". This subject was referred to the Subcommittee on Veterans Affairs on Tuesday, 15 October.

Over the past six weeks, we have heard from several witnesses who have challenged in detail the historical accuracy and likelihood of the account which the film gives of Billy Bishop's career as a World War I pilot. This morning we will be hearing from Mr. François Macerola, Government Film Commissioner of the National Film Board and from Mr. Paul Cowan, listed on the film credits as being responsible for co-editing the film, being the writer, director and producer and for the camera work.

To give you some background, Mr. François Macerola studied at the University of Montreal where he obtained a Bachelor of Arts degree in 1963 and his law degree in 1970. He joined the National Film Board as Executive Assistant to the Director of Distribution and was named head of the Commercial Division in 1974, and director of French production in 1976. In 1979, he became Deputy Government Film Commissioner and General Manager of the NFB and was appointed Acting Government Film Commissioner in January, 1984, a position in which he was confirmed on 29 May, 1984.

As I have mentioned, we also have with us today Mr. Paul Cowan. Mr. Cowan was born in Montreal and studied engineering at Cornell University before studying at the Film and Broadcasting School of Stanford University. He received his Master's degree and the Broadcast Journalism award in 1970.

Mr. Cowan worked for American television before he became associated with the National Film Board where he has worked on a full-time basis since 1977. As the film credits for "The Kid Who Couldn't Miss" suggest, he has wide experience in the various aspects of film production. Many of his films, in addition to "The Kid Who Couldn't Miss", have won international recognition. The film "I'll Go Again" about the 1976 Olympics received the First Jury Award in Budapest in 1977; his 1978 documentary, "Going the Distance", the official film of the Commonwealth Games, was nominated best film of 1980 at the Commonwealth TV and Film Festival in Nicosia and also won him an Oscar nomination. His other films, such as "Stages," a tribute to Canadian performing artists and "Democracy on Trial: the Morgentaler Affair," have received wide circulation.

We also have with us today Mr. Adam Symansky, a producer at the NFB and Ms. Joan Pennyfarthing, the Vice Film Commissioner.

Mr. Macerola, perhaps you would now go ahead with your brief.

———

Mr. François Macerola, Commissioner of the National Film Board:

For close to fifty years now, the National Film Board of Canada has won national and international renown in fulfilling its mandate: to express and reflect the social and cultural realities of this country through film. Our accomplishments have long been a source of pride for the Canadian people. Our films, a precious expression of our culture, are freely available here and abroad; they are the testimony to and tangible proof of our success.

The principal activity of the NFB is to produce films and videos of quality, which can compete in the marketplace, but which never lose sight of the NFB's ongoing preoccupation to create authentically Canadian products, social and cultural in character, and profoundly cinematic in nature.

As in the past, the mandate of the NFB will be to focus its programming and productions on the bilingual, as everyone knows, multicultural, multi-ethnic and regional realities of Canada.

NFB films will not only attempt to present reality, which is also the concern of television journalism, they will also strive to reflect—and reflect on—that reality. Throughout its history, the films of the NFB have encouraged Canadians to question their destiny and their place in the world as individuals and as a nation, in North America and in the international community. The NFB will continue to play a key role in the sustained, collective effort to enrich and enliven Canadian culture.

It is our objective to serve the multi-interests of the Canadian public through film, to present a variety of issues in a variety of ways, to develop filmmaking techniques which enhance our ability to provide Canadians with challenging, innovative, high-quality films which present this country's culture, languages and visions and which respond to the social and cultural needs of all Canadians in all parts of the country.

A film is made with a specific audience in mind and the distribution mechanism provides us with information essential to the planning of film programs at the NFB. It is integral to the institutional programming process. I bring this up because I realize you have expressed interest in why and how we program films at the NFB. How do we manage to assure ourselves that programs are indeed relevant to the social and cultural needs and interests of our various constituencies?

Programming is a continuous activity from concept, through the production to the launching and exhibition of a film. It is essential that, at all stages in the making of a film, the people involved exchange ideas, knowledge, expertise and support. In effect, filmmaking is a collective effort and the programming process of the NFB reflects this fact. There are two programming branches at the NFB, one English and one French, in which production, research and marketing activities are integrated. Programs and individual films are the result of planning sessions involving producers from across the country. Programs are built from public feedback on films completed, on current issues and concerns, and on the ideas brought to them by filmmakers.

Film programs developed in each branch are discussed at the institutional table, before final yearly budgets are granted. Filmmaking is a long process and so considerable lead time is required. During the actual production process, a film goes through several stages before it is finally approved for release. Be it the research, treatment, script or rough cut stages, through to editing, final-cut and test print, there are reviews and critiques by professionals. Standards are thus kept high in what is a demanding and costly craft.

But let us go back to the early stages of an individual film. A filmmaker will discuss his or her idea at length with the producer. Just as important as the subject matter is the style of format the film maker decides to use to render the subject. An appropriate illustration is the film which is the subject of your review "The Kid Who Couldn't Miss."

The film raised important questions about heroism, about legends, about warfare and about the individuals who fought in those wars, and the chosen few who became symbols of that heroism. We felt those were significant questions to put before the Canadian public. In telling this story, Mr. Cowan opted for an approach which combines a number of elements or dramatic devices: Excerpts from the play on Billy Bishop, dramatic sequences and stock shot material. This decision was made in order to better carry the message of the film to the audience.

It is, then, with a great sense of responsibility to film making, to its audiences and its subject matter, that the NFB has developed and carried forward a tradition of creative interpretation, particularly in the documentary, or non-fiction form. This term describes a wide range of films, just as the term "historical writing" describes a wide range of presentation.

Be assured, honourable senators, that no film by the NFB can or should stand as the official word or only viewpoint on any issue.

The docu-drama is one of the techniques which finds its place in non-fiction film making, while pushing the frontiers of both fictional and non-fictional forms.

Mr. Cowan structured his film as a docu-drama to convey a message. He chose to juxtapose specific and often separate events, often out of their chronological order, precisely for the dramatic effect needed to make his point.

Surely, senators, this is what art and cultural enterprise in this country is all about. It is our job to make films which reflect the cultural reality of our country, and sometimes those films are controversial. Controversy means that people will differ, often strongly, even violently. Some of you will come down on one side of the controversy, some on the other. Surely you would not suggest that controversy be eliminated. There is no one here who will deny the importance of preserving freedom of expression. To do otherwise would be to go against a fundamental principle which is one of the underpinnings of democ-

racy in this country. I would certainly hope that the day does not come when our artists start censoring themselves for fear of expressing their point of view, instinctively shying away from troublesome issues. It is extremely important that creators—and, in our case, documentary film makers—force themselves in the other direction constantly. It is a heavy responsibility, and one that we take seriously at the National Film Board of Canada.

The film was conceived as a docu-drama, shot as a docu-drama, and, in our mind, clearly released as a docu-drama. But, as with some other docu-dramas produced and released by the National Film Board, I have decided in the future to label the film as such. The film will carry a statement that it is a docu-drama presenting a perspective on the nature of heroism and the legend of Billy Bishop.

Mr. Paul Cowan, National Film Board: I would just like to say, senator, that we will get into this question in much more detail when I speak. However, I believe that the film is based on actuality. It might be presented in a way which is not that of a traditional documentary, but I think you will see that it is based on actuality.

Senator Everett: Further, is Mr. Cowan saying that the statements in it are true and verifiable?

Senator Barootes:
I ask you, sir, what is that message that you intended to carry to your audience in this film?

Mr. Macerola: I think that I answered that question in my opening remarks.

Senator Barootes: Are you referring to the general remarks about the purpose of the National Film Board?

Mr. Macerola: No, I mean the remarks about why we decided to make the film. The main reason was not to destroy Billy Bishop but, rather, to ask a certain number of pertinent questions on the subject of heroism in this country.

Mr. Macerola: Yes.

Senator Walker: To sum it all up, you have been wrong all the way through, haven't you? It is not a documentary, you admit that. You have said so a dozen times.

Mr. Macerola: Yes, I have said that it is a docu-drama.

Senator Walker: Wasn't one of the reasons that you have slowly come to that conclusion, is that you have three thousand-odd letters protesting what you have done, the kind of film it is and the title of it, and calling it a documentary? Is it not correct that you have three thousand or more letters?

Mr. Macerola: Yes, three thousand letters.

Senator Walker: And most of them in protest.

Mr. Macerola: Oh, yes.

Senator Walker: And most of them in protest on the subjects which we are talking about now.

Mr. Macerola: Yes.

Senator Walker: Having said that, the case is over. As far as the propriety of your film is concerned, it was a horrible, horrible mistake, wasn't it?

Mr. Macerola: I don't agree with you, senator.

Senator Walker: And you have dishonoured the memory of Bishop to the extent that it can never be repaired again. Do you not admit that?

Mr. Macerola: No, I do not admit that, senator.

Senator Walker: What could you say worse about him than you've already said?

Mr. Macerola: Personally, I would not like to discuss the film, sequence by sequence. Mr. Cowan is more competent to do that.

Senator Walker:

Don't you think you should be thoroughly ashamed of yourself? I am saying that in all goodwill to you, because I think you are a bright man within your limits. Aren't you ashamed of yourself? You are head of this Film Board and you have allowed this to happen. Just answer that, yes.

Mr. Macerola: Would you accept a "No", senator?

Senator Walker: I want to shorten the approach.

Senator Walker: By that you are getting around to the truth and the admission of the truth for the first time today.

Mr. Cowan: May I add something?

The Chairman: Mr. Cowan, I have several supplementaries and several questioners.

Mr. Cowan: I will keep it to two sentences. First of all, if you look at the film very closely and at the techniques that were used in the film everything from an actor, to clapper board, to Hollywood footage, to Gary Cooper being in the film, all of those kinds of techniques, I think it is clear to most people that this is not a straight documentary. Whether we called it something else or not I think is irrelevant. It is very clear to people that this is not a straight documentary. I think they understand that now and I think they understood it when they first saw the film.

Secondly, by calling it a docu-drama, I personally am not in any way saying that what the film says is not true. I think what you are trying to do by calling it a docu-drama is that you are somehow trying to make it less true. I do not believe that. Whether we call it a docu-drama or not does not matter to me. What the film says through the techniques, I believe, is true. Whatever we call it, I still believe what the film says is true.

Senator Walker: With that background that you believe that this film is true, are you here this morning to say that despite the experts who have all been in the war and know all about it and they say that you are wrong in 30 important instances.

Mr. Cowan: Yes, I am here to say that this morning, senator, that I believe that the film is true and that is what we are going to debate.

Mr. Macerola: I would like to issue another press release instead of adding a paragraph to this one. At the NFB we worked on that press release yesterday and at a certain point we decided not to add a paragraph to that statement but to wait and see what would happen this morning and eventually to issue another press release on that very point.

Senator Walker: Will you include in your release your errors and your admissions today?

Mr. Macerola: Senator, you can always issue your own press release and I am going to issue mine.

Senator Walker: We want an honest press release.

Mr. Macerola: Honest like the film we made.

Senator Walker: That is a sad commentary.

Mr. Macerola: Nevertheless, last week I delivered a speech in which I said that my objective, as the Film Commissioner, is to put the institution at the service of film-making and the Canadian public. I totally agree with John Grierson's statement. I do not think I am there to administer the NFB for my own pleasure. I do not think that the film makers are at the NFB in order to make their own little films. We are there to answer the cultural and social needs of the public. I totally agree with the statement by Mr. Grierson.

Senator Hicks: You certainly did not act as if you did.

Senator Walker: You should add that you have made a hell of a mess of it.

Mr. Macerola: With one particular film but, nevertheless, we have produced, over the last 49 years, close to 4,000 films at the NFB. and I do not pretend that all these films are balanced.

Senator Lang: When this film was released was it, in your opinion, in the national interest?

Mr. Macerola: Absolutely, yes.

Senator Lang: And what was that national interest?

Mr. Macerola: As I said previously, to ask pertinent questions with respect to being a hero in this country.

Senator Lang: In other words, you are asking the question: "Do we really need heroes"?

Mr. Macerola: Yes.

Senator Sinclair: I will be very short. Mr. Macerola, the mistake you made in regard to the film that is being discussed here today was in labelling it as a documentary, is that correct?

Mr. Macerola: In the first press release that we issued, yes, we defined the film as a documentary.

Senator Sinclair: In the light of what has occurred, you now know that that was a mistake, is that correct?

Mr. Macerola: I would have preferred to have had the word "docu-drama" in that press release, frankly speaking.

Senator Sinclair: Yes, but "docu-drama" is a different kind of a film from a documentary?

Mr. Macerola: Yes, totally different but it does not deal with the truth of the message.

Senator Sinclair: But a documentary is non-fictional, correct?

Mr. Macerola: Yes.

Senator Sinclair: And it is not supposed to mislead?

Mr. Macerola: You are absolutely right.

Senator Sinclair: Thank you.

Mr. Macerola: Like a docu-drama, too. A docu-drama is not supposed to mislead either.

Senator Sinclair: But it has fictional elements?

Mr. Macerola: Absolutely, yes.

Senator Sinclair: And fictional elements can mislead?

Mr. Macerola: But if in this particular field—

Senator Sinclair: But they can mislead? That is what the word means, does it not?

Mr. Macerola: They can, yes.

Senator Sinclair: Thank you.

Mr. Macerola: Obviously the docu-drama is a new form of expression.

There was a time at the Film Board—and I don't have to tell you the history of the Film Board—when they went from the traditional documentary to cinéma vérité and so on.

Currently—and I think this is the NFB's role at present—we're inventing new ways of describing reality. In dramas we're trying to describe new ways of defining our collective imagination.

Senator McElman: At page 9, second paragraph in your brief you say:

> You can question our style, our ways of handling this matter, but there is no room for accusing the National Film Board and the film maker of setting an objective to destroy a Canadian hero. Our objective was rather to question, and to do so in good faith and with a great deal of respect for the events and individuals involved.

Do you feel that it is appropriate under the guise of questioning and through testimony given by the mechanic—which was never given by the mechanic—to use words that were put in the mouth of the actor, that Billy Bishop lied, that he received his decorations from His Majesty under false pretences? Is that a line of questioning that is appropriate to the purposes of your film?

Mr. Macerola: Mr. Cowan can answer these questions.

Senator McElman: I am asking you.

Mr. Macerola: But we are not saying that in the film at all.

Senator McElman: I am quoting what you had to say and I am asking you to answer my question.

Mr. Macerola: I am answering your question by saying that we are not saying that in the film at all.

Senator McElman: You are not?

Mr. Macerola: No.

Senator McElman: You do not think that there is that inference or that suggestion there?

Mr. Macerola: No. It was a more in-depth approach. What we were trying to do was to analyze philosophically what it is to be a hero in this country.

Senator Steuart (Prince Albert-Duck Lake): It is dangerous.

Mr. Macerola: I agree that it is dangerous.

Senator McElman: Would it be appropriate for me to believe that the film attempted to question the veracity of the official Canadian government's recognized record of Billy Bishop?

Mr. Macerola: Yes.

Senator McElman: Good; we finally get a straight answer on one thing.

Mr. Macerola: Excuse me, but if a straight answer for you is "yes", I must say that I have said "no" sometimes, and I think that that is a straight answer, too.

Senator McElman: I said that was a straight answer.

Mr. Macerola: I am trying to answer your questions in good faith. I am trying to give you all of the information that I have.

Senator McElman: Well, many of your answers have been rather rhetorical and voluminous in skating round the questions that have been asked.

Mr. Macerola: That is like some questions that I was asked, too.

Senator McElman: Yes, of course.

Senator McElman: Mr. Chairman, could I ask the witness to turn to what is page 3 of his statement to us? The last paragraph on that page reads:

Senator Molson: Mr. Chairman, I should like to raise the matter of the producer's remarks about the Victoria Cross. I believe that the witness inferred that they did not really do anything that was detrimental to the image of the Victoria Cross. I refer to that point in the film where the King and all of the brass are shown to be waiting for Bishop to come back so as to give him the Victoria Cross. At that point, there was a line in the film which I and a great many other people found completely offensive. The King had apparently expressed the desire to give the three top decorations to one man at one time, and the line to which I refer was to the effect that "the King usually gets what he wants" or "got his way" or "has his way."

Mr. Cowan: "Generally gets what he wants."

Senator Molson: Do you not think that that is simply a snide remark? Was there not another way you could have put that into the film?

Mr. Cowan: First of all, senator, would you disagree with the statement that the King generally gets what he wants? The King, after all, is the highest authority.

Senator Molson: Do not lecture us on that.

Mr. Cowan: I am simply asking you a question, senator.

Senator Molson: That is not an intelligent question. In matters of that sort, if the King expressed his wish, probably people would try to meet it, but the King did not go around "getting his way," no.

Senator Walker: He is a constitutional monarch, son.

Mr. Cowan: In fact, the King's desire to award the three medals at one time to one man was a direct quote from a letter which had been written regarding Billy Bishop.

Senator Molson: Who made the quote? Why do you not state it? Why do you include those words from someone unknown? Those words are simply damaging.

Mr. Cowan: Do you find that an offensive statement?

Senator Molson: I find it offensive in that sense; that, if the King expressed that wish, he usually "gets his way." I find that thoroughly offensive.

Senator Walker: So do I.

Senator Molson: I think that the people of Canada would find it offensive, as well. It is attributing to the King a quality that I do not think people thought was there. I do not think people would think that today about the Queen. I think you are just adding a cheap shot.

Mr. Cowan: I disagree with Senator Molson.

Senator Molson: I knew that.

Senator Sinclair: Do you really believe that you have a mandate to ask the Canadian people whether they want to be free?

Mr. Macerola: Absolutely, yes, it is part of our mandate.

Senator Sinclair: Would you also think it is part of your mandate to ask someone if he would like to be under a dictatorship?

Mr. Macerola: I did not refer to any sort of political regime.

Senator Sinclair: That is what freedom means.

Mr. Macerola: Yes, but I am only answering questions.

Senator Walker: You are not doing very well.

Mr. Macerola: That is your evaluation.

Senator Walker: Although you may be doing your best.

Mr. Macerola: Like you, senator; you are trying to do your best, as well.

Senator McElman:

> In the accounts of the raid, Bishop's claim *(sic)* is described as returning in tatters. This isn't so.

Is that not an attempt to prove that Billy Bishop was lying?

Mr. Cowan: Can I answer that question?

Senator McElman: I am asking the commissioner.

Mr. Macerola: My answer is no.

Senator McElman: It is not an attempt to show that Bishop is lying?

Mr. Macerola: No, but I would like Mr. Paul Cowan to answer that question, senator.

Senator McElman: Do you say no to my question? Are you saying that that is not an attempt to show that Bishop is lying?

Mr. Macerola: Yes.

Senator McElman: You have changed your answer to yes?

The Chairman: No, he is agreeing with you that he said "no."

Senator McElman: Let us make sure that he is. Would the witness please answer my question? Is that not an attempt to show that Bishop lied?

Mr. Macerola: No.

Senator McElman: It is not?

Mr. Macerola: No.

Senator McElman: Can you give that answer to my question after I have read this section from the film that you approved?

Mr. Macerola: I can only say that I would like Mr. Paul Cowan to answer that question.

Senator McElman: No, I am asking you to explain why you would answer "no" to my question after I have read that part. The narrator says, "Bishop's claim," after which it says, "This isn't so." In other words, Bishop lied. You approved that.

Mr. Macerola: Mr. Chairman, I would like Mr. Paul Cowan to answer that question.

Mr. Cowan: If you want to get to the bottom of it, I am the one who made the statement.

Senator McElman: Just a moment, I am dealing with a witness here and I am a parliamentarian and I have the right to ask him to answer that question. I now ask you, Mr. Macerola, to answer the question. Do you refuse to answer?

Mr. Macerola: I would like to consult with the film maker before answering the question.

Senator McElman: Very good.

Mr. Macerola: Is it possible to have a five or 10-minute break and to consult with the film maker?

Senator McElman: The film maker now wants to answer the question. Would the film maker proceed to answer my question?

The Chairman: Mr. Cowan can answer the question now.

Senator McElman: Mr. Cowan is the one I am asking now.

Mr. Cowan: There are three reasons why we said that. There is only one man alive today who was there at that time. His name is Willie Fry. He was there; he inspected the plane when it came down. He said that there was only a small number of bullet holes in the tail. That is not saying that the plane returned in tatters. Secondly, there was no repair report issued on the plane that day in the squadron, no repair report at all. Thirdly, that very same plane flew later that day, with Bishop at the controls, to another squadron. That is in the squadron records. Would you not say that that is sufficient evidence to say, "That isn't so"?

An Hon. Senator: No.

Senator McElman: Indeed, I would say it is entirely possible that there was no report on repair and maintenance. I served in the Air Force, as have others who are here. Such a thing is entirely possible, that there would have been no such report. I simply say to you: Can you justify putting into this film the blunt comment "This isn't so" in contradiction of Billy Bishop's claim? More than 60 years after the event, when you, yourself, say that there is one eyewitness still left alive, do you maintain that that is sufficient evidence for the statement "this isn't so" in contradiction of Billy Bishop's claim?

Mr. Cowan: That, plus the fact that the plane flew again later that day, plus the fact that there was no repair report and the fact that there is an eyewitness who was there who says that. Does that not seem like enough?

Senator McElman: No, it does not.

Mr. Cowan: Then we disagree on that point.

Senator Molson: He said that 70 years afterwards. Willie Fry is the person who refused to go on the raid with Bishop. Right?

Mr. Cowan: That is correct.

Senator Molson: It is in his book.

Mr. Cowan: That is right.

Senator Molson: To my mind, you are using a fairly questionable witness in making your case.

Senator Le Moyne: Was it the tail or the rudder? They are not the same.

Mr. Cowan: It was in the tail section of the plane. I cannot tell you whether it was the elevator or the rudder.

Senator Walker: There is a big difference.

Mr. Cowan: There may well be a big difference; the point is, there was only a small group of bullet holes there. That is—

Senator Molson: He doesn't say "only five" in his book.

Mr. Cowan: I am saying that that is what an eyewitness has said.

Senator Molson: But you did not have an objective eyewitness in the person of Willie Fry. Let's be fair about that at least.

Mr. Cowan: I am not sure that he is or he isn't.

The Chairman: Mr. Cowan, would you please proceed with your opening statement.

Mr. Cowan: First of all, honourable senators, let me thank you sincerely for inviting me to speak to you today.

During your debates over the last few weeks, a lot of testimony has been heard concerning the veracity of my film "The Kid Who Couldn't Miss." That testimony has been heard, in the words of Senator Molson, "to get to the truth about Bishop, and nothing else. We are not censors, nor are we witch hunters."

So, honourable senators, with that in mind, I would like to go back to the beginning when this project was started.

I first got the idea of doing a film about Billy Bishop during the making of a film about the Canadian performing arts. I had filmed segments of the then popular play "Billy Bishop goes to War" for that film, and I was fascinated both by the play itself and by the story of Billy Bishop the man.

I then looked into what films had been made about Bishop, and found that none had — presumably because no footage exists of Bishop during the First World War. So, I decided that I would use the play, which would serve as a kind of personification of Bishop, and, along with archival footage from the war, interviews with those who had known him, et cetera, I would tell the story of Billy Bishop.

What I knew about Bishop at this point was more or less what most Canadians know about the man: that he was a World War One flying ace who shot down a lot of German aircraft.

I had read Billy Bishop's autobiography, his son Arthur's biography of his father, and Stanley Wise's long history of Canada's flyers, all of which told more or less the same story about Bishop.

That story, the story of a great Canadian hero, was the film I proposed to the National Film Board's Program Committee in 1980. I have that proposal here, and I would like it entered into the record. I am sure that upon reading it you will agree that it is clearly not the "hatchet job" that I have been characterized as having set out to make from the very beginning. It is, in fact, quite the opposite.

I next started scripting the film, and during the winter of 1981 I made a research trip to Europe to gather stock shot material and interview people who had known Bishop.

As part of that research, I naturally went to the Imperial War Museum. There I came across the first piece of information that made me think there was, perhaps, something more to Bishop's legend. I was listening to recorded tapes of former Royal Flying Corps pilots when I came across one by Sir Archibald Henry James, KBE, MC. What James stated was the following:

... But of course the best known and most advertised (pilot) was Bishop, the Canadian. Unfortunately, Bishop was fraudulent. He began very well and was genuine, but he was so ambitious to have the highest total that he began claiming successes that were completely mythical.

There was then the following question by the interviewer and answer by James:

Interviewer: How did you know that?

James: Everybody knew it. It became common knowledge ... common knowledge, unfortunately. But it couldn't be proclaimed at the time because the Canadians were so proud of him that it could have been damaging to Allied unity to proclaim it. But it's a sad fact that Bishop did this.

Some testimony before you has stated that James' statements were merely sour grapes and that they should be discounted. They may be sour grapes, honourable senators, or they may not be. Neither I nor anyone else will ever know, as James died some time ago. This much, however, is known: Archibald James was a flyer, and a military man who stayed in the service after the war was over. He was a decorated officer who won the Military Cross and he was stationed in a squadron beside Bishop's — close enough to know what was being said at the time.

I then went to RAF 60 Squadron, which is the present-day incarnation of Bishop's World War I 60 Squadron. There I met two men who were to provide me with the next pieces of information. The two men were Willie Fry, MC., a former 60 Squadron pilot; and Squadron Leader Joe Warne.

Warne, a flyer himself, has been the squadron's historian for more than a decade. Fry had often flown with Bishop and was there the day Bishop returned home from the raid which won Bishop the Victoria Cross. Fry recounted to me how he had inspected Bishop's plane upon its return from the raid, and how he, Fry, had found a small circle of bullet holes in the tail of the aircraft. Fry's version — that of an eyewitness — varies widely from the conventional version that the plane returned in tatters.

Just a small aside here, honourable senators: on something like the condition of Bishop's plane, it was not just Fry's word that I took. There are other substantiating facts. There is the fact, for instance, that there was no Casualty of Repair Report issued on Bishop's plane after it had been inspected that day — and this despite Bishop's account that "everywhere (the plane) was shot about, bullet holes being in almost every part of it."

And then there is the fact, verified by Bishop's own logbook, that Bishop flew later that afternoon in the same plane to another aerodrome on the English side.

How bad could the damage have been?

But back to the sources of my information, honourable senators. Squadron Leader Joe Warne has been 60 Squadron's historian for many years, and in that capacity he has had personal correspondence and discussions with many pilots from 60 who flew with Bishop. Warne has a degree in aeronautical engineering, has written a history pof 60 Squadron, and has been published several times in *Cross and Cockade*. I have no reason to believe that either Warne or Fry has any reason whatsoever to want to destroy Bishop's legend, other than to tell the truth as they see it. These are both military men, both flyers from 60 Squadron, and both admire Bishop.

In their statements, they have always given Bishop the benefit of the doubt wherever possible. Later, honourable senators, if you wish, I can go into the information from these two in much more detail. I think you will find that it is not the evidence of cynical, jealous men bent upon destroying a Canadian hero, but the reasoned, rather reluctant conclusion of two men who believe, as I do, that Bishop was a courageous man and a great fighter despite any blemishes on his record.

You will find, honourable senators, that Warne's conclusions. furthermore, are not merely his personal opinions —

which, if they were, could more easily be discounted; instead, they are conclusions based on information gathered painstakingly over the years from many different sources; sources such as Bishop's fellow pilots, who wrote to Warne at their own instigation, and sources such as researchers, past and present, English and German, who have looked closely at the war records and who have the same doubts about Bishop's record.

When Warne gathered this information, it was never with the intention of using it to shoot down Billy Bishop. Squadron Leader Warne is a reluctant source, whose motives are that of a curious historical researcher and not those of a hero basher. Warne has, in fact, always hoped that someone would come up with some information to corroborate Bishop's record. So far, no one has.

I shall submit Squadron Leader's complete declaration for the record.

In his testimony before this committee, Colonel Bauer has stated that he has no knowledge of any negative opinions expressed by those who flew with Bishop. To quote Colonel Bauer: "I have never discussed it with any of the contemporary pilots in 60 Squadron because I did not meet them, but I cannot imagine it being true."

With the exception of Willie Fry, to whom Colonel Bauer has, surprisingly, not talked, Colonel Bauer could not talk to these men, for the simple reason that they are all dead. But Warne has, and to a man, according to Warne, they all refused to author the commemorative cover which 60 Squadron issued in the early 1960s. They all refused because they doubted that the raid ever happened.

After hearing this information, I then started checking other sources, such as RAF records, 60 Squadron records, German records, and other published and unpublished material to see whether there was any information which would dispute what Warne, Fry and the others were saying.

I had heard about three events which might offer some evidence that the VC raid had in fact taken place, and these I set out to verify. They were: that a pilot by the name of Spencer Horn had later flown over the German aerodrome and verified the damage; that two captured Germans had offered eye-witness accounts of the raid; and that some balloonists had, from afar, witnessed the whole event.

These possibilities were also offered to you, honourable senators, at the beginning of this debate, and reiterated by Senator Molson during the debate in the Senate on February 7, 1984.

As it turns out, however, none of these corroborations has been verified. There is simply no record of any such corroborations ever existing.

In fact, Spencer Horn, far from confirming the raid, was, in Warne's words, "the most anti-Bishop pilot of them all."

The fact that no evidence exists for the raid was finally admitted to you, honourable senators, and this was after a research trip was taken to Europe by Colonel Bauer, and this was after almost three years of distribution of the film, a period during which, if anyone had possessed such corroboratory information, I am sure he or she would have come forward.

But what about this question of lack of corroboration? Wasn't Bishop's word good enough?

That is a difficult question to answer, but this fact might put the question into perspective: There were 19 Victoria Crosses awarded to fliers in World War I. Of those, according to Chaz Bowyer who has written *V.C. for Valour*, Bishop's was the only single action VC with no witnesses and/or corroborators other than his own word.

But, honourable senators, remember that the film does not say that Bishop did not do the raid. It does say that there is no confirmation of the raid, and that the awarding of the VC without confirmation is virtually unheard of.

I think, honourable senators, that one out of 19 qualifies as being "virtually unheard of."

And then, honourable senators, we get to the question of the German war records which might provide some corroboratory evidence, as they often have in other unconfirmed or disputed claims.

The question of German records gets complicated, but it is worth examining. We all seem to admit that many German records were destroyed in the Second World War, and consequently it is hard to prove anything from them today. However, a number of researchers did look at those records while they were available, and these researchers could find no confirmation of many of Bishop's claimed victories, and the Estourmel raid in particular.

German researchers, prior to the destruction of most of the material, also undertook the same process. One of these researchers is a man by the name of Turnuss. A researcher in the United states, William Puglisi, the man who founded the American *Cross and Cockade* had much correspondence with Mr. Turnuss as with several other German researchers. Mr. Puglisi died a few years ago, but before he died, he turned over his records to another researcher in the United States, a man by the name of Ed Ferco. At the time of Mr. Puglisi's death, he and Mr. Ferco had come to the same conclusion: that the German records in no way verify the Estourmel raid. A short summary of Mr. Ferco's information follows. His complete document is also at this time submitted for the record. I quote:

There is no evidence available to prove that W.A. Bishop successfully attacked a German airfield on the morning of 2 June 1917.

Jasta Boelcke, Jasta 6, Jasta 5, Jasta 20 and Jasta 26 records are extensive and quite complete. Kofl records are also available and unassailable. Nothing even remotely suggests there is any evidence W.A. Bishop did what he is said to have done on 2 June 1917.

When I came across this information — which seemed to me to question significant parts of the Bishop legend — I had three choices: I could drop the film entirely; I could retell yet again the legend which I now believe to be questionable; or I could make a film which reflected the doubts which do exist. It was my decision that those doubts were too numerous and their sources too credible to ignore. I felt to do otherwise would have been a lie.

The legend of Billy Bishop may in fact be true, honourable senators — and maybe someday, somebody will prove that it is. But for the moment, I am telling the version that I believe is as close to the truth as is possible, and that version reflects the doubts about Bishop's record.

But I think it is important at this time to remember that destroying a legend is not what the film set about to do, and is not what the film does. Instead, the film is about the reasons why heroes, especially war heroes, are created and why countries feel they are necessary.

That, honourable senators, is why I made "The Kid Who Couldn't Miss", and I would do it no differently today.

Senator Everett: ———

Given the way the character Bourne is used in the film — and you would agree that Bourne never made those statements?

Mr. Cowan: Yes.

Senator Everett: These were statements that were put into his mouth.

Mr. Cowan: Yes.

Senator Molson: You have used a large part of John Gray's play in your film.

Mr. Cowan: No, I do not think I have. In fact, I was contractually allowed only to use less than 15 minutes of it, and it lasted over two hours, so that is not true.

Senator Molson: Fifteen minutes is a good chunk of a play, is it not?

Mr. Cowan: There is probably less than seven or eight minutes of it in the film. Be that as it may.

Senator Molson: Be that as it may, why is it that he thinks your work is flawed because it relies heavily on rumours and people who didn't like Bishop. Why would he say things like that?

Mr. Cowan: I have no idea.

Senator Molson: You read it though?

Mr. Cowan: Yes, I did.

Senator Sinclair: Mr. Cowan, would you accept as a fact that once you designate something as a documentary that it has to be balanced in its presentation?

Mr. Cowan: That is a big statement.

Senator Sinclair: Would you accept it?

Mr. Cowan: No.

Senator Sinclair: If you know there is some evidence available do you think you should make some reference to it?

Mr. Cowan: If there was any evidence on the other side I would have made reference to it. You tell me what that evidence is.

Senator Sinclair: I just want to get some principles established. Let somebody else decide about the evidence. The record will show what the evidence is.

Mr. Cowan: I agree with you on that.

Senator Sinclair: You agree with me. Once you establish and designate a film as being of a certain type, then that puts up flags as to what that film is going to portray; is that correct? If it is a drama, a comedy or—

Mr. Cowan: I am not sure what the flags are that you are talking about.

Senator Sinclair: It is a flag to the public as to what they expect to receive. That is what you put it there for.

Mr. Cowan: Then would you say—

Senator Sinclair: Never mind what I would say, what do you say? I am asking you a question.

Mr. Cowan: Would you repeat that again?

Senator Sinclair: I am saying when you designate a film as a comedy, drama or fiction that says to the public what they may anticipate watching. Is that correct?

Mr. Cowan: I have never seen a film designated comedy, drama or fiction. Do you see comedy written before a film which is supposed to be funny?

Senator Sinclair: I certainly do.

The Chairman: Go ahead.

Senator Walker: Having heard how honest Billy Bishop was and how his friends believed in him right across the board, how can you come here today with the pip-squeak amount of evidence that you have, evidence from nonentities, and try to defend the film that was made, a film that was trying to make a fool and a liar and a scoundrel out of Bishop? Aren't you ashamed of yourself?

Mr. Cowan: Absolutely not, and I do not agree with —

Senator Walker: I think it would take a lot to make you ashamed of yourself. Now, why don't you agree with it?

Mr. Cowan: Because I do not agree with your original statement.

Senator Walker: It is a statement, but it is overwhelming. We have Bishop's own account of it and the support of Bishop's probity by dozens and dozens of people over the last —

Mr. Cowan: By no one who was there. Not one who was there accepted it.

Senator Walker: Bishop was there, and he went into it in great detail.

Mr. Cowan: That is not true, senator. In fact, he said that he wasn't sure where it was.

Senator Walker: Well, whatever he said is on the record.

Mr. Cowan: I know it is.

Senator Walker: He convinced everybody else — everyone but you and one or two others.

Mr. Cowan: He didn't convince very many people in the sqaudron at the time.

Senator Walker: Now, who has said that?

Mr. Cowan: Joe Warne. All of the people that he talked to felt that there were questions about the raid, and those were all the flyers who were alive at that time.

Senator Walker: And who is Joe Warne?

Mr. Cowan: He was the Squadron Leader and the 60 Squadron historian. For the past 15, 20 years he has been the historian for 60 Squadron. He talked to many of these people when they were alive.

Senator Walker: And you take all of that — or the little that there is there — and you knock down Bishop and you make a rogue out of him, do you?

Mr. Cowan: Well, let's look at those things. First of all, you have Bishop's record up to that point. In fact, there was a lot of questions about Bishop's record up to then by people in the squadron. As I pointed out, we have this list of 17 aircraft that he reported as being shot down, of which only two are confirmed, or possibly confirmed. That is quite a low average even by the standards at that time.

I can't remember what else you asked, senator.

Senator Walker: You have convinced me that you do not know anything more than what you have already said, and that satisfies me —

Senator Walker: So, the Germans made a mistake when they fêted him as a hero?

Mr. Cowan: I have no idea why the Germans fêted him.

Senator Walker: Of course you haven't. And you do not know what went on, any more than anybody else does. It is all over and —

Mr. Cowan: It was Goering that fetted him, was it not?

Senator Walker: Yes, Goering was there.

Mr. Cowan: And he is a pretty good authority, is he? I believe that by the time he was fêted, he was already Vice Air Marshall. Was he not?

Senator Walker: He was.

Mr. Cowan: And it was a political dinner. It was a political dinner given by one high-ranking German aviation man to a high-ranking Canadian aviation man.

Senator Walker: Who told you that? You are quite a cynical fellow, aren't you. Do you believe in anything?

Mr. Cowan: Do you believe in Goering?

Senator Walker: Do you believe in anybody's heroism?

Mr. Cowan: I do, actually.

Senator Walker: Well, you certainly do your best to hide it. I have nothing more to say to you.

Senator Lang: Could you have made the same film using a fictional character rather than a real person?

Mr. Cowan: I cannot answer that. I do not know. I suppose so.

Senator Lang: It is because you used a real person that the person is objectionable.

Mr. Cowan: You have to understand that as I progressed in the making of this film, the evidence seemed to me — and maybe I was incorrect — to indicate that there were fairly strong doubts as to whether or not Bishop did do this raid.

At that time, as I said in my opening statement, I had to make a choice. I could either disregard that information — information which I felt was solid and good — and simply go on and make the legend yet again, or reflect that information in the film somehow.

At that time, I was not in the position where I could say that I could do the film with a fictional character, or in some other way. In fact, that is where I was in the film.

It often happens in making a film that at some point along the way things change for you, and it did for me in this instance. The film I started to make was not the film that I ended up filming. I changed it along the way. I felt it would have been less correct to just make the legend one more time than to make what I felt was a more important statement.

Senator Molson: Could that not have been quite enough for you without cutting Bishop off at the knees? That is what I am asking. Most of the people that do not like your film do not like it because of the innuendo, the fictitious creations that actually do the biggest axe job. It seems to me that you could have achieved what you wanted to achieve without doing that; and which you did by putting words into the mouth of an actor which purport to be the words of the mechanic. I know the mechanic was sympathetic.

Mr. Cowan: Let us say, for instance, I had called him "Joe Smith" instead of Walter Bourne and had him say those things; would that have made any difference?

Ottawa, Thursday, December 5, 1985

EVIDENCE

Speaking of American researcher Ed Ferco—this is Mr. Cowan's testimony—.

... the German records in no way verify the Estourmel raid.

Further according to Mr. Ferco's report as presented by Mr. Cowan:

Jasta 20 records are extensive and quite complete.

I have already spoken about the Jasta 20 records as they exist. Mr. Ferco did not receive the totality of the German records as is indicated by Mr. Cowan's testimony. In fact, the records compiled by German researcher Turnuss were split into three portions and were sold to the highest bidders, one, two and three. Mr. Ferco was very interested in the technical side of things and he bid on and owns the technical information of this particular period of time. I re-emphasize he has nothing on Jasta 20 because nothing exists on it.

Senator Molson: For that period, you mean?

Colonel Bauer: Ferco explains it this way: When he got the reports from Turnuss he says that Turnuss made his notes from the original Jasta 20 war diaries and there was nothing of worth there for the period in question.

In other words, it is one man's subjective opinion. Previous researcher Turnuss, says there is nothing of worth there which explains to Ferco's satisfaction why there are no records now. Nothing happened to Jasta 20 during that lengthy period of time and yet we know that they moved, if nothing else.

For the record, the names of those three German pilots who disappeared from the strength of Jasta 20 were Baurose, Geissler and Heiss. Cowan makes a strong point that the German records were meticulous in detail. Theoretically, they were meticulous and detailed but in actual practice they were not always perfect. In any event, there are no German records for Jasta 20 for that period.

I wish to submit for the record a letter dated August 17, 1985, to me from Major E. Guth of the German Military His-
torical Department in Freiburg, Germany. His letter contains the quote "there are simply no documents available", and, finally, "please excuse that we can't give you an official view on Billy Bishop's activities." I sought from the military historians their data regarding Bishop and they do not have it. I sought from them their data regarding Jasta 20 and they do not have it and they know that it does not exist.

Senator Molson: One of the key matters in his evidence was the James tape. You mentioned to me, at least, that in the Imperial War Museum you looked over all the tapes that covered the air activity in the First World War. I believe you told me there was quite a number of tapes. They only used one in making this film. Is there any significance in that?

Colonel Bauer: Quite frankly, the only one that had any mention of Bishop was the James tape.

Senator Molson: How many tapes were there?

Colonel Bauer: There were 44 subjects interviewed and there are 75 hours of tape. Sir Archibald William Henry James was rather more verbose than most. He subjected himself to the interviewer for a total of 17 reels of tape. He covered his complete career and gave his opinion about very many things.

Senator Molson: Did you meet the interviewer?

Colonel Bauer: Yes, I did, sir.

Senator Molson: What was his name?

Colonel Bauer: His name was David Lance. We had a charming pub lunch together. I was anxious to determine his feelings about Archibald William Henry James. Having listened to the tape and having formed my own opinion, I wanted to find out from Mr. Lance his own feelings. I do not have my notes with me, but Mr. Lance used words that expressed that James was the most difficult subject that he had ever interviewed. I wrote down in my notes the words "dictatorial", "self-opinionated", and "a strong individualist", in reference to Sir A.W.H. James.

EVIDENCE

Ottawa, Tuesday, December 10, 1985

[*Text*]

The Subcommittee on Veterans Affairs met this day at 12:15 p.m. to examine and report upon the activities of the National Film Board with respect to the production and distribution of the film "The Kid Who Couldn't Miss".

Senator Jack Marshall (*Chairman*) in the Chair.

The Chairman: Honourable Senators, again complying with our reference from the Senate to the examine and report upon the activities of the National Film Board with respect to the production and distribution of the film "The Kid Who Couldn't Miss", we have with us today Mr. Paul Cowan, the director and producer of the film, and Mr. Adam Symansky, the executive producer of the film.

I will now ask Mr. Cowan to present his brief. Mr. Cowan.

Mr. Paul Cowan, National Film Board: Senators, let me thank you once again for inviting us to come back to Ottawa. What I would like to do today, I think, is to go over exactly what the film says, because I feel that somehow over the last few weeks of debate, the film, and exactly what the film says, is starting to get lost in the impassioned rhetoric.

I realize that probably most of you senators, if not all, have seen the film. Maybe you have seen it more than once. But, I would like, if you would permit me, to once again go back over exactly what the film says about Bishop and about the war, and why it says it.

First of all, I will start with the negative things which the film says about Billy Bishop, and then I will go to the positive things which the film says about Billy Bishop. I know when I go over the negative things that some of them you have heard before because we have talked about them before. But, if I left them out, then you would rightly accuse me of diluting what the film says, and I do not want to do that.

So, just starting from the beginning now, the film says,

"He's cheated on his final exams and is to be expelled". The play, to which few of you seem to have objected thus far, in any case, says:

"Take me for instance, twenty years old, a convicted liar and cheat, I mean I'm on record as the worst cadet R.M.C. (Royal Military College in Kingston) ever had ... all I can say is they must have been scraping the bottom of the barrel".

Next, the film states:

"After three very undistinguished months with 21 Squadron, Bishop's nerves are shot and he is being sent to London to recuperate".

Quoting from Arthur Bishop's book, he says of Billy Bishop:

"He was physically exhausted and his nerves were at the breaking point".

And again, quoting Billy Bishop writing to Margaret, he says:

"We are so relieved not to be dead. Then I go back to the barracks and lie down. A kind of terrible loneliness comes over me. It's like waiting for the firing squad. It makes you want to cry, you are so alone ... .I think all of us who aren't dead think of these things."

In an interview with Cecil Knight, the pilot who knew Bishop in 21 Squadron, Knight describes the trick played on the King. Knight says, "we certainly can't have you here when the King comes to your bed and you say, I fell down the steps at the Savoy. We must put a bandage around your head, then you must use your own inventive genious to tell how you were wounded in the head."

Note here that Cecil Knight says "we". It has been implied in the Senate that this was somehow showing Bishop out to be a trickster or a cheat, or something like that. The interview clearly was in a humerous vein, and he used the word "we" several times. A bunch of them were in this together.

Next, the question of whether Billy Bishop was or was not a lousy pilot and just what the film says about this. The film quotes Arthur Bishop speaking on camera here, who says:

"Bishop wasn't a good pilot to begin with. He was a lousy pilot."

This same sentiment can be found in several other references also, and is, for the most part, referring to Bishop's inability to land a plane without cracking it up. Nobody, and certainly not the film, questions Bishop's ability in the air.

Then the film says:

"Though a good sport, Bishop is anything but an ace as he arrives at his first posting in Northern France. He brings with him a lamentable record; he has only received a slight shrapnel wound; he has never fired on an enemy plane; he has committed numerous acts of insubordination."

In Arthur Bishop's book, he quotes a meeting between General Higgins, who was at Bishop's squadron at the time, and Bishop, after he came back from his first patrol:

"Then he peered gloomily through his monocle at Bishop's undistinguished dossier. Bishop has been in uniform for five and a half years, ever since he entered Canada's Royal Military College at the age of seventeen. He had been on active service almost from the day World War 1 started. But entries on the credit side of the dossier on the desk before General Higgins were few: he had suffered a slight shrapnel wound during a tour of duty as a Royal Flying Corps observer; he had achieved consistently high marks at target practice but had never fired a shot in action, except for a few exasperated bursts of machine-gun fire in the general direction of enemy trenches at extreme range. On the "crime" side, Bishop's record contained more entries: a series of Breach-of-discipline, conduct unbecoming-of-an- officer, encounters with authority, and an unusual ability to get involved in mishaps and accidents"

Next, the film says:

"In his first 60 days, he's had 60 fights and brought down 36 planes. The only dark spot is that some members of 60 Squadron are now whispering that Bishop's getting credit for a lot of kills for which there is no confirmation. This is perhaps due to jealousy over Bishop's decorations, but the rumours persist."

Squadron Leader Warne's response to this was the following:

"For some time before becoming involved with the history of 60 Squadron, I had been made aware of the difficulties in reconciling Billy Bishop's claims made both whilst with 60 and with 85 Squadrons, in that other air historians had tried unsuccessfully to find evidence to support those claims . . . .Thus far it is apparent that R.F.C. records do not help justify many of Bishop's claims in any way . . . .It was by virtue of interviewing his contemporaries, and corresponding with the more remote ones, that I became aware of the strong feelings held among some of the stalwarts. In no case did I bring up the topic for the reasons stated above, but as 60 Squadron pilot-to-60 Squadron pilot, I was privileged to hear and read details not available to more researchers . . . ."

The character Walter Bourne then states:

" . . . the defence patrols have come back..six or seven machines, they hadn't seen anything—nothing. He goes out a little later by himself; comes back in a couple of hours, you know, he's firing off his flare guns like it's bleeding Guy Fawkes Day, claiming he shot down one, two, three planes. Well he claimed he shot them down but it was the C.O. who was Major Scott, he's the one that gave it to him."

And Warne's response:

"The difficulty arises when one attempts to find verification of most of his claims, as they were made as a result of either solo forays or having become separated from his patrol. Hence, no members of 60 were able to confirm the majority of the claims, neither did any other R.F.C. observers airborne at the time and in the vicinity; ground observers, mainly the anti-aircraft gunners, provided remarkably little confirmation despite the fact that the location of the fight should have been visible to someone at the front. Bishop's earlier claims were generally substantiated by other evidence, particularly in view of the fact that he was a member of a patrol. Major Scott was obviously convinced that Captain Bishop's Combat Reports usually merited that description "decisive"—i.e., agreement with the nature of the claim made verbally, despite lack of any corroborating evidence."

I think, Senators, the last time that I was here, I gave you a list of 17 victories that Bishop claimed where there would probably have been a pilot killed or seriously injured as a result of the dog fight, and only two of those were verifiable against German records.

Regarding the perplexing question of the Lewis gun, the film states:

Later there will be many doubts about the Estourmel raid, although no pilot in 60 Squadron will ever publicly discuss the incident. One of the most baffling questions is why Bishop's Nieuport returned with its Lewis gun missing.

This is followed by Walter Bourne, who states—

Senator Molson: Excuse me, Mr. Chairman. Mr. Cowan when you say this is followed by Walter Bourne, would you say It is followed by the actor?

Mr. Cowan: This is followed by the actor, Walter Bourne, who states:

That's a bit of a mystery, isn't it. I mean, it didn't have its Lewis gun, you know. I mean he said he chucked it on the way back, you know, to lighten up the plane for added speed, you see. Well, I mean, I'd like to see somebody take one of those off in the air, you know, while flying. I mean . . . I mean I don't know, you know—I put them on.

Warnes response to this is:

It is well known that Nieuport pilots suffered a grave disadvantage in combat when it became necessary to change ammunition drums on the Foster-mounted Lewis gun; both hands were needed, so the control column was held between the knees! This situation resulted in the loss of several pilots on 60 Squadron alone! . . .

. . . Even if it were possible to remove the gun from its mounting and the trigger cable from the control column in flight, would this have been a logical step? The absence of the gun over the top plane would have been fairly obvious to any keen-eyed JS pilot close enough to consider opening fire, whether the ammunition was exhausted or not. Would any pilot worried about being intercepted with ammunition exhausted really spend time and effort struggling to remove his gun when logically he should have been concentrating on going flat-out for the sanctuary of the lines, beyond which German scouts rarely ventured? Any suggestion of dead weight, or even excess drag, on the performance of the Nieuport under these circumstances must be rejected.

Then the film states:

In the accounts of the raid, Bishop's plane is described as returning in tatters.

This isn't so.

This is followed by the actor, Walter Bourne, who states:

In the tail, there's about seventeen bullet holes, you see . . . all in a nice little group like that, you know. And, well I mean I've seen a lot of planes shot up but I mean nobody can shoot a plane like that, you know. No . . . no. Quite a mystery.

I would like to note there that this is of particular importance, because over the last few weeks of debate, many times we have been accused of saying that Bishop shot up his own plane. The film does not say that he shot up his plane. The film says: "Quite a mystery."

The Chairman: Are you reading from the extracts of the minutes or from what appears in the press?

Mr. Cowan: When I am talking about that, I am reading from the extracts of the minutes. I am not quoting them here, but certainly that was the impression I got from the extracts of the minutes.

Warne's response, in part, was:

Recollections of eye witnesses vary somewhat in terms of the location of the bullet holes and the precise number of holes. There is unanimity, however, in that the holes were in close groups. One does not need to be a gunnery expert to appreciate the improbability of a moving target sustaining such damage from machine guns, either from the air or from the ground . . .

At the same time, eyebrows were raised and dissension arose among members of the squadron. The occurrence has baffled researchers ever since.

Then the film says:

The Germans keep meticulous records at all their aerodromes. Historians will later find Estouemel's records and there will be no mention of any raid.

They will also scour the records of other aerodromes in the area with the same result.

I would like now to quote from the statement of Mr. Ed. Ferko, who has many of these German records in his possession and who has researched the German records over a period of 70 years. He says:

There is no evidence available to prove that W.A. Bishop successfully attacked a German airfield on the morning of 2 June 1917. Extracts from the KTB (war diarys) of Jadgstaffel 2, 5, 6, 20 and 26 as well as Kofl reports for 2, 6 and 4 German armee, all fail to show evidence of such an attack on 2 June 1917. The above material is all in my files and may be examined if necessary. The suggestion that Jasta 20 records fail to show a raid resulting in the loss of 3 or 4 of its aircraft while in transit to 4 armee, because there was no need to keep such records, is preposterous.

Nor is it just the work of German experts that have passed into the hands of Americans that we cite. Again, quoting Squadron Leader Warne:

Wing Commander F.J. Hitchins made a thorough list of German losses in Cross and Cockade Journals; Douglass Whetton did specific research into the matching of German claims and losses with my lists; Alex Revell has had similar difficulty trying to find equivalent German losses; no additional matching evidence has resulted from the publication of the 60 Squadron Claims list in the Journals of Cross and Cockade four years ago as part of the series on 60 Squadron.

World War One historians would have enough to ponder about from the above considerations, but there is more to come. It is noteworthy at this stage that frequently books, booklets and articles about the better-known "aces" appear on the market or in specialist journals, except in the case of Billy Bishop: Cross and Cockade (Great Britain) avoids the controversy by declining to use articles in the Journal with Bishop as a topic.

The film then states:

They (the Brass) will recommend him for the Victoria Cross, even though they can discover no confirmation whatsoever of the raid.

This was confirmed before the Senate in testimony by S.K. Taylor. When asked by a senator if, in fact, there was no confirmation of the raid, Mr. Taylor replied:

No, there was no confirmation.

The film then states:

A recommendation for the V.C. without such confirmation is virtually unheard of.

In his book "V.C. for Valour", author Chas. Bowyer, devotes one chapter to each of the 19 V.C.s awarded to flyers in the First World War. As Bowyer acknowledges:

Bishop's V.C. was the only one with no witnesses and/or collaborators other than his own word. All the others were flying two-seaters and therefore had witnesses or were fighters in formation.

I would now like to go over some of the positive things that the film says about Bishop, since they also seem to have been forgotten over the last few weeks of debate.

The first time we see the character, Walter Bourne, he is talking about the death of one of the squadron's pilots, a man by the name of Wolsley, and the interviewer asks:

What was Bishop's reaction to that death?

Bourne answers:

Well, he bawled his eyes out, I mean we all did, you know.

It would seem to me that that would indicate that Bishop had a soul and a heart; that even though he was involved in a terrible war, he could still feel compassion for his adversary.

I then asked Cecil Knight, a man who had known Bishop during Bishop's time in 21 Squadron:

Do you recall, was he a good shot with his rifle, do you recall that?

Cecil Knight replied:

Yes, certainly.

Now I am interviewing Lord Balfour, who was one of the instructors who taught Bishop to fly. Of Bishop, Lord Balfour says:

He was a good, apt pupil and I would say he was really an outstanding personality. Even though 12 pupils were sitting in a row in front of the hanger waiting for their turn, he was a figure and a personality that stood out amongst the 12.

Next, with regard to Bishop's desire to fly, which has been characterized here in the Senate as implying that Bishop was somehow looking for a way out of the fighting, the film says:

He'll be expected to solo in just four days, and so far, 1,200 students have died trying.

Hardly a good choice if one were looking for a safe occupation.

Again, quoting Lord Balfour in a later interview, he says:

Billy Bishop is one of those whom I always felt did not know fear.

Later, to emphasize just what a courageous act fighting in the air was, there is an interview with another pilot by the name of Willy Lomez who states:

The thought of being shot down in flames, that was my one trouble. We had no parachutes. If we were on fire, we'd had it, and you got 16 gallons of petrol sitting on your lap.

. . . The life of a pilot in France in those days was something like 10 to 20 days, and I think if I hadn't come back, I would have cracked up or crashed. I don't think I would have been alive today.

I have also been accused of making even the Red Baron look good to the detriment of Billy Bishop. I would like to quote the film's statement about Von Richthofen:

After his 31st victory, Von Richthofen writes:

"One's heart beats more quickly when the adversary, whose face one has just seen, goes down in flames. Naturally, little is left of the pilot, but I landed and picked up his I.D. number for my collection.

This is followed by a montage of slow zoom-ins to dead English pilots' mutilated faces. If I were trying to garner support for Von Richthofen, that was a strange way to do it. Imagine if I had cut to mulilated young German pilots' faces to illustrate Bishop's mounting score.

Then to illustrate the strain all the pilots were under, but especially Billy Bishop, after the horrors of "Bloody April", I say:

By the end of Bloody April, most of Bishop's friends are wounded or dead. Bishop is an emotional lad and the losses hurt him deeply:

"Oh, how I hate the Hun,

he writes

I'll make him pay. I swear."

To further emphasize the enormous strain that all of the flyers were working under, the historian, Alexander McKee quotes the pilot with whom Billy Bishop was to have carried out the "Estourmel" raid and McKee states:

Captain Ball said "Anyone out here who fights seriously and sticks it for any length of time cannot get through. They all knew they were doomed."

And later about Bishop the film says:

He is a reckless fighter now.

Bishop expressed the following in a letter to Margaret:

My nerves won't last another 3 months. I find myself shuddering at chances I wouldn't think about six week ago.

And then the film goes on to state:

But he has such confidence he orders Bourne to align his machine guns to a point just a hundred feet from his cockpit. I like to work in very close he says.

And then the narration states:

One journalist observes—"they have all the glory, but they pay for it. They die".

Near the end of the film, the narration states:

Bishop ends the war with 72 victories.

Note here, senators, that the film does not say "72 claimed victories", or "72 supposed victories", but "72 victories".

And of his contribution to World War II, the film says:

—his renown as a hero is used to recruit the young men who will pilot the Spitfires in World War II. Throughout the war, Bishop maintains the gruelling schedule required of his country's most celebrated hero. No other hero from either war can match his appeal.

And what is the final statement from Walter Bourne, the character whom I supposedly used to malign Bishop?

They got what they wanted, you know, when they make him a hero. You know when they put the medals on him, gave him the V.C.—they got what they wanted. He was ready to die like the rest of them. He was ambitious ... maybe too damn ambitious ... I don't know.

And the very last statement in the film is the following:

Every year on Remembrance Day, Billy Bishop is remembered once again. And with the passing of years it becomes harder to know what part of his legend is myth and what part truth. But one thing is clear; heroism, like war itself, is neither as simple or as glorious as we would like.

The Chairman: Thank you, Mr. Cowan.

Before I open the floor to questions, I have the following note from Colonel Bauer:

Mr. Chairman, honourable senators:

May I request that some new information which I received only after your last meeting of December 5th be entered into the record. It concerns the career of Wing Commander A. W. H. James.

On page A-10 of the unrevised transcript, I replied that James was in "England at that time". The time referred to is June 2, 1917. In fact, it has been brought to my attention that James went from England to the 2nd British Army sector in Flanders, on 17 June 1917. That is, James went to France, to a different British army from Bishop's two weeks after Bishop's VC raid.

I believe he just wants to correct what might be taken as a misconception in the transcript of the proceedings. Do I have the agreement of the committee to append this to today's proceedings?

Hon. Senators: Agreed.

(*For text of letter see Appendix "VA-8-A".*)

Senator Gigantès: I suppose, sir, you will reflect, the next time before you do one of these films, that pigeon drops on national monuments are not appreciated by everybody. Re-examining history and finding what was wrong with military leadership, however, is perfectly fine. There is a splendid Hollywood film called *Dreams of Glory*, with Kirk Douglas and

Adolphe Manjou, which deals with the butchery at Verdun, a butchery which has been well criticized by many of the younger participants, among them General deGaulle.

One nice thing you say about Bishop at page 58 of the script is that "He was ready to die." That is really the definition of a hero—someone who is prepared to give one's life for one's country.

At page 35 of the text of the script, in the second paragraph, you say:

> Allied generals who rarely agree on anything now admit privately that the war is a mess. Only one of their rank seems to have a solution, and that general's solution is partly the cause of "bloody April".

Are you suggesting that there were allied generals who wanted to use the publicity generated by these young heros they were sending up without very much training in order to facilitate their tasks in the war and, in a sense, make their mistakes less obvious?

Mr. Cowan: That is certainly what people have said in books. There is no question about that.

Senator Gigantès: At page 32 you pursue the same theme when you mention that a journalist writes that "pilots are like children being sent to slaughter."

Have you seen those words in any books?

Mr. Cowan: Well, the journalist only wrote that once.

Senator Gigantès: In the books have you read anything on this business of sending youngsters out to do things that were not necessarily indispensable militarily, but which generated good publicity and made people feel good?

Mr. Cowan: It was certainly a common feeling amongst many people I talked to in Europe. That was not something that I dreamed up.

Senator Gigantès: As I said, I deplore the fact that you chose this particular national monument to write about, but I should like to say that I have appreciated your equanimity under difficult circumstances.

Thank you, Mr. Chairman.

The Chairman: I now call upon Senator Lang.

Senator Lang: Mr. Cowan, I received a letter from a woman in Toronto this week, and to give you the flavour of the letter, she writes:

> At 94 years of age my memory is not as clear as it was three years ago when my book *But This is Our War* was published by the University of Toronto Press. However, my memory of the feelings of Canadians during that war are very clear.

Then she goes on to state:

> The British were grateful for what Canada had done, but tended to put it aside, especially the wonderful achievements of our airmen. Those who write Canadian history, and especially those who make films, must be sure they are not influenced by the prejudices of their sources.

I note that your main witnesses that appear in the film are all British; they are not Canadians.

Were you aware that there existed a prejudice amongst the British war personnel against the activities and achievements of colonials?

Mr. Cowan: I was aware of that. I was also aware that some people stated there was exactly the opposite feeling, and that one of the reasons the command in the First World War gave out some medals to some colonials at that time was to keep the men coming. That is certainly a feeling which was expressed by several people in books and over there. I was aware of that, and I was also aware of the opposite feeling.

Senator Lang: If that prejudice did exist—and I can say from personal experience that I was aware of that prejudice in World War II—why would you select, exclusively as your witnesses, British people rather than Canadians or other colonials?

Mr. Cowan: I didn't feel that anybody here that I knew of, in any case, had anything to add to it except to say "Well, the official history says that he did it."

You gentlemen and the Billy Bishop Heritage Foundation have gone out and scoured the Canadian records, and it was admitted before this Senate committee that there is no confirmation that the raid exists. So, what would I have found?

Senator Lang: You have to look to find. Did you actually look elsewhere than among the witnesses you have used?

Mr. Cowan: I read, for instance, Sydney Weiss' book on the *First World War of Flyers* which is probably the most comprehensive source in Canada right now. That did not change my mind.

Senator Lang: Did you interview any Canadian witnesses?

Mr. Cowan: Other than Arthur Bishop, no.

The Chairman: Did you have any technical experts, as they do in films, to advise you on the contents of the film?

Mr. Cowan: Not specifically in that role, but, obviously, we talked to many people who were experts in the field inasmuch as they had flown or had made it their job to study the First World War.

Senator Lang: There is a man by the name of Ken Molson who is a Canadian air historian in Toronto. He was contacted by the National Film Board in relation to the film. However, he was not invited to appear on the screen, presumably because he was not sufficiently critical of Bishop's record. Were you aware that this man was contacted?

Mr. Cowan: I cannot recall if he was.

Senator Lang: Of course you could not recall as to why his evidence might not be sought?

Mr. Cowan: I cannot recall that. You also have to understand in a film like this we shoot probably 20 or 30 times what ends up in the film. Just because somebody says something does not mean it is going to get in the film anyway.

The Chairman: Mr. Cowan, the last time you appeared before our committee you made a statement, and I am paraphrasing, "the country needs its heroes, but I think a country should be skeptical about them. They make war more simple and glorious than it is." Why should we be skeptical? Am I misquoting you?

Mr. Cowan: I think that that is right. I think the flyers in World War I are a very good example of that. When we think of flyers in the First World War we think of these young, daring, romantic boys flying around with silk scarves trailing out of the back of their airplanes. We never think of them dying or killing people. It is just a romantic image which has been passed down in history and which sums up for many people what the First World War was about. I think that we should go beyond that. As wars regress into history they tend to be summarized by certain images. One of the images from the First World War is clearly that of the unsullied ace who somehow goes out and never gets blood on his hands and is never hurt himself and conducts a rather sanitized war. It just was not the case.

The Chairman: You cannot be skeptical about the servicemen who went overseas. You cannot make something simple that actually existed.

Mr. Cowan: I am not trying to make it simple. I feel that heroes have been made to be rather simple. They just get up in the morning and go out and do heroic acts and that is all wonderful. What I was trying to say with the film is that it is more complicated than that and that there is a strategic value to them. There is a lot of pressure on them to do certain things which may or may not be strategically worthwhile. When one becomes a hero, there are all sorts of pressures that come to bear which, for the average sod fighting in the trenches, for instance, never exist.

Senator Bonnell: Mr. Chairman, it seems to me in the film it says there is no evidence to prove that Bishop successfully attacked the German airfield on the morning of June 2, 1917.

Mr. Cowan: There is no confirmation, I believe, is the way it was put.

Senator Bonnell: Is the word "confirmation"?

Mr. Cowan: That is correct.

Senator Bonnell: Would it not have been just as easy to say there was no confirmation that he did not successfully attack?

Mr. Cowan: I could have said that, except that medals are given for an event which does happen and not for the absence of any proof that it does not happen.

Senator Bonnell: In the brief you presented today at page 8 in the second paragraph:

There is no evidence available to prove W.A. Bishop successfully attacked a German airfield on the morning of 2 June, 1917.

That is what you said in your brief today.

Mr. Cowan: I will quote you exactly what the film said.

Senator Bonnell: I am quoting from your brief that you presented today.

Mr. Cowan: What we are talking about is the film and what the film says is that they will recommend him for the Victoria Cross even though they can discover no confirmation whatsoever of the raid.

Senator Bonnell: Then today you made it worse by saying there is no evidence available to prove that W.A. Bishop successfully attacked a German airfield on the morning of 2 June, 1917.

Mr. Cowan: If I made it any worse today I was not aware that I was doing that. I certainly was not trying to do that.

Senator Molson: We will come back to Warne a little later.

Mr. Cowan: With regard to whether the plane flew or not, Warne does say:

—eyebrows were raised and dissension arose among members of the Sqn. The occurrence has baffled researchers ever since!

Senator Molson: Is that what Mr. Warne said to you?

Mr. Cowan: Mr. Warne was quoting to me what pilots who were there at the time said to him.

Senator Molson: But that is third-hand information.

Mr. Cowan: Perhaps you might like to call him here and ask him that.

The Chairman: Please do not tell us what to do. I believe you have responded to Senator Molson's questions.

Mr. Cowan:

As a film maker, I am most thankful that I am able to do that. I cannot imagine what it would be like if I had to worry about whether or not the films I made would rub certain segments of the population the wrong way. In that sense, of course, my short answer would be that I am very thankful that the arm's length relationship exists.

Senator Lang: What are the confines, then, of your mandate?

Mr. Cowan: When we make a film, for instance, it has to be truthful or as truthful as we can make it. I think that we did that with this film. Beyond that, we have to answer to the laws of the land such as they exist regarding libel or anything like that. We have to make films which, in their totality, serve the Canadian purpose, or I would assume that Parliament would stop funding us.

Senator Lang: The "national interest" are the words, I think, that are in the statutory mandate of the board. Would you feel that this arm's length role should go so far as to permit the Film Board to produce a film that was not generally agreed to be in the national interest?

Mr. Cowan: I think that the basic answer to that is yes. It is very hard to know what the national interest is. We have done everything from making films to teach Eskimos how to make igloos to much larger films, such as this one, which touched the Canadian population as a whole. Is it in the national interest? I believe that it is. I think that most people out there believe that it is. I suspect that you gentlemen believe that it is not, but who is to say what is in the national interest?

Senator Lang: Do you think it is up to the Film Board itself to decide what is in the national interest in the production of films, without any reference whatsoever to the public at large?

Mr. Cowan: No, I think that, ultimately, it is Parliament that has to decide what the national interest is. Parliament funds us and gives us our mandate.

Senator Molgat: But, Mr. Cowan, I think you would be the first to agree that, in your profession of film-making, there are techniques, methods of work and approaches that you know about which someone who is not in that field would not understand. Would you also agree that, insofar as historical research is concerned, there are also techniques, methods and approaches, entirely apart from the knowledge question, that historians have which may not be available to someone who has not had that training?

Mr. Cowan: I am sure there are.

Senator Molgat: Then, would you agree that possibly your historical research may not have been thorough or have exhausted the field as might that of an historian doing it?

Mr. Cowan: Sure, absolutely. I cannot say that we tapped every source and every resource that is out there. But I would also say that no information has come forward to disprove what the film says.

Senator Molgat: Well, I have heard a great deal around here that disagrees with what the film says.

Mr. Cowan: Well, what the film says in the end is that there is no confirmation for the raid, and I have yet to hear anybody else who can tell me what the confirmation of the raid is.

Senator Molgat: But the film says a great deal more than that, Mr. Cowan.

Mr. Cowan: Yes, it does. I am saying that is the bottom line. Whether or not, for instance, the plane could or could not have flown with the amount of damage that it sustained I will not say is irrelevant, but I will say that that is not the key issue to the film. What it comes down to is that for the one V.C. out of 19 there was no confirmation.

Senator Molgat:
But I want to come back to the question of historical research. Did you then have anyone who was a specialist in historical research as a consultant?

Mr. Cowan: No.

Senator Molgat: This is my last question, Mr. Chairman. If Billy Bishop had been alive, would you have produced this film, or would the Board have been concerned about libel?

Mr. Cowan: Well, I cannot speak for what the Board would have been concerned about. If he were alive and I were making that film today, and I found out that same information half way through it, I hope I would have made it the same way.

Senator Molgat: Does the executive producer agree that they would not have considered it libelous?

Mr. Symansky: I am not sure what your definition of libel would be in this case, senator, but we certainly would have interviewed and attempted to deal with Billy Bishop in the film, if he had been alive; in that way, definitely. If that is the question, yes.

Senator Molgat: Well, it was more the legal question as to whether you would have considered the legal aspects of it.

Mr. Symansky: We consider the legal aspects in any film of this nature, and we consult legal opinion.

Senator Molgat: But, when the individual is dead, it is unlikely that an action for libel would be launched.

Senator Molson: Mr. Chairman, I think we said since we started these hearings that the first question that was raised quite forcibly was whether this film should have been called a documentary. We have made progress, because the Commissioner of the National Film Board has agreed that that was a mistake. It should have been called a docu-drama. We have also had considerable evidence presented that the public of Canada should be smart enough to know the difference between a documentary and a docu-drama and fiction, where most of us who feel more like the public than the film producers would not quite agree because we are a little bit slower on the uptake.

Since then, the producer, the executive producer, and the Commissioner of the Film Board have said that they are only seeking the truth. They are only looking for the truth. That statement was made, first of all, by Mr. Cowan on television, and it was repeated at our committee hearings, and we have heard it said several times. He also admitted, though, that those who were critisizing the film were looking for the truth.

In looking at the film, it is very difficult to believe that only the truth is being sought. Surely, in trying to get at the truth, consultation should have been held with all those who might have some knowledge. In the film, only witnesses who doubt Bishop's record appear to be quoted. They seem to be three; Willy Fry, Archibald James, whose tape recorder he has used, and Squadron Leader Warne. These names are not listed in the film credits.

James was an instructor in England, as you heard. He arrived in France a couple of weeks after Bishop's questionable raid. Willy Fry, who has been a great influence on the film, refused the night before the raid to go with Bishop, and the next morning again. Having refused to go along on the raid which might have made him a hero as well, it would not be unnatural if he is nursing some animosity to the idea that the raid produced for Bishop great recognition and the Victoria Cross. So I think it is fair to assume that Willy Fry is a very questionable witness in this instance. Incidentally, I could add there that, in his own book, he makes no mention of this question. His book was printed and published in 1974, and he goes through the whole business of the Bishop raid; he does not say that he thinks it was fraudulent. He said that afterwards in his older age, for reasons best known to him.

With regard to Sir Archibald James, on his tape he makes the statement that Bishop was fradulent. When asked by the interviewer that how he knew that, he said that "everybody knew it; it was common knowledge". Why then did the producer not check a little bit further to see how true this statement was? Surely, in looking for the truth, he could have spoken to many others who really knew Bishop.

I have to wonder why he consulted only people in England like Fry and Warne. Why did he not speak to any Canadian? There were Canadian airmen from the First World War, and from the same battlefront as Bishop, who associated with Bishop. Many others could have been consulted. For example, there are four WW I veterans in Vancouver who wrote me a letter which I read into the record of committee proceedings of 30th October last. The letter is from Air Vice-Marshal Leigh Stevenson and is shown on page 4:17. It included Don MacLaren, Nick Carter and George Howsam, all who knew Bishop and were on the Western Front at that time. In addition, the writer, Air Vice-Marshal Stevenson was in the Air Force at the end of the War and throughout the peace afterwards into the Second World War. These were air aces who could have given valid evidence on the question of Bishop's integrity. They were not consulted. Why?

I would also refer you to page 3:17 of the minutes of Committee proceedings of October 17 last where Mr. Stewart Taylor, the official historian of Canada's Great War Flyers, speaks about having seen and spoken to some of Bishop's contemporaries. Mr. Taylor says that he personally spoke to five veterans who flew with Bishop. These included Jack Rutherford from Montreal, who, he said, flew with Bishop longer than anyone else. He mentions the name of Crompton, another by the name of Mpolesworth, amongst others. Invariably, he says they were all very favourable to Bishop. Yet his evidence has been completely ignored by the producer.

Dr. S. F. Wise, Dean of Graduate Studies and Research at Carleton University, as Official Historian, with his associates spent ten years of research to produce *Canadian Airmen and the First World War* for the Government. He is critical of the research done for this film. He was not consulted.

I would like to ask the producer why, if he wanted the truth, he did not consult, in addition to Mr. Stewart Taylor, Colonel Bauer and Dr. Wise, some people who actually knew Bishop, instead of giving prominence to a questionable winess, Fry, who refused to go on the raid, or, as the young would say today, "chickened out" of that raid.

The author used statements which are second or third hand from Warne. The word of the ex-cavalry officer James, who obviously detested this young up-start, Bishop, is accepted from his tape recording. Why would he give such great weight to James's opinion and give any less to Lord Balfour, who was a pilot in 60 Squadron and went on to become Under-Secretary of State for Air in the Second World War? He told me he taught Bishop to fly. Surely, if you are looking for the truth, you would look very hard to verify the statement "it was common knowledge". Obviously, it would have been better to go and speak to some of those people I mentioned.

There is another veteran whom I mentioned who has made known his views forcibly, and that is Sir William Stephenson,

known as Intrepid, who was a fighter pilot in the same sector during the First World War. Why would Sir William Stephenson's words be disregarded and James's accepted, I ask you? Why would the words of historian Warne carry so much weight when as much or more research has been done by others? Stewart Taylor, Dr. S. F. Wise and Colonel Bauer end up with a different conclusion. I find this very hard to believe as being a search for truth.

I would also like to remind you that John Gray, the author and producer of the play about Bishop, called "Billy Bishop goes to War", has stated that the film is faulted for the reason that Cowan did not consult any people other than Bishop's enemies. Is Cowan's truth better than Gray's?

Honourable Senators, many of these arguments have been made by me and by others. In my own case, I spoke in the Senate on February 7, 1984, and, on page 198 of Hansard, pointed out many of the untruths in this film. I spoke again in the Senate on the motion to refer the film to this Committee. The record for that will be found on page 1247 of Senate Hansard of September 18, 1985.

I do not want to repeat the arguments put forward then, because they have been well presented by others in the interim: Colonel Bauer, Mr. Stewart Taylor, Dr. Wise and others. However, I just remind Honourable Senators that no attention whatsoever has been paid to the many points of view which disagree with the author's.

I would like to point out that in establishing that Billy Bishop was a fraud or a liar, or both, the author has been guilty also of ignoring or distorting certain matters. He is actually making a liar of either Bishop's son, Arthur, who wrote the book about his father, "The Courage of the Early Morning", or of Bishop's fellow pilot, Spencer Horn.

Arthur Bishop told me only a week or so ago that, when he went over to England to do research for his book, Spencer Horn came up from the country specially and took Arthur Bishop for lunch at the Cavalry Club. There, he told him that he had in fact flown over a German aerodrome behind the lines to inspect the damage that Bishop was reputed to have done and had seen certain damage to aircraft. That information is dismissed by the producer, who delcares flatly that Spencer Horn did not do that, because that would have been shown by the Squadron Record. It is quite possible that Spencer Horn did make a flight and did not have any notation in the Squadron Record. If he became involved in combat, he would have had to make some notes, but if he simply made a flight there is absolutely no reason for it to be in the Squadron Record. It would have been in his own log book if he had chosen to put it in. But to say that it did not occur because it is not shown in the Squadron Record is simply calling either Spencer Horn a liar or Arthur Bishop a liar. It is quite uncalled for. I do not believe that one can gain the truth by suggesting that other people are untruthful.

The producer is also distorting the information given by two of those authorities he quotes: Caldwell and Colishaw. In the case of Caldwell, he said that Caldwell was very critical and did not believe in Bishop. We then turn up an official report of June 30, 1917, where Caldwell signed an inspection report on Bishop's plane which did not agree with the film. His report showed more damage and more bullet holes.

In the case of Colishaw, the author said how critical he was, whereas Colishaw's criticism, which is in writing, is that the type of aircraft Bishop claimed to have shot down was not specified in his reports, which was unusual. That has been explained in that Colishaw was at a different part of the front which had a variety of airplanes and would naturally need to have them specified, whereas where Bishop was the German fighters had been only Albatroses for months on end and continued to be. So it is perfectly understandable that in making his report, he wrote "E.A." or "H.A.", enemy aircraft or hostile aircraft, after any action. The other pilots did the same on that front at the time. So, again there is distortion in the film.

Now I would like, Mr. Chairman, if I may, to say just a few words about Billy Bishop, the man, because it appears that in this vicinity I am one of the few who knew him.

I met Billy Bishop about 1930 or 1931, when he returned to Canada from England and settled in Montreal. He came there to fill an executive polition in the McColl Frontenac Oil Company, which later became part of Texaco Canada.

As far as one could see, he was a perfectly normal businessman who led a normal existence, and had a happy and cheerful family whom I got to know. His wife, Margaret Burden, from Toronto, was a delightful person; his son and daughter were fine children; I even knew his two dogs, chows, who were reasonably good-natured. The whole appearance of that family and of its head, Billy Bishop, was normal. He decided to take up flying again, by getting a refresher course at the Montreal Light Aeroplane Club in 1934. He suggested to me that I should take up flying. This I did, and enjoyed getting my private pilot's license. Both of us were flying at the Montreal Light Aeroplane Club. Contrary to some fables, he did not teach me to fly and we did not fly together. I merely mention it, because this is where I saw him as a pilot. He was flying aircraft not too different in size and character from his Nieuport. While he bounced a little on occasions in landing, he was not a bad pilot, as has been suggested.

The Bishop who is depicted on the screen is very unlike Billy Bishop. The real Bishop was a quiet person. I don't ever remember hearing him raise his voice. This is quite different from the character on the screen. He was determined and firm in having things the way in which he wanted to go, but I saw no objectionable characteristics such as have been suggested by the film. He seemed to be a very quiet, likeable person; one who had a warm family life, normal in every way. He was not boastful; he very rarely spoke about his career, although he still loved flying. That was why he took it up again.

I mentioned earlier that among the people who obviously thought Billy Bishop to be an honourable and a decent person—not a fraud and a cheat—was another of our great Victoria Cross winners, Bill Barker. Bill Barker went into business with Bishop in the 1920-1922 period, when they formed a company to fly from Toronto up to Muskoka, in partnership. I don't know how much flying they did, but they had a lot of fun doing it. I believe that effort went the way of all early flying ventures, in that it collapsed financially very quickly.

I only want to add that I find it very difficult, knowing that man years after the war period, knowing his character, to accept the charges laid in this film, because at that stage in life he did not show the bad qualities suggested. In all the times that he might have done anything for people to criticize—and I am sure that he had as many faults as anybody else in this world—nobody ever suggested, within my hearing, that Bishop was not honourable and truthful. I find it impossible, in view of the evidence, to accept as fact that he cheated in the way suggested. I think if there were cheating in this film, one has to look at the effort made to prove Bishop a cheat, by bringing together a lot of scraps of gossip, putting them together into the mouth of the actor playing Bishop's aeroplane mechanic. The natural result is that in the film the mechanic leaves the impression of being the most critical, the most doubtful of Bishop. This, I suggest to you is completely dishonest, because that mechanic was fond of Bishop, as has been proven by a letter he wrote to Bishop later on, and by other people's words. He never made a single one of those accusatory remarks, which are put together in the mouth of an actor, not the mouth of the mechanic, suggesting that he was a fraud.

To this extent, I think the dishonesty revealed exists more in the way this film was put together and issued as a documentary. Even with this description changed, only now, to a docudrama, all the devious factors used to make proof that Bishop was a fraud beg the truth. I honestly believe that this film should not be allowed to circulate in its present form. I believe the film is dishonest, and not in the national interest.

Thank you very much. The committee adjourned.

The Senators Speak

Below are excerpts from some of the excellent speeches given by the Senators.

Sen. Douglas D. Everett: The whole film is based on the fact that in its early stages World War I—and, by implication, World War II—was fought to preserve an arrogant, almost feudal way of life and that the reason there are wars is because generals train armies and, therefore, they want wars; the reason there are heroes is because generals require them, so they make them out of whole cloth.

This is the basis of Mr. Cowan's philosophy about war. There is nothing at all in the film about the fact that the majority of people who went to war in World War II went because they thought they were protecting their way of life and their society against tyranny. Mr. Cowan does not deal with that.

What he does, in order to prove how horrible and how unnecessary war is, is to denigrate somebody who, so far as we know and so far as the record can tell, was an authentic war hero and somebody whom perhaps we should more likely venerate.

Sen. Jack Marshall (Chairman): Although it is my privilege to lead off the debate, which was interrupted yesterday, Senator Molson's initiative deserves the fullest recognition for his conscientious efforts, even though he was not a member of the committee. I commend him for those efforts, for his support, for his advice and his guidance to me as we progressed in our deliberations.

In order to avoid confusion in the public's mind because of the leak which resulted in the printing of the 3 recommendations in a Toronto newspaper, I feel it my duty to place the three recommendations on the record. They are as follows:

1. that the film be withdrawn from circulation or
2. that the film be re-edited to eliminate its unproven allegations or
3. that a disclaimer be added or attached to its title saying that it is a docu-drama, combining reality and fiction.

I feel it should be recorded also that enthusiastic debate followed, with the consensus in favour of recommendation 3 by the subcommittees, and after similar action, by the main committee, as follows:

RECOMMENDATION
That after the titles of the film, the following disclaimer be added:
"This film is a docu-drama and combines elements of both reality and fiction. It does not pretend to be an even-handed or chronological biography of Billy Bishop.
Although a Walter Bourne did serve as Bishop's mechanic, the film director has used this character to express his own doubts and reservations about Bishop's exploits. There is no evidence that these were shared by the real Walter Bourne''.

During the proceedings, the Commissioner, Mr. Macerola had this to say with repeated emphasis on the word "reality," and I quote:
"The NFB will continue to play a key role in the sustained collective effort to enrich and enliven Canadian culture."
Should we not wonder now, honourable senators, with the creation of the film "The Kid Who Couldn't Miss" as to whether it does answer any of those questions as to our destiny and our place in the nation; does it enrich and enliven Canadian culture?

So, the entire scenario is fiction, constructed by Cowan and the National Film Board to make it look as though the raid was all pre-arranged and that they had a welcoming back party with a brass band, brass hats, and all of the rest. And this is done in the name of "creative freedom" and "creative licence." Why do this to Bishop's memory? Why injure his family today?

There is no record of any act of military insubordination committed by Bishop. Again, Bishop's reputation is being tarnished unjustly in this film. Why make a statement of that kind to defame the memory of one of our great Canadian aces? Why do that? Would Mr. Cowan appreciate an attack of that nature on his grandfather without any prior effort to ascertain what the facts really were, and without speaking to any member of his family?

Among those consulted by researchers on this point between 1983 and 1986 are Roger Neville, Bishop's pilot in 21 Squadron; Tim Hervey, an officer who served on Bishop's flight on 60 Squadron; and J.B. Crompton, another officer who served with Bishop on 60 Squadron.

The only 1917 contemporary of Bishop's who, according to Paul Cowan, now alleges that Bishop was fraudulent, is Wing Commander W.M. Fry M.C., who, significantly, stated in 1974 that everyone believed implicitly in Bishop's honesty. Mr. Cowan in fact does not quote Mr. Fry in this film, nor is he listed in the film credits.

Sen. Raymond Perrault: There is no evidence available to support a claim that anyone in the RFC believed during the Great War that Bishop was cheating. There is much evidence from his remaining comrades that Bishop's record is no less valid than that of any other RFC, RNAS pilot, and just as valid as any of the German records, Austrian records, Italian records, French records or American records in the First World War.

Bishop's file of combat reports in Kew, London, reflects the fact that he made many more claims of victory than those with which he was officially credited, because they checked them out as carefully as possible. If there were any doubt, they would reject those claims. The simple fact is that of those claims made 47 were confirmed and recognized by the Royal Flying Corps in 1917. If Major Scott was in collusion with Bishop and granted him victories without confirmation, how would the skeptics explain those of Bishop's claims which were not recognized by Major Scott or higher authority?

Technicians and historians agree that it would not have been impossible for Bishop to have removed and discarded his Lewis gun in flight. Mr. Cowan's suggestion to the contrary is deliberately misleading. Is it introduced to further erode Bishop's honesty?

The Germans never had any doubt about his greatness. After the war, he was honoured by his former enemies who said what a great airman he was, because they had met him in combat. The people who question his honesty, sadly, are those right in our own country in the person of Mr. Cowan and some of his gaggle of supporters at the National Film Board.

Of further interest, from the point of view of the structure of the film, is the fact that Mr. Cowan testified that he had used less than "seven or eight minutes" of John Gray's Play "Billy Bishop Goes to War" in the film. Mr. Cowan stated that he had been contractually authorized to use 15 minutes or less of the play. In fact, there are some 22 minutes of the John Gray production in Mr. Cowan's film.

In a case of this kind, Mr. Cowan should be reminded that Billy Bishop, rather than being guilty until proven innocent, is innocent until proven guilty. The burden of proof rests not upon Bishop, who has made his honourable mark in history, but upon Cowan, the National Film Board and their shadowy coterie of alleged informants, who cannot be encouraged to come out into the open, into the light of day, where their negative mutterings can be tested.

As I have said, the burden of proof rests not upon Bishop, who has made his honourable mark on history, but upon Cowan and the National Film Board. In his desperate effort to register a protest against what he sees as the insanity of war, it seems to me that Cowan has clearly rigged the evidence against Bishop. I believe that this "rigging" has been blatant and cynical. Recognized historical sources have been bypassed and ignored; Bishop's descendants have been ignored, and military historians have been ignored.

If the case of Billy Bishop and Paul Cowan and the National Film Board were before the courts, Billy Bishop would be acquitted on all counts, with all costs assessed against the board and Cowan and with a formal apology to Bishop demanded by the court. If this were an aerial dogfight in the Great War, figuratively speaking, Cowan would be shot down in flames without a parachute.

Sen. D.G. Steuart: All this from the honest Mr. Cowan, a man who in my opinion stands condemned by his own words.

But enough of Mr. Cowan. I think we have already given him too much publicity, or maybe notoriety is a better word.

I would only remind him and others like him that if it were not for people like Billy Bishop he would probably enjoy very little freedom today, artistic or any other kind.

Sen. Henry Hicks: I wish to point out—because it relates to my few concluding remarks—that those errors virtually—I say "virtually," but I really believe without exception—were all against rather than supportive of Billy Bishop and his reputation; and if this does not show a prejudice on the part of the National Film Board—which Senator Perrault documented for us so meticulously and so carefully the other day—then I do not know what, indeed, would show that.

Honourable senators, I think that it is not good enough for the National Film Board to display and to dramatize only what I have previously referred to as a death wish for Canada. It seems to me that, in authorizing the Senate committee to investigate this film and examine witnesses to disprove the historical allegations contained in the documentary—excuse me, "docu-drama"—"The Kid Who Couldn't Miss," the Senate has done a real service to the people of Canada. I suggest—and I do this in the most generous spirit—that the Senate committee may have done a real service to the National Film Board itself. I hope that the National Film Board will ponder on some of these things and, in the future, it should not put itself in the position where anyone can say that it has a death wish for Canada, its heroes and its history.

Sen. Hartland de M. Molson: Honourable senators, after all of the excellent speeches on the report of the Subcommittee on Veterans Affairs, which considered the film entitled "The Kid Who Couldn't Miss", I find myself faced with the task of summing up and presenting my suggestions for the solution to the national embarrassment that is this film.

I have come to doubt more and more that Mr. Cowan's motives in producing the film were honourable. I believe that if the producer acted with his best personal and professional integrity, the film reflects the fact that those qualities are inconsistent with the standard of the National Film Board.

I am convinced that Mr. Cowan was not honest with the history of World War I, nor was he honest with the recorded facts of the life and times of Billy Bishop, Canada's most decorated serviceman.

Another 60 Squadron member in 1917 is Tim Hervey in Leighton Buzzard, England. He received his pilot wings with Billy Bishop in 1917 and both went to 60 Squadron and flew Nieuports in the same flight. Tim Hervey voiced no doubt whatsoever about Billy Bishop's honesty when Colonel Bauer spoke with him earlier this year. This is in direct contradiction to the evidence used by the Film Board from the tape of Archibald James. He stated that Bishop was known to be a fraud. This statement is a lie. Such a thing was not generally known. In fact, there is no evidence that there was even a suggestion during World War I that Bishop was fraudulent and that he was cheating. I must also tell you that in January of this year Peter Simkins, Chief Historian of the Imperial War Museum, when interviewed on a BBC news program implied that James was not a reliable witness. But the National Film Board does not want to hear that! No! If James' outrageous statement can be used to help condemn Billy Bishop, it will be used.

No one has denied that there can be those who doubt that Bishop did all that he said. Anybody is allowed to doubt any record. But to rewrite history, there must be a convincing weight of supporting evidence. There must be actual historians making statements, and citing actual records, not nameless and faceless individuals who deny existing and accepted history. How elusive is the quality of integrity in this work! None of us wants to dampen creative and artistic effort in this country. But those qualities have to be used responsibly and objectively in historical work. In this film creative and artistic effort were used to advance a personal theme at the expense of truth.

...We do question very seriously the use of public funds, and a large amount—remember, $400,000—and, particularly, use of the prestigious label of the National Film Board of Canada to destroy the reputation of a hero, whether Bishop or any other or, in fact, the reputation of any individual without proof. This is our main objection to the film. It is made to appear as presenting the truth, and it is a lie. We in Parliament cannot condone the dishonesty of any government agency. In this case the known history of Billy Bishop has been distorted and he has been shown falsely as a fraud and a cheat.

The film is simply and totally a mistake.

The report of the Senate committee clearly indicates that damage has been done by the film THE KID WHO COULDN'T MISS. Damage has been done to our national image, to our pride, to all those who served to protect our liberty and our way of life, to the families who gave their lives and, last but not least, to the members of Billy Bishop's family.

Sen. Daniel A. Lang: Honourable senators, I have unearthed a reference which was not produced at our committee hearings regarding the raid made by Bishop on a German airfield and for which he was awarded the Victoria Cross. I should now like to read that reference into the record.

It is found in a book entitled *The Years of the Sky King* written by Arch Whitehouse and published by Doubleday and Company, New York, in 1959. Arch Whitehouse is an historian and writer of repute and, particularly, an authority on World War I flyers, he having been one himself. In that publication it is stated:

It was for this solo feat that he was recommended for the Victoria Cross. After long weeks of careful investigation as to the authenticity of his report the decoration was confirmed on August 11, 1917. Agents inside the German lines discovered that the two seater had been seriously damaged, several of the single seaters had been put out of action and the fourth Albatross pilot had been lightly wounded.

I want to underline that this says, "After long weeks..." Honourable senators, in actual fact, it took nine weeks of careful investigation. British agents went behind the German lines and confirmed the damage and destruction that he had accomplished. How can we possibly conceive of anyone awarding a Victoria Cross without substantiation such as that?

Arch Whitehouse further wrote the following:

The raid on the German airfield became the high point of Bishop's career, although he continued his wild attacks on enemy aircraft and ran his score up to 47. British agents inside the enemy line eventually confirmed that three Fokkers had been shot down. Several of the single seaters had been damaged seriously and a two seater so shot up it had to be completely rebuilt.

He then said:

It is interesting to note that after the war German officials said that no such attack had been made on any of their aerodromes on that date. The British, however, were more than satisfied and by August 11, 1917, Bishop was awarded the Victoria Cross for his efforts.

Of course, the Germans would deny that. I can remember much damage that was done to them in World War II which they denied. Remember, for example, the air raids on London in 1940 and 1941. Many German planes were shot down and the Germans denied that they had lost any planes.

CANADA

Excerpts from

Production and Distribution

of the

National Film Board Production

"The Kid Who Couldn't Miss"

**Report of the Standing Senate Committee on
Social Affairs, Science and Technology**

Membership

The Standing Senate Committee on Social Affairs, Science and Technology:

The Honourable Arthur Tremblay, *Chairman*
The Honourable M. Lorne Bonnell, M.D., C.M., *Deputy Chairman*

and

The Honourable Senators:

Cottreau, Ernest G.	Marsden, Lorna
David, Paul	Marshall, Jack
Gigantès, Philippe D.	Molgat, Gildas L.
LeMoyne, Jean	Robertson, Brenda M.
*MacEachen, Allan J.	*Roblin, Duff
Marchand, Len	Rousseau, Yvette

* Ex Officio Members

The Subcommittee on Veterans Affairs:

The Honourable Jack Marshall, C.D., *Chairman*
The Honourable M. Lorne Bonnell, M.D., C.M., *Deputy Chairman*

and

The Honourable Senators:

David, Paul	LeMoyne, Jean
Gigantès, Philippe D.	*Tremblay, Arthur

* Ex Officio Member

The following senators also served as members of the Subcommittee: The Honourable Senators E.W. Barootes, Robert Muir and Yvette Rousseau.

The following senators also participated in the examination by the Subcommittee: The Honourable Senators James Balfour, Ann Elizabeth Bell, Sidney L. Buckwold, Richard J. Doyle, Douglas D. Everett, Royce Frith, John Morrow Godfrey, Henry D. Hicks, Paul C. Lafond, Daniel A. Lang, Finlay MacDonald *(Halifax)*, John M. Macdonald *(Cape Breton)*, Charles McElman, Gildas L. Molgat, Hartland de M. Molson, Raymond J. Perrault, Ian Sinclair, D.G. Steuart *(Prince Albert-Duck Lake)* and David Walker.

Production and Distribution of the
National Film Board Production

"The Kid Who Couldn't Miss"

Mr. Cowan proposed that the film "Billy Bishop" be comprised of three elements: excerpts from the play "Billy Bishop Goes to War", stock shots, and interviews with those who knew Bishop.

In terms of stock shots Cowan proposed that both archived footage dating from World War I and shots from feature films made about that war be used. Films such as "Wings", "Aces High" and "Dawn Patrol" offered dramatized material on early air combat that in his opinion would be virtually indistinguishable from real stock shots.

In the winter of 1981 Mr. Cowan made a research trip to Europe to gather stock shot material and to interview people who had known Bishop during his service overseas. During this trip he came across material that in his opinion threw doubt on official and accepted versions of the exploits of Billy Bishop, and in particular on the latter's official record of enemy aircraft shot down and the very *fact* of his single-handed raid on a German aerodrome. Mr. Cowan believed that he was left with three choices: he could drop the film entirely; he could retell yet again the legend which he had come to believe was questionable; or he could make a film which reflected his doubts.

Although a "Dominique Parent" is listed on the film credits as being responsible for historical research, this person was not heard from or referred to by those who appeared before the Committee. On the basis of our hearings, it appears that Mr. Cowan was responsible for doing all or almost all of the research.

Mr. Cowan also relied very heavily on interviews with a few selected individuals who had done research into Billy Bishop's record, and into his attack on a German airport in particular. These individuals do not appear on camera to express their reservations and doubts about Bishop's exploits, nor do their names appear on the credits of the film as an important source of information. Nevertheless, their unpublished musings or conclusions are inserted into the film as authoritative evidence.

On the basis of the film credits, it does not seem that Mr. Cowan consulted important collections of documents relating to the air war and to Bishop's participation in it. The British Public Records Office which contains important documentation is not listed, nor is the Directorate of History, Department of National Defence in Canada, which holds the most voluminous records on Bishop and other Canadians who served with the Royal Flying Corps.[1] When asked why he had consulted British experts and witnesses to the exclusion of most Canadian sources, Mr. Cowan replied, "I didn't feel that anybody here that I knew of, in any case, had anything to add to it except to say, 'Well, the official history says that he did it.' "[2]

The only identifiable source of the repeated assertion throughout the film that Bishop's credibitility was at issue is the taped reminiscences of Sir Archibald Henry James.

In the opinion of your Committee, if Mr. Cowan had investigated the background of Sir Archibald Henry James' taped reminiscences, he would have discovered that they have been found to be frequently inaccurate and opinionated — in short, a historical source of scant credibility. For example, on the BBC program "Newsnight", Peter Simpkins, official historian of the Imperial War Museum, noted that James had made dubious statements about other military personalities.[3]

A number of people who have researched the subject of Bishop's military record with 60 Squadron and 85 Squadron have, however, come across rumour, gossip and speculation.

As far as your Committee knows, no reputable historian has ever published such an accusation; rather, the suggestion has been treated with the contempt it almost certainly deserves because there is no evidence to support it.

---

[1]   *Proceedings*, 7 November 1985, p. 5:5-6.

[2]   *Ibid.*, 10 December 1985, p. 8:15.

[3]   "Newsnight" with Ian Smith, 10:45 p.m., 22 January 1986 and *Proceedings*, 5 December 1985, p. 7:16.

According to Sqn. Ldr. Warne, Royal Flying Corps records do not help in any way to justify many of Bishop's claims.

At the same time, it remained impossible to document from German sources Bishop's Victoria Cross attack on a German airfield. To make matters more difficult, the bulk of the relevant German archives were lost or destroyed either in the 1918 retreat of the Germans from the Western front or during World War II. In his summary of the "Billy Bishop Controversy", Warne justly notes: "The absence of all the facts inevitably leads to conjecture, which is a personal matter."[1]

The doubts raised in the film about Bishop's attack on an airfield seem to be based very heavily on Mr. Cowan's uncritical acceptance of Sqn. Ldr. Warne's personal conjectures...

While Mr. Cowan's sources have expressed their scepticism about Bishop's record and exploits, many other historians who have checked Bishop's claims against as many sources as possible have found that a very high percentage can be confirmed.

Dr. S.F. Wise is the author of the first volume of the official history of the Royal Canadian Air Force, *Canadian Airmen and the First World War*, the product of some ten years work by himself and a team of professional historians.

Speaking of Bishop's record, he flatly rejected the allegation of fraudulence as being without foundation. A "very high proportion of Bishop's 'kills', so-called were, in fact, verified as the result of corroborative testimony."[2]

So far as Dr. Wise knows, Bishop's Victoria Cross raid was virtually without parallel among V.C. exploits because there was almost no possibility of corroboration. Bishop could have attacked any one of half a dozen airfields, not just Estourmel as the film suggests. Given the loss or destruction of German records there is today "no possibility ... of proving from German records whether or not Bishop did what he claimed to have done". Faced with such a problem, the historian can only consider the whole combat career of the individual concerned and weigh the relative likelihood of the alternatives.[4] In his opinion it is "very likely that Bishop carried out the attack"; that is, it was "in keeping with Bishop's whole career and behaviour during the war".[3]

---

[1]   *Ibid.*, p. 6A:5.

[2]   *Ibid.*, p. 5:8.

[3]   *Ibid.*, p. 5:12.

Your Committee does not believe that there is creditable historical evidence to support the film's allegations that it was generally known in 1917-1918 that many of Bishop's claims were fraudulent or the repeated assertion that these claims caused noticeable friction or dissension in the Squadron. The exceptional award of a Victoria Cross on "personal evidence only" might be expected to raise eyebrows, and perhaps provoke jealousy and gossip.

Most of the doubts and conjecture raised by Mr. Cowan's sources are placed in the mouth of Bishop's 60 Squadron mechanic, Walter Bourne, who is portrayed by an actor against authentic backgrounds such as an aircraft hangar. The technique used is that of an "interview".

Your Committee finds this technique to be the most offensive aspect of the film. It dishonours the memory of Walter Bourne and the very close relationship that existed between pilot and mechanic.

Thus the doubts that are put in Walter Bourne's mouth are all the more devastating to Bishop's reputation simply because they are expressed by his mechanic.

Throughout the film, the chronology of events is hopelessly scrambled. In general, this may be due to dramatic licence, to the effort to give the film greater audience appeal. In one particular instance, however, the film uses a chronological shift to give Bishop a powerful motive for "faking" the attack on a German airfield.

This supplies a false "motive" for faking an attack — it will be his last opportunity to play the "hero" for the "brass hats" the film says are waiting for his return.

There are many more errors of historical fact and chronology in the film, some of them significant, most minor. Details can be found in the Appendices to our proceedings, together with Mr. Cowan's critique of testimony heard before the Committee.[1]

---

[1]   *Proceedings*, Appendices "VA-2-D" and "VA-2-E", p. 4A:4-78; Appendix "VA-6-E", p. 6A:9-16.

RECOMMENDATION

The Committee has unanimously adopted the following recommendation:

> **That after the titles of the film, the following disclaimer be added:**
>
> > **"This film is a docu-drama and combines elements of both reality and fiction. It does not pretend to be an even-handed or chronological biography of Billy Bishop.**
> >
> > **Although a Walter Bourne did serve as Bishop's mechanic, the film director has used this character to express his own doubts and reservations about Bishop's exploits. There is no evidence that these were shared by the real Walter Bourne".**

Some members feel that this recommendation does not go far enough.

Part III
Malloch-Chadderton:
An Interesting Exchange
of Letters

Malloch-Chadderton:
An Interesting Exchange of Letters

WE BELIEVE YOU WILL WANT TO READ THE FOLLOWING. THE TWO PEOPLE WHO WROTE THESE LETTERS WERE NOT AWARE THAT THEY WOULD BE PUBLISHED. The correspondence was not marked "confidential" though; and we can assume that both parties were expressing views that they wanted heard. The question was raised whether we should provide a "platform" for a viewpoint which supports the production of the Billy Bishop film. The Chief Executive Officer felt, notwithstanding, that we had the responsibility to publish comment on both sides of what is now becoming the "Billy Bishop issue."

June 7, 1986
The War Amputations of Canada
2827 Riverside Drive
Ottawa, Ontario
K1V 0C4

Dear Sirs:

Judging from your organization's stated position on the NFB film *THE KID WHO COULDN'T MISS*, part of what was amputated must have been your brains. If anyone in your organization can prove that Billy Bishop did everything he said he did, (and the honorable Senator who investigated the film could *not* prove it), then you may rightly label the film "an attempt to destroy the reputation of one of the country's finest heroes." If you can't produce any proof, then common sense will lead you to recognize the fact that the film simply records some of the doubts which have been expressed through the years concerning Bishop's claims. You may wish that these doubts did not exist, but they do. Since they exist, there is no reason why they may not be stated (unless, that is, the military wishes to suppress history. I would prefer to leave that tendency to other nations).

Until the War Amps publicly state a change of policy on this matter, I will treat your solicitation of funds as junk mail. I can assure you that I will not be the only one.

Yours truly,

Katie Malloch

June 17, 1986
Ms. Katie Malloch
73 Somerville Avenue
Montreal (Quebec)
H3Z 1J4

Dear Ms. Malloch:

Thank you very much for your letter of June 7, 1986
It would appear to me that it is a relatively simple task to provide the proof concerning the accomplishments of the late Billy Bishop.

As you may know, the procedure for certifying a claim regarding the destruction of enemy aircraft in the Air component of the British Armed Forces in World War I was a stringent one.

The authorities required confirmation by at least one person and, in the case of doubt, the British Army even went to the point of arranging for enemy agents behind the German lines to provide the necessary evidence.

In the instance of the Victoria Cross which was awarded to Billy Bishop we would note a report from retired Air Marshall C.R. Dunlap, a former Chief of the Air Staff of the Royal Canadian Air Force which states: "The process of investigating, confirming and gazetting (the recommendation of the award of the Victoria Cross) occupied more than two months during which time Bishop increased his overall total to 47 victories."

It is common knowledge that the recommendation for an award of the Victoria Cross is subjected to meticulous examination. It is, as you probably know, the highest award for valour which can be given in the British Commonwealth and the greatest possible care is exercised to ensure that this recognition is granted only where there is absolutely no possibility of error in regard to the basis for the recommendation. You may be aware that researchers were, after World War I, unable to find any record of the raid carried out on the German airfield near Cambrai. This should not be considered as unusual in that historians generally accept the fact that a great many German records were destroyed.

Should you require proof of whether the Germans accepted the status of Billy Bishop as a genuine war hero, however, you may be interested to know that Billy Bishop was the only Canadian who was recognized by the German Association of "War Aces." This was in Paris in 1928.

You may be aware that The War Amputations of Canada did not make any statement on the Billy Bishop matter until recently. We were invited to appear before the Senate Sub-Committee on Veterans Affairs but declined last February in that we had not, at that time, completed our own research project.

It has been my privilege, however, to now prepare a 30-page report for our Board of Directors, based on extensive research both in Canada, United States and the United Kingdom. You may be aware that, although our position was made known to the media, our request was confined to a proposal that we be allowed to appear before the Senate Sub-Committee.

Should this occur, I am confident that the Sub-Committee will carefully weigh the information in our report and it will probably be the responsibility of that Sub-Committee to decide whether we are justified in making the demand that the film be withdrawn. I would expect that an opportunity would be afforded, at that time, for those responsible for the production of this film to hear our evidence and respond to it, should they be able to do so. You make reference to "...the doubts which have been expressed through the years concerning Bishop's claims.'' By any standards which might be used to measure gallantry, the accomplishments of Billy Bishop would entitle him to a place of honour among his countrymen. Much has been made of the raid on the German airfield and while it is true that there has been some doubt (I would not argue as to how much) concerning this raid, surely it is impossible to dismiss most, if not all, of the remainder of his victories.

When you make reference to the doubts, I hope you will have an opportunity to review the report which I was able to prepare, if and when that report is referred to the Senate Sub-Committee. The so-called doubts just do not seem to stand up, when compared with the positive proof of Billy Bishop's war record. Your somewhat interesting reference to the fact that ''. . . part of what was amputated must have been your brains.'' is noted. I have the honour to be the spokesman for an organization whose ''membership dues'' require the amputation of at least one limb. You may be right in suggesting that, along with my amputation, there was some brain damage. I would leave that for others to judge.

In the meantime I simply do what I perceive to be my job, part of which is to challenge persons such as those in the National Film Board who somehow seem to have the idea that there must be a sensational angle or aspect to a film if it is to attract public attention. That objective is acceptable enough, I suppose, but surely it would require the filmmakers to prove any allegations which are being made.

I am satisfied, as a former journalist, historian and administrator of long standing, that the NFB film just does not ''stand to muster.''

Finally, you suggest that The War Amputations of Canada cannot count upon you for financial support. I would wish to make it clear, first of all, that the cost involved in our own investigation of this matter came from sources other than the public. In fact, from corporate donations. Secondly, I doubt very much whether the organization I represent (The War Amputations of Canada) would take any position on a public matter of this nature based on the possibility that such position may or may not engender support for the charitable purposes and objects of this Association. We have survived for more than 60 years by doing what we thought was right. I cannot believe that any threat of withdrawal of support from the public would deter this Association from what it considered to be its duty and responsibility.

I might add that, even if we were wrong, I hope you would not consider this as a reason for denying support, when in fact more than 90 per cent of our expenditures are on behalf of persons and programs for the benefit of amputees other than our own members— the vast majority being children.

Should you wish to reply, I would be pleased to hear from you. Yours sincerely,

H. Clifford Chadderton

July 3, 1986
H. Clifford Chadderton
Chief Executive Officer
The War Amputations of Canada
2827 Riverside Drive
Ottawa, Ontario
K1V 0C4

Dear Mr. Chadderton:
Thank you so much for your reply of June 17. Your letter raised a number of points, which I would like to address.

Your first few paragraphs demonstrate an interesting tendency which I have noticed in many public statements and letters to editors since the beginning of the whole Bishop/NFB discussion: namely, the confusion of semantics which occurs when ''acceptance'' is used to mean ''proof.'' For example, you say that it is a relatively simple task to provide proof of Billy Bishop's accomplishments. But, curiously enough, you fail to provide that proof. Instead you reiterate, as several senators and many veterans have done that ''the recommendation for the award of a Victoria Cross is subjected to meticulous examination.'' In other words, if Bishop received the VC, then he must have done what he said he did. Acceptance is supposed to equal ''proof?''

Unfortunately, whatever evidence that meticulous examination might have uncovered seems devilishly hard to find. Senator Molson told his Sub-Committee before the investigation of the NFB film began, that proof of the Estourmel Raid was available from three sources: testimony by captured German pilots who'd witnessed the raid, observation by a balloonist, and an eye witness account of the wreckage by Bishop's Squadron-mate Spencer Horne, who'd flown over the raided aerodrome.

However, when Colonel A.J. Bauer (of the Billy Bishop Heritage Foundation) made a special evidence-gathering trip on behalf of Senator Molson's investigation, those three sources came up empty. It turned out that weather conditions on the morning in question precluded any observation from a balloon. The captured German soldiers had not witnessed any raid and Spencer Horne had *not* left 60 Squadron base that day. In fact, the only flyer to leave the base that day after Bishop's return had been Bishop himself. He took off for a second trip in a plane which, according to the legend, was ''in tatters,'' but which was in fact not even booked in for repairs that day.

So, no proof. In fact, the Sub-Committee was told at least twice (by witnesses not very friendly to the NFB) that no evidence exists that Billy Bishop ever made the Estroumel Raid. This was, let's face it, a forum that wanted to find and hear such proof very badly. If any *could* have been found, I have every confidence that these gentlemen would have found it. They did not.

This fact by itself did not seem to perturb them unduly. On November 11, 1985, the CBC Program, *The Journal*, carried a piece on Billy Bishop, heroism and the debate about the film. Senator Molson was asked what evidence he had that the raid had taken place. He could not produce any, but declared that ''the King's word'' was good enough for him. However, history has shown that even monarch's can be swayed by their own prejudices, desires and blind spots. (It was Queen Victoria, after all, who heartily agreed to legislation outlawing homosexuality for men. But she refused to outlaw lesbianism, because she couldn't believe that such a thing existed!)

Fine. Lack of evidence that the raid took place is one thing. Is there any evidence that the raid *didn't* take place?

Yes, in the form of copies of German war records. As you quite accurately observe in your letter, the originals of those records were destroyed by fire during World War II, but as you may know, in the period between the two wars, copies of the originals were made. They were quite actively traded by amateur historians, notably a German named Tornhuss and an American named Puglisi, founder of the Cross and Cockade, a society of First World War fighters. The records in his possession were later sold, and those pertinent to the Estourmel raid became the property of A.E. (Ed) Ferko, of Ohio. He made those records available to the NFB, whose representatives at the Sub-Committee investigation made them available to the Senators for examination. (The Senators declined, although the records became part of the investigation's *own* record.) Those documents indicate absolutely no raid on the date in question in any of the several areas where the raid *might* have taken place. (You must already know that it has never been entirely clear as to exactly which aerodrome Bishop claimed to have attacked.) The records are very complete, detailing any losses of personnel and aircraft under separate headings. Nothing at all in those records indicate the V.C. worthy venture ever happened.

Another sticky wicket is what those records indicate about some of Bishop's other "accepted kills". During the time period covered, Bishop claimed to have taken out seventeen planes. Confirmation is found for only two. It might be said that the Germans were simply covering up losses, but that does not explain the fact that German corroboration for the claimed kills of *other* pilots (among them Albert Ball and Jimmy McCudden) is very much higher, at about 50 percent.

As I said, the senators didn't seem much interested in these records, a fact which you, as a former journalist may find quite interesting.

Neither did they express interest in hearing testimony from Ed Ferko, owner of the records, nor did they want to hear from Group Captain D.W. (Joe) Warne. Warne is a member of 60 Squadron in England, and for about twenty-five years has been the squadron historian. He has undertaken lengthy investigations of his own, hoping to lay to rest the doubts about Bishop's record. However, over time, and with no little regret, he has came to the conclusion that Billy Bishop *could not* have done the Estourmel raid, and that he had falsified other parts of his record as well. His statement to that effect was made part of the NFB's presentation to the senators but, as is the case of Ed Ferko's documents, was not counted worthy of comment.

You have said that you feel a responsibility to challenge those at the NFB who feel there must be "a sensational angle" to their films. Yet when a film such as *THE KID WHO COULDN'T MISS* questions the sensational angles of the legend of Billy Bishop you, and the senators as well, seem quite prepared to ignore what you don't want to hear. That has been quite evident ever since the investigation began. I had to laugh with astonishment when I read the transcripts from early in the hearings. Senators were falling over themselves to intone that "This is not a witch hunt" and "We only want to get at the truth" while, a minute or two later, labelling the film "a monstrosity" and "pigeon droppings on the statue of Billy Bishop." And all this before anyone from the NFB had been called to speak! I have read extensively from the transcripts which, thank the gods, are available to the public. It is clear that what the senators *want* to consider and examine, they consider and examine. What they *don't* want to, they don't. As one who works in the media (the CBC), I find that very troubling and I hope that, as a former journalist, you do too, whatever else your interests in the case.

As for your not being particularly non-plused by my withdrawal of financial support, I didn't expect you to be. But just as you do what you feel to be right, so must I.

There are plenty of organizations which manage to help children without exposing the suppression of unwelcome history. They will receive my whole hearted support.

I guess what breaks my heart most about this whole business is that it reveals some pretty sad needs of certain old soldiers to have a superhuman hero in order to justify what's happened to them.

If Billy Bishop overstepped the truth, he is still a hell of a pilot to me, and I wouldn't have wanted to go up against him in a Nieuport in any weather. I just feel sorry for anyone whose heroes have to be perfect.

Writers' cramp has felled me—does any of this interest you? I'd be pleased if you would let me know.
Yours truly,

Katie Malloch

July 18, 1986
Ms. Katie Malloch
73 Somerville Avenue
Montreal (Quebec)
H3Z 1J4

Dear Ms. Malloch:

Re: NFB Film
    THE KID WHO COULDN'T MISS

Thank you for your further letter. You ask "...does any of this interest you?" The answer is in the affirmative, very much. I may have been a bit of a "late comer" in the controversy but I am now fully committed to getting at the truth of the situation.

Maybe I am wrong, but the film and some of the media exposure, seem to tell only one side of the story.

Who speaks for Billy Bishop? You are probably aware that there is little or any applicability in the law of defamation.

It is quite clear that the jurisprudence holds that no action lies at the suit of the estate of a deceased person if defamatory things are said about him, or by his friends or relatives for injury to their feelings. In effect, only living persons may be defamed as a matter of law.

There exists a long line of cases supporting this principle with the one minor exception that "an imputation against the dead may reflect upon the living...."

Cases cited in support of this latter proposition do not deal with defamation of the dead but rather with the question as to whether an imputation against one person can reflect on another, such as to be actionable by the living person.

In the context of the Billy Bishop film, even if the Bishop family were inclined to bring an action on their own behalf, they would have to prove that the Bishop family reputation has been sufficiently tarnished by this film so as to impact upon themselves as a matter of legal relief and damages. In my view, this would be extremely difficult in these circumstances and would be opposing the general trend of case law in this area.

In any event, I am not aware that the Bishop family is interested in initiating any proceedings. This means that the initiative is probably left to persons such as myself who have a genuine interest in veterans' matters.

Having been trained as a journalist I think I know what is meant by censorship; and I would fight as hard as anyone to prevent it. I did not take on the Billy Bishop situation lightly. In fact, my own personal investigation into the matter preceded that of the Senate Committee.

The issue here is not censorship—but truth. I may not agree with Paul Cowan, but I would defend his right to say it—if it were true. Unfortunately any information I have would not support his allegations.

You are probably aware that there is a source of information on file in London, England as to the investigation that was carried out prior to the award. So far, I have been unsuccessful in getting access to this information.

You say that I have failed to provide the proof. Surely this would be true of any gallantry award; and particularly one which requires the approval of the Head of State.

Maybe I am wrong, but down through the years an award of the Victoria Cross has been a sacrosanct matter and, before any such award could be challenged, surely the onus would not lie on the deceased William Avery Bishop, but upon the producers of the NFB film.

I have the greatest possible respect for Senator Molson. Notwithstanding, I would not be in a position to accept his testimony.

I found it very interesting that you should recount some of the varied details which might well be the basis of any question which could be raised; that is, the weather conditions on the day of the raid . . . that Billy Bishop took off for a second trip in a plane which was supposed to have been "in tatters" etc.

Yet, is it any more reasonable for you to suggest that you have " . . . every confidence that these gentlemen would have found it (the evidence)" than it is for those supporting the Bishop claim to say that the well-known principles accepted in regard to the award of a VC should be sufficient guarantee that the facts had been investigated and were found to be sufficient to justify the award.

I have, of course, been aware of the documents generally filed under the heading of the "Cross and Cockade." Are they evidence?

Of course, I would not want to get into another area set out in your letter of July 3rd. I refer, of course, to what you suggest as "questionable" information in regard to some of Billy Bishop's other claims. It seems to me that the undeniable facts are that Bishop risked his life on many occasions, flying an antiquated airplane and, single-handedly, inflicted a great deal of damage on the enemy.

I have also heard and read some of the views of Joe Warne. He may be the self-appointed "squadron historian" for 60 Squadron but I wonder about his objectivity.

You refer to the Senate Sub-Committee's failure to look at all of the evidence. My information is that there was no restriction laid down by Senator Marshall's Committee as to the witnesses who would be called. Am I wrong?

You may well accuse me of, as you say, " . . . ignore what you don't want to hear." I think that is a little unfair but I will accept if if that is the way I appear to you.

The Parliamentary process is an interesting one. It is a moot question as to who should put in its evidence first; and referring to the Billy Bishop situation, I see no great harm in the Senators expressing their views, so long as it was generally known that witnesses from the NFB would be called.

As I see it, Paul Cowan, and the others from the NFB, had their opportunity to provide the "evidence" which was needed to support the accusations in *THE KID WHO COULDN'T MISS*. You say that you " . . . laugh with astonishment . . ." at some of the comments of the Senators. Notwithstanding, careful reading of the transcripts of the Senate Sub-Committee fails, at least in my opinion, to indicate that Paul Cowan and the NFB persons were able to justify the slant in the film.

Now, let us get to the meat of the subject. You say " . . . I guess what breaks my heart most about this whole business is that it reveals some pretty sad needs of certain old soldiers to have a superhuman hero in order to justify what's happened to them." Surely, you can-

not be serious! I cannot think that any of us "old soldiers" need any kind of a hero (superhuman or not) to justify the loss of the odd arm or leg or what have you, if that is what you are referring to when you said " . . . what's happened to them."

If you will indulge me for just another line or two, you say, "I just feel sorry for anyone whose heroes have to be perfect." I remember Douglas Bader (an old friend) saying many, many times that the only real heroes were the ones who never came back.

In this whole Billy Bishop matter, words come up like censorship, witch-hunt and, to add one from your own correspondence, hero worship.

I find your correspondence both interesting and valuable. You ask whether any of this interests me and you would be pleased if I would let you know.

Yes, indeed. It is perhaps trite to say that there are two sides to every story and I well remember someone saying that there were in fact three sides—the right side, the wrong side—and his own! I certainly want to avoid the latter and so my quest for the facts will continue.

In the meantime my organization has asked that the film be withdrawn and this may well have taken place. The Film Board has refused to release a copy of the film to us so that I could once again screen it. I am wondering how this refusal sits in regard to our current "Freedom of Information" provisions.

The current status of how I see it is that Paul Cowan, unfortunately, still stands condemned; not only on the grounds of having inadequately supported his theory, but also in regard to some of the statements he has made publicly such as "how heroes are made" and "why a country needs heroes."

With best wishes,
Yours sincerely,

H. Clifford Chadderton

July 25, 1986

Dear Mr. Chadderton:

Thank you so much for your letter. Although we have never met, we seem to be developing a rather respect-worthy correspondence, which can be rare in the age of the omnipresent "Ma Bell!"

You say that the film, and some of the media coverage have told only one side of the story and you ask, "Who speaks for Billy Bishop?" Well, the history books I read in *my* school curriculum certainly spoke for Billy Bishop. Ditto for several books written about him, including the one by his son, Arthur. Nowhere in these books can one read that there *are* fliers and historians who dispute Bishop's claims. Nowhere is it reported that some of those (Bishop's) claims cannot be independently validated. Does that one-sidedness shock and dismay you? Wouldn't you like to see those schoolbooks amended to more accurately reflect "the whole story"?

Certainly, many people continue to speak for Billy Bishop; you are among them, as are many veterans and Senators. As for the injury to the feelings of the Bishop family, they must surely be aware by now that their father, grandfather, father-in-law, or whatever he may be to them, is a public figure. They have doubtless reaped the rewards of that situation—please don't tell me that the Bishop pedigree hasn't opened doors and aroused admiration! Now they're taking the bumps that go with the roses. If they have any evidence that all doubts about the Bishop legend are groundless, then let them

—230—

come forward. If they can't, or won't, that is their choice. Frankly, I can't work up much sympathy for the Bishop clan! (By the way, Arthur Bishop told a friend of mine, who was doing a piece on the whole controversy, that Paul Cowan is "a commie faggot"; those apparently being the two worst things one can be. These exchanges can be highly instructive!)

You go on to say the awarding of the Victoria Cross has always been a sacrosanct matter and if there are people with doubts about Bishop's claims, the onus is on *them* to prove that it didn't happen.

Firstly, the film *never* says that the Estourmel raid *didn't* happen. It does say that there are people who have doubts that it happened. That is a fact. Contemporaries of Bishop's, as well as late-comers like Ferko and Warne, do have doubts, based on research that they have done. A "sacrosanct matter" is purely in the eye of the beholder, and while *you* may be totally satisfied by this "evidence" which is not allowed to be revealed, (why *not*, by the way?) surely you cannot, in a democracy, insist that everybody share your touching faith in governments and Kings (both of which institutions have, after all, been known to "cover things up.") As for your contention that the onus is on the doubters to prove that the raid and/or other kills *didn't* happen: Balderdash!! If I claim to have bought a winning Lotto ticket, but can't produce it, is the onus on Lotto Canada to prove that I *didn't* buy it? If I claim to have broken the Canadian broadjump record in my backyard on some moonless night, with no witnesses about, why should anyone believe I did? And even if the Canadian Olympic Committee were to confer a medal on me for my feat, I doubt it would change anyone's mind, nor should it. In my last letter, I outlined some of the evidence which I, and others, feel to be the basis for doubts about certain of Bishop's reported exploits. I have never said that those exploits *didn't* happen—I feel I must make that clear. But I feel that there *are* grounds for doubts. Doubts would seem to me to be a prerogative of the individual and to make a film which says, in part, that there *are* such doubts is no crime, especially in the light of an outstanding lack of evidence to support Bishop's claim.

My saying that, "if there were any evidence then surely these gentlemen would have found it" was merely a reflection of my belief (valid, I feel) that these men wanted, very badly, to find it. I don't argue with their right to believe what they want to, but unless they can produce the evidence, they are hardly in a position to insist that all doubters be silenced.

You wonder whether or not the "Cross and Cockade" documents are "evidence." It's a very interesting thing: you referred in your first letter to the lack of German war records, saying that since they had been destroyed, they were not available as corroboration for Billy Bishop. The implication (or am I wrong?) was that gee, if those pesky records were there, we'd be able to *prove* Estourmel happened! Yet when the copies of the records *do* surface, but contain no corroboration, suddenly you begin to question their validity. Why? Are the records faked? Did Puglisi get taken? Or do the records simply not serve your purpose?

You've taken a similar tack with Joe Warne. You "wonder about his objectivity." Why? What is there about poor Joe that I don't know? He's not a contemporary of Bishop's, so he can't be professionally jealous. He's a member of Bishop's squadron, so if anything he should be prejudiced in Bishop's favour! Of course, he's a Brit (the Senators didn't like that; jealousy against colonials etc. etc.) but then so was the King and government that awarded

the V.C.!! So please, tell me about the lack of objectivity of Joe Warne.

While we're on the subject, what do you think of the probable objectivity of Col. Bauer? He's the head of the Billy Bishop Heritage Foundation, scarcely apt to take a balanced view of anyone or anything that doesn't buy the legend wholesale. Yet you make no mention of *his* testimony, or its trustworthiness. And he was the man that Senator Molson chose to make that "evidence-gathering" trip to England. (Incidentally, Col. Bauer and the foundation had been sent a copy of Joe Warne's statement even before that trip, yet Col. Bauer made no effort to contact Warne while in Britain. Really, if he keeps deciding what's relevant before he decides not to talk to anybody he doesn't like, the purpose of his trip may be more properly called "evidence ignoring!")

As for restrictions laid down about calling witnesses, there certainly *were* some rather oddly-applied ones. The NFB's Commissioner, François Macerola, asked the committee's permission to call Joe Warne and Ed Ferko, as well as some filmmakers. He was told that none of that evidence would be "necessary." The result was that, aside from Messrs. Macerola and Cowan, the NFB was allowed no witnesses while, as you know, the "other side" had plenty!

You say you see no great harm in the Senators expressing their views about the case. Neither do I, but then those with such obviously-made-up minds shouldn't be in a position to rule on the film! How can these men claim that "this is not a witchhunt" and "we want the truth" when they then proceed to rail against the film, and deny the Film Board the right to call other witnesses? Come on now Mr. Chadderton, if you witnessed a trial which began with the judge calling the defendant "pigeon droppings" and "a monstrosity" would you put money on the defendant's chances of a fair trial? To make it perhaps even clearer, would you expect a fair hearing on a film about abortion from a synod of Catholic Bishops? I believe that the committee's clearly biased way of thinking is the exact reason why that committee should *not* be judging the merits of *THE KID WHO COULDN'T MISS*. (And I would firmly oppose a hearing before the Committee on Filmmakers Affairs too, if there were such an animal! A gang of redoubtable old filmmakers would be too apt to harbour biases in the *other* direction!)

So you don't think I'm correct in believing that some old soldiers need a superhuman hero? I wish you could have sat with me in an auditorium at McGill University in early February, where the RCAF had come to do battle with Paul Cowan during a symposium on the nature of docu-drama. One rather ancient gentleman stood up and intoned that the film represented "an attack on the integrity of Billy Bishop and thus on the integrity of all fighting men." Huh? Since when did Bishop become "all fighting men?" Believe it or not, share it or not, but there's a case of *more* than hero worship going on here. The applause that remark won from the RCAF contingent proved to me that, for a healthy number of old vets, at least a portion of their own egos have becomed enmeshed with that of Billy Bishop's. (Would Bishop laugh, or cry?) Further to this, consider the remark of Senator Lang from the Debates of the Senate of Wednesday, May 14. He accuses Paul Cowan of attempting "designed insult" against Billy Bishop because the film states that Bishop vomited at the sight of a ship going down. Senator Lang says that that statement "brings him into contempt" (Bishop) because it makes him look frightened.

Firstly, *I* don't feel contempt for anyone who feels fear or shock at seeing a ship go down, especially if one is young and new to battle, as Bishop was, on his way across the ocean. Secondly, I find it very ominous that Senator Lang obviously finds vomiting in fear to be an act that is "off limits" (in depiction, if not in fact!) for those soon to be canonized as Saints of War. There seems to be a whole cluster of behavioral traits that define "heroes," and the absence of any of them appears to be almost enough to get a man written off. For instance, it was reported in *The Globe and Mail* that when one of Bishop's fellow fliers was reported to have expressed doubts as to Bishop's record, Senator Molson expressed the view that the man's word could be discounted because he had suffered from "Low Moral Fibre," a truly bizarre designation which, I learned, means shell-shock! In other words, Senator Molson believes that if a guy can't hack it in battle, he's proved he's not a "real man," and you don't have to believe a word he says!!

All of this expresses a rather twisted (in my view) version of what a hero is. And, again, it disqualifies these gentlemen in my opinion, from passing fair judgement on the film in question.

I was baffled by your citing of the old quote that "the only real heroes are the ones who never came back." Really, Mr. Chadderton, are you implying that Billy Bishop wasn't a hero? I'll have to tell Senator Molson how you feel...But seriously, for me, the heroes are the men who never *lost* their fear, who fought, vomited, cried and prayed, and stuck it out anyway. The men who came home, perhaps shell-shocked, perhaps emotionally devastated, perhaps terminally bitter, perhaps addicted to pain-killing morphine and who had to pick up their lives and go on as though nothing had ever happened. They are also the women who lost husbands and children, who were raped and killed and who had to learn to live with the sometimes brutalized strangers who came home to them. Heroes are also the kids who lost everything and everyone. There are never too many heroes, just enough to go around. And heroes are also those who can face the disappointment of accepting the possibility that *their* heroes may not be all they were thought to be.

I'm truly surprised to learn that you have had difficulty in obtaining a copy of *THE KID WHO COULDN'T MISS.* I believe that each branch office of the NFB across the country carries a library of films on cassette. If you still have trouble, why not contact the film's Executive Producer, Adam Symansky? I don't have his office address at the Board, but his number in Montreal is (514) 283-9555.

Please write again if the spirit moves you.

Yours truly,

Katie Malloch

August 6, 1986

Dear Ms. Malloch:

Re: NFB Film
THE KID WHO COULDN'T MISS

This will acknowledge receipt of your very explicit letter of July 25, 1986.

You end your letter with a request to "Please write again if the spirit moves you." This I shall certainly do but your letter arrived as I was catching a plane and I will be away for a week or two. In the meantime, you suggest that copies of *THE KID WHO COULDN'T MISS* are available through NFB offices across Canada. We were told by the NFB in Ottawa that the film had been "temporarily suspended!"

It is several years since I saw the film and, primarily due to some of the comments in your letters, I feel I must look at it once again.

Yours sincerely,

H. Clifford Chadderton

August 14, 1986

Dear Ms. Malloch:

I have now had a bit more time and would like to reply to your letter of July 25, 1986.

It seems that the basic issue here is one of proof. There were no witnesses to confirm that the raid took place. Still, can we say that Paul Cowan can substantiate the thrust of his film, which appears to be suggesting that it did not!

Perhaps we have to proceed here on what might be called "the word" of people who were either involved, or had knowledge of the facts.

I have great personal difficulty in not accepting Bishop's own version, given his established record as a fighter pilot. Another person who was apparantly quite prepared to put his own reputation on the line was Bishop's Squadron Commander Major A.J.L. Scott. If I am not mistaken, Scott, who was in the position to judge, accepted Bishop's version of the raid.

Taking the darkest scenario, Bishop *could* have an ulterior motive in glorifying his account of the raid. What motive could we attribute to his Squadron Commander?

You mentioned the name of Colonel A.J. Bauer who appeared as a witness before the Senate Sub-Committee. Bauer, with a distinguished war record himself, is presumably prepared to support the contention that the raid on the German airfield took place, and earned Billy Bishop the Victoria Cross. Of course, Colonel Bauer did not serve in World War I but he has the conviction that Bishop was telling the truth.

I gather that Bauer made his own investigation. I am trying to keep an open mind, but what possible reason could he have had to argue *for* Bishop if indeed there are any grounds to question the historical version of a raid which made history in regard to Aerial Warfare.

You ask whether I would like to see the school books amended to more accurately reflect "the whole story." What source could an historian use (or anyone for that matter) to tell what you call "the other side of the story"—by which, obviously, you mean that the raid itself may not have taken place and that some of Bishop's other claims may be fraudulent.

I have not been in touch with any members of the Bishop family but I wonder if they are in a position to, as you say, "come forward."

I have been trying, to the best of my ability, to find out what people really think now about Billy Bishop. You state that the film does not say specifically that the Estourmel Raid *didn't* happen; only that there are people who have doubts that it did.

I have travelled extensively in Canada and, to a smaller degree in the United Kingdom in the past fourteen months, during which I have been in contact with many people who have an interest in war...significant numbers are working actively in the campaign to outlaw armed conflict. I have purposely raised the name of Billy Bishop, so I could sample opinions. I was shocked by the response, which usually was to the effect that the man stands condemned by the NFB film.

I have enlisted the aid of a contemporary in England who will be contacting Warne. You also mentioned the name of Ferko, stating that they both have done research which leads them to doubt that the raid took place. Research implies, in my mind, the unearthing of factual evidence. That, I guess, is my problem. I haven't been able to see any factual evidence which substantiates the claims made in the film.

May I conclude with what, in my view, is one of the more interesting facets of an intriguing correspondence with you. I still claim that those who served in the Armed Forces of Canada during time of war do not need what we have been referring to as a "super-human hero." You referred to the meeting in the auditorium at McGill University last February; and the fact that one "rather ancient gentleman" suggested that the NFB film is an attack on the integrity of all fighting men.

Is this not so? If, indeed, Billy Bishop is a fraud what about us lesser mortals who toiled away, far from the limelight. I suppose we *thought* we did a pretty fair job of things but if the name of Billy Bishop can be dragged through the mud then what will our grandchildren think of those of us who came home with a spam medal and maybe a wound strip or two—and nothing else to show for those years (some of them pretty harrowing) between 1940 and 1945?

There is one point upon which I certainly do agree with you. That is the recognition which should be given to the women, including those wives and mothers, who bore the brunt of it all while the Billy Bishops were shooting down enemy aircraft.

Kind regards.
Yours sincerely,

H. Clifford Chadderton

August 24, 1986

Dear Mr. Chadderton

Now it's my turn to acknowledge your letter of August 14, with a promise to write at further length after this coming weekend, when my husband and I will move to a new house which we've been renovating for the past month. (I'm fervently praying that I won't have to smell paint or plaster dust again for many years!)

I spoke briefly with your secretary, to tell her that the NFB distribution office has assured me that copies of the film *are* available. It seems that the film was temporarily withdrawn so that the disclaimer agreed upon by the Senate and the NFB could be edited in.

I'll be writing soon. I hope that your trip was a vacation and that it was good!
Yours truly,

Katie Malloch

September 2, 1986

Dear Mr. Chadderton:

I'm writing to you from a chaos of boxes, unhung pictures, drop-sheets and cartons of clothes and books. I don't know first-hand about *war* but moving is hell! If only they gave medals for renovating houses...

As you so aptly note early in your letter of August 14, there is no proof that the raid of June 2, 1917 did or did not take place.

You add, quite correctly, that it really comes down to an issue of belief, and of whose word one wants to take.

If this is so, then what's wrong with a film that supports the belief that the raid didn't happen? If you have trouble accepting such a film, because it has no proof, then you'd also have to reject a film (or, presumably, book) that suggests that the raid *did* happen, because there's no proof of that either.

Obviously, anyone who wants to believe Bishop's version of events is free to do so. But I would, in a democracy, expect an equal right for the opposing viewpoint. As you must know, there is conflicting testimony about the state of Bishop's plane when it returned; a pilot named Willy Frye (who is still alive) was there when the plane came back on June 2, and his version of the state of the plane is distinctly at odds with Bishop's. Joe Warne, in his disposition which was submitted at the Senate hearings, observes that Bishop's plane did not carry enough fuel to make the raid as Bishop described it! Ed Ferko, who reviewed Bishop's story, as well as maps and the German records I mentioned earlier, stated in *his* letters to the NFB producer and director that Bishop's log of his flight is geographically unsupportable. All of this (as well as other research material) may not amount to "proof" in your eyes, but is certainly at least as strong as the "evidence" of the word of one man, namely Bishop.

You say that you have difficulty in not accepting Bishop's story, given his war record above and beyond the Estourmel raid. Firstly, I'm not of the opinion that a large number of good deeds are absolute assurance that a person is incapable of committing a bad one. Secondly, you are probably also aware that for many of Bishop's other "kills" there is no confirmation either. Aside from the lack of corroboration in the German war records, which I believe I mentioned in a previous letter, there is the fact that, in a large number of instances, Bishop was not able to specify the *kind* of plane he claims to have brought down. (See Warne's disposition for more on that. Both Colonel Bauer and Senator Molson have copies, otherwise, the Film Board would probably be most happy to send you a copy.) So, for a number of people, more of Bishop's war record than just the aerodrome raid is suspect.

You ask what possible motivation Jack Scott or Colonel Bauer could have for supporting Bishop's version of events if that version were not true. I'm sure that Jack Scott *did* believe that the raid took place, and was perhaps able to shut any troublesome ideas to the contrary out of his mind because he simply *wanted* to believe Bishop. There is considerable evidence that Scott was very fond of Bishop, possibly because the two had a lot in common in terms of their approach to aerial warfare. Both, I believe, shared a belief in the solo-pilot, maverick style of search-and-destroy, and so the Estourmel raid, or idea of it, would have appealed tremendously to Scott. But his commendation of Bishop's exploit attests only to his (Scott's) *belief* that it happened. If offers no *proof* of its having happened.

Colonel Bauer's belief in Bishop's story does not surprise me, either. Nor do I find it particularly convincing. At the crassest level, of course, if Bishop ever *were* proven to have lied, Colonel Bauer might see his job (as head of the Billy Bishop foundation) evaporate, along with the organization itself. But all that aside, the fact that Bauer supports Bishop means merely that Bauer believes, along with a lot of other people, that Bishop was a hell of a fellow, and that anyone who doubts it is a disgrace to this country. That may be his opinion, but it *isn't* evidence. And the fact that that opinion exists is interesting, but does not give holders of that opinion any exclusive domain. All the people who trumpet loudly that Billy Bishop was a man of sterling character, who never sought the limelight, and who *couldn't* have been open to the weaknesses and temptations that plague the rest of us mortals, are speaking from the podium of the Character Witness. But what about the Billy Bishop who started writing his memoirs while he was on his honeymoon? *That* was a man with no sense of image in history? What about the Billy Bishop who was famous for falling down drunk at the Sheraton Mount Royal and Ritz Carleton Hotels? Anyone who chooses the route of "strength of character" in defense of Billy Bishop must be aware that it's a two-sided coin that's dangerous to play, as it is when *any* human being is involved. I don't believe that there's a single human being who can be certified as being "beyond" telling a lie, or "above" the realms of self-interest.

I don't mean to say that because Billy Bishop had a drinking problem, he was automatically a liar. Far from it. But he *was* a human being with weaknesses, something one might excusably forget, if all the pro-Bishop character testimonies were taken at face value.

Which brings back the point of the super-human hero. You referred to my comment about the "rather ancient gentleman" at the McGill Symposium. (By the way, you included quote marks around "rather ancient gentleman." I can assure you that he was, by his own testimony, a veteran of the First World War, and that he was by anyone's reckoning, except perhaps Methusela's, a "rather ancient gentleman.")

You claim not to believe in a "super-human hero". Yet you support the claim that "an attack on Bishop is an attack on all fighting men" because, as you state rhetorically "...if Bishop is a fraud, what about us lesser mortals..." To me, this question reveals and illustrates the very epitome of the need for a superhuman hero. You have placed Bishop on such a pedestal that he is, in effect, no longer simply a man, an individual who can be questioned, or found to be lacking, or even simply *human*. You imply that Bishop was so marvellous that if *he* can be "dragged through the mud" then it somehow lessens your accomplishments as well as those of other regular guys who just did the best they could. If *that's* not a "super-human hero", then please tell me what is! I had two grandfathers who fought in the First World War, in fact one of them replaced Dr. McCrae, who wrote "In Flander's Fields", when McCrae died. The other was badly wounded, and was mad as hell when the army wouldn't take him back for the *second* war! If Billy Bishop were to turn out to have been lying through his teeth all along, that would never make me think any less of what my grandpas did, nor would it lessen my reckoning of anybody else but Bishop.

It seems to me to be dangerous to decide that *anyone* is beyond the realm of question or doubt merely because that doubt is unwelcome for a series of complex and emotional reasons. And certainly those complex and emotional reasons are not good enough cause to condemn, out of hand, anyone who *does* that unwelcome questioning.

A couple of last points—you say you can't understand how history books could possibly be amended to reflect "the whole story". Would you have any objections to something along the lines of "On the morning of June 2, 1917, Bishop left the 60 Squadron camp, and returned sometime later claiming to have singlehandedly attacked a German aerodrome at Estourmel, and to have destroyed a number of enemy aircraft. He was subsequently awarded the Victoria Cross, in substantial part for his raid, although no proof or confirmation of the raid has ever been produced." That seems

to me to sum up the facts pretty well. You say that a great number of people believe that Bishop stands condemned by the film. I think that, if you see the film again, you'll agree that it states quite forcefully that there *is* room for doubt, but I don't think that it ever implies that the raid definitively didn't happen. A filmmaker is responsible for the content of his or her film—I don't think he or she can be held responsible for the "impression" that an audience comes away with. We must all exercise a little editorial judgement of our own. After all, if I listened solely to senatorial testimony, I'd have the "impression" that William Avery Bishop was a saint!!

I strongly hope that you will have a chance to look over the documents by Warne and Ferko which were submitted by the NFB at the Senate hearings, and then never subsequently referred to by the Senators. If Senator Molson can't, or won't oblige you, why not try Adam Symansky (Executive Producer) or Paul Cowan, at the Film Board?

One last thought, Mr. Chadderton. I don't really expect to change your mind about Billy Bishop, since you seem to be a strong-minded man possessed of an interesting blend of intelligence and faith. And I can assure you that I will never be convinced that the film in question is criminal, or should be withdrawn. (I confess to a tenacity of my own, which borders, according to my dear husband, on pigheadedness. I believe he overstates things.) But although we may never change each others' points of view, I look forward to your letters.
Yours truly,

Katie Malloch

September 10, 1986

Dear Ms. Malloch:
My Executive Assistant read to me, over the telephone, your very kind letter of September 2, 1986.

I am dictating this letter from the Nassau County Medical Center, Long Island, New York where I am delivering a number of papers on medical and prosthetic problems.

I was not aware that Ed Ferko had written letters to the NFB, I am writing to Mr. Adam Symansky, asking for a copy of these letters.

I will not be back in Ottawa for several weeks but would like to see these particular letters as they may shed more light on the situation.
Kind regards.
Yours sincerely,

H. Clifford Chadderton

September 26, 1986

Dear Ms. Malloch:
Thank you for your further letter of September 2nd, 1986.
As I re-read our correspondence to date, nothing seems to have changed since the beginning.

In your most recent letter, you draw a comparison between the anti-Bishop film and a pro-Bishop book and suggest that if I have trouble accepting the former, I should have trouble as well accepting the latter.

With respect, a book about Bishop's exploits, and particularly the VC raid, would be a reflection of the historical version. On the other hand, the NFB film *challenges* that version; therefore, the *onus is on the challenger*!!

May I deal, next, with some of the specifics. Agreed, there is conflicting testimony about the state of Bishop's plane when it returned from the raid. With respect, Willie Frye's opinion (expressed many years after the event) was not at oods with Bishop's version. (He never gave one!)

It was Jack Scott, the Squadron Commander, who described Bishop's plane as being full of holes. This was the subject of reconfirmation by Grid Caldwell, who replaced Jack Scott, and who was required to give a follow-up report.

We now have new documentary evidence from the Squadron Sergeant Major, who has given a vivid description which indicates there were many bullet holes in the plane.

Next, let us deal with Joe Warne's observation that Bishop's plane did not carry enough fuel to make the raid. Assuming the raid was on an airport in the Cambrai area, the Nieuport Scout, with an average speed of about ninety miles an hour, could have made the round trip of eighty-one miles with fuel to spare. I believe I know why both Warne and Ed Ferko's calculations are wrong. We have the specifications. The Nieuport Scout had a flight endurance of two and a half hours. The Nieuport 17's fuel was enough for only two hours and some of the Spads were one and a half hours.

When the time comes, I will have an opportunity of making public the documentation. I doubt very much whether either Joe Warne or Ed Ferko will be able to argue with the logistics.

You refer next to Billy Bishop's character. To do what he and others did, particularly early in 1917 in those fighter aircraft, day after day, takes character. And not the kind of character who would falsify a raid. You will recall Cecil Knight's remark when it was suggested to him that Bishop had been falsifying his claims. The grand old gentleman replied: "Not in the character of Bishop as I knew him."

Next you mentioned there was no confirmation for some of the other "kills" of Bishop. I realize, of course, that you are at somewhat of a disadvantage here. I have been reading of the "Knights of the Air" since the Thirties. Also, I have watched with fascination as the amateur air historians have had their fun.

There's an old, old story with some of us and we are very much aware that, particularly with the aces in the RFC in the early days, who were carrying the fight across the enemy lines, confirmation of "kills" was very difficult. I have some graphic illustrations of dog fights involving eight and nine aircraft. Most times, it was a real question to determine who shot who.

Naturally, those of us who have a historical interest in aerial warfare from World War I must necessarily have to admit that not all claims could be certified beyond all reasonable doubt. This applied equally to Albert Ball, Mick Mannock, The Red Baron, Nungesser, Guynemer and Bishop.

Do not be swayed too much, however, by the suggestion from Raymond Collishaw that Bishop's combat reports often did not specify the type of plane, but merely said "Hostile Aircraft." Firstly, this was the modus operandi in many of the RFC Squadrons over Flanders in 1917. Secondly, Collishaw may have had something else in mind. More on this later.

I was surprised to see your summation of Jack Scott, suggesting that he was able to support Bishop because he wanted to "shut out any troublesome ideas to the contrary...." I happen to know quite a bit about Jack Scott.

He was a very prominent barrister from an excellent family in the old British tradition. Not the type who would falsify claims, for *any reason*. Have you seen *his* book by the way, written in 1919 just a year or so before he died? I have a copy among my prize possessions. It is called *Sixty Squadron!* He was the type of man who exuded trustworthiness and respect.

I certainly was astonished to see that you felt Colonel Bauer's motives had some relationship to his job as Chairman of the Billy Bishop Foundation. It is not a job with him; it is a hobby. His zeal for the Billy Bishop cause, comes specifically out of his unshakeable and justifiable belief in the man.

In the next part of your letter you asked for evidence that the raid took place. I am sure you will be impressed when you see the amount of evidence we have been able to assemble, both from files in England, from leading articles in the U.K. and U.S. publications which dealt with World War I flyers. The material looks to me like some rather strong rebuttal of the Cowan thesis. Much of the evidence is circumstantial—but not all.

You refer next to "the Billy Bishop who started writing his memoirs while he was on his honeymoon." I have no crystal ball and I doubt that you do. Supposing, for example, that Margaret Burden urged him to do so, knowing he was going back to fight again?

You make further reference to the Billy Bishop who was famous for falling down drunk at the Sheraton Mount Royal and the Ritz-Carleton Hotel! I would not dignify that comment with an answer, except to say that, if I had undergone the same war experiences as he did, perhaps twenty years later—? But then, as you stated in your first letter, I "must have had part of my brains amputated"—so I would have another excuse.

Your obnoxious diatribe about Billy Bishop and the rather vivid "hotel lobby" scenes you describe was the giveaway. When I saw this I became somewhat suspicious. Up to that time, I thought I was corresponding with a member of the public who was exercising her right to criticize the stand being taken by my organization.

I have been gathering research material on Billy Bishop for some little time and when I went to the computer with the name MALLOCH I came up in the media file with a letter to the Editor of *Maclean's*. I did a little more digging and there it was. You were corresponding with me from 73 Somerville Avenue, the same address as I got from the Montreal telephone book for Paul Cowan. In case you had forgotten the *Maclean's* letter, it is appended herewith.

Naturally, this terminates the correspondence. Somehow I get the feeling that I have been "had" and I cannot for the life of me understand why you did not disclose the relationship with Paul Cowan, if in fact one exists.

Kind regards.

Yours sincerely,

H. Clifford Chadderton

Maclean's Magazine, December 16, 1985

Billy Bishop may have been awarded the Victoria Cross for his purported Estourmel raid, but none of his defenders has been able to produce any proof that the raid actually took place. *The Kid Who Couldn't Miss* does not deny that Billy Bishop was a man of courage. The film is about our need for heroes and our over-eager tendency to create them. It simply states that there *are* doubts as to whether or not the Estourmel raid ever took place. That statement may not please veterans or senators, but that does not give those people the right to withdraw the film.

—KATIE MALLOCH,
Montreal

Part IV
Research Documents

WINGED WARFARE

BY
LT. COL. WILLIAM A. <u>BISHOP</u>, v.c., d.s.o., m.c.
ROYAL FLYING CORPS

EDITED BY
STANLEY M. ULANOFF
LT. COL., USAR

Air Combat Classics

DOUBLEDAY & COMPANY, INC.
GARDEN CITY, NEW YORK
1967

BOOKS WRITTEN OR EDITED
BY STANLEY M. ULANOFF

ILLUSTRATED GUIDE TO U.S. MISSILES AND ROCKETS

FIGHTER PILOT

MATS—THE STORY OF THE MILITARY AIR TRANSPORT SERVICE

AIR COMBAT CLASSICS

WINGED WARFARE
by Lt. Col. William A. Bishop

ACE OF ACES
by Capt. René Fonck

FIGHTING AIRMAN—THE WAY OF THE EAGLE
by Major Charles J. Biddle

INTRODUCTION

In writing this introduction to Billy Bishop's classic *Winged Warfare* I feel very much like the toastmaster introducing the great man for whom no introduction is really necessary. I wasn't born until four years after the close of the First World War (in which my father also participated as a second lieutenant with General Pershing's American Expeditionary Force in France), but Billy Bishop, along with my dad, were my boyhood heroes. His exploits and aerial duels above the clouds fired my imagination.

Oh yes, Billy Bishop had some of the human frailties, but nevertheless he was a great man. To me, he was a knight in shining armor who sallied forth daily to perform feats of valor and do battle with the enemy. Together with René Fonck, Jim McCudden, Eddie Rickenbacker, and the other white knights of King Arthur's Round Table, Bishop defeated the black knights led by Manfred von Richthofen, Ernst Udet, Werner Voss, and Hermann Goering (the last of whom went on to become, by far, the blackest knight of them all).

What sort of fellow was my "white knight"? What was his background?

Though a Canadian, Billy Bishop's boyhood was very much like that of any American boy who grew up in the Midwest or plains states during the same period. The similarity between that area and the middle Canadian provinces is remarkably close. Like any youth of high spirit and with a good sense of humor young Billy got into his share of troubles. As a cadet in the Royal Military College he ran afoul of authority there. But the war was on and he received the King's Commission as a Cavalry officer.

Once in France, Lieutenant Bishop found that he didn't care too much for life in the cavalry. He looked to the sky and was inspired by the thought of flight in the clean free air. Before not too long Bishop's transfer came through to the Royal Flying Corps (RFC). Unfortunately, his training gave little indication or promise of his future formidable ability as a fighter pilot. In fact he succeeded in demolishing a couple of British aircraft rather than German ones, and was about to be "washed out" as a flyer. As always, however, the customary Bishop luck prevailed. The RFC sorely needed pilots and the colonel gave him one more chance. Needless to say, Bishop made it.

His dash and daring gave the Allies one of their top fighter aces who participated in more than 170 air battles and emerged with seventy-two confirmed victories to his credit.

His career did not end here, however. Billy Bishop served his country again in World War II as Marshal of the Royal Canadian Air Force (RCAF), and his son fought as a fighter pilot in one of its squadrons.

Billy Bishop is an all-time great, one of that fabulous contingent of First World War Canadian aces that included his close friend and postwar business partner, Billy

Barker; Ray Collishaw, leader of the famed Naval Black Flight; and Roy Brown, credited with shooting down the Red Baron von Richthofen.

Such were the exploits that fired my childish flights of fancy. And they were encouraged by such pulp paper magazines as *Sky Birds, Flying Aces, War Birds,* and *G-2 Battle Aces.* They were enhanced even more by such dramatic motion picture classics as *Hell's Angels* and *Dawn Patrol.* My appetite was further whetted by trading cards—the same kind that kids collect today. They came with a pack of gum and had pictures of the World War I aces and their aircraft, instead of baseball players. We used to toss for them and swap them.

"Hey, I'll give you a Rickenbacker and a Fokker D-VII for a Bishop!"

Let's face it, by the end of World War I the Spad XIII flew at a top speed of 120 miles per hour in level flight. Other Allied and opposing German aircraft flew at comparable speeds or had other advantages of maneuverability to make up for their speed deficiency. When facing each other in combat an SE-5 could dive from out of the sun on to the tail of his Albatross adversary and if he didn't succeed in downing him on that pass could climb again and hit him from below. And the battle would continue in an ever-tightening circle, with each one trying to get on to the tail of the other maneuvering to "draw a bead on him," or loop up and over to get behind his opponent. They faked stalls and simulated spirals, as though crashing to earth, to shake a persistent foe.

These fabulous early fighter planes moved at a speed that enabled them to stick with a protagonist and continue the battle until one was shot down or broke off contact and lit for home.

The World War II Thunderbolts, Spitfires, and Mustangs tore at the Me 109s and Focke Wulf 190s at speeds approaching 400 mph. Their ability to remain with an adversary in a "dog fight" was severely limited by the excessive speed of the aircraft. Such maneuvering became impossible in the first jet war—in the skies over Korea where F-86 Sabrejets and Mig 15s tangled, attaining speeds of 600 mph in level flight where a single pass took the planes miles apart.

Any personal relationship between opposing fliers that might have existed in World War I was lost forever. No longer would a fighter pilot fly over the enemy's aerodrome and drop a note challenging him to an aerial duel. Nor would the victor in battle fly over the lines to drop flowers as a salute to his fallen foe.

Those days of gallantry in battle and high adventure come alive again in Billy Bishop's *Winged Warfare*. Here, in his own colorful words, is the exciting firsthand account of the British Empire's great fighter ace of the First World War.

STANLEY M. ULANOFF

Early Encounters

The weather cleared late in the afternoon of the 5th, and for the first time in my flying career I had the privilege of going out alone in search of a fight. There was not an enemy machine in the air, however, and I returned with nothing to report.

Next morning, bright and early, I was again out "on my own" in search of adventure. I had been flying over the lines for over half an hour when suddenly I spied an enemy machine about a mile over in Hunland, and some distance above me. In these days I no longer had any misgivings as to whether a machine was friend or foe—I had learned to sense the enemy. Our greatest difficulty at the time was drawing the Huns into a close combat. I set out to see what sort of fighting material this particular pilot of the Iron Crosses was made of. Keeping him always within view, I climbed to nearly 15,000 feet, and from that point of vantage dived upon him. I waited until my plunge had carried me to within 150 yards of him before opening fire. I had gotten in a burst of probably twenty rounds, when my gun jammed. The Hun saw me and dived away as fast as he could go. I dived after him, tinkering with the gun all the time, and, finally getting it clear, fired another burst at 100 yards. This drove him into a still deeper dive, but he flattened out again, and this time I gave him a burst at 50 yards. His machine evidently was damaged by my fire, for he now dived vertically toward the ground, keeping control, however, and landing safely in a field.

This fight gave me a new resolve—to devote more time to target practice. I should have destroyed this Hun, but poor shooting had enabled him to escape. Going home, I spent an hour that day practising at a square target on the ground. Thereafter I gave as much time as possible to shooting practice, and to the accuracy I acquired in this way I feel I owe most of my successes. Aeroplane target practice is not without its dangers. The target on the ground is just about the size of the vital spots you aim at in fighting. You have to dive steeply at this, and there is a very little margin of safety when plunging at full speed to within a few feet of the earth.

The Richthofen Flying Circus

One of the distinguished German flying squadrons opposite us was under command of the famous Captain Baron von Richthofen. One day I had the distinction of engaging in three fights in half an hour with pilots from this squadron. Their machines were painted a brilliant scarlet from nose to tail — immense red birds, they were, with the graceful wings of their type, Albatross scouts. They were all single-seaters, and were flown by pilots of undeniable skill. There was quite a little spirit of sportsmanship in this squadron, too. The red German machines had two machine guns in fixed positions firing straight ahead, both being operated from the same control.

The first of my three fights with these newcomers in our midst occurred when I suddenly found myself mixed up with two of them. Evidently they were not very anxious for a fight at the moment, for, after a few minutes of manoeuvering, both broke it off and dived away. Ten minutes later I encountered one of the red machines flying alone. I challenged him, but he wouldn't stay at all. On the contrary, he made off as fast as he could go. On my return from chasing him I met a second pair of red Huns. I had picked up company with another British machine, and the two Huns, seeing us, dived into a cloud to escape.

The Aerodrome Raid

MY RECORD of machines brought down was now in the vicinity of twenty, and I saw I had a rare chance of really getting a lot before going on my next leave—at the end of my second three months at the front.

With this object in view I planned an expedition into the enemy country, to attack an enemy aerodrome. I had carefully thought it out, and came to the conclusion that if one could get to an aerodrome when there were some machines on the ground and none in the air, it would be an easy matter to shoot them down the moment they would attempt to come up. It would be necessary for them to take off straight into the wind, if there was a strong wind at all, so I could not be surprised that way, and would be able to hit them if I came low enough, before they would get a chance to manœuvre or turn out of my way.

I planned this expedition after much thought, and set it for June 2nd, as that was to be my day off. Dawn was the hour I considered advisable, as there would be very few machines in the air, and I would have a great chance of evading trouble on the way to the aerodrome. I spent my spare moments, the next few days, arranging the details.

Now came the day planned for my expedition. I wrote my name on the blackboard, the night before, to be called at 3 o'clock, and sat down for the last time to consider exactly if the job was worth the risk. However, as nothing like it had been done before, I knew that I would strike the Huns by surprise, and, considering that, I decided the risk was not nearly so great as it seemed, and that I might be able to get four or five more machines to my credit, in one great swoop.

At 3 o'clock I was called and got up. It was pitch-black. I dressed, and went in to tell two of my friends that I was off. They were not entirely in favour of the expedition, and said so again. Notwithstanding this, I went on to the aerodrome, and got away just as the first streaks of dawn were showing in the upper sky.

I flew straight across the lines, toward the aerodrome I had planned to attack, and coming down low, decided to carry out my plan and stir them up with a burst of machine-gun fire into their hangar sheds. But, on reaching the place, I saw there was nothing on the ground. Everyone must have been either dead asleep or else the station was absolutely deserted. Greatly disappointed, I decided I would try the same stunt some other day on another aerodrome, which I would have to select.

In the meantime, for something to do, I flew along low over the country, in the hope of coming on some camp or group of troops so as to scatter them. I felt that the danger was nil, as most of the crews of the guns which ordinarily would fire at me would still be asleep, and I might as well give any Huns I could find a good fright. I was in rather a bad temper at having my carefully laid plan fall through so quickly, and nothing would have pleased me better than to have run across a group of fat Huns drilling in a field, or something of that sort. However, nothing appeared, and I was just thinking of turning and going home, or of climbing up to see if there were some Huns in the upper sky, when ahead, and slightly to one side of me, I saw the sheds of another aerodrome. I at once decided that here was my chance, although it was not a very favourable one, as the aerodrome was pretty far back from the lines. To make good my escape from this place would not be as easy as I had hoped. Furthermore, I was not even certain where I was, and that was my greatest worry, as I was a bit afraid that if I had any bad fights I might have trouble in finding my way back. Scurrying along close to the ground, zigzagging here and there, one's sense of direction becomes slightly vague.

Another half-minute and I was over the aerodrome, about 300 feet up. On the ground were seven German machines, and in my first glance I saw that some of them actually had their engines running. Mechanics were standing about in groups. Then I saw a thing which surprised me very much—six of the machines were single-seaters, and one a two-seater. I was not very anxious for the two-seater to come up to attack me, as in taking off he would have a certain amount of protection from behind, with his observer, while the single-seater could have none. However, in this, luck also favoured me, as the two-seater did not move at all.

I pointed my nose toward the ground, and opened fire with my gun, scattering the bullets all around the machines, and coming down to 50 feet in doing so. I do not know how many men I hit, or what damage was done, except that one man, at least, fell, and several others ran to pick him up. Then, clearing off to one side, I watched the fun. I had forgotten by this time that they would, of course, have machine guns on the aerodrome, and as I was laughing to myself, as they tore around in every direction on the ground, like people going mad or rabbits scurrying about, I heard the old familiar rattle of the quick-firers on me. I did not dare go too far away, however, as then I would not be able to catch the machines as they left the ground, so turning quickly and twisting about, I did my best to evade the fire from the ground. Looking at my planes, I saw that the guns were doing pretty good shooting. There were several holes in them already, and this made me turn and twist all the more. Then one machine suddenly began to "taxi" off down the aerodrome. It increased its speed quickly, and I immediately tore down after it. I managed to get close on its tail, when it was just above the ground, and opened fire from dead behind it. There was no chance of missing, and I was as cool as could be. Just fifteen rounds, and it side-slipped to one side, then crashed on the aerodrome underneath. I was now keyed up to the fight, and turning quickly, saw another machine just off the ground. Taking careful aim at it, I fired from longer range than before, as I did not want to waste the time of going up close. For one awful moment I saw my bullets missing, and aimed still more carefully, all the time striving to get nearer. The Hun saw I was catching him up, and pushed his nose down; then, gazing over his shoulder at the moment I was firing at him, he crashed into some trees near the aerodrome. I think I hit him just before he came to the trees, as my tracers were then going in an accurate line.

I again turned toward the aerodrome. This time my heart sank, because two machines were taking off at the same time, and in slightly different directions. It was the one thing I had dreaded. There was not much wind, and it was possible for them to do this. I had make up my mind, before, that if they attempted to do this I would immediately make good my escape, but I had counted on being higher. However, true to my intention, I began to climb. One of the enemy machines luckily climbed away at some distance, while the other made up straight after me. At 1000 feet, and only a few hundred yards from the aerodrome, I saw that he was catching me, so turned on him and opened fire. We made about two circuits around each other, neither getting a very good shot, but in the end I managed to get in a short burst of fire, and his machine went crashing to the ground, where it lay in a field, a few hundred yards from the aerodrome.

The fourth machine then came up, and I opened fire on him. I was now greatly worried as to how I was to get away, as I was using up all my ammunition, and there seemed to be no end to the number of machines coming up. I was afraid that other machines from other aerodromes would also come in answer to telephone calls, and wanted to get away as quickly as I could. But there was no chance of running from this man—he had me cold—so I turned at him savagely, and, in the course of a short fight, emptied the whole of my last drum at him. Luckily, at the moment I finished my ammunition, he also seemed to have had enough of it, as he turned and flew away. I seized my opportunity, climbed again, and started for home.

To my dismay I discovered four enemy scouts above me. I was terrified that they would see me, so flew directly underneath them, for some time—almost a mile, I should think—going directly south. Then, deciding that I must do something, I took the bit in my teeth and slipped away. They did not attempt to attack me at all, so I am not sure whether they even saw me or not.

I now headed in the approximate direction of our lines, and flew in rather a dazed state toward them. I had not had any breakfast, and was feeling very queer at my stomach. The excitement, and the reaction afterward, had been a bit too much, as well as the cold morning air. It seemed, once or twice, that my head was going around and around, and that something must happen. For the only time in my life it entered my thoughts that I might lose my senses in a moment, and go insane. It was a horrible feeling, and I also had the terrible sensation that I would suffer from nausea any minute. I was not at all sure where I was, and furthermore did not care. The thrills and exultation I had at first felt had all died away, and nothing seemed to matter but this awful feeling of dizziness and the desire to get home and on the ground.

By the time I reached the aerodrome, however, I felt much better, and flew over our still sleeping huts, firing off my signal lights frantically, to show them I had certainly had some success. I landed, and my sergeant immediately rushed out and asked me how many I had bagged. When I told him three, he was greatly pleased, and yelled it back to the mechanics who were waiting by the shed. Then, as I crawled out of my machine, I heard the remarks of the mechanics around me. They were looking it over. Everywhere it was shot about, bullet-holes being in almost every part of it, although none, luckily, within 2 feet of where I sat. Parts of the machine were so badly damaged as to take a lot of repairing; but I used the same patched planes in the machine for some time afterward, and always felt great affection for it for pulling me through such a successful enterprise. I personally congratulated the man who had charge of my gun, suddenly realizing that if it had jammed at a critical moment what a tight corner I would have been in.

Within three or four hours I had received many congratulations upon this stunt, and what I had planned as merely a way of shooting down some more of the Huns I found the authorities considered a very successful expedition. It pleased me very much—and, of course, I have always kept the telegrams of congratulations which I received that day. At first I had been disappointed in the net result, for when I started out I had rather hoped they would all take off as the first machine did, and that I would be able to bag, at the very least, four. But, on looking back at it, I think I was overoptimistic, and was very lucky to have brought down as many as I did.

That afternoon I was still suffering from the excitement of the morning and, although tired out, could not sleep, so with one other man I climbed in my machine and flew about fifty miles south, to pay a visit to another of our aerodromes there. We left to return about 5 o'clock and had more excitement, as a rainstorm was coming up, and for the last ten minutes had to plough through a drizzle. It was pretty dreary work, and I was very glad to see the aerodrome again. An hour later I was sound asleep in my bed, and did not awaken until the next morning.

Excerpts from
Canadian Airmen and the First World War, S.F. Wise

It was during this dark period, one of the most critical that the RFC was to undergo during the war, that W.A. 'Billy' Bishop emerged as 60 Squadron's foremost fighter pilot, beginning a career that was to make him one of the most famous airmen of his generation. Of that extraordinary group of Canadian fighter pilots of the First World War—Collishaw, Bishop, MacLaren, Barker, McKeever, Claxton, to name the most prominent—it was Bishop more than any other who caught the public eye. More has been written of him than of any other airman in Canada's history. A decidedly erratic RMC cadet, he left the college to join the Canadian Mounted Rifles. In September of that year, when his unit crossed to France, Bishop was left behind; he had transferred to the RFC, where he was training with 21 Squadron as an observer. After a brief period on the Western Front with that squadron in early 1916 he underwent pilot training in England. In March 1917 he reported to 60 Squadron at Izel-le-Hameau. By that time, according to his logbook, he had a total of seventy-five hours, and experience on BE2s, BE12s, Avro 504s, and Sopwith Pups.

No. 60 Squadron, however, flew Nieuports, and Bishop, a better fighter than he was a pilot, had trouble adjusting to this sensitive aircraft. On 11 March he began practice flying; over the next two weeks he and the ground-crew endured burst tires, strained airframes, and at least one crash-landing. A less discerning squadron commander might well have returned Bishop to the pilot's pool before he had had an opportunity to show what he could do. But Major A.J.L. Scott, one of the RFC's most perceptive leaders, recognized that the ham-fisted young Canadian flew with the calculating aggressiveness that marked the great fighter pilots. After five hours of practice flying in France, he flew his first operational patrol on 17 March. On 25 March he shot down his first enemy aircraft, an Albatros, while flying as rear man in a formation of four Nieuports. The combat began at 9000 feet near Arras and demonstrated that, whatever Bishop's weaknesses as a pilot, he was a first-class shot with the true killer instinct:

While on D(efensive) P(atrol) 3 Albatros Scouts approached us. One, separating from the rest, lost height and attempted to come up behind our second to the rear machine. I dived and fired about 12 to 15 rounds. Tracers went all around his machine. He dived steeply for about 600 ft. and flattened out. I followed him and opened fire from 40 to 50 yards range. A group of tracers went into the fuselage and centre section, one being seen to enter immediately behind the pilot's seat and one seemed to hit the pilot himself. The machine then fell out of control in a spinning nose dive. I dived after him, firing. I reached 1500 or 2000 ft. My engine had oiled up and I glided just over the line... The Albatros Scout when last seen by me was going vertically downwards at a height of 500 to 600 ft....

On 30 March Scott demonstrated his prescience by sending the still inexperienced Bishop out as the leader of a five-man offensive patrol. Within a month of his first operational flight Bishop had become the squadron's 'ace,' and Scott was permitting him to fly roving missions by himself in addition to his normal patrol duties. Like all the great air fighters, Bishop was an expert deflection shot, a skill he maintained by constant practice. His tactics, a subject to which he gave much thought, were built around surprise, which he regarded as the essence of air fighting. In part, his methods were forced upon him because the Nieuport was much slower than the best German fighters; even so, his combat reports from this period show that, once surprise was lost, he was usually willing to break off combat. When that was not possible, his heavy-handedness became a positive advantage in the rough-and-tumble of air combat. He threw the little Nieuport about with complete abandon and a rare tactical sense.

Joined to his skill and drive was a relentless courage that impelled him constantly to seek combat. On 30 April, for example, in a space of two hours before noon, he reported eight distinct combats against a total of nineteen aircraft. As Scott noted at the bottom of his report: "Comment, I think, is unnecessary."

Although Messines was the main centre of air action in the latter part of May and early June, the most publicized event in the air war was the strafing of a German airfield on the Arras front by W.A.Bishop on 2 June. His action brought him a Victoria Cross, the tenth to be won by an airman and the first by a Canadian flyer. The attack had its origin in Bishop's brief association with Captain Albert Ball, recognized at the time as the most outstanding airman in the RFC. During a visit to 60 Squadron on 5 May Ball had invited Bishop to join him in a surprise raid on a German aerodrome with the object of destroying aircraft on the ground. There were obvious hazards, but the aggressive young Briton felt that surprise, in as much as a low-level attack on an aerodrome had never been attempted and would not be expected, would enable them to turn the trick. A few days later, before anything definite had been organized, Ball was killed in action. But the idea kept churning in Bishop's mind.

By the end of May, with the Arras front relatively quiet, 60 Squadron was mainly occupied with answering compass calls. Bishop disliked this kind of work: there were frequent chases but few combats. Moreover, he found the sound of that 'damned Klaxon horn' used to alert the pilots was becoming 'hard on the nerves—and the legs.' It was in this mood that he determined to carry out the proposal which he and Ball had briefly discussed. He chose a free day, 2 June, for his self-assigned mission and took off before dawn in his Nieuport. At the aerodrome he attacked the Germans as they were getting ready for the day's work. Always a key factor in his tactics, surprise worked for Bishop here as it did on so many other occasions. His combat reports tells what happened during the few minutes he was over the enemy airfield:

I fired on 7 machines on the aerodrome, some of which had their engines running. One of them took off and I fired 15 rounds at him from close range 60 ft. up and he crashed. A second one taking off. I opened fire and fired 30 rounds at 150 yards range, he crashed into a tree. Two more were then taking off together. I climbed and engaged one at 1,000 ft., finishing my drum, and he crashed 300 yards from the aerodrome. I changed drums and climbed E(ast) a fourth H.A. came after me and I fired one whole drum into him. He flew away and I then flew 1,000 ft. under 4 scouts at 5,000 ft. for one mile and turned w. climbing. The aerodrome was armed with one or more machine guns. Machines on the ground were 6 scouts (Albatros Type I or II) and one two-seater.

A note appended to the combat report by the squadron commander observed that Bishop 'was several times at a height of 50 ft. over this enemy aerodrome at least 17 miles East of the lines. His machine is full of holes caused by machine gun fire from the ground.' A fellow pilot remembered 'clearly seeing a group of about five bullet holes in the rear half of his tailplane, the elevator, within a circle of not more than six inches diameter at the most. Whatever machine was on his tail must have been very close indeed to achieve that group.'

Although an isolated event and really an episode in the private war which Bishop, like many other fighter pilots, carried on against the German air force, the action did have a wider significance. As the most daring and successful low-level attack yet carried out, it provided an example which was repeated during the Battle of Messines and later. Thus, the orders issued to 9 (HQ) Wing for 7 June included specific reference to low-flying attacks on aerodromes of a kind which had not been attempted before Bishop's exploit. On the announcement of Bishop's having been awarded the Victoria Cross, more than two months later, General Trenchard removed him from operational flying. He was not to return to the Western Front until 1918, when he came back as a squadron commander. Until he left for England in August, however, Bishop continued to take a prominent part in the air war, which now centered upon a major British offensive in Flanders.

Cross & Cockade

THE SOCIETY OF WORLD WAR I AERO HISTORIANS

VOLUME 1   NUMBER 1   SPRING 1960

JOURNAL

Bitterness and hatred was not present in the Air Forces

CHIVALRY
IN THE
AIR

By

Lt.-Col. W. A. BISHOP, V.C., D.S.O., M.C., D.F.C.

CHIVALRY! Of course it existed! The bitterness and hatred between the armies and navies engaged in the war, as well as the intense feeling of the civilians, was not present in the Air Forces of the countries involved. In its place was a healthy respect for and interest in the opposing flying men.

This was of course due to several definite causes. Since the Wrights captured the air there has always been a great atmosphere of romance surrounding it. The war enhanced this. The flying men themselves felt the thrill of conquering a new element and their interest in the development of aviation was always at concert pitch. They like their work; they admired their comrades; and in fairness admired equally their foes. There were no sordid points of contact between the opposing pilots, such as surrounded the troops on the ground. They met in the cold clear air, highly trained, expensively equipped, in battles where their own skill and the quality of their equipment were the two vital factors in deciding their fate. It was a battle of skill and wits, free from animosity of any kind, a game more than a war; and of the hundreds of times I have seen pilots return to their aerodrome badly shot about—and so often having barely escaped with their lives—I have never heard remarks of any kind other than of great admiration for their opponents.

This feeling almost of friendship did exist, and on both sides of the lines. Of this I have ample proof. But to understand it, it is necessary to appreciate that we did—I am now speaking as a fighting pilot—truly regard our work as a game and not as war. Although we always aimed to kill the pilot, we did that as the surest way of destroying an enemy machine, and not with the thought of shooting a man. It was as impersonal as a hard-fought battle on the gridiron or in the boxing ring, and the Germans and Austrians had the same spirit.

From the beginning of air fighting, notes were dropped

Colonel Bishop was the victor of more than 100 sky combats, with an official record of 72 enemy planes destroyed. A native of Ontario, Canada, he is now engaged in banking and finance.

at great personal risk, telling the fate of members of opposing forces who had failed to return to their own lines, and in many cases these were accompanied by messages of admiration for the skill and bravery of the missing airman.

When Boelcke, the great German ace, who was Richthofen's leader and teacher, was killed in a collision, British machines flew over to Cambrai, where he was stationed, and dropped wreaths with notes attached, which read:

> To the memory of Captain Boelcke, our brave and chivalrous foe, from the British Flying Corps
>
> and
>
> To the officers of the German Flying Corps and Services at the front—
>
> We hope you will find this wreath but we are sorry it is so late in coming. The weather has prevented us from sending it earlier. We mourn with his relatives and friends—we all recognise his bravery. Please give our kind regards to Captain Evans and Lieutenant Long of the Morane Squadron.
>
> (signed)—J. Seeman Greene, Lieutenant.

Nor did this feeling exist only while in the air. On the ground when those rare occasions came for us to meet our opponents it was most marked. These opportunities only occurred of course when a prisoner was taken. In nearly all cases, except when they were wounded, we entertained these prisoners in our messes, and great care was taken that they were treated as gentlemen and guests, and not as prisoners. True, of course, that this pleasure was allowed us in the hopes that we could get information of a technical nature from them, but that was not our attitude when they arrived in our midst. The first move was to introduce them to the various officers; the second to offer them enough cigarettes and drinks to quiet their nerves and lessen the heartache of being captured.

In my own squadron, we have had on occasions

officers for several days before passing them on. Although I have seen them so nervous on arrival that in one case an officer jumped to his feet and saluted the mess waiter who was offering him a cocktail, usually at the end of an hour they were comparatively at ease. When the time came to part, they were always sent away properly supplied with clothing and such small comforts as we could give them to help in the dull prospect ahead of a long rest in a prison camp.

In many cases, prisoners on both sides of the lines were allowed to write notes or letters to their relatives or friends in their squadron telling that they were safe and well, or wounded, as the case might be, and these messages were dropped by their captors at some spot over the opposing lines where they were certain to reach their destination. Sometimes as well, messages would be dropped asking for special clothing or equipment which their prisoner did not have with him.

This was often necessary, as pilots were extremely careless about their dress when flying, and I recall that in the summer of 1917, when it was very hot, we in 60 Squadron used to do our dawn patrols in our pyjamas, with nothing over them but flying boots and flying coats. It is not hard, therefore, to picture the predicament in which a pilot found himself when captured by the enemy so inappropriately attired! It was a serious matter for him too, as it was necessary for him to be properly dressed, in order to prove his rank and receive the treatment due to it. I think that we on our side saw the humour of these situations much more than the Germans did, although they seemed equally willing to help out the unfortunate prisoner.

Here is a typical case in point. Early in 1918, Lieutenant Jerrard of 66 Squadron, operating in Italy over the Piave, was shot down in a tremendous fight near an Austrian aerodrome, during which he sacrificed himself to save some of the other members of his squadron. This was such a gallant show that he was awarded the Victoria Cross for it. When he landed on the ground, however, the Germans found him very improperly dressed for a long stay in a prison camp. For one thing, he was not wearing his Sam Browne belt, which to them was the main distinction between an officer and a private. It was therefore vital for him to get one, in order that he would go to an officers' and not to a privates' prison camp. With this in view, his captors flew back to a British aerodrome and dropped a note written in French explaining Lieutenant Jerrard's predicament, and also enclosing an uncensored note from him to his parents, which they asked the British Squadron to forward.

As soon as this note was received at his Squadron, two bundles of clothes were made up—including a Sam Browne belt, shoes, socks, cigarettes and everything that he might require. Aeroplanes then left carrying these bundles, and notes of condolence, which they dropped over the aerodrome where the fight had occurred. It is significant to point out that on the way from the British aerodrome to the German aerodrome these machines were under hot and intense fire from the Austrian anti-aircraft batteries and to note that from the moment they dropped the bundles and started their rush for home not a shot was fired at them, nor did any Austrian machine attempt to attack them. This instance, to my mind, is most conclusive proof that chivalry did exist between the Air Arms.

I have often heard it argued that no friendly spirit could possibly exist between the fighting air forces, when it is acknowledged that both sides have fired upon balloonists who were escaping from their balloons in parachutes. And my answer to this is, that the difference—although a very subtle one—was nevertheless quite distinct in our minds. The first time I heard of balloonists being shot at while descending in their parachutes was in the Spring of 1917 at the Battle of Vimy Ridge. On that day two Germans destroyed five of our balloons, and in several cases stayed to fire at the balloonists while they were parachuting to earth.

We had at this time received strict instructions that when attacking balloons we were to concentrate upon destroying the personnel, as this was more important than the balloon itself—the reason being that trained balloonists were much harder to replace than the balloon, a substitute for which could be in operation in a few hours. I consider, therefore, that those cases, where observers were fired upon while parachuting to earth, were simply operations of war carried out, in almost all instances, under specific orders. As regards parachute descents from

Colonel "Billy" Bishop, when he was a fighting pilot. The machine is a Nieuport.

aeroplanes, these were extremely rare during the war. I have never heard of a man escaping from an aeroplane in a parachute who was fired upon by an enemy machine, and I cannot conceive any pilot doing it.

In fights, machines have frequently been forced to land although they have not actually been shot down. The victor in these circumstances would always if possible fire at these machines upon the ground, in the hopes of completely destroying them, but it was seldom, if ever, that we would fire on the pilot if he was running away from his machine. I have never heard of this being done, but I have often heard of episodes where the escaping aviator had been waved to by his victor and left unharmed.

This business of waving to each other was not confined to episodes like the above, and has actually occurred many times in the air. A most interesting example of it was experienced by Major Maclaren, D.S.O., M.C., D.F.C., a Canadian ace who was accredited with forty-eight enemy machines destroyed.

One day, while flying over the German lines, he engaged an enemy two-seater, and after considerable manœuvring got himself within close range of the enemy machine, and in such a position that he could not be fired upon by the enemy observer. Taking aim, he pressed his triggers, but to his annoyance his guns refused to work.

Pulling out of the fight for a few minutes, he thought he had readjusted them, and after some more manœuvring placed himself in the same position as before. Again he pressed his triggers, but no shot came from his guns. Feeling his ammunition chutes, he discovered that both belts were broken. By this time he had lost his perfect position of being in his enemy's blind spot, but to his astonishment, he saw that the German was not firing at him. He flew closer, and almost alongside, and saw that the observer was standing with his machine gun pointing up into the air, away from him. Suddenly the observer waved to him, and moved his gun up and down, signalling that he had no more ammunition. Maclaren then flew in as close to him as he possibly could without colliding and waved back at him. The German pilot and the observer both returned the greeting, and they parted the best of friends.

Shortly before the Battle of Arras in 1917, there was operating in front of Monchy almost daily a German two-seater which always aroused our greatest admiration. On several occasions, when we got to close quarters, we noticed that the observer of this machine was so big that he could hardly fit into the cockpit. He was, however, very quick in moving about and a good shot, although his pilot was far from being a good pilot. We took such an interest in this huge fat German that he was affectionately nicknamed in our Squadron "The Flying Pig." After one fight in which he escaped by getting down too low to the ground for us to follow—but during which he had put up a very stout-hearted performance—we decided that so far as our Squadron was concerned, he had earned immunity, and we forbade any pilot to shoot to kill him. In other words, we began to look upon him as our own pet mascot. To our great

Colonel Bishop's opposite number. Perhaps the happiest photograph ever taken of Rittmeister Manfred von Richthofen.

horror, ten days later, however, a new young pilot, who had been informed of the story of the Flying Pig but who in his enthusiasm did not recognise him, attacked and shot him down. We held that night, in our Squadron Mess, a dinner in his honour, and drank his health in the same way as we would one of our own pilots.

There are instances and instances of things of this kind which were almost daily occurrences, and although they were frowned upon at Headquarters as not being in keeping with the general policy of conducting a war, in which bitterness and hatred seemed to be as necessary as machine guns and ammunition, this good feeling could not be quelled.

Two instances of people being really badly shot about and bearing no resentment come to my mind here. One is of Major Keith Caldwell, a New Zealander, and the other of myself. In both cases we had very narrow escapes but felt nothing but admiration for our opponents.

In Caldwell's case, I was standing on our aerodrome in France in May, 1917, when I saw him return from the front line, and very gingerly indeed—for him—land his little Nieuport fighter. He taxied slowly up to the hangar and I strolled over to ask him his luck ; before I reached him, however, he was out of his machine and striding away towards the officers' mess. I saw the flight Sergeant follow him, asking for instructions about his machine and I heard a very surly reply from Caldwell —" Burn the bloody thing "—as he continued walking away muttering to himself.

More than curious, I went to look at the machine and found it riddled with bullets. To my astonishment too, the bullets had all come from behind and had evidently in different groups pierced the machine on both sides of the pilot's seat, barely missing him. My surprise was great because " Grid," as we called him, was a wonderful pilot and an extremely courageous fighter.

Still more curious, I was about to follow him to the mess when a telephone message came through from a front line observation post telling of a great duel between a German and a Nieuport which had started at 12,000 feet and been fought all the way down to the ground. The German had the best of it all the way, and all the skill of Caldwell, which was perfect, could not shake the enemy off his tail.

So to the mess I went to hear more particulars. On the way several pilots met me and said, " Don't speak to Grid, he is in a terrific temper." I went up to him, and after three or four questions to which he didn't pay any attention, I said, " That must have been a great pilot you were fighting. How did it happen and who was it ? "

He looked up and grinned—" Hell's own fury in an Albatros Scout!" Here was no bitterness—just praise!

The other incident occurred to me in a fight with Richthofen—

Richthofen was, as I say, at his best at this time, and one afternoon, flying with my Squadron Commander, Major Scott, and seeing four German fighting machines, I led him in to attack them, arriving at approximately the same height at which they were flying. The next few minutes were almost the most hectic of my life, and gave me the biggest surprise I ever got. Three of the Germans cleared off to one side and the leader (Richthofen) took the two of us on. We at that time had both shot down a number of Germans . . . I think my score was around twenty and Major Scott's about twelve, and we were beginning to feel that we knew more about the game than anybody else, and therein lies the humour of this fight. . . . Richthofen promptly gave us the rudest shock we could possibly have had. His three friends stood off to one side in case one of us tried to get away. He at the beginning of the fight got almost on my tail—which is the ideal place to be—and the only way I could avoid being shot down was to turn immediately across him, giving him the most difficult shot in air-fighting, as I was flying directly across at right angles to him at roughly 100 miles an hour. He fired seven bullets in one burst, all of which ripped through the back of my seat and through the folds of my flying coat. The most beautiful shooting I have ever seen. This didn't make me feel any too happy, and, worse still, a few seconds later he had me in a position where the only thing I could do was to give him the same shot again. I suppose he had seen his tracer bullets going a matter of a few inches too far back, and this time allowed for more deflection and another burst of his bullets came right through, cutting my instrument board and instruments to pieces. He had in the meantime also considerably damaged Major Scott, and had shot through part of his engine, with the result that it was operating at reduced power, making it very difficult for him to fly. On the other hand, Richthofen was not having it all his own way; after that second burst I made up my mind that he was not going to get another crack at me, and I managed a few seconds later to get almost directly behind him, and I opened up with my gun as hard as I could. I thought I had shot him down, as he immediately dived straight towards the ground, and unquestionably I must have shot his

machine up very badly, as I was firing at him from less than 40 yards' range. However, our attention was taken by the three other Germans, who attacked immediately, and I do not know what the result would have been in the fight with them, because at that moment another flight of aeroplanes appeared a few thousand feet above, at which the Germans cleared off—and so did we!

We then recognised the flight above as being British and they escorted us home. The last stages of the fight took a few seconds only, and I looked down in the hopes of seeing Richthofen crash, only to see him about 4,000 feet below flatten out and fly towards his aerodrome. He had nearly finished my young life, but no thought other than admiration was in my mind as we flew home.

The burial of von Richthofen behind the British lines in 1918 was a just and fitting tribute to the wonderful career of that great German soldier. He was buried with the fullest of military honours, and not an aviator in the whole of our flying forces but felt a real pang of sorrow that such a great career should be ended—although it goes without saying that the fact that he had been eliminated from the German forces was to us all a tremendous relief. However (although he probably would not have wished it himself), it would have been to us much more satisfactory if he could have been captured and his life spared.

I have met since the war many pilots of the German Flying Corps and these meetings have confirmed my feeling of admiration for them and their good sportsmanship.

A few years ago I was entertained in Berlin by a large number of these German war pilots . . . men against whom my Squadron and I had frequently been engaged in mortal combat. Their reception of me is something which I shall never forget, and an experience which I shall always look back on with great pride and satisfaction.

At this luncheon we discussed in the frankest terms all the serious and amusing sides of our experiences. I had been told so often that these flying men—brave and fine fellows—were usually lacking in a real sense of humour, but I found the reverse to be the case. For instance, the first thing we did was to have a group photograph taken underneath a portrait of the Kaiser!

All round the room in which we were lunching were paintings and drawings of fights in the air, and when the time came for me to reply to their toast, I referred to these pictures. I pointed out that, interesting as they were, to me they did not seem to be technically correct. Many good pictures there were which I had seen of fighting in the air, but never like these, which all showed Allied machines being shot down by German pilots, and I told them that in so far as I knew such a thing had never occurred. They appreciated my point but disagreed with me.

Amongst the points on which I was curious and questioned them was by what nickname they referred to us. I explained that we always called them " Huns," it being the most objectionable-sounding name we could think of. Their answer was quick and to the point. They told me they had no special nickname for us, but merely called us, "Englishers," as they considered that bad enough!

This was the spirit in which we sat down together, and this was the spirit in which we fought our battles in the air.

Cross & Cockade Journal, Winter 1963

WHO IS THE BRITISH ACE OF ACES?

by

George Shiras

This controversial article will undoubtedly lead to further discussion in these pages, which it is hoped will lead to some eventual agreement concerning the top-ranking British ace. To add fuel to the fire, Russell Manning, a Northeast Chapter member, has submitted the following pertinent excerpt from the Encyclopedia Americana, Book 28, page 459:

"The above list of British Aces is incomplete. It is understood that the Official Air Records, while in transit from Field Headquarters in France to the office in London, was destroyed by enemy action at sea. Efforts to reconstruct the records from accounts of survivors, field reports, etc., will probably never adequately replace the records destroyed."

To most World War I historians it is no secret that the "official" victory scores of several of the war's most celebrated aces are inflated. For example: Arch Whitehouse, respected author, aero historian and World War I flyer, himself, has written in his book, "The Years of the Sky Kings":

"Even the British, who were most conservative in their claims, later admitted that several of their top-scoring aces had been credited erroneously with victories to which they were not entitled. I refer to the records of Ball and Mannock in particular........"

Yet, having made this admission, Whitehouse goes on in his book to credit Major Edward Mannock with 73 official victories, top score for British flyers. Today, Mannock is widely accepted as the British Ace of Aces, and of Allied flyers, second only to France's Rene Fonck, the Allied Ace of Aces with 75 official victories.

While correcting errors of the past may sometimes seem to diminish the reputations of brave men and shatter cherished myths, our reputation as a Society of World War I Aero Historians demands we follow where truth leads. Let us, therefore, squarely face the question, "Who is the British Ace of Aces, Mannock or some other pilot?"

Fortunately, Douglass Whetton, writing in the Summer 1961 issue of the Cross & Cockade Journal (page 99-102), has gone a long way toward setting the record straight. Though Whetton did not explain how he went about compiling Mannock's victory record (I assume, however, he went to squadron records), in his compilation Whetton arrived at a total count of 45 1/2 victories for Mannock. If correct, this would move Mannock down from the Number One spot on the British victory list, to Number 10 behind Captains Fullard and McElroy, who are each credited with 46 official victories in the Harleyford publication, "Air Aces of the 1914-1918 War".

Comparing Whetton's figures with those of Mr. J. M. Bruce who compiled the British section of the Harleyford book published in 1959, Bruce credits Mannock with 73 confirmed victories.

Mannock served with three British squadrons: Nos. 40, 74 and 85. It is instructive to compare Mannock's victories, squadron by squadron, as given by Whetton and Bruce:

Mannock's Victories Compiled by:

Squadron	Whetton	Bruce
40	7	23
74	32 1/2	36
85	6	(14)*
Total	45 1/2	73

* No total recorded for No. 85 Squadron,
but 14 needed to bring score to 73 victories.

The discrepancies are obvious. Unfortunately, neither Whetton nor Bruce explain how they arrived at their respective figures. Whetton, however, goes further than Bruce (in print, at least) and records Mannock's victories by date (and type of enemy plane where possible) for Nos. 74 and 85 Squadrons, but not for 40 Squadron. This does not mean that Whetton is right and Bruce wrong, but it does lend more weight to Whetton's figures.

Who is right? For better or worse, I would like to give my personal answer and then hurriedly ask interested readers to add what information they may have to the debate.

I believe Bruce, and the many others, who have accepted Mannock's record of 73 confirmed victories, may have been misled. The gentleman responsible for this error neither did it with malice, nor intent to deceit. He is the late Group Captain J. Ira ("Taffy") Jones, an outstanding World War I ace (44 victories), and devoted friend and admirer of Mannock. Jones not only flew with Mannock in 74 Squadron, but owed his life to Mannock's skill as a pilot. All of this Jones has faithfully recorded in several of his books.

With the publication of Jones' biography of Mannock ("King of the Air Fighters") in 1934, the world fully accepted Jones as Mannock's Boswell. Until Douglass Whetton went to the records, the world also accepted Jones claim of 73 official victories for Mannock.

How did Jones reach the magic figure of 73? I suggest he took Mannock's word for his total victories. Though there is no way of knowing whether Mannock was right or wrong about his own score, it still differs from what should be the official record. (If the same technique, for example, were applied to Rene Fonck, his total would be 127 victories, which he always claimed, instead of the officially confirmed 75.)

That "Taffy" Jones actually did accept Mannock's personal estimate of his own victories is strongly suggested by a statement made to Whetton by Group Captain Jones in an interview appearing in the same issue of the Cross & Cockade. Remarked Jones: "He left for a well-earned leave on June 19th (end of Mannock's services with 74 Squadron, before taking over command of 85 Squadron). According to his own reckoning, he had been victor in sixty-six combats."

If we add to this 66, the six victories that Whetton gives Mannock while with 85 Squadron, we arrive at 72 victories, only one tantalizing victory away from 73. Perhaps that last victory was the one that the New Zealander, Lieutenant Donald Inglis, gave to Mannock on that tragic day that he watched his Squadron Commander, and hero, fall victim to machine gun fire from the ground.

But returning to our main question: Who is the British Ace of Aces? Should the Cross & Cockade set the record right by recording that William Bishop, with 72 confirmed victories, is truly the British Ace of Aces ? ? ?

Cross & Cockade Journal, Winter 1973

Victory Lists of Leading Aces: A Study

By Edward L. Leiser

During the Great War one particular ace usually led all the others in total victories (were there any ties?) and they all stood in relative position to each other at any one time, changing from day to day as luck would have it. This article studies the high-scoring aces whose victory lists are available to the writer and provides a graphic presentation of their relative scores.

It was 1915 before aerial warfare took on individual aspects. French pilot Roland Garros armed his Morane airplane with a machine gun firing straight ahead through the propeller and in April his name thrice appeared in the *New York Times* signalling victorious combats, as a new type of scorekeeping began which kept the grim count of men and aircraft destroyed. About two and a half months after Garros' capture, German airmen Oswald Boelcke and Max Immelmann began scoring in Fokker *Eindeckers* with machine guns synchronized to fire between the propeller blades, a design inspired by the French innovation. Boelcke and Immelmann exchanged the lead seven times during the eight months before Immelmann's death in March 1916. Meanwhile French ace Georges Guynemer, who tied with Boelcke and Immelmann in July 1915, continued collecting victories as the leading Allied ace. A month before Boelcke's death in October 1916 the teenage Englishman, Albert Ball, passed Guynemer and Boelcke to become the leading ace for a few days. After Boelcke's death Ball retook the lead even as he fretted away his time in England, anxious to return to combat. Guynemer passed Ball in February 1917 and assumed the lead with his 32 victories. The nearest German high-scoring ace was Manfred von Richthofen who had recorded 21 officially confirmed victories at this date.

Von Richthofen swept through the Royal Flying Corps in the Spring of 1917. By the end of "Bloody April" he was the unquestioned leader with a score of 52 confirmed victories that made him the top-ranking ace of the war. Guynemer's efforts tapered off and Albert Ball passed the Frenchman in late April but he was second for only a week before entering the clouds over Annouelin, never to be seen alive again. Von Richthofen's rising total stood unsurpassed during the remainder of the war. Guynemer, still in second place, failed to return from an operational patrol in September 1917, like Ball and others too numerous to mention.

As Fate manipulated the Richthofen-Ball-Guynemer triumvirate, three more star-turns rose rapidly to the front ranks in the company of aces: Werner Voss, William A. Bishop and Raymond Collishaw. Collishaw's record shines the brightest; he earned it in a remarkable machine, the Sopwith Triplane. All three were nearly even during July 1917 until Collishaw took a rest. Bishop continued scoring almost one victory a day until he was ordered back to England in mid-August. Voss passed Bishop's 52 victories in September of that year. Pitting his skill alone against the S.E.5's of No. 56 Squadron RFC, Voss lost his life that month after achieving 53 confirmed victories.

Fall and Winter of 1917 passed as low-scoring periods for the leaders Richthofen, Bishop, and Collishaw, all on occasional duty away from the Front. During this period one veteran British pilot climbed to prominence, however: his name was James T. B. McCudden. After a four-month joust for position with the celebrated French ace René Fonck, McCudden shot down 35 enemy aircraft between September 1917 and February 1918 to become the leading Allied ace with 57 victories before returning to England. Von Richthofen's winning streak resumed in March 1918 as the last great German spring offensive began. The Red Baron averaged one aircraft downed every other day until his death on 21 April 1918. His final total read 80 victories.

With the death of Richthofen the new leading surviving ace was James McCudden who was home in England and was preparing to bring his squadron back into action on the Western Front. By now several other swift climbers began to assume prominent positions.

William A. "Billy" Bishop, the fast-rising early starter of 1917, had returned to the Front and he was as sharp a marksman as before. Another "newcomer" was Edward "Mick" Mannock, an old hand at combat and a slow starter. Being only a few days ahead of Bishop in the confirmed victories race, Mannock experienced a slow month in June when victories were elusive. During this same month of June 1918 Bishop had received firm orders to return to Canada where he was to assist in the founding of the proposed Royal Canadian Air Force, but before departure he managed to score five victories on his last day of action to pass Mannock in a rush. The following month, in July 1918, Mannock exceeded Bishop's final total of 72 victories; Mannock now had 73 victories. A few days later Mannock was shot down and killed; he was then the leading British ace of the war. McCudden's victory total rested at 57 as he, too, was dead -- the victim of a tragic air crash. Thus Bishop became the leading surviving ace of the war but he was to score no more as he was already en route to Canada.

American pilots never competed with the leading British, French or German aces; they simply weren't around long enough and had entered combat in April 1918. Edward V. Rickenbacker led the American scoreboard until illness grounded him during the Summer of 1918. Taking advantage of Rickenbacker's incapacity, both George Vaughn and Frank Luke passed Rickenbacker. The most aggressive of these two aces was Luke and he began a metoeric rise by scoring rapidly on balloons and quickly assumed the American lead which he held until his death in late September 1918 -- the same month month in which he scored his initial and final victories. Luke recorded all his victories within the short time span of seventeen days -- from 12-29 September 1918! Returning to action Rickenbacker took over the lead once more, continuing his successes until late October when he reached his 26th and final victory of the war.

Rising to challenge the leaders, four outstanding pilots steadily swelled their records through forty then fifty victories. René Fonck, a deadly marksman in an airplane and an excellent French pilot, had vied for the lead with Raymond Collishaw, an excellent British pilot in the Royal Naval Air Service. Two prominent German aces, Ernst Udet and Erich Löwenhardt, seemed to fight their own duel for the Fatherland's and the war's ranking as the top ace. Udet's score had risen slowly until Löwenhardt caught up with him in May 1918. This feat appeared to galvanize the easy-going Udet whose total then soared dramatically to the lead in June, only to drop back again in July 1918. Löwenhardt managed to stay ahead of Udet as their scores mingled with those of Fonck and Collishaw. A bizarre turn of events soon swung the pendulum in favor of Udet when another mid-air collision proved how great were the risks of aerial combat. On 10 August 1918 Löwenhardt's Fokker D.VII collided in mid-air with that of Alfred Wenz' over the Albert-Bapaume area. Both pilots parachuted towards safety but Löwenhardt's parachute failed to open. His war and his life ended that August day with 54 victories.

Udet continued scoring almost daily. Collishaw found fewer targets and recorded his 60th and last victory in September. Udet and Fonck tied for second place in September and while Udet found no more victims, Fonck continued to score into early November. He surpassed the absent Bishop and ended the war with 75 confirmed victories as the leading surviving ace of the war at the time of the Armistice.

The following graph proportions on the following page are based on the *JOURNAL* page dimensions with no intent to exaggerate or minimize the display.

The writer is grateful to Dick Layman for his editorship of the manuscript.

The sketch of *Rittmeister* Manfred *Freiherr* von Richthofen, the legendary "Red Baron" who emerged as the top-scoring ace of all nations during World War I, was provided by Wayne Douglas Barlowe of Massapequa, New York. Young Master Barlowe is a 15 year old "World War I aero enthusiast of many years" who has been a devoted member of *CROSS & COCKADE* for four years. Of special interest to be noted in Barlowe's art is the map of Corbie and vicinity over which the famed Fokker Dr.I is flying, the celebrated victory cups inscribed with the date of each victory and the type of aircraft downed, and the seldom-seen Richthofen baby portrait coupled with the *Pour le Merite* and a photo of Richthofen as a cavalry officer.

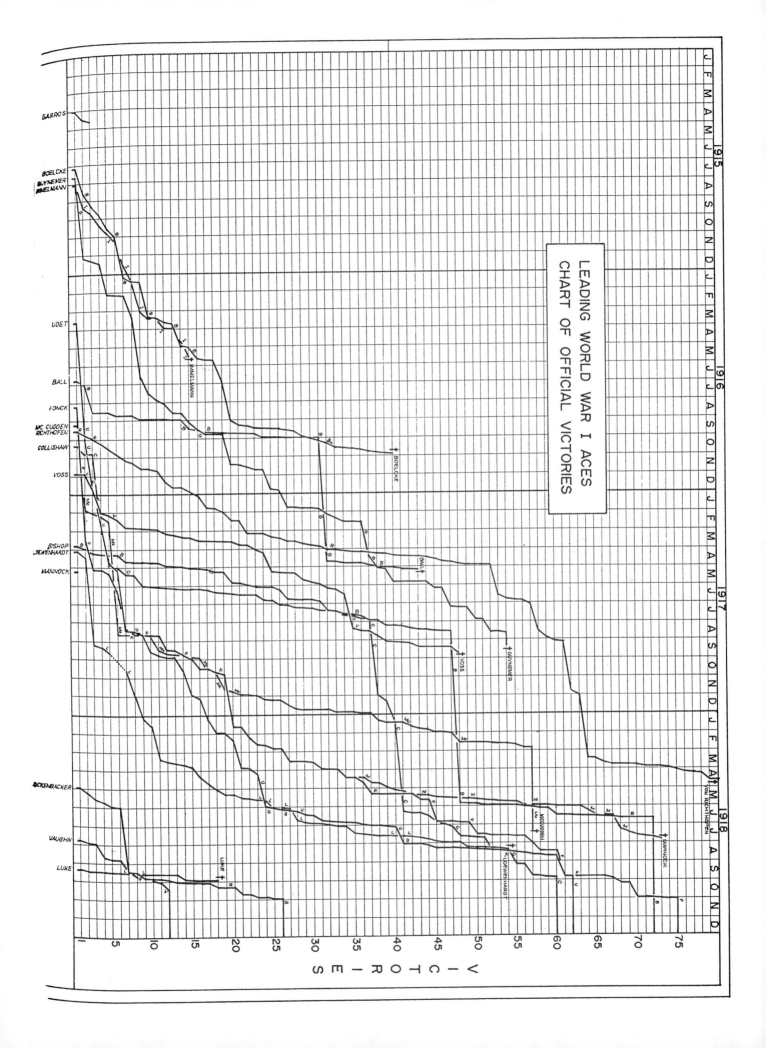

LEADING WORLD WAR I ACES
CHART OF OFFICIAL VICTORIES

THE TWO FACES OF CHIVALRY IN THE AIR WAR

by

GEORGE SHIRAS

Though the First World War is now fifty years old, the tradition of describing World War I flyers as Knights of the Air and their deeds as chivalrous endures today stronger than ever. Only last March the editors of Life magazine opened their essay on the war in the air with this sentence: "The fame and glory that are war's highest wages were paid in the First World War to a new kind of warrior, a gay, chivalric knight-errant--the fighter pilot."

Actually, the Life editors were only borrowing well-worn phrases first employed by journalists and popular writers who reported the war, phrases that wartime politicians were not above using themselves. Speaking before Parliment in 1917, Prime Minister Lloyd George thus eulogized flyers:

"They are the knighthood of this war, without fear, without reproach;
and they recall the legendary days of chivalry, not merely by the
daring of their exploits, but by the nobility of their spirit."

The tradition continued among popular writers after the war. Floyd Gibbons, in 1927, could write in his best seller, The Red Knight of Germany: "Into the grisly story of the World War, there came a refreshing gleam of the chivalry of old, when the pick of the flower of youth on both sides carried the conflict into the skies. Into that Knighthood of the Blue, Richthofen has been given a place of highest merit by those he fought with and against." Thirty years later, the well-known author, Quentin Reynolds, was still writing in the same vein. In his book, They Fought For The Sky, he could say, "But the unique developments...was the fact that the first war in the air unexpectedly returned the ancient concept of the duel to modern warfare, and along with it a code of conduct which had been considered obsolete for centuries." With such a descriptive pattern set so early, it is little wonder that the Life editors would almost automatically describe World War I flyers as chivalrous knights. Yet in returning to the records left by the flyers, themselves, their combat records, their diaries and reminiscences, two very different and distinct faces of the aerial war begin to emerge.

One face reflects kindness, decency and chivalrous behavior and is to the highest credit of the airmen. This code of conduct, however, revolves almost exclusively around non-combat activities. The other face of the air war concerns aerial combat, the actual fighting, and here the record is also clear. Combat was a ruthless, unchivalrous, dog-eat-dog affair in which no aviator expected mercy, and few ever received it from an opponent. These two faces of the aerial war, one chivalrous, reflecting all the fine things that have been said about the first air fighters; the other unchivalrous, reflecting all the ruthlessness of aerial combat as it was truly fought, are summed up in the destruction of Werner Voss, the fourth-ranking German ace, on September 23, 1917. Voss, out alone over the front, was caught by British ace, James McCudden and his flight of six S.E.5's. Skillfully the veteran British pilots boxed Voss in. There was no thought of surrounding him and allowing one of their number, perhaps McCudden, himself, to engage Voss in single combat, a classic duel to the death as knights of yore. Every member of the British flight began firing at Voss and McCudden recalled that at one point Voss was at the apex of a cone formed by the tracer bullets of five planes. Finally Lt. Rhys-Davids secured a favorable firing position above Voss and the German ace started the last, long fall. When the flight landed, Rhys-Davids was showered with congratulations. All he would say, however, was, "Oh, if I could only have brought him down alive." On October 3, a wire arrived from Wing announcing the award of decorations, including a D.S.O. to Rhys-Davids, and a celebration was planned for that evening. As the party heated up, McCudden began chanting for Rhys-Davids to speak. Quiet descended as the young Lieutenant spoke:

> "We are fighting against magnificent men of courage, and I'm
> going to ask you to do an unprecedented thing. I'm going to ask
> you to rise and drink a toast---Gentlemen, I drink to Manfred
> von Richthofen, our most worthy enemy."

It is recorded that everybody present, except for one non-flying officer, toasted von Richthofen.

The manner in which Voss was shot down was hardly chivalrous if the standard Webster dictionary meaning is applied--"valorous and generous to foes." Voss was out-numbered, ganged-up upon and didn't have a chance. In fact a careful reading of the combat report submitted by Rhys-Davids immediately following the fight strongly indicates that young Rhys-Davids, recently out of Eton and considered by his squadron mates the epitome of the true gentleman--kind, loyal, decent--had actually killed Voss as he was gliding helplessly, motor off, and probably badly wounded, toward the British lines. The report reads:

> "Eventually I got east, and slightly above the triplane, and made for it, and
> got in a whole Lewis drum and a corresponding number of Vickers into him.
> He made no attempt to turn until I was so close to him I was certain we
> would collide. He passed my right-hand wing by inches and went down. I
> zoomed. I saw him next with his engine apparently off, gliding west. I
> dived again and got one shot out of my Vickers. However, I re-loaded
> and kept in the dive. I got another good burst and the triplane did a slight
> right-hand turn, still going down. I had now over-shot him (this was at
> 1000 feet), zoomed and never saw him again....."

In the fever and excitement of battle, with all his animal instincts aroused, young Rhys-Davids turned into the cold-blooded killer that all successful pilots became in the air if they were to survive on the Western Front after 1915. On the other hand the non-combat behavior of Rhys-Davids after the fight in wishing he had brought Voss down alive was neither hypocritical nor unusual. In the air war it was kill or be killed or as the English ace, Albert Ball, wrote..."either them or me." But on the ground when the blood cooled, the great majority of young flyers on both sides felt a kinship with each other that came from sharing the same skills, experiences and a common danger in the new element of war---in the air.

The non-combat, chivalrous behavior of Rhys-Davids and the other members of 56 Squadron who toasted von Richthofen was not an isolated incident. Such behavior was standard throughout the war. Upon the death of Boelcke, Germany's great ace, British planes flew high over the German field at Cambrai and dropped wreaths to which were attached such messages as, "To the memory of Captain Boelcke, our brave and chivalrous foe. From the British Royal Flying Corps." Following Richthofen burial, the RAF dropped a note and a photograph of the flower-strewn grave to his German comrades. Richthofen, himself, had dropped a note to the British informing them of the death of British Squadron Commander, Major L.G. Hawker, Richthofen's 11th victim. The practice of keeping each other informed about down airmen was followed throughout the war. Edwin C. Parsons of Lafayette Escadrille fame remembers one list dropped by the Germans in 1918 that contained 37 names! Flyers even dropped clothes over the lines to make their comrades' stay in prison more comfortable. In contrast during the Second World War when the Nazis informed the British that they would honor a lone plane dropping a new artifical leg for Wing Commander

Douglas Bader, Britain's legendary legless ace, the RAF would have none of it. They dropped the leg during a regular combat mission.

It was also a regular custom for the squadron messes of both sides to entertain airmen before they went off to prisoner-of-war camps. The hosts went to great lengths not to embarrass a guest and to make him feel at home. Udet, Germany's second-ranking ace, tells of entertaining a British major brought down by Lothar von Richthofen:

"We discussed the Kiel Regatta, the Epsom Derby, horses, dogs,
and aeroplanes. The war was never mentioned. We had no wish
to make him feel that we were trying to 'pump' him for information."

When it was time to leave the mess, the captured pilot was often given clothing, cigars, cigarettes to take with him. James Norman Hall of the Lafayette Escadrille, shot down near a German field, left his gloves and helmet in a German dugout. Later a German pilot drove 35 kilometers to take them to the American in the hospital. Wounded pilots were often visited in the hospital by their victorious opponents. Boelcke and his fellow ace, Immelman, won the admiration of their foes for such behavior. Lt. L. C. F. Clutterbuck, shot down in his Bristol Fighter by Richthofen on 12 March 1918, recalled, "During my second day in the hospital, a German flying officer came in and said he had been sent by Baron von Richthofen who wished me to accept half a dozen cigars with his compliments. I did, with thanks."

It was from such true incidents as these that the great myth of chivalry in the air grew. The myth was born during the war. Reporters deliberately came to the squadrons seeking colorful, personal interest stories for in a static war dominated by a near-impregnable defense built on machine guns and barbed wire, there was little such "color" to be found with the ground forces. Some flyers took a dim view of reporters who worked the "Knights of the Air" angle. The story is told of one such correspondent who came to No. 74 Squadron, RAF, to interview the British ace, Edward (Mick) Mannock. The shrewd Irishman was soon enthusiastically telling the reporter about a German two-seater going down ablaze with the observer vainly attempting to beat out the fire with his bare hands. Later the reporter angrily tore up his notes. He told the C. O. of the squadron that Mannock was a "monster." But Mannock, in his own inimitable way, was only trying to tell the reporter the truth: that the war in the air was monsterous. Perhaps in the first year and a half of war, when the planes were mostly unarmed, and the pilots waved to each other as they went about their respective reconnaissance tasks, perhaps then the war in the air was chivalrous. Once the planes began carrying machine guns and flying in formation, and as the ace system developed, the air war on the Western Front became ruthless and unchivalrous.

Major Charles J. Biddle, who was later to command America's 13th Squadron, summed up combat tactics on the French front in a letter home dated 15 July 1917: "The flying is generally in groups of 4 or 5... The idea seems to be to try to find one machine by itself or to maneuver one of a group until it is out of touch with its fellows, and then the whole group jumps on the one unfortunate 'isole.' Hardly seems a square deal, but after all, the aim is to put as many of the other fellow's machines out of business as possible." Tactics were no different on the British front. Voss had been killed by this method. Flight and squadron leaders watched carefully for stragglers. Air Marshall Sholto Douglas looking back to the days when he was a young man and led the RAF's 84th Squadron recalls, "We always looked for the Hun that had become separated from his friends, and when we found him we wasted no time. We would pounce and give him two or three short bursts, and if one's shooting was up to scratch he would start the long fall to earth, sometimes on fire."

Another technique of achieving an almost certain kill was to shoot an opponent before he saw you--about as far from the chivalric concept of the duel as one can get. The attack out of the sun became a well-used tactic of successful pilots. Every Allied pilot was warned, "To beware the Hun in the sun." Surprise became a key to victory.

Biddle wrote, "The majority of successful combats are cases of surprise, where you sneak up close behind another machine without his seeing you or where he is busy attacking still another machine, and you can drop upon his rear unawares." James McCudden fattened his score on unsuspecting German observation planes who never dreamed an S.E.5 could climb to 20,000 feet. McCudden, a sensitive, intelligent human being, could never whitewash his occupation. In his book, Flying Fury, he describes himself and his fellow fighter pilots as "hired assassins." As for his successful technique, he wrote: "I hate to shoot a Hun down without him seeing me, for although this method is in accordance with my doctrine, it is against what little sporting instinct I have left." It may seem equally unsporting to shoot up planes whose propellors had stopped and that were trying to land, or unchivalrous to fire on planes and pilots that had been shot down and were on the ground. But both actions were common on the Western Front.

The development of the ace system was responsible for a good deal of such behavior. Young, highly competitive pilots, who measured their skill, or had their skill measured by the number of enemy planes they downed, often went out of their way to make sure of a kill. Add to this the fever of battle, the fear of death, the anger and hatred at seeing a friend shot down and there are ample enough reasons for the war in the sky quickly becoming just as brutal a battlefield as the Somme, the Marne, or Chateau Thierry.

Baron von Richthofen was particularly ruthless about finishing off motorless opponents attempting to land, usually miles behind the lines in Germany. The same sentence reoccurs time after time in his requests for acknowledgement of victories: "I followed the adversary to the ground." On April 2, 1917, Richthofen attacked a Sopwith 1 1/2 Strutter piloted by Lt. Warren, cutting Warren's cartridge belt, knocking his observer to the bottom of his cockpit and stopping the motor. Warren gamely tried to zoom away from his opponent, into a cloud, but his controls were shot away. "There was nothing to do but go down and hope to keep out of a spin as best I could," he writes. "I was busy with the useless controls all the time and going down at a frightful speed, but the red machine seemed to be able to keep itself poised just above me and behind me all the time, and its machine guns were working every minute...I managed to flatten out somehow in the landing." The following day, April 3, Richthofen first killed the observer of an F.E.2d. Then according to the pilot, Lt. McDonald, "It was a matter of seconds before some of the bullets got my engine...The Hun followed me right down to the ground, firing all the time, till he almost shot away every control I had." On 8 April 1917, requesting acknowledgement for his 38th victory, Richthofen again reports following his opponent to the ground. Lt. Heagerty, pilot of the Sopwith 1 1/2 Strutter, vividly recalls the fight: "My controls had been shot away. They must have gone in the same burst that killed Cantle. From a glide we went into a dive. All the way down, the red machine, or some machine, kept right in back of me, ripping burst after burst of machine gun bullets into the plane from the rear."

On 29 April 1917, the Baron, his brother, Lothar, and Wolff met three Spad VII's from 19 Squadron, RFC. Wrote Manfred: "My man was the first to fall. I suppose I smashed his engine. At any rate, he made up his mind to land. I no longer gave pardon to anyone. Therefore, I attacked him a second time, and the consequences were that his whole plane went to pieces." The desire for victory became so aroused in some pilots that they not only finished off cripples, but took rightful victories from their fellow pilots.

Paul Bäumer, a German 43-victory ace, has told of disabling an Allied plane. By hand signals he indicated that the pilot should land below in Germany. As the plane circled to land, another German machine streaked in and with one burst of fire, set the Allied plane afire. Bäumer was incensed at such tactics. Furthermore, the interloper received credit for the kill. In much the same manner, Theo Osterkamp, the leading German naval ace with 32 victories, destroyed a crippled plane being escorted down by another German pilot. Osterkamp also received the victory.

The Germans, of course, had no monopoly on eagerness to score. Captain Edward Rickenbacker tells how, having disabled the motor of a red-nosed Fokker D. VII, he was escorting it back to the Allied lines. The German had begun his landing pattern when suddenly a Spad dove down on the crippled Fokker, firing as it came. Rickenbacker drove the Spad off, but not before it had ruined the Fokker's dead stick landing. Instead of a museum piece, Rickenbacker had a completely wrecked plane.

Albert Ball possessed Richthofen's killer instinct and occasionally followed victims earthward, shooting them up. There were also unpleasant rumors, never substantiated, that some aces, including Mannock, loaded their cartridge belts with extra tracer bullets to better their chances of getting a sure kill, a flamer which was easy to see. Nor were pilots whose guns jammed shown mercy. "If the other fellow's guns jammed, you popped him off if you could," Edwin C. Parsons relates.

Perhaps even less chivalrous than making sure of helpless victims in the air was the practice of shooting up planes and pilots after they had crashed to earth. Sometimes such behavior appears to be sheer battle fever that temporarily possessed a pilot. For example, there is the story of Willi Gabriel and his frantic battle with nine Spads. Having shot one down, he was twisting and turning for his life when an Albatros came to his rescue. All but one of the Spads retreated. Gabriel got off a burst at his lone tormenter and the Spad immediately went down, landing near a German artillery battery. Wild with rage, Gabriel dove several times on the Spad. The pilot never climbed out and Willi turned for home, suddenly sick with shame. Sometimes shooting up a grounded opponent appears to be cruel, unthinking exuberance. "Taffy" Jones, who ended the war with 40 victories, reports in his wartime diary a fight on 19 June 1918. A flight from his squadron, plus part of an Australian squadron, caught two German pilots behind the Allied lines on a balloon strafe. One scampered away, but the other stayed to be engulfed by S.E. 5A's and Camels. In their eagerness to finish off the rash German, the Allied pilots were endangering each other and Jones wisely climbed above the engagements to watch the results:

> "At last a Camel--it turned out to be my pal, Cobby (the Australian ace of aces)--poured a torrent of bullets into the machine from 30 yards range. The Hun zoomed for the last time, turned on its back and spun down invertedly on to the trees of the Nieppe Forest, where it got jammed in the branches.

> "Then followed a sort of target practice. Machine after machine dived and gave a burst at it before zooming steeply upwards.... The body of the Hun pilot was placed in one of our hangars for the night. He must have been 'blotto.' He was dressed in pyjamas and a dinner jacket."

Lt. Sherry of the American 94th Squadron suffered a somewhat similar experience, but lived to tell about it. In late September of 1918, Sherry and Lt. Nott were attacked by eight Fokkers. Nott was killed and Sherry's motor shot out. Sherry glided down followed by four Fokkers with guns blazing. He crashed into No Man's Land and jumped from his plane into a shellhole. The Fokkers weren't through, however. They took turns diving on him and spraying the shellhole with bullets until they grew tired of the sport and flew home.

Both Ball and Mannock are known to have fired on downed pilots. On 21 September 1916 Ball attacked two Roland two-seaters. From 30 yards he got several drums into one and without waiting to see its fate attacked the second which, however, had not stayed in the fight, but cleared out. Ball then spotted his first victim on the ground and coming down to 500 feet put 100 rounds into the wreck--in his own words "to make sure of the passengers." Mannock's behavior, unlike Ball's, seems to have been inspired by simple hatred of the Hun. On 30 April 1918 he was flying with Lt. Dolan of his flight. Dolan crashed a two-seater inside the British lines. Mannock dove on the wreck a half dozen times spraying bullets at the pilot and observer. Back at the field, Mannock was called to account for his monstrous behavior. Replied Mannock, "The swines are better dead--no prisoners for me."

Downed pilots, however, were often shot at because they tried to destroy their planes. German pilots were under orders to prevent Allied pilots from burning their planes, even if it meant killing the pilot. On 30 June 1918, the third-ranking German ace, Erich Loewenhardt attacked a Spad forcing it to the ground. The pilot tried to set fire to his plane. Loewenhardt drove him away once by firing his guns, but when he returned again, Loewenhardt killed him. In turn many Allied pilots believed it their duty to destroy German planes that they had forced down behind German lines. Billy Bishop felt this way, but was careful to add, "It was seldom, if ever, that we would fire on the pilot if he was running from his plane."

Just as orders from higher up resulted in the deaths of downed Allied airmen who attempted to destroy their planes, so orders from higher up were responsible in many cases for possibly the most ruthless behavior by pilots in the air war: the shooting of balloon observers in their parachutes. Not much has been written about this practice, but both sides killed parachutists escaping from their balloons, and probably many more would have been shot than were had not machine guns, ack-ack, and flaming onion batteries stationed around the balloon nests made it very unhealthy for a flyer to linger waiting for a clear shot.

Billy Bishop, a strong defender of chivalry in the air, admitted parachutists were shot up:

> "The first time I heard of balloonists being shot at was in the Spring of 1917 at the Battle of Vimy Ridge. On that day two Germans destroyed five of our balloons, and in several cases stayed to fire at the balloonists while they were parachuting to earth.
>
> "We had at this time received strict instructions that when attacking balloons we were to concentrate upon destroying the personnel, as they were more important than the balloon itself-- the reason being that trained balloonists were much harder to replace than the balloons, a substitute for which could be in operation in a few hours."

Such instructions could come from very high up indeed. Wrote Mannock in his diary dated 2 June 1917: "I had almost forgotten to record the visit of the GOC (General Officer Commanding) Army on the 28th last. He came specially to congratulate us on the success of our last balloon stunt. He was very pleased indeed, and advised us to shoot at the observers as well as the balloons." Willi Gabriel is unable to remember any attacks made by German pilots on parachutists when he was flying with Jasta 11, but he recalls that the French repeatedly fired at parachutists escaping from balloons. The French do not deny this. Lt. Colonel Rougevin-Baville, Director of the Musée de l'Air, Paris, points out, "It would be silly to pretend that there were not orders to attack not only the balloons but their occupants." Willi Gabriel remarks that from a "war" point of view such conduct was correct. "Why," he asks, "destroy a balloon that can be replaced and let an experienced observer get down with his observations?"

Taffy Jones, with or without orders, was of the same mind. He tells of his attack on a German "Drachen" on 19 May 1918:

—271—

"I had opened fire at about 200 yards range and kept at it until
I got to within 40 yards. Two men jumped out of the balloon
and to avoid colliding with it, I turned sharply to the right and
then back to it again. Then, for the first time in my life, I saw
at close quarters a couple of men going down in parachutes. I
immediately attacked them, one after the other. I could see no
point in setting the cumbersome-looking 'sausage' on fire if the
observers were allowed to get away with their information and
their lives. I think I hit them. I hope I did. But I could not pay
too much attention to them. A flaming-onion battery got going
from the ground, and I was soon in a maze of hate."

Taffy Jones' code of behavior did not, however, win complete approval among his
squadron mates. He explained, "My habit of attacking Huns dangling from parachutes
led to many arguments in the mess. Some officers, of the Eton and Sandhurst type,
thought it 'unsportsmanlike' to do it. Never having been to a pulic school, I was un-
hampered by such consideration of 'form.' I just pointed out there was a bloody war
on, and that I intended to avenge my pals." A careful reading of R.A.F. Communiques
will doubtlessly provide other examples of pilots firing on parachutists leaving balloons.
For example, Communique #23, dated 4 September 1918, reports the work of two
pilots of No. 24 Squadron: "Captain T. F. Hazen brought down two balloons in flames
and Lt. E. P. Crossen attacked the observer of one, causing the parachute to collapse."

In the last month of the war, though the Germans were retreating, they were still
able to mount persistent attacks against American balloons. The records show that most
of these actions were fast in-and-out raids that usually left the balloon in flames.
American observers had become skilled in bailing out well before these attacks were
launched and were usually able to get down safely. On 2 October 1918, however, Lt.
Moore of the 7th Balloon Company was alone in his basket just south of Montfaucon
when his balloon was attacked by eight enemy planes, "two of which fired on the balloon, two on the winch crew, and a fifth on the observer's parachute; the remaining
three hovered over the balloon. Lt. Moore landed safely and the balloon was not
burned, although the balloon, parachute, and basket were riddled with holes."

These are but some of the many incidents that can lead to but one conclusion:
taken as a whole, air combat in World War I was ruthless and merciless, just as war
by its very nature, is ruthless and merciless. Yet, in all honesty it must be recorded
that the flyers of both sides viewed one another with more friendliness and treated
each other on the ground with more kindliness than did the pilots of World War II.

And it must also be recorded that occasionally, very occasionally, generosity
and true mercy was shown in combat. Some scoff at the story, but Udet has recalled
meeting the great French ace, Guynemer, in single combat in 1917. At the height of
the wild duel, Udet's guns jammed. Guynemer, watching Udet hammering desperately
on the gun barrels, refrained from shooting. Udet remembered that before banking
for home Guynemer "raised his arm and waved to me." Max Holtzem, who flew with
Jasta 16, remembers Lothar von Richthofen once recounted how a British opponent
stopped his attack when he realized Lothar's guns were jammed. But most vividly,
Holtzem recalls sneaking up on a Spad over the Verdun front in 1917. Though he had
the pilot's head in his sights, Holtzem could not force himself to fire. When he returned to his squadron, he told them what happened. Their reaction to his generous
action best summarizes the whole idea of chivalry in combat: They laughed and called
him a damned fool!

Acknowledgements

I wish to thank Max Holtzem for making available to me the story of his wartime experiences. Alex Imrie provided invaluable information and material about German aces Willi Gabriel, Paul Bäumer, and Theo Osterkamp. Ed Ferko read the first draft of this article and made several important suggestions. My thanks also to Sgt. Harry Creagen of Canada, Larry Penn, and Col. Rougevin-Baville for providing important research material.

Listed below are the major books and articles from which direct references have been taken. The reading of many other works was, of course, required for background purposes and are not listed.

BIBLIOGRAPHY

The Balloon Section of the American Expeditionary Forces, History of the Balloon Company. Edited by Lt. S. W. Ovitt.

Biddle, Major Charles J. The Way of the Eagle. Scribner's Sons, New York, 1919.

Bishop, William Avery. Chivalry in the Air. Popular Flying Magazine, Oct., 1934.

Douglas, Sholto. Years of Combat. Collins. London, 1963.

Gibbons, Floyd. The Red Knight of Germany. Garden City Publishing Co. Inc., Garden City, New York. 1927.

Imrie, Alex. The Gabriel Brothers. Cross & Cockade, Winter 1962, Vol. 3, No. 4.

Jones, Ira. King of the Air Fighters. Ivor Nicholson & Watson. New York and London, 1935.

Jones, Ira. Tiger Squadron. W. H. Allen, London. 1954.

Kiernan, R. H. Captain Albert Ball, V. C., D. S. O. The Aviation Book Club, London, 1939.

Marson, T. B. Scarlet and Khaki. Jonathan Cape. London. 1930.

McCudden, James T. B. Flying Fury. Aviation Book Club, London, 1935.

Parsons, Edwin C. Knights of the Air. (Clip from Pulp Magazine, 1930's).

Rickenbacker, Edward V. Fighting the Flying Circus. Frederick A. Stokes Co., New York. 1919.

Udet, Ernst Ace of the Black Cross. Newnes, London.

MEMORIES OF 60 SQUADRON

By
Major W. E. MOLESWORTH, M.C.

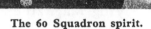

The 60 Squadron spirit.

I ARRIVED at Izel Le Hameau Aerodrome, where 60-Squadron was stationed, at 6 o'clock on a cold, bleak evening in March, 1917.

If it had not been for the flashes of the guns in the east, and the noise of gun fire and bursting shells in the distance, it would have been difficult to realise one was in France within a few miles of the mud and squalor of the Arras battlefield.

As far as comfort was concerned, our camp left little to be desired, owing to the untiring efforts of Major Graves, our Squadron-Commander. An excellent Mess with chairs, tables, papers, and all the amenities of a Home station, was provided, and our sleeping quarters in Nisson huts were as comfortable as one could hope for under the circumstances. So much for the ground.

Now a word about the air.

The machine with which 60-Squadron was equipped was the Nieuport Scout, of French design. This single-seater fighter, one of the most successful in its day which our Allies ever produced, was fitted with an air-cooled 110-h.p. Le Rhone engine and had a ceiling of approximately 20,000 feet. It was a good climber and very handy up to 10,000 feet, but inclined to be

Col. A. J. Scott with Billy Bishop.

The Author of this article—taken at Upavon.

slow as compared with the German Albatros D.3.

Unfortunately, it was only armed with a Lewis automatic gun mounted on the top 'plane, while the enemy machines generally carried two Spandau machine-guns each, tuned to fire between the propeller blades by means of special gearing.

As far as the personnel of the Squadron were concerned, I can only say that no man could wish for better. Trained in the hard school of War, some of them having already served with the ground troops, my comrades were well fitted for the work they were called upon to do.

My first flight across the lines, although not exciting, was extremely interesting.

There was a thin coating of snow on the ground and the wind was bitterly cold. We, that is my Flight-Commander and myself, left the aerodrome at about 3 p.m. and headed for the battle area. Guns flashed here and there, and the ground was marked and pitted with trenches and shell craters. Arras lay below us like a gaunt skeleton in its funeral shroud. Above and around us white clouds floated in the ground mist like great icebergs in a grey-blue sea. No enemy machines were in sight, so after flying

Nieuports of "B" Flight, 60 Squadron, lined up preparatory to starting on an offensive patrol.

backwards and forwards for about half an hour, we turned home and landed in the dusk.

With the arrival of A. J. L. Scott as Squadron-Commander, on the death of Graves, who was brought down in flames, 60-Squadron entered a period of the War which was to prove the stamina and fighting

N.C.O.'s of "B" Flight, 60 Squadron, waiting for the "birds" to come home.

What you often read about, but seldom see depicted—a war-pilot's quarters. Interior of the author's Nisson hut in France.

qualities of its pilots. The Von Richthofen " Circus " of D.3 V Strut Albatros biplanes, worthy opponents and painted red in order to distinguish themselves from the rest of the German Air Force, appeared on the scene and proceeded to create trouble.

Caldwell, Daly, Whitehead, Weidon and Meintzies all did excellent work, but the weather was so bad that only the experts could do much good, while some of our best pilots went " West."

Through this somewhat trying time I managed to survive. Once I got lost in a fog and landed on what I thought was an enemy aerodrome, having run out of petrol, but fortunately I was wrong.

On another occasion I attacked a two-seater and would have got him except that at the critical moment my Nieuport went into a spin, as I had pulled her up too much, and I missed the opportunity. However, everything comes to him who waits, and a few days later I got my first machine and an observation or kite balloon.

It was just about this time that Pope, now a Squadron-Leader in the Royal Air Force, and Bishop were posted to the Squadron. The latter showed great promise as a fighter shortly after he arrived. He soon inspired all those who served with and under him to gain the victories which made the name of " 60-Squadron " famous in the annals of aerial warfare.

To return to balloon straffing, I may say that it was a thrilling if somewhat unhealthy job. Orders would come through for an attack to be carried out by the Squadron on the balloons. We were each detailed to a special balloon and were then left to decide how to bring it down. If the weather was clear, we generally crossed the " lines " at a good height and when over our balloons, dropped on to them. That was when the fun began.

First a barrage of anti-aircraft fire, known as " Archie," greeted us. Then came " Flaming Onions," which consisted of a number of balls of fire fastened together and shot up into the air so as to fall across the attacking machine. Finally we had to pass through a concentration of rifle and machine-gun fire.

Arriving on the scene of action, if we were lucky and the balloon was still in its place, we proceeded to put a drum of Buckingham tracer ammunition filled with phosphorus into it. If our luck still held good, a thin trail of smoke and then flames would reward our efforts ; if not, the performance had to be repeated after a fresh drum had been placed on the gun.

Sometimes, whilst fully engaged in this, there would be a sudden lull in the enemy's fire and a German Scout would drop out of the blue. This meant a scrap in which the enemy started off with everything on his side. Very often the worst part of the show was the difficulty of getting back safely. It was no use climbing, as this meant another barrage of " Archie " and almost certain trouble. The only alternative, a none too pleasant one, was to " hedge hop." Whilst one skimmed over the ground a few feet up, the fire of every conceivable weapon within range seemed to be concentrated on the machine until the front lines were crossed.

On one occasion part of my tail 'plane was blown away by a shell, and I had a bit of trouble landing, as the machine was lopsided. Of course, if the clouds were low and it was possible to make use of the cover they afforded the job was much easier. However, the balloons were not often up in bad weather as the visibility was too poor.

And so the days passed.

One's work consisted chiefly of offensive patrols to keep the air clear of the enemy scouts and two-seaters and to protect our own artillery observation machines. We were also employed on reconnaissance and escort duties to bombing and photographic 'planes.

From March to May, 1917, our losses were very heavy. Thirty-five officers were missing during this period, almost twice the strength of the Squadron, and in three days we lost ten out of eighteen pilots.

One officer, Lieut. Penny, broke his lower 'plane, which fell to pieces in mid-air whilst he was on patrol. In spite of this, he managed to get back to the aerodrome and make a fairly good landing. He reported to his Flight-Commander, on the latter's return, that he was sorry he had left the patrol, but, as one of his 'planes had come off, he thought he had better return.

On June 2nd, Bishop, who was adding to his score almost daily, shot up the German Aerodrome at Cambrai, and bagged four machines, for which he was awarded the Victoria Cross.

It was just about this time, too, that I had a bit of luck, and managed to get three Albatroses, one of them in flames. [You might have told us a bit more about this.—ED.]

I was by now a Flight-Commander and beginning to feel confident that I could compete with any of the " Circus," but pride comes before a fall, and once I nearly fell for good. This was how it happened :—

My flight had been detailed to patrol the area over the Drocourt Switch, a formidable line of German trenches breaking off from the main line at Quiant, and defending Douai.

When we arrived over Vitry I spotted almost a dozen enemy 'planes over the town and, having first climbed into position, I fired a red Very light, the signal for attack, and we dived at the rear machine. Unfortunately I missed him, as he turned under me just as I was about to open fire. I pulled up and followed him while the rest of the flight took on the others.

My man was obviously no novice and I had some difficulty in getting my sights on to him, but eventually I succeeded. The last I saw of him was a trail of smoke streaking towards the ground.

By this time the dog-fight had disappeared, and I made for our own lines to collect my flight, which had been ordered to concentrate over Arras after a scrap.

On my way I spotted two enemy two-seaters working just behind their own lines.

Here was my chance of bagging another to add to my score. I dived at the rear machine and opened fire. Just as I thought I had got him, I heard the sharp crack of bullets round me and, looking round, I saw four or five of the " Circus " and a red Albatros on my tail, about 150 yards away. The latter had loosed off too soon and given me my chance. I swung my Nieuport round in a climbing turn and found myself flying straight towards him. We both fired but missed each other and he passed a few yards over my head. Again we turned and repeated the performance a second and third time, neither of us doing any good. Then the worst happened—I ran out of ammunition. There was only one thing left to do. I put the machine into a spin and, after considerable difficulty, managed to get another drum of ammunition on to my Lewis gun. I was now about three thousand feet up and decided it was time to flatten out. The machine straightened up nicely and, just as I thought everything was O.K. and the Albatros had departed, I heard the sharp crackle of twin Spandau guns. Out of the sky dropped my man with his friends who had come to watch the fun. Bullets were flicking past too close for my liking. One smashed the windscreen, another bored a neat hole in the seat, missing me by a fraction of an inch. One more cut a notch in my joystick just below my hand. Then a pretty little burst punctured my petrol tank in front of me and I thought all was up. Every moment I expected the machine to burst into flames, but by a miracle it did not. Petrol spurted out all over my legs and into the cockpit, but my Nieuport still flew on. The red Albatros shot over my head and did his usual climbing turn. I could see him out of the corner of my eye as he swung upwards. I was certainly in a bit of a fix. Something had to be done, and done quickly, before he could get at me again. As a last resort I shut off the engine, pushed my control fully forward and dived for the ground. The German pilot, thinking he had finished me off, stayed where he was and waited for the crash. Unfortunately for him he was disappointed. At 200 feet I flattened out and tried the engine. It picked up and I headed for home, hoping there would be enough petrol in the carburettor and the bottom of the tank to see me at least across the " lines." I had to risk the chance of fire if I ever wanted to get back, but my luck held good. I scraped over and made for Arras.

As I reached our gun positions, there was a splutter in the engine and I knew that I could not get much further. I looked around for a good landing-place and spotted a strip of ground clear of shell holes, on which I thought I could just land, so I side-slipped to lose height and, by a bit of luck, managed to put the machine down without crashing. Seldom have I been so thankful to feel good solid ground under my feet. I made straight for some guns I could see a few hundred yards away, and asked for the Battery-Commander. He took me to his dug-out, where I had something to warm me up, and then telephoned to the Squadron. A tender was quickly sent out to collect myself and the machine.

Thus we fought and time passed. Pilots came and went. Some gained victories and decorations, others little wooden crosses.

One day I was told that my time had come to be transferred to Home Establishment for training as an instructor. We had a great farewell party in the Mess that night, and the following morning I went round the sheds to say good-bye to my mechanics, who had held my life in their hands, and to my Nieuport, which had carried me so truly in the air, in storm and rain, through cold and heat and at dawn and dusk, when the sun sank beneath the western horizon over a welter of mud, blood and death.

Thus, I close with memories of days which I shall never forget. Days when sorrow filled our hearts at the loss of well-known comrades, and days when one or another of us had done well and we celebrated the occasion fittingly in the Mess.

Farewell to 60-Squadron ! Here's to all those who served in it during the Great War, 1914—1918.

Depressed ? No. Capt. Chidlaw Roberts and Lt. Pope disguised as Russian aviators. St. Marie Capelle. September, 1917.

Capt. " Billy " Bishop, V.C., and Lt. Young. Taken outside their Nissen hut at Filescamp Farm, June, 1917.

Quite happy. Capt. Chidlaw Roberts and Lts. Young and Pope at Marie Capelle. September, 1917.

RE-UNION MEMORIES

By
Sergt.-Major A. A. NICOD (Late of No. 60 Squadron, RF.C., and R.A.F.)

ON April 27th, 1935, in the comfortable dining-room of a London hotel, the survivors of No. 60 Squadron forgathered from all parts of the United Kingdom for their first reunion. Hearty bursts of laughter, accompanied by " do you remember ? " could be heard on all sides.

A well-known air fighter arrived, and after greeting everyone with a warm handshake was suddenly confronted by a one-time ack-emma, who accosted him in these terms :

" You're the blighter who ' put me on the peg ' and gave me seven days C.B."

" Did I ? " smilingly replied the officer. " Never mind, old man, what are you going to have to drink ? " And, suiting the action to the word he placed his arm affectionately round the shoulder of the ack-emma and conducted him to the bar. Glasses were filled, and both exclaimed simultaneously, " Cheerio ! Happy days."

How often I noticed that cheerful phrase in the many letters which I received from officers and other ranks while I was organising the gathering. There is no

The photographs on these pages are not remarkable for their artistic or technical merit. On the contrary, some of them are bad, even for the amateurs whose work they were. Nevertheless, they are of vital interest now, and always will be while tradition is worth while, for they show pictures that have hitherto existed only in the imagination—at least, of the majority. For this collection we are indebted to Sergt. Major Nicod, late of 60 Squadron, R.F.C., the unit which produced so many fearless fighters ; he tells us the story about them in his own way, with a sincerity that rings of truth, which is so much more desirable than the fiction even of a stylist.

doubt that behind the grim reality of war there existed an atmosphere of gaiety such as those who were not there will never understand. Much has been written and photographed of the serious aspect, but little has been done to portray the other side, which we know now was only a safety-valve to relieve the tension.

June, 1916 ! The scene changes swiftly to that famous and now historical aerodrome on the Amiens-Doullens road, where the Squadron, commanded by Major F. F. Waldron, and later by Major R. Smith-Barry, commenced its war-flying activities.

Vert Galand Farm ! Who of those who were there will not experience a thrill when confronted with a picture of this famous rendezvous of airmen ? And who amongst the rank and file has not slept—or tried to sleep—in the rat-infested barn on the main road, when relief from the activities of the rodents was afforded by getting up, going out, and watching the gallant regiments swinging along towards the line.

The officers serving with the Squadron at this early period were Captains Summers, Towers and Gray, and

Vert Galand Farm, of historical importance. No. 60 Squadron workshop lorries in courtyard.

The rat-infested barn on the main road in which thousands of troops passed the night.

Lieutenants Browning, Patterson, Simpson, Portal, Balfour, Armstrong, Smart, Bell-Irving, Ridley, Meintjies, Keddie, Knowles, Williams, Clark, Newton, Harris, Good, Overy, O'Beirne, Bryant, Laurie-Reid and Heenan (Equipment Officer).

The name of Vert Galand Farm will always be associated with one of the most remarkable experiences recorded in the history of the R.F.C., and the hero of it might well reflect with pride on his achievement, for at a critical period he rendered a service of incalculable value. It won the approbation of everyone in the R.F.C. at the time.

On the evening of August 3rd, 1916, Lieut. (now Squadron Leader) Claud A. Ridley took off from Vert Galand Aerodrome with a French agent, who was to be landed over the other side. But things went wrong and he was compelled to make a forced landing, through engine failure, near Cambrai. By the rules of war he would have been shot, with the spy, if they were caught.

For many weeks they moved cautiously about the occupied territory of Northern France, gathering much information of military importance,

Lt. Claude Ridley (now Sqdn.-Ldr., retired) in the " civvies " in which he escaped from German territory. The photo was taken in Mons in 1916, while he was behind the German lines.

and despite many hair-breadth escapes, ultimately succeeded in crossing the frontier. This officer's performance was rendered more remarkable in that he could not speak German, and very little French, but he managed to elude capture by masquerading as a deaf mute, with his head in bandages. On one occasion, still with the French agent, he boarded a tramcar bound from Mons to Brussels. A military policeman on board suspected him, and endeavoured to arrest him, but Ridley promptly knocked him down, jumped off the swiftly moving car and concealed himself in a cornfield, where he discarded his bandages.

Having lost touch with the French agent, he continued his amazing adventures alone, and after suffering many hardships, but still gathering information of immense value, in company with a Belgian from Hal he succeeded in forcing his way through the electrified wire into Holland, setting foot on neutral soil in the early hours of October 8th. On the 13th of the same month he crossed over to England, from Flushing, and in due course landed at Gravesend with a mass of information concerning

Lt. Ridley in his Morane "Monocoupe." Vert Galand, 1916.

The electrified wire through which Lt. Ridley, with a Belgian from Hals, broke through in his dash for liberty.

ALBERT BALL, V.C.

Capt. Albert Ball, V.C., in the greenhouse in which he spent much of his time when on the ground.

Capt. Ball (right) with two unknown officers. Probably taken while he was in No. 11 Squadron.

The greenhouse and small garden which Capt. Ball made whilst with 56 Squadron, April, 1917.

Building his hut on the edge of the aerodrome at Savy, 1916.

"My Garden." The little plot of land which he cultivated, and where he spent many happy hours.

enemy ammunition dumps, depots, billets and aerodromes. The following day he returned to France, where he made his report at R.F.C. Headquarters and afterwards had a special interview with the late Field-Marshal Sir Douglas Haig.

On September 1st, 1916, the Squadron was again moved, this time to Savy, and I do feel at this juncture that the countless admirers of Captain Albert Ball, V.C., should have an opportunity of seeing how this wonderful fighter spent his time between patrols, and on dud days. His hut on the edge of the aerodrome at Savy, where he slept, with "Archie" for his reveille ; his little plot of land where he grew lettuce, carrots, sweet peas, and other flowers ; also his greenhouse.

"Please send me some plants for my garden" he wrote in his letters home. He said he thought it was "great fun" to dive on large enemy formations, and discharge a bunch of blazing rockets into their midst, causing them to panic and dive for home—usually leaving one or more of their number behind. I feel sure that had he survived the war he would have treasured the thoughts of the pleasant hours spent in his garden and greenhouse, and would have regarded them as happy memories.

At this Station we possessed an almost unbeatable Rugby team, composed chiefly of "hardy Colonials,"

An interesting photo of a machine fitted with Le Prieur rockets, which Capt. Ball used with such devastating effect. Probably Capt. Ball's machine, but this is unconfirmed.

The famous and now historical Filescamp Farm, Ixel-le-Hameau, June, 1917.

MEMORIES OF 60 SQUADRON

A famous character. Diciplinary Sergt.-Major J. A. Aspinall (by propeller), one of the outstanding characters of No. 60 Squadron.

More fun. Lt. Young being " forcibly fed " at Breck-Plage by Lts. Armstrong, McColl, Rutherford and Soden. August, 1917.

Off duty. Outside the officers' mess at Filescamp Farm. June, 1917. Captain Bishop, V.C. (centre), and Lts. Horn, Sellars, and Parks.

the leading lights being Lieuts. Middlemas, Bell-Irving, Giles and Meintjies. One of our Sergeants, who fancied himself at the game, challenged them to a match. They accepted. During one of the scrums the officers, apparently out of sheer devilment, stripped every stitch of clothing off his body. Minus all his clothing except his boots, he staggered off the field to the accompaniment of roars of laughter.

In January, 1917, the Squadron was transferred to Filescamp Farm, Izel le Hameau, an ancient and picturesque house, half farm and half chateau, situated amidst charming surroundings. In an orchard adjacent to the farm an almost perfect camp was created, thanks to Major Graves and the indefatigable efforts of the Disciplinary Sergeant-Major, " the Great Man."

Sergeant-Major J. Aspinall was a fine soldier, and possibly the principal humorist of the Squadron, although the humour was often unconscious. He was called with all reverence the " Great Man " by the officers and generally execrated under the nick-name of " Jimmy " by the rank and file. Imported from the Guards, his relentless adherence to military discipline soon earned him a " reputation."

But Guards discipline and the efficient maintenance of aeroplanes did not synchronise in the opinion of the mechanics, and the following are typical of some of the

The hostess of Filescamp Farm, with her little daughter, so well known to the personnel of many squadrons.

Mine host. M. Tetus; a familiar figure to numberless men of the R.F.C., who at some time stayed at this famous camp. July, 1917.

incidents that have been told and told again.

One very wintry day in early February most of the Squadron were frantically endeavouring to put out a fierce conflagration caused by a Hun two-seater that had become lost, and finally landed on the aerodrome, where its pilot had set it on fire with a time-bomb. Meanwhile, the "Great Man" had mobilised everyone not engaged in fire-fighting and armed them with rifles. As the Hun pilot and observer slowly crossed the aerodrome with their hands above their heads, he approached the C.O., and after discharging his inimitable salute, he exclaimed dramatically "Shall we open fire on these Huns, sir?"

The possibility of two half frozen Huns offering any resistance caused the C.O. to laugh. We all laughed. Who could help it? Whipping round at the sound of the laughter, the "Great Man's" eagle eye fell on some unfortunate ack-emmas. "Consider yourselves under arrest" he yelled, this remark causing even greater merriment, as his speech when labouring under provocation became inarticulate and was accompanied by facial distortions that were a joy to behold. The arrival of the Hun prisoners terminated this episode.

One day he was requested to visit a kite balloon section stationed at Arras, to arrange a football match, and on his return to the mess at tea-time he related the following:

"When I arrived I spied a bunch of ack-emmas floating about in space." With his voice taking on a rapid crescendo, he continued: "What a mob!" (He always referred to R.F.C. units as mobs.) The remaining description of his interrogation of the personnel of this K.B.S. is

unprintable, but it quickly dawned upon us that these "spare parts" had treated him with complete indifference, neither standing to attention when addressed, nor answering "sir."

The photo that was taken at great risk. The Hun machine brought down by Lt. Fry at St. Pol, snapped just as it was brought in on the trailer. The Hun pilot, very disconsolate, can be seen standing in centre background

Another photo of the same machine, which officers of 60 Squadron are examining with great interest on Filescamp Aerodrome.

"What did you do?" I asked innocently.

"Do!" he roared, his face white with passion. "I f-f-f-fell the ——s in and gave them half an hour's drill."

We all collapsed in fits of uncontrollable laughter.

If those old grey walls of Filescamp Farm could speak, what stories of rollicking fun they could tell. For many of us the old place is full of unforgettable memories, tragic and gay, for it was here during the summer of 1917 that the Squadron enjoyed such wonderful times, with a hard tennis court, swimming pool, concerts and cinema. And who amongst those who were there will fail to recognise mine host, M. Tetus, his good lady and children? So near to the line and yet so far.

Among the officers serving with us at this period were Captain Bishop, V.C., Captain "Grid" Caldwell, Captain Molesworth and Lieuts. Soden, Young, Pope, Armstrong, Rutherford, McColl, "Zulu" Lloyd and Horn, Binnie, Meintjies, Fry, Penny and Sellars. What names! What memories! What creators of mirth! These destroyers of Huns were commanded by that very gallant officer, Major A. J. Scott.

Occasionally, during the summer, the Squadron performed what was known as a wireless interception patrol, the signal to take off being given by blasts on a hunting horn. On receipt of the message the Major would seize his horn and summon his "hounds" outside the Squadron

REUNION MEMORIES

office. This unique idea of sounding the alarm in a manner reminiscent of rural England caused the following chorus to be composed. It was sung to the tune of "John Peel."

" For the sound of his horn brought me from my bed,
And the roar of his ' grids ' which he oft times led,
Jack Scott's blasts would awaken the dead,
Or the Hun from his lair in the morning."

[In 60 Squadron all machines were known as " grids " at this period, the name having been bestowed by " Grid " Cauldwell.—ED.]

Even our adversaries apparently considered it the thing to enjoy themselves as well, as the following incident will show. Captain Fry forced a Hun scout machine to land at St. Pol. On searching the pilot, what do you think they found? Nothing connected with frightfulness. Only a ticket for the theatre at Cambrai. The photograph taken of this machine, with the Hun gazing disconsolately at it, was only obtained at great risk, as " Jimmy " was on the war-path.

How well I remember the day in June when Major Scott, unshaven and clad only in pyjamas, ventured alone across the line looking for trouble. He found it. Unfortunately it so happened that General Allenby was due to inspect the Squadron that very morning. It transpired, however, that the C.O. had engaged a formation of Huns, and being badly shot about was forced to make a landing near Arras. His anxiety can be imagined when he remembered the inspection.

Anxiously scanning the sky for signs of his machine, for he was long overdue, great excitement and amusement was created when he appeared astride a mule, cantering towards the aerodrome over the sloping ground from Hermaville. He turned up on parade just in time to receive the Brass Hats.

Tennis tournaments were now in full swing, and the swimming pool was the scene of great activity. Many curious bathing costumes were on view, which caused much fun and excitement amongst the troops, and villagers who occasionally ventured far enough to witness the aquatic pastime under active service conditions.

A memorable night that no one who was present will ever forget was the celebration of Captain Bishop's winning the V.C., for his wonderful show at Cambrai. After much celebration, singing and dancing, the Very light experts took command. Thus armed they began to raid the neighbouring squadrons. What actually happened I don't know, but the number of coloured lights that appeared in the sky, in the huts, going through one window and out of the other on the opposite side, created a scene bordering on pandemonium that startled even the rats. I remember rushing over to my shed and switching on the lights, to find it occupied by hundreds of rats that had apparently sought shelter there.

What a night! We thought the whole place was going up in flames. Many of us stood by with troops armed with fire extinguishers, while the " Great Man " whirled about like a piece of paper in a gale.

In early September, after nearly nine months at Filescamp Farm, we moved with deep regret to St. Marie Capelle, where we came under the command of the late Major Patrick. Among other fine pilots with us at the time were Captains Chidlaw-Roberts, Selous, Soden, and Ball.

Should any other war-time Squadron have the good fortune to re-unite, and recapture the spirit that undoubtedly prevailed in those days, I feel sure that the discussion of morbid details will be conspicuous by their absence ; and when glasses are filled, and toasts are exchanged, the one that will strike the most dominant chord will be " Cheerio ! Happy days !"

I should like to acknowledge with gratitude the kindness of Sir Albert Ball, Squadron Leader Ridley, D.S.O., M.C., Captain Young and Flight Sergeant Hacche for granting me facilities for the publication of the accompanying photographs. Members of the old Squadron will learn with interest that I have collected over two hundred photographs, and if possible a publication entitled " The Pictorial History of No. 60 Squadron " will be the result.

AVIATION BOOKSHELF

THE ENCYCLOPEDIA OF AVIATION. Compiled by Squadron Leader C. G. Burge. Pitman. Price, 15s.

Being of an economical turn of mind, my first thought when I opened this book was to see what the reader was going to get for fifteen shillings. A few seconds was sufficient to answer that question. It is more than worth the money ; it is cheap at the price, for its 642 pages say all that there is to be said about Aviation from the beginning up to the present day. From cover to cover it is packed with the most useful and interesting facts and figures, and it is, without a shadow of doubt, one of the most useful reference books on the subject of Aviation ever compiled. Definitely, no bookshelf will be complete without this volume.

THE AIR ANNUAL OF THE BRITISH EMPIRE. Edited by Squadron Leader Burge. Pitman. Price, 21s.

To readers who possess the previous six editions of this work no description will be necessary, and they will automatically put it on the shelf with its predecessors. It contains an incredible amount of information, the compilation of which must have given its editor many a headache. The introduction of a thumb index this year is a great improvement, for in tomes of this size it is not always easy to turn up the information one requires at a moment's notice. The Air Annual deserves its reputation of being the standard work of its kind.

VULTURES OF THE SKY. By Phillip Conde.
Wright & Brown. Price, 3s. 6d.

This book comes in the " light reading " class. It rather lacks conviction here and there, although younger readers are not likely to find fault with it on that score. Spend three-and-six when you see it on the bookstall.

BRITISH AIR MAILS. Produced and Published by Francis J. Field, Ltd., Sutton Coldfield. Price, 3s. 6d.

This is a most useful and interesting book, and one that no student of Aviation can afford to be without, because it is probably the only thing of its kind in the world which deals solely with the air mail from its inception right up to date. Flights are shown in chronological order, the first beginning as far back as 1784, while a large number of illustrations from the author's remarkable collection brighten up the text. A copy of this unique document must certainly go on your shelf.

AIRCRAFT AND ACCESSORIES, 1935. Published by the Business Statistics Co., Ltd., Cardiff. Price, 2s. 6d.

This is a slim but very informative handbook for readers who are interested in investment in Aviation. The financial aspect of British aircraft manufacturing companies is set out in detail.

REGULATIONS FOR UNIVERSITY AIR SQUADRONS. (Air Publication 1401.) Published by the Air Ministry. Price, 4d., postage extra.

Copies of this publication may be obtained from H.M. Stationery Office, or through any bookseller.

Cross & Cockade Journal, Summer 1964
COLLISHAW - CALDWELL COMMENTS
on
"Who Is The British Ace of Aces?"

In the Winter 1963 issue of the Journal, (Vol. 4, No. 4, pp. 333-4) the question of "Who Is The British Ace Of Aces?" was asked by George Shiras. Was it, indeed, Major Edward "Mick" Mannock with 73 victories (*) albeit disputed in part, or was it Colonel Billy Bishop with his 72 victories? To help solve this riddle, Cross & Cockade is presenting two interesting letters that may help Shiras to find his answer. One of the letters came from Canada; the other from Australia. The Canadian letter was sent by Air Vice Marshall Raymond Collishaw, DSO and Bar, DSC, DFC, C de G, formerly of 10, 13 (RNAS) and 203 (RAF) Squadrons. Collishaw, with 60 victories (**) was the famed leader of "Black Flight" and is today the top-scoring surviving ace of all the nations. The Australian letter came from Major Keith L. "Grid" Caldwell, MC, DFC, of 8, 60, and 74 Squadrons, RFC. Caldwell, with 25 victories, was Mannock's C.O., during their service in 74 Squadron. (***)

Shiras prefaces his query with the information that "...it is understood that the Official Air Records, while in transit from Field Headquarters in France to the office in London, was destroyed by enemy action at sea. Efforts to reconstruct the records from accounts of survivors, field reports, etc., will probably never adequately replace the records destroyed." Since all RFC and RAF Squadrons were required to produce a daily War Diary, a copy of which had to be submitted first to the War Office and later to the Air Ministry, these records were forwarded to the Air Ministry Offices in April of 1918. By examining the War Diaries of 40, 74, and 85 Squadrons, RFC, one can check the validity of Mannock's victories as the Air Ministry Offices (Air Historical Branch) has transcripts of all squadrons' War Diaries.

THE COLLISHAW REPORT

I was a fighter pilot continuously in France from August 1916 to November 1918. I mention this to emphasize experience, as the RFC regualry sent fighter pilots home for a rest after about 8 months active service. I commanded four Fighter Squadrons on active service: Seaplane Defence Squadron, No. 13 Naval Squadron, No. 3 Naval Squadron, and No. 203 Squadron, RAF. This paper is being compiled in respect to the claim that Manjor Mannock was credited with 73 victories in the 1914-1918 war; a claim that is not in accordance with the facts as they were known in 1918.

Amongst the principal British fighter pilots in France in 1918, a healthy spirit of competition existed and the scores of each principal were very well known to all concerned. Headquarters, RFC (and later Headquarters, RAF) in France, produced a daily Command Communique in which the General Officer Commanding produced a summary of air operations of the day, and especially those results attained by the principal fighter pilots. The squadrons concerned kept a careful record of these published results, and so it was common knowledge in France, in the autumn of 1918, that the order of merit of victories was as set below:

(a)	Collishaw =	60	Bishop had a record of 72 victories
(b)	Barker =	50	at this time; but he was not in France
(c)	McLaren =	48	in the autumn of 1918. No other
(d)	Mannock =	43	pilot has exceeded a score of 40.
(e)	Proctor =	41	

(*) See Vol. 2, No. 2, Summer 1961 issue, p. 102 for Douglass Whetton's compilation.
(**) See Vol. 2, No. 4, Winter 1961 issue, pp. 357-8 for Frank Yeoman's compilation.
(***) Caldwell is now an Air Commodore, RAF (retired).

It was the custom for the G.O.C. commanding the RAF in France, together with the generals commanding RAF Brigades, to send telegrams of congratulations to those pilots who had accomplished 50 victories. The only telegrams sent out in this way were addressed to Bishop, Collishaw and Barker.

The victory scores of individual British fighter pilots, as given on the preceeding page, were well known to everyone of importance in the RAF in 1918 and these figures were used in the host of war books that were published after the 1914-1918 war. These figures were used in similiar published books for the next 30 years.

Some 20 years after the 1914-1918 war, Group Captain "Taffy" Jones began to publish a series of books in which he claimed that Mannock had accomplished a total of 73 victories, but without giving a detailed account of Mannock's individual victories. The claim for Mannock had not, in any way, been supported by the Headquarters RAF Communiques issued in France in 1918, and without such endorsement, the claim by Group Captain Jones is quite unsupported and it is, therefore, simply one man's contention; bereft of facts or creditable evidence.

Many of the books published in respect to military aviation of the 1914-1918 war, in the past 10 years, have adopted Group Captain Jones' contention of 73 victories for Mannock and no proper investigation has ever been made as to the facts of the matter.

THE CALDWELL REPORT

The Cross & Cockade Journals are extremely interesting and obviously contributors are aware of the standards expected of them in supplying accurate information. A lot of effort must go into your researches on aviation during the First World War; it is very well done.

Interested parties in this business of "how many Huns various people have shot down" should try to realize how difficult it was to judge what aeroplanes went down to crash or not. Especially from a large dogfight when machines were milling 'round in close proximity as they did at the beginning.

If an aeroplane broke up under fire, which they rarely did, or caught alight, which they frequently did in later 1917 and 1918 when explosive ammunition was used (Pomeroy, Buckingham, and Brock), all was well and easy. But if a fellow got good shooting at several Huns at close range he could easily knock down two or three, or more, but would not know for certain because he could not leave the scrap and so weaken his side, to dive down and try to confirm his likely successes. Of course, there was always the chance that some of his side could support his claims, if they happened to see the Huns that he was engaging go down out of control. And again, if the fight was not too far over the lines or too high, the spotters on the ground could sometimes supply evidence on request, which could later be sorted out at the Squadron or Wing Headquarters.

It was always difficult to get decisive results from these large affairs at the start. Soon the scrap would spread out and usually quickly downwards, and when aircraft followed aircraft it was easier to observe crashes if you were quick enough. Another problem was this...later in the war, when the nastier types of ammunition were being used, a machine could leave a scrap in a dive or a spin with a badly wounded pilot who would lose consciousness before getting to the ground, and probably no claim could be made for this one.

My feeling on this matter of claiming victories is that they were largely made in good faith. But a total score attributed to this pilot, or that pilot, could only be approximate...and this would apply to everyone...in every air force! I see no point in these writing fellows trying to get anything definite on this subject as it can be very unfair to the people they single out. Especially in Mannock's case... I don't think that I can recall anyone of the larger scorers who shot down so many when on patrol, and in front of his patrol. When in 74 Squadron he rarely hunted alone; this was not encouraged, mainly because of confirmation difficulties. But on one occasion I do remember (which pleased him no end) was when he attacked a Fokker D.VII from above and behind, pulled up again in case the Hun zoomed, and then never saw him again. He must have gone down vertically, when there is very little to see. Anyhow, Wing were asked to try to get confirmation as Mannock was very sure that he could not have missed it from his position. Later it was confirmed that an S.E. had shot down an E.A. at the right time and place, and no other claims had been put in. He was bucked about this.

When Mannock came to 74 Squadron as flight commander in early 1918, I was informed that his score was 21. He then had an MC and bar, and a very good reputation; and there was no one I would rather have had as a flight commander in my squadron.

In my diary and logs, in which I have recorded the deeds of pilots in the squadron, Mannock's list of successes may not be completely accurate, or balance with squadron records, but it would not be far away.

On looking it over again now I see that one victory, at least, is missing --- the time he and Dolan shot down a two-seater and he shot at it on the ground. In fairness to him I must say that there could be others I have missed. I do not know how many he shot down when with 85 Squadron. Their records, if available, would show this. He was, in my opinion, a most reliable man, and I would place him as a Number One fighter pilot, with McCudden a close second. Close... in order of all around effort and not in victories alone.

It has been said often that Mannock gave credit to one of his juniors for shooting down a Hun that he, himself, had actually hit. I believe this to be true, and actually know of others who have done the same. The team spirit was very strong in some of the better squadrons. In entering a scrap it was usually the leader who fired the first shots, but often his followers would fire on the same aircraft (sometimes needlessly) and this would be a chance for the leader to tell "so-and-so", on returning to the ground, that he got the Hun. His log book, however, might not indicate this generous action. Refer to the ninth entry on the following list: some of these should probably have been to Mannock's credit. His score with 74 Squadron could have been 40 or more for this reason.

Regarding the total figure of 68 in my diary, I just cannot say how reliable this is. The actual figure could be more, or less; 68 was what I evidently believed it to be at the time of Mick's death.........

Hostiles Credited To Capt. E. Mannock Whilst With 74 Squadron
(From the Diary of Major K. L. Caldwell)

April, 1918

12	Destroyed Hun Scout.
12	Destroyed Hun Scout with patrol to help.
21	Helped Dolan against three Triplanes.
22	Got Scout out of control.
23	Crashed enemy scout.
12-23	"Still late on patrol."
29	Got Hun in flames. Led Dolan and Glynn versus 9 E.A.
30	Got observer in Hun two-seater, same time Dolan got Hun.
12-30	Mainly responsible for all E.A. destroyed by A Flight.

May, 1918

3	Led patrol from 1,400 feet to 2,000 feet, 1 mile E of Merville, and crashed Hun two-seater with patrol help.
6	Crashed Triplane.
11	Scout in flames; with Dolan, attacked 8 E.A. five miles over.
12	Attacked by enemy formation and got three; two in pieces and one crashed; excellent show. Recommended for decoration.
13	Several indecisive fights.
15	Two-seater out of control, with Clements and Roxburgh-Smith.
16	Scout in pieces.
17	Enemy Scout crashed; attacked 4 Pfalz alone, excellent show.
17	Two-seater in flames.
18	Two-seater crashed.
19	Missed three good chances, gun trouble. Awarded D.S.O.
20	E.A. driven down with centre section tank on fire.
21	Two-seater crashed.
21	Three Scouts crashed, excellent show.
26	Scout crashed.
29	One Scout crashed, one out of control. Awarded Bar to D.S.O.
29-30	Gun trouble.
31	Pfalz out of control.

June, 1918

1	In dogfight; got one E.A. in pieces, one in flames.
2	One of four Pfalz out of control.
7	Shared two-seater with Young...crashed.
16	One Pfalz (black) crashed and one out of control. Good show.
17	One two-seater crashed.

Took over command of 85 Squadron...killed later, shot from ground after getting 68 Huns. (Note: Also one Pfalz out of control when Mannock and Caldwell engaged nine E.A. Date sometime bewteen May 21-30...date not certain in diary).

'Grid' Caldwell of 74

by

H. H Russell

W. R. Puglisi

In France there's a darned old Squadron
  Though the "Drome's" on the side of a hill,
It's a Squadron of great reputation.
  It is Seventy-four Escadrille.

There was Mannock of fame in the Air Force
  Hunarinos he shot down with ease
As happy as hell round the Aerodrome,
  As he shouted--"All tickets, please."

And Roxburgh, and Youngski & Taffy,
  Men who are who in the Air
And all of the rest in the Squadron
  The best you could find anywhere.

Now, I will offer in closing
  Just one, it could easily be more,
A toast to the C.O. who led us,
  To Caldwell of Seventy-four.

When analyzing the annals of squadrons or autobiographies by those who served in them, there is quite often found some reference to the C.O., either praising or condemning him. They came in a number of types; those who were complete with regulations and discipline and who seldom socialized with the pilots and there was the commanding officer who flew only occasionally and still was respected because he was thoroughly efficient, had everything functioning smoothly, and took care of his pilots' welfare on the ground.

Fifty-six Squadron had such a C.O. in Maj. R. G. Blomfield, and remember what a Squadron they were! McCudden, V.C., has described them perfectly in his book, "Five Years in the Royal Flying Corps." Maj. Blomfield personally saw every patrol depart and arrive, which in summertime meant between 4 and 5 AM and landings from evening patrols around 9 to 10 PM.

The ideal leader was of a quite different caliber and only remotely resembled the first. Maj. Caldwell belonged to the latter species and was, in fact, selected because of his humane qualities. Physically a big man, near the 6 foot mark, he was heavily built with black unruly hair. He won fame in 60 Squadron as a great fighter and patrol leader of unusual daring and loved flying for the satisfaction it gave him. His old C.O. of 60 Squadron, Col. A. J. L. Scott, MC, who above all was a marvelous judge of a man's capabilities as a fighter, reckoned Caldwell would have been the top ranking ace of the War but for his shooting. He had more combats during his patrols than any other man. As a commander, Caldwell had the marvelous gift of leadership and inspiration for his men to give that extra something of which they, themselves, were not aware. In the air or on the ground, he was greatly admired, and throughout the length and breadth of the Western Front was affectionately known as "Grid," since he had coined the saying, "wheel out the grids," while "B" flight leader of 60 Squadron. Caldwell has often been quoted as a poor marksman. [1] A perusal of his personal records of 1917 showed that he certainly missed a lot of victories, but it showed a small percentage of ammunition used in his fights. Against enemy scouts, his average was 50 rounds, and then it was "finis" for the German. Where he lost out was against two-seaters, his consumption of rounds going up to 2 and 3 drums (190-290 per scrap without visible results). Fighting two-seaters was an art and evidently Caldwell never mastered it. He had another burden to bear all too frequently--jammed guns. It has been quoted that no man ever went nearer to an enemy than Caldwell, and although his shots appeared to pierce his opponent's cockpit, the enemy aircraft flew on quite unconcerned. In spite of this, however, during 1918, he was among the top scorers and bagged 17 enemy aircraft, third best in 74 Squadron after Mannock and Jones.

As a pilot, he probably was not outstanding, but neither were many other high-scoring men. He never received a wound in his three years at the front and he fought against the best the German Air Service had to offer. Perhaps, on defense, Caldwell was a tough proposition and had an instinctive insight into his opponent's tactics that saved him time and time again.

---

[1] *"I was certainly a poor shot and it was very frustrating to miss so many opportunities, but I did not know that I was regarded as an indifferent pilot. Russell must have quoted from some unknown source. Actually, I was a very confident pilot (I say this with all due modesty, please understand) and this confidence helped considerably in pulling off a number of forced landings in awkward and confined places. Since I was a rotary pilot, I was chosen to gun test the first Camel sent to France in early 1917, at Omer, even though I had not flown one before. I was also sent to bring the first S.E. 5 to 60 Squadron when we changed from Nieuports. I had to land this A/C a mite short of the aerodrome at Izel-le-Hameau as the engine siezed in the air, but we got down O.K. and the aeroplane arrived by land across fields, pushed by our mechanics. I had only 20 minutes dual before my first solo on a Maurice Farman Longhorn, my first RFC aeroplane. I just mention some of these things to indicate that, with a poor pilot, things might have been different."* (Keith L. Caldwell - 1968)

Keith Logan Caldwell was born at Wellington, New Zealand, in 1895. He attended the Wanganue Collegiate School, and when Britain declared War on Germany, he was employed in the Bank of New Zealand. Attracted by the newly inaugurated flying services, he was one of the first pupils of Walsh Bros. Flying School at Kohimarama, Auckland.

During November-December, 1915, he put in 8 hours on Curtiss Flying Boats and Caudrons, sufficient for his entry to the Royal Flying Corps. He arrived in England early in 1916 and joined the RFC as a Prob. 2/Lt. on April 15, 1916. [2]

He went to Oxford on May 14th for his first dual, and after one month, had completed 7-1/2 hours solo and dual. From Oxford, he departed for 45 Squadron, Sedgeford, to fly Farmans and B.E.s for 6 weeks, and then came the great day in his life--a transfer overseas.

On the 19th of July, he left for France and reported to No. 2 A.D. Candas where he spent a week waiting for his turn to be posted to a squadron. Caldwell finally arrived at No. 8 on July 29th for his first tour of duty, to fly two-seater B.E. 2c's and 2d's. He was engaged in artillery observation and bombing patrols at a height of 8000 feet down to 4000 feet, but mostly ranging batteries. It must have become very irksome for him. To relieve the tedium of his job, on the 23rd of August, he dived at a balloon which was pulled down! Imagine this kind of a stunt in a B.E. 2d! Even then, Caldwell was full of confidence and fight.

The next day, on artillery patrol, he encountered three Fokkers at 7000 feet who fired about five rounds and then went off, and, as Caldwell recorded, "much too fast to catch up." He was forever on the lookout for enemy aircraft and made good use of the element of surprise while on patrol during the 18th of September. He was spotting for enemy gunflashes at 4500 feet over Aichet-le-Petit when he jumped on two Roland two-seaters. He put in three drums of Lewis at one of them after clearing four stoppages, and marked up the first of his 25 victories.

This was exhilarating sport to Caldwell because, a week later, the 26th of September, when doing artillery observation at 9000 feet, he engaged another E.A. at close range. Again, his gun jammed after firing only ten rounds. In return, received shots through his center section struts, cowl, and propeller. Later during the patrol, he dived on three LVG two-seaters who, themselves, dived away, firing over their tails. His gun jammed again, so Caldwell gave up at 4000 feet.

It was not until November 3rd that he recorded another brush with a hostile aircraft, and this he chased over Biez at 1200 feet, only to see it disappear in the low clouds.

Caldwell's aggressive and offensive tactics were evidently noted in the right quarters, for on the 12th of the month, he was sent to No. 1 A.D., St Omer, to fly Morane Parasols and Bristol Scouts for a week. He shaped very well indeed there and was transferred to a crack group of Nieuport Scouts at Savy, No. 60 Squadron, where, as a member of "B" flight, he made his first offensive patrol on the 22nd of November.

His first recorded fight occurred on December 11th [3] when "B" flight, comprised of Lt. A.P.V. Daly, Lt. A.D. Whitehead, Lt. L.S. Weedon, Caldwell, Lt. H. Meintjes, and

_____

[2] *"Another young man, G. G. Callender, and I were the first two pilots to be trained in New Zealand. First on a N.Z. homemade flying boat, built and flown by Vivian Walsh of the Walsh Flying School at a beach near Auckland. This aeroplane was under-powered and would rarely leave the water with two up so that our solos were rather adventurous affairs; but on the old Caudron (they bought and converted to a float plane), we had no difficulties in obtaining our "tickets" and then off to England and the war in the RFC."* (Keith L. Caldwell)

Capt. E. O. Grenfell, were on O.P. at 11,000 feet when he dived on an Albatros C.III two-seater which was flying along at 5000 feet on the Allied side of the lines. The efforts of the leader and the rest of the patrol forced it down at Arras. The pilot was found to have been shot in the foot and the observer badly wounded by two more shots. The Germans blew-up their machine after coming down with the result that the observer collected more wounds from the explosion. The patrol landed along side the E.A. and both Caldwell and Capt. Grenfell damaged their machines, particularly the latter who also broke a leg. [4]

The following are extracts from Caldwell's log-book and give a crisp account of his activities in the latter half of December, 1916:

16.12.16   A.184 Nieuport. "North to Bruay and then east over lines. Climbed to 14,000 ft. after an H.A.* which was going N.W., and after 3/4 hour, got to close range. Scrapped all the way back to the lines, firing 3 drums, apparently without effect. Crossed lines at 4000 ft. after the Hun who had dived from about 7000 ft."

21.12.16   "As escort to F.E. on photography. Went 15 miles over and fought most of the way back with E.A. One green one was shot down to about 3000 ft. where he seemed to gain control again. Engaged at 7000 ft. Guns jammed twice."

25.12.16   "To C flight. A.307, new type Nieuport."

For the next three weeks, it was a repetition of this type of work and then the Squadron moved to Izel-le-Hameau on the 14th of January, with no let-up for Caldwell who was soon in the thick of the fighting:

23.1.17.   "Escort again to photo machines and had 2 fights with Albatros 2-seaters our side and had to force-land. Later in day, on O.P. attacked one of three 2-seaters over Gommecourt. Nil results."

27.1.17   "Engaged H.A. over Hogeaste Wood at 5500 ft. Engine stopped and glided back over our lines, landing 100 yards from the front line trenches. Machine wrecked 20 mins. later by shell fire."

Caldwell acquired a new machine, A.6646 (C.5) from Candas the next day, but he did not keep it very long.

* Hostile Aircraft

[3] *Actually my first combat with 60 Squadron happened the day after I had arrived. When getting the hang of the new Nieuport in practice flying above the aerodrome, I saw our BR AA fire high up. I climbed up and found an E.A. 2-seater well over our side of the lines. I attacked him at close range, got into a short spin, then chase him the whole way down to the enemy trenches, firing all my three Lewis drums on the way. I believe the observer was hit, as he disappeared from view, but the A/C was last seen still flying low, so imagine he got back. Here was, indeed, evidence of poor shooting and I was disgusted. (Keith L. Caldwell - 1968)*

[4] *In my case, I had to get down quickly, somehow, because my bottom left hand wi had turned in its socket from the violent twisting about during the one-sided scrap Grenful crashed from a low down turn while watching the Hun landing. (Caldwell - 1*

60 Squadron, RFC.
Bishop, Molesworth & Young.
(Mladenoff)

74 Squadron, RAF - Clairmais, July 1918. Back Row left to
right: Matheson, Kilpatrick, Luff, Shoemaker. Middle
Row: Bergett, Glynn, Howe, Clements, Roxburgh-Smith,
Wallace, Carew, Gondie, Stidolph, Gordon, Padrè Banks.
Front Row: Spiers (Adj.), Kiddie, Gould, Harrison, Hunt,
Venter, Carlin, Coverdale.   (Mladenoff)

60 Squadron Officers - December 1916.
(Sater)

60 Squadron, RFC.
Roberts, Jenks, and Selous
(Mladenoff)

K. L. Caldwell's
checkered fin S.E. 5a
in an imaginary scrap
with Vee Strutters.
(Caldwell)

60 Squadron Officers - December 1916.
(Sater)

29.1.17   *"With Meintjes and Fry, did O.P. 13,500 ft. and met 8
            Albatros over Biez Wood. We engaged them, Capt. Meintjes
            shooting one down. My petrol tank and other parts of
            grid shot through by explosive bullets so landed at 8 Sq.
            Machine a write-off."* [5]

1.3.17   *"Escort to F.E. Attacked 2 H.A. Albatros over Gommecourt.
            One dived through clouds and the other one with streamers
            on scrapped for about 10 minutes. This machine was a
            little faster and a better climber than C.5, but the pilot
            wasn't very good and did flat turns."*

On the 12th of March, Caldwell was sent to England on sick leave and came back on
May 22nd as leader of "B" flight. He made his first patrol in three months and,
from then on, was right in the thick of the air fighting. The new German models,
Albatros D.III's and D.V's were out in force against the slower British types. Caldwell
and his flight were over Louvain on May 25th when 20 E.A. attacked them. The scrap
lasted half an hour, but without any results. Two days later, again with his flight,
he dived at two two-seaters, but lost them in the sun. The patrol split up and both
Phalen and 2/Lt. W. H. Gunner each got themselves a victim. A later patrol south of
Louvain was indecisive to Caldwell when he fired 45 rounds at a silver Rumpler above
him.

On the 28th, he came up against one of Germany's leading airmen, but let his combat
report and log sum up this scrap.

COMBAT REPORT

PILOT: CAPT. K. L. CALDWELL, 60 SQ.   LOCALITY: NEAR LENS

DATE: 28 MAY 1917   BRITISH
                                               MACHINE: NIEUPORT SCOUT
HEIGHT: 7000 FT TO GROUND   SILVER, MARKING,
                                                           B.3 STREAMER ON RUDDER.

REMARKS ON HOSTILE AIRCRAFT: ALBATROS SCOUT, BLACK AND RED, SHORT STREAMER
FROM BOTH STRUTS. PILOT EITHER WORE BLACK HELMET OR HAD BLACK HAIR.

NARRATIVE: NIEUPORT ATTACKED TWO 2-SEATERS S.E. OF LENS AT 7000 FT. NIEUPORT
WAS IN TURN ATTACKED BY THREE ALBATROS SCOUTS...ONE OF THEM, THE LEADER, WAS
A WONDERFUL PILOT AND VERY AGGRESSIVE.

NIEUPORT TRIED EVERY CONCEIVABLE STUNT TO SHAKE OFF E.A., BUT TO NO AVAIL.
HEIGHT WAS LOST DOWN TO 1000 FT. WHEN NIEUPORT PILOT MADE MACHINE TO APPEAR
OUT OF CONTROL. GERMAN PILOT CEASED SHOOTING AND FOLLOWED DOWN TO WATCH
CRASH. NIEUPORT PULLED OUT JUST ABOVE GROUND AND LUCKILY FOUND AN ATTACKING

---

[5] *I might enlarge on this engagement because the Hun leader's Albatros was mostly
red in color and he flew pretty well. We attacked these 8 E.A., and after the first
hectic skirmish, I saw Meintjes going down after a Hun, but with two on his tail, so
I set off down in a steep spiral to try to help him. On the way down, I noticed a
chattering sound which I thought was caused by a loose fitting chin strap on my
helmet; then a bang in front and out came petrol over my knees and feet, and then
much difficulty shaking off a persistent Hun pilot--the reddish one. This was my
lucky day, as the aeroplane did not catch alight. Flew to the nearest airfield at
La Bellevue and thankfully landed. On inspection, found the Nieuport was like a
sieve; hence, a new Nieuport. (K. L. Caldwell - 1968)*

POSITION FOR THE FIRST TIME. NIEUPORT CHASED E.A. EAST, FIRNG 94 ROUNDS
UNTIL RANGE BECAME TOO GREAT. E.A. FLEW ON, APPARENTLY O.K.

NIEUPORT RETURNED TO AERODROME VERY BADLY SHOT ABOUT, ALSO PILOT'S CLOTHES.

Caldwell's log-book entry of this fight gives added detail and further insight into his
dogged tenacity and fighting determination.

28.5.17 *"Attacked two 2-seaters near Lens at 7000 ft. Was attacked by
three scouts behind; one with streamers was hot stuff and I
couldn't shake him off, until down to 200 ft. My petrol tank,
flying wires, aileron control, struts, and main spar shot
through, so I came home after a brief scrap with another two
Scouts who were pretty dud. Phalen missing from this show."*

Caldwell's own words on this fight confirmed the contention that he had run into Voss...
*"When I returned to Ixel le Hameau from the patrol, an Anti-Aircraft battery west of
Lens had phoned through, reporting this scrap and said that they thought it had been
Voss' machine."*

*"Not long before this fight, we had lost a pilot named Phalen and the same
German pilots may have been responsible." (This, indeed, was a Jasta 5 Kette consist-
ing of Voss, Konnecke, and Schuhmann. Phalen fell to the guns of Schuhmann while
Voss and Konnecke collected their 31st and 2nd victories respectively over two
25 Sq. F.E. 2d's.) (Editor)*

Not content with taking a beating from Voss, he had the audacity to try his hand
with two more enemy aircraft, with a machine shot to bits. Stunts like that were
typical of Caldwell, as will be noted from later combats.

In the following week, there were plenty more scraps, but nothing to show for
them. The C.O., Maj. A. J. L. Scott, joined a "B" flight patrol on the 5th of June
when they engaged three H.A. at 11,500 ft. Caldwell's gun was very erratic, firing
three shots at a time, but the C.O. got one Albatros down in flames on our side with
a short burst of only five rounds. It was attacking a 29 Sq. Nieuport when the C.O.
made his swift coup. The enemy pilot jumped out and was found 1/4 of a mile from the
crashed aircraft. *(Lt. Oskar von Neudorff, Jasta 3. First cousin of Manfred von
Richthofen...Editor.)*

On the 8th of June, Caldwell had several engagements and, with Capt. Molesworth,
attacked a Scout from 50 yards, but the German dived from 10,500 to 2000 feet, flattened
out and made good his escape. Right up to the 14th, Caldwell was recording fights
daily, still without that touch of good fortune as an added spur, and then he came out
on top; his long spell of "nothing to report" was over as he marked up his first
victory in 60 Squadron.

14.6.17 9:55 A.M. *A. & B. flight O.P. 6 Huns seen - I engaged one,
fired 15 rounds at Albatros Scout at 6000 ft.
Buckingham went into cockpit and machine went on
its back and fell out of control 2 miles S.E. of
Drocourt-Queent Line. A/A saw this Hun disappear
through the haze 100 ft. above the ground still
all of a -----!!*

On the 16th, doing an early patrol, he engaged three Albatros C.III's and fired
three drums of Lewis, but, again, without result. These machines were always good
and many skilled Allied pilots took a beating from them. Probably McCudden and
McElroy of the RAF were the only two who really achieved success against them and
they gave much time and thought to their destruction. Later in the day, Caldwell
secured his second victory when he was on patrol with "B" and "C" flights at 11,500
feet over Vitry. Five Albatros D.III's attacked a "B" flight formation of four

machines from above and behind. They were "rather dud," according to Caldwell, and "C" flight drove them down through the lower formation, and, in his own words, "we then did battle..."

> "I fired 50 rounds at 100 yards. Later dived to 4000 ft., followed by Fry and Collier - fired 20 rounds at Hun Scout who dived vertically, Fry and Collier also fired. Couldn't see what happened. Lost Lloyd (2/Lt. D.F.C.) who went down with two E.A. on his tail."

This aircraft was officially confirmed and credited to Caldwell. *(Vzfw. Robert Riessinger, Jagdstaffel 12, collided with Lt. D. R. C. Lloyd and both pilots were killed. Lt. Hermann Becker, Jasta 12, shot down and wounded during this combat, apparently the victim of "Grid" Caldwell...Editor)*

Caldwell's next recorded scrap came on the 24th when he gained a double victory. With eight Nieuports, he dived on 15 E.A. southeast of Douai to get one crashed and one out of control. His log entry is very meager in details and gives no more than the bare facts. He had a close shave with death the next day when taking off from No. 8 Sq. aerodrome. On a sharp climb the engine cut out at 300 feet. He just made the 'drome again, but bent his axle badly on landing (McCudden in 1918 was killed in similar circumstances). It had no effect on him, however, because on the 26th, he did three patrols with several encounters, first against two-seaters at whom he got off 50 rounds. Later he bounced five Scouts who dived away east, getting in with only 40 rounds. His third patrol of the day was against four two-seaters with 100 rounds expended, and again, nil results.

Activity was constant now for Caldwell with hardly a day going by without some sort of scrap against hostile aircraft. The 27th of June found him on a patrol with his flight attacking three Scouts at 8000 ft. when they were, themselves, pounced upon by eight others. A busy 10 minutes was had by all, with honors to the enemy. Lt. D. G. C. Murray went down wounded and was made a prisoner of war. *(Murray brough down by Lt. von Nostitz of Jasta 12...Editor)* This fight was evidently a trap set by the enemy pilots and "B" flight were lucky not to have had other casualties. The occasion of Caldwell's 5th victory in 60 Squadron was a terse entry in his log for 3.7.17:

> "Dawn O.P. Attacked 7 EA over Grandcourt. I fired 50 rounds at one Scout from 30 yards range and he fell out of control, also seen by Jenkins, who also got one out of control."

From this and previous entries, it emerges quite clearly that, against scout machines, his scraps were sharp and decisive with a minimum of rounds fired and that he was generally successful in his attacks; whereas, against two seaters, he was using from 150 to 250 rounds without result. The element of surprise over a two-seater was always at a minimum if the observer was correctly carrying out his duties, and he attempted to attack from below--the observer's blind spot. In the whole of Caldwell's 25 victories, he scored only twice over two-seaters, which about sums up his superiority over the type.

The S.E. 5 made its first appearance with 60 Squadron at the beginning of July with Caldwell having his first flight in one on the 7th of the month. The next day, he went over to 56 Squadron to learn all he could about these great fighting machines as some of them had formerly been in use with 56 before being replaced with later models; but he continued flying his Nieuport for the next three weeks. In that period, he marked up another victory and shared one with Lt. W. E. Jenkins. His log entry reads:

14.7.17   "B" Flight O.P. Scrapped 12 E.A. over Douai and lost Lt. Parkes. Met E.A. on way back and Jenkins and self got him. A/A confirmed. Later I fired 50 rounds at E.A. by Havrincourt

Wood. *Hit petrol tank, but it didn't go off. Don't know if Hun went down or not. Got within 20 yards or so."*

Nevertheless, he did get it as it was later confirmed as out of control.

By the 28th of July, Caldwell had run up quite a bit of flying time in the S.E. 5, but jammed guns caused him much anxiety. Besides having a Lewis gun firing over the top wing, a Vickers was also carried and fired through the airscrew. Caldwell was not used to this extra gun, and to have the pair of them jammed was no joke.

On 29 July, patrolling with Capt. W. A. Bishop and Lt. Gunner, he was involved in a fight of which he recorded in the barest outline, and it was left to Bishop to amplify in his book, "Winged Warfare."

Caldwell's version of the fight as given from his logbook:

29.7.17   *"With Gunner and Bishop, I attacked 4 E.A. over Vitry. We drifted north of Douai and 3 more came up. Both guns jammed--came home escorted by 2 E.A. down to 80 ft. Gunner did not return from this show."*

(2/Lt. W. H. Gunner's S.E. 5 downed by Oblt. von Tutschek of Jasta 12 as his 19th victory...Editor.)

This is Bishop's version of the fight relative to Caldwell:

"In one case, I had a Capt. out of my own squadron, a New Zealander, come eight miles across the lines after both his guns had choked, and he was entirely useless as a fighting unit, just to try to bluff away seven of the enemy who were attacking me. It was unnecessary in this case as I had the upper hand of the few machines that were really serious about this fight, but it was a tremendously brave act on his part as he ran great risks of being killed while absolutely helpless to defend himself in any way."

In the course of the next three weeks, Caldwell had little to report except for the 20th of August and they were the notes he made in testing the relative performances of S.E. aircraft with the 200 HP and 150 HP engines. The tests were made under actual war conditions and gave some idea of the differences between the two engines:

150 HP S.E. 5	to 15,000 ft	38 mins.	82	m.p.h.
	to 10,000 ft.	15 mins.	106	m.p.h.
200 HP S.E. 5	to 13,200 ft.	19 mins.		
	to 12,000 ft.	16-1/2 mins.		
	to 10,000 ft.	12-1/2 mins.		

On the 23rd of September, a 60 Squadron patrol under Caldwell was the direct cause of the epic fight in which Werner Voss was vanquished. It was just after 6:00 P.M. when Lt. H. A. Hamersley, slightly astray from Caldwell's guidance, was pounced upon by an expertly handled Fokker DR.I. Handling his plane to the best of his ability, Hammersley was still forced into a tight spin earthwards, with Voss close on his tail, and in dire trouble when a flight from 56 Squadron came on the scene and gave him relief. Hamersley was the second known escapee from Voss' clutches, and in both cases, it had to be a 60 Squadron member. Caldwell was a spectator of Voss' last great fight against 56 Squadron and recognized the masterly exhibition of flying as identical with his own combat for the 26th of May.[6]

[6] *Cross & Cockade, Volume 8, No. 4, pages 394, 395.*

From the 14th of July, he had carried out offensive patrols without gain, but on the 25th of September, he crashed on an Aviatik two-seater N.E. of Ypres, one mile over the lines. The official comminque on the fight stated:

"AN OFFENSIVE PATROL OF NO. 60 SQUADRON ENGAGED AN ALBATROS SCOUT WHICH WAS DESTROYED BY 2/LTS. J. CROMPTON AND YOUNG. 2/LT. W. JENKINS SHOT DOWN A TWO-SEATER OUT OF CONTROL AND THEN HIS PATROL ATTACKED SEVEN ENEMY AIRCRAFT OVER ST. JULIAN, AND CAPT. K. CALDWELL DROVE ONE DOWN OUT OF CONTROL."

This was his last combat in 60 Squadron, and on 12 October, he returned to Home Establishment and one month's leave. He left the Squadron with the purple and white ribbon of the Military Cross under his "wings" and his citation to the award told how ably it had been won.

"FOR CONSPICUOUS GALLANTRY AND DEVOTION TO DUTY WHEN LEADING OFFENSIVE PATROLS. HE HAS PERSONALLY DESTROYED FIVE HOSTILE MACHINES, AND HAD OVER 50 CONTESTS IN THE AIR, IN ALL OF WHICH HE HAS DISPLAYED SPLENDID SKILL AND FEARLESSNESS, AND HAS SET AN EXCELLENT EXAMPLE TO HIS SQUADRON."

With the expiration of leave, he reported on the 12th of November to Gosport for special flying instruction under Capt. E. J. Gilchrist, who had been in 60 Squadron some time previously, and for 14 days went through the curriculum of this famous school. On the 27th, he arrived at the School of Aerial Fighting, Turnberry, where he had five weeks more of intensive training until the New Year, when he had another spell of three weeks leave from the 24th of January. Caldwell finished off with two weeks at the Central Flying School under his one time commander, Col. Scott, M.C., and to judge from his war record in 1918, must have passed out a polished fighter and capable shot.[7]

At the end of January, he was promoted Major, and on the 8th of March, 1918, assumed command of 74 Squadron from Maj. A. S. Dore, recently promoted. The squadron was then at London Coloney and had begun mobilizing for overseas at the beginning of March, equipped with S.E. 5a's, 180 h.p. Wolsely "Viper" engines.

A wonderful spirit established itself in 74 with such men as Capt. E. "Mick" Mannock, MC. & Bar, later a V.C., and Caldwell, which was displayed in the subsequent history of the squadron after its departure for France on March 30, 1918. In seven months fighting, they created new records for enemy aircraft shot down, some 224 in all, at the cost of 11 killed, 8 prisoners of war, and 6 wounded. 56 Squadron had been the premier scout squadron for the number of aircraft shot down, 100 in three months, but 74 easily exceeded this in two months and one week. A more detailed analysis is as follows:

56 Sq.	23.4.17 to 27.5.17	- 50 E.A.	23.4.17 to 20.7.17	- 100 E.A.
74 Sq.	12.4.18 to 19.5.18	- 50 E.A.	12.4.18 to 17.6.18	- 100 E.A.

_____

[7] *Quite a bit of use of camera gun in mock dog fights with other instructors at Central Flying School, Upavon, and upon return there from 60 Sq., showed up faults in deflection shooting.*
Half-way through 1918, in 74, I had my Lewis gun removed from the top plane where it was pretty useless, really. In a scrap you could not easily change the ammunition drums while trying to maneuver it, and at the same time, the Hun could see what was going on and took advantage (naturally) of the break. The S.E. would have been a much better airplane if it had had two Vickers through the propeller; even then, it would have been no match for a well flown Fokker D.VII (in my opinion), which I flew after the war and liked very much. (Keith L. Caldwell - 1968)

74 Sq. RAF. Rugby X 5 (2 absent).
K. L. Caldwell (3rd left seated),
Taffy Jones (3rd right seated).
(Caldwell)

Keith L. ("Grid") Caldwell
C.O. of 74 Squadron

(Kilduff)

74 Squadron RAF Pilots. Standing from left:
Roxburgh-Smith and Kiddie. Seated from left:
Mannock, Caldwell, Gerrard (Adj.), and Young.
(Caldwell)

Captain Chidlaw-Roberts
& K. L. Caldwell, 60 Sq.
RFC - September 1917.
(Caldwell)

Roxburgh-Smith in his S.E. 5a
(Whetton)

Those who contributed to the laurels of the squadron were Capt. J. I. T. Jones, 40 victories; Capt. E. Mannock, 36 victories; Capt. B. Roxburgh-Smith, 16 victories; and Capts. Kiddie and Carlin with 11 each. The last named had a wooden leg and was later concerned in a collision with Caldwell while diving on enemy scouts. Nine other pilots in the squadron had scores of 5 and more.

The squadron pilots and machines under Major Caldwell left London Colney for Goldhanger, Essex, on March 24th, crossed to St. Omer, France on the 30th, and reached Teteghem on the 2nd of April. In preparation for their debut as a fighting unit, they did line patrols only, from the 5th to the 11th of April, and no aircraft were encountered or sighted. The squadron stayed only a week in the 64th Wing, and on the 11th, moved to Clairmarais Aerodrome where they came under the 11th Wing (Lt. Col. Van Ryneveld), 2nd Brigade.

Contact was made with the enemy on April 12th, the day Earl Haig issued his famous "Backs to the Wall" message, and 74 fought at their best. Five E.A. were shot down in the afternoon patrol; Caldwell, Dolan and Capt. W. E. Young with one each, and Mannock with two. Caldwell's victim was an Albatros D.V with yellow fuselage and green wings and any doubt as to his markmanship could now be forgotten. He dived from 17,000 ft. to 14,000 ft. and fired 15 rounds at close range into the enemy's cockpit. The Albatros fell out of control and Caldwell followed it for 1000 feet, fired a few more rounds, and the E.A. went down to crash along side a balloon in a ploughed field, S.E. of Deulemont. In this fight, he was leading "C" flight composed of Jones, Lt. F. Skeddon, Lt. W. B. Giles, Lt. Begbie, and Capt. W. J. Cairnes.

Until the end of the month, Caldwell was engaged in Offensive Patrols, and while it was not a general practice for a C.O. to do so, he made it a rule to carry out at least one a day. He adhered to this principle during the whole of the squadron's active service in France. Of course, there were squadron duties to be performed such as organization and other onerous jobs which filled his day all too frequently. Nevertheless, Caldwell made a point of getting one hour's flying each day, watching the various flights at work and gaining a thorough knowledge of his pilots.

He did not record another victory until May 7th, on an afternoon patrol at the rather low level of 7000 feet. With Lt. Roxburgh-Smith and three others, he dived on two Fokker DR.I's flying west near Ypres. Caldwell put 70 rounds into one at 30 yards and it went down vertically through the clouds. He never sighted it again. He fired another 70 rounds into the next triplane which was being engaged by Roxburgh-Smith. Hits were observed in the cockpit and petrol tank and down it went out of control on its back, with the nose pointed upwards through the clouds. Although he was credited with this aircraft, Caldwell felt sure that the pilot had been killed by Roxburgh-Smith's fire before he, himself, had commenced firing. *(Possibly Off. Stellv. Waldemar von der Weppen + of Jasta 27...Editor.)*

Two weeks elapsed before Caldwell succeeded in catching up with his score, which now stood at 10 confirmed, and he literally had a chase for it. He was doing an evening patrol just before 7:00 P.M. on May 21st, at a little over 4000 feet, when he observed six Pfalz D.III's attacking our balloons. He dived and engaged a Pfalz from the front, but was immediately attacked from above by another Pfalz, painted all black. Caldwell was kept on the defensive for a short time, then got into a position to fire. The Pfalz dived vertically and made towards the lines with Caldwell in pursuit. He overtook it near Ypres and the Pfalz dived east again and flattened out at 50 feet off the ground, just over the trenches. The enemy pilot zoomed and dived for about a mile, with Caldwell after him firing continuously, then crashed two miles west of Ypres. Altogether, Caldwell fired 240 rounds from both guns, which was somewhat over his usual expenditure of shots. In this scrap, five Pfalz were destroyed; Capt. Young with one and Mannock three. Earlier, Mannock had destroyed another one, giving him 4 for the day.

The next successful combat for Caldwell occurred two days later and is quoted here in its entirety:

SQUADRON: 74   DATE: 23.5.18

TYPE & NO. OF AEROPLANE: S.E. 5a C/5396   TIME: 7:35 P.M.

ARMAMENT: 1 VICKERS, 1 LEWIS   LOCALITY: I. 36.

PILOT: MAJ. K. L. CALDWELL, MC.   DUTY: S.M.

RESULT: OUT OF CONTROL___1___.   HEIGHT: 6000 FEET

REMARKS ON HOSTILE AIRCRAFT (TYPE, SPEED, ARMAMENT, ETC.):
          Pfalz Scouts (silver wings, red tails and cowls)
                       (black wings, red tails and cowls)

NARRATIVE: Observing 4 E.A. flying N. to S. over I. 36., I signaled to three S.E. 5's to follow me and dived on the E.A. The rear E.A. evaded my attack, and I was then attacked by one of the other E.A. who had climbed in front. I fought this E.A. down to 6000 feet from 9000 feet, and after a burst at very close range, he fell over on his back and went down in a spin. I could not follow him down as I was attacked by a lot of E.A., which had come up between me and the line unseen. I fired a few rounds at several of these E.A. without result, and then dived towards the lines.
               (signed) *K. L. Caldwell,* Major
                         Royal Air Force.

As his log book says of this fight, "I was chased home by 15 Pfalz." It has been mentioned earlier in this account of "Grid" Caldwell that he made a practice of watching his pilots at their daily work in the air and to give advice on the tactics they used. One pilot who probably did not forget the 23rd May was Lt. Giles. He was concentrating on the destruction of a silver-gray two-seater when he allowed a black Albatros D.V to pounce on him. However, Caldwell had been keeping a sharp lookout, and driving off the Albatros, saved Giles from taking a beating. Giles kept a weather eye open after that.

The last of May brought Caldwell on the 13 mark with a victory over a Pfalz D.III. He was flying alone in the evening at 11,000 feet over Ploegsteert Wood and sighted five Albatros D.V's. He engaged one of them without apparent result and had to come back to the lines owing to loss of height. At 8:00 P.M., he joined up with Capt. Mannock and, together, they attacked nine Pfalz D.III's. Caldwell tackled one of them nose on and fired 120 rounds until they practically collided. The Pfalz turned over and dived vertically. After falling 1000 feet, it began to sideslip badly and appeared to be hit, but could not be watched further in the presence of other hostile aircraft. Mannock also had one down out of control.

May was Caldwell's best month to date, and that of the Squadron as well. During the 31 day period, they disposed of 66 aircraft and one balloon, a record they were never able to approach by half up to the cessation of hostilities. The principal scorers were:

Mannock - 20; Jones - 15; Kiddie - 5; Roxburgh-Smith - 5; Caldwell - 4; and Clements - 3.

The late evening of June 1st was a successful one for Caldwell. He was on a special mission, east of Dickebusch at 14,000 feet, when he spotted four Pfalz, colored silver with red tails. He dived and attacked one at 100 yards range and it immediately went into left-hand climbing turns. Caldwell flew to cut it off, still firing, and closed to point blank range. He zoomed up and saw the Pfalz still spinning 1500 feet below, but could not watch any further as he was engaged by others of the enemy patrol This Pfalz was confirmed as out of control.

On one of his occasional massed formation patrols, June 6th, he led "B" and "C" flights against 14 Pfalz lurking at 14,000 feet. They drove them eastwards to 4000 feet and got only one crashed during the scrap. As Caldwell recorded at the time, "should have got 5 at least."

He was not exactly a strategist, but believed in getting as close to the enemy as possible, and then tactics too became of secondary importance. Position meant nothing so long as there was something to shoot at. With activity at an ebb, he, on one occasion in June, led a full squadron of 19 machines over the Ypres sector searching for enemy patrols, but not a sign of a single fighter anywhere. Caldwell immediately set off for Roulers with the squadron in full support, flew around the aerodrome there and challenged all to come up. They didn't have long to wait. Airplanes from every 'drome in a radius of 15 miles came along, but not to fight. The closest they approached was about 400 yards and as soon as Caldwell attacked, they all scattered. This kept up for half an hour without either side making contact and, eventually, Caldwell flew off with his men, very disgusted. The Germans must have suspected some colossal trap when they saw this British formation and refused to be taken in, little thinking that is was purely a gesture of defiance.

Later in 1918, full squadron formation flying was tried out by some units; 85 under Mannock, 4 A.F.C., and one or two others, but were not really a success. Capt. A. W. Beauchamp-Proctor, VC, of 84 Squadron used it to great advantage, and his squadron probably was the only one to reap rich rewards by these methods.

On June 7th, Caldwell and Capt. Young took on three LVG two-seaters and forced one to land, but it had brought them down very low and that was how they had to come home to 74's aerodrome. Caldwell was still finding two-seaters far from easy pickings Although he was carrying out his daily patrol, there was little air activity for him. Mannock had left the squadron to command No. 85 in late June and Lt. J. I. T. "Taffy" Jones had taken over as flight commander on the 20th with marked success. In the last ten days of the month, Jones added 6 to his score, taking up where Mannock had left off. The loss of Mannock was a blow to Caldwell and left a big gap in the squadron. He watched over his pilots and kept everything normal until the incident had taken a back seat. Events happened too quickly to worry about the past.

Caldwell led a morning patrol on the 15th of July, south of Roulers, when they tackled five Fokker D.VII's from the east at 16,000 feet. The fight went on down to 6,000 feet with Caldwell jumping one at close range. It turned and dived for 5,000 feet when one of the right-hand wings folded back and the Fokker spun out of control to crash. The patrol also collected two more out of control for the loss of Lt. Gray, later reported a prisoner of war.

From July 1st to the 14th, the squadron had secured only three victories, but in that period, the unit discovered a first class fighting man in their midst, Lt. S. Carlin, MC DCM. He had marked up one confirmed on the 13th of June over a DFW two-seater, but from the 18th of July, started a run on the balloons. By the end of the month, three of them had gone down in flames, plus two Scouts; and before being captured, "Timbertoes," as Mannock called him, had collected five E.A. and six balloons. Capt. Jones also continued to add more to his growing total with seven for July, and Caldwell, himself, gained a double on the 30th.

West of Armentieres, on a late morning patrol, he sighted a Fokker D.VII that dived away. Caldwell chased it from 11,000 to 7000 feet before he could engage it at close range. The Fokker evaded quickly, and while still 500 feet above, Caldwell did a spin turn and got on his opponent's tail. He fired 60 rounds at 50 yards and observed hits in the cockpit. The Fokker fell out of control, turning over and side-slipping. Owing to bad visibility, Caldwell could not follow below 2000 feet and the presence of other aircraft was a hazard not to be disregarded.

His second came late in the day on one of his "special missions." East of Dickebusch, at 13,000 feet, he bounced a Pfalz D.III which had been engaged by our A/A batteries. Caldwell fired 40 rounds at point-blank range and down went the Pfalz. He followed it down to 4000 feet, then had to break off or he would have been in trouble with more E.A. who just wanted him to keep going down. Too many good men were caught that way because they wanted a positive confirmation of a victory. However, the battery that had been firing at the Pfalz watched it down to 100 feet, but could not see it crash owing to trees being in the way. There could have been no chance of the Pfalz surviving under those circumstances and it was con- sidered confirmed out of control. The next day, he did a really high patrol with Capt. Young and Lt. F. S. Gordon. They pushed up to 19,000 feet and spotted 20 E.A. north of Estaires. Three Fokkers were attacked, and in Caldwell's own words, "got good shooting at one fellow who went down, but flattened out." There must have been a dearth of enemy aircraft for that day and Capt. Jones with Lt. Shoemaker, USAS attached to 74, were the only scorers by getting a two-seater each.

The squadron was now at a pitch where Caldwell could take a spell of leave, and from August 6th to the 19th, he was in England. In his absence, with Capt. Jones as acting C.O., the squadron added another 13 to their total, a round 150 victories. Full of zest when he returned, Caldwell wasted no time in getting his 18th victim on August 23rd. Leading a late evening patrol of S.E.'s southeast of Houthulst Forest at 7000 feet, he observed six E.A. north of his own formation. With Capt. Roxburgh-Smith, he attacked the leading Fokker D.VII which dived away eastwards through a thin layer of clouds. As it reached the clouds, Caldwell fired at close range, hit the petrol tank resulting in vapor starting from the cockpit. The Fokker turned over and dived in a northwest direction, followed by Caldwell. At 4500 feet, he again closed to 50 yards and fired a double drum from his Lewis. The enemy pilot never pulled out of his dive and crashed east of Houthulst Forest.

After having lost the services of the original senior flight commander, Capt. W. E. Young, DFC, on August 4th to No. 1 Squadron as their new commanding officer, Caldwell also lost Capt. Jones, DSO, MC DFC & Bar, MM, who had run up 40 victories in the squadron. He departed from the scene on rest in England, but there were plenty of good fighters in the squadron, and quite tough: Lt. Fred Luff, USAS, Lt. F. J. Hunt, G. R. Hicks, Carlin, Kiddie, and Roxburgh-Smith.

During September, they took time out to destroy six balloons, and with 21 E.A. on the slate, had their best month since the previous June. For Caldwell, it was to be his most successful one with five E.A., and, incidentally, the highest individual score for the month in the squadron. His first was a very decisive one in the even- ing of the 4th. South of Lille, he tackled, at 14,000 feet, one of 4 Fokker D.VII's with a quick burst from underneath. The Fokker dropped past Caldwell, who followed to 9000 feet and then broke away to watch his opponent crash. The same day was a successful one for the balloon fanciers; Gordon and Carlin with one and two respectively.

Within 24 hours, Caldwell was to suffer an experience he probably never will forget. The squadron was spending the day around Izel-le-Hameau and a dawn patrol over the south Cambrai sector at 16,000 feet found he and Carlin attacking the same enemy plane. The time was just on 6:00 A.M. They dived together, and Carlin, being above Caldwell, did not see him and struck his upper wing tip. Carlin noticed the impact, but thought he had struck the German machine. It was not so, and Carlin returned to his own aerodrome on half a tail over south Cambrai, unaware of what had really happened. Caldwell's machine had gone diving down over enemy territory and he was unable to control its actions. After falling 2000 feet, the dive developed into a flat spin. Lt. G. R. Hicks had followed down to protect Caldwell and, at 5000 feet, was astounded to see him climb out and rest his right foot on the lower wing. He grasped the left center section strut and manipulated the stick with his right hand, hoping for results. Caldwell waved to Hicks, who took it to be a parting gesture, and rather than watch his C.O. go down to certain death, as he thought, Hicks flew away. With only 500 feet to earth, the position seemed hopeless; but Caldwell, displaying all his skill and resourcefulness, succeeded in guiding his S.E. 5a so that he just cleared his own front lines. When the plane was about to dive into the ground, he jumped and turned a few somersaults on the ground. He came to a stop near a dugout where some of the infantry were watching, spellbound by the swift turn of events, as Caldwell got up and walked towards them.

None the worse for his alarming experience, he returned to the squadron and the next day was again leading patrols. His only remark entered in his log book relative to the occasion was summed up in just three words:

"Very lucky still!!"

Caldwell entered the ranks of those credited with 20 victories when he secured a double on the 17th of September. It was a patrol N.W. of Courtrai at 6:30 P.M. when he led 5 S.E.'s on to 7 E.A. at 15,000 feet. Their quarry lost height to 13,000 feet, but Caldwell left them alone on seeing six Fokkers approaching at a high level, sensing a trap. At that moment, he spotted an S.E. 5a being driven down by three E.A. two miles farther east. He immediately went to the aid of the British pilot and engaged the top Fokker D.VII at 10,000 feet. The enemy pilot never saw Caldwell, who opened up at close range and watched his 20th victim crash northeast of Courtrai. The other two Fokkers were still attacking the lone S.E. 5a (Lt. Hunt of 74 Squadron) and the fight was then down at 7000 feet. Caldwell next jumped the uppermost of the two, who dived away as he stopped 100 rounds at 50 yards range. Up zoomed the Fokker to fall over sideways and dive down southwest. It was most certainly hit, but Caldwell could not waste time in watching for results as the remaining Fokker still had height over Hunt. He attacked this one, which spun down low, but it was seen to flatten out.

They both returned north of Roulers with four E.A. following close behind, one in particular being a little too close, yet it did not bother Caldwell, not at all. He only turned and engaged it with two jammed guns!! (Lewis, broken extractor; Vickers, No. 3.) As he reported at the time, "I could only frighten the E.A. away." What superb confidence he must have possessed and an inversely low opinion of his opponent!

One of the penalties of being C.O. of the squadron was to lose the services of outstanding pilots. It was not good for morale and, in minor ways, was upsetting to others in the squadron, resulting in a falling off of their fighting capabilities. On the other hand, it could sharpen their appetitite for work in a spirit of revenge, but generally speaking, such a loss cast a feeling of gloom over the squadron, especially if the belief was that the pilot concerned had had no chance of surviving. Caldwell was to suffer this loss of a very good pilot on the 21st of September and one he could ill afford to lose.

He was leading a squadron patrol west of Lille just after 6:00 P.M. on his usual evening forage and, at the high level of 18,500 feet, intercepted ten Fokker D.VII's. He fired at seven different machines with time for only a few rounds at each. With a half roll, Caldwell dropped on a Fokker who was diving on an S.E. and fired a short burst at 25 yards. He could see his tracers all about the cockpit as the German went into a vertical dive with engine full on. The presence of the other E.A. prevented him from watching further. Hunt and Glynn knocked down one each and Roxburgh-Smith one out of control, but Carlin had to force land between the lines.

Carlin attempted to reach the British lines on foot, his only one, without luck. He made a good try, but handicapped as he was physically, the German troops got there first and he was made prisoner. In his 3-1/2 months with the squadron, he destroyed five E.A. and six balloons. [8]

It was indeed a loss, yet there were still other good men prominent in the destruction of aircraft:

Capt. B. Roxburgh-Smith, who finished with 16; Capt. A. C. Kiddie with 11; Capt. Glynn with 7; Lt. Hunt with 7; Lt. Luff who had 5; Lt. Hicks with 6; and Lt. Gordon with 5.

Caldwell gained his fifth victory of the month on the 24th against a new type of Scout--the Siemans-Schuckert D.IV. They were highly regarded by those enemy pilots who flew them, yet somehow, either through political error or incompetence in the "aviation cliques," were used only by a few front squadrons. On this occasion, Caldwell was on a morning patrol with three of his men and was three miles east of Armentieres when they dived on seven Siemans flying west from Lille at 12,000 feet. The enemy pilots turned to gain height and Caldwell engaged the leader at right angles, firing until they nearly collided. The Siemans turned to engage and Caldwell was on his tail in a flash. Up zoomed the other for 200 feet, but the speed of the S.E. allowed Caldwell to follow and he fired again at close range. The Siemans hung on its prop for a second and then fell over to the right. He could see the enemy pilot leaning to the right with his head down on his chest before the aircraft began to fall out of control. Although the other squadron members saw it falling, no results were witnessed due to other hostile aircraft nearby.

This was the only Siemans shot down in the fight and the observed performance gave them a lesser speed than the S.E. 5a, but more maneuverable. They had a better rate of climb, although their zoom was not so good. In dog fighting, they were very handy.

During the period of September 25th to October 13th, Caldwell managed only ten hours of flying. The war had speeded up considerably with the enemy retreating and Caldwell flew only to know the state of the line which was rapidly moving eastward.

He was engaged on one of these line patrols during the morning of October 14th near Iseghem. Flying at 18,000 feet, he spotted a Fokker D.VII below him at 15,000 feet. He closed rapidly, and as the enemy turned east to avoid his fire, he let go

---

[8] *I remember this fight well...how badly it turned out to be. Perhaps I might enlarge: Previously we had noticed a Hun patrol of 10 to 12 Fokkers come up to the lines just before dark and after our side had set off for home so I thought I would organize a surprise for them. Took four of our best chaps well behind the lines at 20,000 feet and then flew towards the lines and there, sure enough, were our enemy Fokkers. Our surprise failed, however, because they saw us coming and spread out in climbing turns (obviously old hands). In the dog fight that followed, we did reasonably well for a start, but when another E.A. formation came in from the north, 10 or so strong; we were in dire trouble! I saw Carlin's S.E. going down with explosive ammunition hitting it, but I could not help as I was in the center of several persistent Huns. We had to do just what we could to save ourselves. Carlin crashed, survived to serve again in the last war, to be killed as a 50 year old gunner in a night flying Defiant. Glynn and Hunt (of our five) were forced down on our side of the line and only Roxburgh-Smith and I returned to the aerodrome at Clair Marais North. It was a sad ending to what we had planned would be a successful venture. (I have never known whether we crashed any or not--we certainly had plenty of shooting, but it was very quick, nor do I know who claimed Carlin.)*
                                                      (Keith L. Caldwell - 1968)

a burst of 50 rounds. Caldwell could see his shots taking effect, and in perfect visability with nothing to hinder him, watched the Fokker go down to crash. Later in the day, he joined in a big scrap between 74 Squadron and a corresponding number of Fokkers without anything decisive.

His last and final victory of the war came on the 28th of October. In 20 minutes, he had three different scraps, only the first one being decisive. At 11:35 he was at 16,000 feet over N.E. Tournai when he surprised a black and white tailed Fokker D.VII. Caldwell moved in quickly and fired 100 rounds as he followed his victim down to 12,000 feet. The Fokker went down out of control with engine full on and crashed. He then joined a nearby mix-up of Camels and E.A. with red tails. The Camels most likely came from 70 Squadron. After 15 minutes of scrapping, the fight terminated at 50 feet, northeast of Tournai, without Caldwell becoming seriously engaged in it.

He then climbed toward a two-seater between Roubaix and Tourcoing, which had been engaged by an A/A battery, but found that it had already been taken on by Maj. G. W. Murlis-Green, the C.O. of 70 Squadron, who, by this time, had started a fire in the pilot's cockpit. Caldwell got in close behind the two-seater and fired ten rounds, then his guns packed up. The observer could not be seen at all, but his gun was sticking up. The pilot turned west as though to land in our lines, changed his mind when he saw that Caldwell was not firing, and got back over his own lines at about 50 feet. He was last seen when about to land with his prop just turning over, gliding at a height of 10 feet.

The Squadron kept up a steady rate of scoring and destroyed another 13 from the 28th of October to November 4th, the last one being secured by Capt. Kiddie. Under Caldwell's leadership, they destroyed 140-1/2 enemy aircraft with 68-1/2 out of control, plus 15 kite balloons, for a total of 224 in exactly seven months of war patrols. A truly remarkable record.

Caldwell was awarded the D.F.C. and Bar and the Belgian Croix de Guerre plus two mentions in dispatches for his services in 74 Squadron and remained with the squadron through its various moves and was still in command on January 4, 1919. In August of that year, he was demobilized and returned to his New Zealand homeland where, in 1923, he offered his services to the New Zealand Air Force and was appointed Squadron Leader.

In 1930, the R.N.Z.A.F. was re-organized and Squadron Leader K. L. Caldwell was appointed Honorary O.C. of the New Zealand Territorial Wing with the rank of Wing-Commander, which position he relinquished on the announcement of his retirement in 1937.

At the outbreak of the war in September 1939, he returned for duties with the R.N.Z.A.F. and became a Station Commander. Late in the war, he visited India and reconstituted the RNZAF Liason Office there.

He returned to New Zealand in the New Year of 1946 after six months duties abroad. For his services he was awarded the C.B.E.

+O+O+O+O+O+O+O+O+O+O+O+O+O+O

I wish to express my appreciation to "Grid" Caldwell who reviewed and annotated this brief history, adding many colorful points. Mr. Caldwell writes to me from New Zealand and I find him a very modest and extremely interesting person...W. R. Puglisi

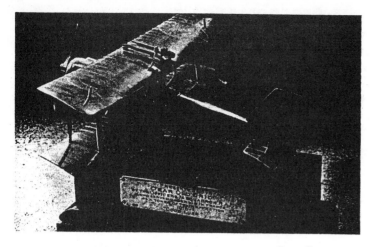

The S.E. 5a silver model presented to "Grid"
Caldwell by the officers of 74 Squadron.

Major Keith L. Caldwell,
as C.O. 74 Squadron RAF,
just before war ended.

Major Caldwell with Captain Glynn (Scotch
Bonnet) and Adj. Spiers in chair. Clairmais,
July 1918.

Major K. L. Caldwell &
Captain S. C. "Timbertoes"
Carlin of 74 Squadron RAF.

Lt. Richardson, a Canadian. "A" Flight,
74 Squadron, RAF, just before war ended.

(All photos Caldwell)

WORLD WAR 1 AIRCRAFT PERFORMANCE CHART

by George R. Evans

The purpose of this chart is to give a quick cross-reference on the general performance of the most widely used World War I aircraft. No pinpoint accuracy is intended; probably none is possible for there are too many variables. Specification sheets on groups of presumably identical production aircraft sometimes show as much as 7 m.p.h. difference in speed, and minutes difference in a 16,000 foot climb. Existing charts which show speed recorded to fractions are from specific tests, of one specific aircraft, and may be far away from the capabilities of production models. Where possible, I have used figures from aircraft in front-line service, which may not be fair, since the rest of the figures are from official tests and/or factory information -- and that last usually gave extremely optimistic performance. Especially Fokker aircraft -- but then the extrovery Tony Fokker told of finagling to run tests with only enough fuel and oil to get through the tests -- and only ammunition enough to fill the machine gun belts where they were visible.

Much of this information will not be new to the avid buffs, but it should put some of the performance figures into focus. For instance, every common report on the Pfalz D.III will indicate, "...Speed: 102.5 m.p.h...." Some other reports will qualify this report by adding, "....at 10,000 feet..." Performance figures on the Albatros D.III will indicate the speed of that aircraft as being "....115 m.p.h...." and will seldom announce the altitude at which that speed was recorded -- which was usually at a very lowe level. The general concensus of opinion is that the Albatros D.III was considerably faster than that of the Pfalz D.III --- yet flown at the same level of 10,000 feet, the speed of the Albatros D.III was approximately 100 m.p.h.....one report placing the figure at 95 m.p.h.

Another oddity in comparing performance figures of these old aircraft was in finding a number of different sources giving the performance of the Fokker Dr.I as "....97 m.p.h. at 9200 feet; increasing to 102.5 m.p.h. at 13,120 feet; then collapsing to 86 m.p.h. at 13,800 feet...." This would represent a decrease of 16.5 m.p.h. at only 700 feet higher altitude! It would appear that someone once had erred in transcribing a test-sheet of data performance figures, and when this test-sheet was later used as reference, the apparent error went unnoticed. The figures are not reasonable: no other rotary-powered aircraft of either side shows the "up-down-up" performance at changing altitude -- not even the *uberkompressed* high-altitude engines, and the Fokker Dr.I had no fancy engine, just the Thulin Le Rhone rotary engine....the Oberursel engine.

The performance figures on the Austrian figures were derived from old magazine clippings. None of the new wave of World War I books have anything listed but a "top speed" figure. But they are in line with the other types, so they are included in this report. The specifications on the Siemens-Schuckert D.III and D.IV were scrounged from notes by other German and Allied pilots that, at this or at that altitude, "...it was not as fast as...." or "...was a good five miles faster than..." If any readers has veried-level test data, such information and correction is welcomed.

The biggest performance factor of all didn't seem possible to put into a chart: how a pilot melded with the best characteristics of any given aircraft. This was the secret that made the Richthofen-Albatros, Voss-Albatross, Guynemer/Fonck/Luke/Rickenbacker-Spad combinations so effective. With the Fokker Dr.I and its tricky handling, the first-line Jastas had picked flyers to cope with it. The Sopwith Camel reversed this process of hand-picked flyers for certain aircraft: those who survived its idiosychrosies soon wore the term "Camel Pilot" like a badge.

Finally, there are aircraft obviously omitted from this report which saw service among the types listed. The Halberstadt D's, the Fokker D's, the Roland D.II and the *Walfisch*. The F.E.8, which saw more service than generally indicated; the widely-sued Moranes, B.E.'s, Bristol Scouts, etc., are not represented herein. They either arrived on the combat scene, or departed same, before performance became much of a factor....or they were used in desperation until better aircraft arrived.

The Bristol Fighters, Hannovers, L.V.G.'s, Breguets and similar types, which were good, tough scrappers and flown with equally tough and scrappy crews, probably deserve consideration also, but in an area other than this.

PERFORMANCE OF WORLD WAR 1 AIRCRAFT

A/C TYPE: H.P.	3280	6560	9840	13120	CEILING	ENDURE	ARM'T	BEST/WORST CHARACTERISTIC (S)
Siemens Schuckert D III 160	114 1¾	113 3¾	113 6'	111.5 9'	26,500	2	2 Spand.	Astonishing altitude performance... almost no fall-off
" D IV 200	119 1¾	118 3¾	117 6½	115 9¼	26,240	2	"	until above 17,000ft. Short engine life due poor Castor oil.
Pfalz D XII 180	115 3¾	112 7¾	106 12¼	103 20½	18,500	1½	..	Very sturdy but heavy handling; tough to land.
Sopwith Snipe 230	134 2½	125 5¼	121 9½	116 14'	20,000	3	2 Vickers	"Camel" handiness without its meanness. Almost too late in use.
ANSALDO A1 [3] 220	136 3'	134 5½	131 8'	128 13'	26,000	1½	2 "	Speedy, good climb, good engine... poor in maneuver.
MACCHI M5 160	115 3½	113 7½	108 12½	100 20'	15,000	3	2 "	Seaplane, but performed up to best Austrian fighters.
BERG D1 185	112 3¼'	— 7'	— 13'	98 19'	20,000	3	2 Schw.	Good A/c handicapped by engine cooling problems. Schwarzlose
BERG D1 200	115 2¼'	— 6'	— 7½'	102 11¼'	20,400	3	2 "	m.g.'s slow-firing, set forw'd of pilot, out of reach to clear
PHÖNIX D II 200	113 3'	109 7	104 12	101 22	19,600	2	2 "	Big, strong, reliable engine. Not too agile.
" D III 230	122 2½'	119 6½'	115 12'	111 18¾'	22,300	2	2 "	Improvement, but too late too see much action.
Austrian 185 ALBATROS D III	116 3'	112 7¼'	110 12'	107 18'	20,600	1½	2 Spand.	In some ways better than Ger. version. Better engine.
FOKKER D VIII 140	2½	114 5¼	112 7½	110 14'	20,600	1½	2 Spand.	Light, agile, pleasant-handling. Wing structure problems.

A/C TYPE (H.P. Symbol)	3280 (min to climb)	6560	9840	13120	CEILING	ENDURE	ARM'T	BEST/WORST CHARACTERISTIC(S)
Fokker E III 100	91 / 5'	83 / 15'	80 / 30'	—	11,500	1½	2 Maxim	Synchronized guns—Mediocre A/c
De H. 2 100	92 / 4½'	89 / 13½'	86 / 26'	70 / 45'	14,000	2¾	1 Lewis	Fairly agile – tricky, fragile
Albatros D II 160	105 / 5'	91 / 9½'	90 / 13½'	88 / 20'	17,000	1½	2 Spand.	Far ahead of Allied fighters of its time. Less agile, however.
Nieuport 11 80	95 / 5'	90 / 11'	88 / 19'	87 / 28'	15,000	2½	1 Lewis	Very agile / very fragile too.
Sopwith Pup 80	107 / 3½'	105 / 8'	101 / 14'	85 / 25'	18,000	3	1 Vickers	Maneuverable, fine A/c but light, Vickers slowed by Sop.-Kauper Synch.
Sopwith Tripe 130	120 / 2½'	113 / 6'	108 / 11½'	103 / 18'	20,500	1¾	1 Vickers	All around 1st Class A/c — but underarmed + needed rigging care.
Albatros D III 160	109 / 3½'	100 / 7'	96 / 12'	93 / 18¾'	18,000	2	2 Spand.	Best at the front over quite a long span. Lower wing trouble.
Nieuport 17 110	109 / 3'	107 / 5½'	101 / 9'	97 / 19½'	17,400	2	1 Lewis + 1 Vickers	Fine in handling + maneuver — not sturdy enough.
De H. 5 110	110 / 3'	108 / 7'	102 / 12½'	94	16,000	2¾	1 Vickers	Available ... poor handling, sluggish.
Spad VII 180 h.p.	125 / 2¾'	119 / 6¾'	112 / 11½'	108 / 19½'	18,000	2¼	1 Vickers	Fast and sturdy...underarmed, less handy than rotary scouts.
SE 5 180 h.p.	122 / 3'	118 / 7'	110 / 13'	105 / 22'	17,500	2½	1 Lewis 1 Vickers	Fast, tough, handy ... weak land. gear, unreliable engines.
Albatros DV-Va 180	116 / 3½'	112 / 7'	103 / 12'	96 / 23'	20,500	2	2 Spand.	Easy handling workhorse A/c... structure of wings weak.
Pfalz D III 160	112 / 3½'	107 / 7½'	103 / 13'	95 / 24'	17,000	2½	2 Spand.	Sturdy built, fast-diving, but heavy-handling, sluggish up high.
Sopwith Camel Clerget 130		115 / 6'	113 / 10'	108 / 15'	19,000	2½	2 Vickers	THE dogfighter of WWI. Not the plane for timid nor
" Le Rhone 110		120 / 5¼'	118 / 9'	110 / 12'	24,000	2¾	"	heavy-handed pilots. Le Rhone) more reliable among
" Bentley 150		125 / 4¾'	121 / 8¼'	117 / 10½'	22,000	2½	"	Bentley} engines used.
Fokker Dr. I 110	113 / 3'	103 / 6¼'	96 / 10'	89 / 15¼'	20,000	1½	2 Spand.	Up with the Camel in overall agility... Structurally weak.
Hanriot H-D 1 [1] 110	115	113 / 5½'	111 / 9¼'	105 / 14¼'	23,600	2½	1 Vickers	Tough and agile...only 1 gun, in 2-gun times.
Spad XIII [2] 200hp	132	126 / 6'	123 / 10'	118 / 15½'	22,500	1¾	2 Vickers	Sturdiest WWI A/c, great in "bounce" attacks. Fast landing
" 220hp	134	130 / 5¼'	128 / 8¾'	125 / 13¼'	23,000	2	"	speed - a "flying brick" if engine failed. Generally
" 235 h.p.	139	135 / 4¾'	134 / 8'	130 / 12¼'	23,000	1¾	"	conceded French aces could do most with a Spad.
Nieuport 28 160		122 / 5½'	120 / 9'	115 / 14'	19,000	1½	"	Maneuverable + available for U.S. purchase...fragile fire-trap.
SE 5A "Viper" 200hp		132 / 6¼'	130 / 10'	126 / 14½'	19,500	3	1 Lewis 1 Vickers	Fast, strong, stable. Engine teething troubles.
Sopwith Dolphin 200		131 / 6¼'	128 / 10½'	121 / 14'	21,000	2	2 Lewis 2 Vickers	Tough and maneuverable. 2 Lewis usually removed at front...eng. trbls.
Fokker D VII Mercedes 160	117 / 4¼'	114 / 8¼'	109 / 13¾'	104 / 18'	19,500	1½	2 Spand.	All around German best...but needing a better engine...
" BMW 185	122 / 2½'	119 / 6'	117 / 9'	115 / 12'	22,900	1½	"	and getting it. Fokker factory specs even better...No complaints.

[1] Hd 1, 110 Le Rhone. 130h.p. gave 3-5 m.p.h. gain along the line, but added weight kept speed of climb about same

[2] Spad VII's had engine h.p. increases too, keeping pace with XIII in some areas. Also, S XII was used, 1st as cannon armed. Performance similar to XIII.

THE LEWIS AIRCRAFT MACHINE GUN: MODEL 1918

by
Howard F. Powders

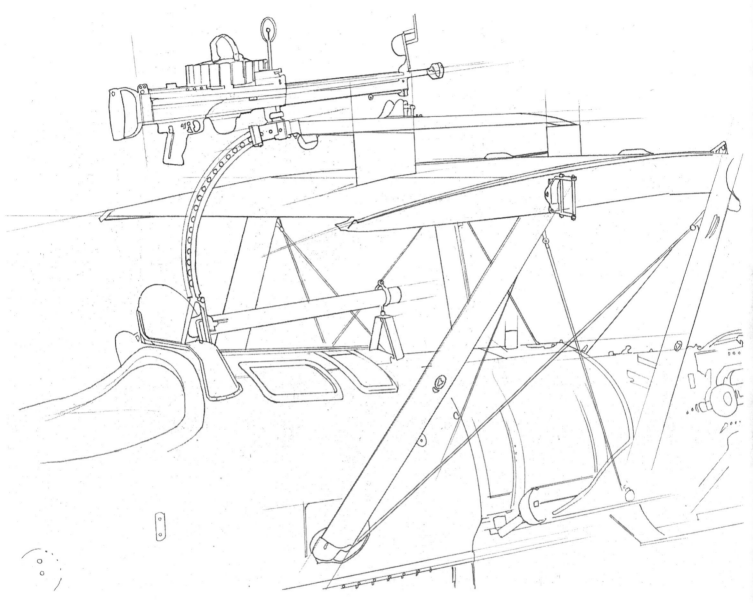

HISTORY OF DEVELOPMENT

The Lewis Aircraft Machine Gun, Model of 1918, flexible mount, was an outgrowth of an original concept of a light (infantry type) machine gun conceived by an American, Samuel McLean. McLean assigned rights of patent of his gun to the Automatic Arms Company of Buffalo, New York, whom he hoped would produce the weapon. Colonel Isaac Newton Lewis, whose name the gun bears, joined the firm in 1910, following retirement from the United States Army.

(Photo Above: A Lewis aircraft machine gun installation on a Foster mount on an S.E.5A. showing method of installation and remote firing by Bowden cable. Note sight arrangement and unique top wing attachments. Photo: USAF Museum, Wright=Patterson AFB).

to study foreign weapons. As a result of his study abroad, our field artillery was reorganized and re-armed accordingly. Col. Lewis remained in service until 1910, during which time he invented various range-finding and electrical instruments, and other developments and improvements on existing ordnance items. His final duty station was the Coast Artillery School at Fort Monroe, Virginia. Here, he held the rank of Lt. Colonel and was chief instructor and director of the school.

Responding favorably to the request to join the Automatic Arms Company of Buffalo, Lewis was assigned the task of developing new weapon concepts and improving existing ones. Having already acquired patent rights to the McLean development, but finding it complicated and cumbersome, the company gave Lewis his first assignment; namely improve the weapon to meet certain standards set forth by the Army Chief of Staff, General Leonard Wood. Other similar prototypes were presented to the Secretary of War and other Army dignitaries in 1911, but no decision was reached on procurement, much to Lewis' annoyance. The following year, 1912, Lewis, acting unofficially, persuaded Capt. Charles deForest Chandler to mount the gun on a Type B Wright airplane and attempt what was to become a significant milestone in mating the machine gun with the airplane for the first time in history.

Chandler, first Army officer detailed to Aeronautic Division, and the first commandant of the flying school at College Park, and his alternate pilot and gunner, Lt. Milling, managed to place some 14 rounds out of a drum of 44 rounds onto a target laid out on the ground. Considering that the gun had no sights on this occasion, plus the somewhat unsteadiness of the Wright B, the firing was impressive, and provided good press at the time. As a result of this, a request was submitted for ten Lewis machine guns to further the development. Ironically, since the Lewis machine gun had not been officially adopted, none were in stock, and several Benet-Mercier machine guns and ammunition were sent to the school as a substitute. These were rejected due to the outsize strip-feed arrangement, which proved too restricted for the confining space allowed in the early military airplanes.

Lewis, as stated, was displeased at the government's lack of decision on the gun, and like other inventors of auto-weapons before him, took the gun to Europe. It was marketed successfully in Belgium and later to the British Small Arms of Birmingham, England. With the demand of World War I becoming too great for producers on the continent, the Savage Arms Company of Utica, New York, contracted to produce the weapon. When the United States entered the war on 7 April 1917, we had on hand 670 Benet-Mercier machine rifles, 282 Maxim machine guns (Model of 1904), 148 Colt guns, and 353 Lewis machine guns (caliber .303--British acquired), even though the earlier gun by Lewis which was offered to the United States was the standard 30-06 caliber, and thus required additional ammunition requirement from standard. There were only two U. S. firms producing machine guns at the time; The Savage Arms Company who supplied the British and Canadians with some 12,500 Lewis machine guns, and the Marlin-Rockwell Corporation who were making the old style Colt machine gun for the Russians.

The standard ground-type Lewis machine gun weighed about 26 pounds, and was supplied in both the British .303 and the U. S. 30-06 calibers. The standard drum (magazine) held 47 cartridges, but was later enlarged to hold 97 rounds in the aircraft version. Gas-operated, the gun fired between 500-600 rounds per minute, depending on the amount of gas released (3 port selection). Its most unique feature was the cooling system comprising a series of aluminium fins which surrounded the barrel. Air, sucked from the rear forward, dissipated the heat, and this system also eliminated the cumbersome water-cooling system required for cooling on most other types. With the emergence of the air service model, the cooling fins were removed, as the air about the aircraft provided sufficient cooling. General John J. Pershing, himself, took an interest in the Lewis machine gun, and in May of 1918 requested that its cyclic rate of fire be improved, which was accomplished to the extent of 1000/minute, however, only a few of the high rate of fire machine guns were delivered.

Recognizing the immediate need for aircraft machine guns, the U. S. government modified the order with the Savage Arms Company to include some 10,000 aircraft types out of an order for 16,000 guns, the remaining 6,000 being delivered to the U. S. Marine Corps. By Armistice Day, we had produced some 34,000 Lewis aircraft machine guns.

Many improvements were made to adopt the gun for flexible aircraft mounting. Since it could not be synchronized, being held in cocked position, it became the main free gun. Some were mounted on the top wing of the Nieuport, and others on the Foster mount of the S.E.5, both, however, fired outside the propeller arc. The most widespread usage occurred on the Tourelle or Scarff Ring, and here it was mounted singly or in pairs and fired simultaneously by a Bowden connection. Other improvements included the removal of the radiator, and electric heater to prevent stoppages at high altitudes, and a shell deflector and cartridge collector bag attached to the ejector. A cartridge counting device was provided so that the gunner would know how many rounds remained in the drum. The sights were improved also to include a wind vane and ring sights to assist the gunner in firing at moving aircraft.

The Lewis machine gun was still on hand at the beginning of World War II and was used extensively at Pearl Harbor, Dunkirk, and other battles early in the war. The Japanese copied both the aircraft and ground gun and produced the latter in 7.7 mm at the Yokosuka Naval arsenal. Colonel Lewis refused all U. S. royalties for his gun, being dissatisfied with the way that the Ordnance Department had handled the development. Lewis had made a great contribution to the U. S. arsenal and to the air service, and it is seemingly even more meritorius when he turned his royalties of over one million dollars to his country.

LEWIS AIRCRAFT MACHINE GUN DESCRIPTION

The Lewis aircraft machine gun is designed for flexible mounting. As may be seen from the photographs, it differs from the Army type, in that the radiator has been removed and a spade grip is used instead of a regular butt stock, and it is fitted with a special mounting yoke and recoil check. The gun is fed from a magazine holding 97 rounds. It weighs 18 pounds and the rate of fire is 600 rounds per minute. The gun is mounted either singly or in pairs on a flexible mount. The gun comes in a wooden case containing one gun and its spare parts. The magazines comes three to a box and each gun is supplied with six magazines or drums.

POINTS TO BE OBSERVED BEFORE A FLIGHT
(Handbook of Aircraft Armament)

The gun must be in perfect operating condition, all parts cleaned and properly oiled. The parts which need particular attention in oiling are:

    Bolt
    Worm of feed operating stud
    Head of piston
    Striker post
    Slot in feed arm for feed operating stud
    Feed pawl (at pivot)
    Stop pawls (at pivot)
    Teeth on mainspring casing and on rack
    Threads on gas chamber and gas regulator cup.

Make sure that the hole in the gas chamber gland registers with the hole in the gas chamber, and the gas cylinder connection is tightly screwed onto the gas chamber. See that the large gas port (No. 4) in the gas regulator cup is turned to the rear, thereby giving the maximum gas pressure on the recoiling parts.

The gun ordinarily operates with a spring tension of from 12 to 14 pounds. Due to the adverse conditions under which the gun works, it may sometimes be necessary to reduce the tension to insure operation, but it should never be made less than 10 pounds. Work the mechanism slowly back and forth several times by means of the charging handle to see that it runs smoothly.

The magazines for the Lewis machine gun should be examined very carefully before being used since a defective magazine is almost certain to give trouble. A little oil should be applied to the bearings and to the magazine latch. The latter should be tested to see that its spring works freely, as cases have been found where the latch did not return to its proper position to lock the magazine to the magazine post. Magazines should be spun on a loading handle to see that they revolve easily. When not in use, magazines should always be kept in containers to prevent them from becoming damaged or dirty.

Make sure that the fixed sight, where supplied, is rigid. See that the gun is firmly attached to its mount. Make sure that the Bowden wire control, if used, will release the trigger. The recoil check is screwed to the muzzle of the machine gun and consists of a disk with an opening for the bullet to pass through. The rear surface of the disk is so shaped as to deflect the gases to the rear.

The gas pressure assists in counter-balancing the recoil of the barrel and limits the recoil to about 4 pounds.

REFERENCE MATERIAL

The Machine Gun, Vol. 1; Chinn.
Small Arms of the World, Smith.
America's Munitions, 1917-1918, Benedict Crowell; Washington, D.C., Govt. Printing Office, 1919.
Aircraft Armament Handbook, 1918, U.S. Air Service.

PHOTO CREDITS

Except where noted, all photos are presented through the courtesy of the U. S. War Department, General Staff, and are in the files of the National Archives.

(Photo at Right: A cutaway view of the Lewis Aircraft machine gun, Model 1918, showing details of firing and loading mechanisms. An alternate wind vane front sight was provided on many models and was interchangeable as shown in this view. The standard 47-round magazine was later enlarged to accomodate 97 rounds of ammunition. The cyclic fire rate was 500-600 rounds per minute; later being stepped up to 1,000 rounds per minute, but the faster-firing models were not completed in time for service and only a few were in combat use.)

Photo: Aircraft Armament Handbook

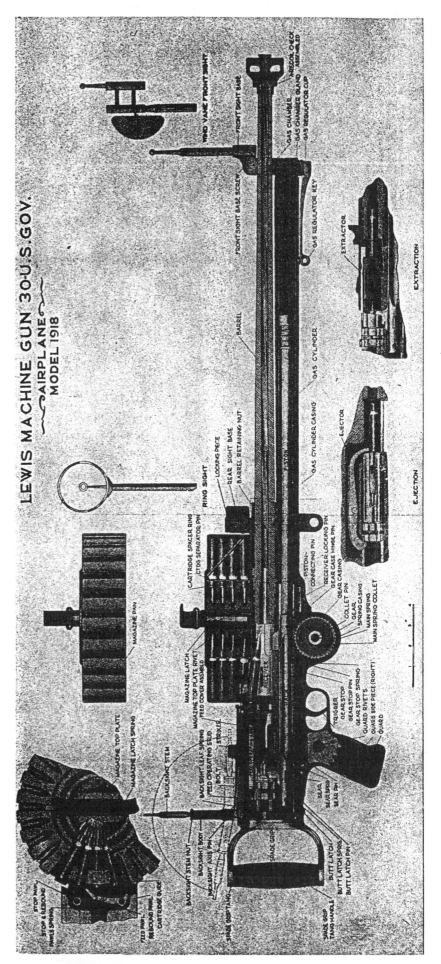

LEWIS MACHINE GUN 30·U.S.GOV.
AIRPLANE MODEL 1918

This photo shows the feeding and extracting mechanism accessories, as well as the rear top plate of the Lewis aircraft machine gun.
National Archives Photo: 165-WW-386F-16

Barrel, piston, compensator, springs, locking pins and miscellaneous accessories of the Lewis aircraft machine gun.
National Archives Photo: 165-WW-385F-17

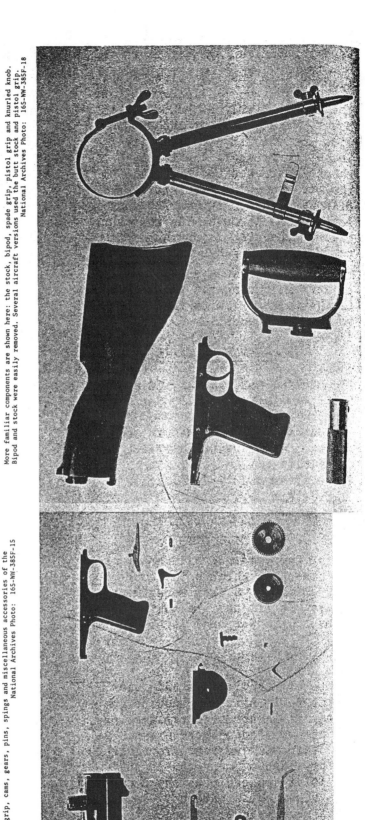

More familiar components are shown here: the stock, bipod, spade grip, pistol grip and knurled knob. Bipod and stock were easily removed. Several aircraft versions used the butt stock and pistol grip.
National Archives Photo: 165-WW-385F-18

Receiver housing group, pistol grip, cams, gears, pins, spings and miscellaneous accessories of the receiver housing.
National Archives Photo: 165-WW-385F-15

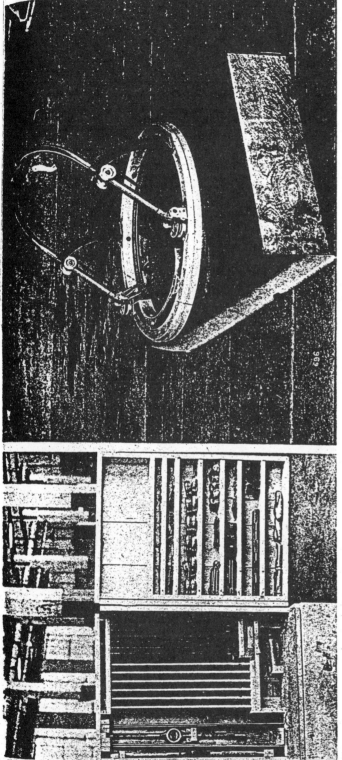

Lewis aircraft machine gun mounted on the top wing of a Curtiss JN-4 and used for aerial gunnery practice. Mechanic is seen in pilot's cockpit, making adjustments to engine; giving good indication of the clearance afforded by top wing. Aircraft refueling tank car in foreground lends atmosphere to scene.

A post-war Martin bomber is fitted with the Lewis gun in the gunner's forward cockpit. Of special interest is the early type U. S. star insignia painted on nose, pilot's headrest, exhaust stacks on engine nacelles, generators on underside of fuselage and landing gear arrangement.

Armament gun mount, raised in oblique view. Also called the Tournelle, or Scarff Ring, it was manufactured by Standard Aero Corporation.
Photo: Smithsonian Inst., Nat'l Air Museum, #A-32 752

Lewis machine gun armorer's chest. Chest contains spare parts and accessories, spare barrels, receivers, springs, etc., as well as tools and lubricating equipment.   National Archives Photo: 165-WW-385F-13

A camera gun, designed by Lewis, and mounted on a JN-4. The camera gun was instrumental in teaching observers the rudiments of aerial gunnery and allowing them visual evidences of their marksmanship. Designed to operate in a manner similar to the machine gun, the observer became well adjusted to the changeover from camera to gun. National Archives Photo: 165-WW-386-C4

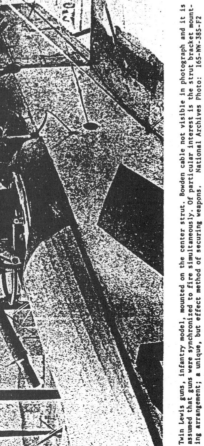

An Army infantry model Lewis machine gun is mounted and employed on the Standard J-1 aircraft. Crew not identified. Of particular interest is the diamond markings on fuselage sides---compare same with Photo #31 of the article, *FAYETTE PRATT'S SCRAPBOOK*, elsewhere in this issue. National Archives Photo: 165-WW-386-C5

A Lewis aircraft machine gun mounted on the barrel of a Davis anti-sub gun. For details of the Davis gun, see *CROSS & COCKADE, Vol. 6, No. 1, Spring 1965, pp. 76-84.* The Lewis machine gun was used to sight the target before firing the Davis gun. Naval officer not identified. National Archives Photo: 165-WW-385-B3

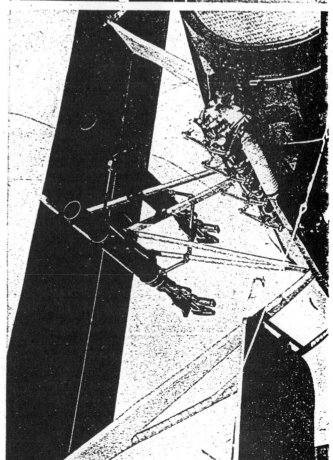

Twin Lewis guns, infantry model, mounted on the center strut. Bowden cable not visible in photograph and it is assumed that guns were synchronized to fire simultaneously. Of particular interest is the strut bracket mounting arrangement; a unique, but effect method of securing weapons. National Archives Photo: 165-WW-385-F2

Loading device employed to arm a full drum of 97 rounds of ammunition. Cartridges are cranked into drum position and are automatically dispersed into proper positioning. Ammunition can be seen in partially loaded drum. National Archives Photo: 165-WW-385F-14

Lewis aircraft machine gun drum (and/or magazine) with automatic ammunition counter. Small arrow in center dial points to remaining rounds in the drum and instantly relays to gunner the need for a full drum when firing. Arrow remains stationary as numbers are clicked off by cam. National Archives Photo: 165-WW-385F-11

Above: The Lewis aircraft machine gun, Model 1918, equipped with regulation front sight., Added accessory is the casing recovery bag. Designed to catch exploded cartridges to prevent them from being blowin in the slip-stream, the bag was unsatisfactory and was discarded in actual operational use in combat aircraft. National Archives Photo: 165-WW-385F-4

Above Right: The Lewis machine gun, infantry model, of the U. S. Army, shown here with its radiator and bipod. Front sight was not needed and a different rear sight was employed from aircraft models in use. National Archives Photo: 165-WW-385F-6

Below Left: Capt. Charles deForest Chandler with an infantry model Lewis machine gun mounted on a Wright B Flyer at College Park in 1912. The pilot is believed to be Lt. Milling. Photo source unknown.
Below Right: Col. Isaac Newton Lewis, who developed the air weapon that bore his name. Photo source unknown.

POPULAR FLYING, *December*, 1934.

A group of R.F.C. pilots (Major Lloyd, D.S.O., in centre) beside a B.E.2C

By
Sergt.-Major
A. A. NICOD

MEMORIES OF 60 SQUADRON R.F.C.

I SUBMIT these reminiscences of 60 Squadron in the hope that surviving members of the Squadron may be encouraged to respond and revive the friendships created during their service with this unit. They must not be regarded as an official history, but rather as a sequence of events that transpired during the active service period of the squadron from Gosport, 1916, to Aux-le-Chateau, 1918.

I arrived at Gosport from Farnborough in the spring of 1916, with other N.C.O.'s, to join 60 Squadron, and reported to Sgt.-Major J. Aspinall, a stern disciplinarian, but with whom some time later I formed a close friendship. A splendid farewell concert was organised the same evening, and two days later we entrained for Southampton, crossed the Channel to Le Havre, and proceeded by steamer up the river to Rouen.

Following the usual medical inspections, organisation of transport, stores, etc., we proceeded by road to Boisenghem Aerodrome, just outside St. Omer, under the command of Major F. F. Waldron; the flight commanders were Captains Smith Barry, Summers and Towers; other prominent pilots were Lieutenants Balfour, Ridley and Armstrong. Lieutenant Heenan, equipment officer, Technical Sgt.-Major Smyth, and a very efficient company of good mechanics completed the personnel of the Squadron.

We immediately settled down for active service conditions. Equipped with Morane "bullets" and

A group of pilots at Beauval, 1916. The machine is a D.H. 2 Scout, with Monosoupape Rotary engine.

Pilot in the cockpit of a Nieuport Scout. December 27, 1917.

Sergt.-Major A. A. Nicod, who served with the famous Squadron for two years.

" parasols," we entered a vigorous period of preparation, and about mid-June we proceeded to Vert Galland Aerodrome to take our place in the line.

The Squadron was soon engaged on offensive patrols and intelligence work, and in early July Major Waldron was killed in combat. He was a very gallant officer. Major Smith Barry was appointed to succeed him. The Squadron suffered heavy losses during July, many excellent pilots being lost ; in fact, the casualties were so great at this period it was deemed advisable to send the Squadron for a rest, and we were forthwith detailed to Herden for recuperation. We spent about three weeks there, everybody participating in recreation arranged with adjacent units, and enjoying the brief rest afforded them. Reinforced with new pilots, and the first of the Nieuport Scouts machines arriving, we were dispatched to a small aerodrome near Le Hameau, about mid-August, to take our place in the line for the second time. Captain Ball joined us here, about a week later, from No. II Squadron, and his arrival laid the foundation of a new 60 Squadron. The courageous deeds of Captain Ball manifested themselves immediately. Inspired by his presence, the remaining pilots took on a new lease of life, and tackled their arduous duties with such zest and vigour that memories of the early disasters at Vert Galland were soon dispelled. Splendid work was achieved by the Squadron, but our stay was short-lived, as on September 1st we were moved to Savy, near Aubigny. It was at Savy that Ball performed some of his most courageous deeds. In conversations I had with him I am firmly convinced he destroyed more E.A. than he was credited with.

He simply wouldn't bother to find out. He was essentially a lone fighter and, when not spraying his opponents with lead, would seek solitude in his hut with his gramophone, his favourite record being Schubert's "Unfinished Symphony." Being of a musical temperament, I often spoke to him about music, and I was the proud possessor

of some of his records (which I lost at Beckendorf Aerodrome in 1919).

During " dud " weather he was constantly inspecting his machine and trying to improve his gun mounting. Lieut. Osmond and myself did our best to please him, but never succeeded in improving the existing mounting introduced by Captain Cooper and Flt.-Sgt. Foster, of No. II Squadron. We would gaze with astonishment at his machine after a scrap—no ammunition, petrol tanks empty—marvelling how he managed to get back. Fabric ripped, struts and longerons shattered, wires

Not so good. An S.E. makes a bad landing at Savy.

Getting his hair off. Jack Rutherford and Billy Bishop, outside their Nissen hut on 60 Squadron's aerodrome.

Wreckage of a German aeroplane brought down near Inchy, Sept. 13, 1918.

broken, bullet holes all over the machine. Yet he would give orders for his tanks to be refilled and ammunition to be replenished, and even jocularly suggest to his rigger (Corporal Henderson) to tie his struts together. He would relate with boyish enthusiasm his experiences with the Le Prieur rockets. Instead of using them for balloons he would fire them at formations of E.A. to disperse them, and then dive on the nearest machine, get underneath, and send the German machine down, either in flames or out of control. He would say, " You should have seen them ' splitairing ' all over the sky, wondering what the hell had struck them."

We lost Captain Summers and Captain Towers here, and Captain Goodrich was killed on the aerodrome and buried with full military honours in a small cemetery near Aubigny. Lieut. A. M. King was also killed on the aerodrome doing target practice. As wintry weather was approaching and flying hours became shorter, efforts were made to provide recreation for the Squadron. This was accomplished, to his everlasting credit, by Sgt.-Major Aspinall. An orchestra was formed, sponsored by Major S. Barry (an excellent musician himself), Lieut. Vincent (O.C. orchestra), Sgts. Hoskins, Billam, Cpl. Vivian, A. McCliffe (violins) ; Cpls. Bunny and Woodward (cornets) ; A. McPolden (drums), and myself at the piano. I am sure these officers, N.C.O.'s and men will reflect with pride on their musical achievements at Savy. Concert parties were arranged and enjoyed. While on the subject of recreation, Sgt.-Major Aspinall's gigantic achievement must be mentioned—the staging of a boxing tournament in " C " Flight shed. Entries were received from all adjacent units. No. 60 Squadron orchestra, mounted on a platform gaily decorated with bunting, a boxing ring erected in the centre of the shed, and hundreds of eager faces, presented an animated picture. A prominent referee was procured and everyone enjoyed a thrilling evening. A. M. Bourne was the hero of the night. A corrugated iron roof was blown off one of No. 13 Squadron sheds the following day, during a gale, and came to rest against the gap in the sheds through which Captain Grenfell and Captain

Modesty ! Who was it ? The photo was taken at St. Omer, June 21, 1918. The machine is an S.E.5a.

Foote performed hair-raising stunts on their Nieuport Scouts. Captain Roderic Hill and Captain Gilchrist joined us here about this time.

Mention must be made here of the farewell dinner given by Major Smith Barry to Brigade Commander General (now Air Marshal Sir John) Higgins, Colonel (now Air Vice-Marshal) Playfair and officers of the Squadron, prior to his departure for Home Establishment. Captain Ball also left us here early in October, after adding more victories to his name, to receive the decorations (D.S.O. and two bars) he so richly deserved, to reappear in sensational fashion the following spring. He bequeathed to the Squadron that indomitable spirit that every pilot sought to emulate.

Major Graves joined us as C.O. Like Major Smith Barry, he was incapacitated through a flying accident. He was adored by all, sympathetic in nature, a courageous man, with a will to do or die, in spite of his physical disability.

Christmas 1916-1917 was spent at Savy, but in February we were transferred to Filles Camp Farm, Izel de Hameau, a few kilometres away, while snow fell heavily. No. 29 Squadron occupied the same aerodrome and we were very grateful for the reception given to us on our arrival. Filles Camp proved to be the scene of our most prosperous period. The coming of Captain Bishop helped matters considerably, and it was here that his memorable exploit over Cambrai gained for him the coveted V.C.

The Battle of Arras (March, 1917) was fast approaching, and it was evident the Squadron were in for a strenuous period. One day a German Halberstadt landed on the snow-covered aerodrome. We rushed excitedly to the spot, to be greeted by pilot and observer gesticulating frantically for us to keep back. Their warning came none too soon, for with a terrific explosion the machine blew up. Urged by the C.O., all ranks made superhuman efforts to subdue the conflagration, but in vain. The machine was destroyed; only a charred skeleton was eventually sent to Headquarters.

The battle of Arras was now in progress (March 10th) and many O.P.'s were successfully led over the lines by Major Graves. A disaster then occurred which threw the whole Squadron into gloom. Major Graves was shot down in flames behind Arras. A party led by Sgt. Rogers, "B" Flight, endeavoured to locate his machine, but it transpired that his body was recovered from the burnt machine by the infantry and buried behind the line.

Captain Black, "A" Flight, was now in charge of the Squadron, but another notable personality in Major A. J. L. Scott arrived to assume command. He also suffered a physical disability similar to his predecessors, Major Barry and Major Graves.

What with the skilful reorganisation by our new C.O., the

All that was left of a German aeroplane (Hannoverana ?) that crashed behind the Canadian lines at Rosières, Aug. 13, 1918. Evidently the number 13 was not the pilot's lucky number.

wonderful deeds of Captain Bishop, and the excellent work performed by Captain "Grid" Caldwell, Lieut. Meintjes, Lieut. Rutherford, Lieut. Fry, and other pilots of this period, we entered upon the most triumphant period of the history of the Squadron. In spite of heavy losses in April, excellent work was performed, particularly in trench straffing. Our leading pilots complained very bitterly about their guns. A remark so often heard was, " I wish someone would invent something to clear these stoppages."

In conjunction with Lieut. Osmond, I made a device for clearing the No. 1 stoppage on the Lewis gun. This was accomplished by pulling a small handle attached below the handle of the gun. This operation caused a sharp decisive withdrawal of the bolt which cleared the stoppage, the piston of the device instantaneously returning by means of a spring, without touching the gun. I recall, with pride and interest, standing in the officers' mess with a Lewis gun on my shoulder, whilst our renowned pilots, who were to make history, were operating the device. Captain Caldwell said, " What a priceless stunt !"

[Careful observation of a photograph of Captain Bishop in a Nieuport Scout in one of our previous issues will

The Morane Parasol Monoplane (1916 type.)

100% BRITISH.

The Badge of Quality

The Quality Car

The BRITISH
SALMSON

" A standard of excellence unusual in the manufacture of cars."

If the British Salmson were a 16 or 20 h.p. car, doing its 70 miles per hour at 20 miles per gallon of petrol, and priced at £750, it would still be outstanding in its class, because of its engine design and construction. But as it is a 12 h.p. car, with a guaranteed speed of 70 miles per hour at 30 miles per gallon, and priced at £395, it marks a new era in the production of high-class cars. It stands alone, especially at its price, in meeting the demand created by modern conditions for an economical high-speed car of medium size and unsurpassed efficiency.

Write for Catalogue :
BRITISH SALMSON AERO ENGINES, LTD.,
RAYNES PARK, LONDON, S.W.20.
London Distributors : Shrimptons Motors Ltd., 38/9, Berkeley St., W.1.

12343

reveal the small handle beneath the Lewis gun.—ED.]

This device was shown to Colonel Pretyman (O.C. No. 13 Wing) and permission was obtained to fit all machines, although later it was improved in the form of a sash and pinion pivoted at the handle. Why this excellent device was not fitted to all machines in the R.F.C. was beyond my comprehension, as every pilot who used it was loud in his praises as to its efficiency.

The weather was now improving rapidly. One fine morning in mid-April a thunderous roar was heard, and a formation of strange machines literally hurtled just over the sheds. It was the famous 56 Squadron led by Captain Ball, with the new S.E.5 machines. One had a glimpse of a black curly mop, a smiling face, a hand in a very graceful gesture over the cockpit paying a compliment to his old Squadron. With a roar of triumph they passed over the lines to challenge the supremacy of the air held by the Germans at that period.

On the death of Major Graves, Squadron Commanders were forbidden to lead patrols, but on many occasions Major Scott went over and gave battle to the enemy. In spite of his physical handicap, he was a wonderful pilot, and in one of his " scraps " he was wounded in the finger. I often wonder how he managed to hide this as Colonel Pretyman and General Higgins visited us frequently. Major Scott set a magnificent example to his pilots, as the following example will show.

Whilst at target practice, a new pilot named Lieut. Harris, for some unaccountable reason, failed to pull out of the dive, and he met a terrible death in full view of the horrified spectators. Realising the moral effect of this disaster on his pilots, Major Scott rushed from the Squadron office, as fast as his disability would allow him, and said quite calmly, " Get my machine out, Flight Sergeant." Going up, he performed the most hair-raising stunts in diving that it has ever been my lot to witness. Diving on the same target again and again with engine full on, and pulling out of the dive only a short distance from the ground, he had us with " our hearts in our mouths." Landing safely, he quietly left his machine and walked back to the Squadron office.

Major Scott took a considerable interest in the welfare of his men. He insisted on all Flight Sergeants recording the number of hours worked by each fitter and rigger, also the number of hours' rest obtained. These lists were handed to him weekly for signature and comments. " A good week's work," " Well done, 'C' Flight," were typical examples of his personal remarks.

The activities of Sgt.-Major Aspinall, appertaining to recreation, created a profound impression at Filescamp. He commenced by forming flower beds between the hangars, started a Squadron canteen for the men, and constructed a tennis court behind the officers' mess. Where he obtained all the red gravel for the tennis court remained a mystery, but eloquent testimony to this achievement will be confirmed by any surviving officers who had the pleasure of playing a game of tennis between patrols. A swimming pool was also constructed behind " C " Flight shed. This was a masterpiece. Although a stern man, Sgt.-Major Aspinall was ever " all out " for the comfort and recreation of officers and men during their hours of relaxation, and his activities in this sphere

MEMORIES OF 60 SQUADRON R.F.C.

will always be remembered and appreciated. I wonder how many of the football team still have the silver medals for winning the Brigade Football League ?

Captain Bishop was now making history. Enjoying a roving commission, he went off any time, and always fired a Verey light on his return to the aerodrome if he had destroyed a German machine. Sometimes he would fire two. Everyone would surge round his machine on landing to hear his account of how he had put paid to a Hun. Captain Bishop developed a style entirely his own. Taking advantage of the sun, he would stalk his victim and send a stream of lead just in front of the enemy machine, using Buckingham tracer ammunition. The German machine would invariably fly straight into this burst of fire, and in the majority of cases, would dive to earth in flames.

Captain Bishop's stupendous feat over Cambrai aerodrome, for which he was awarded the V.C., will ever be remembered. Raiding the aerodrome just after dawn, he destroyed several enemy machines, and I can recall him relating how he dived on the German mechanics starting the machines ; but he had a very warm time returning to the aerodrome, as his machine was badly damaged by anti-aircraft guns and machine gun fire. There were a dozen bullet holes in the radius of a few inches just behind his head as he sat in the cockpit. A miraculous escape. I often wonder if he remembers attending the dinner in the sergeants' mess to celebrate the auspicious occasion of his winning the coveted decoration. He made a very nice speech that night. An official film of the Squadron was taken here.

The Squadron was performing excellent work on E.A. alarm patrols, and were the recipients of many congratulatory messages from Headquarters. Captain Ball landed twice here to rectify gun trouble. Captain Fry also forced a German Albatros Scout to land at St. Pol. This machine was apparently lost and flew right across the aerodrome. Captain Fry gave chase immediately with the above result.

Captain " Grid " Caldwell was awarded the M.C., and he celebrated the event by presenting " B " Flight with a gramophone. " B " Flight will remember the countless hours of amusement derived from Captain Caldwell's generous gift. He called the machines " grids " and would good-humouredly remark, " Get the ' grids ' out, Flight Sergeant." Hence the nickname " Grid " Caldwell. He left us later and was promoted Major in charge of No. 74 Squadron.

At the expiration of a successful period of leadership, Major Scott was recalled to Home Establishment. He departed leaving behind a Squadron who had nought but admiration for a leader who had raised this unit to the pinnacle of success.

Captain Bishop also made his departure to receive his decorations. His brilliant achievements coupled with those of his illustrious predecessor, Captain Ball, created R.F.C. history. The passing of Captain Ball and the departure of Captain Bishop terminated a glorious period of brilliant work, unsurpassed by any Squadron at that period.

MEMORIES OF 60 SQUADRON
R.F.C.

By Sergt.-Major A. A. NICOD

"One of our machines failed to return." A genuine photograph of a British Nieuport Scout down over the wrong side of the lines. This photograph was taken from a German prisoner at the Battle of Messines, by Mr. G. Eddington, of Tottenham, who sent it to us.

ABOUT September, we were paraded on the aerodrome and praised in most eulogistic terms by General Higgins for work accomplished, and we left Files Camp Farm under the command of Major Kennedy Cochran Patrick to commence a new life at St. Marie Capelle.

On arrival at the new aerodrome, we made acquaintance with that famous Squadron No. 20, No. 19 and No. 57 occupying the opposite side of the field. In spite of all our trials and troubles here, surviving members of 20 Squadron and 60 Squadron will recall with pride the wonderful *esprit de corps* that existed between the two Squadrons.

We were fitted out with S.E.5's, with geared Hispano Suiza engines, and experienced a devastating period of bad luck with the new machines. Pilots would return from patrol blinded with oil, petrol pipes leaking, "dud" oil pressure, leaking radiators, choked carburettors, broken gears, half a propeller through faulty C.C. gear, sometimes no propeller at all, due to gears seizing up, fusing and burning the propeller boss, and also due to propeller bosses working loose through faulty grinding of the boss on the shaft.

This deplorable state of affairs existed for some time, and seriously retarded the work of the Squadron in spite of superhuman efforts to rectify the troubles.

The noise of the gears, aggravated by faulty carburettors, created a noise that would have discouraged any aspirants for flying honours.

Captain Hammersly, Captain Duncan, Captain Crompton, Lieuts. Pope, Thornton and Jenkins, were amongst the pilots who experienced these initial troubles.

One "dud" day, in the hangar of "B" Flight, a voice "boomed" out, "Where's the Flight Sergeant?" On rushing out I found General Trenchard questioning the mechanics on the troubles of the new machines. During his interrogations he would remark to his *Aide de Camp*, "Make a note of that." After his visit, matters certainly improved, but it required a considerable time to dispel the bogy of noisy gears, etc.

No. 20 Squadron had meanwhile been fitted with Bristol Fighters and, in conjunction with 60 Squadron, performed excellent work. With the approach of the moonlight nights the Germans began to raid St. Omer and neighbouring districts, and we witnessed some wonderful sights during these hostile visits, although the incessant warnings of "Lights out" seriously hampered the work of preparing for the following dawn patrol.

A detachment of American mechanics joined us here for instruction. Recreation was provided by football matches, concert parties, an occasional film, and a visit by a Canadian band.

A son of the Premier, the late Mr. Bonar Law, was reported missing, and I recall the Premier himself visiting the Squadron, a pathetic figure, seeking information concerning his son.

Another fine pilot we had at this time was Captain Selous, a son, I believe, of the famous big game hunter. This gallant officer was accidentally killed in collision with Lieut. Jenkins over Passchaendale Ridge, returning from patrol. Two very valuable and capable pilots were thus lost to us. Christmas 1917-1918 was spent here, heavy snow falling at this time.

An episode occurred here that must be mentioned—the snow fight with 20 Squadron and 60 Squadron on one side, and 19 Squadron and 57 Squadron on the other.

The fight eventually terminated with Major Patrick shouting "Let's raid 57's mess." A glorious assault was made, gallantly led by the C.O. and Lieut. Pope. I wonder if any of the surviving members of No. 57 Squadron remember that event. I believe it was reported to the Wing Commander, but Colonel Van Ryneveld must have considered that our conduct was not to the prejudice of good order and military discipline.

Major Patrick was recalled to Home Establishment after the turn of the year, and events moved very rapidly on the approach of the big German offensive in the spring. Under the command of Major Moore, our new C.O., we found ourselves suddenly transported to Bailleul, followed by No. 19 Squadron with Dolphins.

We experienced a hectic time here, as we couldn't get things going in our customary manner. There was something wrong at Bailleul, and as events proved, it was not very long before our mysterious forebodings materialised. Shelling of the aerodrome, machine-gun fire on the sleeping quarters at night, German machines taking photographs by day, and proving their work by night, and the shelling of the town with heavy calibre shells which created considerable havoc in the station and the Rue de Lille. Two heavy shells burst just behind the hangars, and pieces of tombstone, etc., fell all around the machines (our hangars were situated just a few yards away from a small churchyard). But these incidents were but a forerunner of the shape of things to come. Our stay at Bailleul was very short indeed, for

MEMORIES OF 60 SQUADRON

suddenly, one morning at dawn, we had to get out. The town was heavily shelled and the lorries passed through the square " between shells."

Arriving at Merville, we were greeted by a crowd of panic-stricken inhabitants exclaiming " The Boche is coming." Leaving Merville, which was being shelled, we passed through St. Pol, where the station was the German objective, and eventually arrived at Belle Vue. There was very little flying done here on account of the misty weather. Everything was confusion, which created a tense feeling of extreme anxiety as to future events. Orders were given and countermanded, transports loaded and unloaded, preparations for a hasty departure were arranged, then cancelled, but, eventually, after a very short stay at Belle Vue, we were moved back to Feinvillers. Chaotic conditions existed here as various types of machines landed one after the other. The Germans had paid a visit here the previous night and " laid their eggs " and some of the hangars were well perforated with the results of the raid.

Beautiful May weather was responsible for many long distance O.P.'s, but very little fighting, as our pilots announced the Germans were becoming rather more difficult to find. At the beginning of June, the Squadron were again moved, this time to an empty field on the Aux-le-Chateau Road. Hangars were erected and accommodation for the Squadron was bell tents. Major Moore was still C.O. and other notable pilots at this time were Captain Belgrave, Captain Saunders, Captain Scholte and Captain Perry. O.P.'s were commenced

immediately on arrival and some fine work was accomplished by these pilots. A large twin-engine Gotha machine crashed near here returning from a raid. It was remarkable the number of objectives marked on the maps found in the machine, and on the fuselage were several small patches with the date written on. Souvenirs of the London Defence.

Periods between patrols were very pleasantly spent here, the officers joining in the cricket games during relaxation periods. Captain Belgrave never returned from an O.P. and Captain Saunders took over command of his Flight.

The Squadron performed good work during June and early July, but E.A. were getting very difficult to find and patrols had to fly far behind the lines to engage them.

At this juncture, I was transferred to No. 79 Squadron under Major Arnold, and bidding farewell to all my comrades, I received the best wishes from the officers, to take my departure to St. Marie Capelle with the new Squadron. But these reminiscences must close with a sad note, as an incident happened which shocked the Royal Air Force. Major J. B. McCudden,* V.C., was killed, whilst flying on his journey to take over command of my old squadron—July, 1918.

* * *

Sergt.-Major Nicod has asked us to say that since the first instalment of his article appeared, he has been the recipient of many messages. He would like to hear from more old comrades. His address is 133, Victoria Road West, Hebburn-on-Tyne, Co. Durham.

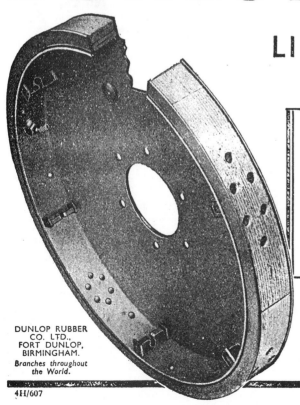

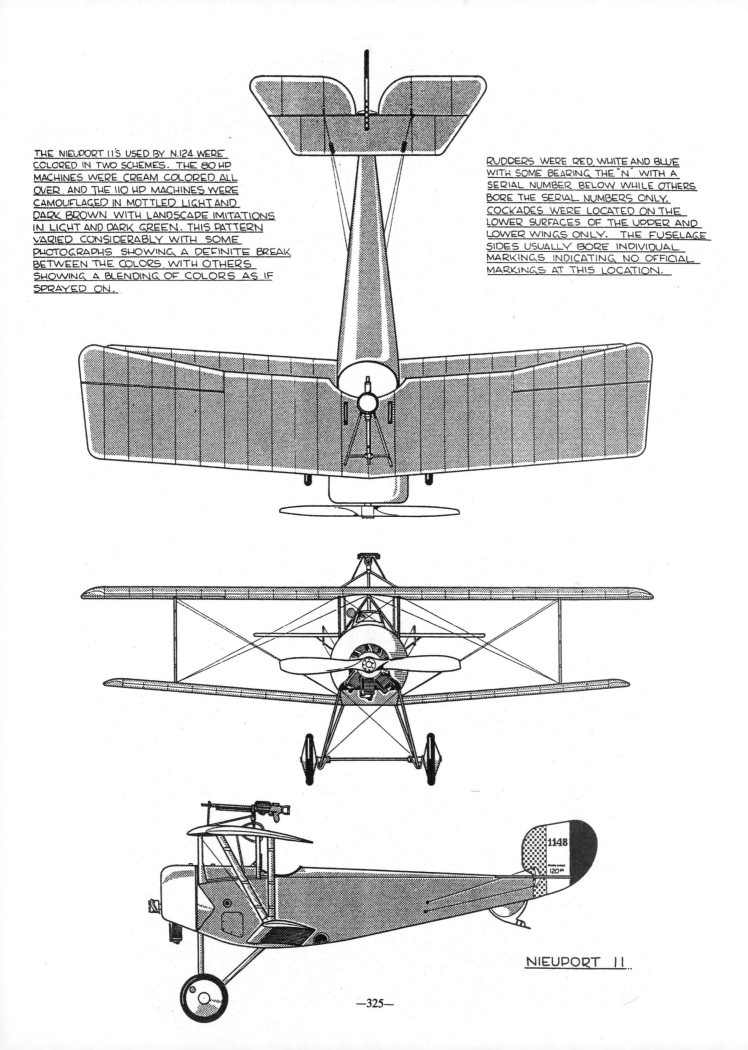

THE NIEUPORT 11'S USED BY N.124 WERE
COLORED IN TWO SCHEMES. THE 80 HP
MACHINES WERE CREAM COLORED ALL
OVER, AND THE 110 HP MACHINES WERE
CAMOUFLAGED IN MOTTLED LIGHT AND
DARK BROWN WITH LANDSCAPE IMITATIONS
IN LIGHT AND DARK GREEN. THIS PATTERN
VARIED CONSIDERABLY WITH SOME
PHOTOGRAPHS SHOWING A DEFINITE BREAK
BETWEEN THE COLORS, WITH OTHERS
SHOWING A BLENDING OF COLORS AS IF
SPRAYED ON.

RUDDERS WERE RED, WHITE AND BLUE
WITH SOME BEARING THE "N" WITH A
SERIAL NUMBER BELOW WHILE OTHERS
BORE THE SERIAL NUMBERS ONLY.
COCKADES WERE LOCATED ON THE
LOWER SURFACES OF THE UPPER AND
LOWER WINGS ONLY. THE FUSELAGE
SIDES USUALLY BORE INDIVIDUAL
MARKINGS INDICATING NO OFFICIAL
MARKINGS AT THIS LOCATION.

1148

NIEUPORT 11

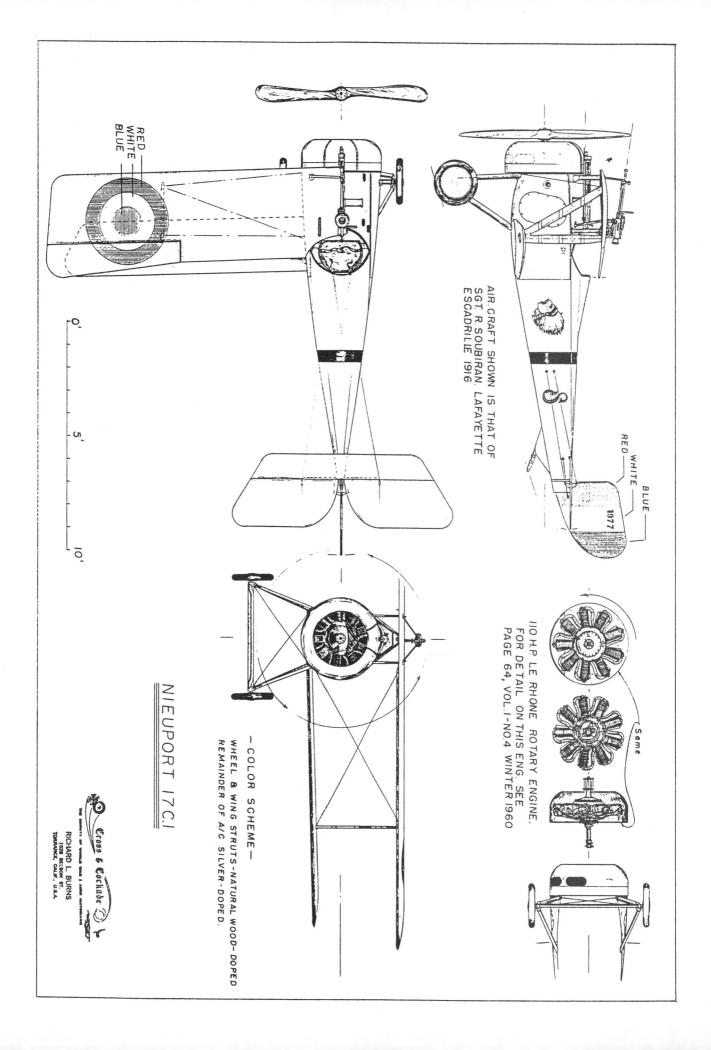

RED
WHITE
BLUE

AIR CRAFT SHOWN IS THAT OF
SGT. R. SOUBIRAN. LAFAYETTE
ESCADRILLE 1916

RED
WHITE
BLUE

1977

110 H.P. LE RHONE ROTARY ENGINE.
FOR DETAIL ON THIS ENG. SEE
PAGE 64, VOL.I-NO.4 WINTER 1960

Same

NIEUPORT 17C.I

—COLOR SCHEME—
WHEEL & WING STRUTS-NATURAL WOOD-DOPED
REMAINDER OF A/C SILVER-DOPED.

0'   5'   10'

Cross & Cockade

THE SOCIETY OF WORLD WAR I AERO HISTORIANS

RICHARD L. BURNS
1026 BELSON ST.
TORRANCE, CALIF., U.S.A.

Knights of the Air

CAPTAIN ALBERT BALL, V.C., D.S.O., M.C.

IN Albert Ball, the first great British Ace, we see a Knight of the Air whose heart and soul were in Aviation, and whose magnificent example set an inspiring standard for those who were to follow.

Born at Nottingham on August 21st, 1896, he was only seventeen when war broke out, but he at once enlisted in the Sherwood Foresters and quickly rose to the rank of Sergeant. Burning with eagerness to get to the Front, he obtained a commission, transferred to the Cyclists Corps and learned to fly at his own expense. He then transferred to the Royal Flying Corps.

Within a few months his name was known to the whole world and he had won the highest honours for gallantry the Allies could bestow. In May, 1917, he was killed in combat by Lothar von Richthofen, brother of the famous Red Knight, when his record stood at 43 enemy planes shot down.

He arrived in France in February, 1916, a time when pilots were desperately needed by the Allies, for the Fokkers were in the hey-day of their fame and the British pilots, flying machines of inferior performance, were hard pressed to hold their own. His arrival in France undoubtedly helped to stem the tide, for the effect of his victories was felt when morale was being tested to the utmost. Germany was ringing with the names of Max Immelmann and his fine pupil, Oswald Boelcke. Where was the British Champion? Ball answered the question and the German stars began to fall.

Among those who fell during the period of Ball's reign were Immelmann (16), Boelcke (40), Frankl (19), Baldamus (18), Wintgens (18), Kirmaier (11), Kendell (11), Theiller (11), Berr (10), Mulper (10), Leffers (9) and Parschan (8). Aces all, and doughty fighters.

It would seem that Ball paid little attention to tactics. He was the Spirit of Fighting. He attacked, fought and killed. Like the Knights of old, he flung himself into combat with such impetuosity and with such utter disregard for personal safety, that he carried all before him by the sheer fury of his attack. The enemy soon learned to avoid the pilot with the mop of black, curly hair, for he seldom wore a helmet. He sometimes returned with his machine so badly damaged that it was surprising it did not fall to pieces in the air.

He flew at all times, and in all weathers. He never refused combat, irrespective of the number of his opponents. He went far into enemy sky looking for antagonists, and certainly shot down many more machines than his record reveals. Reckoned according to Continental or American standards he would probably have been credited with nearer 100 victories. He once admitted that he had not claimed certain victories because they had occurred so far over the lines that confirmation was impossible. In any case he would seldom go to any trouble to confirm them.

When not in the air, he was in the hangar, tuning up his engine or checking his guns, for he was very particular about his machine. His recreation was gardening. He made himself a garden in which he raised vegetables and flowers.

He was first posted to No. 13 Squadron, flying the slow and obsolescent B.E.'s, but the authorities were not slow to see that he was a born fighter, so he was taken off two-seaters and sent as a Flight Commander to No. 11 Squadron, with Nieuport Scouts. On his nineteenth birthday he had five aeroplanes and one balloon to his credit. By September, 1916, his score had risen to twenty-eight, and he was the British Ace of Aces. Guynemer, the French Ace, alone had a higher score. He then went to No. 60 Squadron, and by February, 1917, his score had increased to thirty-two.

He returned to England to receive his decorations, the M.C. and D.S.O., and returned to France to the famous 56 Squadron, which ended the war with a magnificent record of over 400 enemy planes destroyed, a record unequalled by any other Squadron, Escadrille, or Staffel.

He took off on what was to be his last patrol in the evening of May 7th, 1917. Just what happened we shall never know, except that he died fighting against odds. It would seem that he, with one companion, engaged a superior number of machines of the Richthofen Circus. The pilot of the second machine was badly wounded, fell out of the fight, and, by a miracle, reached home, where he lost consciousness. Ball was alone, far over the line, with his enemies. He did not return.

Following a period of silence, Wolff's Agency announced that "Leut. von Richthofen had shot down a triplane flown by Captain Ball. It was the twentieth victory for the German." This raised a controversy which has never been settled. Ball was not flying a triplane (Sopwith Triplane) when he met his death, and no proof was ever produced that he fell under the guns of the German Ace. There were many who thought, and still think, that the victory was credited to Richthofen to add lustre to the name of the famous brothers.

His death was later confirmed. He was buried in the German War Cemetery at Anneoulin, near La Bassée, where a Memorial marks the spot.   W.E.J.

DREAMS

Some fellows are out to make money in shoals
And some to win races and some to shoot goals,
But I sit in my study and breathlessly read
Of McCudden and Mannock and their deathless breed.

Of Boelke and Bishop, Richthofen and Ball,
Yes, by name and by fame I'm acquainted with all;
And sometimes the study fades out from my sight
And high over Flanders I'm swooping to fight.

I've raked a tall Fokker from cockpit to rudder
And drawing away I've bagged yet another.
Then a noise from the engine says something is wrong,
And I'm crashed from the clouds by the old dinner gong!
          J. N. H. Brennan.

KNIGHTS OF THE AIR

Rittmeister Baron Manfred von Richthofen.

MANFRED VON RICHTHOFEN was one of the most romantic figures of the Great War; perhaps more stories have been woven about him than any other individual, and the exploits of his famous circus have become legendary. Books have been written about him, and of these *The Red Knight of Germany*, by Floyd Gibbons (Cassell), and *German War Birds*, by Vigilant (John Hamilton), are probably the best. Before speaking of this striking personality let us glance back at the origin of the German formations, which subsequently became known as " circusses ".

Before 1916 formation flying was crude and little attempt had been made to defeat enemy planes by concerted attack. Germany was fairly and squarely beaten in the air by the R.F.C.; General von Hoeppner, the head of the German Air Service at the time, admits it. The Higher Command decided that this state of affairs must stop, and they sat down to consider ways and means to do it. They noticed that one or two of their pilots who had lived long enough to gain experience were piling up modest scores, and one of these became famous for inventing a stunt which has since been copied by everybody. I refer to Lieut. Max Immelmann.

His *modus operandi* was to pull up as if he was going to loop, then he turned sideways over the vertical and came out in the opposite direction. It was a simple way of gaining height, and at the same time reversing direction, but it so happened that no one else had thought of it. It took a lot of our fellows by surprise and, until the trick became known, he did well, but afterwards his score mounted less rapidly.

Immelmann was the first real ace and more will be said about him on a future occasion. He was shot down in June, 1916, but before he went West he imparted a good deal of his knowledge to Oswald Boelcke who, by the way, took up flying after he had been rejected by the army on account of lung trouble. Boelcke carried on and soon equalled Immelmann's total of 16. The authorities became scared. His luck, they said, will not last, and they sent him back to do some instructing. But Boelcke was soon fed up with that and went to Headquarters with a new idea.

The Boelcke Circus

He prepared a scheme for grouping fighter pilots into " *staffels*," a word which, literally translated, means steps. Each *staffel* consisted of " swarms," which were subdivided into " chains." He called these *Jagd* (hunting) *staffeln*. We called them circusses, and Boelcke was the leader of the first German *Jagdstaffel*, which normally consisted of about twenty machines. Boelcke had an aptitude for spotting likely pilots, and among his first selections were Manfred von Richthofen, Erwin Bohme, Max Muller, and young Immelmann (cousin of the ace), all of whom afterwards became aces.

On August 30 the *Jagdstaffel* took up its quarters at Lagnicourt. On September 17 Richthofen shot down Lieut. Morris (pilot) and Lieut. Rees (observer), and the Red Knight had started on his long line of victories.

On October 28, when his score stood at 40, Boelcke was killed. He was engaged in a fierce duel with a British machine when one of his pupils decided to take a hand and collided with him. Boelcke's machine broke up in the air, but as luck would have it the pupil got away with it. He said that he never even saw Boelcke until they touched, and anyone who has ever sat in a dog-fight will have no difficulty in believing this.

Kirmaier took over the circus, which, by Imperial decree, was still called the Boelcke *Jagdstaffel*. On November 20, in a fierce fight with 70 Squadron (Sopwith Pups) Richthofen brought off a double, but Kirmaier went West. Duels to the death were now the order of the day. Richthofen met Major Hawker, V.C., and for half an hour they fought what must have been one of the most thrilling combats of the War. In the end Richthofen killed Hawker. He modestly put down his success to having a machine of superior performance, which was true enough.

The German Higher Command now grasped the wisdom of the *Jagdstaffel* idea; others were formed, and Richthofen departed to take over his own pack.

Thus was born the Richthofen circus. The original circus operated until the close of the war and its records show many famous names and scores. Bernert (27) and Voss, who, with skull and crossbones blazoned on his fuselage, was shot down by Lieut. Rhys Davis when his score stood at 48. Bohme (24), who fell at Zonnebeke, and Loffler (15), who fought his last fight over Paschendale. Von Bulow (28) and Muller (36), who went down in flames over Morslade. Bolle (36), Gallwitz, Pappenmayer, Plange and Kempt were others. When they handed over their planes to the Allied Forces they had painted on the fuselage of each machine the name of its pilot and the number of his victories.

Manfred von Richthofen

Before the War Manfred von Richthofen was a typical Prussian officer of the Uhlans, whose regimental cap he wore until the time of his death. It would seem that he was not a very good cavalry officer, and after seeing active service on the Russian front he transferred to the Air Service. He admits that he was not an apt pupil, and it is difficult to reconcile his early attempts to fly with the masterly ability that came to him later. It must have dumbfounded his instructors. He was vain, but always fair, proud of his prowess, but a relentless and rather inhuman killer—a very different type from Boelcke, from whom he learned much of the art of air duelling.

In April, 1917, he shot down thirty machines in thirty days; altogether he scored 80 confirmed victories, all British machines. Towards the end of his career he did not dog-fight with his circus, but sat above it and picked off stragglers; he was doing this when he was killed. Most of his victims were two-seater machines, but this was not unusual, for the records of most aces are simply a story of the superiority of the single-seater fighter over the slower and less manoeuvrable bomber or reconnaissance machine.

In March, 1917, Richthofen was shot down by an

unknown British pilot, but he managed to land behind the German lines. In July of the same year, in a duel with Capt. A. E. Woodbridge, of No. 20 Squadron (killed after the War in the air mail disaster at Jask), a bullet grazed his skull and put him in hospital for three weeks. Most of Richthofen's flying was done in an Albatros, but later he used the Fokker Triplane, and it was in a machine of this type that he was killed by Capt. Roy Brown, of Toronto, on April 21, 1918. It may surprise some people to know that Richthofen never looped the loop in his life. Not only did he refrain from indulging in unnecessary aerobatics, but he discouraged other members of his circus from doing so. His motto was : " Go and get your man." " Don't try and shoot holes in the other machine, aim for the man," he advised his pilots. " If you are fighting a two-seater, get the observer; never mind the pilot until you have downed the rear gun." (*German War Birds*, by Vigilant.)

The great secret of his success was probably an outstanding ability to hit what he shot at with his guns.

The Richthofen Circus

At the height of his fame he commanded *Jagdeschwader* No. 1, composed of four *staffels*. With him at this time was his brother, Lothar, who, with 40 victories to his credit, survived the War only to be killed in a cross-country crash in 1922. There was Gussmann (10) and Wolff, not yet an ace, but who lived to score 33. There was Hans Weiss (16), who crashed to eternity about the same time as Wolff. There was the one-armed Karjus, who, since he shot down many two-armed pilots, must have been something of a wizard. There was Erich Lowenhardt, who piled up a score of 56 before a comrade accidentally sent him to his doom, and Wilheim Reinhardt, who scored 20 and led the circus after Richthofen's death. There was Ernst Udet, who bagged 62 and survived to do some sensational flying for the films. He was over here only last year. These were the German fighters pitted against us in the height of the Red Knight's fame.

The circus had some curious superstitions. One was the use of the greeting, " *Hals und Beinbruck* "—in other words, " May you break your neck and legs." " *Gluck auf* " (" Good luck ") would have turned any one of them pale with fright. Calamity, they said, would follow, and not one of them would fly on the day anyone greeted him in this manner. They would not allow themselves to be photographed, and it is curious to note that those of them who succumbed to this natural temptation of vanity did not last long. Richthofen himself broke the rule, and so did Boelcke, and they were both killed shortly afterwards.

After Richthofen had celebrated his fortieth victory there was a strong controversy in Germany. One faction said he must be sent back from the front because his luck could not last and his death would shatter the morale of an idolising nation, and the other party said he must go on because his very presence put new life into every pilot along the line and inspired him to further efforts. Richthofen went on flying, but he admitted nevertheless that he was nervous. He had reached Boelcke's score, and he breathed a sigh of relief when he scored his forty-first victory. Curiously enough he was killed when his score was exactly double—80.

After the death of their leader most of the circus quickly followed him to Valhalla. Lowenhardt went down, like Boelcke, in a collision, but with one of our pilots. There was a tale in France at the time that the British pilot, hard hit, deliberately rammed him, and it may be true. Contrary to the popular idea, Richthofen could not just pick who he liked for his circus. He was sent the same raw material for replacements as any other squadron; he licked them into shape and then complained bitterly when they were taken away to command other *Jagdstaffels*. Naturally, every pilot in Germany wanted to serve under a man who had learnt the game in the Boelcke or Richthofen circus.

Methods Compared

In his reports, Richthofen frequently refers to the " west wind which was fortunately blowing," and this leaves us in no doubt but that he preferred to fight behind his own lines. In a dog-fight, machines lost height rapidly and tended to drift with the wind, so the reason for his partiality becomes apparent. It was an obvious disadvantage for a damaged machine to have to fight its way home against a head wind, and it made confirmation of a victory more certain. It rather looks as though Richthofen was quite as much concerned with his own glorification as with the success of the German cause.

His circus was very rarely seen over the British side of the line and apparently it never had to act as an escort to photographic, artillery, or bombing machines, which was one of the chief duties of the British scout squadrons. It was far more a weapon of defence than offence, waiting as a rule for British machines to cross the lines before attacking them.

Richthofen's own victories comprised 30 single-seaters and 50 reconnaissance and artillery-spotting machines (mostly the slower B.E.'s and R.E.8's), and a few Sopwith 1½ Strutters and Bristol Fighters. He admits that he concentrated his attention upon two-seaters, but whether this was because they were " easier meat " than fighters or because he considered they were doing more harm than the single-seaters is a matter for conjecture, but it seems as though the increase of his own score was the first thing in his mind.

His usual method of attack was the orthodox one of getting under the tail of a two-seater, or above a fighter, and holding his fire until very close. He called his brother Lothar (who scored 40 victories) a "butcher," because he recklessly attacked any machine within sight, and when Lothar was rather badly wounded (his hip was smashed by a bullet), he as good as told him that it was his own fault.

Lothar was credited with having killed Captain Albert Ball, V.C., but it is doubtful if this claim would stand a close investigation; there was a general feeling at the time that this was done purely to enhance the fame of the Richthofen brothers in Germany. It would have been difficult to prove. Lothar was again in hospital when his brother was killed.

Most of the British officers who survived encounters with the Baron bore witness to his flying skill, accurate shooting, and fearlessness.   W. E. J.

NEXT MONTH:
CAPTAIN RENE PAUL FONCK
The French Ace of Aces

MANFRED von RICHTHOFEN

A Necessary Answer to an Incredible Slander on the Dead Hero of the Air

By ERNST UDET

(Courtesy Berliner Börsen-Zeitung)

Translated by Claud W. Sykes

IF there is any time and place for the spiteful tactics of blind hatred to cease, it is surely on an occasion of respect to the majesty of death and silent honour to the fallen foeman. Then some will lower their swords simply from a feeling of tact, but the sincere man obeys an impulse of the heart in so doing.

It has afforded me particular pleasure and satisfaction over and over again to find in the circles of comrades of the air in all countries that a close bond of genuine and honourable camaraderie unites us with our heroic ex-opponents of the Great War, and that this bond is forged solely by the respect each feels for the other's achievements. The English are most especially proud of this fair play, and rightly so, because it is due to their manly, straightforward attitude that former enemies could come together for frank exchanges of views in the years immediately following the war. The German front-line soldiers in general, and we airmen in particular, felt all the more delighted at this, because we had learnt a high esteem for our English opponents in battle and were already aware of the chivalry—a self-evident matter for us too—with which the men on the other side of the lines honoured the fallen foe.

All the greater is, therefore, the indignation we feel at the veritable flood of the meanest slanders on Manfred von Richthofen, our squadron-leader, whom we can never forget, which an English newspaper has not shrunk from publishing. These slanders are all the more shameless in that they preface a series of articles dealing with the gallant life of the famous English airman, Major Micky Mannock, and thus, in our opinion, also besmirch the reputation of this English hero of the air and all his comrades. The author is a certain Lieutenant Jones, who must therefore take the responsibility of these outrageous invectives,

Ernst Udet in his Fokker D.VIII.

A new photograph of Manfred v. Richthofen.

although I can hardly believe that an English comrade of the air would have acted in this incredible fashion of his own free will.

For motives of unmistakable sensation-mongering this series of articles commences with an insult to Richthofen in its assertion that Major Mannock was greater than the valiant Guynemer (a French hero of the air) and greater than " the arrogant Richthofen." The paragraphs which then follow contain one calumniation of my deceased commander, which, as a member of the Richthofen Squadron, I simply cannot leave unanswered. It is not merely for the sake of my fallen friend that my heart impels me to appeal to the honest judgment of the whole world, but I also feel myself bound in the interests of comrades of the air all over the world, and most especially in the interests of those English comrades for whom I cherish so great an esteem, to refute these slanders.

Every child of to-day knows what Richthofen was. The whole world utters his name with respect. It is not only our German boys who give their aeroplane models the name of the heroic German airman ; the American boys do the same. What will the world say, therefore, when all of a sudden an English newspaper asserts that the English airmen were forced to fly over Richthofen's aerodrome to look for him, and when it seeks confirmation for this shameless lie by stating that Richthofen wrote in his diary : " It is better to let one's customers come to one's shop than to go running after them." This unfair quotation out of context characterises the tone of the whole article.

Certainly, the German war airmen could not always take the offensive. We were up against an enormous enemy superiority in men and materials. With odds of ten to one against us, it was self-evident that we had to

Kurt Wolff, Richthofen,s friend and flying partner, who thought the Red Knight was making a tactical error when he chased "Wop" May across the lines on his last flight.

attempt to lure the enemy into a trap. Further comment is superfluous, and the fact that Richthofen was shot down a long way behind the enemy's lines should suffice in itself.

In regard to the further assertion that Richthofen was a purely defensive fighter and seldom fought on the British side of the front, I can vouch that I know of no single combat flight I was permitted to make in his company in which he remained behind the German lines.

But a general vilification of the dead German hero does not suffice, for an attempt is made to disparage Richthofen's individual victories. It is alleged that 50 of his 80 victories were gained against two-seaters, which were as little a match for his fast Albatros as "a sparrow fledgling which had strayed from its nest would be for a hunting falcon." The other 30 were one-seaters which were inferior in every respect to his machine, such as Vickers Fighters, F.E.8's, D.H.2's, Spads, Nieuports and Sopwith Pups. Richthofen is stated to have generally let these machines attack him over his own aerodromes, and so "there was no great song to make about his victories." The only British machines which could be considered equal to his own were the S.E.5, the Sopwith Triplane and the Camel. Of these he "shot down only very few"!

With regard to these assertions, let me first state that in those days a two-seater of the Vickers or Bristol type, for example, was by no means inferior to a German one-seater. Quite the contrary. Generally the attacker found it a far more unpleasant business to shoot down a two-seater, and, moreover, the two-seater had a definite tactical superiority. This lame-wing comparison—in the literal sense of the words—is therefore too idiotic, and contains a severe disparagement of the English aeroplane builders in that it compares their machines with sparrow fledglings

which had strayed from their nests.

The attempt to disparage Richthofen personally by alleging that he was generally conspicuous by his absence, I can answer by my statement that our commanding officer was always the first to haul us out of our beds.

Further incredible attempts to minimise Richthofen's victories are made in the assertion that he always picked out "inexperienced opponents" and that the war service of the victims he shot down in France amounted to 9, 5, 6 and 3 weeks, 2 years, 7 months, and 3 weeks. He sought out these victims with " much discernment " and always lay in wait for the chance of engaging an opponent " who would give him an easy task."

First, as his comrade of the air, I sincerely regret that, apparently, the author does not see his way to put a higher value on his English comrades who were shot down after heroic resistances. Does he think the English airmen were so inexperienced that a victory over one of them was worth less than a victory over a German airman ? In our experience that was certainly not the case, as we can frankly and honourably admit. From such allegations we can divine the direction the path will take when hatred guides the pen.

Naturally, it is very regrettable when one of the victims has been only six weeks at the front, but how can we hold Richthofen responsible for that, when he could not ask his opponents about their length of service ? This is an over-estimation of his powers of penetration ; even Richthofen himself could not tell by looking at an enemy airman whether his war service amounted to 3, 5 or 7 weeks, or 2 years, or 7 months.

Likewise the attempt to disparage his victory over the famous English fighting pilot, Major Hawker, V.C.—which the author seeks to minimise by reference to the inferiority of his machine (D.H.5)—shows a lack

Guynemer, of the Cigognes, who fell with a score of 53, waiting to start on patrol.

This should be sufficent to show what the R.F.C. thought of Manfred von Richthofen. The grave at Bertangles.

MANFRED v. RICHTHOFEN. By Udet

of understanding, because it was not the machine, but the will and skill of the pilot, which decided the issue when two one-seaters fought each other in 1917.

Another accusation which is simply too outrageous is that which asserts that Richthofen first let his own pilots shoot down many of his victims and then followed them down in order to claim them as his own. This assertion is so shameless that it breaks down my cool restraint. In this respect Richthofen set us an example that no other commander could have done. His fighting spirit inspired his entire squadron, which followed his lead with the same whole-hearted loyalty and comradeship which he gave to all of us. I have repeatedly witnessed occasions when he yielded to younger comrades so-called doubtful victories which he could easily have booked to his own account, because he desired to give them encouragement and strengthen their confidence in themselves. He was the very one who never claimed credit for a victory unless he had the complete proof of eye-witnesses that the opponent had been demolished. There were no doubtful victories in any Richthofen Staffel—and least of all to the account of our leader !

In conclusion, I shall quote just one more sentence of this article which renders all refutation unnecessary and shows the trend of the calumny. This Englishman does not hesitate to write the words : " Richthofen betook himself [e.g., when attacking] to a safe post far from the centre of the fray as soon as it started."

After the war I have had frequent opportunities of meeting English comrades of the air ; I have been rescued by them when I have been in tight places, as, for example, in Africa. They have shown by their words and deeds that their spirit is an entirely different one from that which speaks from the scurrilous article in the Sunday paper. They will sympathise with me and understand my indignation, which is shared by the entire German nation. My friend and comrade Bishop, who is the greatest English scouting ace, and his splendid squadron, had many battles with Richthofen. What he has told me of my dead commander is in accordance with the picture of that heroic, undaunted, honourable airman which the whole world honours and esteems in our Manfred von Richthofen.

A SUMMARY OF AIR FIGHTING TACTICS

By FRANK RENAUT

TYPE 1. THE STRAIGHTFORWARD OR "PERFECT CONDITIONS" ATTACK

For this form of attack, it is necessary that the friendly pilot be flying a Spad 13 or better, while the enemy should be in an Albatros C-III with a broken propeller and an observer who is asleep or drunk.

The Spad should first climb to an altitude about one thousand feet higher than the Albatros can possibly attain, then carefully navigate into the glare of the sun. After waiting until the enemy aircraft has ventured at least ten miles on the Allied side of the lines, the Spad pilot may now make his firing run. This form of attack is guaranteed to succeed, provided that the conditions listed above are prearranged and that the ground crew remembered to load the Spad's guns.

TYPE 2. THE HEAD-ON OR "MY FATHER CAN LICK YOUR FATHER" ATTACK

This method is used by a lazy pilot who encounters a lazy enemy
pilot, when both are just too lazy to work out any tactic
whatever. It is best carried out by the fastest single seater
available on the Allied side against its equivalent enemy. These
will cause the most dramatic scrunch as the two aircraft meet.

TYPE 3.

TYPE 3. THE SCIENTIFIC OR "INSTANT ACE, <u>BUT</u> DISCRETION IS THE
         BETTER PART OF VALOR" ATTACK

This method is recommended for newcomers to the front, just up
for the first trip in a Camel, who wish to be able to say, "I
had a run-in with The Baron today" at every opportunity. The
pilot of the Camel should choose a time when a couple of dozen
Fokker Triplanes are almost out of fuel and have decided to go
home for supper. He should catch them as they are going towards
their side of the lines but not have actually reached them. This
is important and ensures that when he turns and runs for it, he
will automatically be pointed in the right direction and already
on his own side of the lines. The Camel should try to approach
from below and behind the Fokkers to retain the element of
surprise. (Not that they wouldn't have been surprised enough
anyway to have one lone idiot attack the lot of them.) Should
any one of the enemy pilots show any sign whatever of having seen
the Camel, the pilot should, of course, break away without making
any attack at all and dive for the protection of the nearest SE5
unit, which he has previously picked out for such an emergency.
This is known as discretion, (and he can STILL say he had a run-in
with The Baron).

TYPE 4.

TYPE 4. THE DASHING OR "ONE U.S. CAVALRYMAN IS AS GOOD AS TEN INJUNS" ATTACK

The friendly pilot is flying an SE 5 when he comes upon a formation of six Albatros D 3, which appear from behind a cloud. The SE should immediately fly right into the middle of the formation at great speed, causing their concentrated crossfire to shoot each other down, with any luck. Without any luck, the SE 5 pilot can expect to have his machine sawed in halves by the hail of lead from ten Spandaus. (The other two belong to the leader of the enemy formation, who is so helpless with laughter that he is unable to fire a shot.)

TYPE 5. THE OVERWHELMING SUPERIORITY ATTACK

This is the best kind, if it can be arranged. It is necessary to gather a striking force of 100 SE 5's flying in line abreast, closely followed by an equal number of Bristol Fighters mounting twin Lewis Guns at the rear. The formation simply flies towards Germany, accompanied, of course, by 100 Spads overhead and 100 Camels underneath, all similarly protected by Bristols; and upon any sign of movement in the sky, all open fire. Since most of the sky over western Germany will become immediately full of flying lead, it is unlikely that any enemy aircraft will be able to stay in the air. This method is used at the ends of wars when the side with all the aircraft has already won anyway, so it does not really influence the battle much, one way or the other. It does, however, help use up all the ammunition which would otherwise lie around until the next war and at last be found to be unfit for use, as some great scientist has invented a better type of gun which unfortunately uses far more expensive bullets.

FOOTNOTE:

We concede that the above may not help our side win the first World War, but in any case, this is unecessary, as we have already done that. What we hope to have done is put a little badly needed humor into a technically excellent journal, which has been more than musty enough and reeking of museums rather than castor oil. Elliot White Springs had fun with his war, and we're with him! We are interested in flying machines, as opposed to rear sear spring retainer keepers and the tensile strength of 18-strand microgage piano wire, etc. etc. etc. etc.

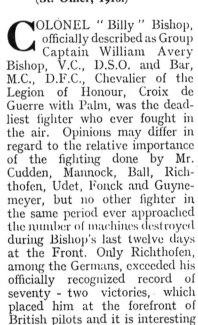

"Bish" lights a soother
after a show.
(St. Omer, 1918.)

All dressed up
and somewhere
to go. Leaving
Hounslow for
France (85
Squadron). (May,
1918)

BILLY BISHOP
AIR FIGHTER

By
COLONEL GEORGE DREW

A short history of the career of the leading British
surviving War Ace by a Canadian friend who is also
an historian

Yours sincerely,

Billy Bishop—his fist.

COLONEL " Billy " Bishop,
officially described as Group
Captain William Avery
Bishop, V.C., D.S.O. and Bar,
M.C., D.F.C., Chevalier of the
Legion of Honour, Croix de
Guerre with Palm, was the deadliest fighter who ever fought in
the air. Opinions may differ in
regard to the relative importance
of the fighting done by Mr.
Cudden, Mannock, Ball, Richthofen, Udet, Fonck and Guynemeyer, but no other fighter in
the same period ever approached
the number of machines destroyed
during Bishop's last twelve days
at the Front. Only Richthofen,
among the Germans, exceeded his
officially recognized record of
seventy - two victories, which
placed him at the forefront of
British pilots and it is interesting
to speculate what might have
happened if he had been permitted
to stay at the Front even a few
days longer at a time when he
was destroying several German
machines every day.

There are a number of rather
striking similarities between the
careers of Bishop and Richthofen.
In 1914 Bishop was twenty and
Richthofen twenty-two. Both had been trained at
military colleges. Both were excellent shots with a rifle
or shot-gun before the war. Both received commissions
with cavalry units and both transferred to the flying
service as observers in 1915, when they became convinced
that mud and horses didn't mix.

Bishop joined the Royal Flying Corps as an observer
in July, 1915, and proceeded to the Front in the autumn.
He then spent four comparatively uneventful months as
an observer until he received his only injury during
the war, when in a bad landing his knee was injured.
After some months in hospital he was given his chance
to become a pilot, and, in March, 1917, was attached
to No. 60 Squadron.

Once more the similarity between Richthofen's and
Bishop's experiences appeared. Six months earlier the
former had joined the famous Jagdstaffel II, under
Boelcke, who was then the idol of the German air force,
while the No. 60 Squadron was being inspired by the
example of Captain Albert Ball, who was at that time
the greatest British pilot. Each, therefore, started his
career as a fighting pilot under the inspiration of belonging to the squadron which claimed the outstanding
fighter of their respective air forces.

At the time of Bishop's arrival, 60 Squadron was
equipped with the Nieuport Scout, a small single-seated
fighter, mounting one Lewis machine gun above the
upper plane. Like most of those who started their
fighting at that time, Bishop had only a few hours'
flying before getting his wings, and it was largely a
question of chance whether he, or any other pilot,
would survive the first few fights, from which alone they
could gain the
vitally necessary
experience in
handling their
machines in action.
The British
superiority in air-
craft of 1916 had
passed, and the
severity of the
British losses in the
Spring of 1917 made
such demands upon
the training schools
for new pilots, that
they received little
or no real training
in aerial gunnery.
For the time being
the principle
followed was the
honoured but some-
what heroic method
of teaching a child
to swim by throwing
him into the water.

At Hounslow.
(April, 1918.)

It was a costly process of instruction in the presence of fighters like those in Richthofen's squadron, and one of the greatest tributes to British pluck is the fact that it did not completely break the spirit of the Royal Flying Corps. In such a stern school previous experience in shooting at moving objects was of incalculable advantage.

After one uneventful observation patrol, Bishop had his first fight and first victory on March 25th. It was also very nearly his last. He was flying at about 9,000 ft. between St. Leger and Arras when he had his first encounter as a pilot. His combat report for the day tells the story in his own words. " While on Defensive Patrol, three Albatross Scouts approached us ; one separating from the rest lost height and attempted to come up behind me, second to the rear machine. I dived and fired about 12 to 15 rounds. Tracers went all round his machine. He dived steeply for about 600 ft. and flattened out. I followed him and opened fire from 40 to 50 yards range, firing 40 to 50 rounds. A group of tracers went into the fuselage and centre section, one being seen entering immediately behind the pilot's seat, and one seemed to hit himself. The machine then fell out of control in a spinning nose dive. I dived after him firing. When I reached 1,500 or 2,000 feet, my engine had oiled up and I glided just over the line. The Albatross Scout when last seen was going vertically downwards at a height of 500 to 600 feet, evidently out of control, and appeared to crash at . . . " Bishop left the place blank. He was too busy at the moment trying to gain his own lines. Less than 2,000 ft. up, with a dead engine, well behind the German front, there was every prospect that the best he could hope for was to spend the rest of the war in a German prison camp. As it was he barely cleared our own trenches, and got away just before the German artillery finished the service of Nieuport Scout A.306.

It was one of those strokes of good luck that played so important a part in every pilot's career. Richthofen had a somewhat similar experience as an observer in Russia, long before he had a victory to his credit. His pilot flew low over a burning town, and the engine apparently became choked with smoke. With little idea of where they were, they barely succeeded in reaching their own front line. In either case, just a little less height, a little less speed, an adverse wind or a lucky shot from the machine guns of the infantry, and the names of Richthofen and Bishop would never have been known.

On March 25th, 1917, Bishop's first

" Bish " in a Bristol Scout.

confirmed victory made an unimpressive showing beside those of the leaders of that time. Earlier that day Richthofen had claimed his 31st victory. Guynemeyer had thirty-five to his credit, and Ball twenty-nine. Bishop was probably the last to think that in a few months he would considerably exceed those figures.

Richthofen's report for March 25th is doubly interesting, as it emphasizes a fact that should be borne in mind in assessing the fighting qualities of opposing pilots. On the day of his first victory, Bishop fought well over the German lines. Richthofen fought over his own territory. With very few exceptions it was the same as long as they were at the front. Bishop sought his foe. Richthofen waited for his. This is no reflection on the courage of a great fighter. It is a simple statement of the policies of the fighting squadrons of the two armies. Richthofen's own reports show that he rarely fought over the British lines and rarely fought alone. This had a very important result on the victories for which a pilot would receive credit. A British pilot might destroy a German machine behind the German lines without any confirmation, but there was no doubt when a pilot waited for the enemy over his own territory. This is Richthofen's report for the 25th :—

" Requesting acknowledgment of my 31st victory.

Date . . March 25th, 1917.   Place . . Tilley.
Time . . 8.20 a.m.   Plane . . Nieuport. Burned.
          Occupant   . .   Lieutenant Gilbert.

"An enemy Squadron passed over our lines. I went up and overtook their last machine. After only a few shots, the enemy's propeller stopped running. The adversary landed near' Tilley, thereby upsetting his plane. I observed that some moments later the plane began to burn. (Signed) BARON VON RICHTHOFEN."

This little pig went to market— wearing the red, white and blue target. (6 0 Squadron.)

An air fighter of note. Rutherford of 60 Squadron (1917).

An historic spot where many battles were re-fought. The fireplace in 60 Squadron's mess, at Izel-le-Hameau, 1917.

Bishop was in heavy fighting daily for the next two weeks, during which the British losses in the air were causing grave concern to those in charge of operations. With many more machines the British losses far exceeded those of the Germans because of the aggressive policy adopted. His was a baptism of fire from which all too few survived. The British artillery was busy all along the line, particularly near Vimy Ridge where the great Canadian attack was to be launched on April 9th.

The fighting squadrons were in the air almost continuously, escorting photographic and observation planes over the German lines.

Bishop was credited with his second victory on March 31st. Flying at 15,000 ft., at 7.30 in the morning, ten miles behind the German lines at Arras, he attacked one of five Albatross Scouts. This was the entry in his combat report :

" While on escort, I went to the assistance of another Nieuport being attacked by an Albatross Scout. I opened fire twice, the last time at 50 yards range, my tracers were seen to hit his machine in the centre section. Albatross seemed to fall out of control, as he was in a spinning nose dive with his engine on. Albatross crashed at 7.30. Ref. 51 B.29.30."

This was confirmed by other pilots and the anti-aircraft observers.

"Richthofen," 60 Squadron's lovable "porker," who carried a streamer on her tail and black Maltese crosses on her back and ears.

May, 1917. Izel-le-Hameau. (Left to right) : Guy (R.O.), Major Jack Scott (O.C. 60 Squadron) and Billy Bishop.

Bishop shot down three more German machines during the following week and then on Saturday, April 7th, was instructed to attempt to destroy an enemy balloon about four miles behind the lines near Vimy. As he was about to dive at the balloon, he was attacked by a German Scout, but after a short fight drove it down in flames. Then he returned to attack the balloon, which, in the meantime, had been pulled down to the ground. He dived at it, set it on fire and fired several bursts at the crew. Again, for the second time in a few days, his engine failed and he was very nearly forced to land, but when only a few feet from the ground, he succeeded in bringing it to life again, and got safely home.

For this exploit Bishop was awarded the Military Cross, thus winning his first decoration within two weeks after starting his career as a fighting pilot.

It was announced in the *London Gazette* on May 26th as follows :—

" His Majesty the King has been graciously pleased to confer the Military Cross on the undermentioned Officers and Warrant Officers, in recognition of their gallantry and devotion to duty on the Field.

" Lt. William Avery Bishop, Can. Cav. and R.F.C. For conspicuous gallantry and devotion to duty. He attacked a hostile balloon on the ground, dispersed its crew and destroyed the balloon, and also drove down a hostile machine which attacked him. He has on several occasions brought down hostile machines."

The following day was Easter Sunday, but it was not to be a day of rest at the Front, for the following day was to see the great attack on Vimy Ridge. It was a busy day for the British scouts, whose duty it was to prevent German observation machines and balloons from detecting the heavy concentration of troops. It was a brilliantly clear day, and at nine o'clock Bishop crossed the lines with an offensive patrol of six machines, under the squadron commander, Major Scott. His combat report for the day briefly describes the busy morning that followed :—

" While on offensive patrol at 9.30, I dived after Major Scott, on a two-seater, opening fire twice as he was already diving. Then I engaged a single-seater. He flew away eastwards after I had fired 40 rounds at him. Tracers hit his machine in fuselage and planes. I then dived at a balloon from 5,000 ft. and drove it down to the ground. It did not smoke. I climbed to 4,000 ft. and engaged an Albatross Scout, fired the remainder of my drum at him, dodged away and put a

Bishop, Molesworth and Guy (holding " Horace ") at Izel, June, 1917).

The tennis court built by 60 Squadron at Izel, June, 1917. The officer on the right is " Poppy " Pope.

new drum on, and engaged him again. After two bursts he dived vertically and was still in a nosedive when about 500 ft. from the ground. I then climbed to 10,000 ft. and 5 miles north - east of Arras I engaged two single-seaters flying toward our lines. Three more machines were above and behind. I fired the remainder of my drum into the pair, one burst of 15 at one and the remainder at the second one. The former turned and flew away with his nose well down, the second one went down in a spinning nose dive. My tracers hit all round the pilot's seat and I think he must have been hit. Then I climbed and got behind the other three about the vicinity of Vitry. I engaged them and one double-seater went down in a nose dive, but I think partly under control. I engaged the remaining two and finished my third drum at them. They both flew away eastwards.''

The destruction of two of these machines was confirmed. His record was mounting fast and he had packed a lot of fighting experience into those crowded two weeks, which stood him in good stead during the heavy fighting following the successful storming of Vimy Ridge on April 9th.

His next confirmed victory came on April 20th. The following is the narrative from his combat report:

" I engaged a two-seater by getting under him and firing with my gun pulled down at a range of 10 to 20 yds. I fired about 10 to 15 rounds, then dived twice, firing from 100 yds. range. I dived a third time, opening fire at 30 yds. range, and looking back after passing saw smoke was coming out around the pilot's seat. In a few seconds flames were visible and the machine fell in a volume of smoke. I fired 80 rounds in all.''

The lengthening days and finer weather increased the activity in the air and Bishop's reports show that he was frequently flying more than seven hours a day. It is well to remember what that meant in machines which were still in the infancy of fighting aircraft and against German scouts, which at that time had the advantage of speed and equipment.

It is impossible in this brief narrative to quote from more than a few of Bishop's combat reports, but some extracts will indicate the extent and nature of his activities. On April 24th, for instance, he reported : " I attacked balloon on ground, firing 20 rounds from 800 ft. Gun stopped and I flew away. I came back about five minutes later and again attacked from 800 ft. to 300 ft., firing remainder of drum. Bullets

were seen hitting balloon, but no smoke or flame was visible.''

That was not satisfactory, so the first chance he got to get away from ordinary patrols, he went back after the same balloon. His report for the 27th describes this flight : " While proceeding to attack the Vitry balloon, I lost my way in clouds. I discovered a balloon 800 yds. west of me about 600 ft. up. I passed over and turned to finish my drum, but saw the balloon smoking. I then fired about ten rounds into the basket. I flew south then for a few minutes and came to Vitry where another balloon was up. I fired the remainder of my drum at it, but cannot say whether I hit it or not.''

The following day he was promoted to the rank of Captain, less than six weeks after going to France as a pilot. The next day he shot down another machine in flames. This was his report :—

" (1) While flying at 17,000 ft., I saw one hostile aircraft 3,000 ft. below me. I dived at home from the sun side opening fire at 150 yards. I fired in bursts of threes and after about 12 shots he went down in a spin. I followed and fired the remainder of my drum with the exception of about 10 rounds at him. At about 11,000 ft. he burst into flames.

" (2) I climbed again to 15,000 ft., and dived at another single-seater. He dived away and I fired about 30 shots at him with no apparent result.

Izel. 60 Squadron, 1917. (Left to right) ——, Jenkins, Bishop, Molesworth, and Soden.

" (3) I then saw another hostile aircraft on my own level. I climbed above him and dived from the sun, but he dived away before I could get within 400 yards. I fired the remainder of my drum at long range, but could observe no apparent result."

It all sounds so ridiculously easy when reported in this way that it is necessary to recall how few pilots destroyed more than five or six enemy machines, and in what constant danger even these indecisive fights placed the very best of pilots. Bishop's report for the following day, April 30th, gives interesting evidence which required no elaboration to show the almost incredible amount of fighting through which he came unscathed, also the number of fights in which the best of pilots engaged without decisive results on either side.

"At 10 a.m. South of Lens at 10,000 ft., while leading offensive patrol, dived at hostile aircraft and fired 15 rounds with no apparent result. Hostile aircraft dived away Eastwards.

"At 10.10. North of Lens, at 11,000 ft., climbed up to two two-seater hostile aircraft on our side of the line. I fired at one from underneath, firing 15 rounds. Wire cocking device caught in slide, and I returned to aerodrome to adjust it.

"At 11.08. South of Lens, not having found the patrol, I attacked two two-seaters doing artillery observation. I dived on the leader and fired 10 rounds at him. He dived away and flew under five Halberstadt Scouts. I was above those, so I attacked from above, firing 20 rounds. I then flew away, as they had almost reached my level.

"At 11.15. South of Lens, at 8,000 ft., the three hostile aircraft doing artillery observation returned. I attacked them, firing 20 rounds into second machine. He went into a spin and I turned and attacked the last machine. He dived away and I followed, finishing my drum into him. He continued diving eastwards. I could not see second machine still in a spin and only about 1,000 ft. from the ground. The last one evidently landed, as he didn't come back.

"At 11.25. East of Monchy at 6,000 ft., I attacked from above five Halberstadt Scouts, who were flying as if to attack the B.E.'s. I dived at them three times, and fired about twenty rounds. They flew away east.

"At 11.30. East of Wancourt, at 5,000 ft. I attacked two machines doing artillery observation, firing at the rear one. They flew away east. I followed them to Vitry and again opened fire with no result. They came back to east of Monchy and I again attacked, finishing my drum into one.

"At 11.41. North of Monchy. I attacked one of the above pair, firing at him head on. He flew away east, losing height and neither of them came back.

"At 12.08. South of Lens, at 11,000 ft., I dived on one hostile aircraft doing artillery observation, and fired about 60 rounds, finishing my last drum into him. He dived away east and landed about Sheet 36 C. V.19. in a field.

"At 3 p.m. I attacked four Albatross Scouts from behind and above. I fired two bursts of five rounds each at the leader, who had turned. I then fired ten rounds at the rear man, with no apparent result. Seeing four more machines diving from above, I zoomed up and found they were triplanes. The four hostile aircraft then disappeared."

A report such as this gives some indication of the number of fights represented by any substantial number of decisive victories. The important jobs of driving away enemy scouts from our own observers, or driving enemy observers to the ground, might be well done, and in the process many hits might be scored, but it took a lot of flying and a lot of fighting to destroy completely an enemy machine.

May 2nd was perhaps one of Bishop's busiest days at the Front. It must be remembered that he was flying a machine much inferior to the latest German scouts, and that although he had nearly twenty victories to his credit, it was only five weeks since his first fight, and good though he already was he had not yet become the deadly killer of his later days at the Front. These extracts from his three combat reports turned in that day tell their own story.

"At 9.50 at 13,000 ft., N.E. of Monchy, while returning from photographic escort, I attacked one single-seater and fired two bursts of five rounds each. I was unable to catch him and evidently did not hit him.

"Later I saw five hostile aircraft about 5,000 ft. doing artillery observation. I manœuvred to catch one party of three when just west of the Queant-Drocourt line, as that was the nearest they were coming to our lines. I attacked the rear one, and after one burst of 15 rounds he fell out of control and crashed near V. 1 or 2, just east of Queant-Drocourt line.

"While watching him, another two-seater came up under me and opened fire. I attacked him, firing about forty rounds. He fell out of control and I followed him to about 1,500 ft., finishing my drum. He was in a spinning nose-dive and my shots could be seen entering all around the pilot's and observer's seats. Three more hostile aircraft being above me, I returned.

"At 12.15. East of Lens, at 8,000 ft. I attacked two hostile aircraft doing artillery observation, firing twenty rounds into one. Then they escaped. Watching five minutes later, I saw only one, the other evidently having been forced to land.

"At 12.35. East of Monchy, at 6,000 ft. I attacked two hostile aircraft doing artillery observation, but only succeeded in driving them away.

"At 12.40. Over Monchy, at 9,000 ft. I attacked from underneath a two-seater returning from our lines. I fired a whole drum into him, but there was no apparent result.

"At 1.05. Over Peloes, at 6,000 ft. I attacked the same two hostile aircraft as before and fired a drum from long range. I returned to the aerodrome as I had no more ammunition.

"At 3.45. South of Vitry, at 11,000 ft. While leading the offensive patrol I attacked two hostile aircraft, firing into the rear one. He turned and I fired sixty rounds at him. He dived on me while I was correcting a stoppage. I then turned and finished my drum at him.

"At 4.30 at Wancout. I attacked one hostile aircraft from above, firing seventy rounds at him. He turned on me while I was changing my drum and I fired a whole drum with the exception of five to ten rounds at him.

"At 5 o'clock. I fired the remainder from long range at six hostile aircraft attacking one of our machines."

For this busy day's work, during which the observers confirmed the destruction of two German machines, Bishop was awarded the Distinguished Service Order.

BILLY BISHOP

He next destroyed a two-seater on May 4th and shot down one of the new Albatros Scouts in flames on May 7th.

But although May 7th was fortunate for Bishop it was a black day for the 60th Squadron and the whole Royal Flying Corps, because Captain Albert Ball was killed late in the afternoon during a fight with Richthofen's squadron. With forty-three victories to his credit, he was an inspiring figure to Bishop and the other junior pilots and was the first officer to be awarded the Victoria Cross, Distinguished Service Order and Military Cross.

A few days later Bishop went on leave with twenty victories to his credit. When he rejoined the Squadron late in May the air fighting had increased in activity as a result of the German retreat to the Hindenburg line, and the resulting necessity for air co-operation in ranging the artillery on both sides. Bishop shot down three more machines in the first week after his return and then on June 2nd found the chance to carry out an expedition he had planned for some time. He hoped, by arriving alone at dawn at an enemy aerodrome, to surprise them as they were preparing to take off for their morning's work.

He rose well before sunrise and, just as the first light of dawn was brightening the sky, he was on his way over the enemy lines. He flew to the aerodrome he had chosen, but on reaching it was disappointed to find no sign of activity. He decided to try another one and, after flying three miles south-east, he found just what he wanted. Flying over this aerodrome at about three hundred feet, he saw seven machines out of their hangars, with busy groups of mechanics getting them ready for flight. The engines of several of the machines were already running. He turned and dived, raking the length of the aerodrome as he passed over it. When he turned he saw that one of the enemy was about to take off. This was the chance for which he had hoped when planning the flight. As it rose he swung in behind it and a burst of fifteen rounds sent it crashing to the ground. As he turned back over the aerodrome another machine had taken off. This time he fired thirty rounds at a range of over 100 yards, and the German crashed into a tree at the end of the landing field. Turning to the attack again, he found two machines in the air. Attacking one at a height of 1,000 ft., he finished his drum of ammunition before he shot it down close to its own aerodrome. He then turned on the other machine as soon as he had placed a new drum in his gun, but it escaped after he had fired the whole drum at it.

In his first attack, he hit several of the mechanics on the ground and damaged some of the machines. His Nieuport, during the fight, was literally riddled with bullets both from the air and the ground, and he was more than twenty miles from his own aerodrome. He was followed by four enemy scouts, but, in spite of heavy rifle and machine-gun fire as he flew low over the trenches, he landed without a scratch.

This daring exploit, which was confirmed in the next few days by German pilots, who were taken prisoner, won for Bishop the greatest of all decorations for valour, the Victoria Cross. He continued to add to his victories through June, July and August, and when he left the Front on leave in the middle of August his official record of victories stood at forty-five. He was promoted to the rank of Major and awarded a bar to the Distinguished Service Order. The official announcement of this award in the *London Gazette* was as follows:—

"Awarded a Bar to the Distinguished Service Order. Captain William Avery Bishop, V.C., D.S.O., M.C., Canadian Cavalry and Royal Flying Corps. For conspicuous gallantry and devotion to duty when engaging hostile aircraft. His consistent dash and great fearlessness have set a magnificent example to the pilots of his squadron. He has destroyed no fewer than forty-five hostile machines within the past five months, frequently attacking enemy formations single-handed and on all occasions displaying a fighting spirit and determination to get to close quarters with his opponents which have earned the admiration of all in contact with him."

In speed of promotion and victories, Bishop's record was probably unequalled during the war. In the same length of time, after he became a pilot, Richthofen had thirty victories to his credit.

Bishop returned to Canada in September, 1917, to assist in recruiting pilots for the training organisation that had just been established there. His speeches and attractive personality had a great deal to do with the truly astonishing number of young Canadians who joined the Royal Flying Corps in Canada.

Returning to England early in 1918, he was attached to the School of Aircraft Gunnery, and acted in an instructional capacity until he again went to the Front on May 22nd, 1918, in command of the 85th Squadron. The great German offensives of the spring of 1918 were in full swing and every experienced fighter was needed at the Front, as the dominance in the air might well decide the issue on the ground.

Under instructions, he flew very little during his first ten days at the Front, but even though he confined his activities largely to executive duties, he added two more victories to his list. Then he threw caution to the winds and in the next twelve days demonstrated beyond all question that he was the greatest aerial fighter the world has known. In those twelve days he destroyed twenty-five German aircraft, twelve of them falling under his guns in the last three days. He was then ordered to return to England immediately and appointed to the staff of the Air Ministry. Those in authority decided he was too valuable as a living example to young pilots to take any more chances with his life. One cannot help wondering what would have happened if he had been at the front even a few days longer.

Those heroic twelve days won for him the Distinguished Flying Cross and the announcement in the *Gazette* had the following citation:—

"A most successful and fearless fighter in the air, whose acts of outstanding bravery have already been recognised by the awards of the Victoria Cross, Distinguished Service Order, Bar to the Distinguished Service Order and Military Cross.

"For the award of the Distinguished Flying Cross now conferred upon him he has rendered signally valuable services in personally destroying twenty-five enemy machines in twelve days—five of which he destroyed in the last day of his service at the Front.

"The total number of machines destroyed by this distinguished officer is seventy-two, and his value as a moral factor to the Royal Air Force cannot be over-estimated."

BILLY BISHOP

It is perhaps only by comparison that one can understand what twenty-five victories in twelve days really meant.

Few—very few—pilots achieved that number during the war and the total victories of Rickenbacker, the leading American pilot, was twenty-one.

The most amazing part of this achievement is the fact that Bishop's log book shows that his total time in the air during those twelve days was only thirty-six and a-half hours.

Bishop now lives in Montreal and is Vice-President of McColl-Frontenac Limited, one of Canada's most important oil companies. He is also associated with air transport operations in Quebec and has recently given great impetus to civil flying in Montreal by becoming one of the most active pilots at the Montreal Flying Club.

One of the most prized possessions among the interesting collection of war trophies in his library is the bullet-riddled instrument board from one of his machines.

This is a precious souvenir of an encounter with Richthofen, when a burst of fire from the great German fighter missed him by inches. Another interesting thing he will show you with pride is his badge of membership in the German Aces Association. He has a photograph taken in Berlin at the time he became an honorary member a few years ago in which he is seated between Goering and Udet.

Bishop has been sucessful in peace as in war, but he is still the same cheerful and lovable " Billy " Bishop that he was during those hectic years when the Royal Air Force was made up of mere boys, and in days of single combat a pilot's life was pitched on a higher plane of excitement than will probably ever be possible again.

The passing of the years has in no way dimmed the glory of his achievement, and to-day, as in 1918, " his value as a moral factor to the Royal Air Force cannot be overestimated."

King George V talking to a pilot during the war.

Excerpts from *Knights of the Air*
by John Norman Harris
MacMillan, Toronto 1963

on March 7, 1917, he crossed over to France to join his squadron.

He had been fortunate in receiving far more training and more air experience than many of the replacement pilots who came after him. If he had not, it is quite likely that he, too, would have fallen an easy victim to the pouncing tactics of Richthofen's pilots.

As it was, he was none too sure of himself on his first patrols in the beautiful little Nieuport Scout. He tells how he desperately tried to keep station at the rear of a flight of six on his first patrol; how everything was new and strange and a little frightening; how he saw other formations, but could not for the life of him tell if they were hostile or friendly; how he saw a British machine go down in flames, but did not know exactly what had happened; how his attention would wander for a moment, and how he would then suddenly see the other machines a quarter of a mile away, so that he would have to go full throttle to catch up.

No. 60 Squadron had a brilliant record. Just before Bishop's arrival, the squadron's most famous member, Captain Albert Ball, had been posted as a flight-commander to 56 Squadron. The fledgling pilot must have been inspired in his early days by tales of Ball's exploits.

It is very unlikely that anyone on the squadron, in late March, 1917, suspected that the new, uncertain young pilot would, within two months, be the deadliest fighting unit in the air over France; that the awkwardness and uncertainty would give way to a bold aggressiveness such as had never been seen; that the newcomer would be called "the incredible Billy Bishop", and would take on the mantle of the great Ball, who was so soon to die in action.

Bishop's combat reports for those days often contain the words "fired a long burst without apparent result", and several times he mentions that his guns jammed at the crucial moment. Complete honesty was one of the features of all Bishop's reports, and this enables us now to see the manner in which he developed.

Though not a natural pilot—and he himself stated that he was the straightforward type of pilot rather than the aerobatic specialist—he mastered flying in a severely practical way. He could somehow always manoeuvre the machine well enough to get into an attacking position. Many pilots who could handle their machines with much greater skill could get nothing like Bishop's results.

Much of his success depended on superb marksmanship: he was a dead shot, and he practised constantly, firing at ground targets whenever possible. Much also depended on the care he took with his guns and his plane. Disappointed by early experiences with guns which jammed, he took over personally the job of cleaning and maintaining his guns in first-class fighting condition. He also made a careful inspection of his plane before every flight.

By April 5, Bishop had already ceased to be the uncertain newcomer, and he was permitted to go out alone and look for a fight. His experience that day shaped much of his career, for after finding an enemy and engaging him, he was foiled because his gun jammed at the vital moment, and several times he fired from close range and failed to destroy the German plane, which flattened out and landed safely in a field. This was the experience which made Bishop decide to engage in target practice and maintain his guns, and also to get in to the closest possible range in every fight.

When Bishop went on leave a few days later, he knew that he had inherited the grim task which Ball had left behind, for already Bishop was in the front rank of the British fighter pilots. In six weeks he had scored 17 victories, and won the D.S.O. and M.C.

It was only a few days after his return from leave that Bishop performed the most famous of his many exploits. On the morning of June 2, he was called from his bed at three a.m., in accordance with his own pre-arranged plan. Friends in the squadron had tried to dissuade him. They said that the attack he contemplated was sheer suicide. Nevertheless, Bishop had conceived the plan, and was determined to carry it out. It was simply to fly over the lines before dawn, and attack a German aerodrome just as the sun rose.

Billy Bishop took off in the chill darkness, without breakfast, and was soon flitting over the strangely silent trenches and across No-Man's-Land. The aerodrome he had selected was completely silent when he arrived. There was no sign of a plane or a human being anywhere, and he suspected that it might have been abandoned. He was bitterly disappointed to find no target after all his careful planning, so he began to search the countryside, in the hope of finding troops on the march, whom he could strafe with his gun.

For a few minutes he flew about aimlessly, but suddenly, in the grey light, he picked out the outlines of hangars: he had found another aerodrome, and as he approached he saw seven machines on the tarmac, some with their propellers turning. Mechanics were bustling about getting them ready to take to the air. Bishop noted that one was a two-seater, the others single-seaters. He did not want the two-seater to get airborne, because it would have a rear gun to defend it on take-off; his plan was to shoot down the German machines one by one as they left the ground.

He began his attack by a dive towards the standing planes, and a long burst which sent the angry sparks of tracer bouncing between the machines. One man on the ground was hit, and others rushed to pick him up. Bishop turned, and saw a plane taking off. He wheeled, came in behind it, and fired a 15-round burst. The plane staggered, side-slipped and crashed, catching fire on the ground.

By now all the ground-defence machine-guns were in action, and Bishop's Nieuport was riddled with bullets—he could see the holes appearing in the wing—so he began weaving and dodging to confuse the gunners' aim. A second machine was now taking off, so Bishop attacked it as he had the first, but this time he opened fire at greater range. For a moment he thought he had missed, and he fired again, as the German pilot put his nose down to gain speed. At the wrong moment the German glanced round to look at his attacker, and he crashed into some trees near the boundary, just as Bishop's second burst hit him.

As Bishop turned back, he saw that two more machines were taking off—in different directions. There was practically no wind, so that they could take off any way they liked. Bishop at once turned for home, but one of the newly airborne machines climbed after him, and was rapidly overtaking him, so he turned back and began to "waltz" with it. Luckily the other plane had climbed away in another direction, so that Bishop had only one to contend with. After some circling, Bishop got in a burst and sent the German plane crashing to the ground a few hundred yards from the aerodrome.

Now the fourth plane reappeared and attacked him, and he used up all the rest of his ammunition in a futile dogfight with it. Luckily, just as his bullets were used up, the enemy flew away, and Bishop turned for home.

He was now deep in enemy territory, with a bullet-riddled machine and no ammunition, and when he looked up, he saw that four enemy Scouts were flying above him. The light was still bad, so Bishop reasoned that the enemy had not seen him, and he continued to fly directly underneath them, evidently unspotted, for a mile or so, after which he broke away and flew home at low level.

Telegrams of congratulation poured in on Bishop when details of his exploit became known through the Flying Corps. Bishop's dawn raiding tactics were to be repeated many times before the war was over, by Collishaw, by Barker and by MacLaren, among others. The little Nieuport, darting about the enemy aerodrome under a hail of machine-gun fire, picking off the helpless enemy planes before they could get airborne, and gambling on getting them all before any could come up and get the attacker, appealed to the imagination of the entire service.

A few weeks later Bishop was called to the telephone to talk to General Trenchard, who was Commander-in-Chief of the Flying Corps. The General wanted to inform him that he had been awarded the Victoria Cross for his dawn raid on the aerodrome, which had taken place less than ten weeks after his first fight.

Excerpt from
Heroes and Aeroplanes of the Great War 1914-1918
by Joseph A. Phelan

AIR MARSHAL WILLIAM AVERY BISHOP
V.C., C.B., D.S.O. and Bar, M.C. and D.F.C., was the one who said it most unequivocally: "It was the mud, I think, that made me want to fly." He said it in his wartime autobiography, *Winged Warfare*. Bishop, a native of Owen Sound, Ontario, Canada, went to England with the Seventh Canadian Mounted Rifles in June 1915, and had enough of mud while stationed at Shorncliffe camp near Folkestone without even going to France. He applied for the R.F.C. and was accepted for training as an observer. He first went to France with No. 21 Squadron in the fall of 1915 and served as an observer until the beginning of May 1916. He was unlucky at all times except under fire. He was in auto crack-ups, aeroplane crack-ups and things fell on him. Once he nearly suffered a fractured skull when a steel cable hit him on the head as he stood in a hangar. He was unconscious for two days. Enemy bullets came close but never touched him. When he finally went to the hospital, it was to recover from the knocks of bad luck, not as a result of enemy action.

Through the intercession of an influential patroness, Bishop won a chance to train as a pilot. He came through with colors not exactly flying, but with himself and most of his aeroplanes in one piece. He was never a brilliant pilot, and at times he was barely adequate, but when it counted most, in closing with German fighters, he suddenly became magnificent. Perhaps he was not interested in flying for its own sake and did not really try to fly unless it was for the immediate purpose of shooting down an enemy machine.

He returned to France in March 1917 as a member of No. 60 Squadron and was soon promoted to the command of "C" Flight. He was known as a wheel-smasher in the unit because of his frequent bad landings, but by the end of the first week of May when he went on a two-week leave he had nineteen confirmed victories.

Albert Ball had hunted up Bishop just before he disappeared and suggested that from what he, Ball, had heard about him, Bishop was just the man he was looking for to join him on a private little adventure. He had the idea that a couple of single-seaters could slip over the lines at dawn and shoot up a German aerodrome and get away before the Germans knew what hit them. It was the kind of show that appealed to Bishop, so like Ball in temperament. Both were pilots of indifferent skill, moody and depressed after a victory, whose sole tactic was to rush straight in and blaze away at point blank range.

Bishop was shocked at the news of Ball's disappearance, and soon after returning to duty with No. 60 Squadron decided to go ahead alone with the show he and Ball were to have staged together. He took off before 4:00 a.m. on 2 June, a morning of cloud and rain, and headed toward Cambrai. The aerodrome he came across was the base of *Jasta 5* at Estourmel, south-east of Cambrai. He dived on the field in the first light of dawn and fired his first burst at a string of machines lined up before the tent hangars. Four Albatros pilots tried to take off to get at him. He shot one of them up as its wheels left the ground. He turned back over the field and fired at a second one. He missed, but the pilot crashed anyway. The other two Albatros took off in opposite directions, one of them flying away and one of them scrapping with Bishop for a moment before being shot down near the field. Bishop got away from the fourth machine and cleared out.

Ball had erred on the side of optimism when he calculated that the Germans would be so surprised at this kind of attack that they would not be able to put up any resistance. Bishop had had his hands full for a few minutes. But that was when he flew best—when he was thinking about shooting, not flying.

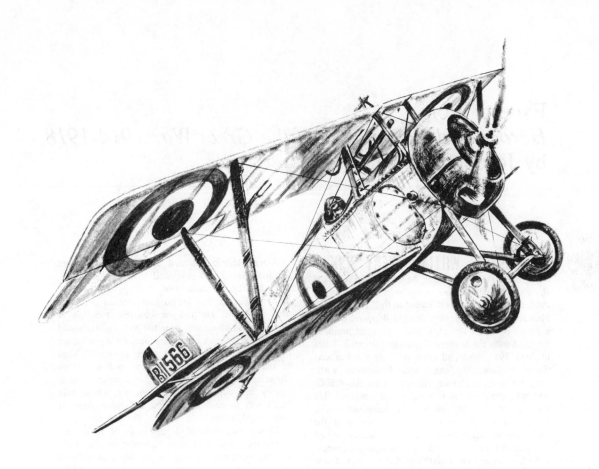

Part V
From *The FRAGMENT:*
A Commentary in
The War Amps' quarterly

Hanging A Legend: Billy Bishop's Continuing Battle

A Commentary by H. Clifford Chadderton

This is a story which must be told. It is a story of deception of the worst possible type, perpetrated by a National Film Board (NFB) writer-director. His victim: a World War I fighter pilot and hero of gigantic proportions, the late Air Marshall William Avery Bishop, VC, DSO and BAR, MC, DFC. We hope everyone in Canada will see how the NFB attempted to do what skilled enemy fliers couldn't do: shoot down Billy Bishop!

The film attempts to do just this very thing, but in a most cowardly fashion by casting a shadow of suspicion over Bishop's most dangerous and finely executed combat mission: the pre-dawn raid on a German airfield on June 2, 1917.

The Fighting Man According to the NFB

It is bad enough that the government-financed film board, which admits that it has had very few combat people in its ranks,

---

H. Clifford Chadderton, OC, CAE is the Chief Executive Officer of The War Amputations of Canada.

---

should dare to challenge the record of one of Canada's finest fighting men.

What is perhaps even worse, is that the filmmaker, Paul Cowan, stated publicly (before a hearing of the Senate Sub-Committee on Veterans Affairs) that in telling the story of Billy Bishop he was, in fact, talking about most men who have gone to war. Cowan used terms like, "The naive kids, gleeful at the prospect of encountering the enemy. . .the bloodthirsty killer. . .the man numbed by fear and the human being finally horrified by the futility of war."

Cowan stated of his film: "It is the very intimate story of a rather special hero — it is also the lament of all fighting men."

We can certainly agree with the last part of Cowan's statement. The fact that he was ever allowed to make the film — and that it is still in circulation — is in our opinion certainly "the lament of all fighting men." Based on his efforts in this film, one is entitled to doubt whether Cowan would know a "fighting man" if he fell over one.

I have known quite a few in my day. Very few of them could ever be described as "the naive kid gleeful at the prospect of encountering the enemy." And, most as-

Photos of Billy Bishop provided by the Public Archives of Canada.

suredly, very few of them could be described as "bloodthirsty killer(s)."

Maybe it is not for us to say but neither is it for Cowan to say that the metamorphosis of most men who went to war can be described as "men numbed by fear as the ground around him is being torn up by shell-fire." Where does he get off using the word "numb"?

In my mind, "numbed with fear" would be the description for that very few who, despite orders, remained hunkered down in slit trenches, or froze at the controls of an aircraft, or on the gunsights of an anti-craft gun on the fantail of a fighting ship. Sorry, but I never met any, and I doubt whether Cowan has either.

In Cowan's final statement at the hearing, he described the fighting man as a "human being finally horrified by the futility of war." At last we have some common ground, but we would argue vehemently with Cowan in regard to the time frame.

Most fighting men came back from the war harbouring a great deal of concern for what they had seen. Like Billy Bishop, however, while the war still raged they couldn't let their concern get in the way of the job they had to do. Billy Bishop may well have, in the post-war years, given a great deal of thought to the futility of war but there is no evidence to indicate that these thoughts were uppermost in his mind while he was doing the job for which he volunteered and/or was assigned to do: that of fighting a very skillful and determined enemy in combat. An endeavour which can be described as kill or be killed.

The Kid Who Couldn't Miss

The Kid Who Couldn't Miss was released by the NFB in 1982. The film has been the subject of controversy ever since, and no wonder! Most recently the film was reviewed by the Senate Sub-Committee on Veterans

Affairs in the hearings which I referred to earlier. The hearings took place over the fall of 1985 and the early part of 1986 and as a result the Sub-Committee provided a report in April of 1986.

The report makes for most interesting reading. A short summary of the historical facts indicate that Cowan submitted a proposal to the NFB and was then given the authority to proceed with production. What bothers me, perhaps as much as anything, is that in the evidence given to the Senate Sub-Committee, Cowan indicated that his proposal was basically to tell what he called "the very intimate story of a rather special hero."

In his testimony, Cowan claimed to have found important information, which in his mind indicated some question about the official version of the exploits of the late Air Marshall Billy Bishop.

It is necessary to wonder openly about the utter ridiculousness of the whole issue. You will have noted the decorations of Billy Bishop. Many of us in our childhood knew him as a fighting ace and a hero of the Great War. Yet Cowan and the National Film Board seem to want to insult and vilify this great man and stain his memory based on some very doubtful comments, comments that question the raid that won Bishop the Victoria Cross, the Commonwealth's highest award for valor.

According to the Senate Sub-Committee Report, Cowan said he encountered evidence which threw doubt on the documented verson of Bishop's raid. He stated he was faced with three choices and he set them out before the Senate Sub-Committee:
1) He could drop the film entirely;
2) He could retell yet again the legend which he had come to believe was questionable;
3) He could make a film which reflected his doubts.

Cowan told the Senators at the hearing that he was unable to proceed with the film based on the version which historians have investigated and found to be correct and which was accepted as the basis for his award of the Victoria Cross. Instead, Cowan proceeded to ignore everything that had created the legend of Billy Bishop and make a film which reflected (and I quote from the report) "his doubts."

Once he realized that he might get away with debunking one of our greatest war heroes, I suggest that Cowan saw the possibility of not making just an ordinary film but a blockbuster! As we used to say in the newspaper business: "twist it around." "Man bites dog." Everyone knows that's the kind of story that gets attention!

And so, with what would seem to be the thinnest possible grounds to proceed, Cowan and the NFB made *The Kid Who Couldn't Miss*. And in doing so, probably thought they'd have a chance at the big brass ring.

Cowan and the NFB did succeed in creating a climate in which their film would be seen by those who would ordinarily not have chosen to. But in the end they didn't get the brass ring and only managed to anger many people in their attempts to destroy the legend of Billy Bishop.

Billy Bishop, fighting ace and hero of the Great War.

The Senate Debates

We often hear talk about the role of the Senate, and even the suggestion that is either ineffective or irrelevant in today's world. Those who have studied the now-famous Senate report entitled "They Served — We Care," can refute any such suggestion. The report has, in fact, served as the basis of some far reaching improvements in veterans' legislation in the past few years.

We now have another example. One wonders whether there would have been any real public debate about *The Kid Who Couldn't Miss* if our Senators hadn't pushed the issue. In any event, the media realized that the Senators were on to something substantial, and moreover, the Senate Committee had the power to call witnesses including the Chairman of the NFB and the producer of the film.

It is important to review some of the statements in the Senate after the Sub-Committee's report came out. For example, in Senator Douglas D. Everett's speech to the

Cowan and the NFB seem to want to insult and vilify this great man and stain his memory, based on some very doubtful comments about one very particular episode.

Senate on April 16, he cites two passages from the Senate Committee Report wherein Mr. Cowan "denies that his object became to destroy a legend" and further ". . .Mr. Cowan. . .sought to make the film reflect his personal convictions in his own way."

Senator Everett then goes on to say, and it seems to me quite rightly:

It seems to me that there is a certain contradiction in terms. On the one hand, the Senate Report says the Senators were convinced that 'in the conception and execution of the film Mr. Cowan acted with personal and professional integrity.' However, it goes on to say that 'he sought to make the film reflect his personal convictions and express these convictions in his own way.

As Senator Everett states it:

That, Honourable Senators, is the basis for my disagreement with the Committee's Report. I think it was a personal conviction of Mr. Cowan that was reflected in this production.

I think Mr. Cowan set out to make an anti-war film and he used the sequence of events that took place and he manipulated them in order to prove his personal thesis.

Senator Everett pointed out that Mr. Cowan did most of his own research for the film. He also quoted the Senate Sub-Committee Report which suggests that:

Common prudence, in the opinion of your committee, should have raised serious questions about whether making such a film was in the public's interest and, if so, what

Billy Bishop's wife Margaret.

"I think Mr. Cowan set out to make an anti-war film and he used the sequence of events that took place and he manipulated them in order to prove his personal thesis." (Senator Everett)

precaution should be taken to ensure historical accuracy, particularly since the film would be released as a documentary.

Senator Everett also reviewed the circumstances surrounding the Estourmel raid, noting that it was a solo mission in which it has been accepted that Billy Bishop attacked an airfield behind the German lines and destroyed a number of enemy planes. It was for this that he was awarded the Victoria Cross. In Senator Everett's opinion, it would seem that Mr. Cowan came to his conclusion because no one saw Bishop do it, and there was no corroboration that the raid had actually taken place. Also, German records at the end of the war were largely

The Honourable Senator Hartland de M. Molson was acquainted with Bishop and has taken a personal interest in the controversy.

destroyed. Cowan concludes that there is some considerable doubt as to whether or not Bishop ever made the raid.

In introducing his evidence, Cowan uses what could only be considered as film trickery. He shot a fake black and white interview with Bishop's mechanic, Walter Bourne (a man no longer alive), that casts doubt on the accuracy of Billy Bishop's account.

There is no proof that Mr. Bourne ever uttered one word of criticism concerning Billy Bishop's raid. To the contrary, there is much evidence that Bourne was a great admirer of Bishop. During World War II, when Billy Bishop was an Air Marshall in charge of the development of the Commonwealth Air Training Plan, he fell seriously ill. His confinement in a hospital in Montreal was a news item around the world. When Bourne heard of Bishop's illness, he wrote a letter to Bishop from the RAF Training Base where he was stationed. The letter, as it is recorded in the *Courage of the Early Morning**, reads:

> Get well soon, Sir. Train us the men and we'll beat them as we did in the old days. Here is good luck — I am enclosing something which has travelled with me all these years. Remember the time your gun jammed and you had to get away? Well, Sir, here's the bullet that might have ended your career. You can see the mark on it where I gripped it in the vice to get it free.

Corporal Bourne was referring to an incident on April 30, 1917, when the then Captain Bishop attempted to attack two giant gothis, the mammoth planes built to bomb London. Bishop had to break off the attack when his gun jammed. Bishop was unaware, at the time, that these gothis had machine guns mounted in such a way that they could be fired downwards through an opening in the door. Accordingly the "blind spot" that Bishop thought existed below the planes was, in fact, a trap. The favourite attack zone for allied airmen at that time was toward the so-called "blind zone" in the belly of the German

---

* For further details, see the excellent book by Billy Bishop's son, William Arthur Bishop, entitled, *The Courage of Early Morning*.

aircraft. The point being made here, of course, is that the real Walter Bourne must have thought very highly of Bishop. It is too much to ask anyone to believe the NFB's version which shows the same Walter Bourne questioning the honesty of the gallant pilot.

Another fact which is hardly in keeping with the attemps to paint Bishop as a fraud, is that his final month of combat in June 1918 — nearly a year after the Estourmel Aerodrome — Bishop earned yet another gallantry award, the Distinguished Flying Cross. The citation read:

> A most successful and fearless fighter in the air whose acts of outstanding bravery have already been recognized by the awards of the VC, DSO, a bar to the DSO and MC. For the award of the DFC now conferred upon him he has rendered valuable service in personally destroying 25 enemy aircraft in 12 days, 5 of which he destroyed on the last day of his service at the front. The total number of machines destroyed by this distinguished officer is 72 and his value as a morale factor to the Royal Air Force cannot be over-estimated.

His son Arthur stated ". . .my father expressed little interest in the statistics of his fighting days. . . ." It is true that in 1917, when he returned to Canada after his first tour of duty, the British War Office admitted that in addition to his 47 confirmed victories (at the time), he had 23 single "probable but unconfirmed single kills."

If Cowan had balanced his evidence with that of the evidence that the raid was genuine, ". . .that would have given the viewer the right to determine which interpretation was correct," stated Senator Everett. It doesn't matter whether Bishop shot down 72, 62 or 52 planes. He was nevertheless a great war ace.

As for the decision to have the film labelled a docu-drama, Everett is wary. He said he has been unable to find a definition for docu-drama: "Some members feel that this recommendation (i.e., that the film be called a docu-drama and that there was no evidence

"It doesn't matter whether Bishop shot down 72, 62, or 52 planes. He was nevertheless a great war ace." (Senator Everett)

that the real Walter Bourne shared the views attributed to him in the film) does not go far enough," stated Senator Everett.

Senator Everett is not satisfied with the recommendation:

> Every trick of the trade is used to create the feeling of authenticity. Any reasonable person viewing that movie will come to the conclusion that Bishop's claims were false; that he did not deserve the Victoria Cross and that he was a fraud.
>
> There is nothing in this film that indicates that the people who go to war go because they believe they are defending some sort of concept. The whole film is based on the fact that in its early stages World War I — and by implication, World War II — was fought to preserve an arrogant, almost feudal way of life and that the reason there are wars is because Generals train armies and, therefore, they want wars; the reason there are heroes is because Generals require them, so they make them out of whole cloth.
>
> This is the basis of Mr. Cowan's philosophy about war.

He goes on to say, "what he (Cowan) does in order to prove how horrible and how unnecessary war is, is to denigrate somebody who so far as the record can tell, was an authentic war hero and somebody whom perhaps we should more likely venerate."

"I do not think we should allow either Mr. Cowan or the National Film Board to get away with it," concluded Everett.

The Debate Continues

The following day in the Senate, Senator Jack Marshall of Corner Brook, Newfoundland, spoke on the report of the Sub-

Committee of which he was chairman. In his address he indicated four legitimate grounds for criticizing the film:

- The historical contentiousness of the suggestion that Billy Bishop's record was substantially fraudulent;
- The film techniques used to convey and reinforce this suggestion;
- The existence of many errors of fact and chronology in the film and its transcript;
- The description of the film in promotional material as a full-length documentary.

Senator Marshall also related to the Senate the actual citation concerning Billy Bishop's Victoria Cross:

> His majesty the King has been graciously pleased to approve of the award of the Victoria Cross to Captain William Avery Bishop, DSO, MC, Canadian Cavalry and Royal Flying Corps. For most conspicuous bravery, determination and skill, Captain Bishop, who had been sent out to work independently, flew first of all to an enemy aerodrome; finding no machine about, he flew on to another aerodrome about three miles south east, which was at least twelve miles the other side of the line. Seven machines, some with their engines running, were on

The Honourable Jack Marshall, Senator and Chairman of the Sub-Committee on Veterans Affairs.

the ground. He attacked these from about 50 feet, and a mechanic, who was starting one of the engines, was seen to fall. One of the machines got off the ground, but at a height of 60 feet Captain Bishop fired fifteen rounds into it at very close range, and it crashed to the ground.

> A second machine got off the ground, into which he fired 30 rounds at 150 yards range, and it fell into a tree.

> Two more machines then rose from the aerodrome. One of these he engaged at the height of 1,000 feet, emptying the rest of his drum of ammunition. This machine crashed 300 yards from the aerodrome, after which Captain Bishop emptied a whole drum into the fourth hostile machine, and then flew back to his station.

> Four hostile scouts were above him for about a mile of his return journey, but they would not attack.

> His machine was very badly shot about by machine gun fire from the ground.

Then Senator Marshall went on to say what is in the minds of many Canadians:

> So we ask the question: given that there is doubt of his VC exploit, is it fair to blot out some 70 or 60 less victories and to destroy the authenticity of his other awards and those of thousands of other heroes to satisfy a questionable purpose for producing a film? For what purpose?

Senator Marshall suggested three optional recommendations:

- That the film be withdrawn from circulation or;
- That the file be re-edited to eliminate its unproven allegations or;
- That a disclaimer be added or attached to its title saying that it is a docu-drama, combining reality and fiction.

It seems unfortunate that the Senate Standing Committee on Social Affairs, Science & Technology, which the Sub-Committee reported to, apparently felt that the first two recommendations were not justifiable. Hence, the Sub-Committee was left with the third recommendation. The official recommendation stated that after the titles of the film, the following disclaimer be added:

This film is a docu-drama and combines elements of both reality and fiction. It does not pretend to be an even-handed or chronological biography of Billy Bishop. Although Walter Bourne did serve as Bishop's mechanic, the film director has used this character to express his own doubts and reservations about Bishop's exploits. There is no evidence that these were shared by the real Walter Bourne.

The Man and His Exploits

Billy Bishop was a Royal Military College graduate and one of 18 Victoria Cross winners among airmen in World War I. Billy Bishop went overseas with the Canadian Army in the infantry corps and transferred to the British Royal Flying Corps in September 1915. After several hazardous months of flying as an air observer on battlefield reconnaissance he was returned to Britain for pilot training.

On March 17, 1917, he joined Number 60 Squadron in France. His arrival coincided with a period of intense activity both on the ground and in the air, at a time when losses on both sides were devastating and when the life expectancy of the average pilot was less than one month.

Before March ended, Billy Bishop had scored two victories and by April 8, his total was six. By mid April, in the span of two weeks, his squadron had lost 13 pilots. Suddenly Bishop found himself not only one of the squadron veterans, but the one with the most victories. As a result, he was made Commander of his flight.

At that time, action became even more intense and over the next three weeks he destroyed two hostile aircraft a day. Then came the famous single-handed raid against the German aerodrome. For this action, he was recommended for, and won, the Victoria Cross. It is interesting that the process of

investigating and confirming his award for the Victoria Cross took two months. During this time, what did Billy Bishop — *The Kid Who Couldn't Miss* — do?

In this two-month period the intrepid fighter ace continued to shoot down enemy aircraft and historically he was given a credit for another seventeen victories which included one six-day period when he destroyed two German aircraft a day.

At this point, he was returned to Canada to support a victory bond drive. He had acquired great national value from a public relations viewpoint and he might well have rested on his laurels, but not Billy Bishop. He indicated to senior officers, in no uncertain terms, his desire to get back to the front line.

In fact, he did just this. Returning to Britain in 1918, he was given the task of developing a new squadron and by late May, he was back in action. The official record shows that by May 27 he scored the first victory for his new unit. The next day he got two more, followed by three and then two on successive days.

On June 19, in twelve minutes, he accounted for five enemy aircraft. This brought his grand total to 72 confirmed, plus two possibilities. These are the facts and it is sad to relate that, although the facts would have been available to Cowan, he decided to ignore them and zero in on one raid, and in so doing, attempted to demolish the remarkable record of this great fighter pilot of another era.

The German Airfield

It would seem that the reports of what actually took place in regard to Billy Bishop's single-handed raid on the German airport portray a deed of valor that, undeniably, deserved the award of the Victoria Cross. It is interesting to read Billy Bishop's own account of the raid. When one reads this, it is necessary to consider that these are the words of a man who was a hero many, many times over and had already been not only an infantry man, but a fighter ace: surely one of the most dangerous occupations in World War I. Bishop reported:

I fired on seven machines on the aerodrome, some of which had their

The film seems to dismiss the idea that the raid ever took place at all.

engines running. One of them took off and I fired 15 rounds at him from close range sixty feet up and he crashed. A second one took off, and I opened fire and fired 30 rounds at 150 yards range; he crashed into a tree. Two more were then taking off together. I climbed and managed one at 1,000 feet, finishing my drum and he crashed 300 yards from the aerodrome. I changed drums and climbed east. A fourth hostile aircraft (H.A.) came after me and I fired one whole drum into him. He flew away and I then flew less than 1,000 feet under four scouts at less than 5,000 feet for one mile and turned west climbing. The aerodrome was armed with one or more machine guns. Machines on the ground were six scouts (Albatros type I or II) and one two-seater.

Billy Bishop's commanding officer, Major Jack Scott, gave the following official report on the raid:

I wish to make a special report on an extremely brilliant individual attack on a German Aerodrome near Cambrai, planned and executed by Captain W.A. Bishop DSO, MC on 2/6/17.

He left the ground before daylight and flew intending to attack the aerodrome at Newville, but on arriving there found the hangars closed and no signs of any activity. He then flew south and east of Cambrai until he arrived at an aerodrome where seven machines were on the ground, of which three or four had their engines running. On the first one taking off he fired 15 rounds from very close range and

the machine crashed; a second one he similarly engaged and it flew into a tree. Two more were then taking off together, he finished his drum on one of these and it fell 300 yards from the aerodrome. The fourth machine pursued him and he fired a whole drum into it but observed no result. The above took place at heights varying from 40 to 1,000 feet. He then observed four scouts at 5,000 feet, climbed to 4,000 feet underneath them and flew thus for a mile. Finding the scouts were climbing at least as fast as he was himself, he turned west and returned safely.

The Cowan/NFB Version

The film alleges that it was known back in 1917 and 1918 that many of Bishop's claims were fraudulent. The film seems to dismiss the idea that the raid ever took place at all. As for holes in Bishop's aircraft, the film implies that there is evidence that Bishop landed somewhere, took off his own machine gun, fired the holes in his own aircraft, threw the machine gun away and then flew back to the aerodrome that he had left earlier in the morning.

The Senate Sub-Committe's report makes interesting reading concerning the NFB film generally. It states:

Throughout the film, the chronology of events is hopelessly scrambled. In general, this may be due to dramatic licence in the effort to give the film greater audience appeal. In one particular instance, however, the film uses a chronological shift to give Bishop a powerful motive for "faking" the attack on a German airfield.

In reality, Bishop carried out the raid toward the middle of his first tour of duty as a pilot in France. When he returned to Canada and married his fiancee, he had already received the Victoria Cross. The film, however, deliberately changes the chronology of events so that the raid appears to take place in the last week of Bishop's front line service. This supplies a false "motive" for faking an attack; it will be his last opportunity to play the hero for the brass hats the film says are waiting for his return.

There are many more errors of historical fact in the film, some of them significant, most minor.

The Condemnation

The Senate Sub-Committee couldn't accept Mr. Cowan's version and in fact, condemned his film in some very strong words:

Whatever the abstract validity of a film questioning our need for heroes, members of the Committee and other Honourable Senators who attended our meetings were upset because the elaboration of this theme involved casting doubt, not on a fictional character or characters, but on the personal integrity and service records of an individual veteran and war hero, one of the few whom all Canadians could admire.

This concern does not mean that we feel that the NFB should help to create, prop up, or fail to disclose fraudulent heroes. It does mean, however, that we were surprised to discover that no technical experts or professional historians were retained to assist in the production of the film. There was an obligation on the part of the National Film Board to ensure absolute historical accuracy. . . .

Although Dominique Parent is listed on the film credits as being responsible for historical research, this person was not heard from or referred to by those who appeared before the Committee. On the basis of our hearings, it appears that Mr. Cowan was responsible for doing all or almost all of the research.

Mr. Cowan also relied very heavily on interviews with a few selected individuals who had done research into Billy Bishop's record, and into his attack on a German airport in particular. These individuals do not appear on camera to express their reservations and doubts about his exploits, nor do their names appear for information. Nevertheless, their unpublished musings or conclusions are inserted into the film as authoritative evidence.

On the basis of the film credits, it does not seem that Mr. Cowan consulted important collections of documents relating to the air war and to Bishop's participation in it. The British Public Records Office which contains important documentation is not listed, nor is the Directorate of History, Department of National Defence in Canada, which holds the most voluminous records on Bishop and other Canadians who served with the Royal Flying Corps. When asked why he had consulted British experts and witnesses to the exclusion of most Canadian sources, Mr. Cowan replied, "I didn't feel that anybody here that I knew of, in any case, had anything to add to it except to say, 'Well, the official history says that he did it.'"

We believe that the National Film Board should have insisted on far higher standards of research and of the "admissibility of evidence," or the close association of professional historians with the project, before permitting work to continue on the film. We also believe that the proposed format of the film should have been changed to a traditional documentary study to avoid the additional controversy that might be caused by the "avant-garde" techniques and dramatic licence involved in the modern "docudrama."

The Media Speaks

Toronto Star
January 3, 1986

In a recent letter to the *Globe and Mail* Pierre Berton lambasted the "national newspaper" and journalists generally for not getting "off their butts long enough to look at the evidence in the case of Billy Bishop."

I know Berton slightly and admire him a lot, particularly as an effective popular historian. But in this case of the National Film Board movie, *The Kid Who Couldn't Miss*, produced by Paul Cowan, Berton himself hasn't examined the matter very well. His defence of Cowan's treatment of Bishop in the film is embarrassing.

To start, there's been a lot of reportage on the film and the critical inquiry into it mounted by a Senate sub-committee on veterans affairs. My file on the case has clips representing some 40 different stories or comments on the issue and the hearings. A file kept in the Library of Parliament is much fatter. I'd say young Cowan's been treated more fairly in most reports than have the senators as inquisitors.

Berton says that no one dug into the evidence which Cowan has to defend his treatment of Bishop. If or when Berton reads the proceedings of the sub-comittee he may shift this opinion. Yes, a few senators were verbally contemptuous of Cowan. Those who serve the committee, however, did a thorough job — a parade of witnesses and papers showing that any evidence Cowan had was flimsy or fiction.

Take just one example . . . research. Cowan claimed to have "researched" the subject thoroughly, going through voluminous records of World War I, including a close search of German records. He insisted that the Germans have no record of the exploit which brought the Victoria Cross to Bishop. This supports his dramatization of events. Nothing heroic happened to contradict the lines in his script alleging Bishop shot up the tail of his own plane to make credible daring deeds.

I don't know of any book by a Canadian historian so favourably reviewed in Britain and the U.S. as *The Royal Canadian Air Force, Canadian Airmen and the First World War*. It's by S.F. Wise, now dean of graduate studies and research at Carleton after a decade as director of history for the department of national defence.

Wise was a witness for the Senate sub-committee and, as he told it: "I was affronted by *The Kid Who Couldn't Miss*."

By the time Wise finished it was clear Cowan hadn't checked the richest sources of records on air actions of the First War: one in London, the other in Ottawa.

Wise blew away Cowan's claim that German records indicate Bishop's feat never happened. No one has seen such records, including Wise and others who've searched for them. As Wise put it. "They disappeared long ago, well before WW II . . . There is, in fact, no possibility, of proving from German records whether or not Bishop did what he claimed to have done."

If Berton or the NFB think Wise a patsy for the senators consider that he's the historian who wrote that available evidence showed Manfred von Richthofen, the Red Baron, was not shot down by Canadian pilot Roy Brown but by ground-fire from Australian troops. He's also the man who footnoted the official score of enemy planes credited to "Intrepid" or Sir William Stephenson.

Berton argues in his letter as though the central point of the film and the criticism of it turns on the aerodrome-strafing attack which led to the VC. It wasn't normal to give the VC for deeds without Allied eyewitness but this unique factor has been known since the award was made.

Once forced to defend his film, producer Cowan used the lack of witnesses to the VC deed as sky-hook for his whole fabric. It justifies his themes that heroes fabricate and the authorities fabricate heroes. Such themes can be accepted as generalities by most of us but the purpose of this film is to do it by putting down or ridiculing a particular man. And so a fellow Canadian, Billy Bishop, is presented at the taxpayer's expense, as an unsavory character given to cheating and lying.

To fit the film's themes better Cowan twisted facts or incidents in Bishop's life, even out of chronology. He has imagined much, a lot of it nasty. The result is a mean-minded fiction which Pierre Berton should be sad about, not defending.

Douglas Fisher
Syndicated Columnist

Toronto Star
April 7, 1985

Almost 70 years after Billy Bishop became a legendary fighter pilot, it's difficult to sort fact from fancy in the controversial National Film Board movie that suggests he was a liar.

The movie also suggests that Bishop never carried out the solo raid on a German airfield in 1917 for which he was awarded the Victoria Cross, highest award in the British Commonwealth.

With it he wore the Companion of the Bath, two Distinguished Service Orders, the Military Cross, the Distinguished Flying Cross and an assortment of foreign decorations. He was a legend in his own time and became a hero to generations of youngsters around the world.

Col. Brit Smith, a Kingston lawyer and president of the Royal Military College Club of Canada, told The Star that on behalf of former RMC cadets he sent a letter of protest to (then Communications Minister) Fox. Enclosed were references to documents containing "lots of confirming evidence" about the raid, including interogations of German prisoners-of-war.

"The Germans admired Bishop, too, remember," Smith said. "And these were contemporary accounts. The NFB accounts are pure conjecture. The movie hasn't attempted to document anything and has used a lot of poetic license. Bishop has been accepted as one of our few national heroes for nearly 70 years and we need all we have. The negative attitude of the NFB should be stomped on."

However, Macdonald (an aid to Fox) said that Fox, in a reply to Smith, felt successive governments have held that cultural agencies must be able to fulfill their mandates free from direct adminstrative intervention.

"Each agency is accountable ... to Parliament and discharges its responsibilities before the appropriate House standing committee," she quoted Fox's letter to Smith.

"We Canadians can be proud, thanks in part to people such as Billy Bishop, that we live in a free country in which individuals have the right of freedom of speech and the right to express a different point of view from that held by the government of the day. This right extends to reviewing heroes in the context of a film-maker's hypothesis about nations at war."

Cowan had told The Star that one source for the doubts about Bishop was Squadron Leader Joe Warne, a Royal Air Force officer and for the past 25 years historian for 60 Squadron, Bishop's old outfit. Warne confirmed this in a telephone interview with The Star.

"I find it hard to believe that his own squadron, in which he was so proud to serve, would vilify his record and desecrate his memory in this fashion," wrote Billy Bishop's son Arthur Bishop (to 60 squadron leader John Maddocks), author of *The Courage of the Early Morning Dawn*, a biography on Bishop.

An upset Maddocks replied that 60 Squadron has "no doubt whatsoever" about Billy Bishop's integrity and bravery and "we are very proud that he was on our squadron."

Maddocks said he'd talked to Warne, who told him "the producers' opinions are entirely their own."

"It does seem to me perhaps to be another case of the media trying to do down the name of a great man, when he is no longer around to defend his corner," Maddocks wrote Art Bishop. "I'm sure there were occasions when your father's gallantry went unrecorded and undocumented, occasions which would have merited further recognition."

When Warne was reached at his Melton Mowbray home and questioned about Cowan's movie, he said that there were "many errors in it." "He gets his timing all wrong on the Red Baron (the German ace, Manfred von Richthofen). Of course, I'm looking at it purely from the historical point of view."

Warne said he hasn't published anything detrimental to Bishop, but merely started with "what it says in the records." "Mr. Cowan's conclusions are, of course, his own."

But he added that the most acid critic was the late Spencer Horn, who Bishop took with him when he switched from 60 to 85 Squadron.

Art Bishop says it was Horn who confirmed to him, when writing his father's biography, that on the orders of 60 Squadron's commanding officer, Major Jack Scott, he flew over Estourmel the same afternoon and saw the destroyed aircraft.

"Horn said they had to have confirmation for a decoration, in this case the VC," Art Bishop said. "My book was the authentic version of my father's life and it was cleared by the RAF and the RCAF (Royal Canadian Air Force) plus historians past and present. All his claims are listed in the back."

Bishop's combat report is endorsed by Scott, who said: "Capt. Bishop has been encouraged to catch the H.A. (hostle aircraft) referred to in 7 Corps' daily intelligence summary No. 151 . . . He was several times at a height of 50 feet over this enemy aerodrome at least 17 miles east of the lines. His machine was full of holes caused by machine-gun fire from the ground."

Ron Lowman
Columnist

Toronto Star
July 1985

Opponents of the maddening movie from the National Film Board that suggested World War I air ace Billy Bishop lied about some of his exploits haven't given up.

And you have it on the word of Stewart K. Taylor that the remarkable feats of the Victoria Cross winner, who was credited with 72 serial victories, are true, despite the movie's suggestions to the contrary.

Taylor made a careful study of German records and concludes that the planes belonged to Jasta 20 which, like many other squadrons, was in transit from the St.

The How and Why of Heroes

Cowan took it upon himself, obviously with the support of the National Film Board, to examine: "the reasons why heroes, especially war heroes, are created and why countries feel they are necessary."

Is this the real key to Paul Cowan's thinking? Was he merely using the story of Billy Bishop to join those who seem to delight in what is sometimes called *"hero bashing?"*

You will be intrigued by Cowan's rather peculiar statement to the effect that he was

Quentin front to the Flanders sector, where a big allied offensive was expected.

A large gap in the records of Jasta 20 between May 24 and the second week of June, 1917, "reinforces arguments favoring the involvement of this particular jasta."

Taylor says it was an indifferent squadron led by an indifferent *Oberleutnant* named Fritz Heising. The Germans were loath to admit defeat in the air and jasta commanders often tried to disguise their casualties, something that would account for a lack of German records of Bishop's daring behind-the-lines raid.

Despite Taylor's expert verdict, the NFB film, *"The Kid Who Couldn't Miss,"* produced and directed by Paul Cowan, has been circulating for two years now as a documentary and questioning the Bishop legend. It roused the wrath of the Royal Canadian Air Force (RCAF) Association, the Royal Canadian Legion, Group Capt. (Col.) A.J. Bauer, chairman of the Billy Bishop Heritage at Owen Sound, and assorted senators.

The verdict (that the film be labeled a "docu-drama") isn't good enough for Senator Hartland Molson, a World War II Battle of Britain pilot. He financed a research trip last Spring by Bauer to Britian, France and Germany.

"The Heritage doesn't have the kind of taxpayers' funds available to the film board," growled Molson. "I haven't given up on this because the whole bloody thing makes me so angry. The film board has used public funds to destroy a man's character without proof."

Ron Lowman
Columnist

Toronto Star
September 15, 1985

The trouble is that he (Paul Cowan) took far too much artistic license and bent the fact to fit. His research was superficial and his knowledge of war flying is on a par with my Aunt Sarah's, who found it difficult to accept the automobile.

After all, when Cowan refers to one of his British sources as Group Captain Joe Warne, despite the fact that Warne is a retired squadron leader, you have to wonder about the accuracy of the rest.

At one point in the chronologically warped production (*The Kid Who Couldn't Miss*) Cowan implies that Bishop didn't really carry out the solo raid on a German airfield, for which he received the Victoria Cross.

In a six-page report after visiting Britian's Public Records Office and consulting historians and files of the German and French air forces, Col. A.J. Bauer says:

"There is . . . absolutely no evidence that the (Bishop) attempted to become the leading . . . ace by falsifying his combat record."

Bauer says that like some of his contemporaries, Bishop may have been somewhat cocky and brash, and, intensely competitive. He may, in fact, have boasted that he intended to become the leading ace of the Royal Flying Corps. But fraud? No!

Communications Minister Marcel Masse, who has declined to interfere with the internal affairs of the NFB, should be told by Prime Minister Brian Mulroney to withdraw and destroy all copies of the offending movie.

Ron Lowman
Columnist

looking for reasons "why heroes are created. . ."; an unusual statement to say the least. But when you see Cowan's movie, assuming you can follow the drift, he is blatantly suggesting that Canada badly needed heroes during WWI, and that the powers-that-be deliberately set out to create a hero, with Billy Bishop being the chosen candidate.

This all seems very far-fetched but maybe not in the mind of a writer like Cowan. He seems to feel that, for example, if a government needed a hero to run back home and head up a war bond drive to buoy up the flagging spirits of a civilian population, it would only be necessary to select the right type of person, create the right kind of circumstances, wait for the opportunity, write up the proper citation and Presto! We have an instant hero. Surely Cowan doesn't think the Canadian people so naive? And what he also may not realize is that anyone who went to war was already considered valiant and brave, albeit without killing anyone.

Another Defender

According to the film, there is every reason to believe that Billy Bishop faked his reports, even with the connivance of his superior officer and his government. A person who sees this film might well think that it is not about one of Canada's war heroes whose story should be told as an inspiration. Rather, one could be led to believe that the film is an exposé, a story of a gigantic fraud exposed by a brilliant, investigative film reporter.

It seems obvious that we just cannot let Mr. Cowan and the NFB get away with this. As of May 1986, the whole issue was re-opened. On Tuesday, May 13, Senator Hartland Molson made an inspired address to his fellow Senators. It should be remembered that Senator Molson is extremely well known both within and beyond the borders of Canada. He was, also, personally acquainted with Billy Bishop and (thank heavens) has taken a personal interest in this matter.

"The most objectionable feature in the film is the use of rumours and statements purported to have been made to an unofficial historian D.W. Warne", said Senator Marshall (These are the same statements that in the film are attributed to Walter Bourne. Bourne was played by an actor and said things the real Walter Bourne obviously never did.)

Senator Molson gives a graphic description of the Nieuport 17 flown by Billy Bishop. It weighed only 825 pounds and as Senator Molson says: ". . .it is hard to believe that a man could go up in the air for approximately 200 sorties and engage in all of the battles in which he engaged." Interestingly enough,

Senator Molson compares this with the hurricane fighter he flew in World War II, which weighed nearly 8,000 pounds.

Senator Molson zeroes in on the fact that Paul Cowan, in the film, shifts the actual date of the raid which was June 2, 1917, to later in the war and Cowan describes the raid as being the climax of Bishop's career. As Senator Molson says, "This is misleading and dishonest." It ignores the fact that Bishop returned to action in 1918 and added 25 more victories to his score, nine months after he had received the VC.

Senator Molson then goes on to quote a statement by Adam Symansky, the Executive Producer of the film, who criticized the Senate Committee for refusing to hear witnesses from NFB sources including Willie Fry who, according to Symansky was "the only living pilot who flew with Bishop." Senator Molson says this an absolute falsehood. Molson reported that there are several others still alive who flew with Bishop (and obviously would have refuted any of the film's allegations) who were not consulted during the filmmaker's research.

Senator Molson makes reference to statements made by Stewart Taylor, the official historian of World War I flyers who "strongly supports the honesty of Bishop."

In his address he makes further reference to a statement from Air Vice-Marshall Stevenson in Vancouver who had talked with three fighter pilots who flew with Bishop — Don MacLaren, Nick Carter and George Howsam — all of whom spoke highly of Billy Bishop and his exploits.

Senator Molson also referred to a letter from Sir William Stephenson, a man called "Intrepid" who was (and still is) one of the most credible sources of information on World War I and World War II. Sir William served at the Front with Bishop and was apparently "incensed that such charges should be made in the film sponsored by the Canadian government."

Senator Molson states that the Film Board used as evidence a tape made by Mr. Archibald James. Presumably, James has been discredited a number of times as a reliable source, and even by no less an authority than

Peter Simkins, Chief Historial of the Imperial War Museum in London, England.

Senator Molson concludes: "The film is simply and totally a mistake."

As a result of Senator Molson's speech, the Senate agreed to refer the report back to the Sub-Committee.

The next day Senator Daniel A. Lang, a highly respected lawyer, spoke to the Senate. He referred, in particular, to the legal aspects of the matter and stated: "If this matter were before a court of law, the National Film Board would have no defence whatsoever."

As Senator Lang suggests, "This film is defamatory libel." He is referring, of course, to the manner in which the film besmirches the reputation of Billy Bishop and unduly distresses the Bishop family.

Senator Lang goes on to criticize the film in a number of specific areas. He states that the film is really "hate literature" in terms of suggesting hatred against Billy Bishop because he fought in a war. As the Senator states: "That extends not just to World War I but, in fact, it tends to bring hatred and contempt to all of us who are veterans of World War I and World War II."

The Senator states further: "What defence does the NFB have? It has that one powerful, cowardly defence: the man is dead."

Senator Lang has also done some research of his own. He quotes from a book entitled *The Years of The Sky King*, written by Art Whitehouse and published in 1959. Mr. Whitehouse is described as a historical writer of repute and an authority on World War I fliers, having been one himself. Concerning Billy Bishop's award of the Victoria Cross, White states:

The raid on the German airfield became the high point of Bishop's career, although he continued his wild attacks on enemy aircraft and ran his score up to 47. British agents inside the enemy line eventually confirmed that 3 Fokkers had been shot down. Several of the single-seaters had been damaged seriously and a two-seater so shot up it had to be completely rebuilt.

It was for this solo feat that he was recommended for the Victoria Cross.

After long weeks of careful investigation as to the authenticity of his report the decoration was confirmed on August 11, 1917. Agents inside the German lines discovered that the two-seater had been seriously damaged, several of the single-seaters had been put out of action and the fourth Albatross pilot had been lightly wounded.

In Conclusion

The War Amputations of Canada has, for more than a year, been engaged in the production of a four-part film series (for schools, cable stations and networks) entitled NEVER AGAIN. The message of the series is simple. We, who experienced war firsthand, are in a position to tell about the horrors, the futility and the cost of war. Costs not only in terms of the lives of those who gave the supreme sacrifice, but also of the continuing grief of loved ones, to say nothing of the loss to Canada as a nation.

Our idea was to show what might be called "the other side of war" and that is: the brutality, the inhumanity, the senselessness and the slaughter. If we are to make any impact, however, on the youngsters of this country, we need some real heroes to talk about. The younger generation, to a certain extent at least, has been brainwashed to think that heroes depicted in the movies and television are the real thing. If you ask them to name a hero, they are just as likely to come up with somebody such as *Rambo* or a member of the *A-Team*.

To counteract this, it is very obvious that we have to show war as it really was. One way to do this, of course, is through actual use of war film footage. In our film series NEVER AGAIN we have had the co-operation of many countries including Russia and Yugoslavia, to the use of original film footage. It is sad but true that our war heroes are not known to the younger generation. Had they been, perhaps our task would have been easier as we could have assuredly gained their co-operation in appearing in the film and explaining to the youngsters that there's no glory or glamour in war.

What we are saying of course, is that a

country certainly does need heroes, not to glorify war but to represent a credible source of information, a person whom the younger generation will listen to when they say that war is a tragic and degrading experience that sets man against man and legalizes murder.

And so, if Cowan is looking for the reasons why a country needs heroes, I suggest he and the NFB take a good, hard look at the film fare being served up to young Canadians today most of which comes across from below the 49th parallel.

Current television and movie heroes have achieved almost a god-like status with our younger generation. How frightening when you know they are preaching violence and terror that is backed by sophisticated weaponry, explosives and fast-moving and dangerous vehicles. To counteract this, would it not make better sense even to lionize those whose valorous deeds were recognized by gallantry awards? To leave it to these men to tell future Canadians about the real cost of war, especially in terms of human suffering? Then, a man such as Billy Bishop, if he were given the proper status in his country as a hero, could use his influence to counteract the hogwash that has been coming through films and books and through the television screen.

At the date of this writing, the issue is still squarely before the Senate. Let us all hope that, this time, their recommendation will be much stronger.

I would like very much to compliment the Senate Sub-Committee for tackling a difficult and onerous task. One hopes the report is only a starting point and others will take up the fight. We should examine very seriously whether this film should be allowed to remain in distribution.

Our recommendation is that the film should be withdrawn and destroyed. Anything less is an unforgiveable attempt to destroy the well-deserved legend of Billy Bishop and an insult to all war veterans.

The War Amps Takes Action

The War Amputations of Canada has asked the federal government to ban distribution of the controversial National Film Board production, *The Kid Who Couldn't Miss.*

The film, which depicts the flying exploits of World War I fighter pilot Billy Bishop and his subsequent winning of the Victoria Cross, has been the subject of much controversy.

The Senate Sub-Committee of Veterans Affairs, chaired by Senator Jack Marshall, began an extensive examination of the production and distribution of the film. The Sub-Committee concluded that the authenticity of the film was in serious doubt and recommended that a disclaimer be added to the title, labelling it as a "docu-drama."

In a release dated June 6, H. Clifford Chadderton, Chief Executive Officer of The War Amps, stated that the Sub-Committee did not go far enough and has requested a hearing with the Committee to put forth The War Amp's recommendations.

"We feel that the recommendation of the Senators, to the effect that the film should be labelled as a docu-drama, is far too lenient," stated Mr. Chadderton.

"Our membership has today authorized the release of a letter to the Honourable George Hees, Minister of Veterans Affairs, demanding that the film be withdrawn and all prints be destroyed."

"Moreover," Mr. Chadderton stated, "If we allow a government agency to debunk our heroes, changing history in the process, younger generations may never know the instrumental role our volunteer forces played in both World Wars."

The Association feels that war heroes are the best people to communicate the tragedy and horrors of war to the younger generation.

The Silent Witnesses

Locked away in the dusty vaults of the British War Office in London, England there is a dossier which would settle for all time the doubts (if there really are any) about Billy Bishop's Victoria Cross.

It is a certain bet that the file will not be opened—for any reason. As John Percival says, in his definitive book *For Valour:* "The process whereby a Victoria Cross is awarded is always shrouded in mystery . . . it is just as well that it should be."

It would be ridiculous, all the same, to assume that Billy Bishop's award was not the subject of thorough investigation.

For one thing, it took two months to get approval for the award. Also, in George Drew's book, there are reports from captured pilots about the raid; a reference to balloonists seeing the raid; and one report suggests British Agents behind the enemy lines did the confirmation.

Every authoritative historical source agrees on one point of information: the Victoria Cross would not have been awarded without proof. The fact that Billy Bishop's aerodrome raid was not confirmed officially by eyewitnesses would have ensured that the normal British military advisers would be all the more careful in assembling the facts supporting the recommendation for the British Empire's award, described by Percival as ". . .the supreme award for valour, and no other nation has an exact equivalent to it."

H.C.C.

About the Author

H. Clifford Chadderton has been at the heart of the veterans movement in Canada since his return to civilian life, after overseas service with the Royal Winnipeg Rifles in World War II. He is the Chief Executive Officer of The War Amputations of Canada and the Chairman of the National Council of Veteran Associations in Canada. His other veteran affiliations include: Patron of the Hong Kong Veterans Association of Canada; Honorary President of the Sir Arthur Pearson Association of the War Blinded; Honorary Vice President of the Canadian Corps Association and Honorary Member, Dominion Command, Royal Canadian Legion.

He has appeared before more than 30 Parliamentary Committees in Ottawa as a veterans' spokesman.

He was made a Member of the Order of Canada for his work among amputees, including development of CHAMP, a program especially for child amputees in Canada. He was elevated to Officer rank in the Order of Canada in the mid-year Honours List this year for his continued contribution to the rehabilitation of the disabled and his work with veterans.

He was raised in Winnipeg, Manitoba and was employed, prior to his military service, as an Editor with The Canadian Press. He has studied law and accounting and has a degree in Association Management.